Between Flexibility and Disintegration

Between Flexibility and Disintegration

The Trajectory of Differentiation in EU Law

Edited by

Bruno De Witte

Professor of European Union Law, Maastricht University, the Netherlands, part-time Professor, European University Institute (EUI), Italy and Co-director of the Maastricht Centre for European Law

Andrea Ott

Associate Professor of European Union Law, Law Faculty of Maastricht University, the Netherlands and Jean Monnet Chair in EU Law

Ellen Vos

Professor of European Union Law, Law Faculty of Maastricht University, the Netherlands and Co-director of the Maastricht Centre for European Law

Edward Elgar
PUBLISHING

Cheltenham, UK • Northampton, MA, USA

Published by
Edward Elgar Publishing Limited
The Lypiatts
15 Lansdown Road
Cheltenham
Glos GL50 2JA
UK

Edward Elgar Publishing, Inc.
William Pratt House
9 Dewey Court
Northampton
Massachusetts 01060
USA

A catalogue record for this book
is available from the British Library

Library of Congress Control Number: 2016953912

This book is available electronically in the **Elgar**online
Law subject collection
DOI 10.4337/9781783475896

MIX
Paper from
responsible sources
FSC
www.fsc.org
FSC® C013056

ISBN 978 1 78347 588 9 (cased)
ISBN 978 1 78347 589 6 (eBook)

Typeset by Columns Design XML Ltd, Reading
Printed and bound in Great Britain by TJ International Ltd, Padstow

Contents

Contributors

Vestert Borger is a PhD Fellow at the Europa Institute at Leiden Law School, the Netherlands, conducting research on the debt crisis and EMU.

Deirdre Curtin is Professor of European Union Law at the European University Institute, Florence, Italy.

Mark Dawson is Professor of European Law and Governance at the Hertie School of Governance, Berlin, Germany.

Maartje de Visser is Associate Professor of Law at the Singapore Management University, Singapore.

Wouter Devroe is Full Professor of Law at KU Leuven, Professor of Competition Law at Maastricht University, Member of the Brussels Bar (Allen & Overy, EU and Competition) and part-time member ('Assessor') of the Belgian competition authority.

Bruno De Witte is Professor of European Union Law at Maastricht University, the Netherlands and part-time Professor at the European University Institute (EUI) in Florence. He is Co-director of the Maastricht Centre for European Law.

Alieza Durana is a Policy Analyst in the Better Life Lab at New America, USA. She provides research, analysis, and programmatic support for the Family-Centered Social Policy Initiative and Care Index.

Nadine El-Enany is Senior Lecturer in Law at Birkbeck School of Law, University of London, United Kingdom.

Cristina Fasone is Assistant Professor of Comparative Public Law at LUISS Guido Carli University, Rome, Italy.

Eilís Ferran, FBA, is Professor of Company and Securities Law and JM Keynes Fellow at the University of Cambridge, United Kingdom.

Ester Herlin-Karnell is Professor of EU Constitutional Law and Justice and has a University Research Chair at VU University Amsterdam, the

Netherlands. She is the Director and founder of the VU Centre for European Legal Studies.

Christoph Herrmann is Professor of Public and Administrative Law, European Law and European and International Economic Law at the University of Passau, Germany.

Suzanne Kingston is Professor of Law at University College Dublin, Ireland, and a barrister.

Panos Koutrakos is Professor of European Union Law and Jean Monnet Professor of European Law at City University, London, United Kingdom.

Andrea Ott is Associate Professor of European Union Law at the Law Faculty of Maastricht University, the Netherlands. Since 2011 she holds a Jean Monnet Chair in EU Law.

Steve Peers is Professor of EU Law and Human Rights Law at the University of Essex Law Department and Human Rights Centre, United Kingdom.

Daniel Thym is Professor of Public, European and International Law at the University of Konstanz, Germany.

Pieter Van Cleynenbreugel is Professor of European Law at the University of Liège, Belgium.

Stefaan Van den Bogaert is Professor of European Law and director of the Europa Institute at Leiden Law School, the Netherlands.

Anne Pieter van der Mei is Associate Professor in EU Law at Maastricht Faculty of Law, the Netherlands. He is Academic Director of the Master's programmes European Law School, Globalization and Law and International Laws.

Ellen Vos is Professor of European Union Law at the Law Faculty of Maastricht University, the Netherlands. She is Co-director of the Maastricht Centre for European Law of Maastricht University.

Maria Weimer is Assistant Professor in EU Law at the Law Faculty of the University of Amsterdam, the Netherlands, and a senior researcher at the Amsterdam Centre for European Law and Governance (ACELG).

Preface

The chapters of this book are based on contributions made by their authors to an academic conference organized by the Maastricht Centre for European Law, at Maastricht University. The conference was made possible by the funding provided by the European Commission's Jean Monnet Programme for our project *Flexibility or Disintegration? Differentiation of the Rights and Obligations of the EU States after the Lisbon Treaty and the Euro Crisis (FLEXIDIS)*. In addition to the European Commission, thanks are owed to the contributors for their commitment to this publication project. Special thanks go to Marina Jodogne, who provided invaluable assistance through her able and patient work in the formatting and editing of the book, as well as to Carol Ní Ghiollarnáth for her thorough and expert language revision of the book. We would also like to express our gratitude to Gloria Bozyigit, student-assistant at Maastricht University, for her support in the editing process. The publication process was greatly facilitated by the smooth cooperation with Edward Elgar Publishing.

The editors

Introduction

Bruno De Witte, Andrea Ott and Ellen Vos

Some 15 years ago, we edited a book entitled *The Many Faces of Differentiation* together with Dominik Hanf, in which the various facets of flexibility in EU law, following the Treaty of Amsterdam, were examined.[1] The 2001 volume addressed the topic of flexible and differentiated integration that started to receive increased political and scholarly attention[2] around that time, after the introduction of closer cooperation into the Amsterdam Treaty in 1997. This Treaty-based recognition of differentiation took place against the backdrop of the preparation for the Union's enlargement and for a more heterogeneous institutional future.[3] We defined differentiation in 2001 as 'the facilitation and accommodation of a degree of difference between Member States or regions in relation to what would be otherwise common Union policies'.[4] Differentiation was a new concept denoting a long-established reality. Certain forms of differentiation had existed from the very beginning of the Communities as, for instance, safeguard clauses in the Treaties, Benelux *inter se* cooperation and flexible arrangements in EU legislation. Differentiation took many legal forms, ranging from primary Community law to secondary law and soft law instruments, and from external agreements with third states to 'internal' agreements between the Member States themselves.

Differentiation became a politically relevant topic as of the 1970s and more obviously from the 1990s onwards in the context of the Maastricht

[1] Bruno De Witte, Dominik Hanf and Ellen Vos, *The Many Faces of Differentiation in EU Law* (Intersentia 2001).

[2] See e.g., Filip Tuytschaever, *Differentiation in European Union Law* (Hart Publishing 1999); Gráinne de Búrca and Joan Scott (eds), *Constitutional Change in the EU. From Uniformity to Flexibility?* (Hart Publishing 2000).

[3] See on this: Andrea Ott, 'Fundamental and Basic Principles on the EC and the EU', in Andrea Ott and Kirstyn Inglis, *Handbook on European Enlargement* (TMC Asser Press 2002) 25–6.

[4] See (n 1) XII.

Treaty and its aftermath. At first it was not perceived as a threat to European integration, but rather as a tool to promote further integration, by allowing a group of Member States to forge ahead with closer cooperation while leaving the door open for the remaining Member States to join later. The Schengen and Prüm Conventions and social policy can be highlighted as successful examples of this multi-speed concept, while the Economic and Monetary Union (EMU) (and in particular the adoption of a common currency), although built on that same multi-speed logic, soon developed in a different direction towards a more permanent division of two sets of Member States.

Today, 15 years after the publication of that earlier volume on the *Many Faces of Differentiation*, differentiated integration has developed much further and now arguably is a defining feature of the European Union polity. More EU policies than ever are marked by concentric circles of integration, implying a lack of uniform application of those EU policies in the various states. The internal market provides a good example. It is a core policy for all EU Member States and is extended to the EEA countries Norway, Iceland and Liechtenstein, but it also includes significant temporary derogations for new accession states. The Area of Freedom, Security and Justice is a fragmented 'area' with special arrangements for Denmark, the UK and Ireland and temporary exceptions for Schengen candidates. Remedying the deficiencies of the EMU resulted in intergovernmental constructions such as the European Stability Mechanism and the Fiscal Compact. And finally, the general mechanism of flexibility introduced by the Treaty of Amsterdam and now renamed as 'enhanced cooperation' has emerged from the shadows since 2010 and has now been used in relation to divorce law, patents, and financial transaction tax, thereby resulting in important jurisprudence by the CJEU clarifying the legal regime.

This volume takes stock of the many faces of the 'EU law of differentiation' that exist today. It is divided into two parts dealing respectively with the general institutional and the policy-specific aspects of differentiation. Part I is devoted to the general institutional aspects, with chapters dealing with the nature and characteristics of the various institutional and extra-institutional forms of differentiation. Part II takes a policy-oriented perspective, zooming in on the most important areas of EU law and policy in which differentiated integration is prevalent or particularly intriguing, such as EMU, the internal market, justice and home affairs, and foreign policy. The overall question underlying this exploration was whether differentiated integration serves the EU integration process and the core values of the supranational entity by introducing a useful degree of flexibility in the complex EU machinery among so many EU Member States or whether the multiplication of those forms of differentiation threatens to lead to the disintegration of the European Union.

The first, institutional, part of the book starts with a chapter in which *Bruno De Witte* sketches the general evolution of flexibility in EU law, from one Treaty revision to the next, and notes the paradox that, whereas the negotiations leading up to the Constitutional Treaty and the Lisbon Treaty paid relatively little attention to the legal regulation of flexibility, the post-Lisbon years have seen a remarkable upsurge of the practice of flexibility in its different guises of enhanced cooperation, opt-outs and *inter se* agreements between Member States. In the following chapter, *Daniel Thym* emphasizes the 'legality' of differentiated integration in the sense that the many, often quite adventurous, forms of flexibility that we have witnessed in the past years were basically compatible with the constitutional rules and principles of EU law. The main challenge, in his view, is therefore not the legality of differentiation, but its legitimacy, as widespread flexibility contributes to make Europe more distant and impenetrable for the citizen. *Steve Peers* then examines the differentiation mechanism *par excellence*, the enhanced cooperation procedure originally introduced by the Amsterdam Treaty, and compares it to Cinderella: after a promising early life, it was neglected for a long time and has only recently been revived, although still rather timidly. Peers argues that a more frequent use of the mechanism could increase the EU's input and output legitimacy. *Mark Dawson* and *Alieza Durana* discuss flexible legal instruments as modes of differentiation. They argue that the increasing 'hardening' of soft law instruments may not necessarily upset the ability of soft law to accommodate diversity but requires a re-evaluation of the legal framework in which these instruments operate. *Deirdre Curtin* and *Cristina Fasone* address a novel institutional question, namely whether there is a need for differentiated representation within the European Parliament to reflect the fact that an increasing part of EU legal norms do not apply across the whole EU territory. They argue that a move towards such a 'flexible' European Parliament would affect that institution's overall institutional credibility. *Andrea Ott* examines differentiation through accession treaties in relation to free movement, particularly their impact on European citizens' rights. She argues that differentiation by accession treaties was a necessary precondition to achieve enlargement, although it is doubtful whether it serves to deepen integration and it rather leads to two classes of EU citizens. *Maartje de Visser* and *Anne Pieter van der Mei* discuss the protection of fundamental rights in EU law and plead for more flexibility in this domain. They argue that the European Court of Justice should be more liberal in allowing the

Member States to offer a higher level of protection of fundamental rights within their domestic legal orders in situations falling within the scope of EU law.

The book subsequently turns to the discussion of differentiated integration in various policy sectors, starting with two conceptualizations of differentiation in economic and monetary policy. *Stefaan Van den Bogaert* and *Vestert Borger* discuss the many forms of differentiation in EMU law. While noting the dangers of this fragmentation, their analysis underlines the dynamism of differentiation and the EU's unique transformative capacity that allows it to adapt to new challenges. *Christoph Herrmann* delves into the use of (semi)extra-legal instruments in the euro-crisis and the limits of existing mechanisms of differentiated integration. He proposes to insert a new Treaty article allowing for amendments of Article 139(2) TFEU by euro-area Member States only, a so-called *inter se* Treaty amendment. This flexibility, he argues, would be the only way to repatriate the legal and constitutional framework of the euro area under the umbrella of the Treaties and of EU law. *Eilís Ferran* examines the specific forms of flexibility that characterize the European Banking Union, which straddles the borderline between (essentially uniform) internal market law and (essentially differentiated) EMU law, and she argues that the institutional arrangements that were adopted in this area may have both centripetal and centrifugal effects.

Turning to internal market law, *Pieter Van Cleynenbreugel* and *Wouter Devroe* analyse the EU's financial transaction tax proposal as an example of 'fast track' enhanced cooperation provided for by the Treaties. They conclude that this proposal may in fact constrain the regulatory freedom of non-participating Member States. *Ellen Vos* and *Maria Weimer* discuss institutional instruments allowing for derogations from internal market harmonization measures. They show that the opt-out procedures laid down in Article 114 TFEU (but originally created by the Single European Act) have not been resorted to often by the Member States and, when they were used, were frequently rejected by the European Commission or the Court. In view of the ongoing conflict on the acceptance of genetically modified organisms (GMOs), they plead for a rethinking of the ways in which the internal market paradigm of uniformity may be combined with a respect for regulatory diversity between the states. *Suzanne Kingston* discusses the flexibility that has been embedded in EU environmental law since the 1970s. She explains flexibility as a response to the natural complexity and indeterminacy of the topic. She nevertheless stresses the need for clarity in defining the outer limits of flexibility.

Nadine El-Enany analyses formal differentiated integration arrangements and informal flexibility which, on the one hand, have enabled the UK to adopt a cherry-picking approach to participation in the Common European Asylum System (CEAS) and, on the other hand, have led to vast differences in practice between Member States in their treatment of asylum seekers. She argues that differentiated integration, either in the form of official agreements or in the form of informal flexibility, is not appropriate in the field of asylum. *Ester Herlin-Karnell* explores flexibility in the field of EU criminal law, in particular the emergency brake and accelerator procedures laid down in Articles 82 and 83 TFEU. She considers that too much flexibility in criminal law is likely to challenge the legality principle and the possibility for citizens to claim their rights in cross-border situations. *Panos Koutrakos* addresses flexibility in what used to be known as the EU's 'second pillar', namely Common Foreign and Security Policy; this policy domain is marked by a wide range of cooperation arrangements which groups of Member States rely upon in practice, combined with a heavily proceduralized, but little used, formal framework for closer cooperation laid down in the TEU. He argues that, paradoxically, while this field would be most suitable for accommodating differentiation, it also seems to be the less amenable to a process-oriented management of differentiation.

In *The Many Faces of Differentiation* book, published in 2001, we observed that 'differentiation may be the opposite of uniformity, but that it may well – if handled with care – actually strengthen European unity'.[5] Today, when the European Union is faced with multiple challenges which often amount to true crises, and with discussions on a possible decrease of its number of Member States, the term disintegration is becoming ubiquitous in the public discourse. The question arises whether the proliferation of mechanisms of flexibility over the years has contributed to this newly fragile state of the integration project or whether, on the contrary, differentiation has been able to keep the impetus of European integration going despite the heterogeneity of national interests and priorities. There are good arguments to support that geographical widening and policy deepening can only be reconciled by allowing a sufficient degree of flexibility in EU law and policy. This is true for specific policy areas (as discussed in the single contributions to this book), but it may be equally true in more general terms, as a condition for the continued existence of the EU and of the whole integration process and for inhibiting a process of disintegration. Differentiation and flexibility seem

---

[5] See (n 1) xii–xiii.

essential components to address tensions and reconcile differences between Member States. In this manner, differentiation may indeed truly strengthen European unity. Finally, the question whether flexibility is a tool for disintegration or integration can only be answered by establishing what are the core institutional and policy elements, the core principles and values from which the Union of all EU Member States cannot deviate without putting the essence and functioning of the supranational entity at stake. Practical suggestions have been put forward, such as excluding the internal market from variable geometry and preserving the distinctive features of EU law like primacy, direct effect, centralized judicial enforcement and unity in the EU's external relations. The message that this book seeks to convey is that differentiation is a necessary tool to help prevent a breakdown of the European integration project. It is no longer an anomalous feature of the progress towards an ever-closer union, but rather a structural characteristic of the European Union project. Therefore, the question for the future is not so much whether differentiation and flexibility are good things per se, but rather which *forms* of flexibility are preferable from democratic and efficiency perspectives and which *limits* should be set to the range and depth of flexibility arrangements in order to protect the core principles and values of the European integration project.

REFERENCES

De Witte B, Hanf D and Vos E, *The Many Faces of Differentiation in EU Law* (Intersentia 2001).

de Búrca G and Scott J (eds), *Constitutional Change in the EU. From Uniformity to Flexibility?* (Hart Publishing 2000).

Ott A, 'Fundamental and Basic Principles on the EC and the EU', in Ott A and Inglis K, *Handbook on European Enlargement* (TMC Asser Press 2002) 13–28.

Tuytschaever F, *Differentiation in European Union Law* (Hart Publishing 1999).

PART I

Institutional dimension

1. Variable geometry and differentiation as structural features of the EU legal order

Bruno De Witte

1. INTRODUCTION: FROM ANOMALY TO A STRUCTURAL FEATURE OF EU LAW

Until the adoption of the Treaty of Maastricht, there was a growing sense of the unity of a single integrated Community legal order, despite the existence of three different Communities. That *unitary* legal order was also *uniformly* applicable to all the Member States, except for some limited derogations provided by primary or secondary law, which exempted single countries from specific rules of Community law. The Court of Justice set great store on this uniform application. For example, in a judgment of 1972, it held that:

> [T]he attainment of the objectives of the Community requires that the rules of Community law (...) are *fully applicable at the same time and with identical effects over the whole territory of the Community* without the Member States being able to place any obstacles in the way.[1]

This ambition of uniform application was backed by the duty for national courts to apply directly effective EC law and by the infringement actions the Commission could launch against non-complying Member States. However, there were also inherent limits to this aspiration of uniform application. The main limit was, and is, that EU law is applied most of the time by national authorities and courts that do not *actually* apply EU law faithfully and correctly on many occasions. But there was another limit, inherent in Community law itself; namely the fact that there were

[1] Case 48/71 *Commission v Italy,* ECLI:EU:C:1972:65, para. 8 (emphasis added).

forms of European law and policy that contained an inherent permission for differential application. The most obvious example is the fact that directives could be transposed by the Member States with the freedom to decide the 'form and methods' of that transposition and further application (as the current Article 288 TFEU still holds).

Nevertheless, those instances of territorially-based differential application of EC law could be seen as anomalies which would be gradually eliminated by the further development of the Community legal order. This is, quite clearly, no longer the dominant perception today. Not only is the gap between the goal of uniform application and the messy practice within the Member States now accepted as an unavoidable feature of the multilevel nature of the application of EU law, but the EU legal order itself has gradually moved away from the ideal of unity and now accommodates various forms of uneven application across its Member States, whereby these states are allowed to derogate from the common norms, or, more radically, they are allowed not to participate in the making of EU law norms and are consequently not bound to apply those norms either. The latter form of differentiation is sometimes called *variable geometry*, pointing to the fact that the territorial design of a certain EU policy is modified from the outset, due to the absence of some Member States.

Strong functional and normative reasons explain this evolution and make it very likely that this complex regime of differentiation is here to stay and probably to expand further. The *functional* reason is that variable geometry has proved essential for allowing European integration to proceed. Widening, deepening and uniformity could not go together. The choice for widening-with-deepening of the integration process, a choice that was repeatedly made in the past 25 years of the EU's existence, led to sacrificing the aspiration to a uniform legal order. But differentiation is also *normatively* attractive since it allows for the diverse preferences of national governments and national public opinions to be accommodated. Some countries can decide to move ahead with the European integration process in a given field without being stopped by the more reluctant countries, but also without forcing the latter to participate in new cooperation ventures.

A wide variety of forms of differentiation currently exist, and some policy areas are more clearly marked by their use than others. At the introductory stage of this volume, a rapid panorama will be offered, based on a simple distinction between the mechanisms of differentiation laid down in the Treaty text, and which therefore have a formal constitutional status (section 2), and the forms of differentiation that were developed beyond the text of the Treaties, through the practice of the EU institutions and the Member States (section 3). To this picture of *internal* differentiation, one should add the numerous examples of *external* differentiation, whereby third countries are associated with the adoption and application of EU law.[2]

2. FORMS OF DIFFERENTIATION IN THE TREATY TEXT

2.1 The Gradual Spread of Opt-outs

The Single European Act introduced a potential mechanism of differentiation at the heart of Community law, namely the single market, by creating a complex procedure allowing for country-specific environmental derogations from internal market harmonization in what was then Article 100a EEC (the current Article 114 TFEU). At the time, the new mechanism was criticized for disrupting the unitary ethos of the common market, but it was, in fact, rarely invoked by the Member States. Moreover, the Commission, helped by the Court's case law, kept a tight control on the potential for country-specific derogations which was opened up. The new mechanism, which is still included in the TFEU, albeit in modified form, proved to be a useful safety valve allowing the Member States to pursue more progressive environmental policies, rather than a Trojan horse within internal market law.[3]

The Treaty of Maastricht innovated by allowing some Member States not to *participate* at all, or in limited ways, in crucial areas of Community law such as Economic and Monetary Union (EMU). The major advance in the scope of activity of the EC/EU, brought about by the Maastricht Treaty, had to be paid for by abandoning the notion of a unitary Community legal order that applied evenly in all its Member States. Instead, new mechanisms were put in place allowing some countries not to participate in the development of Community law in certain areas and, consequently, not to be bound by that Community law either. This new institutional complexity was noted at the time and criticized by many observers.[4]

This structural differentiation was a functional necessity to allow the Treaty of Maastricht to be adopted in the first place. The urge to

---

[2] See the chapter by Ott in this volume.

[3] See the chapter by Vos and Weimer in this volume.

[4] Most famously by Deirdre Curtin, 'The Constitutional Structure of the Union: A Europe of Bits and Pieces' (1993) 30 *Common Market Law Review* 17.

neutralize the obstructive power of single countries (that is, their power to prevent the others from deepening their cooperation) had become very acute during the twin intergovernmental conferences (the EMU and EPU conferences) that eventually led to the Treaty of Maastricht. Until the very end, the United Kingdom (UK), in particular, opposed essential elements of the package that the other countries came to support, namely the creation of the EMU and the rather less spectacular plan to transfer new competences in social policy. In both cases, a compromise was brokered at the very final stage of the negotiations, and this was indeed crucial to reaching the final agreement on the text of the Treaty.[5] In the case of EMU, an opt-out was agreed to for the UK but also for Denmark; this opt-out was presented as temporary, although no timeline was laid down for those countries to join the EMU. As regards social policy, the legal construction was seemingly the opposite, as the Maastricht Treaty comprised a Protocol by which all the Member States enabled 11 of them (that is, all members except the UK) to opt-in to a separate Social Policy Agreement laying down new competences in the field of social policy. Both stratagems had one major element in common: they allowed for the creation of new norms of secondary EC law that would be adopted by the Council in a *reduced* composition, but with the participation of the other institutions acting in their *normal* composition and resulting in EC law that had all the qualities of 'normal' EC law, except that it did not apply in the dissenting Member States. The Maastricht Treaty thus set the legal model for the way in which variable geometry is still practised today: structural differentiation exists between Member States both at the time of law making and at the time of its application. The Maastricht Treaty also set the tone for the legal modelling of Treaty opt-outs: they tend not to be very visible in the main text of the Treaties, but they are half-hidden in annexed Protocols and Agreements. The Treaty of Maastricht was accompanied by 17 Protocols, eight of which contained country-specific derogations of one kind or another.[6]

---

[5] The compromise on social policy, in particular, was only achieved at the Maastricht Summit itself. See Derek Beach, *The Dynamics of European Integration: Why and When EU Institutions Matter* (Palgrave Macmillan 2005) 100, and Giorgio Maganza, 'Jean-Claude Piris, un seul homme pour cinq traités' in *A Man for all Treaties – Liber Amicorum en l'honneur de Jean-Claude Piris* (Bruylant 2012) 407, who evokes a draft being written in the cafeteria of the provincial government building in Maastricht, where the Summit took place.

[6] Isabelle Bosse-Platière, 'Annexes aux Traités européens et différenciation', in Ségolène Barbou des Places (ed.), *Aux marges du traité: déclarations, protocoles et annexes aux traités européens* (Bruylant 2011) 115, 117.

Since Maastricht, opt-outs have multiplied and have become a major feature of the EU legal order. The Amsterdam Treaty 'repatriated' the Schengen regime within the legal order of the European Union,[7] but the price that had to be paid for this move – given the lack of unanimous support among all Member States – was a new opt-out Treaty regime for the UK and Ireland, and another one for Denmark.[8] A system of differentiation between EU Member States that had existed *outside* the EU legal framework was thus brought *inside* that framework, but without modifying the degree and content of the differentiation and creating, indeed, a number of frictions in the institutional functioning of the EU's immigration and border control policies.[9] This vast new opt-out area established by the Amsterdam Treaty joined the Maastricht-based opt-out regime for the EMU. It 'replaced', so to speak, the social policy opt-out which was terminated at Amsterdam in view of the fact that the Labour government, which had recently come to power in the UK, had agreed to join the other Member States in their post-Maastricht regime of social policy law making.

Interestingly, the Convention on the Future of the Union of 2002–3, despite its general ambition to simplify and consolidate the existing

---

7 That regime was laid down in the Protocol integrating the Schengen *acquis* into the framework of the European Union, annexed by the Treaty of Amsterdam to the EC and EU Treaties. That Protocol was somewhat modified by the Treaty of Lisbon and has now become Protocol No 19 annexed to the Treaties.

8 As Monar put it, in the title of his analysis of the new mechanism, the Amsterdam Treaty had achieved 'reform at the price of fragmentation' (Jörg Monar, 'Justice and Home Affairs in the Treaty of Amsterdam: Reform at the Price of Fragmentation' (1998) 23 *European Law Review* 320). For a detailed analysis of the post-Amsterdam opt-out regime, see Georgia Papagianni, 'Flexibility in Justice and Home Affairs: An Old Phenomenon Taking New Forms' in Bruno De Witte, Dominik Hanf and Ellen Vos (eds), *The Many Faces of Differentiation in EU Law* (Intersentia 2001) 101.

9 The special position of those countries was laid down partly in special Protocols applying to them (known today, after the Lisbon Treaty, as Protocols No 21 and 22 annexed to the Treaties) and partly in special provisions within the Schengen Protocol (No 19). On the ultra-complex legal position of the opt-out countries in relation to the Schengen *acquis,* see Julian Schutte, 'UK v EU: A Continuous Test Match' (2011) 34 *Fordham International Law Journal* 1346. For an example of the institutional frictions caused by the Schengen opt-out, see the judgment of the Court of Justice in Case C-482/08, *United Kingdom v Council,* ECLI:EU:C:2010:631, as to whether a contested measure came within the development of the Schengen *acquis* (in which the UK does not take part) or within the field of police cooperation (in which the UK fully participated at the time).

constitutional law of the EU, did not seriously attempt to absorb the existing opt-out mechanisms. They were kept practically intact in the Constitutional Treaty, first, and in the Lisbon Treaty later. In the end, the Lisbon Treaty even added a major new opt-out regime in the field of police cooperation and criminal justice where, in return for the adoption of the 'Community method' within that policy area, the UK obtained an opt-out from future developments and even a right to unilaterally pull out from *existing* third pillar instruments by which the UK was bound. As before, in Maastricht and in Amsterdam, the creation of a new opt-out regime in Lisbon was a deal-making bargain without which the Lisbon Treaty would not have seen the light.[10]

The UK's right to pull out from its existing obligations under the former Third Pillar was a constitutional novelty, since, for the first time in the EU's history, it allowed a Member State to free itself from existing EU law obligations. The right had to be exercised in relation to *all* existing third pillar instruments taken together, hence the commonly used expression of a *block opt-out*. It was not to be exercised immediately upon the entry into force of the Lisbon Treaty, but 'at the latest six months before the expiry of the transitional period' of five years.[11] Despite many misgivings expressed on the home front,[12] the UK government decided to make use of that block opt-out option and duly notified the Council of this on 24 July 2013, well before the expiry of the transitional period. On 27 November 2014 (four days before its expiry), the Council adopted a Decision setting out the 'consequential and transitional arrangements' deriving from the UK's pull-out. However, on 1 December 2014 (on the fifth anniversary of the Lisbon Treaty), both the Commission and the Council adopted Decisions allowing the *re-entry* of the UK to a selected number of pre-Lisbon third pillar measures (35 all together, including the European Arrest Warrant, Europol and Eurojust).[13] Indeed, the privileged treatment which the UK had meted out to itself

---

[10] David Phinnemore, *The Treaty of Lisbon – Origins and Negotiation* (Palgrave Macmillan 2013) 164–7.

[11] Protocol No 36 on Transitional Provisions, OJ 2008, C115/322, Art. 10(4).

[12] See in particular the Report of the European Union Committee of the House of Lords, 'EU police and criminal justice measures: The UK's 2014 opt-out decision' (2012–13, HL 159).

[13] See respectively OJ L343/11, L345/1 and L345/6. For a short discussion of what happened, legally speaking, on those days of November and December 2014, see Steve Peers, 'The UK Opts back in to the European Arrest Warrant – and other EU Criminal Law' (2014) *EU Law Analysis*, http://eulaw analysis.blogspot.co.uk.

when signing the Lisbon Treaty consisted not only of having a block *exit* option, but also a selective *re-entry* option for those EU measures that it liked to keep – namely the ones that seemed most useful from the point of view of the UK's domestic justice and home affairs policy. The re-entry option depended, according to the Transitional Protocol, on decisions by the Commission (for most matters) or the Council (for the Schengen-related police cooperation measures), but the EU institutions happily obliged and let the UK continue to participate in as many former third pillar measures as it wished. Note, however, that the UK's 'revolving doors' operation came at a price: the third pillar EU acts by which the UK still accepts it is bound are, since 1 December 2014, subject to the normal enforcement powers of the Commission and to the normal jurisdictional powers of the Court of Justice.[14]

2.2 The Slow Development of Enhanced Cooperation

The institutional asymmetries created by the Maastricht Treaty in the fields of EMU and social policy were presented at the time as, possibly temporary, exceptions and were not vindicated as a new structural way of addressing the problem of 'unity in diversity' in European integration. Not long after the entry into force of the Maastricht reforms, however, the debate on the constitutional codification of a general regime of 'flexibility' or 'variable geometry' began rather abruptly with a series of speeches and papers presented by leading politicians in the summer of 1994. Right from the start, this debate was linked to enlargement, flexibility being seen in some quarters as a means of sidelining unknown and possibly unpredictable newcomers. However, the debate was also linked, more immediately and pressingly, to the fear of irreconcilable differences of views between the existing Member States. In his William and Mary Lecture given in Leiden in September 1994, John Major, the then British Prime Minister, welcomed the enlargement of the EU to the east and stated that the continuing growth in size and diversity of the Union should lead to greater *à la carte* flexibility, whereby overlapping groups of countries would be allowed to cooperate in specific fields of common interest *outside* the main EU institutional framework.[15] Around the same time, other countries, particularly France and Germany, started canvassing the alternative idea of enabling a *stable core group* of countries to cooperate across a broad range of policy fields, either within

---

[14] Protocol No 36 (n. 11), Art. 10(1) and (3).

[15] John Major, 'Europe, A Future that Works' (William and Mary Lecture, Leiden Town Hall), *Agence Europe*, No 6312, 10 September 1994.

or outside the institutional framework of the EU. In particular, the so-called Lamers-Schäuble paper presented by the CDU-CSU fraction of the *Bundestag*, while never put forward as official German government policy, became a key document in this political debate, as it canvassed the idea of a core Europe (*Kerneuropa*) composed of a 'pioneer group' of countries.[16]

As a result of those debates in 1994, most governments saw both options (*à la carte* cooperation outside the EU framework and a structured core group either inside or outside) as threats to the cohesion of the EU and to the principle of uniform rights and duties of states, which was still seen as a central principle of the EU regime despite the opt-outs that were agreed in the Maastricht Treaty. The consensus emerging from the 1996 Intergovernmental Conference (IGC), after long and extenuating negotiations, was that some general mechanism of institutional flexibility could be put in place, but it would be encapsulated within the existing EU framework and made subject to rather strict conditions.[17] Agreement was eventually reached, in the Treaty of Amsterdam, on a very cautious institutional experiment whereby a group of 'willing' states would be able to undertake closer cooperation among themselves, while using the institutional mechanisms of the EU, but, crucially, this could only be successful if the others would allow them to do so.[18] Therefore, this was neither *à la carte* cooperation nor the creation of a fixed vanguard group. Indeed, according to one observer:

> [M]uch of the debate about flexibility during the IGC focused on a set of regulatory conditions which were designed to prevent the creation of a *directoire* or an *avant garde* group which would forge ahead towards deeper integration, leaving behind those which were either not willing or not able.[19]

In fact, the conditions for closer cooperation imposed by the Amsterdam Treaty were so rigid that, only one year after the Treaty's entry into force,

---

[16] CDU/CSU Group in the *Bundestag*, *Reflections on European Policy*, 1 September 1994.

[17] For a political analysis of the negotiation of the Amsterdam flexibility regime, see Alexander Stubb, *Negotiating Flexibility in the European Union. Amsterdam, Nice and Beyond* (Palgrave Macmillan 2002) Ch. 4.

[18] For a legal analysis of the original Amsterdam rules, see, among others, Helmut Kortenberg [a pseudonym], 'Closer Cooperation in the Treaty of Amsterdam' (1998) 35 *Common Market Law Review* 833; Giorgio Gaja, 'How Flexible is Flexibility under the Amsterdam Treaty?' (1998) 35 *Common Market Law Review* 855.

[19] Stubb (n. 17) 49.

and before the new regime had even been tested in practice, the Member State governments started a process of reviewing and, ultimately, redrafting the relevant rules during the IGC that led to the Nice Treaty. The substantive and procedural conditions for launching an enhanced cooperation project were later softened again by the Treaty of Lisbon,[20] and the general regime of enhanced cooperation has finally been used several times in the past few years. A first and rather uncontroversial application dealt with conflicts of law on divorce. More controversial applications related to the new EU patent system and the financial transaction tax, and the legal challenges to which those initiatives gave rise, allowed the Court of Justice to give guidance on the interpretation of the conditions for recourse to enhanced cooperation.[21] In particular, the Court confirmed that enhanced cooperation could indeed be used to circumvent the veto power possessed by small groups of states in areas where the TEU and TFEU continue to require unanimity in the Council. This feature of enhanced cooperation, in particular, would seem to suggest its more frequent use so as to overcome the unanimity lock; however, such side-lining of recalcitrant states goes against the grain of the Council's decision-making culture, which is still marked by the search for overall consensus among all national delegations. This could help to explain why enhanced cooperation remains, for now, a rather rarely used instrument of differentiation – despite the high hopes put in it ever since its 'invention' during the Amsterdam IGC. The painfully slow process for the enactment of a financial transaction tax directive is testimony to the fact that cooperation between states, even when formally 'enhanced', can remain substantively problematic.[22]

Apart from relaxing the conditions for the use of the general enhanced cooperation regime, the Lisbon Treaty put in place two policy-specific mechanisms of enhanced cooperation. During the Convention on the European Constitution, much attention was devoted to the question of facilitating closer cooperation in the field of CFSP and particularly defence. Whereas the latter policy field was previously off limits for closer cooperation initiatives, it has now been turned into a privileged area for experimentation with a range of flexibility regimes, denoting a greater acceptance of the EU as a policy-making venue for military

---

[20] See the chapter by Peers in this volume, tracing the changes made with each Treaty revision.

[21] See, ibid.

[22] On this particular enhanced cooperation project, see the chapter by Devroe and Van Cleynenbreugel in this volume.

matters.[23] The post-Lisbon developments have not, however, concretized these possibilities offered by the Treaty text, since no attempts at setting up 'permanent structured cooperation' within the EU's defence policy have been made. On the contrary, we saw new instances of ad hoc coalitions, patchy multilateralism and bilateral ententes,[24] such as the Lancaster House agreements concluded between France and the UK in November 2010.[25]

Another specific regime of enhanced cooperation created by the Lisbon Treaty, which was less prominently discussed in its preparatory phase, but proved to be more important in practice, concerns the field of economic governance, where it was grafted upon the existing variable geometry between euro-area and non-euro-area countries. The legal basis allowing for the adoption of euro-area specific legislation on economic governance (Article 136(1) TFEU) was used for important parts of the 'six-pack' and 'two-pack' economic governance reforms;[26] and, more recently, unprecedented forms of variable geometry were experimented with for banking supervision, where the new ECB-centred mechanism, while legally mandatory only for euro-area states, is opened up for 'closer cooperation' with non-euro states who wish to join.[27]

---

[23] See, for an analysis of the Lisbon changes in this policy area, Marise Cremona, 'Enhanced Cooperation and the Common Foreign and Security and Defence Policy' (2009) EUI Working Papers LAW 2009/21; Hervé Bribosia, 'Les nouvelles formes de flexibilité en matière de défense', in Giuliano Amato, Hervé Bribosia and Bruno De Witte (eds), *Genesis and Destiny of the European Constitution* (Bruylant 2007) 835. See, for further details, the chapter by Koutrakos in this volume.

[24] Those three terms are borrowed from *More Union in European Defence*, Report of a CEPS Task Force, February 2015, p. 7.

[25] See Benoit Gomis, 'Franco-British Defence and Security Treaties: Entente While it Lasts?', Chatham House Programme Paper ISP PP 2001/01, March 2011.

[26] See, for a detailed discussion, the contributions by Herrmann and Van den Bogaert/Borger to this volume.

[27] See the chapter by Ferran in this volume.

3. DIFFERENTIATION THROUGH INSTITUTIONAL PRACTICE

3.1 Secondary EU Law: Derogations, Formal and Informal Flexibility

The oldest form of differentiation in EU law is still ubiquitous today: EU legislation adopted with the participation of all the Member States may allow individual states (whether named or not) to opt out from some of its provisions. This practice is linked to the processes of consensus building in the Council and compromise building between the Council and the Parliament under the codecision procedure. Often, this search for consensus and compromise is considered to allow for two routes: either a general agreement on a lowest common denominator norm or a decision to set a higher standard while allowing some states to derogate from it. There are many examples of the latter approach, some of which are mentioned in the chapters by Kingston and by Vos and Weimer in this volume. A further example is the Working Time Directive, which set some quite ambitious norms of social protection, but the price to be paid for this was the enactment of a series of derogatory clauses; in fact, half of the text of this directive is devoted to the definition of those derogations.[28]

In addition, we also find a large number of EU legal instruments intended from the outset, and deliberately, to apply only to a limited set of Member States. Sometimes those states are not named, although their identity is clear from the political context. A recent example is the Council Regulation of 15 March 2016 on emergency support within the EU.[29] Although no specific Member State is named, either in the text of the regulation or in its preamble, it is clear to all that this measure was adopted so as to create a basis for channeling humanitarian assistance to Greece to deal with the massive influx of migrants and refugees in that country. In other cases, the beneficiary countries are spelled out. Recent examples, also from the domain of migration and asylum policy, are the two Council decisions of 2015 on the relocation of asylum seekers from Greece and Italy.[30] In some policy areas, country-specific measures are ubiquitous and outnumber the acts with general territorial application.

---

28 On this directive, see the chapter by Dawson and Durana in this volume.

29 Council Regulation 2016/369 of 15 March 2016 on the provision of emergency support within the Union, OJ 2016, L70/1.

30 Council Decision 2015/1523 of 14 September 2015 establishing provisional measures in the area of international protection for the benefit of Italy and of Greece, OJ 2015, L239/146; Council Decision 2015/1601 of 22 September

This is the case in macro-economic and fiscal governance, where the EU institutions adopt a myriad of decisions and recommendations addressed to individual countries, sometimes with major implications for their domestic policies.[31]

This phenomenon of territorial differentiation in EU legislation has become so common that one tends to forget how typical it is for the EU legal order; such frequent renunciation to the uniform application of common norms is rare in unitary states and even in federal states.

3.2 Decline and Revival of *Inter Se* Agreements

In contrast to differentiation in EU secondary legislation, flexibility is also occasionally sought through the intergovernmental cooperation of groups of Member States *outside* the EU legal order. This form of flexibility has existed since the early days of the European integration process. Indeed, it was clear from the outset, in the 1950s, that the new Community institutions would not provide the exclusive framework for the relations between the (then) six Member States. The EEC Treaty did not terminate any of the existing bilateral or multilateral treaties between them. During the negotiation of the EEC Treaty, and in the period immediately afterwards, several *inter se* agreements[32] were concluded, also on matters related to those covered by the EEC Treaty; a prominent example was the Treaty establishing the Benelux Economic Union which was concluded on 3 February 1958, that is, only one month after the entry into force of the EEC Treaty. In anticipation of this, Article 233 EC stated – and Article 350 TFEU still states today – that the Treaty does not preclude 'the existence or completion of regional unions between Belgium and Luxembourg, or between Belgium, Luxembourg and the Netherlands …'.

Benelux cooperation was not the only form of international cooperation between small groups of states. We can find numerous examples of international agreements concluded between Member States

establishing provisional measures in the area of international protection for the benefit of Italy and of Greece, OJ 2015, L248/80.

[31] As for example the Council Implementing Decision 2015/1411 of 19 August 2015 approving the macroeconomic adjustment programme of Greece OJ 2015, L219/12.

[32] I use the term '*inter se* agreements' as a synonym for agreements concluded between less than all the Member States of the EC/EU. The term is traditionally used in international law for agreements concluded between some, but not all, parties to an earlier agreement.

of the Community and the Union, ever since the 1950s, in areas such as tax law, environmental protection, defence, culture, and education. Such *inter se* agreements could also serve the purpose of allowing a group of Member States to move European integration forward in the face of the opposition of other Member States. One clear pre-Maastricht example of such a 'pioneer group initiative' was the Schengen cooperation regime, composed of a first Agreement signed in 1985, an implementing Convention adopted in 1990, and numerous specific decisions adopted by the Schengen Executive Committee after that. Schengen cooperation was started at a time when a general consensus on abolishing the controls on persons at the intra-Community borders could not be reached. The same reasons which justified the rule of Article 233 EEC Treaty, whereby the Benelux countries were allowed to adopt more advanced measures of integration, could be applied to Schengen. Yet, from the start, there was a concern that Schengen could develop from a transitional laboratory into a stable institutional regime functioning *alongside* the EU in a durable fashion, which seemed unattractive due to its important deficits in terms of transparency and judicial protection and also due to its proximity, content-wise, to the core idea of the internal market. The Schengen experiment therefore focused the minds of Europe's institutions and governments on how to institutionalize closer cooperation *within* rather than *outside* the main legal framework of the founding Treaties. The fact that the Amsterdam Treaty managed to terminate the separate legal life of the Schengen Agreement and Convention, by transforming their content into EU law, and that it had also established a system of enhanced cooperation within the EU institutional framework, could be seen as relegating *inter se* agreements to the margins of the European integration story. That impression could be reinforced by the fact that the Lisbon Treaty deleted some existing Treaty provisions which had previously invited the EU Member States to conclude international conventions among themselves to help advance the EU's integration agenda (former Articles 293 EC and 34(2)(d) EU).

Yet, the post-Lisbon practice shows that the EU Member States consider that they have retained the capacity and the right to conclude international treaties among themselves, even when the subject matter of their agreement is closely connected to EU policies. The conclusion of the 'Fiscal Compact' between 25 Member States and of the Treaty establishing the European Stability Mechanism between the then 17 euro-area states are recent and spectacular examples of the use of international law as a mechanism of differentiated integration.[33] They were followed more recently (in May 2014) by the signature of yet another international agreement in the sphere of EMU law, namely the Agreement on the Single Resolution Fund, which is the intergovernmental part of the banking union package.[34] This Agreement was signed by 26 Member States (all except the UK and Sweden) and entered into force on 1 January 2016. The original Commission proposal for a Europe-wide banking resolution mechanism was split in two by the Council, with one part (the resolution mechanism itself) forming the object of an EU regulation, whereas the other part (the building of a fund to be used for resolution operations) was left to be created by the Member States by means of a separate international agreement. This split was requested by Germany for a mixture of legal and political reasons which were not explained in a transparent way,[35] and it has been criticized in the literature.[36]

---

[33] On the political and legal circumstances explaining this recourse to extra-EU international agreements in the context of the euro crisis, see Bruno De Witte, 'Using International Law in the Euro Crisis – Causes and Consequences', ARENA Working Paper No. 4 (2013), http://www.sv.uio.no/arena/english/research/publications/arena-publications/workingpapers/working-papers2013/wp4-13.pdf; among the many critical assessments, highlighting the threat to the EU's institutional integrity, see Angelos Dimopoulos, 'The Use of International Law as a Tool for Enhancing Governance in the Eurozone and its Impact on EU Institutional Integrity', in Maurice Adams, Federico Fabbrini and Pierre Larouche (eds), *The Constitutionalization of European Budgetary Constraints* (Hart 2014), 41.

[34] Agreement on the Transfer and Mutualisation of Contributions to the Single Resolution Fund, [2014] Council doc. 8457/14.

[35] In its press release on the day of the signature of the agreement, the Council enigmatically stated that 'using an intergovernmental agreement to establish rules on the transfer and mutualisation of contributions is intended to provide maximum legal certainty. The Council decided on this approach in December [2013], given legal and constitutional concerns in certain member states'. Council press release, Member States sign agreement on bank resolution fund, [2014] 10088/14. For some clarification of those 'concerns', see Alberto de Gregorio Merino, 'Reflexiones preliminares sobre la unión bancaria', (2014) 33 *Revista General de Derecho Europeo* 1, 7–8.

[36] See the critical discussion of the Agreement: Federico Fabbrini, 'On Banks, Courts and International Law – The Intergovernmental Agreement on the Single Resolution Fund in Context' (2014) 21 *Maastricht Journal of European and Comparative Law* 444; see also Jean-Victor Louis, 'La difficile naissance du mécanisme européen de résolution des banques' (2014) *Cahiers de droit européen* 7.

A further international agreement closely connected with the functioning of the EU, but in a very different domain, was signed on 19 February 2013 between 25 Member States (all except Croatia, Poland and Spain), namely the Agreement on a Unified Patent Court.[37] That court's main task is to adjudicate an EU law instrument, namely the Regulation on the creation of unitary patent protection, which is itself, as mentioned above, the outcome of an enhanced cooperation initiative. There was no legal reason why this adjudication task could not have been entrusted to the Court of Justice (or a newly created specialized intellectual property court within it), but the 'patent community' apparently persuaded the Member State governments that it would be preferable to create a separate and allegedly more expert court instead.[38] The Agreement on the Unified Patent Court will enter into force as soon as it is ratified by 13 of its Contracting Parties,[39] which will lead to a curious case of 'enhanced cooperation within enhanced cooperation':[40] 25 out of the 28 Member States are bound by the patent regulation, but a smaller number of those could end up participating in the adjudication mechanism of that regulation, depending on whether or not they will ratify the Agreement.

4. CONCLUSION: TOOLS OF FLEXIBILITY OR SEEDS OF DISINTEGRATION?

The existence of a controlled system for differentiation between Member States has now become a stable characteristic of EU law. As rightly noted by Rosas and Armati, it is 'one of the defining features of the EU, setting it apart from established nation states. It is crucial to a description of

---

[37] Agreement on a Unified Patent Court, OJ 2013, C175/1. For a discussion of the very idiosyncratic nature of this (still to be created) international court, see Manuel Desantes Real, 'Le paquet européen des brevets, paradigme du chemin à rebours: de la logique institutionnelle à la logique intergouvernementale' (2013) *Cahiers de droit européen* 577, 654–61; and Franklin Dehousse, 'La juridiction unifiée du brevet: le nouvel oxymoron du droit européen', in Inge Govaere et al (eds), *The European Union in the World. Essays in Honour of Marc Maresceau* (Brill 2014) 259.

[38] See Dehousse (n. 37) 269.

[39] Article 89(1) of the Agreement. Those 13 states must include Germany, France and the UK, which is yet another form of status differentiation between EU Member States. Those three countries are coyly referred to, in the Article, as 'the three Member States in which the highest number of European patents' have effect.

[40] Desantes Real (n. 37), 641.

what the Union legal order is'.[41] Although it has rightly been observed that territorial differentiation is more prevalent in what used to be 'core state powers', namely money, migration, criminal law, and defence,[42] forms of flexibility have also spread into more traditional areas of EU competence, such as internal market law. Nor is the commonly used term of 'multi-speed integration' appropriate any more, in view of the fact that the Member States have ceased to pursue common goals at a different pace. Rather, they have fundamentally different views of the appropriate degree and scope of integration, and these different views are considered by the others to be both legitimate and durable.

Indeed, each of the elements of the flexibility design seems likely to last and to flourish. First, there is no reason to think that the major *opt-out areas*, namely EMU, immigration and criminal law, will become more uniform any time soon. In addition, now that *enhanced cooperation* has been experimented with a few times, one can expect it to become a more regularly used instrument in the EU's law-making toolbox, in particular in order to circumvent single country veto positions in policy matters where the unanimity rule applies. Thirdly, recourse to *international agreements* between groups of Member States outside the EU legal framework has been confirmed to be a valid option, particularly through its use in the context of the euro crisis, with the adoption of the ESM treaty and Fiscal Compact. Finally, we might see a continued and increasing use of the omnipresent *micro-flexibility* that has been part of Community law for decades, namely the recourse to minimum harmonization, to soft law and to tailor-made derogations.[43]

---

[41] Allan Rosas and Lorna Armati, *EU Constitutional Law: An Introduction* (Hart Publishing 2010) 98. Similarly, for the author of a recent Italian textbook of EU law, variable geometry has become one of the three fundamental characteristics of the EU legal order: Jacques Ziller, *Diritto delle politiche e delle istituzioni dell'Unione europea* (Il Mulino 2013) 283 ff.

[42] Berthold Rittberger, Dirk Leuffen and Frank Schimmelfennig, 'Differentiated Integration of Core State Powers', in Philipp Genschel and Markus Jachtenfuchs (eds), *Beyond the Regulatory Polity? The European Integration of Core State Powers* (Oxford University Press 2014) 189.

[43] For an earlier discussion of this kind of differentiation in secondary EU law, see e.g. Gráinne de Búrca, 'Differentiation within the "Core"? The Case of the Internal Market' in Gráinne de Búrca and Joanne Scott (eds), *Constitutional Change in the EU – From Uniformity to Flexibility?* (Hart Publishing 2000) 133 and Ellen Vos, 'Differentiation, Harmonisation and Governance' in Bruno De Witte, Dominik Hanf and Ellen Vos (eds), *The Many Faces of Differentiation in EU Law* (Intersentia 2001) 145.

As a result, the contours of the EU legal order have become rather fuzzy. In principle, there are firm criteria to determine whether a legal norm belongs to the EU legal order or not. Thus, measures of enhanced cooperation are part of EU law, although they are binding only upon, and within, the Member States that participated in their adoption. Similarly, legal measures from which some countries opt out are also part of the EU legal order, despite their limited geographical scope. Also, what is still called 'Schengen law' colloquially has become regular EU law after the incorporation of the Schengen regime in Amsterdam. On the contrary, international agreements concluded by a limited set of Member States (such as the ESM treaty and the Fiscal Compact) are not part of the EU legal order, and the Court of Justice cannot review the decisions adopted by organs set up under such an agreement. However, the institutional practice has led to a number of intertwinements between organs and legal norms of EU law and non-EU law. Examples of this fuzziness are the fact that EU institutions are being 'borrowed' by the Member States when setting up and operating an *inter se* regime, as is the case with the European Stability Mechanism;[44] and the fact that the entry into force of norms of secondary EU law is conditioned on the prior entry into force of a satellite agreement, as we have seen in recent years with the unified patent regime and the banking resolution mechanism.

If the formal criteria for deciding what belongs to the EU legal order still function well, the content of that EU legal order presents a very unusual shape. Its degree of fragmentation, in terms of the participation of states in decision-making and of the applicability of legal norms across the EU territory, is rather unique and sets the EU firmly apart from the federal constitutional systems which it resembles in other respects. The Court's old ideal of EU legal rules being 'fully applicable at the same time and with identical effects over the whole territory of the Community'[45] has become unattainable. This, in itself, may not be such a great loss; but the easy and almost insouciant recourse to variable geometry also comes with a lack of transparency, complicated accountability mechanisms, and a neglect of intra-state solidarity, and these are

---

[44] This 'borrowing' of the EU institutions to accomplish non-EU tasks is legally controversial. See discussion by Paul Craig, '*Pringle* and Use of EU Institutions outside the EU Legal Framework: Foundations, Procedure and Substance' (2013) 9 *European Constitutional Law Review* 273; and Steve Peers, 'Towards a New Form of EU Law? The Use of EU Institutions outside the EU Legal Framework' (2013) 9 *European Constitutional Law Review* 37.

[45] See the citation from *Commission v Italy* in the introduction of this chapter.

serious challenges for the constitutional integrity of the EU. There is thus a danger that the mechanisms of differentiation, rather than serving as useful instruments of flexibility, may turn into contributory factors in the disintegration of the EU.

REFERENCES

Beach D, *The Dynamics of European Integration: Why and When EU Institutions Matter* (Palgrave Macmillan 2005).

Bosse-Platière I, 'Annexes aux Traités européens et différenciation', in Barbou des Places S (ed.), *Aux marges du traité: déclarations, protocoles et annexes aux traités européens* (Bruylant 2011) 115–32.

Bribosia H, 'Les nouvelles formes de flexibilité en matière de défense', in Amato G, Bribosia H and De Witte B (eds), *Genesis and Destiny of the European Constitution* (Bruylant 2007) 835.

Craig P, '*Pringle* and Use of EU Institutions outside the EU Legal Framework: Foundations, Procedure and Substance' (2013) 9 *European Constitutional Law Review* 2, 263–84.

Cremona M, 'Enhanced Cooperation and the Common Foreign and Security and Defence Policy' (2009) EUI Working Papers LAW 2009/21.

Curtin D, 'The Constitutional Structure of the Union: A Europe of Bits and Pieces' (1993) 30 *Common Market Law Review* 1, 17–69.

De Búrca G, 'Differentiation within the "Core"? The Case of the Internal Market' in De Búrca G and Scott J (eds), *Constitutional Change in the EU – From Uniformity to Flexibility?* (Hart Publishing 2000) 133–72.

De Gregorio Merino A, 'Reflexiones preliminares sobre la unión bancaria' (2014) 33 *Revista General de Derecho Europeo* 1, 7–8.

Dehousse F, 'La juridiction unifiée du brevet: le nouvel oxymoron du droit européen', in Inge Govaere et al (eds), *The European Union in the World. Essays in Honour of Marc Maresceau* (Brill 2014) 259–74.

Desantes Real M, 'Le paquet européen des brevets, paradigme du chemin à rebours: de la logique institutionnelle à la logique intergouvernementale' (2013) 49 *Cahiers de droit européen* 3, 577–670.

De Witte B, 'Using International Law in the Euro Crisis – Causes and Consequences', ARENA Working Paper No. 4 (2013), http://www.sv.uio.no/arena/english/research/publications/arena-publications/workingpapers/working-papers2013/wp4-13.pdf.

Dimopoulos A, 'The Use of International Law as a Tool for Enhancing Governance in the Eurozone and its Impact on EU Institutional Integrity', in Adams M, Fabbrini F and Larouche P (eds), *The Constitutionalization of European Budgetary Constraints* (Hart 2014) 41–64.

Fabbrini F, 'On Banks, Courts and International Law – The Intergovernmental Agreement on the Single Resolution Fund in Context' (2014) 21 *Maastricht Journal of European and Comparative Law* 3, 444–63.

Gaja G, 'How Flexible is Flexibility under the Amsterdam Treaty?' (1998) 35 *Common Market Law Review* 4, 855–70.

Gomis B, 'Franco-British Defence and Security Treaties: Entente While it Lasts?', Chatham House Programme Paper ISP PP 2001/01, March 2011.
Kortenberg H [a pseudonym], 'Closer Cooperation in the Treaty of Amsterdam' (1998) 35 *Common Market Law Review* 4, 833–54.
Louis Jean-Victor, 'La difficile naissance du mécanisme européen de résolution des banques' (2014) 50 *Cahiers de droit européen* 1, 7–20.
Maganza G, 'Jean-Claude Piris, un seul homme pour cinq traités' in *A Man for all Treaties – Liber Amicorum en l'honneur de Jean-Claude Piris* (Bruylant 2012) 399–420.
Major J, 'Europe, A Future that Works' (William and Mary Lecture, Leiden Town Hall), *Agence Europe*, No 6312, 10 September 1994.
Monar J, 'Justice and Home Affairs in the Treaty of Amsterdam: Reform at the Price of Fragmentation' (1998) 23 *European Law Review,* 320–26.
Papagianni G, 'Flexibility in Justice and Home Affairs: An Old Phenomenon Taking New Forms' in De Witte B, Hanf D and Vos E (eds), *The Many Faces of Differentiation in EU Law* (Intersentia 2001) 101–28.
Peers S, 'Towards a New Form of EU Law? The Use of EU Institutions outside the EU Legal Framework' (2013) 9 *European Constitutional Law Review* 1, 37–72.
Peers S, 'The UK Opts back in to the European Arrest Warrant – and other EU Criminal Law' (2014) *EU Law Analysis*, http://eulawanalysis.blogspot.co.uk.
Phinnemore D, *The Treaty of Lisbon – Origins and Negotiation* (Palgrave Macmillan 2013).
Rittberger B, Leuffen D and Schimmelfennig F, 'Differentiated Integration of Core State Powers', in Genschel P and Jachtenfuchs M (eds), *Beyond the Regulatory Polity? The European Integration of Core State Powers* (Oxford University Press 2014) 189–210.
Rosas A and Armati L, *EU Constitutional Law: An Introduction* (Hart Publishing 2010).
Schutte J, 'UK v EU: A Continuous Test Match' (2011) 34 *Fordham International Law Journal* 1346-1376.
Stubb A, *Negotiating Flexibility in the European Union. Amsterdam, Nice and Beyond* (Palgrave Macmillan 2002).
Vos E, 'Differentiation, Harmonisation and Governance' in De Witte B, Hanf D and Vos E (eds), *The Many Faces of Differentiation in EU Law* (Intersentia 2001) 145–79.
Ziller J, *Diritto delle politiche e delle istituzioni dell'Unione europea* (Il Mulino 2013).

2. Competing models for understanding differentiated integration

Daniel Thym

1. INTRODUCTION

Debates about differentiated integration are among the rituals of European integration. Whenever the EU enters a critical stage, politicians and academic observers evoke the option of 'multiple speeds', 'concentric circles' or related terminology and call upon some Member States to proceed towards closer integration without the participation of others. More recent arguments about differentiated integration replicate earlier debates and, yet, there is something novel about them. It is true that the experience with various forms of differentiated integration over the past two decades has been fairly positive: defence policy, justice and home affairs and the generic mechanism for enhanced cooperation demonstrate that differentiated integration within the EU framework may proceed rather smoothly in practice. Also, the crisis of monetary union does not originate primarily in the asymmetric non-participation of some Member States but in the structural deficits of both the Treaty design and its implementation. This shows that differentiated integration can support the integration process.

What is new about recent developments, however, is the pertinence and visibility of differentiated integration as a result of the euro crisis. It is no longer a peripheral occurrence, but it takes centre stage in legal and political debates. The assessment of the constitutional implications of differentiated integration has become a vital question for the future of Europe: Does it undermine the supranational rule of law? Is Union law capable of domesticating 'satellite treaties' outside the EU framework? What are the consequences for the institutional balance and the role of Member States? In addressing these questions, this chapter will defend the proposition that legal difficulties can be contained – both in the case of intra-EU differentiation and satellite treaties under public international law (3). Differentiated integration may stabilise the rule of law by accommodating internal tensions and heterogeneities, while it may, at the same time, undermine the legitimatory infrastructure of the European project (4).

2. THE CONCEPT OF DIFFERENTIATED INTEGRATION AND ITS REALISATION

Whenever the EU enters a critical stage, politicians and academic observers usually evoke 'multiple speeds', 'concentric circles' or related terminology and call upon some Member States to proceed towards closer integration. This section distinguishes three conceptual ideal types underlying these debates: 'multiple speeds', 'federal core Europe' and 'flexibility à la carte' (2.1). Most existing Treaty provisions on differentiated integration are not a clear-cut realisation of the three concepts. They regularly pursue limited ambitions and they stem from political compromises at intergovernmental conferences. They are pragmatic instruments, which provide for the asymmetric realisation of specific policy projects among a limited number of Member States, thereby allowing the Union to move ahead in spite of fundamental disagreement about the future course of the European project (2.2).

2.1 Political Debate

Our generation is not the first to discuss differentiation. In political and academic circles, the topic was discussed prominently in the late 1970s, in the early 2000s and, more recently, during the euro crisis. Throughout these debates, we may identify three ideal types of models of European integration that proponents of differentiation pursue. They are ideal types in a Weberian sense, are modelled upon individual opinions as real-life phenomena and accentuate certain features for analytical purposes. In this chapter, I shall distinguish between three ideal types: 'multiple speeds', 'federal core Europe' and 'flexibility à la carte'. They are not mutually exclusive and the positions by individual actors will often reflect a blend, combining elements of different ideal types. Nevertheless, their juxtaposition demonstrates that behind the façade of rather pragmatic Treaty provisions on differentiated integration lurks a fundamental disagreement about the course of European integration.

2.1.1 Multiple speeds: reflection of economic differences

The debate started in earnest during the 'eurosclerosis' of the 1970s, when proponents of further integration became frustrated with the lacklustre advance of the integration project and perceived multiple speeds as an elegant way out. In November 1974, during a speech in Paris, the German Chancellor Willy Brandt observed that 'stark differences in the economic situation argue against the mechanic equal treatment of the Member States' rights and obligations which might seriously impede the cohesion of the nine members.'[1] One year later, the Belgian Prime Minister Leo Tindemans followed along this path in his 'Report on European Union' to the European Council, in which he presented the blueprint for the realisation of monetary union: 'It is impossible at the present time to submit a credible programme of action, if it is deemed absolutely necessary that … all stages should be reached by all the States at the same time.'[2] Both were careful to present the 'new approach' as a response to objective differences. Instead of 'permanently decoupling'[3] different groupings of Member States, 'it is only the timescales for achievement which vary'.[4] Their approach is about a Europe of 'multiple speeds', since all Member States will be bound by the final objective, whose realisation is phased in gradually.[5]

It is a characteristic feature of 'multiple speeds' to conceive differentiation as a transitional phenomenon in response to allegedly objective distinctions. Economic discrepancies, not political will, are meant to guide the distinction among Member States. At the time, this reflected the dominant vision of European integration. The law of the common market was defined by an inbuilt aversion to protectionism and was often presented as a depoliticised economic project.[6] In a system based on the

---

[1] Willy Brandt, 'Rede vor der Organisation Française du Mouvement Européen' (1975) *Europa-Archiv* D33-8, D36 (own translation).

[2] Leo Tindemans, 'European Union. Report to the European Council' (1976) Suppl. 1, *Bulletin of the E.C.*, 20.

[3] Brandt (n 1) D36.

[4] Tindemans (n 2) 21.

[5] For similar positions see Ralf Dahrendorf, 'A Third Europe?', Jean Monnet Lecture at the EU, 26 November 1979; Eberhard Grabitz and Bernd Langeheine, 'Legal Problems Related to a Proposed "Two-Tier System" of Integration within the European Community' (1981) CML Rev 334; and Jean-Claude Piris, *The Future of Europe. Towards a Two-Speed EU?* (Cambridge University Press 2012) 66–7.

[6] See the overview by Armin von Bogdandy, 'A Bird's Eye View on the Science of European Law: Structures, Debates and Development Projects of Basic Research on the Law of the European Union in a German Perspective' (2000) 6(3) ELJ 227–8.

elimination of barriers to trade through harmonisation and mutual recognition, the invocation of national interests or differences appeared illegitimate. Both the depoliticised vision of the integration project and the aversion to protectionism explain why the project of multiple speeds accepts differentiation in response to allegedly objective differences. Most academic commentators assumed that European primary law required derogations to be temporary exceptions, which would have to be phased out, reflecting the approximation of economic realities.[7]

The concept of multiple speeds was put into practice in the Treaty of Maastricht with the gradual realisation of the monetary union on the basis of the convergence criteria, which assess Member States' macroeconomic performance.[8] Similarly, transitional periods in Accession Treaties, such as the phased realisation of the free movement of workers, remain limited in time and may be perceived as an expression of multiple speeds.[9] By contrast, the British and the Danish opt-out of monetary union follow a different rationale. Even if they fulfil the convergence criteria, both the UK and Denmark retain the freedom to 'notify the Council whether [they] intend to move to the third stage [of monetary union]'.[10] There is no guarantee that any of them will ever catch up with the avant-garde; their choice, whether to do so, is political in nature. The

---

[7] See Claus-Dieter Ehlermann, 'How Flexible is Community Law?' (1984) 82(5/6) MLR 1291–2; Grabitz and Langeheine (n 5) 38–44; and, today, Christine Guillard, *L'Intégration différenciée dans l'Union européenne* (Bruylant 2007) 324-352; see also, on the original art. 226(2)(3) EEC, Case C-19/07 *Paul Chevassus – Marche v Groupe Danon* [2008] ECLI:EU:C:2008:23, Case C-212/96 *Paul Chevassus-Marche v Conseil régional de la Réunion* [1998] ECLI:EU:C:1998:68: 'It follows that the Council cannot, on any view, authorise a system of general or systematic exemptions' (para. 37); Community institutions may 'authorise only strictly necessary derogations for limited periods' (para. 41).

[8] Cf, art. 121(1) TEC as amended by the Maastricht Treaty (OJ [1992] C224/36) and today's art. 140(1) TFEU, which are complemented by Protocol (No. 13) on the Convergence Criteria (OJ [2008] C115/281) and Protocol (No. 12) on the excessive deficit procedure (OJ [2008] C115/279), which establishes the 3 per cent resp. 60 per cent threshold for annual/accumulated public deficits; for detail see also Erich Vranes, 'The "Internal" External Relations of EMU' (2000) 6 *Columbia Journal of European Law* 364–72.

[9] See Alan Dashwood, 'Position Paper' in Alan Dashwood (ed.), *Reviewing Maastricht, Issues for the 1996 IGC* (Sweet & Maxwell 1996) 159; and Ulrich Becker, *EU-Erweiterung und differenzierte Integration* (Nomos 1999) 29; they were proposed first by the Commission Communication, Enlargement of the Community, COM(78) 190 of 24 April 1978 Suppl. 2, Bulletin of the E.C.

[10] Art. 1 of Protocol (No. 15) on Certain Provisions Relating to the United Kingdom of Great Britain and Northern Ireland (OJ [2008] C115/284); similarly,

domestic decision to let the people decide in national referenda underlines this political character. Their opt-out is not about multiple speeds in response to real or perceived economic differences but rather about political choices.

2.1.2 Federal core Europe

In the early 2000s, the political debate about differentiated integration gained momentum. Politicians assumed that the asymmetric introduction of the euro and increasing heterogeneities after forthcoming enlargements would result in further differentiation. Moreover, continued reticence against closer integration in the UK and the negative referenda on the Treaties of Maastricht and Nice in Denmark and Ireland indicated that the unanimity requirement for Treaty change would be difficult to achieve. As a result, the 'core Europe'[11] idea became popular among French and German politicians. Their motivation was to retain the momentum in support of closer integration and to forge ahead with those who are willing to do so. Instead of generally re-orientating the European project according to the national interest, the integration method should be salvaged by granting an opt-out to certain Member States,[12] thereby moving towards 'ever closer union'[13] in line with the ultimate objective of the original Schuman declaration, which presented the Coal and Steel Community as 'a first concrete foundation of a European federation'.[14]

Protocol (No. 16) on Certain Provisions Relating to Denmark (OJ [2008] C115/287).

[11] See the initial proposal by two conservative German politicians: Wolfgang Schäuble (then Minister of the Interior) and Karl Lamers (President of the Parliament's foreign affairs committee), *Überlegungen zur europäischen Politik* (CDU 1994), 7: 'hard core of the five (Germany, France, Benelux)'.

[12] The orientation according to common values and the supranational integration method mirror constructivist and neo-institutional accounts of integration theory in political science; see Dirk Leuffen et al, *Differentiated Integration. Explaining Variation in the European Union* (Routledge 2013) 77–83 and 99–103.

[13] Recital 1 of the Preamble of the original EEC Treaty of 1957 and the present TFEU.

[14] Robert Schuman, Declaration of 9 May 1950 (own translation); the federal objective was mentioned explicitly by Schäuble and Lamers (n 11) 5; Jacques Delors, 'Ma vision d'une Fédération des États-nations' (Juillet/Août 2000) Le Monde des Débats, 5; and Joschka Fischer, 'Vom Staatenverbund zur Föderation' in Walter Hallstein-Institut (ed.), *Verfassungsrechtliche Reformen zur Erweiterung der Europäischen Union* (Nomos 2000) 171, para. 56.

In a wider sense, the Common Market may in itself be understood as an expression of the 'core Europe' idea, since it forged economic bonds beyond the regular obligations of the international trading system of the time.[15] Similarly, the six founding members had indirectly rejected earlier attempts to promote European integration within the framework of the Council of Europe by establishing the European Communities as an avant-garde.[16] If all that is correct, the 'core Europe' project tries to realise long-standing objectives in changing political environments. The German Finance Minister, Wolfgang Schäuble, reiterated this approach during the euro crisis: 'In order to achieve further integration, we will have to depend on pragmatic – i.e., suboptimal, but feasible – solutions, including differentiated integration ... Such second-best-solutions are suboptimal, but they are better than inertia and they will often pave the way for more coherent solutions at a later stage.'[17]

Notwithstanding differences between positions,[18] the 'federal core Europe' has surfaced regularly. After the initial proposal by Wolfgang Schäuble and Karl Lamers in the aftermath of the Maastricht Treaty,[19] it played a prominent role in the debate about institutional reform in the early 2000s, which paved the way for the constitutional reform process, when the German Foreign Minister Joschka Fischer and the French President Jacques Chirac supported a 'centre of gravity'[20] or 'pioneer groups'.[21] A few years later, the Belgian Prime Minister Guy Verhofstadt took up the idea as a possible way out of the impasse after the failure of

---

15 Cf, art. XXIV sect. 5 GATT 1947.

16 For a historic account see Heinrich Schneider, 'Kerneuropa – ein aktuelles Stichwort und seine Bedeutung' (2004) 12 Journal für Rechtspolitik 136–61.

17 Wolfgang Schäuble, 'Institutioneller Wandel und Europäische Einigung' *Frankfurter Allgemeine Zeitung* (Frankfurt, 12 January 2013) 14 referring to the twofold compromise of (1) international satellite treaties instead of supranational law and (2) the non-participation of some Member States.

18 On different 'core Europe' theses, see Daniel Thym, *Ungleichzeitigkeit und Europäisches Verfassungsrecht* (Nomos 2004) 28-38 (<http://www.ungleichzeitigkeit.de>); the chapter by Bruno De Witte in this volume; and Claus Giering, 'Vertiefung und Differenzierung' (1997) Integration 72–83.

19 See Schäuble and Lamers (n 11).

20 Fischer (n 14), who borrowed central elements from the 'Quermonne Report' of the French Commissariat Général du Plan, *L'Union européenne en quête d'institutions légitimes et efficaces* (Documentation française 2000).

21 Jacques Chirac, 'Notre Europe. Discours devant le Bundestag' *Le Monde* (Paris, 28 June 2000).

the Constitutional Treaty.[22] During the euro crisis, the idea became pertinent when the reform of both macroeconomic governance and the stability and growth pact focused on the euro area and were complemented by the ESM Treaty and by the Fiscal Compact outside the EU framework.[23]

Proposals on how to implement the 'federal core Europe' idea are often pragmatic. They usually either focus upon an activation of the general mechanism for enhanced cooperation, support Treaty change in order to deepen integration (in combination with opt-outs for reticent Member States) or call for the adoption of international satellite treaties outside the EU framework.[24] Occasionally, proposals are more radical – such as the call by Fischer for a 'revolutionary renewal' among some Member States beyond the present Treaty regime.[25] Also, international satellite treaties can have diverse functions in practice; while supporting and buttressing EU integration politically, they can also be a mechanism to sideline the supranational institutions.[26] Such ambiguity does not render the juxtaposition of analytical ideal types irrelevant. The principled idea to move towards an (often vague) vision of federal Europe distinguishes the 'federal core Europe' model ideal typically from 'flexibility à la carte', even if the specific proposal often combines elements of both models.

2.1.3 Flexibility à la carte

Advocates of 'federal core Europe' and 'flexibility à la carte' may agree on the way forward (differentiation), but they disagree fundamentally in their understanding of the driving forces and the ultimate objective of the European project. While the 'core Europe' camp pursues an (often vague) vision of a *finalité fédérale*, supporters of 'flexibility à la carte' want to orientate European integration at the national interest. Most prominently,

---

22 See Guy Verhofstadt, *Die vereinigten Staaten von Europa* (Grenz-Echo Verlag 2007); and, among the academic observers, Buno De Witte, 'The Process of Ratification of the Constitutional Treaty and the Crisis Options' (2004) 16 EUI Working Paper Law.

23 Prominent support for differentiation was voiced by Schäuble (n 17); Piris (n 5); and Jürgen Habermas, *Zur Verfassung Europas – Ein Essay* (Suhrkamp 2011) 75–82.

24 See section 3.2 below.

25 See Fischer (n 14) paras 41, 47; arguably, it was a rhetorical trick to forge a compromise on the way ahead within the EU framework, see Thym (n 18) 36–8; and De Witte (n 18).

26 Cf, the interpretation of the Fiscal Compact by Nicolas Sarkozy, 'Entretien: Le sommet de Bruxelles' *Le Monde* (Paris, 12 December 2011).

British conservative politicians have voiced their support for the underlying rationale of 'flexibility à la carte'. Due to negative connotations, they do not usually use the 'à la carte' vocabulary and instead speak of 'flexibility'[27] or 'network Europe'[28] (I use the term nonetheless to emphasise that the national interest is guiding principle[29]). Their core impetus is to reject the federal vision and to emphasise a principled freedom of the Member States to decide upon the degree of participation in the EU, mirroring intergovernmental international relations theory.[30] The Union appears as a forum of international cooperation, in which Member States may participate if it suits their mutual interests or from which they may abstain if that is not the case.

It was first formulated by the British Prime Minister John Major as a constructive proposal on the way forward after domestic struggles over the ratification of the Treaty of Maastricht. He considered that it was not right 'to characterise Britain's opposition to some policies as anti-European'; the vision of the founding fathers 'was proved right for its age. But it is outdated. It will not do now. We must all adjust our vision.'[31] His successor David Cameron underlined the renunciation of federal objectives by suggesting abandoning the objective of an 'ever closer union'.[32] He could convince the European Council that the EU would have embarked on a move in this direction in case the British had voted in favour of remaining in the European Union.[33] Pleas for more

---

27 John Major, 'Speech at Leiden University' (Leiden, 7 September 1994, <http://www.johnmajor.co.uk/page1124.html>); David Cameron, 'Speech at Bloomberg' (London, 23 January 2013, <https://www.gov.uk/government/speeches/eu-speech-at-bloomberg>).

28 The former party leader William Hague, 'Harmonization or Flexibility' in Martin Rosenbaum (ed.), *Britain and Europe* (Oxford University Press 2001) 287–92; and the former shadow foreign minister Francis Maude, 'Networks and Nations' in Walter Hallstein-Institut (ed.), *Die Reform der europäischen Institutionen* (Nomos 2002) 27–40.

29 Note that supporters of core Europe do not regularly employ the adjective 'federal' either.

30 See, in the context of political theory, Leuffen et al (n 12) ch 2; among academic observers, see Giandomenico Majone, *Europe as the Would-be World Power* (Cambridge University Press 2009) Ch. 8.

31 Major (n 27).

32 Cameron (n 27); the European Council of 26/27 June 2014, Conclusions, EUCO 79/14, para. 28 noted that 'the concept of ever closer union allows for different paths of integration for different countries'.

33 The political arrangements in preparation for a post-referendum settlement according to European Council Conclusions, doc. EUCO 1/16 of 19 February 2016, Annex 1 listed a Decision of the Heads of State or Government,

flexibility are usually combined with a commitment to stand by existing obligations, especially in the field of the internal market.[34] In other policy areas, such as justice and home affairs or social policy, Member States should have more freedom to participate or not: 'We believe in a flexible union of free member states who share treaties and institutions … This vision of flexibility and co-operation is not the same as those who want to build an ever closer political union – but it is just as valid.'[35] Like the proponents of a 'federal core Europe', the supporters of 'flexibility à la carte' often refrain from designating precise scenarios for future implementation. However, the influence on the British opt-outs is palpable, especially in justice and home affairs.

2.2 Pragmatism of the Treaty Regime

Political concepts about integration at multiple speeds have rarely been translated without modification into specific Treaty provisions. Existing examples of differentiation usually stem from political compromises at intergovernmental conferences and were regarded as pragmatic instruments that provide for the asymmetric realisation of specific policy projects among a limited number of Member States. In the analysis of existing expressions of differentiation, this chapter concentrates on a specific legal pattern: differentiation in situations of general non-application of certain legal acts to one or more Member States. By focusing on this specific phenomenon, this chapter evades the pitfall of an overtly wide understanding of differentiation, which would cover various forms of national discretion in primary and secondary Union law and thereby be too broad to allow for accurate conclusions.

If we adopt an expansive reading of differentiation as based on the differential treatment of Member States in primary or secondary law, multiple instruments of flexibility have been an integral part of the European legal order since its inception. Primary law contains safeguard clauses allowing Member States to maintain or introduce more stringent

---

meeting within the European Council, concerning a New Settlement for the United Kingdom within the European Union, sect. C had promised to enshrine in primary law the statement that the objective of 'ever closer union' does not apply to the United Kingdom; the decision would have been activated after a vote to remain in the European Union, which never took place.

[34] Cf Major (n 27); Maude (n 28) paras 41–42; Cameron (n 27).

[35] Cameron (n 27).

national laws[36] and it accepts national derogations from the fundamental freedoms.[37] Numerous protocols attached to the EU Treaties grant manifold exceptions and privileges[38] and are complemented by differential treatment in secondary legislation, among which the 'British exemption' from the Working Time Directive may be the most prominent example.[39] Such a wide understanding of differentiation would embrace central aspects of single market rules.[40]

Flexible differentiation of the European legal order extends even further, when we broaden our view to the level of national implementation and application. From the point of view of the citizens and companies concerned, the late or imperfect transposition of directives, national differences in the implementation of framework rules and the factual non-application of European law by national authorities may result in differentiated realities on the ground.[41] That is not the end of the list. With regard to third states, association agreements may provide a mode for asymmetric participation in certain EU policies, since these states 'must, at least to a certain extent, take part in the Community system'[42] – or it may even be argued that national constitutional caveats on *ultra vires* acts result in differentiation.[43] As a matter of principle,

---

36 See, for example, arts 114(4)–(10), 153(4) and 193 TFEU and the chapter by Ellen Vos and Maria Weimer in this volume.

37 Case C-36/02 *Omega* [2004] ECLI:EU:C:2004:614, para. 31 recognises: 'specific circumstances which may justify recourse to the concept of public policy may vary from one country to another'.

38 One 'minor' example: the 1992 Protocol on the Acquisition of Property in Denmark.

39 Cf, art. 22 of Directive 2003/88 (OJ [2003] L299/9).

40 See Gráinne de Búrca, 'Differentiation within the "Core"?' in Gráinne de Búrca and Joanne Scott (eds), *Constitutional Change in the EU: From Uniformity to Flexibility?* (Hart 2000) 133–72.

41 See the chapter by Mark Dawson in this volume.

42 Case C-12/86 *Demirel* [1987] ECLI:EU:C:1987:400, para. 9; see also Sandra Lavenex, 'Concentric Circles of Flexible "EUropean" Integration' (2011) 9 *Comparative European Politics* 372–93; association was considered, from the very beginning, to provide a bridge between the EEC and states, such as the UK, which did not originally want to join the supranational avant-garde; cf. the first Commission President Hallstein, *Der unvollendete Bundesstaat* (Econ 1969) 209–12.

43 See the German Federal Constitutional Court (*Bundesverfassungsgericht*), judgment of 30 June 2009, 2 BvE 2/08 *et al*, *Treaty of Lisbon*, BVerfGE 123, 267, para. 340: 'if exceptionally, and under special and narrow conditions, the Federal Constitutional Court declares EU law inapplicable in Germany'.

there is nothing wrong with adopting such an expansive understanding, which, as a result, would embrace various policy areas and instruments.

Moreover, Member States have always cooperated on the basis of international law outside the EU framework. Such 'old flexibility'[44] concerns international 'satellite' treaties which were particularly prominent in the early years, when the Communities had limited competencies. Many examples of complementary treaties, such as the WEU, the Schengen Agreements, the Brussels Convention or the specific case of Maastricht's Agreement on Social Policy, have in the meantime been incorporated into the supranational legal order; they originally served as laboratories for closer cooperation.[45] It is widely known that international satellite treaties gained new momentum during the euro crisis with the ESM Treaty and the Fiscal Compact.[46]

Academic writing has proposed various systematic approaches to analyse and structure the aforementioned variety of flexibility instruments: In 1984, Eberhard Grabitz coined the generic term differentiated integration (*abgestufte Integration*),[47] which Alexander Stubb later broke down to the triad of differentiation along the dimensions of time, space and substance.[48] In his monograph, Filip Tuytschaever specified various degrees of 'actual and potential', 'inter-state and intra-state', 'temporary and non-temporary', and 'general and specific' differentiation.[49] From a legal point of view, all these examples of flexibility have one thing in common: as a matter of principle, most legal instruments concerned apply to all Member States with only their legal effects being suspended or modified, either in law or factually, with regard to some Member

---

[44] Bruno De Witte, 'Old Flexibility' in de Búrca and Scott (n 40 31–58).

[45] See section 3.2 below and, on the specific case of Social Policy Agreement, Philippa Watson, 'Social Policy after Maastricht' (1993) 30 CML Rev 481–513.

[46] See Steve Peers, 'Towards a New Form of EU Law?: The Use of EU Institutions outside the EU Legal Framework' (2013) 9 *European Constitutional Law Review* 37–72; and Robert Uerpmann-Wittzack, 'Völkerrecht als Ausweichordnung – Am Beispiel der Euro-Rettung' in Armin Hatje (ed.), *Die Einheit des Unionsrechts im Zeichen der Krise* (Nomos 2013) 49–60.

[47] Eberhard Grabitz (ed.), *Abgestufte Integration* (N.P. Engel 1984).

[48] See Alexander Stubb, 'A Categorisation of Differentiated Integration' (1996) 34 JCMS 283, 287–8; this categorisation has been taken up by various authors.

[49] See Filip Tuytschaever, *Differentiation in European Union Law* (Hart 1999); and, similarly, Guillard (n 7) 24–8; and the contributions to Bruno De Witte, Dominik Hanf and Ellen Vos (eds), *The Many Faces of Differentiation in EU Law* (Intersentia 2001).

States. Such outcome-oriented differentiation embraces various aspects of the EU legal order.

Supranational differentiation as the focus of this chapter follows a more specific pattern: differential effects do not emanate from the contents of the law, but are the direct result of its general non-application. Differentiation in this meaning is defined by the limited geographic scope of Union law and the corresponding suspension of the voting rights of the non-participating Member States in the Council. Monetary union, the Schengen law and the general mechanism for enhanced cooperation are the most prominent examples of supranational differentiation. This input-orientated pattern was first introduced by the Treaty of Maastricht, where Member States agreed upon the asymmetric realisation of monetary union on the basis of the convergence criteria and political opt-outs for the UK and Denmark.[50] This legal construct was taken up by the Treaty of Amsterdam, which formalised the Danish opt-out from defence and justice and home affairs.[51] More importantly, the Treaty of Amsterdam also introduced the general mechanism for enhanced cooperation.[52] At the same time, the incorporation of the Schengen law established a first example of enhanced cooperation – complemented by the British-Irish opt-out/opt-in from the legislative realisation of the area of freedom, security and justice.[53] In addition, specific forms of differentiation exist in security and defence policy.[54]

Differentiation has always been a projection sphere for different visions of the future of Europe. Supporters and opponents consider it a symbol of divergent ideas. This explains emotional reactions, which invocations of differentiation sometimes provoke. While these visions are relevant in the long run, the immediate motivation for Treaty reform was often more pragmatic[55] – as the example of the Maastricht Treaty

---

[50] See ns 8–10 above and accompanying text.

[51] See Daniel Thym, 'Supranational Differentiation and Enhanced Cooperation' in Takis Tridimas and Robert Schütze (eds), *The Oxford Principles of European Union Law. Vol. I* (Oxford University Press 2017 forthcoming), section 3.2 forthcoming; these rules formalised political compromises after the negative Danish referendum on the Maastricht Treaty analysed by Deirdre Curtin and Robert van Ooik, 'Denmark and the Edinburgh Summit: Maastricht without Tears' in David O'Keeffe and Patrick Twomey (eds), *Legal Issues of the Maastricht Treaty* (Wiley Chancery Law 1994) 349–65.

[52] See section 3.1 below.

[53] See Thym (n 51) section III.C (forthcoming).

[54] See Thym (n 51) section III.D (forthcoming).

[55] Similarly, Allan Rosas and Lorna Armati, *An Introduction to EU Constitutional Law* (Hart 2010) 112; and Sébastien Roland, 'La Différenciation,

illustrates. The initial introduction of a supranational differential neither stemmed from a desire to establish a 'hard federalist core' nor was designed to move towards a general à la carte-logic. Granting political opt-outs to two Member States, while obliging the others to participate in monetary union on the basis of the convergence criteria, was the only compromise on which the UK, who opposed monetary union in principle, and its continental partners, who argued for the equal participation of all, could agree.[56] The situation was similar to the communitaurisation of the Schengen Agreements and the former third pillar in the Treaty of Amsterdam. Member States sleepwalked towards differentiation without having taken a conscious decision about what it means for the European project.

For political or economic analysis, questions of legal structure are not particularly relevant. They might consider, therefore, our focus on supranational differentiation to be too narrow. From the perspective of European constitutional and institutional law, however, the limited geographical scope and the suspension of voting rights in the Council matter, since they deviate from the orthodoxy of the supranational method with its quest for unity and equal treatment. Differentiation touches upon core assumptions of legal integration. The resulting tension between differentiation and the supranational integration method will be the focus of this chapter. It will be demonstrated that, from a legal perspective, the tension can be resolved and, rather, the main danger is a structural weakening of the political legitimacy.

3. THE PRACTICE OF SUPRANATIONAL DIFFERENTIATION

The introduction, 20 years ago, of the general mechanism for enhanced cooperation was called a 'Copernican revolution'[57] and was hailed as a way 'to strengthen the Union from within, an instrument of integration,

nouvelle frontière?' in Claude Blumann (ed.), *Les frontières de l'Union européenne* (Bruylant 2013) 249, 270–74.

[56] For the negotiation history of the Maastricht opt-out on monetary Union see Jean-Victor Louis, 'L'Union économique et monétaire' in *Commentaire Mégret, Le droit de la CE, Vol. 6* (2nd edn, Editions de l'Institut d'études européennes 1995) 1, 148.

[57] Renaud Dehousse cited by Vlad Constantinesco, 'Les clauses "de coopération renforcée"' (1997) 33 RTD 751, 752.

not exclusion'.[58] In comparison, other commentators warned of 'constitutional chaos',[59] a 'blatant assault on'[60] and 'natural contradiction with'[61] the uniform application of Union law. This sharp contrast in opinion may be explained by the fact that differentiation may be seen as serving as a projection sphere for hopes and fears about the future of Europe. Notwithstanding these expectations, manifestations of supranational differentiation in the EU Treaties have functioned rather smoothly over the past two decades. This is illustrated by the practical experiences with the general mechanism for enhanced cooperation (3.1), the area of freedom, security and justice (3.2), economic and monetary union (3.3), and defence cooperation (3.4). Neither high expectations nor deep concerns materialised. Differentiation is neither a magic potion for continued dynamism nor a deadly poison leading to a constitutional heart attack. Instead, it appears as a pragmatic institute for limited asymmetrical progress in specific scenarios when Member States cannot agree on a joint action.

3.1 Generic Model: Enhanced Cooperation

Given that enhanced cooperation is not limited to certain Member States or specific policy areas, its rules are crucial for the overall assessment of differentiated integration. Closer inspection of the Treaty rules illustrates that the mechanism has been deliberately designed on the basis of the supranational integration method. As a pragmatic instrument, it provides for the asymmetric realisation of specific policy projects among some Member States within the existing legal and institutional framework of the EU. First introduced by the Treaty of Amsterdam under the name of 'closer cooperation', the legal bases were reformed fundamentally by the Treaty of Nice and then modified again by the Lisbon Treaty in line with the former Constitutional Treaty.[62] Generally speaking, enhanced

---

[58] Former Belgian Prime Minister Guy Verhofstadt, 'A Vision for Europe' (Speech to the European Policy Centre, Brussels, 21 September 2000, a few weeks before the IGC on the Treaty of Nice).

[59] Deirdre Curtin, 'The Constitutional Structure of the Union: A Europe of Bits and Pieces' (1993) 30 CML Rev 17, 67, albeit not with regard to enhanced cooperation.

[60] Steven Weatherhill, 'If I'd Wanted You to Understand I Would Have Explained It Better' in David O'Keeffe and Patrick Twomey (eds), *Legal Issues of the Maastricht Treaty* (Wiley Chancery Law 1994) 21, 22.

[61] Constantinesco (n 57) 758.

[62] On the intermediate changes in Nice see Stéphane Rodrigues, 'Le Traité de Nice et les coopérations renforcées au sein de l'Union européenne' (2001) 444

cooperation provides for the adoption of European laws with limited geographical scope and the suspension of voting rights of the *outs* in the Council. In contrast to other commentators, I do not consider the Treaty regime to be overly restrictive. Neither the substantive constraints (3.1.1) nor the procedural provisions (3.1.2) stifle enhanced cooperation.

During the first decade of existence, Treaty rules on enhanced cooperation have been modified thrice, but they have not been activated a single time (other than the specific case of the Schengen Protocol[63]). Recent years have only seen four activations. In January 2013, the Council authorised 11 Member States to agree upon a Directive on the Financial Transaction Tax (FTT),[64] the small print of which resulted in protracted discussions in the Council for more than three years until the Commission decided to withdraw the draft, since it concluded that there was no realistic chance of adoption.[65] Nevertheless, the sequence of events shows the underlying idea of enhanced cooperation: after the Commission had tabled a first proposal it became evident that unanimity in the Council could not be reached. Instead of aborting the project or realising it outside the EU framework (as in the case of the fiscal compact), the EU institutions supported the initiative of 11 Member States forging ahead. The same occurred in respect to the law applicable to divorce and legal separation in 2010[66] and the unitary patent system in 2011[67] as well as with regard to property regimes of international couples in 2016, which resulted in legally binding measures within weeks, once the resistance of certain Member States had been overcome in the

---

RMCUE 11–16; and Tobias Bender, 'Die Verstärkte Zusammenarbeit nach Nizza. Anwendungsfelder und Bewertung im Spiegel historischer Präzedenzfälle der differenzierten Integration' (2001) 61 *Heidelberg Journal of International Law* 729–70.

[63] See section 3.2.1 below.

[64] Recital 6 Decision 2013/52/EU (OJ [2013] L22/11) lists 11 Member States, which all use the euro, although non-euro-states could have joined them in line with art. 328.1 TFEU.

[65] See the original Commission Proposal, COM(2011) 594 of 28 November 2011, which was officially repealed on 30 April 2016 (OJ [2016] L155/3); the legal basis, art. 113 TFEU, would have required unanimous consent among the participating Member States.

[66] Cf, Decision 2010/405/EU (OJ [2010] L189/12) and Regulation (EU) No. 1259/2010 (OJ [2010] L343/10); originally, 14 Member States listed in Recitals 5–6 took part.

[67] Cf, Decision 2011/167/EU (OJ [2011] L76/53) and Regulation (EU) No. 1257/2012 (OJ [2012] L361/1), in which all Member States except for Italy and Spain participate.

framework of enhanced cooperation.[68] Future instances of enhanced cooperation could include the Common Consolidated Corporate Tax Base (CCCTB) as a first step towards the harmonisation of corporate taxation,[69] the Common European Sales Law[70] or the establishment of the office of the European Public Prosecutor.[71]

3.1.1 Substantive constraints

Substantive constraints for enhanced cooperation in the EU Treaties have often been described as strict.[72] This is only correct if we expect differentiation to allow Member States to break free from the regular constraints of the supranational legal order. Closer inspection of the substantive requirements outlined in Article 20 TEU and Articles 326–334 TFEU show that they are, in essence, declaratory confirmations of general principles of supranational Union law.[73] The only true limitation is the minimum threshold for the participation of at least nine Member States,[74] which may pre-empt an elite collaboration of the six founding members, but it ensures that there is no excessive fragmentation of European law.

Declaratory confirmations of general principles of Union law include the obligation, in Article 20(1) TEU, 'to further the objectives of the Union' and to 'reinforce its integration process'.[75] Likewise, the obligation to comply with the Treaties and to respect the existing *acquis*, which

---

[68] Cf, Decision (EU) 2016/954 (OJ [2016] L159/16) as well as Council Regulation (EU) 2016/1103 (OJ [2016] L183/1) on matrimonial property and Council Regulation (EU) 2016/1103 (OJ [2016] L183/30) on registered partnerships, in which 17 Member States participate.

[69] Agreement upon the Commission Proposal, COM(2011) 121 of 16 March 2011 requires unanimity in accordance with art. 115 TFEU.

[70] See Commission Proposal, COM(2011) 635 of 11 October 2011 based upon art. 114 TFEU.

[71] See Commission Proposal, COM(2013) 534 of 17 July 2013; in addition to the distinct opt-outs of the UK, Ireland and Denmark, other Member States might object the proposal, which requires unanimity under art. 86 TFEU.

[72] See, among many, the criticism of the Treaties of Amsterdam and Nice by Giorgio Gaja, 'How Flexible is Flexibility under the Amsterdam Treaty' (1998) 35 CML Rev 855, 870; Wolfgang Wessels, 'Die Vertragsreform von Nizza'(2001) *Integration* 8, 15; and Jo Shaw, 'The Treaty of Nice: Legal and Constitutional Implications' (2001) 7 *European Public Law* 195, 202.

[73] See the examples discussed below and Thym (n 18) 62–76.

[74] Cf, art. 20(2)(1) TEU.

[75] Any EU instrument is bound to respect the objectives under art. 3 TEU, thereby promoting the process of integration, which is defined by these objectives.

was adopted for the Union as a whole and which some Member States cannot modify unilaterally,[76] reflects established EU law principles. This conclusion extends to the requirement to respect the limits of the Union powers in line with the principle of conferral (although one may want to modify this hurdle in the future[77]). Along similar lines, compliance with the 'competences, rights and obligations' of the non-participating Member States is inherent in the limited geographical scope of any enhanced cooperation and does not require additional safeguards beyond the respect for primary law and the non-application of legislative acts to the *outs*.[78] The latter implies a limitation of the Union's implied external treaty-making power, which the ECJ ignored in Opinion 1/03 where it referred to an exclusive external Union competence despite the Danish opt-out from the internal measure in question.[79]

Since many Community policies, such as social affairs, tax harmonisation, the environment or consumer protection, have an economic dimension, Article 326(2) TFEU is an important bottleneck for more enhanced cooperation. The obligation 'not (to) undermine the internal market' is still relatively easy to define, since an earlier version of that provision referred explicitly to Article 26(2) TFEU.[80] If it is read in

---

[76] See art 20(1)(1) TEU, art 326(1), art 327 TFEU; Case C-503/03 *Commission v Spain* [2006] ECLI:EU:C:2006:74, para. 34 considers art. 134 Schengen Implementing Convention (OJ [2000] L237/13), which obliges the Schengen countries to respect the EU *acquis*, to be 'a specific expression of the principle laid down in' today's art. 20(1) TEU.

[77] The euro crisis demonstrates that certain reform projects, such as the ESM Treaty, could not be realised within the EU framework due to the lack of EU competence.

[78] See art. 327 TFEU, which also emphasises that the non-participating Member States 'shall not impede' enhanced cooperation; the unclear obligation, under the Treaty of Amsterdam, to respect the 'interests' of non-participating Member States was deleted by the Treaty of Nice.

[79] Opinion 1/03 *Lugano Convention* [2006] ECLI:EU:C:2006:81, para. 135 notes that Denmark is not bound by Regulation (EC) No 44/2001 (OJ [2001] L12/1) and concludes, nonetheless, that the Union has an exclusive external competence to enter into agreements with third states on the matter; instead, it should have clarified that the EU institutions are under an obligation, in line with art. 327 TFEU, to ensure that such agreements do not bind Denmark; see Thym (n 18) 270–74; and Catherine Schmitter, 'Coopérations renforcées et compétences externes de la Communauté européenne' in Marianne Dony (ed), *L'Union européenne et le monde après Amsterdam* (Université libre de Bruxelles 1999) 77, 97–9.

[80] Cf, art. 43(e) TEU as amended by the Treaty of Nice (OJ [2006] C321E/5); the Constitutional Treaty and, on its basis, the Treaty of Lisbon

combination with this reference, the Treaty commands compliance with the fundamental freedoms, whereas harmonisation measures under Article 26(1) TFEU are not generally excluded.[81] Again, this does not establish additional hurdles. Member States are always bound by the fundamental freedoms additionally when they cooperate on the basis of international law;[82] the same applies to EU institutions.[83] Again, enhanced cooperation is treated no better or no worse than regular Union law.

The additional prohibition in Article 326(2) TFEU not to 'constitute a barrier to or discrimination in trade between Member States' may be perceived as being more restrictive. Yet, the drafting history supports a different conclusion. The original formulation of the prohibition took up the wording of today's Article 36 TFEU and the famous *Dassonville* formula, where it obliged enhanced cooperation not to constitute a 'discrimination or restriction of trade between the Member States'[84] – a criterion which was generally interpreted as a reference to the free movement of goods.[85] Only the French language version used different wording. Comprehensibly, the French presidency based its reform proposal on the French text of the Amsterdam Treaty during the IGC drafting of the Treaty of Nice and the presidency aligned other language versions with it, thereby eliminating the textual reference to free movement and the *Dassonville* judgment.[86] If the provision is still understood

---

streamlined the wording without intending to change underlying rules; see the explanation of the new version in the European Convention Presidium: Draft on Enhanced Cooperation, Convention doc. CONV 723/03 of 14 May 2003.

[81] The argument extends to the additional prohibition, in art. 326(2)(1) TFEU, not to undermine economic, social and territorial cohesion, since the earlier Treaty version (see ibid.) explicitly invoked Title XVII TEC, thereby guaranteeing the continuity of regional policy and funds.

[82] See, for double taxation agreements, Case C-307/97 *Saint-Gobain* [1999] ECLI:EU:C:1999:438, and, for cooperation in the field of culture, Case C-235/87 *Matteuici* [1988] ECLI:EU:C:1988:460.

[83] See Case C-240/83 *ADBHU* [1985] ECLI:EU:C:1985:59, para. 9.

[84] Art. 11(1)(e) TEC as amended by the Treaty of Amsterdam (OJ [1997] C340/173) and, similarly Case C-8/74 *Dassonville* [1974] ECLI:EU:C:1974:82, para. 7.

[85] See, by way of example, Helmut Kortenberg (pseudonym), 'Closer Cooperation in the Treaty of Amsterdam' (1998) 35 CML Rev 833, 849, Rainer Hofmann, 'Wie viel Flexibilität für welches Europa. Gedanken für künftigen Entwicklung der europäischer Integration' (1999) Europarecht 713, 724; and Constantinesco (n 57) 761.

[86] There is no indication that the French delegation wanted to change underlying rules; the same applies to the Constitutional Treaty and, on its basis,

to command respect for the fundamental freedoms, it will generally not impede the harmonisation of national legislation; only rules which fall foul of the free movement of goods would be incompatible with the Treaties. Further limits do not flow either from the additional obligation not to 'distort competition', since a 'distortion' requires more than a simple difference in the legal environment.[87] The realisation of the EU patent among 26 Member States demonstrates that most harmonisation measures will respect these standards. It establishes more commonality than the continued co-existence of 28 national systems.[88]

3.1.2 Procedural requirements

It is reasonably simple to establish enhanced cooperation for a specific project. Whenever it appears unrealistic to adopt a measure among all Member States, nine or more Member States may ask the EU institutions to authorise the initiative. Such authorisation is granted when the Commission supports the initiative and both the Council and the European Parliament give their consent.[89] This supranational authorisation procedure is no coincidence. It ensures a thorough exchange of the political pros and cons of asymmetric progress and there is no guarantee that the initiative will be given the green light. Even if all the legal requirements are met, the Commission, the Parliament and the Council retain political discretion whether or not to authorise differentiation.[90] Against this background, procedural requirements are no more restrictive

---

the Lisbon Treaty, which continue the wording of the Treaty of Nice; for detail, see Thym (n 18) 69–72.

[87] This conclusion is supported by a comparison with art. 114(6) TFEU, where the option of legislative harmonisation (art. 114(5)) is broader than the criterion of 'distorting' (art. 116); moreover, practical assessments should be handled similarly to competition cases, i.e., the Commission has to assess potential distortions in its decision (not) to authorise enhanced cooperation, while judicial review of such complex economic assessment is regularly limited; see Thym (n 18) 71–2.

[88] See also Joined Cases C-274/11 and C-295/11 *Spain and Italy v Council* [2013] ECLI;EU:C:2013:240, paras 76–77; of course, a detailed analysis of the rules may come to the conclusion that certain provisions fall foul of the economic freedoms and need to be altered; as a matter of principle, however, harmonisation among some Member States does not deteriorate the competitive environment.

[89] Cf, art. 20(2)TEU and art. 329(1) TFEU.

[90] Any Member State or institution may challenge the authorisation (not) to establish enhanced cooperation in accordance with the rules on access to the Court; for detail see Matthias Pechstein, 'Herausforderungen für den Rechtsschutz in einer flexiblen Union' (2013) 2 Europarecht 71–87.

than the substantive constraints. The original criticism of a procedural 'straitjacket'[91] no longer has any hold, since the veto option for non-participating Member States has been abolished.[92] The authorisation procedure is neither restrictive nor loose but, as is often the case in Europe, it is a vehicle for compromise, which supports the emergence of a basic political consensus about the suitability of differentiation.

In contrast to the ordinary legislative procedure, the political initiative for enhanced cooperation rests with Member States,[93] who may invite the Commission to table a formal proposal to authorise enhanced cooperation – or to decide not to do so.[94] If the Commission presents a proposal, both the Council and the European Parliament will have given consent, irrespective of whether they act as equal co-legislators within the framework of enhanced cooperation.[95] All Member States participate in the decision on whether to authorise enhanced cooperation in the Council by qualified majority (irrespective of whether the adoption of the legislation concerned requires unanimity).[96] Once the authorisation has been granted, the legislative procedure on the proposal in question continues in accordance with the applicable Treaty rules, i.e., consent on the FTT Directive will require unanimous agreement among the participating Member States.[97] This means that there will always be at least two decisions: one authorising enhanced cooperation in the abstract and another (or several) adopting more specific legislative instruments on the proposal in substance.

---

[91] Josef Janning, 'Dynamik in der Zwangsjacke – Flexibilität in der Europäischer Union nach Amsterdam' (1997) Integration 285; see also Gaja (n 72) 870.

[92] In contrast to art. 11(2) TEC in the Amsterdam version (n 84), art. 20(2) and art. 16(3) TEU foresee a vote by qualified majority.

[93] The Commission supported this modification of its monopoly of initiative in order to lay the potentially divisive initiative for differentiation with Member States, thereby buttressing its function as neutral arbiter in the common interest; see Tuytschaever (n 49) 58–9.

[94] Art. 329 (1)(1) TFEU emphasises that the Commission 'may submit' a proposal, i.e., it has political discretion whether (not) to follow the request; see Thym (n 18) 48–50.

[95] Art. 329(1)(2) TFEU reinforces the role of the Parliament in line with art. III-419 Constitutional Treaty (OJ [2004] C310/1) and covers situations where the adoption of legislation will not require parliamentary consent, such as agreement on the FTT on the basis of art. 113 TFEU.

[96] See art. 20(2) TEU, art. 329(1)(2) TFEU, art. 16(3) TEU; this means, for instance, that the Council decided by a qualified majority among all Member States to authorise the FTT cooperation.

[97] See art. 20(2), (3) TEU, art. 330 TFEU.

In accordance with Article 20(3) TFEU enhanced cooperation 'shall be adopted by the Council as a last resort, when it has established that the objectives of such cooperation cannot be attained within a reasonable period by the Union as a whole'. This procedural safeguard ensures that pan-European projects take precedence and, in doing so, entrusts the Council with discretion to assess the political situation; the wording and structure of the Treaty do not require a formal failure of the legislative procedure for the Union as a whole before the Council may authorise enhanced cooperation.[98] This was reaffirmed by the ECJ in the judgment on the EU Patent.[99] It follows from the 'last resort' criterion, however, that the scope needs to be defined clearly and will regularly not cover more than a cluster of related instruments. Enhanced cooperation concerns the adoption of selected instruments and cannot generally exempt some Member States from the realisation of certain EU policies.[100]

At the same time, the absence of any 'exit' procedure underlines that (voluntary) participation is a one-way street and that participating Member States are bound by instruments adopted within the framework of enhanced cooperation in the same manner as they are bound by regular Union law.[101] By contrast, the later participation of the initial *outs* is subject to a simple Commission decision (without the involvement of the other EU institutions).[102] This guarantees that the 'essential principle of

---

[98] It is the responsibility of the Council to 'establish' whether the project can 'be attained', thereby spelling out more clearly than the Treaty of Amsterdam that a formal vote need not to be taken; see Christian von Buttlar, 'Rechtsprobleme der "verstärkten Zusammenarbeit" nach dem Vertrag von Nizza' (2001) Zeitschrift für Europarechtliche Studien 649, 665–6; and Hervé Bribosia, 'Les coopérations renforcées' in Giuliano Amato, Hervé Bribosa and Bruno De Witte (eds), *Genèse et destinée de la Constitution européenne* (Bruylant 2007) 623, 631–3; too restrictive Steven Peers, 'The Constitutional Implications of the EU Patent' (2011) 7 EuConst 229, 250–51.

[99] See CJEU (n 88) paras 47–54.

[100] See Thym (n 18) 52–4.

[101] EU institutions remain free to repeal all instruments adopted within the context of enhanced cooperation; once such a *tabula rasa* has been established, a different grouping may theoretically reapply for enhanced cooperation on the same matter; see Thym (n 18) 244–5; moreover, one might accept a retreat of Member States as long as the authorisation has not been granted – as in the case of Greece according to Recital 5 of Decision 2010/405/EU (n 66).

[102] Cf, art. 329 TFEU; and, by way of example, Decision 2012/714/EU (OJ [2012] L232/18).

openness'[103] is realised to the greatest extent possible. In a nutshell: enhanced cooperation is meant to support the realisation of EU objectives among as many Member States as possible and is firmly embedded into the supranational integration method.

3.2 Containment of International Satellite Treaties

With international 'satellite' treaties, I designate agreements among Member States, which complement EU integration but which are located outside the supranational legal and institutional framework. They are not a novel phenomenon. There used to be many examples of some (or all) Member States collaborating alongside EU integration, including Benelux cooperation, the Brussels Convention, bilateral double taxation agreements, the original Schengen Agreements, the organisation for the safety of air navigation Eurocontrol, the multilateral Eurocorps[104] or, more recently, the Franco-German agreement on an elective 'community of accrued gains' matrimonial property regime.[105] Satellite treaties gained new momentum during the euro crisis, in particular through the ESM Treaty and the Fiscal Compact. From a legal perspective, these satellite treaties do not belong to the supranational order; their negotiation, ratification, interpretation, and termination follows the international law of treaties. There may be good reasons for recourse to public international law (1) and, yet, Member States are not free when they act outside the EU legal order. There are legal constraints, which they are bound to obey (2). Like satellites in the earth's orbit, international treaties are kept in their path by the gravitational pull of Union law.

3.2.1 (Dis-)advantages of international cooperation

Why should Member States have recourse to public international law treaties, considering that they could amend the EU Treaties instead? The core motivation is simple. Cooperation outside the EU framework has procedural advantages, including simplified entry into force. If the ESM Treaty or the Fiscal Compact had been brought about by means of EU Treaty change, all Member States would have had to consent to the

---

103 Cf, Claus-Dieter Ehlermann, 'Differentiation, Flexibility, Closer Co-operation. The New Provisions of the Amsterdam Treaty' (1998) 4 ELJ 246, 254.

104 For an overview see De Witte (n 44); and Thym (n 18) Ch. 6.

105 Cf, the Agreement of 4 February 2010 (German Federal Law Gazette/ *Bundesgesetzblatt* 2012 II 178), whose art. 21(1) invites all EU Member States to accede.

amendment and ratify it in accordance with national constitutional requirements, which are often stricter for EU law than for 'ordinary' international treaties.[106] Most Member States were not willing to take the inherent risk of ratification delay or failure. Neither the ESM Treaty nor the Fiscal Compact required universal ratification, not even among Eurozone members.[107] Streamlined ratification procedures were not the only motivation. It seems that the German Government, in particular, was eager to sideline the supranational institutions through the use of public international law;[108] the heads of state or government were supposed to remain at the helm.

Recourse to international law is not a one-way street that only brings about advantages. At the same time, it implies that the benefits of supranational law making do not materialise. This includes the arbitratory and supervisory function of supranational institutions, in particular the Commission and the ECJ, which smaller Member States tend to appreciate as a protective shield against (Franco-German) dominance by larger states.[109] Moreover, international treaties do not normally have supranational legal weight, including primacy and direct effect, which does not foster compliance. If Member States have confidence that common rules will be enforced, this, according to the prisoner's dilemma of game theory, is a crucial motivation for supranational law making.[110]

---

[106] Cf, art. 48 TEU and corresponding national constitutional rules.

[107] Art. 12(2) Treaty on Stability, Coordination and Governance in the Economic and Monetary Union of 2 March 2012 (Fiscal Compact) requires 12 ratifications; art. 48(1) Treaty establishing the European Stability Mechanism of 2 February 2012 (ESM Treaty) sets out that all ratifications must represent 90 per cent of national capital subscriptions.

[108] See Matthias Ruffert, 'Die europäische Schuldenkrise vor dem Bundesverfassungsgericht' (2011) Europarecht 842, 844; for the French perspective Sarkozy (n 26); and, more generally, Michael Schwarz, 'A Memorandum of Misunderstanding – The Doomed Road of the European Stability Mechanism and a Possible Way-out: Enhanced Cooperation' (2014) 51 CML Rev 389–423.

[109] Cf, Karen Alter, 'Who Are the "Masters of the Treaty"?' in Karen Alter, *The European Court's Political Power: Selected Essays* (Oxford University Press 2009) 109, 125–6.

[110] See Alec Stone Sweet, 'The European Court of Justice' in Paul Craig and Gráinne de Búrca (eds), *The Evolution of EU Law* (2nd edn, Oxford University Press 2011) 121, 124–5.

Parliamentary involvement may also be compromised, if national parliaments cannot always effectively control the action of governments and if the European Parliament has no decision-making or control prerogatives.[111]

Public international law may promise quick results, but the supranational integration method is often more successful than recourse to public international law in the long run. It does not come as a surprise, therefore, that both the Commission and the German Government call for the medium-term supranationalisation of the ESM Treaty and the Fiscal Compact[112] (like in the case of the Schengen Agreements[113] or the former third pillar on justice and home affairs[114]). This objective even found its way into the Fiscal Compact[115] and has already, to a certain extent, been put into operation when the so-called Six- and Two-Packs on budgetary surveillance and macroeconomic coordination incorporated certain elements of the Fiscal Compact by means of secondary law making.[116] This demonstrates that the euro crisis will not necessarily

---

111 For a criticism of euro rescue operations, see Christian Joerges, 'Europas Wirtschaftsverfassung in der Krise' (2012) 51 Der Staat 357, 371–3; and Uerpmann-Wittzack (n 46).

112 See Commission Communication, COM(2012) 777 of 28 November 2012, 16, 39; European Parliament, Resolution on Constitutional Problems of a Multitier Governance in the European Union, doc. P7_TA-PROV(2013)0598 of 12 December 2013, No. 35; and the (German) Coalition Agreement 2013-2017, 156 (the agreement is politically, not legally, binding).

113 Cf, the Protocol (No. 19) on the Schengen *acquis* integrated into the framework of the European Union (OJ [2008] C 115/290) and the predecessor (OJ [1997] C340/93); see also the incorporation of the plurilateral 'Prüm Treaty' on police cooperation by Decision 2008/615/JHA (OJ [2008] L210/1).

114 On long ratification periods of conventions, such as the Europol Convention, under the old intergovernmental third pillar at the time of the Maastricht Treaty, see Thym (n 18) 182–7.

115 See art. 16 Fiscal Compact (n 107).

116 See Carlino Antpöhler, 'Emergenz der europäischen Wirtschaftsregierung. Das Six Pack als Zeichen supranationaler Leistungsfähigkeit' (2012) 72 *Heidelberg Journal of International Law* 353, 362–81, 392; and Christian Calliess and Christopher Schoenfleisch, 'Auf dem Weg in die europäische "Fiskalunion" – Europa– und verfassungsrechtliche Fragen einer Reform des Wirtschafts- und Währungsunion im Kontext des Fiskalvertrages?' (2012) Juristenzeitung 477, 478–80; further deepening has been proposed by the Commission, COM(2013) 165 and 166 of 20 March 2013.

result in the long-term decline of supranationalism.[117] Moreover, there seems to be a general consensus that the ESM Treaty and the Fiscal Compact are meant to strengthen the integration process through public international law instruments.[118] They serve as a 'bypass' and do not resemble a 'heart attack' of the supranational integration method.

3.2.2 Protective shields for the supranational legal order

It is usually accepted that the Member States may cooperate outside the EU legal order as a matter of principle. According to the principle of conferral, the Member States retain a residual competence for powers, which have not been transferred to the EU, and they may exercise these powers by means of international cooperation (not much different from agreements among sub-units, which most – but not all – federal states tend to permit[119]). In its *Pringle* judgment, the CJEU also assumed the permissibility of international cooperation without further discussion[120] and focused, instead, on the limits which protect the supranational legal order.

First, Union competences create a hurdle. International satellite treaties are unproblematic in areas without EU competence, such as the organisation of national armed forces, where Member States may follow the example of the multilateral Eurocorps and cooperate on bilateral or plurilateral bases.[121] In these fields, Member States act on their own behalf as autonomous subjects of international law. By contrast, there is no room for inter-state cooperation whenever there is an exclusive Union competence, including instances of shared competences, which the Union has exercised.[122] EU activities pre-empt inter-state cooperation outside

---

[117] But see Frank Schorkopf, 'Finanzkrisen als Herausforderung der internationalen, europäischen und nationalen Rechtsetzung' (2012) 71 Veröffentlichungen der Vereinigung Deutscher Staatsrechtslehrer 183, 209–11.

[118] I do *not* argue that the 'simple' supranationalisation of the ESM Treaty and/or the Fiscal Compact is sufficient to save monetary union; additional and/or different reform steps are necessary.

[119] For a comparative analysis see Hans Schneider, 'Verträge zwischen Gliedstaaten im Bundesstaat: Schranken nichthoheitlicher Verwaltung' (1961) 19 Veröffentlichungen der Vereinigung Deutscher Staatsrechtslehrer 1–33.

[120] Cf Case C-370/12 *Pringle* [2012] ECLI:EU:C:2012: 756, para. 68; and Daniel Thym and Mattias Wendel, 'Préserver le respect du droit dans la crise' (2013) 48 Cahiers de droit européen 733, 738–9.

[121] For a typology see Maxim Kleine, 'Integrated Bi- and Multinational Units in Europe' in Georg Nolte (ed.), *European Military Law Systems* (De Gruyter 2003) 889–908; see also art. 42(3)(1) TEU.

[122] As is laid down explicitly in art. 2(1), art. 3(2) TFEU.

the EU framework. Against this background, the ESM Treaty was legally permissible, precisely because it did not interfere with the Union's exclusive competence for monetary policy.[123]

One could argue, however, that the abstract possibility of realising potential projects among some Member States within the framework of enhanced cooperation blocks inter-state cooperation outside the EU framework. Satellite treaties would be prohibited in situations without uniform EU policy, if asymmetric process could theoretically be achieved for some Member States within the supranational framework.[124] I have argued elsewhere that the wording, the structure and the drafting history of the current Treaty regime argue against this position.[125] It is true that the introduction of enhanced cooperation pursued the political objective, among others, to provide an alternative to extra-EU arrangements.[126] This does not, however, entail that recourse to this mechanism is mandatory from a legal perspective.

Secondly, when acting outside the EU framework 'Member States may not disregard their duty to comply with European Union law'.[127] One example is that the ESM Treaty is bound to respect the so-called 'no bail out' provision in Article 125 TFEU[128] in the same way as bilateral agreements on double taxation or cultural cooperation, which need to respect the fundamental freedoms and the principle of non-discrimination.[129] This duty flows directly from the autonomy and primacy of Union law over national laws, thereby reiterating that the classic position of public international law on treaty collisions under Article 30(4) of the Vienna Convention on the Law of Treaties cannot be extended to the interaction between EU primary law and subsequent satellite treaties, which some Member States have concluded outside the EU framework. From the perspective of EU law, supranational obligations have primacy over international satellite treaties irrespective of

---

[123] Cf, CJEU (n 120) paras 93–98.

[124] In *Pringle*, the CJEU (n 120) paras 166–168 noted that recourse to enhanced cooperation was impossible, since there was no EU competence for the substance of the ESM Treaty.

[125] For detail see Thym (n 18) 304–8.

[126] Cf, Kortenberg (n 85) 835.

[127] CJEU (n 120) para. 69; Thym (n 18) 311–2; De Witte (n 44) 45–52; and Robert Schütze, 'EC Law and International Agreements of the Member States – An Ambivalent Relationship?' (2007) 9 CYELS 387, 420–25.

[128] See CJEU (n 120) paras 129–147.

[129] In this sense Case C-307/97 *Saint-Gobain* [1999] ECLI:EU:C:1999:438, paras 57–59; and Case C-55/00 *Gottardo* [2002] ECLI:EU:C:2002:16, para. 33.

whether the latter expressly recognises this explicitly, like in the case of the Schengen Agreements and the Fiscal Compact.[130]

Thirdly, the CJEU emphasises throughout the *Pringle* judgment that Member States are under an obligation 'not to affect' the rules of primary or secondary Union law.[131] Such a prohibition on negatively affecting Union law mandates more than the disapplication of national or international rules in cases of conflict; rather, it guarantees the *effet utile* of EU rules in a broader sense. It goes beyond the prevention of vertical conflicts between different layers of compound legal orders by means of the US constitutional doctrine of pre-emption or the German concept of *Sperrwirkung*.[132] In *Pringle*, the CJEU refrained from establishing the prohibition not to affect the Union *acquis* explicitly in the structure of Union competences.[133] One reason for this more flexible approach is the softer edge of the obligation not to affect, since Member States may act either unilaterally or collaboratively in areas of shared powers, as long as their activities do not undermine the effectiveness of Union law.[134]

In the context of the obligation not to affect Union law, the CJEU asked, in *Pringle*, whether the ESM Treaty called into question the effectiveness of the supervision and coordination function of the EU institutions, in particular the prerogatives of the Commission and the Court of Justice.[135] By doing so, the Court rejected a strict reading of institutional powers; satellite treaties may entrust EU institutions with tasks which reach beyond their functions under the EU Treaty. On the

---

[130] Cf, art. 2 Abs. 2 Fiscal Compact (n 107) and art. 134 Schengen Implementing Convention (n 76).

[131] See in particular CJEU (n 120) paras 101, 113, 119; it is not convincing that ibid., para. 101 invokes art. 3(2) TFEU in order to substantiate this claim, since art. 3(2) TFEU concerns the existence of exclusive EU competences, not substantive limits for international satellite treaties outside the scope of exclusive Union competence; see AG Kokott, ibid., Opinion of 26 October 2012, ECLI: EU:C:2012:756, paras 96–99.

[132] For instructive reading see Robert Schütze, 'Supremacy without Pre-Emption? The Very Slowly Emergent Doctrine of Community Pre-emption' (2006) 43 CML Rev 1023, 1032–44; and Armin von Bogdandy, 'Founding Principles' in Armin von Bogdandy and Jürgen Bast (eds), *Principles of European Constitutional Law* (2nd edn, Hart 2009) 11, 29–32.

[133] The second sentence of art. 2(2) TFEU is not mentioned, i.e., Member States may act, but they have to respect the effectiveness of EU law; see Thym and Wendel (n 120) 741–3.

[134] This corresponds to earlier ECJ case law; see Schütze (n 132) 1039–44; De Witte (n 44) 41–2; and Thym (n 18) 313–14.

[135] See CJEU (n 120) paras 153 et seq.

basis of earlier judgments and academic writing, this was not a foregone conclusion and one could have expected a stricter position.[136] The Court did not follow this line, however, and opted for a flexible solution. To insist that the effectiveness of institutional prerogatives of EU institutions under the EU Treaties are not affected requires an assessment of the specific circumstances of the scenario in question; there are no general red lines.

Finally, the principle of loyal cooperation directs the everyday interaction of international satellite treaties and the EU legal order.[137] One may expect, for example, that Member States investigate the feasibility of creating new projects within the supranational context, if necessary on the basis of differentiated integration, before embarking upon the negotiation and conclusion of international satellite treaties.[138] Moreover, the principle of loyalty prohibits the formation of 'voting cartels', when, for instance, Members of the euro group coordinate their position on an informal basis and present other Member States with a *fait accompli*, where the question is 'discussed' and formally decided in the Council. To apply this rule to specific scenarios will always require an assessment of the circumstances of each case, since some degree of informal coordination short of 'voting cartels' is certainly permitted.[139] Ideally, clever institutional design during the negotiation of new projects will prevent such 'friendly takeovers' of EU institutions by some Member States.[140]

---

[136] Cf, Thym (n 18) 315–18; De Witte (n 44) 45–52; and Paul Craig, 'The Stability, Coordination and Governance Treaty: Principle, Politics and Pragmatism' (2012) 37 ELR 231, 243–4.

[137] Cf, indirectly at least, CJEU (n 120) paras 148–152.

[138] See De Witte (n 44) 52–4; Thym (n 18) 309–10; and Calliess and Schoenfleisch (n 116) 483.

[139] Two examples: the euro group 'agreed' upon the suspension of the excessive deficit procedure against Germany and France during 2002/2003 before the Council took a formal position (see Thym (n 18) 144, 312–13); another problematic case were euro group discussions before the European Council of 24 October 2012, when David Cameron 'vetoed' the realisation of the Fiscal Compact within the supranational framework, see Allegra Stratton and David Gow, 'Nicolas Sarkozy tells David Cameron: shut up over the euro' *Guardian unlimited* (London, 23 October 2011); and Nicolai von Ondarza, 'Auf dem Weg zur Union in der Union: Institutionelle Auswirkungen der differenzierten Integration in der Eurozone auf die EU' (2013) 1 *Integratio*n 24–5.

[140] Cf, the debate about voting cartels of Eurozone members in the future European Banking Authority (EBA) and other elements of the banking union discussed by Alex Barker and Richard Milne, 'Eurozone "outs" fear banking union plan' *Financial Times* (London, 2 October 2012).

4. CONSTITUTIONAL IMPLICATIONS

The 'unity dogma' has long characterised European law discourse. In many of its landmark judgments, the European Court of Justice resorted to the 'unity argument' – such as in *Costa v E.N.E.L.*, where it rightly stated that 'the executive force of Community law cannot vary from one state to another ... without jeopardising the attainment of the objectives of the Treaty'. Unilateral national deviations could not be tolerated without the common rules 'being deprived of their character as Community law and without the legal basis of the Community itself being called into question'.[141] Other expressions of the 'unity dogma' include the principle of non-discrimination or the uniform composition of EU institutions. Many legal experts on EU law remain sceptical about differentiation precisely because it seems to call into question cherished principles of Union law.

It seems to me that this scepticism is not justified. To be sure, the supranational legal order continues to depend upon unity-building elements, but this requirement is not being called into question by the various examples of differentiation in the EU Treaties. They are firmly embedded in the supranational legal order. Or, to put it otherwise, they do not provide for an exit from the supranational integration method. Procedural and substantive constraints ensure that differentiation is an integral part of the EU legal order and respects its constitutional credentials (4.1) in the same ways as it does not impede the functioning of EU institutions (4.2). Its main benefit is the accommodation of political diversity (4.3), while it may result, at the same time, in a structural weakening of political legitimacy (4.4).

4.1 Unity of the Legal Order

The EU is, more than the nation-state, a creation of the law whose abstract equality and normative neutrality have always been essential tools in overcoming political differences between Member States. That is what the CJEU hints at when it qualifies the integration project as a 'Community based on the rule of law'.[142] To emphasise the credentials of legal integration accepts, indirectly at least, that the Union may rely upon

---

141 Case C-6/64 *Costa v E.N.E.L.* [1964] ECLI:EU:C:1964:66, at 594.

142 Opinion 1/91 *European Economic Area*, Opinion [1991] ECLI:EU:C:1991:490, para. 21.

a lesser degree of political and identificatory cohesion.[143] When it comes to legal unity, however, the importance of equal treatment stands out, as the first Commission President Walter Hallstein highlighted 40 years ago: 'equality results in unity – this is the rationale behind the Treaty of Rome'.[144] As mentioned at the beginning, this chapter defends the proposition that differentiation can be accommodated with the core achievements of legal integration.

The situation appeared different 20 years ago, when Deirdre Curtin wrote her seminal article on a 'Europe of Bits and Pieces',[145] which captured the prevalent mood at a time when the Agreement on Social Policy,[146] special arrangements for Denmark with dubious legal character[147] and the novelty factor of the intergovernmental pillars[148] presented formidable challenges to the orthodoxy of the supranational integration method – and differentiation seemed part of the challenge. Today, we may conclude that the fear did not materialise, at least insofar as the rule of law is concerned. Contemporary examples of differentiation were introduced by means of a formal Treaty change and were ratified by national parliaments.[149] With regard to the former third pillar, differentiation even facilitated communitarisation, since British Governments would probably not have consented to gradual supranationalisation in the Treaties of Amsterdam, Nice and Lisbon without the opt-out as a softener.[150] In short: differentiation is an integral part of primary law.

---

143 Cf, Christoph Möllers, 'Pouvoir Constituant, Constitution, Constitutionalisation' in Armin von Bogdandy and Jürgen Bast (eds), *Principles of European Constitutional Law* (1st edn, Hart 2006) 227; similarly, Jiri Přibáň, 'The Self-Referential European Polity, its Legal Context and Systemic Differentiation' (2009) 15 ELJ 442, 449 et seq.

144 Hallstein (n 42) 33 (own translation).

145 Curtin (n 59); see also Anne Peters, *Elemente einer Theorie der Verfassung Europas* (Duncker & Humblot 2001) 449 who extends Curtin's argument to the Treaty of Amsterdam, including enhanced cooperation, without considering its different form and substance.

146 See Watson (n 45); and Curtin (n 59) 52–61.

147 See Curtin and Van Ooik (n 51); and David Howarth, 'The Compromise on Denmark and the Treaty on European Union: A Legal and Political Analysis' (1994) 31 CML Rev 765–805.

148 See Curtin (n 59) 22–30.

149 The Labour Government under Tony Blair agreed to integrate the Social Policy Agreement into the EU framework in the Treaty of Amsterdam; at the time, the Danish exception was also formalised.

150 See Daniel Thym, 'Einheit in Vielfalt' in Armin Hatje and Peter-Christian Müller-Graff (eds), *Enzyklopädie Europarecht. Vol. 1 Europäisches Organisations- und Verfassungsrecht* (Nomos 2014) § 5 paras 45–48.

Considering the formal unity of legal orders, Hans Kelsen recognised the potential need for differentiation a century ago:

> When individual rules of one legal order do have a divergent geographic scope of application, different normative regimes apply to different parts of that order. The formal unity of a legal entity does not necessarily entail substantive uniformity ... Among the various reasons calling for differentiated geographic treatment ... greater geographic reach and heterogeneity of living conditions usually entail more differentiation.[151]

Along similar lines, the French *Conseil constitutionnel* had no doubts that the Treaty of Maastricht respected the French constitutional requirement that EU obligations are 'subject to reciprocity', since reciprocity was ensured among the members of the Eurozone despite the British opt-out.[152] Similarly, reciprocity under public international law does not require international treaties to lay down identical obligations for all parties.[153]

Examples of differentiation discussed in this chapter not only respect the formal unity of the EU legal order, but also preserve the distinctive features of supranationalism.[154] There are just two variations: legislative acts adopted within the framework of differentiated integration have limited geographic scope and, correspondingly, the voting rights of non-participating Member States are suspended in the Council. All other supranational legal characteristics apply without modification; EU institutions regularly adopt directives and regulations, which may be interpreted by the Court of Justice, which prevail over national laws in cases of conflict and which may give rise to Francovich-style damages.[155] To provide an example: if Austria did not transpose an EU directive on asylum correctly, which does not apply to the UK, the legal consequences would be the same as with any other EU directive; national courts are under an obligation to interpret Austrian laws in conformity with the

---

[151] Hans Kelsen, *Allgemeine Staatslehre* (Springer 1925) 165 (own translation).

[152] French *Conseil constitutionnel*, Decision of 2 September 1992, No. 92-312 DC.

[153] See Bruno Simma, *Das Reziprozitätselement im Zustandekommen völkerrechtlicher Verträge* (Duncker & Humblot 1972).

[154] For a similar conclusion, see Michael Dougan, 'The Unfinished Business of Enhanced Co-operation' in Andrea Ott and Ellen Vos (eds), *Fifty Years of European Integration: Foundations and Perspectives* (TMC Asser Press 2009) 157, 160; Jo Shaw, 'Flexibility in a "Reorganised" and "Simplified" Treaty' (2003) 40 CML Rev 279, 295; and Guillard (n 7) 107 et seq.

[155] On the preservation of these principles, see Thym (n 18) Chs 8–9.

directive and can make preliminary references to the ECJ; the Commission may initiate infringement proceedings and, later, may ask the Court to impose penalty payments.[156]

At first sight, supranational differentiation is difficult to reconcile with the principle of non-discrimination on grounds of nationality. Some commentators have even argued that it 'turn(s) what the ECJ would normally consider as illegal discrimination into permissible differentiation'.[157] The argument is not convincing. Asymmetric legislation may have a limited geographic scope, but within the latter it applies like any other law and Article 18 TFEU must be respected. Spain, for instance, is obliged to treat British citizens on an equal footing with its own nationals or Portuguese visitors when it applies rules of monetary union or rules on border controls. As the Court has argued as early as 1969:

> (Article 18 TFEU) is not concerned with any disparities in treatment or the distortions which may result … from divergences existing between the laws of the various Member States, so long as the latter affect all persons subject to them in accordance with objective criteria and without regard to their nationality.[158]

This position reaffirms the essence of differentiation, which shares the same legal-normative effects of other Union law in the Member States to whom it applies. Differentiation is about freedom of choice in the participation of law making, not about arbitrariness in (dis-)respecting supranational rules, to which one has subscribed. From a doctrinal perspective, this conclusion extends to international satellite treaties, such as the ESM Treaty or the Fiscal Compact, which must respect the primacy of Union law and shall not impede the prerogatives of EU institutions.[159] They are, from a legal perspective, no *Verfassungsdurchbrechung* in the Schmittian sense, which, in an emergency situation, overcome constitutional constraints to prevent, by extra-legal means, the

---

[156] Cf, art. 260(2), (3) TFEU; Sebastian Zeitzmann, 'Das Verfahren der Verstärkten Zusammenarbeit und dessen erstmalige Anwendung' (2011) Zeitschrift für Europarechtliche Studien 87, 98 does not give any reasons why these rules should not apply to enhanced cooperation.

[157] Tuytschaever (n 49) 57; similarly, Kieran Bradley, 'Institutional Design in the Treaty of Nice' (2001) 38 CML Rev 1095, 1116.

[158] Case C-14/68 *Wilhelm* [1969] ECLI:EU:C:1969:4; para. 13; on the application of art. 20 Charter of Fundamental Rights, when regular EU rules (without differentiation) distinguish between Member States see Case C-101/12 *Schaible* [2013] ECLI:EU:C:2013:661, paras 76–87 and Thym (n 18) 254–8.

[159] See section 3.2.2 above.

legal order from collapsing.[160] From a legal perspective, the rule of law remains intact in the face of differentiation. Supranationalism is preserved.

4.2 Single Institutional Framework

The legal birth certificate of today's European Union, the Preamble of the Treaty establishing the European Coal and Steel Community, declares the objective 'to lay the bases of institutions capable of giving direction to their future common destiny'.[161] In doing so, it refers to a core component of European constitutionalism, since questions of institutional design have always been instruments of organisational unity building. Political science shows that institutional arrangements can support the gradual approximation of national interests and the formation of a collective impulse.[162] It is essential, therefore, that the examples of differentiation in the EU Treaties are firmly embedded in the supranational legal order. This applies to the authorisation of enhanced cooperation in the same way as it does to the adoption of legislative acts with limited geographic scope.[163] The only exception is the suspension of voting rights of the *outs* in the Council;[164] other institutions sit and decide without modification.[165] Contrary to international satellite treaties, supranational differentiation is not a backdoor to an exit from supranational decision making.[166]

---

160 See Thym and Wendel (n 120) 734–7 against Joerges (n 111) 377–81 and Frank Schorkopf, 'Gestaltung mit Recht: Prägekraft und Selbstand des Rechts in einer Rechtsgemeinschaft' (2011) 136 Archiv des Öffentlichen Rechts 323, 336–43.

161 Recital 5 of the Preamble of the 1951 ECSC Treaty, which expired in July 2002.

162 In political science, both neo-functional approaches, historic institutionalism and constructivism emphasise the relevance of institutions for EU integration; see the contributions to first part of Erik Jones, Anand Menon and Stephen Weatherill (eds), *The Oxford Handbook of the European Union* (Oxford University Press 2012).

163 Cf, art. 20(2) TEU, arts 328–329 TFEU; and section 3.1.2 above.

164 See art. 20(3) TEU, art. 330 TFEU and, for monetary union, art. 139(4) TFEU.

165 For detail see Thym (n 18) Ch. 7.

166 At first glance, the wording of art. 20(1) TEU could be understood wrongly to permit institutional experiments, when it allows Member States to 'make us of its institutions' – albeit 'by applying the relevant provisions of the Treaties.'

The uniform institutional framework may help explain why differentiation has, in recent years, proceeded smoothly in justice and home affairs. Equal participation of British ministers and civil servants in debates about legislative proposals in the Council and its working groups may have supported the British decision to participate in many legislative measures.[167] For precisely the same reason, it is problematic that the euro group has established independent working arrangements outside the Council. Parallel institutions support political fissures – most prominently in situations of a 'voting cartel', when the euro group takes a political decision behind closed doors, which is then turned into a formal vote in the Council without meaningful debate.[168] This negative example demonstrates why it is important that differentiation is regularly embedded into the single institutional framework. Permanent dialogue facilitates that differentiation does not lead to political rupture and that it does not contradict the common interest of the EU at large.

Enhanced cooperation, in particular, has functioned as a 'veto buster' in practice. Recourse to the mechanism may overcome an impasse in decision making, in particular when the Treaties prescribe unanimity. This veto-busting function was evident in three cases in which enhanced cooperation had been authorised hitherto,[169] and the function supported EU decision making in a different manner before the agreement on the European Arrest Warrant, when the resistance of the Italian Prime Minister Silvio Berlusconi was overcome in part by the 'threat' of activating the enhanced cooperation mechanism without Italy.[170] In its judgment on the EU patent, the ECJ emphasised in welcomed clarity that the move towards enhanced cooperation to overcome difficulties in reaching unanimity is not abusive.[171] The situation is quite similar at intergovernmental conferences, where unanimity for Treaty change can only be obtained when some Member States are given an opt-out.[172] It

---

167 See Funda Tekin, *Differentiated Integration at Work* (Nomos 2012) 234–8; and Rebecca Adler-Nissen, 'The Diplomacy of Opting Out: A Bourdieudian Approach to National Integration Strategies' (2008) 46 JCMS 663, 675.

168 See (n 139) above; and Thym (n 150) para. 65.

169 See the introduction to section 3.1 above; and Guillard (n 7) 496.

170 See the letter to the editor by the chairman of the EP-Committee Graham Watson, 'Go Ahead on Arrest Warrant Without Italy' *Financial Times* (London, 8 December 2001).

171 See CJEU (n 88) paras 33–36; the 'last resort' criterion ensures that institutions strive for a compromise among all beforehand; see art. 20(2) TEU, section 3.1.2 and ibid., para. 49.

172 See the political science analyses by Kenneth Dyson and Angelos Sepos, 'Differentiation as Design Principle' in Kenneth Dyson and Angelos Sepos (eds),

seems that the British Government pursues a similar strategy, when it hopes to obtain further concessions before a referendum on British membership in return for its consent to potential Treaty changes in response to the euro crisis.[173] The experience of earlier IGCs indicates that this strategy might work, in particular if Treaty change was perceived to be necessary for solving the euro crisis.[174]

Supranational differentiation was given a potentially significant boost when the European Convention drafting the Constitutional Treaty introduced a modification at the very last minute,[175] which later became Article 333 TFEU. The Council may adopt a decision, within the framework of enhanced cooperation, to move towards the ordinary legislative procedure, including qualified majority voting in the Council. Crucially, the voting rights of the *outs* will be suspended when this decision is taken.[176] One hypothetical example illustrates what this means: after having established an enhanced cooperation on the harmonisation of the Common Corporate Tax Base,[177] participating Member States could adopt a simple Council Decision to move towards qualified majority voting. On this basis, tax harmonisation and social policy coordination for the Eurozone would be feasible. Those calling for a *gouvernement économique européen* could achieve much (but not anything) if they continued down this road. Not to do so is the result of a lack of political support.[178] The Treaty regime for enhanced cooperation is more flexible than many observers think.

Which Europe? The Politics of Differentiated Integration (Palgrave 2010) 3, 8–9; and A Kölliker, 'The Functional Dimension' in ibid., 39–53.

173 Cf, rather bluntly, Cameron (n 27).

174 See, for the Treaties of Maastricht and Amsterdam, section 2.2 above and, for the reinforced British opt-outs in the Lisbon Treaty, Clemens Ladenburger, 'Police and Criminal Law in the Treaty of Lisbon' (2008) 4 EuConst 20, 28, 36–7.

175 The proposal was submitted to the *last* working session, one day before the solemn agreement on the Draft Constitution by consensus; see Daniel Thym, 'United in Diversity – The Integration of Enhanced Cooperation into the European Constitutional Order' (2005) 6 *German Law Journal* 6, 1731, at 1746–7.

176 Art. 333 TFEU refers to art. 330 TFEU.

177 For this example see (n 69) above.

178 On the occasion of the enhanced cooperation applicable to divorce (see n 66 above), the European Parliament called for such a move, but it did not ultimately insist upon it before it consented under art. 329(1)(2) TFEU; see Jan-Jaap Kuijpers, 'The Law Applicable to Divorce as Test Ground for Enhanced Cooperation' (2012) 18 ELJ 201, 216; and, more generally, European Parliament (n 112) No. 20.

It has often been criticised that the composition of the European Parliament is not modified in situations of geographic differentiation[179] if, for instance, British MEPs vote on the future of the Eurozone[180] (not very different from national constitutional settings with asymmetric federalism or devolution[181]). In the European context, the European Parliament itself has vehemently opposed an initial proposal to proceed in this direction.[182] Recent proposals to split the Parliament as a result of potential Treaty reform to help overcome the euro crisis might be met with similar opposition.[183] The assessment of these proposals will also depend on how one construes the legitimatory structure of European integration: those who emphasise the continued relevance of the national state will tend to support a reorganisation of the assembly along national lines in situations of differentiation,[184] while proponents of neo-federal models will emphasise the representative function of the European Parliament for all citizens of Europe, including those outside the Eurozone.[185]

4.3 Cohesion: United in Diversity

More than 40 years ago, Hans-Peter Ipsen, the founding father of European law doctrine in post-war Germany, warned against 'prejudicing the Community's future or even its final appearance: the unity of its legal structure as it allegedly (has to) emanates from the rationale of its

---

[179] See, e.g., the criticism by Ehlermann (n 103) 255; Kortenberg (n 85) 847; Peter Michael Huber, 'Differenzierte Integration und Flexibilität als neues Ordnungsmuster der Europäischen Union?' (1996) Europarecht 347, 360; and Martin Hedemann-Robinson, 'The Area of Freedom, Security and Justice with Regard to the UK, Ireland and Denmark' in David O'Keeffe and Patrick Twomey (eds), *Legal Issues of the Amsterdam Treaty* (Hart Publishing 1999) 289, 301.

[180] There is no provision mirroring art. 330 TFEU for the Parliament.

[181] In Britain, there is a debate about the voting rights of Scottish MPs whenever the House of Commons decides issues which fall within the substantive reach of the Scotland Act; see Robert Hazell, *The English Question* (UCL/The Constitution Unit 2006).

[182] See the EP Resolution, doc. A4-0102/95 of 17 May 1995 (OJ 1995 C151/56), No. 16; and Tuytschaever (n 49) 65.

[183] A 'Euro Chamber' has been suggested as an option in the Commission Communication, COM(2012) 777 of 28 November 2012, p. 45; and the Franco-German Declaration 'Gemeinsam für ein gestärktes Europa der Stabilität und des Wachstums', 30 May 2013; rather open Herman Van Rompuy, Interim Report to the European Council of 5 December 2012.

[184] See, by way of example, Dougan (n 154) 174–7; and Piris (n 5) 128–9.

[185] Cf, art. 10(2)(1) TEU and European Parliament (n 112) No. 29, 31.

construction and its tasks'.[186] Supranational differentiation is such a manifestation of the integration process that transcends the original assumptions about legal uniformity. In the early years, the political and legal fragility of the integration project and the focus on economic integration resulted in a healthy emphasis on unity-building principles.[187] Nowadays, the situation is different. Policy areas such as justice and home affairs, foreign and defence policy or economic and social policy are closely associated with the concept of political union and, for this reason, feature prominently in discussions about differentiated integration.[188] In these policy fields, divergent degrees of integration may align the pro-integrationist dynamics of some with the political desire of others to abstain. It is based on the national political decision (not) to participate in certain projects.

Differentiation combines different visions of the future of Europe. The UK and Germany may agree on the instrument (differentiation) but they disagree on the objective. Proponents of a 'federal Europe' will consider monetary union as a springboard for further integration, whereas British conservatives will present the opt-out as a hallmark of Europe becoming a flexible club of nation states.[189] Both are right and wrong at the same time. Supranational differentiation allows Member States to leave their fundamental disagreement about the *finalité* of European integration unresolved by recognising that the Union may proceed separately. By accepting that the Union be 'united in diversity'[190] in legal, institutional and ideological terms, this pragmatism is the core achievement of supranational differentiation. It introduces a counterpoint to the presumption of 'more Europe'[191] and complements the principle of subsidiarity in preserving and fine-tuning the federal balance of power.[192] It underlines

---

[186] Hans-Peter Ipsen, *Europäisches Gemeinschaftsrecht* (Mohr Siebeck 1972) 1050 with a view to the state – confederation dichotomy.

[187] See Armin von Bogdandy, 'Constitutional Principles' in von Bogdandy and Bast (n 132), 3, 36–42; and section 2.1.1 above.

[188] This argument was already put forward in Daniel Thym, 'The Political Character of Supranational Differentiation' (2006) 31 ELR 781, 785–7.

[189] See sections 2.1.2 and 2.1.3 above.

[190] This would have become the EU's official motto under art. I-8 Constitutional Treaty (n 95).

[191] As argued by Jo Shaw, 'Constitutionalism and Flexibility in the EU: Developing a Relational Approach' in Búrca and Scott (n 40) 337, 341.

[192] See Neil Walker, 'Sovereignty and Differentiated Integration in the European Union' (1998) 4 ELJ 355, 375–8; and Armin Hatje, 'Grenzen der Flexibilität einer erweiterten Europäischen Union' (2005) Europarecht 148, 151 et seq.

the political maturity of the integration project, if supranational differentiation allows for division without fundamental rupture.

This positive outlook does not conflict with recent experiences during the euro crisis. The malaise of monetary union resulted from construction deficits of the Treaty regime and the institutional practice at the national and supranational level – not differentiated integration. The crisis would have unfolded in similar ways if all Member States had belonged to the Eurozone from the beginning. Similarly, the crisis would not be resolved if the UK and the other non-participating Member States joined the euro.[193] It rather seems that differentiation provides the Union with some of the instruments that are necessary to overcome the difficulties. Cooperation among euro members within and outside the EU framework lays the groundwork for crisis resolution, as demonstrated by the examples of the ESM Treaty and the Fiscal Compact as well as enhanced economic policy coordination. Differentiation allows the Eurozone to act, even if the British Government does not (always) consent. In this respect, it is a decidedly European instrument, which allows for compromise and crisis resolution in the face of fundamental disagreement.

It is not a foregone conclusion that differentiation will facilitate the co-existence of divergent visions about the finality of European integration in perpetuity. Success of this venture will depend on contextual conditions, which supranational differentiation cannot guarantee. That lesson may be learned from other (quasi-)federal entities with internal differentiation, which were, at the height of the nation-state, often associated with secession and eventual break-up. During the final years of the Austro-Hungarian Empire, Georg Jellinek concluded that asymmetric arrangements were 'elements of an incomplete or disorganised state',[194] which may pave the way for either the formation of uniform statehood or decentralisation and break-up. Modern experiences with asymmetric federalism or regionalism in the UK, Canada, Spain, Belgium, or Finland are

---

[193] A common denominator may be the weight of political vision, which conceived both the euro and differentiated integration as instruments for the realisation of 'ever closer union' and may, as a result, have paid less attention to economic or political arguments, which had warned against the pitfalls of the Treaty regime for monetary union from the beginning.

[194] Georg Jellinek, *Das Recht des modernen Staates. Vol. 1* (2nd edn, O. Häring 1905) 642 (own translation).

more positive and show that they may – notwithstanding difficulties – result in enduring constitutional settlements.[195]

4.4 Drawbacks for Identity and Legitimacy

It is widely acknowledged that supranationalism has a dual character, since it combines advanced legal-institutional centralisation with a political confederation, in which democratic legitimacy and citizens' identification primarily rest with the nation states.[196] In other words, the core challenge for the EU is legitimacy, not legality. From a legal perspective, differentiation may be compatible with the supranational integration method. This does not, however, imply that it supports the legitimacy of the European project. Insofar as legitimacy is concerned, differentiation is much more than a legalistic-technical undertaking; it may influence the perception of and the identification with the European project.[197] Respect for the EU Treaties and the single institutional framework underlines the supranational legal credentials of differentiation, but respect does not guarantee legitimacy. The latter requires some degree of social and political assimilation on the basis of shared feelings of mutual belonging and some degree of identificatory infrastructure.[198]

In this respect, differentiation may have negative drawbacks. Contemporary social sciences and cultural studies demonstrate that identities are not fixed. Identities, both individual and collective, change over time and the process of identity-formation is influenced by political practices and symbols.[199] The impact of political symbols and practices may be

---

[195] See the comparative overview by Annette Schrauwen (ed.), *Flexibility in Constitutions: Forms of Closer Cooperation in Federal and Non-Federal Settings* (2nd edn, Amsterdam University Press 2002).

[196] See the classic position of Joseph Weiler, 'The Community System: The Dual Character of Supranationalism' (1981) 1 Y.E.L. 257, 272 et seq.

[197] Similarly Neil Walker, 'Flexibility within a Metaconstitutional Frame' in de Búrca and Scott (n 40) 9–10.

[198] For a critical account see Joseph Weiler, 'Deciphering the Political and Legal DNA of European Integration' in Julie Dickson and Pavlos Eleftheriadis (eds), *Philosophical Foundations of European Union Law* (Oxford University Press 2012) 137, 139–44.

[199] See Jürgen Habermas, 'Die postnationale Konstellation und die Zukunft der Demokratie' in Jürgen Habermas, *Die postnationale Konstellation – Politische Essays* (Suhrkamp 1998) 91, 115–16.

particularly significant in 'constitutional moments' that define the political self-image of a generation.[200] Arguably, the financial crisis is such a constitutional moment for European integration and, at this juncture, identity-formation is complicated as a result of differentiation. It seems to me that feedback loops with the identificatory infrastructure are the 'Achilles' heel' of differentiation integration. It may thwart the emergence of a common identity and it may even, at times of crisis, call into question the existing legitimacy.

First, when speaking to British citizens, one may realise that opt-outs may reinforce a self-perception of being different. To be sure, the UK may have already headed towards the exit door 20 years ago if it had not obtained an opt-out from monetary union. However, this constructive pedigree of differentation does not entail that the opt-outs are irrelvent to the identification with the European project; arguably, they promote a perception of distance by means of negative demarcation, thereby being one element among many which paved the way for the Brexit referendum. British citizens are proud of the pound, their border controls and the veto against the fiscal compact – also because the Belgians and the Dutch do not have these symbols of national singularity any more. This buttresses national self-confidence and weakens European identity.[201]

Secondly, the same holds, to a lesser degree, for any example of differentiation. Enter search terms such as 'Schengen', 'EU Patent' or 'Fiscal Compact' into Google (or any other search engine) and you will sooner or later find references to (non-)participating Member States. This has repercussions for the perception of political debates about these issues. In situations of differentiated integration, political debates will rarely be perceived as transnational arguments among different political or social groups across national borders. Rather, the perception of law making is reminiscent of diplomatic inter-state negotiations.[202] This weakens transnational democracy (institutionally within the European Parliament) and buttresses intergovernmental bargaining (institutionally within the European Council). In line with intergovernmental accounts, the national interest seems to guide the integration process.

---

[200] On the re-orientation of US constitutionalism in situations of fundamental change, see Bruce Ackerman, *We, the People. Vol. 2 Transformations* (Harvard University Press 1998).

[201] See also Thomas Risse, 'The Euro Between National and European Identity' (2003) 10 *Journal of European Public Policy* 487, 492–5, 499–500.

[202] For a similar perspective, see Jiri Přibáň, 'Legal Flexibility, Governance and Differentiated Integration' in Dyson and Sepos (n 172) 24, 27–31; and Shaw (n 191) 352–3.

Thirdly, all these factors are amplified when Member States negotiate and agree upon international satellite agreements, such as the Fiscal Compact. Many Greeks and Germans know these agreements, connecting them to summits of heads of state or government or rulings of the German Constitutional Court. Few, however, have the heard of the Six-Pack or the *Pringle* judgment. International satellite treaties are a pure form of intergovernmentalism in the dual legal-institutional and political-identificatory meaning of the term. A focus on inter-state bargaining and international satellite treaties in the national media compromises, in the eyes of the citizens, the continued confidence in the merits of the supranational integration method[203] – irrespective of whether the ECJ subordinates international treaties to the rules of Union law.[204] The lack of faith in supranationalism seems to extend to the head of state or government, who probably do not realise that they could have fulfilled most elements of the Fiscal Compact through secondary law making.

5. CONCLUSION

Over the past 20 years, differentiated integration has become a reality. Monetary union, the area of freedom, security and justice, the general mechanism for enhanced cooperation and security and defence policy define the *acquis* of integration at multiple speeds. In contrast with other instruments of flexible policy making, these expressions of supranational differentiation are defined by the limited geographic scope of Union law and the corresponding suspension of voting rights of the non-participating Member States in the Council. Enhanced cooperation, in particular, was always meant to serve as an instrument to overcome an impasse in decision-making and to support the resolution of potential crises, which cannot be solved with the participation of all Member States. In doing so, the euro crisis example demonstrates that differentiation is more than a technical exercise. It has ramifications for the integration project, which concerns, in particular, the co-existence of different visions of the future of Europe, the compatibility with the

---

[203] See also Nicole Scicluna, 'EU Constitutionalism in Flux: Is the Eurozone Crisis Precipitating Centralisation or Diffusion?' (2012) 18 ELJ 489, 493–5; Walker (n 197) 12; and Kaarlo Tuori, 'The European Financial Crisis: Constitutional Aspects and Implications' (2012) 28 EUI Working Papers Law sect. IV.

[204] See, again, section 3.2.2 above.

supranational integration method and the repercussions for the legitimatory infrastructure.

Proponents of differentiation may agree on the instruments, whenever country-specific opt-outs or the general mechanism for enhanced cooperation allow for the realisation of certain policy projects among a limited number of Member States. However, this agreement will often manifest itself in diverging objectives about the *finalité* of European integration. British conservatives, in particular, perceive different speeds as a hallmark of Europe becoming a flexible club of nation states that pursue certain projects in common, whenever it suits their national interests. In contrast, many continental Europeans want to retain the historic and often vague objective of quasi-federal unity. Differentiation allows these positions to co-exist despite their incompatibility as a matter of principle. To recognise that the Union may proceed non-simultaneously allows Member States to leave fundamental disagreement unresolved. Pro-integrationist dynamics are constructively combined with the desire to abstain.

From a legal perspective, differentiated integration raises a number of doctrinal and constitutional questions about how to accommodate enhanced cooperation and other expressions of differentiation with the supranational integration method. This chapter maintains that these questions can be resolved satisfactorily. The general mechanism for enhanced cooperation, in particular, respects general principles of Union law and does not impede the prerogatives of the supranational institutions – as the substantive constraints and procedural requirements for enhanced cooperation in the EU Treaties demonstrate. With the exception of voting rights of the non-participating Member States in the Council, the other institutions sit and decide without modification in situations of asymmetric law making. Supranational differentiation, at present, is firmly embedded in the supranational legal order. In essence, this conclusion extends to international treaties, which are, like satellites in the earth's orbit, kept in their path by the gravitational pull of Union law. They serve as a 'bypass' and do not result in a 'heart attack' for supranationalism.

Respect for the EU Treaties and the single institutional framework is not sufficient to guarantee the legitimacy of the European project. If differentiation complicates the identification with the EU and the emergence of a robust European identity, the main challenge of differentiated integration is not its legality but rather its negative drawbacks for the legitimacy of the integration process. Identities, both individual and collective, change over time and are influenced by political practices and symbols – particularly in times of crisis. It seems that differentiation may entail negative feedback with the identificatory infrastructure of European integration. It reinforces a sense of national belonging through means of negative demarcation and it complicates transnational debates among political or social groups across national borders. Supranational law making is perceived as inter-state negotiations, most prominently in the case of international satellite treaties. The euro crisis appears not to be a catalyst for pan-European debate or the hour of birth of Europe as a political community. Instead, differentiation brings about the discursive strengthening of national identity; it is a building block for Member States re-imagining themselves as political communities. For that reason, differentiation may be compatible with supranationalism and the rule of law, but it endangers the legitimacy of the European project.

REFERENCES

Ackerman B, *We, the People. Vol. 2 Transformations* (Harvard UP 1998).

Adler-Nissen R, 'The Diplomacy of Opting Out: A Bourdieudian Approach to national Integration Strategies' (2008) 46 JCMSt. 663–84.

Alter K, 'Who Are the "Masters of the Treaty"?' in Alter K, *The European Court's Political Power: Selected Essays* (OUP 2009) 109–38.

Antpöhler C, 'Emergenz der europäischen Wirtschaftsregierung. Das Sis Pack als Zeichen supranationaler Leistungsfähigkeit' (2012) 72 *Heidelberg Journal of International Law* 353–93.

Barker A, and Milne R, 'Eurozone 'outs' fear banking union plan' *Financial Times* (London, 2 October 2012).

Becker U, *EU-Erweiterung und differenzierte Integration* (Nomos 1999).

Bender T, 'Die Verstärkte Zusammenarbeit nach Nizza. Anwendungsfehler und Bewertung im Spiegel historischer Präzedenzfälle der differenzierten Integration' (2001) 61 *Heidelberg Journal of International Law* 729–70.

Bradley K, 'Institutional Design in the Treaty of Nice' (2001) 38 CML Rev. 1095–123.

Brandt W, 'Rede vor der Organisation Française du Mouvement Européen' (1975) *Europa-Archiv* D33-8, D36 (own translation).

Bribosia H, 'Les coopérations renforcées' in Amato G, Bribosia H, and De Witte B (eds), *Genèse et destinée de la Constitution européenne* (Bruylant 2007) 623–44.

Calliess C, and Schoenfleisch C, 'Auf dem Weg in die europäische "Fiskalunion"? Europa – und verfassungsrechtliche Fragen einer Reform des Wirtschafts- und Währungsunion im Kontext des Fiskalvertrages' (2012) Juristenzeitung 477–87.

Cameron D, 'Speech at Bloomberg' (London, 23 January 2013), https://www.gov.uk/government/-speeches/eu-speech-at-bloomberg).

Chirac J, 'Notre Europe. Discours devant le Bundestag' *Le Monde* (Paris, 28 June 2000).

Constantinesco V, 'Les clauses de "coopération renforcée"' (1997) 33 RTD 751–67.
Craig P, 'The Stability, Coordination and Governance Treaty: Principle, Politics and Pragmatism' (2012) 37 ELRev. 231–48.
Curtin D, 'The Constitutional Structure of the Union: A Europe of Bits and Pieces' (1993) 30 CML Rev 17–69.
Curtin D, and Van Ooik R, 'Denmark and the Edinburgh Summit: Maastricht without Tears' in O'Keeffe D, and Twomey P (eds), *Legal Issues of the Maastricht Treaty* (Chancery Law 1994) 349–65.
Dahrendorf R, 'A Third Europe?' (Jean Monnet Lecture at the EU, 26 Nov. 1979).
Dashwood A, 'Position Paper' in Dashwood A (ed.), *Reviewing Maastricht, Issues for the 1996 IGC* (Sweet & Maxwell 1996) 145–66.
de Búrca G, 'Differentiation within the "Core"?' in de Búrca G, and Scott J (eds), *Constitutional Change in the EU* (Hart 2000) 133–72.
Delors J, 'Ma vision d'une Fédération des États-nations' (Juillet/Août 2000) Le Monde des Débats, 5.
De Witte B, 'Old Flexibility' in de Búrca G, and Scott J (eds), *Constitutional Change in the EU* (Hart 2000) 31–58.
De Witte B, 'The Process of Ratification of the Constitutional Treaty and the Crisis Options' (2004) 16 EUI Working Paper Law.
De Witte B, , Hanf D, and Vos E (eds), *The Many Faces of Differentiation in EU Law* (Intersentia 2001).
Dougan M, 'The Unfinished Business of Enhanced Co-operation' in Ott A, and Vos E (eds), *Fifty Years of European Integration: Foundations and Perspectives* (TMC Asser Press 2009) 157–79.
Dyson K, and Sepos A (eds), 'Differentiation as Design Principle and as a Tool of Political Management in European Integration' in Dyson K, and Sepos A (eds), *Which Europe? The Politics of Differentiated Integration* (Palgrave Macmillan 2010) 3–23.
Ehlermann C-D, 'How Flexible is Community Law?' (1984) 82 *Michigan Law Review* 1274-1293.
____'Differentiation, Flexibility, Closer Co-operation: The New Provisions on the Amsterdam Treaty' (1998) 4 ELJ 246–270.
Fischer J, 'Vom Staatenverbund zur Föderation' in Walter Hallstein-Institut (ed.), *Verfassungsrechtliche Reformen zur Erweiterung der Europäischen Union* (Nomos 2000) 171.
Gaja G, 'How Flexible is Flexibility under the Amsterdam Treaty' (1998) 35 CML Rev 855–70.
Giering C, 'Vertiefung und Differenzierung' (1997) Integration 72–83.
Grabitz E (ed.), *Abgestufte Integration* (N.P. Engel 1984).
Grabitz E, and Langeheine B, 'Legal Problems Related to a Proposed "Two-Tier System" of Integration within the European Community' (1981) 18 CML Rev 33–48.
Guillard C, *L'Intégration différenciée dans l'Union européenne* (Bruylant 2007).
Habermas J, 'Die postnationale Konstellation und die Zukunft der Demokratie' in Habermas J, *Die postnationale Konstellation – Politische Essays* (Suhrkamp 1998) 91–169.

Habermas J, *Zur Verfassung Europas – Ein Essay* (Suhrkamp 2011).
Hague W, 'Harmonization or Flexibility' in Rosenbaum M (ed.), *Britain and Europe* (OUP 2001) 287–92.
Hatje A, 'Grenzen der Flexibilität einer erweiterten Europäischen Union' (2005) Europarecht 148–61.
Hazell R, *The English Question* (UCL/The Constitution Unit 2006).
Hedemann-Robinson M, 'The Area of Freedom, Security and Justice with Regard to the UK, Ireland and Denmark' in O'Keeffe D, and Twomey P (eds), *Legal Issues of the Amsterdam Treaty* (Hart Publishing 1999) 289–302.
Hofmann R, 'Wie viel Flexibilität für welches Europa: Gedanken für künftigen Entwicklungen der europäischen Integration' (1999) *Europarecht* 713–35.
Howarth D, 'The Compromise on Denmark and the Treaty on European Union: A Legal and Political Analysis' (1994) 31 CML Rev 765–805.
Huber PM, 'Differenzierte Integration und Flexibilität als neues Ordnungsmuster der Europäischen Union?' (1996) *Europarecht* 347–61.
Ipsen H-P, *Europäisches Gemeinschaftsrecht* (Mohr Siebeck 1972).
Janning J, 'Dynamik in der Zwangsjacke – Flexibilität in der Europäischen Union nach Amsterdam' (1997) 20 *Integration* 285–91.
Jellinek G, *Das Recht des modernen Staates. Vol. 1* (2nd edn, O Häring 1905).
Joerges C, 'Europas Wirtschaftsverfassung in der Krise' (2012) 51 *Der Staat* 357–85.
Jones E, Menon A, and Weatherill S (eds), *The Oxford Handbook of the European Union* (OUP 2012).
Kelsen H, *Allgemeine Staatslehre* (Springer 1925).
Kleine M, 'Integrated Bi- and Multinational Units in Europe' in Nolte G (ed.), *European Military Law Systems* (De Gruyter 2003) 889–908.
Kölliker A, 'The Functional Dimension' in Dyson K, and Sepos A (eds), *Which Europe? The Politics of Differentiated Integration* (Palgrave Macmillan 2010) 39–53.
Kortenberg H (pseudonym), 'Closer Cooperation in the Treaty of Amsterdam' (1998) 35 CML Rev 833–54.
Kuijpers J-J, 'The Law Applicable to Divorce as Test Ground for Enhanced Cooperation' (2012) 18 ELJ 201–29.
Ladenburger C, 'Police and Criminal Law in the Treaty of Lisbon' (2008) 4 EuConst 20–40.
Lavenex S, 'Concentric Circles of Flexible "EUropean" Integration' (2011) 9 *Comparative European Politics* 372–93.
Leuffen D, Rittenberger B, and Schimmelfennig F, *Differentiated Integration. Explaining Variation in the European Union* (Routledge 2013).
Louis J-V, 'L'Union économique et monétaire' in *Commentaire Mégret, Le droit de la CE, Vol. 6* (2nd edn, Editions de l'Institut d'études européennes 1995) 1–198.
Majone G, *Europe as the Would-be World Power. The EU at Fifty* (CUP 2009).
Major J, 'Speech at Leiden University' (Leiden, 7 September 1994), http://www.johnmajor.co.uk/-page1124.html).
Maude F, 'Networks and Nations' in Walter Hallstein-Institut (ed), *Die Reform der europäischen Institutionen* (Nomos 2002) 27–40.

Möllers C, 'Pouvoir Constituant, Constitution, Constitutionalisation' in von Bogdandy A, and Bast J (eds), *Principles of European Constitutional Law* (Hart Publishing 2006), 183–226.
Pechstein M, 'Herausforderungen für den Rechtsschutz in einer flexiblen Union' (2013) 2 *Europarecht* 71–87.
Peers S, 'The Constitutional Implications of the EU Patent' (2011) 7 EuConst 229–66.
Peers S, 'Towards a New Form of EU Law? The Use of EU Institutions outside the EU Legal Framework' (2013) 9 EuConst 37–72.
Peters A, *Elemente einer Theorie der Verfassung Europas* (Duncker & Humblot 2001).
Piris J-C, *The Future of Europe. Towards a Two-Speed EU?* (CUP 2012).
Přibáň J, 'The Self-Referential European Polity, its Legal Context and Systemic Differentiation' (2009) 15 ELJ 442–61.
Přibáň J, 'Legal Flexibility, Governance and Differentiated Integration' in Dyson K, and Sepos A (eds), *Which Europe? The Politics of Differentiated Integration* (Palgrave Macmillan 2010) 24–38.
Risse T, 'The Euro Between National and European Identity' (2003) 10 *Journal of European Public Policy* 487–503.
Rodrigues S, 'Le Traité de Nice et les coopérations renforcées au sein de l'Union européenne' (2001) RMCUE 11–16.
Roland S, 'La Différenciation, nouvelle frontière?: Quelques réflections sur les fonctions de la différenciation dans le système juridique de l'Union européenne' in Blumann C (ed.), *Les frontières de l'Union européenne* (Bruylant 2013) 249–77.
Rosas A, and Armati L, *An Introduction to EU Constitutional Law* (Hart 2010).
Ruffert M, 'Die europäische Schuldenkrise vor dem Bundesverfassungsgericht' (2011) Europarecht 842–55.
Sarkozy N, 'Entretien: Le sommet de Bruxelles' *Le Monde* (Paris, 12 December 2011).
Schäuble W, 'Institutioneller Wandel und Europäische Einigung' *Frankfurter Allgemeine Zeitung* (Frankfurt, 12 Jan. 2013) 14.
Schäuble W, and Lamers K, *Überlegungen zur europäischen Politik* (CDU, 1994).
Schmitter C, 'Coopérations renforcées et compétences externes de la Communauté européenne' in M Dony (ed.), *L'Union européenne et le monde après Amsterdam* (Université libre de Bruxelles 1999) 77–106.
Schneider H, 'Verträge zwischen Gliedstaaten im Bundesstaat: Schranken nichthoheitlicher Verwaltung' (1961) 19 *Veröffentlichungen der Vereinigung Deutscher Staatsrechtslehrer* 1–33.
Schneider H, 'Kerneuropa – ein aktuelles Stichwort und seine Bedeutung' (2004) 12 *Journal für Rechtspolitik* 136–61.
Schorkopf F, 'Gestaltung mit Recht: Prägekraft und Selbstand des Rechts in einer Rechtsgemeinschaft' (2011) 136 *Archiv des Öffentlichen Rechts* 323–44.
Schorkopf F, Finanzkrisen als Herausforderung der internationalen, europäischen und nationalen Rechtsetzung' (2012) 71 *Veröffentlichungen der Vereinigung Deutscher Staatsrechtslehrer* 183–225.

Schrauwen A (ed.), *Flexibility in Constitutions: Forms of Closer Cooperation in Federal and Non-Federal Settings* (2nd edn, Amsterdam UP 2002).
Schuman R, Declaration of 9 May 1950 (own translation).
Schütze R, 'Supremacy without Pre-Emption? The Very Slowly Emergent Doctrine of Community Pre-Emption' (2006) 43 CML Rev 1032–48.
Schütze R, EC Law and International Agreements of the Member States – An Ambivalent Relationship?' (2007) 9 *Cambridge Yearbook of European Law Studies* 387–440.
Schwarz M, 'A Memorandum of Misunderstanding – The Doomed Road of the European Stability Mechanism and a Possible Way Out: Enhanced Co-operation' (2014) 51 CML Rev 389–423.
Scicluna N, 'EU Constitutionalism in Flux: Is the Eurozone Crisis Precipitating Centralisation or Diffusion?' (2012) 18 ELJ 489–503.
Shaw J, 'Constitutionalism and Flexibility in the EU: Developing a Relational Approach' in de Búrca G, and Scott J (eds), *Constitutional Change in the EU* (Hart 2000) 331–58.
Shaw J, 'The Treaty of Nice: Legal and Constitutional Implications' (2001) 7 *European Public Law* 195–215.
Shaw J, 'Flexibility in a "Reorganised" and "Simplified" Treaty' (2003) 40 CML Rev 279–311.
Simma B, *Das Reziprozitätselement im Zustandekommen völkerrechtlicher Verträge* (Duncker & Humblot 1972).
Stone Sweet A, 'The European Court of Justice' in Craig P, and de Búrca G (eds), *The Evolution of EU Law (*2nd edn, OUP 2011) 121–53.
Stratton A, and Gow D, 'Nicolas Sarkozy tells David Cameron: shut up over the euro' *Guardian unlimited* (London, 23 October 2011).
Stubb A, 'A Categorisation of Differentiated Integration' (1996) 34 JCMS 283–95.
Tekin F, *Differentiated Integration at Work* (Nomos 2012).
Thym D, *Ungleichzeitigkeit und Europäisches Verfassungsrecht* (Nomos 2004).
Thym D, United in Diversity – The Integration of Enhanced Cooperation into the European Constitutional Order' (2005) 6 *German Law Journal* (2005) 1731–47.
Thym D, 'The Political Character of Supranational Differentiation' (2006) 31 ELR 781–99.
Thym D, 'Einheit in Vielfalt' in Hatje A, and Müller-Graff P-C (eds), *Enzyklopädie Europarecht. Vol. 1 Europäisches Organisations- und Verfassungsrecht* (Nomos 2014) 259–310.
Thym D, 'Supranational Differentiation and Enhanced Cooperation' in Tridimas T, and Schütze R (eds), *The Oxford Principles of European Union Law. Vol. I* (OUP 2015 forthcoming).
Thym D, and Wendel M, 'Préserver le respect du droit dans la crise' (2013) 48 *Cahiers de droit européen* 733–57.
Tindemans L, 'European Union. Report to the European Council' (1976) Suppl. 1, *Bulletin of the E.C.*, 20.
Tuori K, The European Financial Crisis: Constitutional Aspects and Implications (2012) 28 *EUI Working Papers Law* sect. IV.
Tuytschaever F, *Differentiation in European Union Law* (Hart 1999).

Uerpmann-Wittzack R, 'Völkerrecht als Ausweichordnung' (2013) 2 *Europarecht* 49–60.
Verhofstadt G, 'A Vision for Europe' (Speech to the European Policy Centre, Brussels, 21 September 2000).
Verhofstadt G, *Die vereinigten Staaten von Europa* (Grenz-Echo Verlag 2007).
von Bogdandy A, 'A Bird's Eye View on the Science of European Law: Structures, Debates and Development Projects of Basic Research on the Law of the European Union in a German Perspective' (2000) 6 ELJ 208–38.
von Bogdandy A, 'Constitutional Principles' in von Bogdandy A, and Bast J (eds), *Principles of European Constitutional Law* (1st edn, Hart 2006) 13–52.
von Bogdandy A, Founding Principles' in von Bogdandy A, and Bast J (eds), *Principles of Constitutional Law* (2nd edn, Hart 2009) 13–72.
von Buttlar C, 'Rechtsprobleme der "verstärkten Zusammenarbeit" nach dem Vertrag von Nizza' (2001) 4 *Zeitschrift für Europarechtliche Studien* 649–88.
von Ondarza N, 'Auf dem Weg zur Union in der Union: Institutionelle Auswirkungen der differenzierten Integration in der Eurozone auf die EU' (2013) 1 *Integration* 17–33.
Vranes E, 'The "Internal" External Relations of EMU' (2000) 6 *Columbia Journal of European Law* 361–72.
Walker N, 'Sovereignty and Differentiated Integration in the European Union' (1998) 4 ELJ 355–88.
Walker N, 'Flexibility within a Metaconstitutional Frame' in de Búrca G, and Scott J (eds), *Constitutional Change in the EU* (Hart 2000) 9–30.
Watson G, 'Go Ahead on Arrest Warrant Without Italy' *Financial Times* (London, 8 December 2001).
Watson P, 'Social Policy after Maastricht' (1993) 30 CML Rev 481–513.
Weatherhill S, 'If I'd Wanted You to Understand I Would Have Explained It Better' in O'Keeffe D, and Twomey P (eds), *Legal Issues of the Amsterdam Treaty* (Hart Publishing 1999) 21–40.
Weiler J, 'The Community System: The Dual Character of Supranationalism' (1981) 1 *Yearbook of European Law* 267–306.
Weiler J, 'Deciphering the Political and Legal DNA of European Integration' in Dickson J, and Eleftheriadis P (eds), *Philosophical Foundations of European Union Law* (OUP 2012) 137–58.
Wessels W, 'Die Vertragsreform von Nizza – Zur institutionellen Entscheidungsreife' (2001) *Integration* 8–25.
Zeitzmann S, 'Das Verfahren der Verstärkten Zusammenarbeit und dessen erstmalige Anwendung' (2011) *Zeitschrift für Europarechtliche Studien* 87–113.

3. Enhanced cooperation: the Cinderella of differentiated integration

Steve Peers

1. INTRODUCTION

A Martian who was (for some alien reason) interested in differentiated integration within the EU would probably start by reading the EU Treaties. He, she or it would likely conclude that enhanced cooperation was the most common type of differentiated integration – since, unlike the other types, it is neither limited to certain Member States nor to certain policy areas. But our Martian would be wrong. For despite its potentially broad scope of application, of all the forms of differentiated integration forming part or linked to the EU legal order, the enhanced cooperation procedure has been used the least, and disappointed the supporters of differentiated integration the most. It could be said that enhanced cooperation is the 'Cinderella' of differentiated integration, left behind while its glamorous step-sisters (Justice and Home Affairs and Economic and Monetary Union) go to the flexibility ball.

Why is this? This chapter will answer that question by looking at the past, present and possible future of the EU's enhanced cooperation rules.

2. THE HISTORICAL BACKGROUND[1]

Like Cinderella herself, the enhanced cooperation process had a promising early childhood. After a lengthy discussion of the principle of establishing various forms of flexibility or differentiation among Member

[1] The following two sections are adapted from Steve Peers, 'Divorce, European Style: The First Authorization of Enhanced Cooperation' (2010) 6 *European Constitutional Law Review* 339.

States as regards European integration,[2] and the launch of several projects involving fewer than all Member States outside the scope of the Community process (for instance, the Schengen system), the original Treaty on European Union (TEU) provided for opt-outs for certain Member States within the Community legal order as regards specific policy areas: social policy and economic and monetary union. The Treaty of Amsterdam rescinded the first of these opt-outs but introduced various opt-outs relating to Justice and Home Affairs (JHA) issues, as well as the general possibility of authorising opt-outs in the form of 'closer cooperation'.[3]

The rules on potential closer cooperation comprised general rules set out in Title VII of the TEU (Articles 43–45, previous TEU), along with specific rules for the 'first pillar' (Community law) set out in the EC Treaty and for the 'third pillar' (policing and criminal law) set out in Title VI of the TEU.[4] There was no provision for closer cooperation as regards the 'second pillar' (EU foreign policy), but rather the possibility of 'constructive abstention'.[5]

However, the crucial point was that the conditions for authorizing closer cooperation were as strict as Cinderella's step-mother. The general rules included requirements that closer cooperation could only be authorized as a 'last resort', must involve a majority of Member States, could not affect the '*acquis communautaire*' or any measures adopted on the basis of other provisions of the Treaties, could not 'affect the competences, rights, obligations and interests of those Member States which do not participate therein', and had to be open to all Member States.[6] There were further specific rules applicable to the first and third pillars; as regards the first pillar, closer cooperation could not concern areas within EC exclusive competence (not defined), could not 'affect Community policies, actions or programmes', 'concern the citizenship of the

---

[2] See, for instance, Chs 1 and 2 of Filip Tuytschaever, *Differentiation in European Union Law* (Hart 1999) and Ch. 3 of Alexander Stubb, *Negotiating Flexibility in the European Union: Amsterdam, Nice and Beyond* (Palgrave Macmillan 2002).

[3] On these rules, see, for instance, Ch. 3 of Tuytschaever (n 2) and Ch. 4 of Stubb (n 2), as well as Stephen Weatherill, '"If I'd Wanted You to Understand I Would Have Explained it Better": What is the Purpose of the Provisions on Closer Cooperation Introduced by the Treaty of Amsterdam?' in David O'Keeffe and Pattrick Twomey, *Legal Issues of the Amsterdam Treaty* (Hart 1999) 21.

[4] See respectively art. 11 EC and art. 40 TEU, before the entry into force of the Treaty of Nice.

[5] Art. 23(1), previous TEU.

[6] Art. 43(1) TEU, before the entry into force of the Treaty of Nice.

Union or discriminate between nationals of Member States', 'constitute a discrimination or a restriction of trade between Member States' or 'distort the conditions of competition between the latter'. Any closer cooperation measures also had to remain within the limits of EC powers.[7]

Authorization for closer cooperation would in either the first or third pillar be granted by the Council, acting by a qualified majority vote (QMV), but any Member State could oppose this vote 'for important and stated reasons of national policy', in which case the Council, acting by QMV, could refer the issue to Member States' leaders for a decision by unanimity.[8] Within the first pillar, the proposal to launch closer cooperation would have to be made by the Commission after a request from a group of Member States; the European Parliament (EP) would have to be consulted.[9] There was a special procedure for Member States to join closer cooperation in progress.[10]

The closer cooperation provisions set out in the Treaty of Amsterdam were never used in practice.[11] Due to misgivings about their feasibility, these provisions were renegotiated as part of the Treaty of Nice, at which point they were redubbed the 'enhanced cooperation' rules.[12] The revised provisions abolished the possible 'emergency brake' which could be pulled by any Member State to block the authorization of first or third pillar enhanced cooperation;[13] included rules on enhanced cooperation in

---

7 Art. 11(1) EC, before amendment by the Treaty of Nice.

8 Art. 11(2) EC and art. 40(2) TEU, before amendment by the Treaty of Nice.

9 Art. 11(2) EC, before amendment by the Treaty of Nice. The third pillar rules (ibid.) provided for a more limited involvement of the EP and Commission.

10 Art. 11(3) EC and art. 40(3) TEU, before amendment by the Treaty of Nice.

11 See Jo Shaw, 'Enhancing Cooperation After Nice: Will the Treaty Do the Trick?' in Mads Andenas and John Usher (eds), *The Treaty of Nice and Beyond: Enlargement and Constitutional Reform* (Hart 2003) 207, at 217.

12 The revised general rules were still set out in Title VII (arts 43–45) of the previous TEU, which now included arts 43a, 43b and 44a. The revised first pillar rules were set out in arts 11 and 11a EC, while the revised third pillar rules were set out in arts 40, 40a and 40b of the previous TEU. On the Nice provisions, see Shaw (n 11); Stubb (n 2), Ch. 5; and José M De Areilza, 'The Reform of Enhanced Cooperation Rules: Towards Less Flexibility?' in Bruno De Witte, Dominik Hanf and Ellen Vos (eds), *The Many Faces of Differentiation in EU Law* (Intersentia 2001) 27.

13 Art. 11(2) EC and art. 40a(2), previous TEU. It was still possible for an individual Member State to insist upon discussion of a proposal to launch enhanced cooperation at the European Council, but the latter body had no power to block the authorization.

the field of foreign policy;[14] gave the EP power of assent over the authorization of any first pillar enhanced cooperation which fell within the scope of the co-decision procedure; altered the threshold to launch enhanced cooperation from a majority of Member States to eight Member States;[15] and softened the substantive conditions to which the authorization of enhanced cooperation was subject.

On the last point, this meant in particular that enhanced cooperation measures only had to 'respect' the *acquis communautaire* and other EU measures, rather than 'not affect' them;[16] that enhanced cooperation measures could not 'undermine' the internal market or economic or social cohesion, in place of the prior requirements that it not 'affect' EC policies et al., concern EU citizenship or discriminate between the nationals of Member States;[17] and that enhanced cooperation no longer had to avoid affecting the 'interests' of non-participating Member States.[18] The requirement that enhanced cooperation could only be undertaken as a 'last resort' was retained, but further explained.[19] It was also specified that enhanced cooperation measures did not form part of the EU's *acquis*.[20]

Despite the softening of the substantive and procedural conditions needed to authorize enhanced cooperation, as well as the enlargement of the Union in 2004 and 2007 (which had triggered advance fears among some Member States that enhanced cooperation would be necessary in

---

14 Arts 27a–27e, previous TEU. Enhanced cooperation in foreign policy is not discussed in this chapter.

15 Art. 43(g) TEU (Nice); see previously art. 43(1)(d) TEU (Amsterdam). This change had no immediate impact, since eight Member States anyway constituted a majority of the 15 Member States; rather it was obviously aimed at facilitating enhanced cooperation once the EU enlarged further, as it did in 2004 and 2007.

16 Compare art. 43(1)(e) TEU (Amsterdam) with art. 43(c) TEU (Nice).

17 Art. 43(e) TEU (Nice); see previously art. 43(1)(b) and (c) EC (Amsterdam). The condition relating to trade barriers or discrimination in trade, or distortions of competition, was retained (art. 43(f) TEU (Nice); compare to art. 11(1)(e) EC (Amsterdam)).

18 Art. 43(h) TEU (Nice); see previously art. 43(1)(f) TEU (Amsterdam). Enhanced cooperation still had to 'respect' (rather than 'not affect') the 'competences, rights and obligations' of the non-participants.

19 Art. 43(a) TEU (Nice), replacing art. 43(1)(c) TEU (Amsterdam). The revised provisions now specified that this condition was satisfied when it was 'established within the Council that the objectives of such cooperation cannot be attained within a reasonable period' by (as before) applying the normal rules in the Treaties.

20 Art. 44(1) TEU (Nice).

order to avoid a slowdown in EU integration), the enhanced cooperation rules in the Treaty of Nice were never used. Their use was seriously considered in 2007 when a qualified majority of Member States supported the adoption of a proposal on Framework Decision on criminal suspects' procedural rights,[21] but a small group of Member States exercised a veto on the proposal. However, there was insufficient support among the Member States supporting the proposal to go ahead with the measure on the basis of enhanced cooperation.[22]

Even though no enhanced cooperation was ever approved before the entry into force of the Treaty of Lisbon, the EC Treaty provisions on the authorization of Member States to join enhanced cooperation in progress *were* used,[23] because those provisions applied also to the authorization of the UK or Ireland to join immigration, asylum or civil law measures which had already been adopted, pursuant to the special 'Title IV' Protocol on those Member States' opt-outs from this area. In practice, the Commission quickly authorized those Member States' participation in such measures on five separate occasions.[24]

3. THE CURRENT LEGAL FRAMEWORK

The Treaty of Lisbon amended the enhanced cooperation provisions again. Now, since that Treaty entered into force on 1 December 2009, the relevant provisions comprise a single Article of the TEU and a special Title in the Treaty on the Functioning of European Union (TFEU).[25] In summary, Article 20 TEU provides that Member States can use the EU

---

21 COM(2004) 328, 28 April 2004.

22 Press Release, June 2007 JHA Council.

23 Art. 11a EC (Nice).

24 The Commission authorized Ireland to participate in Dir. 2001/55 on temporary protection (OJ [2001] L212/12), Reg. 1030/2002 on uniform residence permits (OJ [2002] L157/1), and the Decision establishing a Migration Network (OJ [2008] L131/7). See respective Commission Decisions: OJ [2003] L251/23; Decision C(2007)4589/F of 11 October 2007 (not published in the OJ); and OJ [2009] L138/53. The Commission authorized the UK to participate in Regs 593/2008 on conflict of law in contract (Rome I Reg.) and 4/2009 on maintenance (respectively OJ [2008] L177/6 and OJ [2009] L7/1), by means of Decisions in OJ [2009] L10/22 and OJ [2009] L149/73.

25 Art. 20, revised TEU (Title IV of that Treaty) and arts 326–334 TFEU (Title III of Part Six of that Treaty). For comments on the new provisions, see Michael Dougan, 'The Unfinished Business of Enhanced Cooperation: Some Institutional Questions and their Constitutional Implications' in Andrea Ott and

institutions to adopt enhanced cooperation measures within the scope of the EU's non-exclusive competences (Article 20(1), first sub-paragraph).[26] That process must 'aim to further the objectives of the Union, protect its interests and reinforce its integration process', and must also be 'open at any time to all Member States', in accordance with Article 328 TFEU (Article 20(1), second sub-paragraph).[27] Enhanced cooperation must involve at least nine Member States, and can only be authorized by the Council 'as a last resort, when it has established that the objectives of such cooperation cannot be attained within a reasonable period by the Union as a whole', in accordance with Article 329 TFEU (Article 20(2) TEU). All Member States may take part in discussions, but only participating Member States may vote on the measures implementing enhanced cooperation, in accordance with Article 330 TFEU (Article 20(3) TEU). Also, enhanced cooperation measures only bind participating Member States, and new Member States do not have to accept them (Article 20(4) TEU).

The TFEU further specifies that enhanced cooperation must: 'comply with the Treaties and Union law'; 'not undermine the internal market or economic, social and territorial cohesion'; 'not constitute a barrier to or discrimination in trade between Member States', or 'distort competition between them' (Article 326); and 'respect the competences, rights and obligations' of non-participants, who must however 'not impede' the enhanced cooperation (Article 327). It must follow a request to the Commission by a group of Member States, and a proposal from the Commission.[28] The Council must approve that proposal, with the consent

---

Ellen Vos (eds), *Fifty Years of European Integration: Foundations and Perspectives* (TMC Asser Press 2009) 157, and Fabian Amtenbrink and Dimitry Kochenov, 'Towards a More Flexible Approach to Enhanced Cooperation' in ibid., 181.

[26] Since the entry into force of the Treaty of Lisbon, the EU's 'exclusive competence' is defined in art. 3 TFEU.

[27] This is subject to 'compliance with any conditions of participation laid down in the authorising decision'. Later participation is subject to both those conditions and participation in the implementing acts (art. 328(1) TFEU). The Commission and the participating Member States must also promote participation by other Member States (ibid.). Details of the procedure to join enhanced cooperation in progress are set out in art. 331 TFEU.

[28] The Commission is not obliged to make a proposal ('may'), but it must explain why if it does not (art. 329(1), first sub-paragraph).

of the EP.[29] The costs of enhanced cooperation are borne by participating Member States only (Article 332); it is possible to change the voting rules on the measures concerned, again for participating Member States only (Article 333);[30] and enhanced cooperation measures must be consistent with other EU measures (Article 334).

These revised rules retain the previous text, except that: the threshold for the number of participating Member States was increased to nine;[31] the specific rules for the third pillar were merged into the first pillar rules;[32] the EP gained the power of consent over all authorizations of enhanced cooperation (except those relating to foreign policy);[33] in the event that the Commission does not approve a Member State's application to join enhanced cooperation in progress, the Member State concerned can (in effect) appeal to the Council for authorization to join;[34] and the possibility of changing the voting rules is new. Also, the Treaty of Lisbon provides for fast-track authorization of enhanced cooperation as regards certain criminal law and policing issues, in the event of either a veto or the use of an 'emergency brake' as regards a proposal in the relevant areas.[35]

The rules on authorization of enhanced cooperation can be divided into three categories. First, there are rules on participation as such: the minimum number of Member States; openness to all Member States; and the lack of obligation of existing or new Member States to join. Secondly, there are procedural rules, namely the requirements for: a

---

[29] Art. 329(1), second sub-paragraph. The Council votes by qualified majority (the default voting rule). The EP must also be informed about enhanced cooperation in practice (art. 328(2)).

[30] Art. 333 TFEU. The participating Member States must be unanimous making this decision, but there is no requirement of consent by the EP or control by national parliaments (compare to art. 48(7), revised TEU). This provision has not been used.

[31] Art. 20(2), revised TEU.

[32] There are still some distinct rules for enhanced cooperation in foreign policy (arts 329(2) and 331(2) TFEU), which are not further discussed here.

[33] Art. 329(1) TFEU. The possibility of a Member State demanding a discussion at the European Council was dropped.

[34] Art. 331(1) TFEU; the Treaty also now specifies that the Commission 'shall' authorize participation if the relevant conditions are met.

[35] Arts 82(3), 83(3), 86(1) and 87(3) TFEU. These provisions have not yet been used. According to these procedures, enhanced cooperation would automatically be authorized (if requested) if decision-making is blocked and if a dispute settlement process in the European Council is unsuccessful. Only the requirement of a minimum of nine participating Member States would apply.

Member State request; a Commission proposal; approval by the Council; consent by the EP; and the 'last resort' rule. Thirdly, there are substantive rules: the limit to non-exclusive competences; the obligation to aim to further the objectives of the Union, protect its interests and reinforce its integration process; compliance with the Treaties and Union law; the related bans on undermining the internal market or economic, social and territorial cohesion, constituting a barrier to or discrimination in trade between Member States or distorting competition between them; and the obligation to 'respect the competences, rights and obligations' of non-participants.[36]

Legally speaking, the interpretation of the first two categories of rules is mostly straightforward, although of course there may be *political* difficulties satisfying the 'minimum number' rule or the procedural requirements in practice. There is one exception here: the correct interpretation of the 'last resort' requirement is hardly self-evident. In contrast, all of the substantive rules require legal interpretation.

4. APPLICATION IN PRACTICE

The third attempt to adopt enhanced cooperation rules for the EU has been more successful than the previous efforts, since at least the rules have been used in practice. However, they have been used so infrequently that it would still be fair to say that Cinderella is not yet going to the ball.

More specifically, the enhanced cooperation rules, as amended by the Treaty of Lisbon, have been used only three times. First of all, they were used to authorize enhanced cooperation as regards choice of law on divorce, in July 2010 (the 'Rome III Regulation').[37] This followed an inability to agree on a proposal dating back to 2006,[38] even though (since it was a JHA measure) the UK, Ireland and Denmark were already non-participants in the proposal. The implementing measure was adopted by the Council later in 2010.[39] Initially, 14 Member States participated: Spain, Italy, Hungary, Luxembourg, Austria, Romania, Slovenia, Bulgaria, France, Germany, Belgium, Latvia, Malta and Portugal. Two Member States joined later,[40] bringing the total to 16.

---

[36] The parallel obligation on non-participants not to impede enhanced cooperation does not relate to authorization of enhanced cooperation as such.

[37] OJ [2010] L189/12.

[38] COM(2006) 399, 17 July 2006. For details, see further Peers (n 1).

[39] Reg 1259/2010, OJ [2010] L353/10.

[40] Lithuania (OJ [2012] L323/18) and Greece (OJ [2014] L23/41).

Secondly, in 2011 the Council authorized enhanced cooperation as regards unitary patent protection.[41] This followed an inability to agree on a Commission proposal on translation of patents from 2010, although in fact this replaced a prior proposal dating from 2000, and there had been negotiations on EC patent measures beginning in the 1950s.[42] There were two implementing measures, adopted at the end of 2012.[43] Every Member State participates, except Spain and Italy (and subsequently Croatia).[44]

Finally, in 2013, the Council authorized enhanced cooperation as regards a financial transaction tax (FTT).[45] This followed an inability to agree on a Commission proposal dating back to 2011.[46] So far, however, the Council has not been able to agree on the measure implementing enhanced cooperation.[47] Of the Member States 11 participate: Belgium, Germany, Estonia, Greece, Spain, France, Italy, Austria, Portugal, Slovenia and Slovakia.

5. LEGAL CHALLENGES

There were no legal challenges to the first implementation of enhanced cooperation (the Rome III Regulation), but both the unitary patent and FTT decisions have been challenged in the EU courts. Spain and Italy challenged the authorization of enhanced cooperation as regards the unitary patent in the CJEU, losing in 2013.[48] Spain then challenged the two measures implementing enhanced cooperation, losing in 2015.[49] As for the FTT, the UK challenged the authorization of enhanced cooperation, but lost in 2014.[50]

---

[41] OJ [2011] L76/53.

[42] For details, see Steve Peers, 'The Constitutional Aspects of the EU Patent' (2011) 7 *European Constitutional Law Review* 229–71.

[43] Regs 1257/2012 ([2012] OJ L361/1) and 1260/2012 ([2012] OJ L361/89).

[44] In May 2015, the Italian government announced its intention to participate: see <http://www.out-law.com/en/articles/2015/may/italy-drops-opposition-to-eu-unitary-patent-reforms/>.

[45] OJ [2013] L22/11.

[46] COM(2011) 594, 28 September 2011.

[47] COM(2013) 71, 14 February 2013.

[48] Joined Cases C-274/11 *Spain v Council* and C-295/11 *Italy v Council* [2013]ECLI:EU:C:2013:240.

[49] Cases C-146/13 *Spain v Council* [2015] ECLI:EU:C:2015:298 and C-147/13 *Spain v EP and Council*, judgments of 5 May 2015, not yet published.

[50] Case C-209/13 *UK v Council* [2014] ECLI:EU:C:2014:283.

Of these three Court judgments, only the legal challenge against the authorization of enhanced cooperation as regards the unitary patent sheds much light on the enhanced cooperation rules in the Treaties. In that case, the CJEU interpreted the 'last resort' test, as well as a number of the substantive conditions for enhanced cooperation.

In its 2015 ruling on the measures implementing enhanced cooperation as regards the unitary patent, the CJEU did not have to consider arguments about the enhanced cooperation criteria as such, because Spain only argued issues such as the lack of legal base, infringements of the rule of law and autonomy of the EU, and discrimination as regards languages. The latter argument could have been based on the substantive rule in Article 326 TFEU, but Spain did not plead its argument in that way.

As for the FTT judgment, the UK government argued that the authorization of enhanced cooperation on the tax breached Article 327 TFEU, because it would have extraterritorial effects and therefore impinge on the competences of non-participants, as well as Article 332 TFEU, because it would impose costs upon non-participating Member States by means of the application of other EU legislation on mutual assistance in tax matters. The CJEU ruled that a challenge to the authorization of enhanced cooperation could not be confused with a challenge to the implementation of that enhanced cooperation. It was too early to challenge the authorization of FTT on these grounds, because the final shape of the tax had not yet been agreed in the form of a measure implementing the authorization. Furthermore, the authorization decision made no reference to the EU's legislation on mutual assistance regarding taxation.

6. ANALYSIS

The following analysis looks at six separate issues relating to the law of the enhanced cooperation rules:

(1) the 'last resort' test;
(2) the competences rule;
(3) the 'further objectives of the EU' rule;
(4) the requirement to comply with EU law;
(5) the criteria relating to the internal market and competition; and
(6) the obligation not to affect the position of the non-participating States.

6.1 The Last Resort Rule

In its patent judgment, the CJEU ruled against the 'misuse of powers' argument raised by Italy and Spain to say that there was no circumvention of the rule of unanimous voting on language arrangements for patents. More generally, the Court ruled that the enhanced cooperation procedure could apply where the normal rule was unanimous voting, justifying this by a reference to Article 333 TFEU, which refers to the possible move away from unanimity in the context of enhanced cooperation. The Court did not mention the more obvious argument that Article 330 expressly refers to unanimity (and qualified majority) voting as regards the implementation of enhanced cooperation.

Furthermore, the Court ruled that enhanced cooperation satisfied the 'last resort' rule not only where a Member State was 'not yet ready' to participate in an EU measure, but also where there was a 'lack of interest' or 'the inability … to reach agreement'. This is a non-exhaustive list ('for example').

Next, the Court stated that the rule was 'particularly important' and linked it to the requirement to further the Union's objectives, et al. (discussed below). This meant that 'only those situations in which it is impossible to adopt such legislation in the foreseeable future may give rise' to enhanced cooperation. The Council is 'best placed to determine' if there is 'any willingness to compromise' and whether there are likely to be proposals which would lead to the adoption of EU legislation in the foreseeable future. The Court has to examine whether the Council has 'carefully and impartially examined' these issues, and whether it has given 'adequate reasons' for its conclusion.

Applying those principles to the facts of the case, the Court ruled that there was a long process since proposals were tabled in 2000, and there was no sign of agreement on a compromise. The plaintiff Member States had not shown that an agreement was likely at the time when the Council authorized enhanced cooperation.

On the whole, the Court's approach considerably relaxes the possible stringency of the 'last resort' rule. It can be used in cases of unanimity, where the prospect of enhanced cooperation is most likely to be relevant. Obviously it is easier in practice to find sufficient votes to adopt a measure by a qualified majority, since it is impossible for only one or two Member States to block such a proposal. It is arguable that the principles in the Court's judgment are therefore easier to satisfy in the case of unanimity, since a deadlock will necessarily be harder to break by means of a potential compromise. Moreover, since enhanced cooperation needs a QMV to be approved, if there is a blocking minority against the legislation in the first place, the same group of Member States might block the authorization of enhanced cooperation too.

The Court's openness to the various circumstances in which a proposal might be blocked show that even a willingness to participate in principle cannot prevent the EU going ahead with enhanced cooperation if there is not an agreement in prospect nonetheless. It is arguable, however, that further efforts at finding a compromise must be made in such cases, as compared to cases where a Member State declares from the outset that it is entirely opposed in principle to the adoption of EU legislation on a particular topic. And the obligation to attempt a compromise must mean that an EU measure must at least have been tabled and discussed by the Council before enhanced cooperation is considered.

6.2 The Competences Rule

Based on the CJEU's first judgment on the patent rules, it is clear that the competences rule relating to enhanced cooperation is not actually distinct from the general legal rules relating to EU competence. Rather, in the context of enhanced cooperation, it is simply necessary to establish the existence of EU competence in the first place, and the nature of that competence (ie, it must be non-exclusive). The Court's ruling in that case makes clear that enhanced cooperation can in principle take place within the scope of EU rules on the internal market, those rules conferring a non-exclusive competence on the EU. Moreover, the Court took a broad definition to the scope of the 'internal market' (as distinct from competition, an area of exclusive EU competence) in that judgment.

This is significant because a substantial portion of EU legislation falls within the scope of internal market competences, and the possible relevance of enhanced cooperation is therefore increased. Indeed, if enhanced cooperation could not apply to the internal market, some of the conditions (distorted competition, et al.,) would be redundant. However, the adoption of enhanced cooperation measures in the field of the internal market bears a greater risk of falling foul of those substantive conditions than measures in other areas of EU law would.

6.3 Furthering EU Objectives

As for the requirement that enhanced cooperation must further the EU's objectives, protect its interests and reinforce its integration process (Article 331(1) TFEU), the CJEU ruled in the first patent judgment that an enhanced cooperation measure would contribute to the integration process if enhanced cooperation could be authorized despite the inability of Member States to agree on the proposal. However, it also ruled that the EU's interests and integration process 'would, quite clearly, not be protected if all fruitless negotiations' led to enhanced cooperation, 'to the detriment of the search for a compromise' which could apply to the EU as a whole.

So the application of these principles is closely linked to the 'last resort' rule, discussed above. But subject to that principle, effectively the Court agrees here with the 'half a loaf is better than none' principle: EU integration can, by its very nature, in principle be carried forward by some Member States, rather than all. Indeed, this is inherent in the very existence of enhanced cooperation, and this interpretation is buttressed by the Treaty amendments simplifying the use of this process. It is also consistent with the development of other forms of differentiated integration in the Treaties.

The rationale for this approach is that in the absence of enhanced cooperation, there would either be no steps taken toward the objective at all, or they would be taken outside the EU framework, where there is no explicit requirement that they would then be open to all Member States. The absence of any action to accomplish a particular EU objective by *any* Member States can hardly be said to promote the EU's objectives, and the development of cooperation outside the EU framework clearly does not reinforce the EU's integration process, but rather detracts from it. Equally the development of integration processes outside the EU framework damages its interests, rather than protecting them.

6.4 Compliance with EU Law

Like the criterion relating to competence, the requirement to comply with EU law is not really substantively any different for enhanced cooperation measures than it is for any other EU measures. The CJEU discussed it in the particular context of the patents legislation, where it considered and rejected the argument that the details of the EU plans in this area infringed Article 118 TFEU, the legal basis for the planned implementing measures concerned. It was sufficient that the planned measures would apply in all the participating Member States: Article 118, in light of the enhanced cooperation measures, did not require them to apply in all Member States.

The most awkward issue here may be the relationship between the enhanced cooperation measures and other EU measures – given that the Treaties also require coherence. *Prima facie* it is arguable that an enhanced cooperation measure cannot amend EU legislation which is applicable to all Member States. At the very least, it could only amend that legislation as regards the Member States participating in enhanced cooperation only. It was notable that when tabling legislation to implement enhanced cooperation as regards divorce and banking taxation, the Commission dropped the provisions in its original proposals which would have amended other EU legislation.

6.5 Internal Market and Competition

According to the CJEU's patents judgment, the authorisation of enhanced cooperation as regards the EU unitary patent laws did not breach the relevant provisions of the Treaties. This was because (as the Court had ruled already) Article 118 TFEU, in the context of enhanced cooperation, did not require that enhanced cooperation apply in all Member States. The language arrangements could not be challenged at that stage because they had not been adopted. As noted above, the later challenge to the language rules did not rely on the enhanced cooperation rules in the Treaties as such.

The application of the 'half a loaf' principle to this criterion suggests that it will fairly easily be satisfied, which is a crucial point as regards the use of enhanced cooperation in the field of the internal market. Notably, the Court did not require that the Council prove that the measure enhance the internal market, et al., – only that the plaintiffs prove that there was an interference with it.

6.6 Non-participating States

According to the CJEU, the enhanced cooperation in the area of patents did not breach the non-participating States' rights. While EU enhanced cooperation measures could not affect non-participants' rights, et al., that did not mean that there was a legal obligation to refrain from adopting measures that the non-participants disagreed with. Also, the plaintiffs did not disprove the arguments made in the EU decision – that Spanish and Italian right-holders would still have access to the EU unitary patent.

There could be questions raised if the use of enhanced cooperation has an external effect. Clearly the EU could not exercise its external competence in such cases in a way which interferes with the non-participants' external competences, for instance by somehow requiring them to (not) participate in a treaty against their will. But it should be recalled that the non-participants can equally not impede enhanced cooperation.

7. THE FUTURE OF ENHANCED COOPERATION

Two years after the Court judgment generally liberalizing the rules relating to enhanced cooperation, and five years after the second Treaty amendment which liberalized the rules, the procedure is still rarely used. Does this matter? Obviously it matters little as regards EMU and JHA, where there are alternative processes of differentiation in place which Member States are happy to use. But it does matter in other areas, where there have been significant proposals blocked by the objections of a small number of Member States – for instance the proposal for a European Private Company, or the common consolidated tax base. The existence of unanimity, coupled with the rarity of enhanced cooperation, may also be deterring the Commission from putting other proposals forward.

So enhanced cooperation would be a useful method for adopting proposals which many Member States find attractive, without compelling the Member States which object to them to participate. Indeed, the use of the procedure could serve to reinforce the legitimacy of the EU in the eyes of those who object to Member States being required or talked into participating in so many measures.

Can anything be done to encourage the use of enhanced cooperation? There could be a further Treaty amendment, which could for instance eliminate or restrict the use of the 'last resort' clause. The clause could be waived automatically (say) three years after a proposal was originally made, deeming that to be a case where there is a last resort. More radically, the Treaties could be amended so that proposals are automatically transferred into an enhanced cooperation process if they have not been agreed within a certain time.

Treaty amendments are notoriously difficult to agree, however. So could enhanced cooperation be used more within the existing legal framework? It would be possible for Member States (or a sufficiently large group of them) to agree in principle that they will always consider the use of enhanced cooperation if a proposal has not been agreed within a certain period of time. Another approach would be to agree that the Council should pay greater heed to Member States that have very serious stated objections to particular proposals. The secondary rules on Council voting could be amended to specify that if no agreement has been found within a certain period of time after such an objection is expressed, then the Council will consider the use of enhanced cooperation in such cases. It might be objected that if there are sufficient votes to pass such measures, the 'last resort' rule should not apply, but that concern could be addressed by limiting Member States' possibility to raise objections to the rules specifically mentioned in the Treaties (such as the protection of national identity, or the Treaty principles applying to the adoption of employment law measures).[51]

Either approach (and surely others are conceivable) could lead to greater use of enhanced cooperation. This would in turn increase the EU's output and input legitimacy at the same time: resulting in more EU integration for the Member States which support it in a particular field, alongside less imposition of obligations upon Member States which have serious objections to those particular measures. If such a new approach can be agreed, perhaps Cinderella will go to the ball after all.

REFERENCES

Amtenbrink F and Kochenov D, 'Towards a More Flexible Approach to Enhanced Cooperation' in Ott A and Vos E (eds), *Fifty Years of European Integration: Foundations and Perspectives* (TMC Asser Press 2009) 181–200.

De Areilza JM, 'The Reform of Enhanced Cooperation Rules: Towards Less Flexibility?', in De Witte B, Hanf D and Vos E (eds), *The Many Faces of Differentiation in EU Law* (Intersentia 2001) 27–40.

Dougan M, 'The Unfinished Business of Enhanced Cooperation: Some Institutional Questions and their Constitutional Implications', in Ott A and Vos E (eds), *Fifty Years of European Integration: Foundations and Perspectives* (TMC Asser Press 2009) 157–79.

Peers S, 'Divorce, European Style: The First Authorization of Enhanced Cooperation' (2010) 6 *European Constitutional Law Review* 339–58.

Peers S, 'The Constitutional Aspects of the EU Patent' (2011) 7 *European Constitutional Law Review* 229–71.

Shaw J, 'Enhancing Cooperation After Nice: Will the Treaty Do the Trick?' in Andenas M and Usher J (eds), *The Treaty of Nice and Beyond: Enlargement and Constitutional Reform* (Hart 2003) 207–38.

Stubb A, *Negotiating Flexibility in the European Union: Amsterdam, Nice and Beyond* (Palgrave Macmillan 2002).

Tuytschaever F, *Differentiation in European Union Law* (Hart 1999).

Weatherill S, '"If I'd Wanted You to Understand I Would Have Explained it Better": What is the Purpose of the Provisions on Closer Cooperation Introduced by the Treaty of Amsterdam?' in O'Keeffe D and Twomey P (eds), *Legal Issues of the Amsterdam Treaty* (Hart 1999) 21–40.

---

[51] For further details of how this might work, see my blog post, 'Is it possible to reform the EU without amending the Treaties?': <http://eulawanalysis.blogspot.co.uk/2015/05/is-it-possible-to-reform-eu-without.html>.

4. Modes of flexibility: framework legislation v 'soft' law

Mark Dawson and Alieza Durana

1. INTRODUCTION

How does the EU achieve the goal once announced as the official motto of the Union – of unity in diversity? One way of doing so may be to further develop many of the options of 'differentiation' discussed in other chapters in this book. One can imagine differentiation being forwarded either 'negatively' or 'positively' i.e. either by exempting reluctant states from particular provisions of EU law or by allowing Member States, through enhanced cooperation or other means, to go forward into new fields of integration without the need for universal agreement.

What, however, if we reject this option? What if cooperation and integration is to proceed in unison, while still seeking to accommodate significant national differences, or even bring certain states into a set of rules where they either doubt the merits of EU regulation altogether or resist particular norms? One of the principle ways of achieving this task of accommodating diversity may be through flexible legal instruments (FLIs). Before examining these instruments, it may be useful to make one preliminary remark – what do we mean when we speak of 'flexibility'? There are both many varieties of 'flexibility' and many reasons why it may be seen as desirable. It may be useful in this introduction to already distinguish between four different aspects of FLIs.

The first aspect is precision. Rules that simply lay out broad principles, which can be interpreted in different ways by different 'implementing' actors, may be one way of accommodating diversity in legal instruments. Principles often lay out goals and purposes for legislation but do not describe in detail the exact obligations they entail or the means by which they ought to be delivered. Delegation may be another such feature: a sign of flexible rule-making may also be where the power to elaborate and define particular rules is 'contracted out', either to lower-level administrations or to 'other' social actors, such as private standard-setting bodies or social partners. A third feature may be voluntarism: flexible legal instruments can carry both binding rules and non-binding elements, in which national administrations are encouraged to act a certain way but not obliged to do so. Finally, flexible rules may carry a 'framework' character. A characteristic of many of the FLIs we will look at it is their iterative nature. Rather than establish a set of rules 'once and for all', flexible rules may instead establish procedural frameworks or institutions, with the possibility of the initial rules being gradually re-evaluated or re-drawn altogether. These characteristics should be seen as non-exclusive: as we will see, while many 'flexible' EU instruments carry some of these characteristics, few carry all.

How then is flexibility incorporated in the EU's legislative instruments? The ordering of Article 288 TFEU, and the discussions on regulatory simplification conducted through the 2003 Convention on the Future of Europe, suggests a basic, hierarchical classification. As every first-year student of EU law is taught, regulations seem the least accommodating of diversity.[1] Their presence as a single legal standard, and direct effect in national legal orders, seemingly leaves little room for national governments to tailor regulations to national preferences. Directives seem to be more accommodating but nevertheless carry features that limit the capacity for flexibility. On the one hand, the need for national incorporation of directives would be meaningless were national governments not given some leeway in the 'form and methods' by which directives are included in the national legal order. On the other hand, doctrines like vertical direct effect and the duty of consistent interpretation have been developed by the EU Courts precisely to limit the capacity of governments to use that leeway to deviate significantly from a directive's original rules and content.

Finally, soft law seems the most accommodating of diversity. Soft law's non-binding form in effect leaves national executives as the primary 'legislatures', with the capacity to determine themselves what particular guidelines mean in a given national context. In this realm, judicial review is stripped away as a constraint to re-impose 'unity' from above, while norms are often sufficiently open-ended to be met by a wide variety of legal and political reforms. 'Diversity' in implementation is often

---

[1] On efforts at regulatory simplification following the CT, see Armin von Bogdandy, Felix Arndt and Jürgen Bast, 'Legal Instruments in European Union Law and Their Reform: A Systematic Approach on an Empirical Basis' in Piet Eeckhout and Takis Tridimas (eds), *Yearbook of European Law* 23 (Oxford University Press 2004).

embraced by proponents of soft law as a sign not of their weakness but of their responsiveness and experimentalism.[2]

How real – and how useful – however is this hierarchy in practice? Exploring this question will be the guiding task of this chapter. Already in the case of Regulations we know that many Regulations, while they do not require national legal incorporation, may still involve further implementing measures by national agencies and administrations. This reversal of legal expectations also, however, applies to the other two main categories. As sections 2 and 3 of this chapter will explore, the distinction between directives – which seek to marry unified rules with flexible incorporation – and soft law, which seems to allow even non-compliance with its norms, may be far less stark than first imagined.

The story will start by analysing the evolution of EU directives. As section 2 will explore, the generation of EU directives in social and environmental policy that emerged from the mid-90s carry many of the features of imprecision, delegation, non-bindingness and 'framework' elements, which have often previously been attributed to soft law. They leave significant scope for national governments to tailor their provisions to diverse national contexts. Levels of compliance with this legislation has been notoriously low, suggesting that 'diversity' may be being accommodated in a further, more cynical way – by decisions on the part of national governments to 'selectively disregard' EU law, leaving a patchwork of national and regional provisions in its place.

While this element of the FLI story has been told before, the most telling breakdown in the hierarchy may emerge in the case of soft law. While soft law methods – such as the Open Method of Coordination – were designed to be highly open-ended, the onset of the euro crisis has seen a growing formalization of soft law methods. Procedures that were previously voluntary increasingly carry real sanctions for non-compliance, with demands for fiscal austerity and central EU level control outpacing the original soft law design. The 'de-flexibilization' of soft law will be elaborated in section 3.

The chapter will conclude (in section 4) by drawing some conclusions from the increasing inversion of the distinction between 'hard' and hierarchical legal instruments on the one hand, and 'soft' hierarchical ones on the other. While the EU Courts have been hesitant to extend procedural and legal guarantees under the Treaties into the realm of soft

---

[2] See e.g. Charles F Sabel and Jonathan Zeitlin, 'Learning from Difference: The New Architecture of Experimentalist Governance in the EU' (2008) 14(3) *European Law Journal* 271–327.

law, their increasing precision and legal effects demands a re-evaluation of the assumption that soft law methods merely 'supplement' or run parallel to 'proper' EU law-making. As long predicted, 'soft law' may be less soft and flexible than we assumed just as hard law may be taking on a more procedural and framework character.[3] The remedies available under EU law, and the approach of the EU Courts towards 'soft norms', may require re-evaluation in order to reflect this.

2. DIRECTIVES AND 'FRAMEWORK' LEGISLATION

Despite political attempts to decrease the use of formal legislative instruments, the last three decades have witnessed an increase in the use of the directive – in the case of social policy, a near doubling each decade.[4] The answer to why such legal proliferation has taken place is rooted in the form and use of the directive. The Treaties state that the directive is 'binding, as to the result to be achieved, upon each Member State to which it is addressed, but shall leave to the National Authorities the choice of form and methods' (Art. 288). While national transposition is therefore required, no specifications are given as to the form and manner of this transposition.

This lack of definitional precision has led the directive to be bound by three conflicting factors: the expectation that binding legal acts be universal and enforceable, the doubt surrounding how prescriptive and uniform such laws should be, and the ambiguity surrounding the bounds of Member State sovereignty.[5] Both the form of recent directives and the case law interpreting them have placed different weights on each of these elements. Case law, for example, offers conflicting perspectives: directives may be flexible, or require complete uniformity depending on the aim of the directive in question.[6] In the 2003 *Jaeger* case, for example, the Court explicitly re-defined the rest-period in the Working Time

---

[3] David M Trubek and Louise G Trubek, 'Hard and Soft Law in the Construction of Social Europe: The Role of the Open Method of Co-ordination' (2005) 11(3) *European Law Journal* 343–64.

[4] The period of 1970–79 witnessed the passing of seven directives and/or amendments to directives, 1980–89 – 16, 1990–99 – 36, and 2000–09 – 48. The directives cited here do not include directives addressing the free movement of people or goods.

[5] Gerd Winter, *Sources and Categories of European Union Law* (Nomos 1996) 488.

[6] See Case 38/77 *Enka BV v Inspecteur der Invoerrechten en Accijnzen Arnhem* [1977] ECLI:EU:C:1977:168.

Directive, limiting the margin of appreciation for national authorities in interpreting the definition of 'what counts' as rest time.[7] Similar judgments have been drawn in relation to Parental Leave,[8] Waste,[9] and Water Framework Directives.[10] Therefore, while legislative flexibilization is significant, so is the ability of the Court to define and 'harmonize' particular legal elements.

Through the examples below, this section will explore the 'flexibilization' of the directive at a legislative level. While – as in *Jaeger* – the EU Courts may derive rather strong individual rights even from directives that are flexibly framed, the set of directives developed from the mid-90s in the field of social policy were designed to combine a desire for 'minimum' levels of social protection with significantly divergent national systems for delivering social policy. As we will see, these conflicting demands for both partial harmonization and maintaining national 'social' sovereignty drove the initial development of FLIs in the social field.

2.1 The Working Time Directive

One of the first and most exemplary of these FLIs is the Working Time Directive (WTD),[11] which aims to ensure the health and safety of workers by creating minimum standards for the organization of working time. Based on Article 137 EC, the WTD sets 12 encompassing minimum standards while also containing one of the highest numbers of

---

[7] Despite the Treaty provision prohibiting harmonization under art. 137-based legislation, the more recent case law demands all professionals should be able to take rest periods during on-call periods. See Case C-151/02 *Landeshauptstadt Kiel v Norbert Jaeger* [2003] ECLI:EU:C:2003:437, para. 89.

[8] In the 2010 *Chatzi* case, the Court determined that the Parental Leave Directive 'cannot be interpreted as conferring an individual right to parental leave on the child' (Case C-149/10 *Chatzi* [2010] ECLI:EU:C:2010:534), para. 76.

[9] To prevent eutrophication (or the excess of nutrients in water sources), in Case C-438/07 *Commission v Sweden* [2009] ECLI:EU:C:2009:613 the Commission brought charges against Sweden and Finland, to ensure that all their treatment plants from a certain size reduce the proportion of nitrogen in treated waste water.

[10] In Case C-525/12 *Commission v Germany* [2012] ECLI:EU:C:2014:2202, the Commission brought changes against Germany and extended the definition of 'water services' to impoundment which is intended for hydroelectric power production, navigation and flood protection.

[11] Council Directive 93/104/EC of 23 November 1993 concerning certain aspects of the organization of working time [1993] OJ L307/18–24.

exemptions and derogations (14).[12] Most importantly, the WTD introduces two soft law provisions.[13] Although the European Court of Justice annulled the first soft provision urging Member States to include Sunday in the 'weekly rest period' (Art. 5), the second provision remains as one of the first examples of directive-based voluntarism, encouraging Member States to guarantee special provisions for night workers: 'Member States may make the work of certain categories of night workers subject to certain guarantees, under conditions laid down by national legislation and/or practice, in the case of workers who incur risks to their safety or health linked to night-time working.'[14]

The WTD acted as the first of many stabilizing forces in labour law. While the WTD does not uniformly impose specific rules, it sets a precise base line for worker safety standards, bringing legal outliers into line and creating new protections for workers in forgotten sectors. New standards address the overwork and maltreatment of health care practitioners, night workers, and agricultural workers, for example. Despite these 'innovative' (at the time) standards, the WTD leaves significant room for national legal diversity, prompting conflict over the directive from those seeking higher levels of worker protection. The combination of precision and voluntarism can account for the diversity in European working conditions and working-time regulations in France, the Netherlands, and Great Britain.[15]

2.2 The Parental Leave and The Part-time Work Directives

While the WTD was an important model, it was 'traditional' in the sense of being largely a product of inter-governmental bargaining. By contrast, the next generation of social policy directives delegated legislation to the social partners: the Parental Leave[16] and Part-Time Work Directives[17] are direct transpositions of agreements between federations of management and labour. The Parental Leave Directive (PLD) aims 'to set out

[12] Ibid., arts 3, 4, 5, 6, 7, 8, 9, 12, 13.

[13] Ibid., arts 4, 5, 17, 18.

[14] Ibid, art. 10.

[15] See e.g. Gerda Falkner et al, *Complying with Europe: EU Harmonization and Soft Law in the Member States* (Cambridge University Press 2005).

[16] Directive 96/34/EC of 3 June 1996 on the framework agreement on parental leave concluded by UNICE, CEEP, and ETUC [2006] OJ L145/4–9.

[17] Directive 97/81/EC of 15 December 1997 concerning the framework agreement on part-time work concluded by UNICE, CEEP, and ETUC [1998] OJ L14/9–14.

minimum requirements on parental leave and time off from work on grounds of *force majeure*, as an important means of reconciling work and family life and promoting equal opportunities and treatment between men and women'.[18] The PLD is comprised of seven compulsory minimum standards[19] and five exemption and derogation possibilities.[20] Most importantly, the PLD stands out for its high number of non-binding soft-law provisions.[21] Even though the minimum standards set are relatively low, the PLD created adaptational pressure for delegation of legislation to the social partners and for additional legislative volunteerism in all states – in most cases demanding qualitative improvements to existing parental leave schemes. The PLD states: 'Member States shall adopt the laws, regulations and administrative provisions necessary to comply with the Council decision [...] or shall ensure that social partners introduce the necessary measures by way of agreement by the end of this period.'[22]

For the first time, the PLD prompted national parental leave legislation to address male parents (Austria and Italy), and accommodate single-income families (Austria, Germany, Greece, and Portugal). Almost all states had to change or adapt their legislation with regard to *force majeure* leave (Denmark, Ireland, Luxembourg, the UK, Finland, France, Greece, Spain, and Sweden). Most interesting, though, is the difference in national policy innovation across Member States. In Luxembourg, a state in which no leave system had previously existed, the PLD was interpreted as a measure that could reduce unemployment: temporary on-leave parents could be replaced with unemployed persons, giving such persons a chance to reintegrate into the labour market. As a result, Luxembourg ultimately doubled the length of parental leave to six months and increased the amount of benefits. In Belgium, an 'implementation race'[23] between Labour Minister Miet Smet and the social partners took place: Minister Smet argued for an expansion of the 'career break' system she had initially piloted, while the social partners proposed a new collective agreement between industry, labour, and management. Both systems were eventually pushed through, and today Belgians can choose between both systems. Germany went beyond the minimum requirements to create both a right to part-time work during parental

18 Parental Leave Directive (n 16) preamble.
19 Ibid., arts 2, 3.
20 Ibid., art. 2(3).
21 Ibid., arts 2, 4, 8 9, 10, 11.
22 Ibid., art. 8(4).
23 Falkner et al (n 15) 149–52.

leave, and a right to take parental leave simultaneously. In sum, the directives created a system with precise 'minimum standards', which were to be further elaborated at the national level, often to produce higher levels of protection.[24]

With one compulsory minimum standard,[25] four exemptions,[26] and 11 non-binding provisions,[27] the Part-Time Work Directive (PTWD) allows for even greater policy freedom and volunteerism. The core provision of the PTWD is a non-discrimination clause: 'part-time workers may not be treated less favourably than comparable full-time workers unless such unequal treatment is objectively justified'.[28] The PTWD's goals are twofold: to address the equal treatment of part-time workers, and to improve their performance in the labour market.[29]

Given its high emphasis on soft-law provisions, the transposition of the PTWD is not all that different from the volunteerist Open Method of Coordination (OMC) process – introduced in the field of employment from 1997. The PTWD relies on national policy initiative for larger social policy shifts. In practical terms, the flexibility of the PTWD can be seen in the diversity of national interpretation. While Great Britain chose to limit the extent of the directive and simply comply with the minimum standard, in the case of Ireland, partners from industry, labour, and management continued discussions from the Social Partners Pact to find a solution for the Irish transposition of the PTWD. The German case took the PTWD one step further by formalizing the soft provisions in amendments to pre-existing labour law addressing 'the binding legal right to part-time work'. Following suit, the Portuguese Government drafted part-time work legislation for the first time, actively integrating the soft provisions of the directive.[30]

When considering the Working-Time, Parental Leave, and Part-Time Work Directives in tandem, a legislative pattern appears: all three were spearheaded by stakeholders in industry, labour, and management, and all expanded the use of soft-law provisions more progressively than its predecessor. The decreasing ratio of compulsory minimum standards to

---

24 Ibid., 156–8.

25 Directive 97/81/EC (n 17) art. 4.

26 Ibid., arts 2(2), 4(4).

27 Part Time Work Directive (n 17) arts 5(1)(b), 5(2), 5(3), 6(2).

28 Ibid., art. 4.

29 This reference is generally aimed at female caregivers who are statistically more inclined to work part-time.

30 Falkner et al (n 15) 168–71.

derogations and soft-law provisions indicates an initial trend towards integrating FLIs into the legal structure of directives.

2.3 Anti-discrimination Law

Changes in anti-discrimination law mark a further step in the directive's evolution – the development of the directive not just as a series of imprecise or non-binding rules, but as a set of 'framework' provisions, that delegate particular norm-elaborating functions to either local actors, or those operating 'beyond the state'. Beyond the 'framework' provisions, though, the Equality Directives also incorporate precision mechanisms. This development could also be described as a shift from government to governance, marking a more prominent role for non-governmental actors (private firms, representative associations, civil society groups, and other lobby organizations) in policy-making and implementation.[31] Though anti-discrimination law was founded upon a clear, hierarchical definition of discrimination as related to equal pay (Art. 157 TFEU, ex Art. 119 EEC, ex Art. 141 EC), by the 1990s the concept of discrimination was extended to include treatment in the workplace and employment-related social security.[32]

The creation of the European anti-discrimination regime is meant to round out judicial anti-discrimination efforts by (1) designating (or delegating) roles for non-state actors; (2) creating and financing transnational stakeholder networks; (3) encouraging informational approaches, alternative remedies, and alternative dispute-resolution processes; (4) broadening understandings of anti-discrimination norms; and (5) moving from a system of negative to positive obligations.[33] For example, Article 9 of the Race Directive states:

---

[31] See e.g. Ben Page and Maria Kaika, 'The EU Water Framework Directive: Part 2. Policy Innovation and the Shifting Choreography of Governance' (2003) 13 *European Environment* 328–43.

[32] Council Directive 79/207/EEC of 9 February 1978 on the implementation of the principle of equal treatment for men and women as regards access to employment, vocational training and promotion, and working conditions [1976] OJ L39/40; Council Directive 79/7/EEC of 19 December 1978 on the progressive implementation of the principle of equal treatment for men and women in matters of social security [1979] OJ L6/24.

[33] Gráinne de Búrca and Susan Sturm propose that discrimination is best addressed when 'normative elaboration occurs through a fluid, interactive relationship between problem solving and problem definition within specific workplaces and in multiple other arenas, including but not limited to the judiciary'. The new European policy regime attempts to foster such fluid,

> Member States shall introduce into their national legal systems such measures as are necessary to protect individuals from any adverse treatment or adverse consequence as a reaction to a complaint or to proceedings aimed at enforcing compliance with the principle of equal treatment.[34]

To that end, non-state actors have been provided with official roles in anti-discrimination policies such as the Race Directive (Arts 7(2), 11(2), 12, 13, 16), the Framework Employment Directive (Arts 9, 13, 14, and 18), and the Equal Treatment Directive (Arts 8(a), 8(b), and 8(c)). Parallel clauses in each Directive lay out the following responsibilities of Member States:

- to ensure that interested parties are able to participate in judicial and administrative procedures (on behalf of themselves or others);
- to encourage labour and industry to create local agreements to address discrimination;
- to foster dialogue with relevant NGOs;
- to create new 'Equality Bodies' to promote equal treatment of all persons; and
- to constitute collective agreements with social partners for the implementation of the directive.

Having conducted interviews to measure the effects of the new policy regime, Gráinne de Búrca has concluded that the Commission has actively 'used the information provided by the various groups in order to target its policies, to focus its activities under the various EU action programs and funds, and to promote further policy developments in these fields'.[35] This newfound dependency on information gained from transnational networks of civil society organizations and other relevant stakeholder networks has spurred a controversial development: the Commission has taken on the role of a local, anti-discrimination policy watchdog both in legislative and judicial terms. On the one hand, the Commission has begun proposing 'new extensions and developments of

transnational problem solving through new articulations of art. 137 in new directives. See e.g. Gráinne De Búrca, 'Stumbling into Experimentalism: The EU Anti-Discrimination Regime' in Charles F Sabel and Jonathan Zeitlin (eds), *Experimentalist Governance in the European Union*, (Oxford University Press 2010) 221.

[34] Council Directive 2000/43/EC of 29 June 2000 implementing the principle of equal treatment between persons irrespective of racial or ethnic origin [2000] OJ L180, art. 9.

[35] De Búrca (n 33) 230.

the law even in areas where there is no particular interest or support from the Member States at the political level'[36] based on information from relevant civil society stakeholders. On the other hand, the Commission has demanded stakeholder participation in the local transposition and interpretation of anti-discrimination efforts in leading 14 infringement proceedings addressing Member States' excessively narrow definitions of local anti-discrimination legislation.[37] The combined mandate for diverse anti-discrimination policy initiatives and a Commission willing to ensure problem-solving efforts is just one example of the rise and extension of the directive as a multi-level policy framework carrying both judicial and governance elements.

2.4 Environmental Policy

While it may be easy to categorize the changes in labour and anti-discrimination law as a mere social policy fad, the hybridization of the directive in environmental law indicates otherwise. 'Flexibilization' here arises from a related, yet distinct, set of reasons. Beyond the goal of normative or organizational diversity, two forces drive environmental policy change: the significant complexity of the environmental framework and the need to adapt rules to constantly changing risks and technologies.

This is best seen in the case of the Water Framework Directive (WFD),[38] whose policy structure set a strong precedent in environmental law. Beyond the changes witnessed in social policy, the WFD establishes a transnational policy framework that links Member States in pursuit of precise European environmental goals. More than any other directive, the WFD demonstrates how a legislative act can work as the cornerstone of a vast policy regime focused on public participation and administrative cooperation.

The purpose of the directive is to establish 'a framework for the protection of inland surface waters, transitional waters, coastal waters and groundwater' (Art. 1) so as to achieve 'good ecological and chemical status' for all Community waters by 2010 (Art. 9). The directive lays out detailed recommendations for administrative changes and environmental evaluations. As in labour and anti-discrimination law, this directive

---

[36] Ibid.

[37] Commission Press Release IP/07/928 of 27 June 2007; Commission Press Release IP/08/155 of 31 January 2008.

[38] Directive 2000/60/EC of 23 October 2000 establishing a framework for Community action in the field of water policy [2003] OJ L327/1.

suggests Member States tailor local administrative and economic solutions to each unique environmental context (Arts 30–31). Two processes measure the success of the directive: 'information, consultation and involvement of the public, including users' and 'close cooperation and coherent action at community, Member state, and local level' (Art. 14). Yet unique to this precedent is its emphasis on the progressive, incremental nature of the directive implementation. The directive envisions itself as one piece of an ongoing policy regime to be revised every six years according to agreements between European and local state and non-state actors (Art. 4(3)(b)).

In accordance with this incremental, stakeholder-based model, the WFD has been amended multiple times by Decision No. 2455/2001/EC, Directive 2008/32/EC, and Directive 2009/31/EC.[39] In addition to the amendments, the Commission produced several documents to provide optional, concrete policy suggestions for the implementation of the WFD in local river basins such as the *Common Implementation Strategy for the WFD* and the *Guidance on Public Participation in Relation to the WFD*.[40] Based on Article 14 of the WFD, the Guidance acts a horizontal document meant to assist in the implementation of the WFD through the following strategies: by defining and illustrating the (precise) European understanding of public participation and its usefulness, by demonstrating the need for quality public participation through new legislative delegation, by identifying key factors to successful public participation, by analysing Article 14 in greater detail, and by creating procedural framework for the practical implementation of these provisions.

Within the context of the WFD, the Guidance document defines public participation as processes which involve the public and stakeholders in the planning, decision-making, and implementation of the preferred

---

[39] Following the 2009 revision, the European Commission issued the following statement:

> In 2009, nine years after the Framework Directive entered into force, management plans were produced for each river basin district, taking account of the results of the analyses and studies carried out. These plans cover the period 2009–2015. They shall be revised in 2015 and then every six years thereafter.

[40] Common Implementation Strategy for the Water Framework Directive (2000/60/EC), Strategic Document as Agreed by the Water Directors under Swedish Presidency, 2 May 2001 <http://ec.europa.eu/environment/water/water-framework/objectives/pdf/strategy.pdf>; Guidance on Public Participation in Relation to the Water Framework Directive Final version after the Water Directors' meeting December 2002 <http://www.eau2015-rhin-meuse.fr/fr/ressources/documents/guide_participation-public.pdf>.

policy option.[41] The use of public participation is meant to address the complexity of river basin management, but also of the cultural, economic, and other environmental issues underpinning water health. To that end, the WFD describes three processes in which the public may comment and amend policy proposals: the timetable and work programme for policy proposals (data collection, assessment, definition of objectives, decision regarding measures); the preliminary and interim overviews of the major water management issues; and draft versions of the River Basin Management Plan.[42] The precisely defined use of public participation throughout the policy-making process should be understood in contrast to previous models in which the public was consulted as a mere formality at the end of legislative procedures.

Thus, the WFD creates a procedural legal framework for integrated environmental standards, delegation for public participation, and national volunteerism.[43] The subsequent North Sea Regional and Local Implementation of the Water Framework Directive (NOLIMP-WFD) follows this framework by establishing a regional information network for water policy solutions. Between 2000 and 2006, the National Water Institute (Norway) and districts of Aberdeenshire (Scotland), Nort Jutland (Denmark), Wästra Götaland (Sweden), Weser-Ems (Germany), and Frylan (the Netherlands) organized the NOLIMP-WFD collective to evaluate and compare policy solutions for better water health. In testing various methods of reducing nutrients in water, and preventing toxic run-off substances from agriculture and sewage, the cooperative addresses the implementation of the WFD in the North Sea context. Actively involving stakeholders was seen as an active ingredient in the NOLIMP-WTD's success. In the case of the Aberdeenshire Council in Scotland, the population living near tributaries of the River Dee (the areas of Tarland Burn, Loch Davan, and Elricht Burn) involved farmers,

---

[41] Sharon Hophmayer-Tokich, 'Public Participation under the EU Water Framework Directive – Processes and Possible Outcomes', Preparatory Paper for the NOLIMP Workshop on Public Participation and Cost-effectiveness Analysis. Available at: http://doc.utwente.nl/95377/.

[42] Ibid., 6.

[43] The understanding of public participation is still highly contested today. European legal scholars explain the extent of participation based on the type of government, number and types of actors involved, number of government sectors involved, costs and benefits of policy changes, and other factors. Katerina Linos, 'How Can International Organizations Shape National Welfare States? Evidence from Compliance with European Union Directives' (2007) 40(5) *Comparative Political Studies* 547–70.

landowners, and inhabitants in educational projects and wetland refurbishment. Although the project officially ended in 2006, many of the projects were appropriated by local municipalities or EU institutions and continue to this day. The idea behind the North Sea Region Programme was therefore akin to many volunteerist soft law processes, i.e. to establish 'best practices' to be shared with other river basins throughout Europe.[44]

In sum, the framework character of the directive created a new legal basis for broad procedural mechanisms and revisability. The effect of the WFD, in particular, also acts as a model for further EU initiatives. The directive's structure soon expanded to other environmental policy arenas with the creation of the Waste Incineration Directive, the Directive on Environmental Quality Standards, Framework Waste Legislation, the Waste Electrical and Electronic Equipment Directive (WEEE Directive), the Recast of the WEEE Directive, and the Directive on the Use of Certain Hazardous Substances also following a similar model. The concept of environmental 'health' is now based on local stakeholder involvement in the creation and application of European environmental principles.

Through these examples, we see all four elements of the 'varieties of flexibility' outlined in the opening section. While these examples all constitute 'hard law', they attempt to accommodate functional and political diversity through 'imprecise', principle-based norms, through delegating the elaboration of norms downwards, through embracing soft and non-binding elements, and through carrying a framework or revisable character. While all directives certainly do not carry this 'framework' quality, these examples illustrate some of the close continuities between 'hard' and 'soft' law.

3. FLEXIBILITY AND SOFT LAW

3.1 Soft Law 'Before the Fall'

In what ways does 'classical' soft law (if one can use that term) accommodate differentiation and pluralism? Part of this relates to the very reasons and fields in which soft law mechanisms have arisen. Let us begin with the social example discussed above. Two particular factors may have made social policy a fertile breeding ground for soft law

---

[44] Interreg IIIB North Sea Programme Website <http://www.northsearegion.eu/iiib/-projectpresentation/details/&tid=57&theme=4>.

methods. One is a legal factor: while the EU has agreed a number of measures in the social field, the EU's social policy competences remain limited. These competences are not only tied to specific fields, with certain areas – such as collective bargaining or pensions – explicitly excluded from the EU's ambit, but are often operated under high decision-making hurdles. In these circumstances, soft law methods – OMC – can be used to create a structure of cooperation in circumstances where a more binding legal alternative is simply unavailable.[45]

The second factor relates not to legal but structural limits. Partly as a consequence of the significant diversity of national systems of social protection, social policy is an area seemingly unsuitable for harmonization of standards beyond 'minimum' levels. These differences can relate to capacity – such as the ability to deliver and pay for certain social goods – or to procedures: Sweden, the UK and Greece have very different actor configurations in the delivery of employment policy, requiring (even as a matter of constitutional law) particular actors to be consulted in the creation of employment rules. In this context, soft law's openness – both in terms of the norms which states must pursue and the actors they must include when doing so – could be seen as well suited to the task of delivering trans-national social policy (or so the theory goes).

Soft law methods attempt to accommodate this diversity in various ways. If we examine the European Employment Strategy set up in 1997, all of the classical features of FLIs mentioned in the introduction to this chapter are present. In terms of precision, the employment guidelines are typically broad, setting targets and broad normative orientations, but leaving their provisions open ended enough to include various national political choices. Take for example Guideline 17 of the 2005–08 Employment Guidelines, which was to:

> Implement employment policies intended to achieve full employment, improve quality and productivity at work, and strengthen social and territorial cohesion. These policies should help to achieve an average employment rate for the European Union (EU) of 70% overall, at least 60% for women and 50% for older workers (55 to 64), and to reduce unemployment and inactivity. Member States should set national employment rate targets.[46]

---

[45] See e.g. Kerstin Jacobsson, 'Soft Regulation and the Subtle Transformation of States: The Case of European Employment Policy' (2004) 14(4) *Journal of European Social Policy* 355–70.

[46] Council Decision 2005/600/EC of 12 July 2005 on guidelines for the employment policies of the Member States.

This guideline sets particular targets, but even these can be deviated from through national targets, reflecting different national starting points (i.e. a 60 per cent female employment rate is little problem for Sweden but highly ambitious for Italy). The guideline is also vague and aspirational in terms of normative content – more liberally minded Member States, such as the UK, and more Nordic states have ample room to disagree on the types of measures necessary to 'improve quality and productivity at work'. Arguably, the level of precision of such guidelines is so broad as to be practically meaningless, with few national policies clearly excluded.

The second element of FLIs is also present, namely delegation. One of the elements of the European Employment Strategy (EES), as with other OMC style processes, is to encourage Member States to include civil society actors, particularly the social partners, in the preparation of National Progress Reports (NPRs).[47] Non-bindingness and 'framework' elements are also clear. EES obligations are non-binding at both a substantive and a procedural level, with little to no references to the EES in the case law of the Court of Justice.[48] To this end, the quality and depth of national reports has tended to vary wildly, with some seeing reporting largely as a box-ticking exercise, and others taking reporting obligations seriously.[49] 'Enforcement' is conducted not through financial penalties or court enforcement but largely through peer review, or the soft power of 'naming and shaming' (with even this being absent from most OMC processes).

Finally, the framework element of the OMC is provided via its cyclical nature. When 'integrated guidelines' for both the EES and economic policy surveillance were agreed in 2005, they were developed on a three-year cycle, with Member States under a duty to report annually to the EU level on progress in meeting these targets. The explicit design was therefore intended to anticipate policy learning, with new developments, or even the failure of the initial guidelines to anticipate national practice, driving later reforms. Substantive and procedural iteration has thus been a common feature of the OMC with the 'Lisbon 2020' process adopted in late 2010 carrying an amended policy focus, reflecting some

---

47 On the empirical limits of this effort, see Sandra Kröger, 'The End of Democracy as We Know It? The Legitimacy Deficits of Bureaucratic Social Policy Governance' (2007) 29(5) *Journal of European Integration* 565–82.

48 See e.g. Stijn Smismans, 'From Harmonization to Coordination? EU Law in the Lisbon Governance Architecture' (2011) 18(4) *European Journal of Public Policy* 516–19.

49 Mark Dawson, *New Governance and the Transformation of European Law* (Cambridge University Press 2011) 211–215.

(but by no means all) of the criticisms emerging from the 'Integrated Guidelines' preceding it.[50]

In this way, soft law could be seen as an attempt to accommodate diversity, perhaps even to a foolhardy degree. As with the example of the social directives discussed before, the main criticism levelled at the OMC has been its unproven ability to deliver meaningful policy change.[51] This is not a criticism confined to the field of social policy. Many have pointed, for example, to the weak monitoring instruments used in the context of fiscal policy monitoring – the centre-piece of which, the Broad Economic Policy Guidelines (BEPG), is another OMC process – of doing little to promote the necessary level of competitiveness and budgetary discipline needed to safeguard Monetary Union.[52] In fields where adopting a particular guideline is likely to have severe fiscal consequences, it is unclear how soft law processes can achieve effective compliance with their norms.

3.2 Soft Law and the Crisis

It is for precisely this reason that the story outlined above should be treated with caution. The last five years has seen a significant 'hardening' of soft law, questioning its easy association with diversity, flexibility and differentiation in law-making.[53] This can be seen in three senses: as a consequence of a hardening of soft law processes which already carried

---

[50] On the 2020 reforms (and their limits), see Mark Dawson, 'Learning from Past Failures? New Governance in the European Union from Lisbon 2000 to Lisbon 2020' (2010) 17(2) *Maastricht Journal of European & Comparative Law* 389–440.

[51] See e.g. Sandra Kröger, 'The Effectiveness of Soft Governance in the Field of European Anti-poverty Policy: Operationalization and Empirical Evidence' (2009) 11(2) *Journal of Comparative Policy Analysis* 197–211; (for a more positive yet still critical account) Martin Heidenreich and Jonathan Zeitlin 'Introduction' in Martin Heidenreich and Jonathan Zeitlin, *Changing European Employment and Welfare Regimes. The Influence of the Open Method of Coordination on National Reforms* (Routledge 2009) 1–9.

[52] See Servaas Deroose, Dermot Hodson and Joost Kuhlmann, 'The Broad Economic Policy Guidelines Before and After the Re-launch of the Lisbon Strategy' (2008) 46(4) *Journal of Common Market Studies* 827–48.

[53] See e.g. the accounts provided in Sonja Bekker, 'The EU's Stricter Economic Governance: A Step towards a more Binding Coordination of Social Policies?' (2013) WZB Discussion Paper SP IV 2013-501; Desmond Dinan, 'Governance and Institutions: Impact of the Escalating Crisis' (2012) 50 *Journal of Common Market Studies* 85–98.

'hard' elements ('hardening'); as a consequence of policy fields monitored under soft law increasingly being brought under the umbrella of hard coordination ('spill-over'); or finally, as a result of a decrease in the 'flexibility' of soft law instruments, with vague and 'principle' based provisions increasingly being replaced by detailed and more uniform recommendations or demands ('prescription').

The first element, 'hardening', can be seen most clearly in the area of economic policy coordination. Even prior to the crisis, this area could most accurately be characterized as a hybrid area of governance, including both hard and soft law elements.[54] The soft law element of the pre-crisis system was the BEPG, which attempted to coordinate fiscal policy without harmonization and with few possibilities for sanction beyond non-binding Council 'recommendations' for economic reform. The hard element was the Stability and Growth Pact (SGP), which from its inception allowed for deposits and eventually fines if its 3 per cent limit on structural governments deficits were breached.

The adoption by the Council and Parliament of a 'six-pack' of legislative measures designed to strengthen EU economic governance in 2011 significantly strengthened this system.[55] As a result of the six-pack, we see far higher levels of hierarchical steering. Whereas under the old SGP, Member States were permitted to set their own Medium-Term budgetary objectives, within which deficits could be gradually corrected; under the new regime, these objectives are quantitatively defined at the European level.[56] Failure to meet these objectives can trigger fines not

---

[54] Imelda Maher, 'Economic Governance: Hybridity, Accountability and Control' (2007) 13(3) *Columbia Journal of European Law* 679–703.

[55] Regulation (EU) No 1173/2011 of the European Parliament and of the Council of 16 November 2011 on the effective enforcement of budgetary surveillance in the euro area; Regulation (EU) No 1174/2011 of the European Parliament and of the Council of 16 November 2011 on enforcement measures to correct excessive macroeconomic imbalances in the euro area; Regulation (EU) No 1175/2011 of the European Parliament and of the Council of 16 November 2011 amending Council Regulation (EC) No 1466/97 on the strengthening of the surveillance of budgetary positions and the surveillance and coordination of economic policies; Regulation (EU) No 1176/2011 of the European Parliament and of the Council of 16 November 2011 on the prevention and correction of macroeconomic imbalances; Council Regulation (EU) No 1177/2011 of 8 November 2011 amending Regulation (EC) No 1467/97 on speeding up and clarifying the implementation of the excessive deficit procedure; Council Directive 2011/85/EU of 8 November 2011 on requirements for budgetary frameworks of the Member States.

[56] See Bekker (n 53) 6.

just in the 'corrective' stage, i.e. where severe deficits have been identified, but also in the SGP's 'preventive' stage, where Member States have not made steps to meet corrective plans drawn up by the Commission and endorsed by the Council. Finally, the material scope for fines has been increased – sanctions under the Excessive Deficit Procedure can now be initiated for states failing to meet the debt criterion as well as the deficit limit.[57] The reforms are designed both to lengthen and extend the reach of central budgetary surveillance and to increase the penalties on Member States who fail to comply with central rules.

The second element of the post-crisis system, 'spill over', has been to increasingly monitor social policy (that was previously subject to 'soft' coordination) under the roof of the less flexible processes of Monetary Union.[58] An example of this is another reform to emerge from the 'six-pack' from 2011. Acknowledging that many of the Member States (such as Spain) who had suffered most from the crisis carried healthy government deficits prior to 2008, the six-pack also established a further procedure for economic coordination – the macro-economic imbalances procedure (MIP).[59] This procedure is extremely broad – covering any element of national policy with the potential to produce larger economic imbalances, from high private debt to unsustainable pension and social security systems. This procedure also carries the possibility for binding recommendations, 'corrective plans', deadlines for meeting those plans and an interest bearing deposits of 0.1 per cent of GDP (convertible into fines), where Member States deviate from agreed upon rules.

As a consequence of its broad ambit, the MIP allows EU 'coordination' – with the possibility of binding recommendations and sanctions – of areas of policy that normally would be seen as sitting on the limits of EU competence. In its 2012 employment package for example, the Commission argued that:

> Better EU employment governance and coordination has become essential for at least two reasons. First, labour market participation, unemployment and labour cost play a role in macro-economic stability and are taken into consideration in the new regulation on the prevention and correction of macro-economic imbalances.[60]

---

[57] Regulation (EU) No 1175/2011 (n 55) art. 5.

[58] See Bekker (n 53) 9–10.

[59] Regulation (EU) No 1176/2011 (n 55).

[60] European Commission, 'Towards a Job-rich Recovery', COM(2012) 173 final, at 20.

This speaks to a long-standing criticism of the 'social' OMC processes – namely that social policy is in danger of being subsumed under overarching and more strictly binding economic coordination processes.[61] Certain procedural aspects of the post-crisis reforms may encourage this. One change, for example, is the adoption of the European Semester, designed to streamline reporting under the Lisbon 2020 process (the umbrella process for 'soft' economic and social policy) with the reporting cycles for the Stability and Convergence programmes of Monetary Union. This streamlining, in combination with the 'six-pack' reforms, suggests the increasing tendency to monitor and coordinate particular policy fields through several, overlapping EU processes.

The final element of the post-crisis soft law regime – 'prescription' – also suggests a coordination regime less accommodating of diversity. While earlier 'first generation' OMC processes, such as the EES, permitted the Council to mandate specific recommendations to states, notable in recent years is an increase in the volume, scope and precision of these country-specific recommendations (CSRs). One way of observing is quantitative growth – Bekker for example points to 23 CSRs being issued to four prominent states (Germany, Poland, UK and Spain) in 2011 compared to 11 issued in 2009.[62] Another is qualitative growth in CSRs, i.e. recommendations that are increasingly precise and intrusive.

As highlighted by Bekker, Poland's bland 2009 recommendation to 'develop an integrated flexicurity approach' for its labour and pension systems contrasts its highly prescriptive 2011 recommendation to:

> Raise as planned the statutory retirement age for uniformed services, continue steps to increase the effective retirement age, such as linking it to life expectancy. Establish a timetable to further improve the rules for farmers' contributions to the social security fund (KRUS) to better reflect individual incomes.[63]

By referencing specific policies and programmes, which the CSR asks Poland to adopt or develop, the margin of manoeuvre for the state to 'interpret' the CSR or adapt it to changing policy preferences seems to be more limited.

Finally, we see a higher level of procedural prescription. While Member States under previous NRPs and CSRs were given discretion to

---

[61] See Dawson (n 50) 215.

[62] Bekker (n 53) 15.

[63] Council Recommendation on the National Reform Programme 2011 of Poland and delivering a Council Opinion on the updated Convergence Programme of Poland', 2011/C217/02 of 12 July 2011 at 7.

implement planned reforms in their own time, the new round of post-crisis CSRs contain explicit deadlines for implementation, with the UK for example expected to deliver a strategy for early school leavers by 2012 and a normal implementation deadline across the Member States of 12 to 18 months.[64] What was once a procedure based on open suggestions, broad principles, and flexible goals – while not morphing completely into a process of 'hard' law – has at least become increasingly prescriptive and precise.

3.3 Unity in Austerity?

What do these gradual post-crisis reforms to EU coordination processes mean for the general levels of policy prescription in EU soft law? The outcome may be a less politically diverse policy-making landscape than prior to the crisis. In short, if part of the rationale for the emergence of soft law was its ability to avoid a 'one size fits all' approach to 'implementing' EU policies, there is some evidence that post-crisis soft law is coalescing around one in particular: austerity. Sonia Bekker develops this point in her recent study of social policy coordination. In their 2011 'National Progress Reports' on employment reforms, for example, we see a gradual shift in the social policy orientations of Member States with many seeing significant reforms and 'haircuts' to their social security and welfare systems as a necessary ingredient for fiscal consolidation.[65] Even states that suffered little from the crisis, such as Poland, remark that the phasing-out of some active labour market programmes and significant amendments to the pension system are now necessary to avoid excessive government deficits.[66]

This can be observed across several policy areas. In the area of pension policy, for example, during the period from 2011 to 2013 17 countries received CSRs on pensions; 15 of them receiving almost identical recommendations on raising the statutory retirement age and linking that age to life expectancy.[67] These recommendations were also remarkably uniform in rejecting national schemes – such as invalidity pensions, differentiated retirement between men and women, and income indexation – that could inhibit the long-term solvency of the public pension

---

[64] Bekker (n 53) 16.

[65] Ibid., 10–14.

[66] Ibid., 12.

[67] Mark Dawson, 'The Legal and Political Accountability Structure of "Post-Crisis" EU Economic Governance' (2015) 53(5) *Journal of Common Market Studies*, 976–93.

scheme, or the public treasury more generally. Recommendations in other areas with deep fiscal impact – such as tax and social security – similarly coalesced around the goal of fiscal consolidation.

The austerity drive is of course starker still in states with poorer fiscal health.[68] The Irish Government, in its 2011 Memorandum of Understanding with the EU, designed to facilitate European Financial Stability Facility (EFSF) funding, promised to cut by one euro per hour its minimum wage and to repeal a number of collective agreements inhibiting 'wage adjustment' in the labour market.[69] In Portugal's Memorandum of the same year, it committed to reducing severance and bonus salary payments in the public sector, to limiting the entitlement period for unemployment benefits, to reducing state subsidies of pharmaceuticals, and to reform its labour code to ease the grounds under which workers could be dismissed.[70] For states requiring financial assistance, the opportunities for 'diverse' implementation of EU recommendations seem decidedly limited. Centralized EU intervention in areas far beyond the normal reaches of EU competence is not only a reality for these countries but backed up by a sanction potentially above and beyond the 'hardness' of even the most hierarchical form of EU law: withdrawal of bail-out funding and potential economic catastrophe.

Of course, not all Member States are subject to the same level of prescription. This is certainly one way in which 'diversity' *is* emerging in the post-crisis EU: the creation of new surveillance mechanisms for euro-zone states, as well as the presence of financial conditionality, means that at a procedural level different states are subject to different obligations.[71] At the same time, the trajectory of the crisis, and the significant economic inter-dependencies it has exposed, are leading more and more states to become subject to some form of economic monitoring. The number of states in excessive deficit procedures for example has grown for only two (Hungary and the UK) as late as April 2009, to a

---

[68] On the impact of the crisis on national labor law, see Catherine Barnard, 'The Financial Crisis and the Euro Plus Pact: A Labor Lawyer's Perspective' (2012) 41(1) *Industrial Law Journal* 98–114.

[69] Council Implementing Decision on granting Union financial assistance to Ireland, 2010/0351 (NLE) of December 10 2011 <http://register.consilium.europa.eu/pdf/en/10/st17/st17211.en10.pdf>.

[70] Portugal Memorandum of Understanding on Specific Economic Policy Conditionality <http://ec.europa.eu/economy_finance/eu_borrower/mou/2011-05-18-mou-portugal_en.pdf>.

[71] See the concept of 'assymetric sovereignty transfer' discussed in Dawson (n 67).

significant majority (20 states) who were under some kind of budgetary surveillance in 2013.[72] Unless the euro-zone economy significantly improves in the coming years, the 'hard effects' of soft law are likely here to stay.

4. CONCLUSION

This chapter has primarily been interested in categorizing how 'flexibility' and 'differentiation' is expressed in the EU's legislative instruments. As it has attempted to show, initial categories can be misleading. While the distinction between 'hard' and 'soft' law may be an attractive starting point in considering the levels of flexibility which EU measures can accommodate, the last two decades of EU policy-making has seen an increasing blurring of the boundaries between these two categories. Imprecision, delegation, non-bindingness, and 'framework' elements are apparent in both directives and soft law processes in varying configurations. What, however, does this insight mean for the larger legal architecture of the Union?

It may be useful to make one concluding point, which relates to the role of EU law, and of the EU Courts, in patrolling legislative norms. As has been indicated, while the EU Courts have often been highly active in defining the terms of particular directives, and ensuring that Member States do not use flexibility to deprive EU legislation of its normative content, they have largely stayed away from soft law. Soft law has, for understandable reasons, often been viewed as non-coercive and intergovernmental: a bundle of policy preferences, with little hierarchical force or individual obligation. Why therefore extend the normal guarantees of due process and judicial review to its procedures?

If the story of 'hardening' indicated above is to be believed, there may be good reason to reconsider this approach. In so far as soft law 'coordination' increasingly takes on binding and hierarchical elements, the idea that it merely runs 'parallel' to the EU's normal legal architecture is increasingly difficult to sustain.[73] This is particularly so when two further factors are brought into the equation. The first is the policy fields in which soft coordination now operates. While processes like the OMC were extended to social policy on the basis that the balance of EU-Member State competence should not be subverted, the crisis has

---

[72] See the EDP score-board <http://ec.europa.eu/economy_finance/economic_governance/sgp/-deficit/index_en.htm>.

[73] Dawson (n 49) 87–92.

seen an increasing penetration of processes of economic policy coordination into the field of social policy. As another recent paper of the author has argued, this has the potential to significantly upset the 'substantive balance' between policy outcomes that the EU can legitimately deliver and fields where EU intervention is highly contested (and likely to remain so in the future).[74]

The second consideration is power. While the 'absence of law' and of judicial review was often justified on the basis that states could easily 'exit' soft law regimes, or were free to interpret them as they wished, the realities of Monetary Union have increased soft coordination's level of coercion. A state seeking to sign a Memorandum of Understanding, or even a state in an excessive deficit procedure receiving a CSR, may not be in a position to deviate significantly from 'central' norms, whether provided for through 'hard' law or soft. These two considerations, in combination, suggest that the ability of soft law processes to be judicially contested and challenged (e.g. on grounds of conflicts with general principles of EU law, including fundamental rights) ought to be taken more seriously in the future.

Legal contestation of soft law could be done in a variety of ways. Legal controls could either extend to the framing of soft recommendations per se or to the process by which soft law is agreed, demanding for example a certain baseline of social, parliamentary and civil society participation as a pre-condition for a coercive soft law regime to take hold.[75] The increasing prescriptiveness of soft law regimes need not per se frustrate soft law's ability to accommodate diversity in an ever-larger EU. It may, however, demand a re-evaluation of the surrounding legal framework within which soft law is developed and policed.

REFERENCES

Barnard C, 'The Financial Crisis and the Euro Plus Pact: A Labor Lawyer's Perspective' (2012) 41(1) *Industrial Law Journal*, 98–114.

Bekker S, 'The EU's Stricter Economic Governance: A Step towards a more Binding Coordination of Social Policies?' (2013) *WZB Discussion Paper* SP IV-501.

---

[74] See Mark Dawson and Floris de Witte, 'Constitutional Balance in the European Union After the Euro Crisis' (2013) 76(5) MLR 817–44.

[75] See e.g. the suggestions in Dawson (n 49) 254–65. See also Joanne Scott and Susan P Sturm, 'Courts as Catalysts: Rethinking the Judicial Role in New Governance' (2007) 13(3) *Columbia Journal of European Law* 565–94.

Dawson M, 'Learning from Past Failures? New Governance in the European Union from Lisbon 2000 to Lisbon 2020' (2010) 17(2) *Maastricht Journal of European & Comparative Law*, 389–440.

Dawson M, *New Governance and the Transformation of European Law* (Cambridge University Press 2011).

Dawson M, 'The Legal and Political Accountability Structure of "Post-Crisis" EU Economic Governance' (2015) 53(5) *Journal of Common Market Studies*, 976–93.

Dawson M and De Witte F, 'Constitutional Balance in the European Union After the Euro Crisis' (2013) 76(5) *Modern Law Review*, 817–44.

De Búrca G, 'Stumbling into Experimentalism: The EU Anti-Discrimination Regime' in Sabel C and Zeitlin J (eds), *Experimentalist Governance in the European Union* (Oxford University Press 2010) 215–35.

Deroose S and Hodson D, 'The Broad Economic Policy Guidelines Before and After the Re-launch of the Lisbon Strategy' (2008) 46(4) *Journal of Common Market Studies*, 827–48.

Dinan D, 'Governance and Institutions: Impact of the Escalating Crisis' (2012) 50 *Journal of Common Market Studies*, 85–98.

Falkner G, Treib O, Hartlapp M and Leiber S, *Complying with Europe: EU Harmonization and Soft Law in the Member States* (Cambridge University Press 2005).

Heidenreich M and Zeitlin J, 'Introduction' in Heidenreich M and Zeitlin J (eds), *Changing European Employment and Welfare Regimes. The Influence of the Open Method of Coordination on National Reforms* (Routledge 2009).

Hophmayer-Tokich S, 'Public Participation under the EU Water Framework Directive – Processes and Possible Outcomes', Preparatory Paper for the NOLIMP Workshop on Public Participation and Cost-effectiveness Analysis.

Jacobsson K, 'Soft Regulation and the Subtle Transformation of States: The Case of European Employment Policy' (2004) 14(4) *Journal of European Social Policy*, 355–70.

Kröger S, 'The End of Democracy as We Know It? The Legitimacy Deficits of Bureaucratic Social Policy Governance' (2007) 29(5) *Journal of European Integration*, 565–82.

Kröger S, 'The Effectiveness of Soft Governance in the Field of European Anti-poverty Policy: Operationalization and Empirical Evidence' (2009) 11(2) *Journal of Comparative Policy Analysis*, 197–211.

Linos K, 'How Can International Organizations Shape National Welfare States? Evidence from Compliance with European Union Directives' (2007) 40(5) *Comparative Political Studies*, 547–70.

Maher I, 'Economic Governance: Hybridity, Accountability and Control' (2007) 13(3) *Columbia Journal of European Law*, 679–703.

Page B and Kaika M, 'The EU Water Framework Directive: Part 2. Policy Innovation and the Shifting Choreography of Governance' (2003) 13 *European Environment*, 328–43.

Sabel C and Zeitlin J, 'Learning from Difference: The New Architecture of Experimentalist Governance in the EU' (2008) 14(3) *European Law Journal*, 271–327.

Scott J and Sturm S, 'Courts as Catalysts: Rethinking the Judicial Role in New Governance' (2007) 13(3) *Columbia Journal of European Law*, 564–94.
Smismans S, 'From Harmonization to Coordination? EU Law in the Lisbon Governance Architecture' (2011) 18(4) *European Journal of Public Policy*, 502–22.
Trubek D and Trubek L, 'Hard and Soft Law in the Construction of Social Europe: The Role of the Open Method of Co-ordination' (2005) 11(3) *European Law Journal*, 343–64.
Von Bogdandy A, Arndt F and Bast J, 'Legal Instruments in European Union Law and Their Reform: A Systematic Approach on an Empirical Basis' in Eeckhout P and Tridimas T (eds), *Yearbook of European Law* 23 (Oxford University Press 2004) 91–136.
Winter G, *Sources and Categories of European Union Law* (Nomos 1996).

5. Differentiated representation: is a flexible European Parliament desirable?

Deirdre Curtin and Cristina Fasone

1. INTRODUCTION

Adapting the composition and the functioning of the European Parliament (EP) to the increasing flexibility and differentiation in the EU legal and political systems is not an entirely new problem in comparative terms. The issue has also arisen in federal states such as the United States in periods of crisis and times of divided positions among the States.[1] A problem that is similar, although it is not framed in identical terms as in the EU context, is the West Lothian Question in the United Kingdom (UK). Following devolution in the UK, MPs elected in the Scottish, Welsh and Northern Irish constituencies still vote in the House of Commons for Acts that only apply to England. In contrast, in the same Chamber, MPs elected in English constituencies are no longer entitled to vote on a series of Acts that are now regularly passed by the regional legislative Assemblies in Scotland, Wales and Northern Ireland. The debate about limiting the voting rights of the MPs elected in the devolved regions, however, has never led to the actual adoption of measures to operationalize a voting limitation in practice.[2]

---

[1] See further, for example, John Kincaid, 'The United States of America. From Dualistic Simplicity to Centralized Complexity' in John Loughlin, John Kincaid and Wilfried Swenden (eds), *Routledge Handbook of Regionalism and Federalism* (Routledge 2013) 159.

[2] See, for example, the written evidence by Professor David Phinnemore, Queen's University Belfast, on 'The Future of the European Union: Forms of Membership' before the Foreign Affairs Committee of the UK House of Commons about *The Future of the European Union: UK Government Policy*, First Report of Session 2013–14, vol. I, 68, § 139. See also Michael Dougan,

Following the creation of the EMU the problem was discussed by the EP itself, although no measures were adopted to take account of the different degree of participation of Member States in specific policy areas, such as monetary policy and Schengen. This was very different from what happened in the Council where voting rights for non-participating countries were restricted.[3] Since 1995 the EP has in fact explicitly rejected any asymmetric participation of its MEPs in the deliberative processes according to the policy area concerned.[4] The idea of a flexible composition for the EP has been discussed more generally[5] but was never implemented in practice. The EP has recently confirmed its opposition with regard to the Eurozone of any asymmetric participation

'The Unfinished Business of Enhanced Cooperation: Some Institutional Questions and Their Constitutional Implications' in Andrea Ott and Ellen Vos (eds), *Fifty Years of European Integration: Foundations and Perspectives* (TMC Asser Press 2009) 170–71 and 175. However, at present the Government's proposal for Standing Order changes in the UK House of Commons to implement Government policy on English Votes for English Laws (EVEL), presented on 14 July 2015 and directly affecting the West Lothian Question, is subject to a parliamentary inquiry (at the time of writing the second evidence session is under way): <http://www.parliament.uk/business/committees/committees-a-z/commons-select/procedure-committee/inquiries/parliament-2015/english-votes-for-english-laws/>, accessed 10 September 2015.

[3] Jean-Louis Bourlanges, *Draft Report on the Operation of the Treaty on European Union with a View to the 1996 Intergovernmental Conference. Implementation of the Union*, European Parliament, Committee on Institutional Affairs, PE 211.920/A, 10 April 1995, and Claus-Dieter Ehlermann, 'Increased Differentiation of Stronger Uniformity' (1995) EUI Working Paper – Robert Schuman Center no 95/21, 30.

[4] See, for example, the European Parliament Resolution of 12 May 1995 on the functioning of the Treaty on European Union with a view to the 1996 Intergovernmental Conference – Implementation and development of the Union, A4-0102/95, § 16; the European Parliament Resolution of 16 January 1997 on the general outline for a draft revision of the Treaties, B4-0040/97; recently, the European Parliament Resolution of 20 November 2012 with recommendations to the Commission on the report of the Presidents of the European Council, the European Commission, the European Central Bank and the Eurogroup 'Towards a genuine Economic and Monetary Union', A7-0339/2012. Compare Jean-Claude Piris, *The Future of Europe: Towards a Two-Speed EU?* (Cambridge University Press 2012) 119, note 11.

[5] See for example, in the framework of the intergovernmental Conference for the Treaty of Amsterdam (doc. CONF 3914/96, 26.09.1996).

of its members as constituting a violation of the principle of the equality of all Union citizens.[6]

The Eurozone crisis and the European and Member States' institutional response to it can be considered a turning point in the debate on this issue.[7] The economic crisis has shown the weaknesses of the current system of representation in the EU and, arguably, pushes for a structural change of the traditional understanding of representation in the EP. In other words, it is the seriousness and the transformative nature of this crisis and of the Eurozone measures adopted in that context that make the issue of revisiting representation within the EP particularly urgent. Eurozone governance, as a form of two-tier governance, is, in this view, destined to become a permanent feature of the EU, which requires the deeper structural problem to be addressed, namely the current 'discrepancy between the problem structure and the decision-making structure'.[8] At present, the problem – the governance of the euro – mainly affects the 19 Eurozone countries, whereas the decision-making structure in the EP involves the representatives elected in *all* 28 Member States equally. The fact that MEPs from non-euro area countries participate in the deliberations on the Eurozone, which in turn are not applied to their electors, may undermine the democratic legitimacy of those decisions.

This chapter focuses on the possibility of 'differentiated representation' within the EP, depending on the Eurozone or non-Eurozone origin of its MEPs. It analyses the wisdom and appropriateness of the different institutional arrangements that could be adopted to implement such differentiation in practice. Our argument is that the position of the EP cannot be properly understood outside the wider context of the multilevel parliamentary field of the EU. This surrounds the EP with a

---

[6] Resolution of the European Parliament of 12 December 2013 on the constitutional problems of multi-tier governance in the European Union, A7-0372/2013, § 29.

[7] See for example Giandomenico Majone, 'Rethinking European Integration After the Debt Crisis' European Institute-University College London Working Paper no 3/2012, 19-26 and Piris (n 4) 56 and 119.

[8] See John Erik Fossum, 'The Structure of EU Representation and the Crisis' in Sandra Kröger (ed.), *Political Representation in the European Union: Still Democratic in Times of Crisis?* (Routledge 2014) 62. The Dutch Council of State in its Report presented, upon request for information, on the embedding of democratic control in the reform of economic governance in Europe to combat the economic and financial crisis by the President of the Senate of the States General, no W01.12.0457/I, The Hague, 18 January 2013, 16 argues that the principle of institutional indivisibility can no longer be maintained in the EP in the present context.

complex network of inter-parliamentary relationships with national parliaments. Several provisions of the European Treaties (Article 12 TEU and Protocol No. 1) and Article 13 of the Fiscal Compact in fact make clear that it takes both the EP and national parliaments together to reconcile the European and the national dimensions of parliamentary representation in the EU.[9] This inevitably influences the debate on the nature of MEPs' mandates and the potential 'flexible' composition of the EP. This chapter thus first focuses on the issue of plural parliamentary representation in the European constitutional system, namely the extent to which citizens' representation in the EP is different from that of the national parliaments and how these two 'representations' complement each other (section 2). In section 3 some reflections are offered on the possible ways the internal bodies and procedures of the EP in the framework of Eurozone governance can be institutionally (re-)organized. The proposal to establish a new parliamentary Chamber for the Eurozone is considered in section 4. Finally, is any form of 'differentiated' representation desirable and why (section 5)?

2. PLURAL PARLIAMENTARY REPRESENTATION IN THE EUROPEAN UNION

2.1 A Multi-level Parliamentary Field

The pluralism underpinning the EU constitutional system requires a continuous interaction among different instances of democratic and parliamentary representation, which by no means resembles the typical structure of representation characteristic of federal systems.[10] According to Article 14 TEU, the EP in very general terms 'represents' the European citizens while national parliaments individually represent Member States' citizens both in the national arena, when they scrutinize the activity of the national government in the EU, as well at the European level in a number of specific procedures that enable them to take a position on the Union's measures, for instance, in the framework of the early warning mechanism on the principle of subsidiarity (Protocols no. 1 and 2). National parliaments are thus not limited to involvement only at the

---

[9] See, on this point, the Report by Jean-Claude Juncker, in close cooperation with Donald Tusk, Jeroen Dijsselbloem, Mario Draghi and Martin Schulz, on Completing Europe's Economic and Monetary Union, Brussels, 22 June 2015, 17.

[10] See Fossum (n 8) 55.

national level when ratifying amendments to the European Treaties and some EU-related international agreements or in controlling their government's activities at the EU level; in addition, national legislatures have been conferred powers to represent citizens directly at the European level.[11]

Parliamentary representation in the EU includes all forms of direct and indirect involvement of the EP *and* of national parliaments, through which European citizens can influence and control EU decision making. Article 10 TEU is explicit that parliamentary representation is a crucial aspect of representative democracy in the EU and that it has two components: the EP *and* the national parliaments.[12] The actions of the EP and of the national parliaments do not take place within two separate and parallel arenas of representation. They are rather complementary[13] and together comprise a 'multilevel parliamentary field'.[14]

At the same time, by means of inter-parliamentary cooperation, national legislatures collectively represent the interests of national citizens in the supranational arena. This is a collective exercise that is 'particularly important to obtain information about the positions of other member state governments that can then be used to enable national parliaments to put together different bits of the puzzle and to begin redressing the informational advantage that all governments enjoy'.[15] Inter-parliamentary cooperation can reconcile the exclusively national dimension of representation, the *raison d'être*, of parliaments for centuries, with the supranational dimension that demands so much time and resources of national legislatures because of their new European powers. In order to understand what really happens at the European level,

---

[11] On 27 February 2012, in his Speech to the Inter-parliamentary Committee meeting on the European Semester for Economic Policy Coordination, the President of the European Council, Mr Herman Van Rompuy, affirmed that: 'Maybe not formally speaking, but at least politically speaking, all national parliaments have become, in a way, European institutions', <http://www.consilium.europa.eu/uedocs/cms_data/docs/pressdata/en/-ec/128208.pdf> accessed 10 May 2014, 2.

[12] The other pillar of EU democratic legitimacy is the principle of participatory democracy (art. 11 TEU), which however is beyond the scope of the present chapter since it only marginally affects the problem of parliamentary representation in the EU and the composition of the European Parliament.

[13] See Deirdre Curtin, 'Challenging Executive Dominance in European Democracy' (2014) 77(1) MLR 1, 22.

[14] This notion has been proposed by Ben Crum and John Erik Fossum, 'The Multilevel Parliament Field: A Framework for Theorising Representative Democracy in the EU' (2009) 1(2) *European Political Science Review* 249.

[15] Curtin (n 13) 30.

national parliaments need to speak to each other and most importantly – for the purpose of the present chapter – need to be continuously engaged in a conversation with the EP.[16]

2.2 Representation by the EP: National or European

The EP has been directly elected for the past 36 years and as such is the only European institution that enjoys, in formal terms, direct democratic legitimation by the European citizens. This democratic character has justified the gradual but constant extension of its powers with every revision of the Treaties. It is exactly the tension between the EP's functional role and powers in the EU institutional framework, on the one hand, and the imperatives of its parliamentary 'integrity', on the other, that has become a source of controversy over its composition following the Eurozone crisis. There is a functional pressure on the EP which, in the specific context of economic governance, could undermine its institutional credibility. This is the issue that has led to the proposal for a flexible composition of the EP.

Given the strengthening of the other EU institutions, from the European Council to the European Central Bank (ECB), in the aftermath of Eurozone crisis, the European Commission argues that:

> It is the European Parliament that primarily needs to ensure democratic accountability for any decisions taken at EU level, in particular by the Commission. A further strengthened role of EU institutions will therefore have to be accompanied with a commensurate involvement of the European Parliament in the EU procedures.[17]

However, as long as most euro-crisis procedures only concern Eurozone countries, an institution such as the EP, which represents all European citizens regardless of their origins and the policy at stake, arguably cannot be considered the institution best suited to oversee the ECB, the implementation of economic surveillance and the follow-up to the bailouts. Due to the mismatch between the scope of the policies and the composition of the EP, the idea of differentiated representation in the EP was launched to restore the effectiveness of parliamentary action in a democratically accountable manner.

---

[16] See European Commission, Communication on A blueprint for a deep and genuine economic and monetary union: Launching a European Debate, COM(2012) 777 final/2, Brussels, 30.11.2012, 35, <http://ec.europa.eu/commission_2010-2014/president/news/archives/2012/11/pdf/blueprint_en.pdf>.

[17] Ibid.

In addition to its decision-making powers and its scrutiny role, the EP has a highly symbolic function in the EU. This symbolic function can dictate preserving the 'integrity' of the EP as a whole. The decision to make this institution a directly elected assembly was made in 1976 with the aim of countering the problem of the democratic deficit and of building up 'a Parliament for Europe' as a whole.[18] The EP 'has been a powerful symbol of a continent turning away from its past divisions and conflicts'.[19] It has also been one of the most significant advocates for the deepening of the process of European integration and for the constitutionalisation of the EU.[20]

Article 14.2 TEU states that the EP is 'composed of representatives of the Union's citizens' – in sharp contrast to the wording of Article 189 TEC pre-Lisbon, according to which MEPs were 'representatives of the peoples of the States brought together in the Community'. The new article provides quite literal support for the symbolic function of the EP as the representation of the European citizenry as a whole. This new Treaty article basically reverses the earlier case law of the Court of Justice in *Spain v United Kingdom*, where the Court did not find a Treaty basis for a common European definition of the persons entitled to vote and to stand as a candidate in EP elections.[21] Now it is clear that only citizens of the EU Member States, as European citizens, enjoy active and passive suffrage in the EP elections, and this supports the view that the EP ensures supranational representation. There is only one exception: the UK.[22]

---

[18] See David Marquand, *Parliament for Europe* (Jonathan Cape 1979) 36–9.

[19] See David M Farrell and Roger Scully, 'The European Parliament: One Parliament, Several Modes of Political Representation on the Ground?' in Peter Mair and Jacques Thomassen (eds), *Political Representation and European Union Governance* (Routledge 2011) 36.

[20] See Luciano Bardi, Beligh Nabli, Cristina Sio Lopez and Olivier Costa, *Building Parliament: 50 Years of European Parliament History (1958–2008)*, work produced by the European University Institute, Florence, under the direction of Yves Mény, for the European Parliament, Luxembourg, 2009, 111–26.

[21] See Case C-145/04 *Spain v United Kingdom* [2006] ECLI:EU:C:2006:543 and Dougan (n 2) 176–8. In that decision the Court stated that it is for the Member States to decide 'in compliance with Community Law' who was entitled to vote and to be elected in the EP.

[22] See Declaration no 64 by the United Kingdom of Great Britain and Northern Ireland on the franchise for elections to the European Parliament annexed to the consolidated version of the TEU and the TFEU after the Treaty of Lisbon. British overseas territories' citizens can vote for the EP based on national

In practice, Article 14 TEU has not made the EP immune to national pressures. First of all, the seats within the EP are still assigned pro-quota to the Member States, on the basis of their population and of their contribution to the process of integration (e.g. whether they were founding countries or not) although the principle of digressive proportionality tries to balance this strictly national criterion of allocation (Article 14.2 TEU).[23] The European Council's decision of 28 June 2013 (2013/312/EU) establishing the composition of the European Parliament clarifies that the minimum (six) and the maximum (96) number of seats per country set by the Treaties shall be fully utilized and that an MEP 'from a more populous Member State represents more citizens than each Member from a less populous Member State and, conversely, that the larger the population of a Member State, the greater its entitlement to a large number of seats (Article 1)'. Thus the representation in the EP is disproportionately in favour of the smaller countries – a fact that led the German Constitutional Court to qualify the EP as an institution lacking democratic credentials, because of the fact that its composition violates, in the Court's view, the principle of equality among European citizens (Article 9 TEU).[24]

A uniform procedure for the election of the EP has never been adopted, even if some minimum 'common' elements now apply to all Member States.[25] The proposal to elect at least a quota of MEPs by a transnational constituency, which would have emphasized the European quality of the vote, has never been put into practice.[26] The absence of a

---

law. On this point see Michael Dougan, 'The Treaty of Lisbon 2007: Winning Minds, Not Hearts' (2008) 45(3) CML Rev 617, 634–5.

[23] See Dougan (n 2) 633.

[24] See the decision of the Second Senate of the German Constitutional Court of 30 June 2009 on the constitutionality of the Laws accompanying the Act of ratification of the Lisbon Treaty, no 2 BvE 2/08, 2 BvE 5/08, 2 BvR 1010/08, 2 BvR 1022/08, 2 BvR 1259/08, 2 BvR 182/09, in particular §§ 279–289, and its critique: Christopher Lord and Johannes Pollack, 'Unequal but Democratic? Equality According to Karlsruhe' (2013) 20(2) *Journal of European Public Policy* 190.

[25] See for example, Council Decision 2002/772/EC, Euratom of 25 June 2002 and 23 September 2002 amending the Act concerning the election of the representatives of the European Parliament by direct universal suffrage, annexed to Decision 76/787/ECSC, EEC, Euratom, art 1 (OJ L283/01, 21.10.2002).

[26] See the Report by Georgios Anastassopoulos adopted by the EP plenary on 15 July 1998 (OJ C292, 21.9.1998) and the Report by Andrew Duff (2009/2134(INI)), adopted by the EP Committee on Constitutional Affairs on 1 February 2012.

truly European party system has not helped the EP to be perceived in the eyes of the European citizens as an institution fulfilling a European common good, but rather as pervaded by national cleavages.[27] While some scholars argue that the voting behaviour of MEPs is mainly influenced by their affiliation to a political group,[28] others contend that national delegations *de facto* count to a great extent, also in the allotment of key positions in the EP such as Committee Chairs.[29]

There are, however, signs of a turn towards conceiving the EP mandate in truly *European* terms, detached from the national origins of its representatives. The new formulation of Article 14.2 TEU is one such indication. This trend started in the Treaty of Maastricht of 1993 when Article 13 TEC, establishing European citizenship, entitled European citizens to elect their representatives and to be elected to the EP, regardless of their nationality but rather based on their legal residence in one of the Member States. The latter might potentially be different from their country of origin and national citizenship. The abolition of the dual parliamentary mandate, which survived the direct election of the EP, constituted a further step in shielding the European mandate from national pressures.[30]

The turn towards a *European* mandate of MEPs is further supported by the institutional design of the EP, which makes it structurally different

---

[27] See Simon Hix and Christopher Lord, *Political Parties in the European Union* (Basingstoke 1996) and, more recently, Luciano Bardi, Edoardo Bressanelli, Enrico Calossi, Wojciech Gagatek, Peter Mair and Eugenio Pizzimenti, *How to Create a Transnational Party System* (Brussels 2010) <http://www.europarl.europa.eu/meetdocs/2009_2014/documents/afco/dv/etude-departement thematique_/etude-departement-thematique_en.pdf> accessed 9 July 2014.

[28] See Roger Scully, Simon Hix and David M. Farrell, 'National or European Parliamentarians? Evidence from a New Survey of the Members of the European Parliament' (2012) 50(4) *Journal of Common Market Studies* 670 and Richard Rose and Gabriela Borz, 'Aggregation and Representation in European Parliament Party Groups' (2013) 36(3) *West European Politics* 474.

[29] See Amie Kreppel, *The European Parliament and Supranational Party System: A Study in Institutional Development* (Cambridge University Press 2002) 206 et seq. and Olivier Costa and Julien Navarro, 'Le mandat parlementaire européen. Qui représentent les députés européens?', in Sabine Saurugger (ed.), *Les modes de représentation dans l'Union européenne* (L'Harmattan 2003) 123–52.

[30] See Council Decision 2002/772/EC, Euratom, amending the Act concerning the election of the representatives of the European Parliament by direct universal suffrage (n 25) introducing the new art. 2A.

from institutions such as the Council, where Member States are represented *par excellence* (Article 10 TEU). By contrast, the activity of MEPs is protected by the principle of the 'free mandate', as is the case for all national legislatures. 'Constitutionalized' by the Statute for Members of the EP since 2005, this principle ensures that MEPs are free and independent and vote on a personal and individual basis, thus prohibiting any instruction and binding mandate (Articles 2 and 3). Agreements concerning the resignation and the exercise of the mandate by an MEP are null and void.[31]

The prohibition of the binding mandate is a cornerstone of the EP's position in the constitutional architecture of the EU. Given the origins of the process of European integration and the initial composition of the EP, it appears that the free mandate of this institution was instrumental in protecting the elective assembly from national interferences (and today also from the strong control exerted by political groups over individual MEPs). The EP is deemed to be the opposite of 'a congress of ambassadors'; it is rather 'a *deliberative* assembly of *one* polity [nation], with *one* interest, that of the whole',[32] compared to the many different interests of the Member States. In the words of Edmund Burke, '[y]ou choose a member indeed; but when you have chosen him, he is not member of Bristol, but he is a member of *parliament*'.[33] We will now explore whether the existence of a free mandate for MEPs and a 'trustee model' of representation is influential in the current debate on the composition of the EP for the governance of the Eurozone.

3. AN INTERNALLY DIFFERENTIATED EUROPEAN PARLIAMENT

The idea of 'differentiated representation' in the EP is based on the assumption that the Eurozone measures produce effects only within the countries of the euro area. For example, this appears to be the background of the preventive and corrective arm of the Stability and Growth

[31] See the Decision of the European Parliament of 28 September 2005 adopting the Statute for Members of the European Parliament (2005/684/EC, Euratom), OJ L262, 07.10.2005.

[32] See, Edmund Burke (1774), 'Speech to the Electors of Bristol', in Philip B Kurland and Ralph Lerner (eds), *The Founders' Constitution* vol. 1, Ch. 13, doc. 7 (The University of Chicago Press 1987) <http://press-pubs.uchicago.edu/founders/documents/v1ch13s7.html>.

[33] Ibid.

Pact. Although the relevant measures are targeted at individual Member States, there is a common interest within the euro area that each Eurozone country complies with the objectives and standards set in the Pact so as to preserve the stability of the currency. In theory, this interest is specific to Eurozone Member States.

While this is certainly true in legal terms – only the States that are part of the EMU are bound to comply with tighter rules and their citizens are consequently subject to specific rights and duties – doubts can be expressed about the economic and the political effects of those measures in non-Eurozone countries. Euro-crisis measures also appear to produce 'spillover effects' on countries outside the EMU. In other words, European citizens outside the euro area are affected, although to a lesser degree, by those measures; therefore, institutions in non-Eurozone Member States are accustomed to taking those measures into consideration, even though euro-crisis measures do not introduce legal obligations upon them in this regard.[34] A recent example is the ongoing construction of the Banking Union. Non-euro members are formally exempt from, for instance, the Single Supervisory Mechanism,[35] and none of them have opted in so far. Nevertheless, it would be difficult to consider non-Eurozone countries as indifferent towards the ECB's supervision of the banking sector, due to the indirect consequences it has on their national banks.[36]

---

[34] On the effect of the Euro-crisis measures in non-Eurozone countries, see the report on the Czech Republic and on Latvia published in the framework of the 'Constitutional Change through Euro Crisis Law' Project, EUI Law Department, and available at <http://eurocrisislaw.eui.eu>.

[35] See Regulation (EU) 1022/2013, Amending Regulation (EU) No 1093/2010 establishing a European Supervisory Authority (European Banking Authority) as regards the conferral of specific tasks on the European Central Bank pursuant to Council Regulation (EU) No 1024/2013 and Regulation (EU) 1024/2013, Conferring specific tasks on the European Central Bank concerning policies relating to the prudential supervision of credit institutions, OJ L287, 29.10.2013, 5–14, and 63–89.

[36] See UK House of Lords, European Union Committee, 'European Banking Union: Key issues and challenges', *Seventh Report*, 10 December 2012, §§ 58–65. <http://www.publications.parliament.uk/pa/ld201213/ldselect/ldeucom/88/88 05.htm#a13>. This objection has been raised repeatedly by the UK, also with regard to measures linked to the cooperation in criminal matters for which the UK has not exercised the selective opt-in: see, for example, the reasoned opinions issued by the UK House of Commons on the draft Regulation for the establishment of the European Public Prosecutor's Office (COM(2013) 534) <www.ipex.eu>.

However, even if, for the sake of argument, we accept the view that European citizens from non-Eurozone countries are not legally affected by the euro-crisis measures and, thus, that they do not have a right to be represented in the EP, when it deals with the EMU, a second problem arises. Is it reasonable or desirable to treat European citizens and MEPs elected in non-Eurozone countries equally or are further levels of differentiation required with regard to non-euro area MEPs?[37] There are after all divergent degrees of commitment on complying with European fiscal rules and for orienting national economic policies towards more competitiveness, employment and sustainability of public accounts. For example, the Euro-Plus Pact was 'signed', not only by the (then) 17 Eurozone countries, but also by Bulgaria, Denmark, Latvia, Lithuania, Poland, and Romania. Some Member States – mainly those that acceded to the EU in 2004 and 2007 – are definitely engaged in improving and strengthening their fiscal policies with the aim of joining the euro area. In contrast, other countries, such as Denmark, Sweden and the UK, have deliberately chosen to remain outside the EMU, although in principle they could participate. While the latter countries have chosen to opt out of the euro, the eastern countries that supported the Euro-Plus Pact, as confirmed by the case of Latvia and Lithuania,[38] are willing to be a part of the Eurozone, but they have not (yet) been admitted as their economic and fiscal credentials are not strong enough. If one accepts that MEPs represent the interests of their national electorates, it is unreasonable to exclude MEPs elected in those countries that in a few years' time will most likely be part of the Eurozone. Rather, the ongoing involvement of precisely these MEPs can be considered as fostering compliance with stricter fiscal rules and prompt adaptation even before they become legally binding upon the Member States in question. The enlargement of the Eurozone is, after all, seen as inevitable in the provisions of the treaties of accession to the EU.

3.1 Differentiated Representation According to the Rights of MEPs

In implementing a system of differentiated representation within the EP, it is necessary to define the level at which the limitation of the rights of

---

[37] See Cristina Fasone, 'European Economic Governance and Parliamentary Representation. What Place for the European Parliament?' (2014) 20(2) *European Law Journal* 164, 182–3.

[38] Latvia joined the Eurozone on 1 January 2014; Lithuania has become the 19th Eurozone country as of 1 January 2015.

MEPs elected outside the Eurozone should occur.[39] Are only voting rights to be constrained or also the right to take part in parliamentary debates about the Eurozone measures, thus limiting MEPs' freedom of expression? If their participation rights are to be constrained, should this happen in general or should it be more limited? For example, limited participation rights might include not assigning non-Eurozone MEPs to specific positions within the EP, such as Committee Chair, President of a political group or group coordinator.[40]

The idea of limiting certain rights of some members of the Parliament is however problematic. It creates second order MEPs and implicitly recognizes second order European citizens represented in the EP. There are serious concerns about its impact on the very nature of the Parliament as a democratically elected assembly of representatives protected by a free mandate. Precisely for this reason, there are no examples of parliaments which assign a different status to their members on the basis of their origins and constituency. The limitation of the right of non-Eurozone MEPs to participate in parliamentary debates can be considered a disproportionate constraint that would completely exclude some legitimately elected MEPs from the discussion, regardless of their right to vote. This would constitute the demise of the EP as a parliamentary assembly, not only because of the denial of the rationale behind a free mandate, but also due to severely limiting the freedom of expression of 'second order' MEPs who would not be able to contribute to the debate.[41]

Differentiated EP representation is generally proposed for voting rights, i.e. preventing non-Eurozone MEPs from voting on euro-related

---

[39] With this regard, different organizational options have also been examined in the Report of the Dutch Council of State presented, upon request for information, on the embedding of democratic control in the reform of economic governance in Europe to combat the economic and financial crisis (n 8) 18–24 and by Andreas Maurer, 'From EMU to DEMU: The Democratic Legitimacy of the EU and the European Parliament' (2013) IAI Working Paper no 1131, 7–13 <http://www.iai.it/pdf/DocIAI/iaiwp1311.pdf>.

[40] By playing these roles, MEPs are able to affect the EP agenda and procedures decisively. For example, the Conference of the Presidents of political groups is able to set the agenda of business of the EP, the timeframe of the EP decisions and the priorities of the institution.

[41] Without entering into detail about procedural issues within the EP, it may also be worth mentioning that if differentiated representation is applied to the EP under this format, then the current arrangement for the participation in committees between full members and substitutes must be replaced since it is based on the affiliation with the same political groups rather than on the country of election (art. 200 EP Rules).

measures. As is customary in the Council, the voting rights of MEPs elected in certain countries would, under this approach, be temporarily suspended *ratione materiae* both in plenary and in committees. It can be argued, however, that voting in plenary or in committees has very different implications. While standing committees are politically very important and have become more and more crucial during the trialogues of the ordinary legislative procedure, committee members are not entitled to take final decisions and can be replaced by a substitute from the same group if they do not attend a committee meeting. In contrast, the MEPs in plenary do not have a substitute and adopt binding decisions for the entire Parliament. The dynamics within standing committees are moreover characterized by a higher degree of informality and, although group coordinators tend to play a significant role, MEPs in committees are certainly more autonomous than in the plenary. It follows then that it is more logical to limit voting rights only in the context of the plenary.

3.2 Differentiation within the Committee System: A Sub-committee for the Eurozone

A reasonable limitation of the right of participation of non-Eurozone MEPs can be achieved without any amendment of the Treaties or of the rules of procedure of the committees, according to some proposals from the EP itself. For example, key positions in the field of Eurozone governance could simply be assigned only to MEPs elected in the Eurozone area, without formally excluding the other MEPs from participating in parliamentary activities. Thus, the rapporteurs, the shadow rapporteurs and the drafters of opinions on the dossiers affecting the Eurozone, as well as the chairs of the committees on economic affairs, on social affairs and on the budget, would be appointed from within the pool of Eurozone MEPs.[42] It is well known that behind these key positions lie not only the interests of political groups but also the preferences of the national delegations within each group.[43] The possibility of achieving a minimal differentiation in the EP, if (and only if) a political consensus

---

[42] During the seventh parliamentary term (2009–14) the Chairwoman of the committee on economic and monetary affairs was an MEP elected in the UK, Sharon Bowles (ALDE), although she took a pro-integrationist position. By contrast, during the eighth parliamentary term (2014–19) the Chairman of ECON is Roberto Gualtieri, an MEP elected in a constituency of a Eurozone country, Italy.

[43] See Virginie Mamadouh and Tapio Raunio, 'The Committee System: Powers, Appointments and Report Allocation' (2003) 41(2) *Journal of Common*

exists among the groups, has been endorsed by the EP in its Resolution of 12 December 2013: 'the internal rules of the European Parliament offer a sufficient margin of manoeuvre to organize specific forms of differentiation on the basis of political agreements within and among political groups in order to provide for appropriate scrutiny of the EMU'.[44]

There are also further potential developments at committee level that could improve the EP scrutiny of Eurozone measures but which have not yet been prioritized by the standing committee on economic and monetary affairs (ECON). This committee has had an increasing workload in the last few years and in particular an extensive number of legislative dossiers. As ECON is often involved in several ordinary and special legislative procedures at the same time, it has had a limited amount of time available to scrutinize the implementation of euro-crisis measures. Given the complexity of many of the legal measures and of the multiplicity of the institutions involved in the 'new' European economic governance, the EP has argued that its role in this field must be strengthened in order to protect the democratic accountability of the overall system.[45] The idea of creating a sub-committee for the Eurozone within the ECON committee appears to be a plausible solution, although the EP has refrained from establishing sub-committees. Setting up sub-committees requires the prior authorization of the Conference of the Presidents, and their operation is subject to strict control and is dependent on the main committee (Article 203 EP Rules).[46] In the early 1990s, the ECON committee established a sub-committee on monetary policy, which played a very important role in holding hearings and in scrutinizing the policy, although it could only issue recommendations to the ECON committee and the rapporteurs were appointed by the chair of ECON.

Market Studies 333; and Richard Corbett, Francis Jacobs and Michael Shackleton, *The European Parliament* (8th edn, John Harper Publishing 2011) 147 et seq.

[44] Resolution of the European Parliament of 12 December 2013 on the constitutional problems of multi-tier governance in the European Union (n 6) § 31.

[45] Ibid.

[46] The degree of autonomy of a sub-committee has varied over time. So far, only the EP standing committee on foreign affairs and security, which is devoid of legislative power, is divided into two sub-committees, on common foreign and defence policy and on human rights, and both have only a preparatory role in relation to the decisions taking place in the main committee. See Corbett, Jacobs and Shackleton (n 43) 166.

There are different views on the desirability of a sub-committee for the Eurozone and on the possible composition of such a sub-committee. Should it be composed only of members of the ECON committee or should it include members coming from other standing committees dealing with euro-related issues (such as the committee on the budget and the committee on social policy and employment), thereby becoming a cross-sectional committee with a mixed composition?[47] All these positions, however, have a significant point in common: the sub-committee should be composed of MEPs coming from all over the EU and not only from the Eurozone. The idea of differentiated representation within this (prospective) sub-committee is explicitly rejected.

The most structured proposal for a Eurozone sub-committee, to be established within the ECON committee, came from within the committee itself in January 2014 with the intention of being adopted by the new Parliament after its election in May 2014, although at the time of writing no further steps had been taken in this direction. The chair of the ECON committee during the seventh parliamentary term (2009–14), Sharon Bowles (ALDE, UK), sent a letter to the President of the EP on behalf of the group coordinators, outlining the committee proposal 'on the structure and modalities within the Parliament for the Euro area governance'.[48] Different proposals put forward by the ECON committee in June 2013, asking for additional resources, staff and time to devote to 'high profile' hearings on the Eurozone measures were then considered insufficient and a more structural solution was advocated.[49]

According to the new proposal of the coordinators, while the ECON committee should remain competent for examining all draft legislative acts and for the scrutiny of non-Eurozone specific affairs – e.g. on the EU financial supervision authorities – the new sub-committee should be entrusted with the scrutiny of all EMU-related issues. The 'EMU sub-committee' (no official name has been proposed for this new body) would do the preparatory work for the ECON committee with regard to

---

[47] This latter idea has been proposed by Yves Bertoncini, 'Les Parlements de L'UE et la gouvernance de l'UEM. Quelle dimension parlementaire pour "l'Union politique"?', *Notre Europe – Institut Jacques Delors*, 11 April 2013, 4.

[48] See the letter sent on 23 January 2014 as a recommendation to the EP President, Martin Schulz, upon request of the Conference of the Presidents, by the Chairwoman of the ECON Committee, Sharon Bowles, (no 301355), http://sylvie-goulard.eu/articles2014/Annex-3a-Chair-s-Announcements-ECON-structure.pdf.

[49] See the Report of the group coordinators of the ECON committee of 28 June 2013.

non-legislative acts affecting the functioning of the Eurozone. The decision-making power (adoption of reports, of resolutions, of recommendations) would remain firmly in the hands of the ECON committee as a whole. The prospective EMU sub-committee would scrutinize inter alia the functioning of the Banking Union, the ESM and the Fiscal Compact and would hold hearings with the President of the Euro Group, the President of the ECB, the Commissioner for Economic and Monetary Affairs and the Euro and the chairs of the single supervisory mechanism (SSM) and of the single resolution mechanism (SRM). It would also organize inter-parliamentary meetings with national parliaments on EMU-related issues. Nothing could of course prevent the ECON committee from organizing hearings and inter-parliamentary meetings on the Eurozone, should this be necessary to fulfill its legislative tasks.

The letter to the future Parliament on the euro governance reaffirms the 'dogma' in relation to the composition of the EMU sub-committee, where, in principle, all MEPs can be asked to serve. Although the sub-committee is conceived as a sort of counterpart of the Eurogroup in the EP, it is not the same. Unlike the Eurogroup, which is an intergovernmental body representing the national interests of the Eurozone countries (Protocol no. 14 on the Eurogroup), the proposed EP sub-committee will also allow the participation of non-Eurozone MEPs. While confirming that the existing Treaties forbid differentiated representation within the EP according to the origins of MEPs, the letter stresses the margin of manoeuvre for political groups to get to a 'sustainable' differentiation in Parliament. According to this analysis, political groups could informally pursue enhanced scrutiny of the EMU by utilizing the role of Eurozone MEPs in the EMU sub-committee – as rapporteurs, chairs and vice-chairs, etc. – to the maximum. Yet the challenge will be to ensure that the discretion enjoyed by political groups and the Conference of the Presidents will be used in a manner that avoids the imposition of the will of the two major groups, EPP and PES, on the others, including the euro-sceptics. At the same time, the fundamental principles of equal representation of European citizens in the EP and of the EP's free mandate will have to be upheld. It remains to be seen, at the time of writing, whether the new parliament will take up any of these ideas and suggestions in practice.

4. A NEW PARLIAMENTARY CHAMBER FOR THE EUROZONE

The idea, under various labels, of a new Parliament for the Eurozone has been frequently discussed and publicly supported by the French-German axis since the beginning of the euro crisis. Almost at the same time as the signature of the Fiscal Compact, the Arthuis Report of March 2012 launched the idea of setting up a new body to deal with Eurozone issues.[50] The proposal is not entirely new, since the French Parliament, well before the financial crisis, was in favour of creating a new inter-parliamentary body in the EU where national parliaments could be permanently represented and of transforming the Conference of parliamentary committees on EU affairs (COSAC), established under French influence in 1989, into a 'third Chamber' of the Union alongside the Council and the EP.[51] The proposal never succeeded because of the lack of support of other national parliaments, including the German *Bundestag*, and because of the fierce opposition of the EP, which saw such a prospective 'third Chamber' as a potential countervailing power and a challenge to its legitimacy. The Arthuis Report proposed to establish a type of Euro Public Accounts' Committee composed of MEPs elected in all the Member States and MPs from the Eurozone countries. They would be appointed by each Parliament from within the standing committees on financial and budgetary matters. The Member States that, at that time, were not part of the euro area but had not negotiated the opt-out from the EMU (like the Eastern countries part of the convergence process) would be allowed to send their own parliamentary delegates as observers, in anticipation of their accession to the Eurozone. According to the Arthuis Report, the differentiated representation did not directly concern the composition of the EP but rather the 'externalization' of differentiation into a new body. The aim was not to create a new institution so as to impair the position and the role of the EP. The general supervisory and investigatory functions on the EMU – e.g. on the ECB and on the Euro group – and the power to draft own-initiative reports, to adopt opinions

[50] See Jean Arthuis, Rapport on *l'Avenir de la Zone Euro: l'integration politique ou le chaos*, commissioned by the French Prime Minister, March 2012, esp. 62 et seq., <http://www.ladocumentationfrancaise.fr/var/storage/rapports-publics/124000129/0000.pdf>.

[51] See, for example, the contribution presented by the French National Assembly and Senate to the XII COSAC held in Paris on 27 and 28 February 1995 and the debate during the XXVII COSAC of Copenhagen on 16 and 17 October 2002. Compare <www.cosac.eu>.

and resolutions that the report assigned to the Euro Public Accounts Committee, would in fact limit the control of the EP as an institution on the implementation of all Eurozone measures. While the adoption of euro-related legislative acts would firmly remain in the hands of the EP, the Arthuis Report foresaw *shared authority* between the EP and Eurozone national parliaments on scrutiny and oversight through the new Committee.

The formulation of Article 13 of the Fiscal Compact and its weak implementation in 2013, 2014 and, so far, 2015 – given the lack of agreement on the composition[52] – has not permitted the application of the idea proposed in the Arthuis Report of setting up a new inter-parliamentary body. Noting the deadlock encountered in establishing a new inter-parliamentary body for the Eurozone where national parliaments of the countries of the euro area could take the lead for the control on euro-related issues, the French and the German Governments put forward a new proposal with wider implications beyond Eurozone governance. The French-German contribution of 30 March 2013 on strengthening competitiveness and growth in Europe, presented at the European Council of June 2013, sought to enhance the position of national parliaments at the EU level by establishing a permanent representation for the Member States' legislature in Brussels on the model of the German *Bundesrat*.[53] At the same time, given the democratic problems arising from the mismatch between institutional decision making in the EP and the effect of its decisions on Eurozone countries, the French-German contribution and, in particular, the French Senate and Germany's finance minister Wolfgang Schäuble have strongly advocated differentiated representation in the EP. The view expressed by the French

---

[52] The new inter-parliamentary Conference provided for in art. 13 of the Fiscal Compact is composed of a delegation of the EP (composed of MEPs also from outside the Eurozone) and delegations of all national parliaments, including those of the UK, the Czech Republic and Croatia that have not signed this Treaty. The Conference meets twice a year in line with the European Semester. However, it is not clear what size the different delegations should be and what functions are to be carried out. See Valentin Kreilinger, 'Inter-Parliamentary Cooperation and its Challenges: The Case of the Economic and Financial Governance' in Federico Fabbrini, Ernst Hirsch Ballin, Han Somsen (eds), *What Form of Government for the European Union and the Eurozone?* (Hart Publishing 2015) 271 et seq.

[53] See Sénat français, Rapport d'information fait au nom de la commission des affaires européennes (1) sur *les perspectives de l'Union européenne, par* M. Pierre Bernard-Reymond, no 407, session ordinaire 2013–2014, 26 February 2014, 100.

Senate is that, when dealing with the Eurozone measures, the EP should meet according to the Eurozone 18-format, allowing the participation in parliamentary activities only of MEPs elected in the euro area.[54]

4.1 A Directly Elected Eurozone Parliament

As for the institutional design and the functioning of parliamentary institutions in the governance of the Eurozone, there are several other proposals, some more radical than others. The most radical proposal is the idea of setting up a new elected Parliament representing only Eurozone constituents – an idea with many drawbacks.[55] First, this proposal does not take into account the already complex architecture of the EU. Should a new Eurozone Parliament be elected, it would add another institution directly elected by European citizens alongside the EP. Secondly, this new institution risks creating further confusion for the channels of democratic representation and for the relationship between the two Parliaments and towards the voters. Thirdly, the EP has successfully enhanced its democratic credentials throughout the process of European integration, but its democratization took decades and is still ongoing. A new Parliament is very likely to face the same challenges in terms of legitimacy as the EP and thus to duplicate the criticism directed at the EP. Increasing the number of elections and of the Parliaments in the EU does not necessarily lead to improving the democratic quality of the EU and of Eurozone governance if a consistent institutional framework is not in place.

4.2 A Eurozone Parliament of Eurozone National Parliaments

A second proposal for the democratic control of national budgetary procedures within the European Semester, given the spillover effects that they can create across the Eurozone Member States, is to create a new conference of national parliaments within the EMU entitled to exercise

---

[54] Ibid., 107. See also the speech of the German Finance Minister Wolfgang Schäuble at the College of Europe, Bruges, on 27 March 2014 <http://www.bundesfinanzministerium.de/Content/EN/Reden/2014/2014-03-27-bruges.html>.

[55] This idea has been proposed by the French economist, Thomas Piketty, 'Il faut donner un parlement à l'euro', *Le Monde* (20 May 2014) interviewed by Claire Gatinois et Alain Salles.

oversight powers.[56] This proposal highlights the need for more horizontal cooperation among the national legislatures, but it does attempt to marginalize the EP because of its very limited powers within the European Semester, according to the six-pack and the two-pack. Although the proposal rightly points to the existing division of competence between national parliaments and the EP, it appears to disregard Article 9 of the Protocol on the role of national parliaments in the EU, which does not allow the EP to be excluded from inter-parliamentary cooperation. Also, the proposal does not seem desirable given the 'multi-level parliamentary field' in the EU, where the role of national parliaments and that of the EP cannot be separated for the sake of the overall legitimacy of EU representative democracy, as each of them contributes to the European decision making from its own peculiar but complementary perspective.[57]

4.3 A Eurozone Parliament with 'Enhanced' Inter-parliamentary Cooperation

Finally, other proposals, in line with the French-German contribution, suggest the establishment of a special Parliament for the Eurozone, either composed of MEPs elected in the Eurozone countries or as a third chamber of Eurozone national parliaments.[58] The powers can include veto powers on certain decisions taken by the Euro group, the Euro summit and the Commission. This proposal does not consider the two interlocked dimensions, national and European, of the EU parliamentary system. Furthermore, assigning veto powers to national legislatures on ordinary decisions (i.e. beyond the 'extra-ordinary' decisions to amend the Treaties under Article 48 TEU) could result in dramatic consequences. This is the case even if it would be a suspensive veto (i.e. able to delay the decision although not to prevent it) or a final veto supported by a quorum of at least one-third of national parliaments. The individual exercise of a veto power by a national parliament could cause a deadlock in decision making, while a collective exercise of veto powers by

---

[56] See Alexandre De Streel, 'The Confusion of Tasks in the Decision-Making Process of the European Economic Governance', in Fabbrini et al. (n 52) 79 et seq.

[57] See Crum and Fossum (n 14).

[58] See Loukas Tsoukalis, *The Unhappy State of the Union. Europe Needs a New Grand Bargain* (Policy Network 2014) 77; and Christian Calliess, 'The Governance Framework of the Eurozone and the Need for a Treaty Reform' in Fabbrini et al. (n 52) 37 et seq.

national parliaments[59] is highly unlikely to occur since it is virtually impossible for all of them to agree to disagree on the same issue. Moreover, the action of national parliaments as veto players bringing the national interests within the governance of the euro area, similar to the intergovernmental institutions and bodies of the Eurozone, could impair the fulfilment of the European common interest, a problem that the reform of economic governance has tried to solve by means of tools such as reverse qualified majority in the Council.

The position of the EP on the establishment of a new Parliament for the Eurozone is quite clear. While the EP has always been in favour of intensifying cooperation with national parliaments in the governance of the euro area, in particular at the committee level, it has always expressed its opposition to the establishment of an *ad hoc* inter-parliamentary body.[60]

In the light of the multiple proposals on the table and of the EP's reaction, the problem of the best institutional design for the democratic governance of the Eurozone could find a compromise solution in the trajectory of 'enhanced' inter-parliamentary cooperation, an idea which appears to be endorsed by the 'Five Presidents Report' published in June 2015.[61] While preserving the current composition of the EP and the participation of MEPs from all the Member States as representatives of the European polity, 'enhanced' inter-parliamentary cooperation on the

---

59 For example, parliaments in Eurozone debtor countries pursue quite different interests than those in the Eurozone creditor countries. See Arthur Benz, 'An Asymmetric Two-level Game: Parliaments in the Euro Crisis' in Ben Crum and John Erik Fossum (eds), *Practices of Inter-Parliamentary Coordination in International Politics. The European Union and Beyond* (ECPR Press 2013) and Sonia Piedrafita, 'National Parliaments' Say on the New EU Budgetary Constraints: The Case of Spain and Ireland' in Maurice Adams, Federico Fabbrini and Pierre Larouche (eds), *The Constitutionalization of European Budgetary Constraints* (Hart Publishing 2014) 319–40.

60 See the European Parliament resolution of 1 December 2011 on the European Semester for Economic Policy Coordination (2011/2071(INI)), §§ 45, 46, 47, and the European Parliament resolution of 12 December 2013 on constitutional problems of a multitier governance in the European Union (n 6) § 32, in which the EP states that establishing a new inter-parliamentary body:

> would be both ineffective and illegitimate from a democratic and constitutional point of view, and reaffirms that there is no substitute for a formal strengthening of the full legitimacy of the European Parliament, as a parliamentary body at Union level, with a view to reinforcing the democratic governance of the EMU.

61 Juncker et al (n 9) 17.

EMU could involve only the national parliaments of the Eurozone. As regards national parliaments, differentiated representation may be desirable since they represent the interests of their national constituents, who are directly affected by the Eurozone measures, whereas the common European interest is protected by the representation of the EP as a whole. Without creating any new institution or conferring any veto power, the MEPs and Eurozone MPs can meet several times during the European Semester.[62] They can intensify the frequency of the so-called 'European parliamentary weeks' and exercise together the scrutiny and oversight on euro-related issues. None of this would interfere with the legislative power of the EP or with the existing monetary and economic dialogue in which it actively takes part.

5. HOW FLEXIBLE SHOULD THE EUROPEAN PARLIAMENT BE?

The controversy on the desirability of a flexible composition for the EP, in particular of the exclusion of non-Eurozone MEPs from certain procedures and bodies, stems from the tension between functional effectiveness, which the EP has to show by also holding the other EU institutions accountable within EU economic governance and its institutional integrity as the 'Parliament for Europe'. Based on a comparison of the possible institutional arrangements, this chapter argues that the avoidance or the limitation of a prospective differentiation in the EP's representation enhances its overall institutional credibility.

First of all, a free mandate is a distinctive feature of every Parliament that is worthy of this name. Secondly, one should ask what the consequences will be within the EU institutional architecture if MEPs are deemed to have a national mandate. If that is the case, the EP will duplicate the role of other European institutions, like the Council and the European Council, that base their activities on national belonging and claim their democratic credentials based on the relationship with national parliaments and citizens (Article 10 TEU). In contrast, if the EP does

---

[62] At present the European parliamentary week takes place once a year in January, in Brussels, and includes the organization of one of the two Interparliamentary Conferences on Stability, Economic Coordination and Governance in the European Union (art. 13 Fiscal Compact), which take place every year, plenary sessions so as to discuss the ongoing European Semester, and interparliamentary committee meetings between the relevant committees on budget, economic affairs and the social policy of the EP and national parliaments.

have a symbolic function, then that function is to represent the European citizenry and the European 'common good'.

The debate on a Parliament for the Eurozone is usually reduced to a mere descriptive assessment of what the MEPs' mandate often looks like – if they represent the 'collective European interest' or just the parochial interest of their voters[63] – rather than questioning what an MEP is supposed to represent in the light of the Treaties and of the parliamentary nature of the institution. In the end, whether the organization and the working methods of the EP should be revised in the context of Eurozone governance depends on how the mandate of the MEPs is conceived. The 'trustee model' of representation, on which the concept of the free parliamentary mandate is based, favours a truly European mandate of MEPs, at least as an aspiration.

Furthermore, the issue of the desirability of differentiated representation and the problem of its political feasibility for the EP cannot be disregarded. In fact, since the change in the composition and in the voting or in the participation rights of the MEPs would require an amendment of the existing European Treaties, the possibility of having such an amendment ratified in the UK, in Denmark, in Sweden, and perhaps in some non-Eurozone Eastern European countries is very unlikely. Furthermore, at present, while some appear to favour the creation of a new Parliament for dealing with Eurozone issues,[64] the EP has always been opposed to it. Since 1995, the EP has also stated its aversion to the idea of making the composition of EP bodies and its procedural arrangements flexible according to the national origins of MEPs. The EP's opposition is based on the principle of equality of Union citizens and the prohibition of discrimination based on nationality (Article 9 TEU).

Should the idea of a differentiated representation translate into a political reality, then a series of technical problems would have to be solved so as to limit differentiation. The most difficult issue will be to clarify how to define whether a certain procedure dealing with economic

---

[63] See Dougan (n 2) 178 and also Thomas Beukers, 'Flexibilisation of the Euro Area: Challenges and Opportunities' (2014) Max Weber Working Paper MWP 2014/01, 8.

[64] See, recently, the position of the French President, François Hollande, who, in a letter published on 19 July 2015 in *Le Journal du Dimanche* in hommage of Jacques Delors, put forward again the idea to establish a Government and a Parliament for the Eurozone as well as a Eurozone budget. However, no details are provided in the letter concerning the composition of such a Eurozone Parliament.

governance only affects Eurozone countries. In strict legal terms, there are no doubts, except for the case of legislative proposals that deal only with Eurozone countries in some provisions and with all Member States for the remaining part. Even where a draft legislative act is formally addressed to the countries of the euro area, in practice it is almost impossible to exclude that either the adoption of EU draft legislative acts in this field or the oversight of their implementation will indirectly produce effects on non-Eurozone countries. These effects may be on, for example, the circulation of capitals and goods within the entire internal market.

However, if the transformation into a flexible EP becomes politically unavoidable, then a minimal option for sustainable differentiation is to be preferred. Indeed, the Five Presidents Report leaves to the discretion of the EP the organisation of the role it will assume 'in matters pertaining especially to the euro area', i.e. by adapting its own rules of procedure, if needed, without any reshaping of the EP composition and functioning from the outside.[65] For example, a Eurozone committee within the ECON committee could be set up to examine legislative proposals and measures only dealing with the Eurozone. This committee would not have binding powers on the whole ECON committee and, furthermore, there are technical problems, as described above. Another sustainable option, which would not require any amendment of the EP rules of procedure, could be to limit the selection of rapporteurs and the appointment of key committee chairs to MEPs from Eurozone countries. This option has in fact been used for the appointment of the chairs of the Committees on economic and monetary affairs and on employment and social affairs in the newly elected EP.

Finally, the tension between the functional effectiveness of the EP in the Eurozone crisis and its institutional 'integrity' is mitigated if one takes into account the broader context in which the EP is called to act.

As has been highlighted, the very nature of the EP is structurally different compared to the representation of national interests provided by other EU institutions. The representation of national interests by parliamentary institutions is ensured in the EU by national parliaments. Since each of them represents European citizens as nationals of a specific Member State, a differentiated participation of national parliaments in the governance of the euro area would not only be feasible but also desirable. The position of the EP in this context has to be assessed in the light of its

[65] Juncker (n 9) 17.

overall relationship with national parliaments. The functional effectiveness of the EP in the governance of the Eurozone has been improved and complemented by its cooperation with national parliaments.

On some Eurozone measures, for example, where the EP is only consulted or informed, the EP needs the support of national parliaments for effective democratic control by means of additional documents and information that the latter have access to because of the national budgetary procedures during the European Semester.[66] In contrast, whenever crucial decisions on EU economic governance are taken at the European level, with little or no information given to national parliaments, as, for example, in relation to the Banking Union, the information provided to them by the EP could enhance the democratic control of each national parliament over its own executive. In this manner, the European and the national dimensions of parliamentary representation can be fully reconciled without the symbolic function and the institutional integrity of the 'Parliament for Europe' being impaired.

REFERENCES

Arthuis J, Rapport on *l'Avenir de la Zone Euro: l'integration politique ou le chaos*, commissioned by the French Prime Minister, March 2012, <http://www.ladocumentationfrancaise.fr/var/storage/rapports-publics/124000129/0000.pdf>.

Bardi L, Beligh N, Sio Lopez C, and Costa O, *Building Parliament: 50 Years of European Parliament History (1958–2008)* (European Communities 2009).

Bardi L, Bressanelli E, Calossi E, Gagatek W, Mair P, and Pizzimenti E, *How to Create a Transnational Party System*, 2010, <http://www.europarl.europa.eu/meetdocs/2009_2014/-documents/afco/dv/etude-departementthematique_/etude-departement-thematique_en.pdf>.

66 It is not by chance that in the latest resolution adopted by the EP in this field at the moment of writing, the European Parliament Resolution of 24 June 2015 on the review of economic governance framework: stocktalking and challenges (2014/2145(INI)), § 57(a), the EP does not even mention the issue of its potential internal differentiation, according to the Eurozone – non-Eurozone ratio, and besides advocating for the adoption of the convergence guidelines by ordinary legislative procedure and the formalization of its scrutiny role by means of an Inter-Institutional Agreement, the EP also argues in favour of 'ensuring that all Euro area national parliaments follow each step of the European Semester process'.

Benz A, 'An Asymmetric Two-level Game: Parliaments in the Euro Crisis', in Crum B, and Fossum J (eds), *Practices of Inter-Parliamentary Coordination in International Politics. The European Union and Beyond* (ECPR Press 2013) 125–42.

Bertoncini Y, 'Les Parlements de L'UE et la gouvernance de l'UEM. Quelle dimension parlementaire pour «l'Union politique»?', *Notre Europe – Institut Jacques Delors*, 11 April 2013.

Beukers T, 'Flexibilisation of the Euro Area: Challenges and Opportunities', *Max Weber Working Paper*, MWP 2014/01.

Bourlanges J-L, *Draft Report on the Operation of the Treaty on European Union with a View to the 1996 Intergovernmental Conference. Implementation of the Union*, European Parliament, Committee on Institutional Affairs, PE 211.920/A, 10 April 1995.

Burke E, (1774), 'Speech to the Electors of Bristol', in Kurland PB and Lerner R (eds), *The Founders' Constitution*, Vol. 1, Ch. 13, Document 7 (The University of Chicago Press 1987). Available at: <http://press-pubs.uchicago.edu/founders/documents/v1ch13s7.html>.

Calliess C, 'The Governance Framework of the Eurozone and the Need for a Treaty Reform', in Fabbrini F, Hirsch Ballin E, and Somsen H (eds), *What Form of Government for the European Union and the Eurozone*? (Hart Publishing 2015) 37–56.

Corbett R, Jacobs F, and Shackleton M, *The European Parliament*, 8th ed. (John Harper Publishing 2011).

Costa O, and Navarro J, 'Le mandat parlementaire européen. Qui représentent les députés européennes?', in Saurugger S (ed.), *Les modes de représentation dans l'Union européenne* (L'Harmattan 2003) 123–52.

Crum B, and Fossum JE, 'The Multilevel Parliament Field: A Framework for Theorising Representative Democracy in the EU' (2009) 1(2) *European Political Science Review* 249–71.

Curtin D, 'Challenging Executive Dominance in European Democracy' (2014) 77(1) *Modern Law Review* 1–32.

De Streel A, 'The Confusion of Tasks in the Decision-Making Process of the European Economic Governance', in Fabbrini F, Hirsch Ballin E, and Somsen H (eds), *What Form of Government for the European Union and the Eurozone*? (Hart Publishing 2015) 79–94.

Dougan M, 'The Treaty of Lisbon 2007: Winning Minds, Not Hearts' (2008) 45(3) *Common Market Law Review* 617–703.

Dougan M, 'The Unfinished Business of Enhanced Cooperation: Some Institutional Questions and Their Constitutional Implications', in Ott A, and Vos E (eds), *Fifty Years of European Integration: Foundations and Perspectives* (TMC Asser Press 2009) 157-180.

Ehlermann C-D, 'Increased Differentiation of Stronger Uniformity', *EUI Working Paper – Robert Schuman Center,* No. 95/21, 1995.

Farrell DM, and Scully R, 'The European Parliament: One Parliament, Several Modes of Political Representation on the Ground?', in Mair P, and Thomassen J (eds), *Political Representation and European Union Governance* (Routledge 2011) 36–54.

Fasone C, 'European Economic Governance and Parliamentary Representation. What Place for the European Parliament?' (2014) 20(2) *European Law Journal* 164–85.

Fossum JE, 'The Structure of EU Representation and the Crisis' in Kröger S (ed.), *Political Representation in the European Union. Still Democratic in Times of Crisis?* (Routledge 2014) 52–68.

Hix S, and Lord C, *Political Parties in the European Union* (Basingstoke 1996).

Kincaid J, 'The United States of America. From Dualistic Simplicity to Centralized Complexity', in Loughlin J, Kincaid J, and Swenden W (eds), *Routledge Handbook of Regionalism and Federalism* (Routledge 2013) 157–71.

Kreilinger V, 'Inter-Parliamentary Cooperation and its Challenges: The Case of the Economic and Financial Governance' in Federico Fabbrini, Ernst Hirsch Ballin, Han Somsen (eds), *What Form of Government for the European Union and the Eurozone?* (Hart Publishing 2015) 271–88.

Kreppel A, *The European Parliament and Supranational Party System: A Study in Institutional Development* (Cambridge University Press 2002).

Lord C, and Pollack J, 'Unequal but Democratic? Equality According to Karlsrhue' (2013) 20(2) *Journal of European Public Policy* 190–205.

Majone G, 'Rethinking European Integration After the Debt Crisis', *European Institute-University College London Working Paper*, No 3/2012.

Mamadouh V and Raunio T, 'The Committee System: Powers, Appointments and Report Allocation' (2003) 41(2) *Journal of Common Market Studies* 333–51.

Marquand D, *Parliament for Europe* (Jonathan Cape 1979).

Maurer A, 'From EMU to DEMU: The Democratic Legitimacy of the EU and the European Parliament'. *IAI Working Paper* No. 1131, 4 April 2013, <http://www.iai.it/pdf/DocIAI/iaiwp1311.pdf>.

Piedrafita S, 'National Parliaments' Say on the New EU Budgetary Constraints: The Case of Spain and Ireland' in Adams M, Fabbrini F, and Larouche P (eds), *The Constitutionalization of European Budgetary Constraints* (Hart Publishing 2014) 319–40.

Piketty T, 'Il faut donner un parlement à l'euro', interviewed by Claire Gatinois et Alain Salles, *Le Monde*, 20 May 2014.

Piris J-C, *The Future of Europe: Towards a Two-Speed EU?* (Cambridge University Press 2012).

Rose R, and Borz G, 'Aggregation and Representation in European Parliament Party Groups', (2013) 36(3) *West European Politics* 474–97.

Scully R, Hix S, amd Farrell DM, 'National or European Parliamentarians? Evidence from a New Survey of the Members of the European Parliament' (2012) 50(4) *Journal of Common Market Studies* 670–83.

Tsoukalis L, *The Unhappy State of the Union. Europe Needs a New Grand Bargain* (Policy Network 2014).

6. Differentiation through accession law: free movement rights in an enlarged European Union

Andrea Ott*

1. INTRODUCTION: DIFFERENTIATION CAUSED BY ACCESSION TREATIES

This chapter aims to illustrate the differentiation in law resulting from the last generation of accession treaties in a core area of the Internal market and having immediate consequences for Union citizens. With the growing complexity of EU law, and the already existing differentiation resulting from the Economic and Monetary Union (EMU) and the area of freedom, security and justice, accession treaties have triggered extensive temporary differentiation between existing and incoming Member States in the recent accessions of 2004 (Poland, Hungary, Czech and Slovak Republic, Slovenia, Latvia, Lithuania and Estonia[1]), 2007 (Romania and Bulgaria) and 2013 (Croatia). Not all forms of flexibility mechanisms resulting from the recent accession treaties can be discussed here, with

* The author would like to thank Gillian More, legal officer at DG Employment, Social Affairs & Inclusion. European Commission, Brussels, for her valuable comments. The usual disclaimer applies.

[1] This chapter will leave out accession countries Malta and Cyprus. In the case of Malta, the existing Member States did not apply restrictions but Malta could apply restrictions due to Annex XI of the Maltese arrangements. In the case of Cyprus, in relation to the area of Northern Cyprus, for which the Greek part does not exercise effective control but which is not considered an external border of the EU, see further Protocol No 10 on Cyprus and so-called Greenline Regulation 866/2004. Consequently, the question arises how far Turkish Cypriotes fall under EU citizenship and, once these citizens enter the southern Republic of Cyprus, to what extent they can exercise their rights. See further Nikos Skoutaris, *'EU Citizenship in Hibernation'. The Cyprus Issue: The Four Freedoms in a Member State under Siege* (Hart Publishing 2011) 111.

temporary derogations agreed in half of the over 30 chapters of *acquis* covered in the pre-accession process and during the accession negotiations.[2] The focus will instead rest on the temporary arrangements that limit access to the labour market of the existing EU Member States for migrant workers in all the three recent waves of enlargement. These temporary exceptions from market access for new Member States' citizens and their families can be also applied by Norway, Iceland, Liechtenstein, and Switzerland as a result of the extension of the Internal market to the European Economic Area and due to the EU-Swiss bilateral agreement on the free movement of persons.

In the wake of the end of this maximum seven-year restriction on Romanian and Bulgarian workers and their families under the Accession Treaties 2007, on 1 January 2014, a political discussion erupted, especially in the United Kingdom, Germany, Austria and the Netherlands, on 'benefit tourism'.[3] It even sparked an open debate being launched by the former British premier David Cameron to restrict Internal market rights of Romanian and Bulgarian citizens and change the national rules on benefits.[4] In this emotional and politically charged discussion, it could be easily forgotten that, even before the end of 2013, Romanian and Bulgarian work-seekers and their families could be treated differently under the temporary differentiation deriving from the accession treaty but had, in principle, equal rights as EU citizens. National restrictions are not only influenced by the temporary accession treaty arrangements and their restrictions but also by the growing case law of the European Court of Justice (CJEU) in the field of EU citizenship rights. Hence, EU citizens originating from incoming Member States have a 'split identity' or 'multiple personalities', with different rights depending on their personal situation in the host Member State. While access to the labour market for migrant workers and their families can be restricted, the right of self-establishment is not restricted and no limits on EU citizenship rights

---

[2] Andrea Ott, 'EU Constitutional Boundaries to Differentiation: How to Reconcile Differentiation with Integration?' in Andrea Ott and Ellen Vos (eds), *Fifty Years of European Integration: Foundations and Perspectives* (TMC Asser Press 2009) 117–18.

[3] 'EU ministers target benefit tourism', 7.3.2013, <EUobserver.com> accessed 2 April 2014.

[4] 'EU migrants: David Cameron sets out more benefit restrictions', *The Guardian*, 27.11. 2013; 'UK vows to control immigration as Bulgaria, Romania curbs end', 2.1.2014, <EUobserver.com> accessed 3 April 2014; 'Mooted UK migrant cap would be illegal', 16.12.2013, <EUobserver.com> accessed 3 April 2014.

are imposed on the primary law level. This leads to the paradoxical situation that EEA and Swiss nationals have better access to the Internal market than EU citizens falling under the national derogations.[5]

2. ACCESSION LAW AS A TOOL FOR DIFFERENTIATION AMONG EU MEMBER STATES

Accession law consists of a very short accession treaty containing the conditions of accession[6] and adjustments to the treaties accompanied by more detailed conditions fleshed out in the act of accession[7] and provisions relating to the implementation laid down in technical detailed annexes.[8] The accession treaties and acts of accession between incoming and existing Member States are characterised by their hybrid legal nature. They constitute multilateral international agreements among the contracting parties but also belong, once ratified, to primary EU law, amending and derogating from the *acquis communautaire*.[9]

---

[5] While the Internal market is extended to the EEA, it does not participate in the dynamic reading of the EU citizenship status by the CJEU. However, the EEA applies the EU citizenship Directive 2004/38/EC. See on this and the difference for Switzerland: Marc Maresceau, 'On the External Dimension of Directive 2004/38/EC' in Inge Govaere and Dominik Hanf (eds), *Scrutinizing Internal and External Dimension of European Law, Liber Amicorum Paul Demaret* (Peter Lang Publishing 2013) 773–5.

[6] In the case of Croatia consisting of four articles, OJ 2012 L112/10-20.

[7] In the case of Croatia containing 55 articles, Act concerning the conditions of accession of the Republic of Croatia and the adjustments to the Treaty on European Union, the Treaty on the Functioning of the European Union and the Treaty establishing the European Atomic Energy Community, OJ 2012 L112/21. In the previous enlargement rounds 2004 and 2007 called protocol, see for instance Protocol concerning the conditions and arrangements for admission of the Republic of Bulgaria and Romania to the European Union, OJ 2005 L157/29–202.

[8] See further: Kirstyn Inglis, *Evolving Practice in EU Enlargement* (Martinus Nijhoff Publishers 2010) 147–52.

[9] See on this: CJEU, Joined Cases 31 and 35/86 *LAISA v Council* [1988] ECR 2285 (para. 12); Andrea Ott, 'Unity in Diversity? – Differentiation in EU Law and Policy in an Enlarged European Union', *Natolin Paper* 14 (2004). Available at: <http://www.natolin.edu.pl/pdf/zeszyty/NatolinZeszyt15_Ott.pdf> accessed 3 October 2015; Christophe Hillion, 'EU Enlargement' in Paul Craig and Gráine de Búrca (eds), *The Evolution of EU law* (2nd edn, Oxford University Press 2011) 212.

As a consequence of this hybrid legal nature, Member States have a determining role in defining accession conditions which have to be accepted by incoming Member States. The European Commission is assigned an important role to monitor the ongoing pre- and post-accession process. While the starting point is the equality between Member States, including the same rights and obligations under EU law,[10] the Union needs to respect essential national diversities in a Union of 28.[11] It is generally recognised that this enlarged Union cannot function without the policy tool of differentiated integration.[12] Accession treaties with incoming Member States have been accommodating differences and enabling a smoother adaptation process among the Member States in successive accession waves since the 1970s.[13] However, by recognising the deepening and widening nexus of EU integration, the pivotal question arises as to how much diversity the Union can tolerate among Member States without sacrificing the common interests and values[14] of the supranational European integration model. In contrast to the 'Europe of bits and pieces'[15] since Maastricht with increased integration among some Member States in areas such as border control (Schengen), Euro currency, new Member States commit themselves to apply and implement the complete *acquis communautaire* consisting of primary, secondary EU law, international agreements concluded by the Union, and the fundamental principles developed by the Court through case law.[16] It might be a misleading concept in light of all the forms of differentiation covered in this book that some EU scholars speak of a

---

[10] See on this concept Jan Wouters, 'Constitutional Limits to Differentiation: The Principle of Equality' in Bruno De Witte, Dominik Hanf and Ellen Vos (eds), *The Many Faces of Differentiation in EU Law* (Intersentia 2001) 319.

[11] The diversity among Member States is now also explicitly reflected in the sincere cooperation clause (art. 4.2 TEU: The Union shall respect the equality of Member States).

[12] Allan Rosas and Lorna Armati, *EU Constitutional Law: An Introduction* (2nd edn, Hart Publishing 2013) 111; Walter van Gerven, *The European Union* (Hart Publishing 2005) 31; Ott (n 2) 113.

[13] See on the history of the enlargement process Frank Hoffmeister, 'Earlier Enlargements' in Andrea Ott and Kirstyn Inglis (eds), *Handbook on European Enlargement* (TMC Asser Press 2002) 87.

[14] See Pierre Pescatore, *The Law of Integration* (Sijthof 1974) 26.

[15] Deirdre Curtin, 'The Constitutional Structure of the European Union: A Europe of Bits and Pieces' (1993) 30(1) CML Rev 17.

[16] Andrea Ott, 'Die anerkannte Rechtsfortbildung des EuGH als Teil des gemeinschaftlichen Besitzstandes (Acquis communautaire)' (2000) EuZW 293.

principle of EU law unity.[17] Nevertheless, this concept is also reflected in the extensive use of the consistency or coherence principles in the Lisbon TEU and TFEU Treaties. Consequently, a common legal order depends on common institutions and the equal and uniform application of EU law in the main EU policies, especially in the policy field of the Internal market.

Intergovernmental differentiation[18] through accession law challenges this concept of coherence in EU law but reflects the necessary political compromise of combining the widening and deepening of EU integration. It results in differentiation between receiving and incoming EU Member States. This differentiation in the application of primary and secondary EU law is – however, and with a few small exceptions – of a temporary nature. Extraordinary permanent exceptions are, for instance, for Finland the status of its Swedish speaking Åland Islands, Denmark's permanent derogation for EU nationals to buy secondary homes in Denmark[19] and the Swedish chewing tobacco (snus) exemption for marketing and sale in Sweden.[20] It is debated in academia whether EU law impedes Member States from derogating from EU law in a permanent form in substantial fields of EU policies and especially in the field of the Internal market *acquis*. This feeds into the debate whether Member States, as the master of the Treaties, when concluding an international agreement with a third country on accession to the EU, are precluded from altering the fundamental values and principles of EU primary law.[21] This discussion arose with the Member States' negotiation mandate to commence negotiations with Turkey in 2005. This negotiation mandate openly discussed possible scenarios of specific arrangements and permanent safeguard clauses for any future Turkish accession treaty.[22]

General derogations, especially for the complex Common Agricultural Policy and state aid, have been applied since the first enlargement wave. Similarly, specific safeguard clauses to suspend rights and obligations

---

[17] Armin von Bogdandy, 'Founding Principles of EU Law: A Theoretical and Doctrinal Sketch' (2010) 16(2) ELJ 108.

[18] See further on the different forms of differentiation: Ott (n 2) 121.

[19] Protocol No. 16 on certain provisions relating to Denmark, OJ 2008 C115/287. This Protocol also includes the permanent decision of Denmark not to participate in the EMU ('... its intention not to participate in the third stage of economic and monetary union').

[20] See Jean-Claude Piris, *The Future of Europe Towards a Two-speed EU?* (Cambridge University Press 2012) 76; Inglis (n 8) 50.

[21] On this with further details: Ott (n 2) 120.

[22] Council of the European Union, Accession negotiation with Turkey: General EU Position, 12823/1/05 REV 1, Brussels, 12 October 2005, at 11.

under certain circumstances of economic difficulties have been employed in previous enlargements in 1972, 1979 and 1985. These safeguard clauses were modelled on the safeguard clause found in the original EEC Treaty.[23] And the common market regarding fundamental freedoms, including free movement of workers, was only progressively liberalised by 1968.[24] However, since the southern enlargement in the 1980s with Greece, Spain and Portugal was extended with the 'big bang enlargements' of 2004/2007 and was followed by the accession of Croatia in July 2013, derogations and transitional arrangements in major areas of the *acquis* have increased in quantity and quality for several reasons. Policies and pillars have been introduced and extended with new forms of differentiation. Certain derogations have practical motivations to prepare new Member States for accession to the Schengen system or the Eurozone but other derogations are fuelled by political and economic considerations, as can be seen in the limiting access to the Internal market for migrant workers and their families from Southern or Eastern Europe to more affluent Western European Member States. Consequently, the temporary accession treaty flexibility can be divided into temporary derogations from EMU[25] and Schengen,[26] temporary provisions applying to the Internal market *acquis*, safeguard clauses and transitional regimes[27] applicable in the common agricultural policy.[28]

In addition, new forms of flexibility mechanisms were introduced by safeguard clauses which extend the applied pre-accession conditionality

---

[23] Former art. 226 EEC. See Andrea Ott, 'The Principle of Differentiation in an Enlarged European Union' in Kirstyn Inglis and Andrea Ott (eds), *The Constitution for Europe and an Enlarging Union: Unity in Diversity?* (Europa Law Publishing 2005) 112–13.

[24] The original Rome Treaty provision foresaw a 12-year transitional period which was shortened to ten years in 1968, see further Anne Pieter van der Mei, *Free Movement of Persons Within the European Community: Cross-border Access to Public Benefits* (Hart Publishing 2003) 22–5.

[25] Currently the following countries have not yet qualified for the EMU: Bulgaria, Croatia, Czech Republic, Hungary, Lithuania, Poland, Romania, and the special case of Sweden preventing its participation.

[26] Currently Bulgaria, Croatia, Cyprus, and Romania do not qualify for Schengen.

[27] See Kirstyn Inglis, 'The Union's Fifth Accession Treaty: New Means to Make Enlargement Possible' (2004) 41(4) CML Rev 937, 947.

[28] The new Members have to meet the quality, production, processing, and hygiene standards under the CAP but were excluded from the financial benefits and revisions of the CAP were organised in parallel with the enlargement process of 2004, see on this Inglis (n 8) 186.

for up to three years after accession.[29] The economic safeguard clause is the classical safeguard clause which can be taken by new and existing Member States after authorisation by the Commission in the case of economic difficulties. Novelties since 2004 are the Internal market safeguard clause and Justice and Home Affairs (JHA) safeguard clause. The Commission employs an extra tool, apart from the existing cumbersome infringement procedure under Articles 258 and 260 TFEU, to react to failures in the commitments undertaken during the accession negotiations which cause an imminent risk or a serious breach of the functioning of the Internal market or serious shortcomings or risks thereof during transposition, implementation or application of the *acquis* in the area of freedom security and justice (Article 38 or 39 Croatian Act of Accession respectively, see Table 6.1 below). This was aided by a new cooperation and verification mechanism established by the Commission in December 2006 to monitor progress after accession and without time-limit according to individual benchmarks to be achieved by Romania and Bulgaria in the fields of judicial reform, the fight against corruption and organised crime.[30] In addition, in the 2007 accession treaty, an accession postponement clause was introduced (Article 39 Act of Accession) and in the case of Croatia a pre-accession monitoring clause (Article 36 Act of Accession). The wording of the safeguard provisions leaves open what appropriate measures are; Article 38 of the Croatian Accession Treaty explains that the proportionality principle must be applied. Despite the lingering threat to use the safeguards clauses on Poland,[31] Romania and Bulgaria over the first three years, the only example in practice until now is the case of Bulgaria between 2006 and 2008. The Commission invoked the Internal market safeguard clause concerning the Bulgarian aviation sector by not recognising airworthiness and maintenance certificates issued by

[29] See generally Inglis (n 8) 187.

[30] See latest reports on 22 January 2014, <http://ec.europa.eu/cvm/progress_reports_en.htm#thirteen> accessed 10 February 2014. On this Martina Spernbauer, 'Benchmarking, Safeguard Clauses and Verification Mechanisms – What's in a Name? Recent Developments in the Pre- and Post-accession Conditionality and Compliance with EU Law' (2007) 3(3) *Croatian Yearbook of European Law and Policy* 273.

[31] In the case of Poland, the threat had already been used in March 2003. See Ott (n 9) 16.

the Bulgarian authorities and did not qualify Bulgarian air carriers as EU air carriers.[32]

Table 6.1 Accession Treaty and Act of Accession Provisions inducing flexibility

	2004 enlargement	2007 enlargement	2013 enlargement
2 + 3 + 2 years	Temporary provisions market access labour market	Temporary provisions market access labour market	Temporary provisions market access labour market
Up to 3 years after accession	Economic safeguard clause Art.37	Economic safeguard clause Art.36	Economic safeguard clause Art.37
	Internal market safeguard clause Art.38	Internal market safeguard clause Art.37	Internal market safeguard clause Art.38
	JHA safeguard clause Art.39	JHA safeguard clause Art.38	JHA safeguard clause Art.39
	Transitional measures for CAP Art.41	Transitional measures for CAP Art.41	Transitional measures for CAP Art.41
	Transitional measures for veterinary, phytosanitary and food safety rules, Art.42	Transitional measures for veterinary, phytosanitary and food safety rules, Art.42	Transitional measures for veterinary, phytosanitary and food safety rules, Art.42
Special clauses		Accession postponement clause Art.39 one year	Pre-accession monitoring clause, Art.36

32 Commission Regulation 1962/2006 OJ 2006 L408/8 and Commission Regulation 875/2008 OJ 2008 L240/3, see also Spernbauer (n 30) 286 and Inglis (n 8) 192.

3. MIGRANT WORKERS RESTRICTIONS SINCE THE SOUTHERN ENLARGEMENTS UNTIL THE EASTERN ENLARGEMENTS

The Internal market with its four freedoms forms the main showpiece of the effective functioning of EU law and provides EU citizens with directly effective rights but, due to economic and political considerations, as outlined above, incoming and existing Member States have insisted on transitional arrangements in this policy field. While the existing Member States restricted the access to labour markets and, concerning the posting of workers (in certain listed services sectors), in the framework of the free movement of services,[33] the incoming Member States restricted temporarily the free movement of capital (in respect to the acquisition of secondary homes and/or agricultural land).[34]

3.1 Migrant Workers Restrictions in the Southern Enlargement 1981 and 1986

Restrictions for migrant workers and their access to the labour market of the existing Member States through accession treaties date back to the southern enlargement of Greece, Portugal and Spain in 1981 and 1986 respectively, in which a fixed period was agreed. In the case of Greece a six-year period and in the cases of Spain and Portugal a seven-year period for workers was applied,[35] which was later reduced to six years.[36] Overall the feared massive migration from these states did not take place;

---

[33] Since the first enlargement wave, the neighbouring countries Austria and Germany apply more extensive restrictions on the free movement of services in certain sensitive service sectors. See for the Croatian Annex V to the act of accession, para. 12.

[34] In the case of Croatia (Annex V) up to seven years for agricultural land, in the case of Bulgaria up to five years from the acquisition of secondary residences. See for details and country-specific differences: Andrea Ott, 'Grundfreiheiten' in Franz Merli and Stefan Huster (eds), *Die Verträge zur EU-Osterweiterung: Kommentar mit systematischen Erläuterungen* (Berliner Wissenschaftsverlag 2008) 166.

[35] See for instance Hoffmeister (n 13) 88–9.

[36] Council Regulation (EEC) No 2194/91 of 25 June 1991 on the transitional period for freedom of movement of workers between Spain and Portugal, on the one hand, and the other Member States, on the other hand, OJ 1991 L206/1.

either the migrants had already established themselves in the Northern European countries in the 1950s and 1960s or they returned after some years when economic opportunities improved in their home countries.[37] Consequently, in the Commission communication on problems of the enlargement of 1982, the labour market was not even addressed as a problem.[38]

3.2 Migrant Workers Restrictions in the Accession Treaties 2004, 2007 and 2013

In contrast to the southern enlargements with Spain, Portugal and Greece, the Eastern enlargement was a qualitative step in deepening accession differentiation.[39] Not only have the areas covered expanded, but also the number of safeguard measures has increased, including an option of an accession delay clause and post-accession verification measures in the case of Romania and Bulgaria as highlighted above. An underlying fear of the existing Member States in the 'big bang' enlargement was the existing or publicly perceived fear of 'migrations floods' from Central and Eastern European (CEEC) countries to Western Europe. The negotiation chapter on the free movement of workers became a central issue and was an intensely debated matter with studies indicating a steady flow of migrants from the CEEC since 1999 and a majority residing in Germany, followed by Austria, the UK, and Italy.[40] In response to this, Germany and Austria insisted on long transitional periods, while the Commission introduced an information note in 2001 in which five options were presented to the Member States, varying from no restriction

---

[37] Joanne van Selm and Eleni Tsolakis, 'EU Enlargement and the Limits of Freedom' (2004) Migration Policy Institute, available at: <http://www.migrationpolicy.org/article/eu-enlargement-and-limits-freedom/> accessed 15 February 2016.

[38] Problems of enlargement – Taking stock and proposals. Commission communication to the European Council, Copenhagen, 3 and 4 December 1982. COM(82) 757 final, 15 November 1982. Bulletin of the European Communities, Supplement 8/82.

[39] See also: Kirstyn Inglis, 'Treading the Tightrope between Flexibility and Legal Certainty' in Dominik Hanf and Rodolphe Muñoz (eds), *La libre circulation des personnes: États des lieux et perspectives* (Peter Lang Publisher 2007) 100.

[40] Andrea Ott, 'Case Note on *Deutscher Handballbund* v. *Kolpak*' (2004) 10 *Columbia Journal of European Law* 380.

to flexible transitional arrangements and a complete derogation for a fixed period of time.[41] The European Commission in the end, after feedback from the Member States, presented a 5+2 years model which was changed by Member States into a more flexible 2+3+2 years model which found its way into the accession rules. The 2+3+2 model enables receiving Member States to apply their existing national measures in place at the moment of accession in the first two years and states can continue to apply these measures unilaterally for another three years subject to a requirement to notify the Commission. At the end of the five-year period (para. 5 of the Croatian Annex V, Act of Accession), Member States can only maintain their restrictions in cases of serious disturbances of its labour market or the threat thereof and after notifying the Commission. A special safeguard clause applies according to paragraph 7 referring to a seven-year period for any existing Member State encountering serious disturbances on its labour market which could seriously threaten the standard of living or level of employment in a given region or occupation. In these cases, the Member State can apply to the Commission, which decides on the suspension and duration of the free movement rights. The last option can be applied by Member States which did not apply derogations against incoming Member States from the date of accession but considered them necessary during the seven-year period. This case arose with Spain, which had applied the free movement for workers rights since 2009 in relation to Bulgarian and Romanian citizens but applied for authorisation to restrict free movement temporarily from August 2011 until 31 December 2013.[42] In practice, for

---

[41] See on this and background: Georg Ziegler, 'The Accession Negotiations on Free Movement of Workers' in Andrea Ott and Kirstyn Inglis (eds), *Handbook on European Enlargement* (TMC Asser Press 2002) 131.

[42] Commission Decision of 11 August 2011 authorising Spain to temporarily suspend the application of Articles 1 to 6 of Regulation (EU) No 492/2011 of the European Parliament and of the Council on freedom of movement for workers within the Union with regard to Romanian workers, OJ 2011 L207/22-24; see also Commission Decision 2012/831/EU of 20 December 2012, OJ 2011 L356/90-92 authorising Spain to extend the temporary suspension of the application of Articles 1 to 6 of Regulation (EU) No 492/2011 of the European Parliament and of the Council on freedom of movement for workers within the Union with regard to Romanian workers.

the 2004 enlargement, Sweden, the UK[43] and Ireland opened their labour market with Finland, Greece, Italy, Spain and Portugal joining in 2006, while Germany, Austria, and the Netherlands (decided to lift restrictions on 1 May 2007), Belgium, France, Luxembourg, Spain and Denmark decided to keep restrictions until 2009. In the case of the accession of Romania and Bulgaria in 2007, 11 (Czech Republic, Cyprus, Estonia, Finland, Latvia, Lithuania, Poland, Slovakia, Sweden, Ireland and Slovenia) out of 25 Member States provided immediate access and Denmark, Greece, Hungary and Spain provided access in 2009.[44] The national provisions among Member States imposing restrictions also varied in their details.[45] In the case of Croatia, in 2013, 13 out of 27 Member States for the first two years decided to keep national restrictions in place.[46] By 1 July 2015, when the second time period started, only five (Austria, Malta, the Netherlands, Slovenia and UK) out of 27 Member States notified the Commission that they would keep their restrictions in place.[47]

---

43 In the UK, open access was given under the condition of the workers' registration scheme in the case of the first enlargement wave; in the second and third one this was changed into a workers' authorisation.

44 Restrictions were in place in July 2012 in Belgium, Germany, France, Spain, see Table 6.2 (due to later invoked safeguard clause).

45 Communication from the Commission to the European Parliament, the Council, the European Economic and Social Committee and the Committee of the regions, The impact of free movement of workers in the context of EU enlargement, Report on the first phase (1 January 2007 – 31 December 2008) of the Transitional Arrangements set out in the 2005 Accession Treaty and as requested according to the Transitional Arrangement set out in the 2003 Accession Treaty, COM(2008) 765 final. See, for a good overview, Iris Goldner Lang, 'Transitional Arrangements in the Enlarged European Union: How Free is the Free Movement of Workers?' (2007) 3(3) *Croatian Yearbook of European Law and Policy* 251.

46 Report from the Commission to the Council on the functioning of the transitional arrangements on free movement of workers from Croatia (First phase 1 July 2013–30 June 2015), Brussels, 29.5.2015, COM(2015) 233 final.

47 See: European Commission Employment, Free movement: end of the first phase of transitional period for Croatian workers, available at: <http://ec.europa.eu/social/main.jsp?langId=en&catId=1067&newsId=2253&furtherNews=yes> accessed 31 October 2016.

Table 6.2 Access to labour market and transitional arrangements (2+3+2 years)

	2004 enlargement: EU-8	**2007 enlargement: Romania and Bulgaria**	**2013 enlargement: Croatia**
Austria	Restrictions until 2009	Restrictions until 2013	Restrictions
Belgium	Restrictions	Restrictions	Restrictions (access since 1 July 2015)
Cyprus	No restrictions	Access	Restrictions (access since 1 July 2015)
Croatia	n/a	n/a	Reciprocal measures
Czech Republic	No reciprocal measures	Access	Access
Denmark	Restrictions	Access from 1 May 2009	Access
Germany	Restrictions	Restrictions	Restrictions (access since 1 July 2015)
Estonia	Access	Access	Access
Ireland	Access	Access	Access
Greece	Restrictions until 2006	Access from 2009	Restrictions (access since 1 July 2015)
Spain	Restrictions until 2006	Access from 2009, restrictions reintroduced between 08.2011 until 12.2013	Restrictions (access since 1 July 2015)
France	Restrictions	Restrictions	Restrictions (access since 1 July 2015)
Italy	Restrictions until 2006	Access from 2012	Restrictions (access since 1 July 2015)
Latvia	No reciprocal measures	Free access	Access

	2004 enlargement: EU-8	2007 enlargement: Romania and Bulgaria	2013 enlargement: Croatia
Lithuania	No reciprocal measures	Free access	Access
Luxembourg	Restrictions	Restrictions	Restrictions (access since 1 July 2015)
Hungary	Reciprocal measures	Access from 2009	Access
Malta	Access but reversed restrictions	Restrictions	Restrictions
Netherlands	Restrictions until 1 May 2007	Restrictions	Restrictions
Poland	Reciprocal measures	Access	Access
Portugal	Restrictions until 2006	Access from 2009	Access
Slovenia	Reciprocal measures	Access	Restrictions
Slovak Republic	No reciprocal measures	Access	Access
Finland	Restrictions until 2006	Access	Access
Sweden	Access	Access	Access
United Kingdom	Access with registration	Restrictions	Restrictions
Bulgaria	n/a	No reciprocal measures	Access
Romania	n/a	No reciprocal measures	Access

4. THE PARADOX OF ACCESSION DIFFERENTIATION: A LOOK AT THE LEGALITY OF DEROGATIONS

4.1 Transitional Restrictions against Croatian Citizens in Light of EU Law

We have already explained that transitional restrictions divide into a 2+3+2 years model, but we will now take a closer look at the application of these legal provisions. As explained above, differential treatment of EU migrant workers and their families is in principle permitted for up to seven years from the moment of accession. Equal treatment is required when it comes to the citizenship rights of EU migrants and national restrictions applied post-accession are not allowed to discriminate against these EU migrants. Croatia and the other 27 Member States may derogate from the Citizenship Directive 2004/38/EC only as far as this is necessary for the application of the national transitional restrictions.[48] Despite the introduction of EU citizenship rights by the Maastricht Treaty and its scope of application detailed by secondary law, it was only the case law and later introduced secondary regulation (especially the EU Citizenship Directive)[49] which changed the concept of a market citizen to a Union citizen by guaranteeing rights to move and equal treatment for an economically inactive EU citizen.[50] In a joint declaration by the present Member States, they stressed with regard to all acceding countries a high

---

48 See para. 9 of the Annex V.2 to the Act of Accession of Croatia:

> insofar as the provisions of Directive 2004/38/EC which take over the provisions of Council Directive 68/360/EEC of 15 October 1968 on the abolition of restrictions on movement and residence within the Community for workers of Member States and their families (2) may not be dissociated from those of Regulation (EU) No 492/2011 whose application is deferred pursuant to paras 2 to 5 and 7 and 8, Croatia and the present Member States may derogate from those provisions to the extent necessary for the application of paras 2 to 5 and 7 and 8.

49 Directive 2004/36/EC, to be implemented by 30 April 2006, OJ 2004 L158/77.

50 See Koen Lenaerts, 'The Concept of EU Citizenship in the Case Law of the European Court of Justice' (2013) ERA Forum 570, available at: <http://download.springer.com/static/pdf/53/art%253A10.1007%252Fs12027-013-0279-y.pdf?auth66=1396012097_aee645ee385f0d9d93b1d1ccbfde7b1a&ext=.pdf> accessed 6 May 2015.

degree of differentiation and flexibility in these derogations.[51] This flexibility in the application of these provisions leads at the same time to an intransparent, complex coexistence of national measures next to EU law, as demonstrated in Table 6.2 above. It results in legal questions related to the limits the EU sets such national restrictions.

4.1.1 The transitional restrictions: a complex arrangement

These transitional restrictions create a complex arrangement when taking the Croatian Annex V (in combination with Article 18 Act of Accession) on free movement of persons as an example. Transitional provisions can be applied by Member States which derogate from Articles 1 to 6 of Regulation 492/2011 on migrant workers from Croatia. Regulation 492/2011 is the successor regulation to 1612/68, which further specifies the rights of workers and their families.[52] Member States can apply their national measures, including the measures based on bilateral international agreements already in existence between Croatia and the restricting Member States which regulate access to the labour market (subpara.2).[53] Therefore, even if national measures apply, they can vary among Member States. According to subparagraph 10 of the annex, Croatia also can apply reciprocal derogations on nationals of existing Member States and Croatia has made use of this right.

Furthermore, a classical example of differentiation in individual rights results from this legal situation. Currently, for instance, Sweden applies the free movement rights on Croatian workers and their families while Austria (see Table 6.3 below) and the Netherlands apply their national measures. However, the individual position of a Croatian worker, in addition, depends on whether they already have access to the labour market of Austria or the Netherlands before or after the date of accession,

---

[51] Joint declaration by the present Member States 1. Joint declaration on the free movement of workers: Bulgaria: The European Union stresses the strong elements of differentiation and flexibility in the arrangement for the free movement of workers. Member States shall endeavour to grant increased labour market access to Bulgarian nationals under national law, with a view to speeding up the approximation to the *acquis*. As a consequence, the employment opportunities in the European Union for Bulgarian nationals should improve substantially upon Bulgaria's accession. Moreover, the EU Member States will make best use of the proposed arrangement to move as quickly as possible to the full application of the *acquis* in the area of free movement of workers.

[52] Regulation No.492/2011 on freedom of movement for workers within the Union, OJ 2011 L141/1.

[53] In some bilateral agreements fixed quotas of an influx of workers were regulated. Ott (n 34) 148.

1 July 2013. According to subparagraph 2 of the free movement of persons annex, a Croatian worker who either already works legally in a present Member State at the date of accession or was admitted to the labour market of that Member State for an uninterrupted period of 12 months or longer will enjoy access to the labour market of that Member State. The workers will lose this right, however, if they voluntarily leave the labour market of the concerned Member State. This provides for a gradual difference in the rights acquired under EU law according to Article 45 TFEU. According to subparagraph 8, another differentiated right applies to family members (spouse of worker, their descendants under 21 or dependants) of the Croatian worker and this also depends on whether their working spouse was legally working in the respective Member State at the moment of accession or thereafter. In the former case, the family members have immediate access to the labour market, while in the latter case they have access to the labour market only after 18 months. This status for family members also differs from the status that a new Member State citizen could acquire before accession under the association agreement provisions (further discussed in section 4.3). A definition for legally residing or working is not given in the accession provisions and, as such, reference can be made to interpretations by the Court of Justice. An identical formulation of 'legally residing' is (and was) to be found in the associations agreement provisions with Turkey and CEEC countries under the Europe Agreements.[54] As national measures still apply in connection with the accession derogations, a situation comparable to before accession arises. Therefore, legality is determined according to national migration rules and legal rights to reside, however, the proportionality principle limits the application of national law.[55] In addition, and this is especially relevant for the post-accession situation, these provisions have to be interpreted in light of EU citizenship rights. Especially in the context of citizenship rights, the Court has linked the right to non-discrimination to the condition that Union citizens remain lawfully in a host Member State. Member States can impose certain conditions, such as sufficient resources and health insurance or link entitlement to benefits to the existence of a genuine link between the

[54] Ott (n 34) 152.

[55] Case C-1/97 *Birden* [1998] ECLI:EU:C:1998:568; Case C-327/02 *Panayotova* [2004] ECLI:EU:C:2004718. See generally: Alan Dashwood, Michael Dougan, Barry Rodger, Eleanor Spaventa and Derrick Wyatt, *Wyatt and Dashwood's European Union Law* (6th edn, Hart Publishing 2011) 464.

claimant and the host Member State, but again this is under scrutiny of objectivity and the principle of proportionality.[56]

Table 6.3 Differentiation in practice

	Sweden	**Austria**
Croatian citizen	Access under EU law	Restrictions
Croatian citizen access to labour market at the date of accession	No limits	Access to this labour market and family member access
Access to labour market for 12 months or longer	No limits	Access but family member only after 18 months
SAA agreements Access to labour market	No limits	Access by both if legally in the country

These national measures restricting free movement have to be examined against three principles from the annexes to the Croatian Act of Accession and the overarching non-discrimination principle under primary law. The first one is the standstill clause found in paragraph 13 (first subparagraph) of annex V.[57] Application of these national measures cannot result in conditions for access of Croatian nationals which are more restrictive than those prevailing on the date of the signature of the Treaty of Accession. The second one is the Union preference, found in the same subparagraph. Although national measures are applied, preference should be given to workers who are nationals of the Member State over workers who are nationals of third countries as regards access to their labour market. Legally residing and working Croatian migrant workers shall not be treated in a more restrictive way than those from third countries that are resident or working in that Member State (both other principles are also found in paragraph 13, second and third subparagraph). In addition, as explained above, the non-discrimination principle, applicable to EU citizens according to Article 18 TFEU, must be respected. Since the *Martínez-Sala* case from 1998, a right of equal treatment for EU nationals has been based on Article 18 TFEU and made

[56] See case law C-224/98 *D'Hoop* [2002] ECLI:EU:C:2002:432.

[57] Art. 18 of the Act of Accession in combination with Annex V. 2, free movement of persons, OJ 2012, L1112/67.

conditional upon legal residence.[58] This right also includes access to social benefits in light of Regulation 492/2011[59] and rights can even be relied on without a cross-border link according to newer case law.[60] This equal treatment right exists independently whether EU citizens are economically active or not. Member States can limit these rights only, respecting the principle of proportionality and non-discrimination, by requiring that the individual does not become a financial burden for the host Member State.[61]

4.1.2 Restrictions in light of market access and non-discrimination of EU citizens

National measures can restrict the market access of Croatian workers and their families. The accession treaty allows temporary derogations from Article 45 TFEU and Articles 1 to 6 from the Regulation 492/2011 defining details of workers' rights. The rights under EU citizenship and the EU Citizenship Directive 2004/38 are largely applicable. In addition, Article 7(1) of Regulation 492/2011 gives workers equal treatment rights regarding working conditions, remuneration and dismissal; and Article 7(2) guarantees the same social and tax advantages. These provisions limit action by Member States in cases of their application of national measures.[62] Market access, which is restricted, is not explained in the

---

58 Case C-85/96 *Martínez-Sala* [1998] ECLI:EU:C:1998:217; Case C-184/99 *Grzelczyk* [2001] ECLI:EU:C:2001458; Case C-413/99 *Baumbast and R* [2002] ECLI:EU:C:2002:493, see overview at Dashwood, Dougan, Rodger, Spaventa and Wyatt (n 55) 461.

59 See Case *Martínez-Sala* [1998] ECLI:EU:C:1998:217.

60 Founded on EU citizenship as a fundamental status: see Case C-34/09, *Ruiz Zambrano* [2011] ECLI:EU:C2011:124; Case C-434/09 *McCarthy v Secretary of State for the Home Department*, [2011] ECLI:EU:C:2011:277; Case C-256/11 *Dereci and Others v Bundesministerium für Inneres*, [2011] ECLI: EU:C:2011:734. However, see for a more restrictive approach, now: CJEU, Case C-333/13, Elisabeth *Dano and Florin Dano v Jobcenter Leipzig*, [2014] ECLI: EU:C:2014:2358.

61 See art. 7 Citizenship Directive: 'sufficient resources for themselves and their family members not to become a burden on the social assistance system of the host Member State during their period of residence and have comprehensive sickness insurance in the host Member State'. In the first three months of residence any Union citizen can enter another Member State without any conditions and formalities (art. 6 Citizenship Directive). See also Case C-140/12 *Pensionsversicherungsanstalt v Peter Brey*, [2013] ECLI:EU:C:2013:565para. 53.

62 See also Inglis (n 27) 970; and Michael Dougan, 'A Spectre is Haunting Europe … Free Movement of Persons and the Eastern Enlargement' in Christophe Hillion (ed.), *EU Enlargement* (Hart Publishing 2004) 126.

accession treaty but it is discussed in the literature in which various definitions are suggested,[63] but it can only be understood when put into the context of the workers' rights granted under EU law. These rights can be defined by being able to accept offers of employment actually made, moving freely within the territory of the Member States for this purpose and having an implicit right of residence and a work permit. Also, as highlighted above, any national measure is restricted by the standstill clause, Union preference and the non-discrimination principle and rights flowing from the autonomous concept of EU citizenship.[64]

How difficult it is to assess the legality of national measures to manoeuvre around these restricting conditions is demonstrated by the UK provisions. While the UK in the 2004 enlargement decided not to restrict market access, the fear of abuse of welfare benefits led to new provisions on welfare benefits and a workers' registration scheme for new Member States' citizens to monitor their influx into the UK being introduced on 23 April 2004. In addition, a new right to reside test was added to the existing habitual residence test in the case of assessing the entitlement of EU citizens to income-related benefits.[65] For citizens from the new EU Member States, this right to reside was determined on the basis of a work relationship registered under the workers' registration scheme. Where workers lost, or had to give up, their jobs before they had completed 12 months of work, the UK legislation removed their right to retain worker status. In effect, this limited the possibility for the workers to satisfy the new right to reside test until after 12 months of registered work and this resulted in limited access to social benefits.

This scheme was in place until 2011 for the first wave but, with the second wave of accession with Bulgaria and Romania and now with Croatian workers, a variation applies with a worker authorisation scheme.[66] These workers have to apply for a worker authorisation

---

[63] See on this Catherine Barnard, *The Substantive Law of the EU* (4th edn, Oxford University Press 2013) 21.

[64] See on this further: Lenaerts (n 50) 582.

[65] The right of residence test applied to social security benefits within the scope of Regulation 883/2004, such as income support, state pension credit, income-related employment and support allowance, as well as to social advantages under Regulation 492/2011 such as housing benefits and housing assistance, social fund crisis loans and council tax benefits. See further Eva-Maria Poptcheva, *Freedom of Movement and Residence of EU Citizens. Access to Social Benefits,* EP Research Service, 2014, 16.

[66] The Accession of Croatia (Immigration and Worker Authorisation) Regulations 2013, available at: <http://www.legislation.gov.uk/ukdsi/2013/9780111539156> accessed 15 February 2016. Croatian workers require an accession

document, but they also only have the same rights to benefits and tax credits if they have worked without interruption for 12 months in the UK.[67] It could be argued that a breach of the standstill clause and citizenship rights occurred in 2004 when the British government opened their job market to acceding Member States but accession Member States workers were required to register since May 2004. According to the standstill clause, the effect of national measures shall not result in conditions for market access which are more restrictive than those prevailing on 16 April 2003, the date of signature of the Treaty of Accession. In addition, a different treatment between EU/EEA citizens and new Member States' citizens occurred in which the new Member States' citizens had only a right to welfare benefits if they were registered and had at least worked for 12 months in the UK.[68] This made it even more difficult for these citizens to fulfil the right to reside test. Another interpretation argued that this action of coupling workers registration with a habitual residence test and income-related benefits with the 12-month waiting period would be allowed as a national restricting measure under accession law.[69] Yet, the UK never notified the Commission of any derogation before the accession of Bulgaria and Romania and legal questions remain on the correct application of non-discrimination and proportionality principles. It can be considered discriminatory if the right of residence test is only applied to EEA/EU citizens[70] but not to UK citizens.

In practice, two legally problematic scenarios unfolded. The first would arise if a new Member State citizen registers correctly and works but then the worker loses his or her employment before the completion of the 12 months (or works for another employer but is not registered for

---

worker authorisation document but no habitual residence test different from EEA workers.

[67] Steven Kennedy, 'EEA Nationals: 'The Right to Reside' Requirement for Benefits, 5 December 2011, available at: <http://researchbriefings.files.parliament.uk/documents/SN05972/SN05972.pdf> accessed 15 February 2016.

[68] The Social Security (Habitual Residence) Amendment Regulation 2004, See further: Ott (n 34) 154 and Desmond Rutledge, 'Cases' (2009) *Journal of Social Security Law Digest* 96, 101.

[69] See Robin C A White, 'Residence, Benefit Entitlement and Community Law' (2005) *Journal of Social Security Law* 10, 22.

[70] And EEA citizens were automatically treated better, which also raises the issue of Union preference, which is addressed in detail below in section 4.4.

whatever reason)[71] and the second scenario is of the migrant who came into the UK as a self-employed person, encountered no restrictions, worked legally for four years but then lost his business. In both cases income-related benefits were denied[72] and benefits for self-employed persons in the UK can include contribution-based jobseeker's allowance, tax credits or employment and support allowances. The CJEU had already ruled, in *Collins*, that such a residence requirement under the citizenship rights has to be proportionate and rest on objective criteria and must not exceed what is necessary in order for the national authorities to be able to satisfy themselves that the person concerned is genuinely seeking work in the employment market of the host Member State.[73]

The Commission argues that an additional condition such as a right of residence test goes beyond a habitual residence test and consequently infringes Article 11 of Regulation 987/2009 laying down the procedure for implementing Regulation (EC) 883/2004 on the coordination of social security systems.[74] While an infringement procedure by the Commission was started against aspects of the workers' registration scheme, it was not further pursued when the scheme ceased on 30 April 2011. However, after several cases before national UK courts in which the applicants were unsuccessful in arguing that this test infringed EU law, in 2010 the Commission started an infringement procedure against the UK concerning the right to reside test with the argument that it was indirectly discriminatory and a breach of Regulation (EC) 883/2004. In principle, the UK rules aggravate the conditions for EU nationals and infringe non-discrimination if an extra condition of a right of residence test is

---

[71] In this case, a Polish worker was employed between 9 July 2004 and 7 January 2005 in a UK company and was registered but then she changed employers twice and was no longer registered, House of Lords, Opinion of the Lords of Appeal of judgment *Zalewska v Department for Social Development (Northern Ireland)*, 12 November 2008, available at: <http://www.publications.parliament.uk/pa/ld200708/ldjudgmt/jd081112/zalew.pdf> accessed 15 February 2016.

[72] House of Lords, Opinion of the Lords of appeal of judgment *Zalewska v Department for Social Development (Northern Ireland)*, 12 November 2008, available at: <http://www.publications.parliament.uk/pa/ld200708/ldjudgmt/jd081112/zalew.pdf> accessed 15 February 2016.

[73] Case C-138/02 *Collins* [2004] ECLI:EU:C:2004:172.

[74] Thomas Horsley and Stephanie Reynolds, *Union Citizenship: National Report on the UK*, FIDE XXVI Congress, Copenhagen 2014, 14-15. Available at: <http://www.ukael.org/upcoming_events_155_719225124.pdf> accessed 5 June 2015.

introduced. However, this argument was not followed in the CJEU judgment and the court argued that it could only be considered an indirect discrimination and can be justified on the ground of protecting the finances of the host Member States in a proportionate way.[75] This complex situation results in paradox situations of discrimination which are not perceived *per se* as illegal and sanctioned by primary law but could have repercussions in the situation that national restricting measures apply or do not apply. In both cases the non-discrimination principle under EU citizenship is applicable. In case of the application of national rules, additionally, the three limiting principles found in the annexes of the Act of Accession need to be respected.

4.3 The Standstill Clause and Union Preference in Light of the Stabilisation and Association Agreement

The standstill clause applies from the moment the respective accession treaty is signed. Until the moment of accession, the association provisions between the existing Member States and new incoming Member States apply. All of the Europe Agreements with the CEEC and the Stabilisation and Association Agreement (SAA) with the Western Balkan states included and include a right to non-discrimination regarding working conditions, remuneration or dismissal and included access to the labour market for family members during the period of the worker's authorised stay of employment (Article 45.1 SAA with Croatia).[76] Paradoxically, this right granted to workers and their family members is more favourable under the association agreement than under accession law, where access is only granted to workers depending on whether they are legally in the labour market of this Member State at the date of accession. In case of access to the labour market post-accession, the migrant worker has to be admitted to the labour market of the Member State for an uninterrupted period of one year, with family members having to remain for another six months (see Table 6.3 above).

In the literature it was argued that this worsening of the migrant workers' legal status under the applicable national restrictions breaches the standstill clause.[77] In its practical guide on the application of these provisions, the Commission remained silent on this issue and only

[75] Case C-308/14, *European Commission v UK*, [2016] ECLI:EU:C:2016:436.

[76] Stabilisation and Association Agreement with Croatia, OJ 2005 L26/1.

[77] See Steve Peers, Statewatch analysis of the EU accession treaty, available at: <http://www.statewatch.org/news/2003/feb/accession.pdf> accessed 15 April

explained that the rights of access to the labour market of a given Member State cannot fall behind the current status.[78] However, it was correctly rebutted by other scholars arguing that this standstill clause has to be read together with the Union preference and in light of national measures and bilateral agreements between existing and incoming Member States (both subparagraph 13 of the annex V Croatia) but not in light of the Association Agreement which ceased to apply on the day of accession.[79] This reading is also confirmed by the wording of paragraph 6, which spells out the workers' and their families' rights, stating at the end that 'these provisions shall be without prejudice to more favourable measures, whether national measures or measures resulting from bilateral agreements'. However, it is undeniable that the outcome of this interpretation could result in practice in paradoxical situations giving third-country nationals in the EU, such as Serbian citizens falling under the SAA with Serbia, better access to the labour market than EU citizens from Croatia.

4.4 Union Preference and Non-discrimination Principle in Light of the EEA Agreement and Swiss Bilateral Agreement on Persons

Part of the consequences of what could be coined external differentiation is that the EU governance model of differentiated integration is extended to third countries in varying degrees. These third countries are either linked to the Union due to special international agreements preparing for accession or offered participation in the Internal market (EEA area) and opt in, as in the case of Switzerland, to certain policies without the dynamics of the EEA-EU twin pillars system.[80] Primarily, this differentiated integration enables third countries to participate in EU policies

2014; Philipp Tschäpe, 'Das Zugangsrecht zum Arbeitsmarkt für Familienangehörige vor und nach dem Beitritt als Verstoß gegen die Standstill-Klausel aus dem Beitrittsvertrag 2004' (2003) EWS 511-513.; Monika Byrska, *The Unfinished Enlargement* (2004) 15, available at: <http://edz.bib.uni-mannheim.de/daten/edz-k/gde/04/498.pdf> accessed 14 April 2014.

[78] Free movement for persons – A practical guide for an enlarged European Union, European Commission, available at: <http://ec.europa.eu/enlargement/archives/pdf/press_corner/publications/55260_practica_guide_including_comments_en.pdf> accessed 15 February 2016.

[79] Inglis (n 39) 111–12.

[80] The bilateral agreements are characterised by a guillotine clause joining together the seven agreements. If one of the seven is terminated, the other agreements fall with it.

(from Internal market to even individual CFSP missions), EU programmes and EU agencies as observers.[81] However, this external differentiation also creates implications for EU citizens working in the EEA and Switzerland in comparison to third-country citizens in the EU, which are directly linked to the accession treaty differentiation.

Caused by these parallel legal orders, the EEA and EU have concluded EEA enlargement agreements in 2004, 2007 and 2013 which extend the EEA to incoming EU Member States.[82] According to the annexes to the EEA enlargement agreements, the transitional arrangements can be applied to the free movement of workers and also the safeguard clauses apply.[83] In practice, there is no difference between EU and EEA nationals in regard to the free movement rights connected to the Internal market in the EU. If transitional arrangements apply, the paradox situation arises that EU citizens from new Member States are in a less favourable position than EEA citizens, despite the fact that EEA citizens are not EU citizens and do not fall under the privileged interpretation of citizenship rights by the CJEU.[84] This appears as a breach of the Union preference, which is one of the limiting conditions for these transitional arrangements outlined in section 4.1. However, this is not correct. A point of reference for the application of the Union preference is not the comparison of the status of EEA citizens with EU citizens under EU law. Instead, and in line with the situation concerning other association agreements discussed at section 4.3, the position of EU citizens under the national rules is decisive for the interpretation of the rules and it is considered whether no preference is given to third county nationals under national rules.

The EU and Swiss relations in regard to free movement rights of workers are more complex, almost beyond comprehension. Switzerland

---

[81] See Andrea Ott, 'A Flexible Future for the European Union: The Way Forward or a Way Out?' in Steven Blockmans and Sacha Prechal (eds), *Reconciling the Deepening and Widening of the EU* (TMC Asser Press 2007), 142 and Adam Lazowski, 'Box of Chocolates Integration: The European Economic Area and the Swiss Model Revisited' in Blockmans and Prechal, ibid., 87.

[82] EEA Enlargement agreement, the 2004 and 2007 EEA enlargements agreement text, available at: <http://www.efta.int/legal-texts/eea-enlargement> accessed 3 May 2015.

[83] Norway, when ratifying the EEA enlargement agreement for Croatia, has decided not to apply restrictions, see Norwegian Ministry of Foreign Affairs, 7.3.2014, available at: <http://www.regjeringen.no/en/dep/ud/press/news/2014/croatia-eea.html?id=752716> accessed 4 May 2015.

[84] However, the EU citizenship directive is applied on EEA citizens.

decided against participation in the EEA and instead the relations with the EU are governed by bilateral agreements (primarily the bilateral agreements I and II).[85] These agreements prescribe specific rights and obligations analogous, in some respects, to those laid down in the TFEU.[86] One of these sectoral agreements covers free movement of persons between Switzerland and the EU and came into force on 1 June 2002.[87] In contrast to the EEA, however, the *acquis* is not automatically extended. While since 1 June 2004 the EU gives Swiss nationals access to the EU labour market, the Swiss labour market only opens gradually over 12 years since the ratification of the agreement. In principle, two different legal regimes in three different country groups of the EU-28 Member States currently apply. These country groups are the EU-17 (old Member States + Cyprus and Malta), the new EU Member States in 2004 (EU-8), and the recent accession countries Romania, Bulgaria and Croatia. For the first and second group, restrictions have been phased out or phased out over a 12-year period and in different timelines since 2007 – depending on the ratification of the agreement or the date of accession. In the third-country group, Croatia is currently treated *de jure* as a non-EU Member State, which does not fall under the EU-Swiss bilateral agreements due to the latest political developments following the Swiss referendum against migration in February 2014.

During the very restrictive opening of the Swiss labour market, the first wave of enlargement in 2004 took place and the European Commission could not convince Switzerland to extend the existing regime to new EU Member States' citizens. Instead, Article 10 of the bilateral agreement on persons was amended by a protocol in such a way that Switzerland could differentiate between the EU-15 citizens and keep its restrictions in place for the new EU-8 (excluding Cyprus and Malta) according to the 2+3+2 years rule.[88] Since 1 May 2011, EU-8 citizens benefitted from the full free movement of persons, which was four years later than for the existing Member States (including Cyprus and Malta). The restrictions against Romanian and Bulgarian citizens remain in place until 31 May

---

[85] See further Adam Lazowski, 'Switzerland' in Steven Blockmans and Adam Lazowski, *The European Union and its Neighbours* (TMC Asser Press 2006) 154.

[86] So the CJEU in Case C-656/11 *UK v Council*, [2014], ECLI:EU:C:2014:97.

[87] OJ 2002 L114/6-72.

[88] Protocol I to the bilateral agreement, OJ 2006 L89/28-44 (entered into force 1 June 2006).

2016.[89] However, in the meantime, Switzerland invoked the general safeguard under Article 10 paragraph 4 of the bilateral agreement against first the EU-17 (including the EEA), in 2012 and then, in 2013, against the new Member States EU-8. This allows for unilateral limits to residence permits to EU nationals in Switzerland.[90] After the conservative Swiss People's Party launched an initiative to restrict immigration and a narrow majority of the electorate accepted this in a referendum in February 2014, Switzerland decided not to sign the Croatian protocol (Protocol III to take account of the Croatian accession). Between July 2013 and July 2014 Croatian citizens were treated like third-country nationals by the Swiss authorities.[91] The Swiss Federal Council subsequently followed a two-track approach, primarily seeking the renegotiation of the Swiss-EU bilateral agreement on persons but also trying to accommodate the urgent adaptation to the Swiss-EU bilateral agreement on persons with the Croatian accession. In June 2014 the Swiss government requested that the Union, in light of the amended Swiss constitution, revise the bilateral agreement on persons.[92] However, the EU High

---

[89] On the basis of the Protocol II to the bilateral agreement, OJ 2009 L124/53-62. Available at: <https://www.bfm.admin.ch/content/bfm/en/home/themen/fza_schweiz-eu-efta.html> (entered into force 1 June 2009) accessed 6 May 2015.

[90] Art. 10, para. 4:

> Notwithstanding the provisions of paragraph 3, the Contracting Parties have agreed on the following arrangements: if, after five years and up to 12 years after the entry into force of the Agreement, the number of new residence permits of either of the categories referred to in paragraph 1 issued to employed and self-employed persons of the European Community in a given year exceeds the average for the three preceding years by more than 10%, Switzerland may, for the following year, unilaterally limit the number of new residence permits of that category for employed and self-employed persons of the European Community to the average of the three preceding years plus 5%. The following year, the number may be limited to the same level.

[91] Proposal for a Council Decision, 1.10.2013, COM(2013) 673 final.

[92] According to art. 197 Ziff. 9 Abs. 1 of the Swiss constitution are international agreements which contravene art. 121a of the amendment to be renegotiated and amended within three years. However, it has been disputed that this applies for the adaptation of the existing bilateral agreements, see Astrid Epiney, 'Zur rechtlichen Tragweite der Art. 121 a, Art. 197 Ziff. 9 BV' April 2014, available at: <www.vd.ch/…_/avis_de_droit_Epiney_art._121a_général_Deutsch.pdf> 6 May 2015.

Representative denied this request in July 2014 as unacceptable[93] and this stance was confirmed by the Council in December 2014, which considered the free movement of persons as a fundamental pillar of EU policy.[94] Under the second track, the Swiss Federal Council decided to apply Protocol III *de facto* from 1 July 2014, which would result, according to the Swiss government, in the same quotas as Croatia would have received if Protocol III would have been signed.[95] The EU Council rebutted at the end of 2014 that these unilateral measures fall short of the provisions of Protocol III and hinder Croatian nationals from relying on bilateral international agreement between the EU and Switzerland.[96]

EU citizens from new Member States are discriminated against in relation to non-EU nationals, namely EEA and Swiss citizens, in the broader Internal market (including EEA and Switzerland) and this also results in reverse discrimination in which Swiss and EEA citizens have immediate access to the labour market in the EU in contrast to Croatian citizens. This external discrimination is problematic under political and moral considerations and creates differentiated treatment for EU citizens. From a legal perspective, such external discrimination is irrelevant. This reverse discrimination, treating EEA and Swiss nationals better than EU citizens, materialises only on the territory of non-EU Member States. Discrimination and differentiation occurring on the EU territory have been agreed to in the legal framework of primary law and are to be considered legal as long as these differences meet the general conditions

---

93 See exchange of letters between Switzerland and the High Representative Ashton, available at: <http://www.europa.admin.ch/themen/00500/00506/00519/index.html?lang=en&> accessed 5 May 2015.

94 Council conclusions on a homogeneous extended single market and EU relations with Non-EU Western European countries, Brussels, 16 December 2014, para 45, available at: <http://www.consilium.europa.eu/uedocs/cms_data/docs/pressdata/en/er/146315.pdf> accessed 5 May 2015.

95 Bundesrat der Schweizerischen Eidgenossenschaft, Declaration of the Federal Council pertaining to non-discrimination of Croatian citizens, available at: <http://www.news.admin.ch/NSBSubscriber/message/attachments/34637.pdf> accessed 6 May 2015. This *de facto* application would not violate *de jure* the February 2014 referendum, S. Schürer, Eine Sonderlösung für Kroatien, 24.2.2014, *Berner Zeitung*, available at: <http://www.bernerzeitung.ch/schweiz/standard/Eine-Sonderloesung-fuer-Kroatien/story/31097079> accessed 6 May 2015.

96 Council conclusions on a homogeneous extended single market and EU relations with non-EU Western European countries, Brussels, 16 December 2014, para 47.

outlined in sections 4.1 and 4.2. This is another paradox deriving from intergovernmental differentiation.

4.5 Summary

Over the last ten years since the first enlargement wave in 2004, national measures were applied by most receiving EU Member States, which restricted the access of migrant workers and their families under EU primary law. These restrictions were limited by a standstill clause, Union preference and non-discrimination, which have led in practice to problematic and legally disputable scenarios as highlighted above. In this process differentiation is used as a political tool to enable enlargement and not as a legal tool to further integration aims by letting some Member States forge ahead.

5. CONCLUSIONS AND OUTLOOK

Accession differentiation in the domain of the Internal market freedom for workers leads to paradoxical situations in practice. This situation results in legal complexity and differentiating legal regimes between EU Member States but also involving the privileged partners of the EEA and Switzerland. The provisions of the act of accession annex on migrant workers imply gradual and different rights depending on the Member State and depending on whether migrant workers already reside in the existing Member States. Transitional measures are restricted by four principles including the rights provided under EU citizenship which should secure the position of migrant workers but further complicate their situation in receiving Member States. The standstill clause and the Union preference do not apply to all accession situations but only in connection with existing national measures. In principle, Union citizenship rights are fully applicable, but there are grey areas as to the extent to which rights provided by the Citizenship Directive 2004/38 may be restricted in the context of national measures to restrict access to labour markets and how far the equal treatment rights under Regulation (EC) 883/2004 on social benefits are violated. However, practice has shown how difficult it was in the case of the UK to remedy infringements, also due to lack of involvement of the European Commission at an earlier stage.

Accession differentiation serves the aim of deepening integration in an indirect way. Differentiation by EU accession treaties was and is a necessary political tool and a precondition to achieving the widening of the Union without sacrificing the deepening of the process. Without strong forms of conditionality and temporary derogations, the receiving Member States would not have moved forward with the recent three enlargement waves.[97] It resulted and still results – for a substantial number of years – in two-class EU citizenship and cases of discrimination with different layers of applicable law in EU Member States. Transitional derogations restricting labour market access have resulted in transparent rules which have not been interpreted until now by the CJEU. This contributes to the existing difficulties in the enforcement of rights of migrant workers and EU citizens.[98] Additionally, differentiated integration has been externalised and it haunts the EU in its privileged relations with the EEA and Switzerland by extending the *de facto* two classes of EU citizenship to the outer circles of the EU legal space. From a legal perspective, fortunately, this chapter of differentiation with all its complexities and opaque rules will soon come to an end but it is to be expected that in any future enlargement process, it will come to play a role again.

REFERENCES

Barnard C, *The Substantive Law of the EU* (4th edn, Oxford Universtiy Press 2013).

von Bogdandy A, 'Founding Principles of EU Law: A Theoretical and Doctrinal Sketch' (2010) 16(2) ELJ 95–111.

---

[97] Whether transitional restrictions limiting rights of migrant workers were really necessary in practice, is difficult to assess on a Union-wide level but studies have been made on Sweden and the UK which gave immediate access in 2004. Sweden never had any problems and opened its job market in all accession rounds while the UK received more CEEC migrants in comparison to all other existing Member States. In the direct comparison between the two countries, the UK labour market is more attractive due to language and greater flexibility of its labour market. See Briefing Migration Flows from A8 and other EU migrants to and from the UK, the migration observatory, 10.4.2014; Martin Ruhs, 'Swedish Exceptionalism', available at: <http://compass.ox.ac.uk/2011/swedish-exceptionalism>, accessed 13 December 2016.

[98] This is taken up by the draft Directive 9124/13 to facilitate the exercise of rights of migrant workers ensuring appropriate means of redress and allow associations to secure the enforcement of rights. And the Commission has taken up the incorrect transposition and application of the Citizenship directive in the infringement procedure. Report form the Commission for the EP, the Council, the ECOSOC and the Committee of Regions under Art. 25 TEU on the progress towards effective EU citizenship 2011-2013, Brussels, 8.5.2013 COM(2013) 270 final, 4.

Byrska M, *The Unfinished Enlargement* (2004, <http://edz.bib.uni-mannheim.de/daten/edz-k/gde/04/498.pdf>.

Curtin D, 'The Constitutional Structure of the European Union: A Europe of Bits and Pieces' (1993) 30(1) CML Rev 17–70.

Dashwood A, Dougan M, Rodger B, Spaventa E and Wyatt D, *Wyatt and Dashwood's European Union Law* (6th edn, Hart Publishing 2011).

Dougan M, 'A Spectre is Haunting Europe … Free Movement of Persons and the Eastern Enlargement' in Hillion Ch (ed.), *EU Enlargement* (Hart Publishing 2004) 111–41.

Epiney A, 'Zur rechtlichen Tragweite der Art. 121 a, Art. 197 Ziff. 9 BV' April 2014, <www.vd.ch/…_/avis_de_droit_Epiney_art._121a_général_Deutsch.pdf>.

Goldner Lang I, 'Transitional Arrangements in the Enlarged European Union: How Free is the Free Movement of Workers?' (2007) 3(3) *Croatian Yearbook of European Law and Policy* 241–71.

Hillion C, 'EU Enlargement' in Craig P and de Búrca G, *The Evolution of EU Law* (2nd edn, Oxford University Press 2011) 187–216.

Hoffmeister F, 'Earlier Enlargements' in Ott A and Inglis K (eds), *Handbook on European Enlargement* (TMC Asser Press 2002) 87–9.

Horsley T and Reynolds S, 'Union Citizenship: National Report on the UK' FIDE XXVI Congress, Copenhagen 2014, <http://www.ukael.org/upcoming_events_155_719225124.pdf>.

Inglis K, 'The Union's Fifth Accession Treaty: New Means to Make Enlargement Possible' (2004) 41(4) CML Rev 937–73.

Inglis K, 'Treading the Tightrope between Flexibility and Legal Certainty' in Hanf D and Muñoz R (eds), *La libre circulation des personnes. États des lieux et perspectives* (Peter Lang Publisher 2007) 99-124.

Inglis K, *Evolving Practice in EU Enlargement* (Martinus Nijhoff Publishers 2010).

Kennedy S, 'EEA Nationals: 'The Right to Reside' Requirement for Benefits' 5 December 2011, <http://researchbriefings.files.parliament.uk/documents/SN05972/SN05972.pdf>.

Lazowski A, 'Switzerland' in Blockmans S and Lazowski A, *The European Union and its Neighbours* (TMC Asser Press 2006) 147–84.

Lazowski A, 'Box of Chocolates Integration: The European Economic Area and the Swiss Model Revisited' in Blockmans S and Prechal S (eds), *Reconciling the Deepening and Widening of the EU* (TMC Asser Press 2008) 87–110.

Lenaerts K, 'The Concept of EU Citizenship in the Case Law of the European Court of Justice' (2013) ERA Forum, available at: <http://download.springer.com/static/pdf/53/art%253A10.1007%252Fs12027-013-0279-y.pdf?auth66=1396012097_aee645ee385f0d9d93b1d1ccbfde7b1a&ext=.pdf>.

Maresceau M, 'On the External Dimension of Directive 2004/38/EC' in Govaere I and Hanf D (eds), *Scrutinizing Internal and External Dimension of European Law, Liber Amicorum Paul Demaret* (Peter Lang Publishing 2013) 761–77.

Ott A, 'Die anerkannte Rechtsfortbildung des EuGH als Teil des gemeinschaftlichen Besitzstandes (Acquis communautaire)' (2000) EuZW 293–298.

Ott A, 'Unity in Diversity? – Differentiation in EU Law and Policy in an Enlarged European Union', *Natolin Paper* 14 (2004). Available at: <http://www.natolin.edu.pl/pdf/zeszyty/-NatolinZeszyt15_Ott.pdf> accessed 14 April 2014.

Ott A, 'Case note on *Deutscher Handballbund* v. *Kolpak*' (2004) 10 *Columbia Journal of European Law* 379–80.

Ott A, 'The Principle of Differentiation in an Enlarged European Union' in Inglis K and Ott A (eds), *The Constitution for Europe and an Enlarging Union: Unity in Diversity?* (Europa Law Publishing 2005) 105–31.

Ott A, 'A Flexible Future for the European Union: The Way Forward or a Way Out?' in Blockmans S and Prechal S (eds), *Reconciling the Deepening and Widening of the EU* (TMC Asser Press 2007) 133–56.

Ott A, 'Grundfreiheiten' in Merli F and Huster S (eds), *Die Verträge zur EU-Osterweiterung: Kommentar mit systematischen Erläuterungen* (Berliner Wissenschaftsverlag 2008) 129–77.

Ott A, 'EU Constitutional Boundaries to Differentiation: How to Reconcile Differentiation with Integration?' in Andrea Ott and Ellen Vos (eds), *Fifty Years of European Integration: Foundations and Perspectives* (TMC Asser Press 2009) 113–38.

Peers S, Statewatch Analysis of the EU Accession Treaty, <http://www.statewatch.org/news/2003/feb/accession.pdf>.

Pescatore P, *The Law of Integration* (Sijthof 1974).

Piris JC, *The Future of Europe Towards a Two-speed EU?* (Cambridge University Press 2012).

Poptcheva EM, *Freedom of Movement and Residence of EU Citizens. Access to Social Benefits*, EP Research Service 2014.

Rosas A and Armati L, *EU Constitutional Law: An Introduction* (2nd edn, Hart Publishing 2013).

Ruhs M, 'Swedish Exceptionalism', <http://compasoxfordblog.co.uk/2011/11/swedish-exceptionalism/>.

Rutledge D, 'Cases' (2009) *Journal of Social Security Law Digest* 96–103.

Schürer S, 'Eine Sonderlösung für Kroatien', 24.2.2014, *Berner Zeitung*.

Skoutaris N, *"EU Citizenship in Hibernation". The Cyprus Issue: The Four Freedoms in a Member State under Siege* (Hart Publishing 2011).

Spernbauer M, 'Benchmarking, Safeguard Clauses and Verification Mechanisms – What's in a Name? Recent Developments in the Pre- and Post-accession Conditionality and Compliance with EU Law' (2007) 3(3) *Croatian Yearbook of European Law and Policy* 273–306.

Tschäpe Ph, 'Das Zugangsrecht zum Arbeitsmarkt für Familienangehörige vor und nach dem Beitritt als Verstoß gegen die Standstill-Klausel aus dem Beitrittsvertrag 2004' (2003) EWS 511–13.

van der Mei AP, *Free Movement of Persons Within the European Community: Cross-border Access to Public Benefits* (Hart Publishing 2003).

Van Gerven W, *The European Union* (Hart Publishing 2005).

van Selm J and Tsolakis E, 'EU Enlargement and the Limits of Freedom' (2004) Migration Policy Institute, http://www.migrationpolicy.org/article/eu-enlargement-and-limits-freedom/.

White RCA, 'Residence, Benefit Entitlement and Community Law' (2005) *Journal of Social Security Law* 10–25.

Wouters J, 'Constitutional Limits to Differentiation: The Principle of Equality' in De Witte B, Hanf D and Vos E (eds), *The Many Faces of Differentiation in EU Law* (Intersentia 2001) 301–45.

Ziegler G, 'The Accession Negotiations on Free Movement of Workers' in Ott A and Inglis K (eds), *Handbook on European Enlargement* (TMC Asser Press 2002) 131–42.

7. Flexibility and differentiation: a plea for allowing national differentiation in the fundamental rights domain

Maartje de Visser and Anne Pieter van der Mei

1. INTRODUCTION

The subject of the protection of fundamental rights today is a mainstay in EU legal studies, as a cursory glance at the table of contents of leading textbooks and journals in the field attests. Debates about the proper role of the Union institutions, and in particular that of the Court of Justice (CJEU), in respecting and upholding such rights have been taking place ever since the seminal rulings in *Stauder*[1] and *Internationale Handelsgesellschaft*,[2] which established that the EU institutions must heed the fundamental rights that form an integral part of the general principles of Union law. The Lisbon Treaty has given a fresh impetus to the academic discourse on EU fundamental rights, by prescribing the Union's accession to the European Convention on Human Rights (ECHR)[3] and by granting the Charter of Fundamental Rights, first proclaimed at Nice in December 2001, binding force.[4]

---

[1] Case C-26/69 *Erich Stauder v City of Ulm* [1969] ECLI:EU:C:1969:57, para. 7.

[2] Case C-11/70 *Internationale Handelsgesellschaft mbH v Einfuhr- und Vorratsstelle für Getreide und Futtermittel* [1970] ECLI:EU:C:1970:114, 3–4.

[3] On accession, see e.g., Jean-Paul Jacqué, 'The Accession of the European Union to the European Convention on Human Rights and Fundamental Freedoms' (2011) 48 CML Rev 995; Tobias Lock, 'EU Accession to the ECHR: Implications for Judicial Review in Strasbourg' (2010) 35 ELR 777.

[4] Generally on the genesis and early case law on the Charter see Sara Iglesias Sanchez, 'The Court and the Charter: The Impact of the Entry into Force of the Lisbon Treaty on the ECJ's Approach to Fundamental Rights' (2012) 49

In keeping with the theme of this book, the aim of the present chapter is to consider whether, in a legal landscape characterised by the presence of several interlocking rights instruments, it is desirable for the CJEU to allow the Member States to offer a *higher degree* of fundamental rights protection than is required under EU law.[5] To this end, the chapter opens with a *tour d'horizon* of modalities for interaction and conflict resolution envisaged by each of the different rights regimes that co-exist within the European legal sphere, against the backdrop of insights from the literature on constitutional pluralism (Section 2). The chapter continues by scrutinising the Court's interpretation of Article 53 of the Charter in *Melloni*[6] and discusses some of the problems that may arise if the line of reasoning set forth therein is continued in future case law (Section 3). Lastly, the chapter explores possible avenues that can be pursued in the quest to accommodate a certain degree of flexibility in the judicial enforcement of fundamental rights at the national level (Section 4). The law is correct as at 1 January 2015.

2. THE CO-EXISTENCE OF MULTIPLE FUNDAMENTAL RIGHTS REGIMES IN EUROPE AND CONSTITUTIONAL PLURALISM

A useful starting point is to consider how the protection of fundamental rights is presently guaranteed within the European legal space and how differences of opinion concerning the scope and meaning of particular rights are or can be managed. This will provide both the background and the conceptual framework for an inquiry into opportunities for divergence in fundamental rights law.

CML Rev 1565; David Anderson and Cian Murphy, 'The Charter of Fundamental Rights' in Andrea Biondi, Piet Eeckhout and Stefanie Ripley (eds), *EU Law After Lisbon* (Oxford University Press 2012); Paul Craig, *The Lisbon Treaty: Law, Politics, and Treaty Reform* (Oxford University Press 2010) Ch. 6.

[5] This chapter will accordingly not examine the opt-out of the Charter secured by the UK, the Czech Republic and Poland, which can be considered as a 'negative' form of differentiation. On this opt-out, see e.g., Anthony Arnull, 'Protocol (No 30) on the Application of the Charter of Fundamental Rights of the European Union to Poland and the United Kingdom' in Steven Peers, Tamara Hervey, Jeff Kenner and Angela Ward (eds), *The EU Charter of Fundamental Rights – A Commentary* (Hart Publishing 2014).

[6] Case C-399/11 *Stefano Melloni v Ministerio Fiscal* [2013] ECLI:EU:C:2013:600.

There is no single, overarching fundamental rights regime within Europe: victims of alleged rights breaches may be able to rely on up to three different systems in order to obtain redress. Each of these regimes has moreover made its own decisions as to the precise range and scope of the fundamental rights considered to warrant protection and has its own guardians entrusted with the task of ultimately upholding the relevant catalogue of rights.

As self-proclaimed liberal democracies based on the Rule of Law, each of the Union's Member States has a domestic bill of rights,[7] enforced by a variety of national actors such as Parliaments, special bodies with a general or specific rights mandate (such as equality commissions) and courts, including constitutional courts. For obvious reasons, the reach of national rights instruments is in principle coterminous with the respective borders of the State concerned.

A second regime for fundamental rights protection has been established under the aegis of the Council of Europe. The aim of the ECHR and its Protocols is to prescribe a common minimum standard of rights protection that must be respected by all the countries that are parties to this Convention,[8] a group that includes all EU Member States. The Strasbourg Court, as a court of last resort, can determine whether Convention rights have been infringed, while national courts and governments are first in line to prevent or remedy breaches of ECHR rights within their territory.[9]

Turning lastly to the EU itself, it too has its own list(s) of fundamental rights that are considered to warrant protection, which are enshrined in the Charter of Fundamental Rights and/or constitute unwritten general principles of Union law that have been gradually 'discovered' by the CJEU. Designed specifically for the EU, the Union rights system applies in situations that come within the scope of EU law, which means that many, but not all, actions taken by Member State authorities can be scrutinised for compliance with the Charter or unwritten principles. Responsibility for upholding the Union fundamental rights regime is shared among a host of European and national political and judicial bodies, with the CJEU considering itself to be the final arbiter on interpretation and enforcement questions.

---

7 These bills of rights are typically found in the national constitution, but can also appear as separate statutes: consider for instance the UK's Human Rights Act 1998.

8 Art. 53 ECHR.

9 Cf. arts. 1 and 13 ECHR.

It is clear, then, that there are overlaps in territorial coverage among the different fundamental rights systems in Europe. The corollary is that two or more systems can be concurrently applicable in a given situation, such as when national authorities are called upon to implement or apply EU law. The co-existence and intertwinement of a plurality of fundamental rights systems invites a consideration of the way in which their interaction is envisaged and takes place in practice.

In the academic literature, constitutional pluralism has risen to a position of prominence as an approach which provides an attractive conceptual framework for thinking about relationships among a plurality of legal orders.[10] The constitutional pluralism discourse asserts that the co-existence of multiple legal orders should be rationalised in a heterarchical instead of a hierarchical fashion, whereby a premium is placed on constructive interaction and mutual accommodation. Given that each legal order is entitled to have its autonomy respected, notions of mutual respect, dialogue and cooperation are considered instrumental in regulating the interplay between the legal orders. Importantly, adopting a collaborative attitude should enable the supreme judicial guardians in the various legal orders to foster substantive coherence between their decisions and thereby reduce the occurrence of conflicts.

The pluralism discourse has a certain measure of normative and descriptive accuracy when looking at the practical reality of today's multi-layered fundamental rights landscape. Substantively speaking, we observe growing convergence and openness among national and European rights regimes. Courts and legislatures often use sources of fundamental rights emanating from the other systems as inspiration in the development and interpretation of their own catalogue of fundamental rights.[11] For instance, in giving effect to the constitutional command to interpret the Spanish bill of rights in accordance with human rights

---

[10] For a useful overview of the approaches taken by leading scholars in this field see Matej Avbelj and Jan Komárek (eds), *Constitutional Pluralism in the European Union and Beyond* (Hart Publishing 2012). The intellectual father of this discourse within the context of European integration was Neil MacCormick, who first introduced the idea of constitutional pluralism in 'The Maastricht Urteil: Sovereignty Now' (1995) 1 *European Law Journal* 259.

[11] In more detail, see, inter alia, Maartje de Visser, *Constitutional Review in Europe – A Comparative Analysis* (Hart Publishing 2014) Ch. 6; Giuseppe Martinico and Oreste Pollicino (eds), *The National Judicial Treatment of the ECHR and EU Laws: A Comparative Constitutional Perspective* (Europa Law Publishing 2010); Helen Keller and Alec Stone Sweet (eds), *A Europe of Rights: The Impact of the ECHR on National Legal Systems* (Oxford University Press 2008).

treaties,[12] the *Tribunal Constitucional* considers the ECHR and the Charter as instruments that have interpretative value in this regard.[13] Similarly, the CJEU for its part has recognised common national constitutional traditions and the ECHR as principal sources of inspiration in uncovering and fleshing out the EU's unwritten bill of rights.[14] Some national courts have gone even further and accepted the ECHR or rules of EU law as self-standing grounds of review in domestic litigation. For example, the Austrian *Verfassungsgerichtshof* ruled in early 2012 that the rights enshrined in the Charter 'may also be invoked as constitutionally guaranteed rights' in proceedings before it.[15]

The engagement with substantive sources of fundamental rights originating from the other regimes is facilitated by the institutional relationships that exist between national actors and the CJEU or Strasbourg Court, respectively, and between the two European courts. The Union system forges a direct formalised link between the CJEU and national courts in the form of the preliminary reference procedure laid down in Article 267 TFEU, and similar formal mechanisms for judicial interaction are envisaged for the interplay between the Strasbourg Court and the courts within the EU and national systems.[16] In addition, judges in all three systems of fundamental rights also communicate with each other in more informal and indirect ways, such as through their judgments or during personal encounters. The importance of such judicial dialogues has been underscored by European courts as well as by national highest judges alike, who increasingly regard such contacts as crucial in breeding understanding and respect for their respective views.[17] One measure of

---

12 Spanish constitution, art. 10(2).

13 See in particular *sentencia* 303/1993 of 25 October 1993; *sentencia* 53/2002 of 27 February 2002; *declaración* 1/2004 of 13 December 2003.

14 See especially *Internationale Handelsgesellschaft* (n 2); Case C-4/73 *Nold, Kohlen- und Baustoffgroßhandlung v Commission* [1974] ECLI:EU:C:1974:27. The Charter endorses this judicial approach in art. 52(3) and (4).

15 Joined cases U 466/11-18 and U 1836/11-13 of 14 March 2012.

16 See in particular Protocol No. 16 to the Convention for the Protection of Human Rights and Fundamental Freedoms (Council of Europe Treaty Series – No. 214, 2 October 2013), on which e.g., Janneke Gerards, 'Advisory Opinions, Preliminary Rulings and the New Protocol No.16 to the European Convention on Human Rights – A Comparative and Critical Appraisal' (2014) 21 *Maastricht Journal of European and Comparative Law* 630.

17 See e.g., the 'Dialogue between Judges' that the Strasbourg Court has been hosting on an annual basis since 2005; the Opinion of AG Ruiz-Jarebo Colomer in Case C-303/05 *Advocaten voor de Wereld VWZ v Leden van de Ministerraad* [2005] ECLI:EU:C:2005:552, notably para. 28; Andreas Voßkuhle, 'Multilevel

this willingness to engage is the change in attitude of constitutional courts vis-à-vis the preliminary reference procedure: the recent years have seen the Italian, Spanish, French and most recently the German courts overcome their initial disinclination to use this procedure and enter into an institutionalised dialogue with the CJEU.[18] In sum, in a great many cases, the plurality of interlocking systems of rights operates in a harmonious fashion, with a fair degree of convergence as regards the meaning and scope to be given to specific fundamental rights.

Nevertheless, there will be instances where conflict cannot be avoided and a divergence in approach is inescapable. In such cases, the constitutional pluralism discourse, however, does not appear to offer much guidance. Recall that these accounts reject hierarchy as an ordering criterion, which necessitates the need for other types of conflict norms. For example, Kumm has suggested using core tenets of constitutionalism to resolve conflicts, one of which focuses on the effective protection of the fundamental rights of citizens:

> If, and to the extent that, fundamental rights protection against acts of the EU is lacking in important respects, then that is a ground to insist on subjecting EU law to national constitutional rights review. If, however, the guarantees afforded by the EU amount to structurally equivalent protections, then there is no more space for national courts to substitute the EU's judgment on the rights issue with their own.[19]

This begs the question of who is ultimately to decide whether such effective protection of fundamental rights is available and which criteria

---

Cooperation of the European Constitutional Courts: Der Europäische Verfassungsgerichtsverbund' (2010) 6 EuConst 175.

[18] Case C-169/08 *Presidente del Consiglio dei Ministri v Regione Sardegna* [2009] ECLI:EU:C:2009:709; *Melloni* (n 6); Case C-168/13 PPU *Jeremy F v Premier ministre* [2013] ECLI:EU:C:2013:358; BVerfG, 2 BvR 2728/13 of 14 January 2014.

[19] Mattias Kumm, 'The Jurisprudence of Constitutional Conflict: Constitutional Supremacy in Europe before and after the Constitutional Treaty' (2005) 11 ELJ 262. See also e.g., Daniel Halberstam, 'Constitutional Heterarchy: The Centrality of Conflict in the European Union and the United States' in Jeffrey L Dunnoff and Joel P Trachtman (eds), *Ruling the World? Constitutionalism, International Law, and Global Governance* (Cambridge University Press 2009); Pavlos Eleftheriadis, 'The European Constitution and Cosmopolitan Ideas' (2001) 7 *Columbia Journal of European Law* 21; Gareth Davies, 'Constitutional Disagreement in Europe and the Search for Pluralism', in Avbelj and Komárek (n 10).

are to be used in making this determination.[20] At present, the constitutional pluralism discourse does not seem to provide closure in a complete and satisfactory manner in the event of conflicts between legal orders.

Moving from constitutional theory to legal reality, each of the national and European fundamental rights systems typically decides its own rules of engagement with the other, and the 'rules of conflict' to regulate differences in approach are accordingly not mutually agreed upon or necessarily the same.[21] In light of the overall perspective of this volume, the emphasis will be on the systemic relationship between the EU system and the Charter, on the one hand, and national systems on the other hand. More particularly, and leaving aside for the moment European and national understandings of the doctrine of primacy, Article 53 of the Charter merits attention. In its relevant parts, this provision reads as follows:

> Nothing in this Charter shall be interpreted as restricting or adversely affecting human rights and fundamental freedoms as recognised, in their respective spheres of application … by the Member States' constitutions.

On its face, Article 53 appears to countenance the possibility of the Charter setting a floor, a minimum threshold of protection that must at all times be guaranteed, with national regimes being able to offer more extensive protection to fundamental rights in situations that fall within the scope of Union law. In other words, according to this reading of Article 53, the EU rights regime would, *in a systemic manner*, accept some degree of flexibility and differentiation in the fundamental rights domain, which could include a relaxation of, or exception to, the traditional hierarchical conceptualisation of the relationship between EU and national (constitutional) law. This would be a tantalising prospect for those studying the evolution of the Union legal order, who, in the wake of the Charter obtaining binding force, were awaiting CJEU clarification of Article 53.

---

20 It furthermore does not deal with situations where the act in relation to which redress is sought on fundamental rights grounds was adopted by *national* authorities.

21 We will leave aside cases in which rights guardians insist on diversity by means not envisaged by the systems themselves (i.e., instances of resistance).

3. A CRITICAL ANALYSIS OF THE JUDICIAL APPROACH TO ARTICLE 53 OF THE CHARTER

3.1 Article 53 of the Charter before the CJEU

Article 53 of the Charter was interpreted by the CJEU for the first time in the 2013 ruling in *Melloni*.[22] The case concerned the execution of a European Arrest Warrant (EAW) issued by the Italian authorities to their Spanish counterparts for the execution of a prison sentence imposed on Stefano Melloni, an Italian national who had been convicted of bankruptcy fraud following a trial held in his absence. Mr Melloni sought to prevent his surrender to Italy by claiming a violation of the requirements flowing from the Spanish *Tribunal Constitucional*'s interpretation of the constitutional right to a fair trial.[23] This case law requires that the surrender of persons convicted *in absentia* of serious offences is conditional on whether they are able to have their conviction reviewed. Framework Decision 2009/299 concerning the European Arrest Warrant,[24] which has amended the original Framework Decision 2002/584,[25] however provides in Article 4a(1) that the execution of an EAW for serving a sentence imposed *in absentia* cannot be refused when the person concerned was aware of the forthcoming criminal proceedings or was duly represented by counsel during the trial. As this appeared to be the case in Mr Melloni's situation, the Spanish *Tribunal Constitucional* was confronted with the question whether it could nevertheless continue to apply its constitutional standards for protecting the right to a fair trial

---

[22] *Melloni* (n 6). On this judgment, see e.g., Nik De Boer, 'Addressing Rights Divergence under the Charter: *Melloni*' (2013) CML Rev 1083; Maartje de Visser, 'Dealing with Divergences in Fundamental Rights Standards' (2013) *Maastricht Journal of European and Comparative Law* 576; Maja Brkan, 'L'arrêt Melloni: nouvelle pierre dans la mosaïque de la protection des droit fondamentaux dans l'Union européenne' (2013) 1 Revue des affaires européennes 139; Aida Torres Pérez, '*Melloni* in Three Acts: From Dialogue to Monologue' (2014) 10 EuConst 308.

[23] Art. 24(2) of the Spanish constitution.

[24] Council Framework Decision 2009/299/JHA of 26 February 2009 amending Framework Decisions 2002/584/JHA, 2005/214/JHA, 2006/783/JHA, 2008/909/JHA and 2008/947/JHA, thereby enhancing the procedural rights of persons and fostering the application of the principle of mutual recognition to decisions rendered in the absence of the person concerned at the trial [2009] OJ L81/24.

[25] Council Framework Decision 2002/584/JHA of 13 June 2002 on the European arrest warrant and the surrender procedures between Member States [2002] OJ L190/1.

in situations coming within the scope of EU law. It referred this matter to the CJEU under Article 267 TFEU, asking whether, if Article 4a would be interpreted as precluding the imposition of additional conditions before persons are surrendered and was considered compatible with the rights to a fair trial and defence guaranteed by the Charter, Article 53 of that text would nevertheless allow it to afford those fundamental rights a higher degree of protection as a matter of national constitutional law.[26]

The CJEU firmly rejected a reading of Article 53 of the Charter that would result in this provision being seen as the functional equivalent of Article 53 of the ECHR, whereby national courts are free to enforce higher constitutional standards of human rights protection in situations that fall within the scope of EU law, as long as they do not fall below the Charter standard. According to the Luxembourg judges, such an interpretation would be fundamentally at odds with core tenets of EU law, that is to say, its 'primacy, unity and effectiveness'. While national authorities and courts may concurrently apply the Charter and their own constitutional fundamental rights standards in cases that fall within the scope of Union law, doing so cannot undermine or detract from the fundamental doctrines of EU law just mentioned or the level of fundamental rights protection guaranteed by the Charter as established in CJEU case law; and whether that is the case will ultimately be determined in Luxembourg. The upshot is that, in situations where Union law applies, national actors will typically have to refrain from applying domestic standards that offer more protection for fundamental rights.

There are good reasons to treat the Court's proclamations on the meaning of Article 53 of the Charter in *Melloni* as general statements of principle, rather than musings pertinent only to the area of law in question. The judgment was delivered by a Grand Chamber with nine Member States as well as the Commission and Council having submitted their observations for judicial consideration. Arguably more telling is the fact that in *Åkerberg Fransson,* another important decision handed down on the same day, in which the question when Member States must act in accordance with the Charter was addressed for the first time, the CJEU reiterated its conclusion in *Melloni* that the primacy, unity and effectiveness of EU law must be safeguarded when national actors apply domestic rights standards.[27]

---

[26] On this reference, see Aida Torres Pérez, 'Spanish Constitutional Court, Constitutional Dialogue on the European Arrest Warrant: The Spanish Constitutional Court Knocking on Luxembourg's Door' (2012) 8 EuConst 105.

[27] Case C-617/10 *Åklagaren v Hans Åkerberg Fransson* [2013] ECLI:EU:C:2013:105, para. 29 and, more recently, see Case C-206/13 *Cruciano Siragusa*

3.2 Assessing the Importance of Primacy, Unity and Effectiveness in the Domain of Fundamental Rights

The significance attributed to the primacy of Union law, including as regards conflicting constitutional rules, has been a recurring theme in CJEU case law since *Internationale Handelsgesellschaft*,[28] and the CJEU expressly relied on this judgment as a precedent in *Melloni*.[29] In fact, in the past five years there have been several occasions that the Court has underscored the importance ascribed to the supremacy doctrine at the expense of national procedural rules regulating the position of constitutional courts and the authority of their decisions for other State bodies.[30] Moreover, looking at the drafting history of Article 53 of the Charter, Liisberg concludes that the drafters did not intend for this provision to circumscribe the primacy of Union law; rather, the aim was to reassure State bodies that the Charter is not intended to displace national bills of rights.[31] Against this backdrop, it is unsurprising that the Court held that its absolute primacy thesis also applies in the context of the Charter. The rulings in *Melloni* and *Åkerberg Fransson*, taken together with the earlier case law, also demonstrate that the CJEU does not subscribe to one of the principal claims put forward by advocates of constitutional pluralism, namely that the relationship between the Union and national legal orders ought not to be analysed in hierarchical terms. As alluded to, one of the main reasons offered by the Court for its staunch defence of the primacy of Union law is practical in nature and concerns the need to safeguard the

---

v Regione Sicilia – Sprintendenza Beni Culturali e Ambientali di Palermo [2014] ECLI:EU:C:2014:126, para. 32 and Case C-198/13 *Victor Manuel Julian Hernández and others v Reino de España (Subdelegacíon del Gobierno de España en Alicante) and others* [2014] ECLI:EU:C:2014:2055, para. 47.

[28] *Internationale Handelsgesellschaft* (n 2), para. 3.

[29] *Melloni* (n 6), para. 59.

[30] See in particular Case C-409/06 *Winner Wetten GmbH v Bürgermeisterin der Stadt Bergheim* [2010] ECLI:EU:C:2010:503, paras 60–61; Joined Cases C-188/10 and C-189/10 *Aziz Melki and Sélim Abdeli* [2010] ECLI:EU:C:2010:363, paras 52–57; Case C-416/10 *Jozef Križan and Others v Slovenská inšpekcia životného prostredia* [2013] ECLI:EU:C:2013:8, para. 70. For discussion, see De Visser (n 11) 417–27.

[31] Jonas B Liisberg, 'Does the EU Charter of Fundamental Rights Threaten the Supremacy of Community Law?' (2003) 38 CML Rev 1171. See also Bruno De Witte, 'Article 53' in Steve Peers, Tamara Hervey, Jeff Kenner and Angela Ward (eds), *The EU Charter of Fundamental Rights – A Commentary* (Hart Publishing 2014).

efficacy of EU rules. In the specific case of *Melloni*, the Court reasoned that if Spain were allowed to enforce its higher domestic standards of rights protection for persons convicted *in absentia*, the *effet utile* of the EAW regime would be compromised.[32] Familiar policy reasons are at play here: leaving aside an observed tendency on the part of the Court to practise restraint when reviewing Union legislative measures, a pro-integration commitment can be discerned. The Luxembourg judges were keen to bolster – rather than detract from – the efforts by the Union legislature to establish a fully operational Area of Freedom, Security and Justice (AFSJ), undergirded by mutual recognition and mutual trust among Member State authorities, as a complement to the traditional 'economic' pillars of the Union edifice. Placing the realisation of the principles of supremacy and uniformity within their historical context reminds us that these legal tools were conceived in large part to support the achievement of 'ever closer integration' in the economic sphere. Supremacy was necessary to combat economic protectionism at a time when the common market was in its incipiency and uniformity dovetails with the traditional undertaking to give effect to non-discrimination and equality among business and individuals from the various Member States.

It is difficult to overstate the significance of the primacy doctrine and the related notions of *effet utile* and uniformity for the success of European integration. The approach in *Melloni* appears to countenance extending the full force of these principles from the classic domain of market-making to the area of fundamental rights. The question arises whether this is the right way forward or whether more differentiation and greater room for flexibility in the latter domain would be preferable or even necessary. In our view, there are at least two reasons that militate in favour of embracing some measure of 'unity in diversity' when it comes to ensuring respect for fundamental rights, notably in non-economic areas.

The first concerns the legitimacy of the EU's forays into these fields. It could be argued that since non-economic areas, such as the AFSJ, are as yet far from complete, a premium ought to be placed on a firm endorsement of supremacy and uniformity to deliver the objectives pursued in such areas. It is clear that mutual trust and mutual recognition, for instance, are more easily achieved when Member States are restricted in their ability to make use of derogations to otherwise generally applicable EU rules. Yet, the economic logic underlying the idea of *effet utile* applies to a lesser degree in these fields as compared to the classic

32 *Melloni* (n 6), para. 63.

internal market area. The rights and freedoms of individuals in these fields take on greater significance given that the situations at issue are typically those where States, representing the public interest, seek to enforce disadvantageous or coercive measures against alleged or confirmed wrongdoings perpetrated by individuals. The context, in other words, is very different: AFSJ matters are surrounded by a greater degree of political sensitivity, the regulation of many of these matters is still mainly in the hands of the Member States and involves a huge variety in choices made by the Member States as to where to strike the balance between enabling State action against crime and the protection of fundamental rights.[33] In a related vein, allowing Member States to invoke domestic fundamental rights (as compared to other grounds of justification for derogation) to restrict the full force of Union rules, permits the Member States to safeguard a particularly worthy objective: protecting the rights and freedoms of persons on their territory. The prospect of countries using this possibility to covertly achieve undesirable ends, such as economic protectionism, would appear to be slim. Writing about the application of the principle of mutual recognition in the context of the Area, Möstl observes:

> If mutual recognition is only achievable at the expense of either too big a loss of protection of rights and liberties of the individual or too big a loss for the autonomy and legal identity of the Member States, the Union legislature must refrain from establishing it. What results, are competential limits on the Union legislature in the criminal law context which are considerably greater than those in the internal market context – a striking difference which results from the fact that in the internal market context, individual freedom (free movement) acts as a centralizing force, counterbalancing subsidiarity, whereas here, in the criminal law context, freedom (fundamental rights and liberties) joins up with subsidiarity to limit the powers of the EU legislature.[34]

While Möstl's concern is with legislative approximation and harmonisation, it is submitted that his call to show respect for the Member States' autonomy and legal identity should also be heeded by the CJEU to eschew all too eagerly assuming or imposing a judicial harmonisation of the meaning to be given to fundamental rights.

The second reason for accepting some degree of flexibility in relation to the protection of fundamental rights is not specific to non-economic areas. Even before the Charter acquired binding force, the Court had

---

[33] See e.g., art. 82(2) last sentence TFEU.

[34] Markus Möstl, 'Preconditions and Limits of Mutual Recognition' (2010) 47 CML Rev 405, 420–21.

already accepted in some instances that Member States could derogate from internal market rules for the purpose of protecting domestically guaranteed fundamental rights.[35] In doing so, the Luxembourg judges accepted that the legal and economic benefits associated with uniformity in the application of EU law across the then 27 Member States could not be fully achieved. There is no evidence that this has caused major impediments to the *effet utile* of Union law at the national level. More generally, from an economic perspective, inroads to fundamental freedoms in the name of fundamental rights protection are not likely to be a frequent occurrence and consequently would not appear to place the success of the overall integration process in jeopardy. Lastly, as some of the other contributions to this volume demonstrate, complete unity in the implementation and application of Union law is a mirage. It is well known that not insignificant differences and inconsistencies remain in the way that national actors (courts, executive bodies and legislatures) give effect to European rules.[36]

Changing perspective somewhat, the reasoning advanced in *Melloni* was arguably not solely motivated by a concern to ensure respect for the classic doctrines of primacy, *effet utile* and uniformity in the application of Union law, but it simultaneously enabled the Court to strengthen its own institutional position. In *Melloni* (and *Åkerberg Fransson*)[37] the CJEU recognised that national authorities and courts are able to apply the Charter and their own constitutional fundamental rights standards concurrently in cases that fall within the scope of EU law.[38] However, the use of national standards is precluded when this would compromise the protection offered by the Charter, as established in CJEU case law. Whether this is the case will ultimately be determined in Luxembourg. We thus see a Court eager to assert that it – rather than for instance national constitutional courts – has the final authority to decide on the meaning of the rights guaranteed by the Charter and, as a consequence, on the scope

---

35 The *locus classicus* is Case C-36/02 *Omega Spielhallen- und Automatenaufstellungs-GmbH v Oberbürgermeisterin der Bundesstadt Bonn* [2004] ECLI:EU:C:2004:614.

36 See e.g., Tobias Nowak, Fabian Amtenbrink, Marc Hertogh and Mark Wissink, *National Judges as European Union Judges: Knowledge, Experience and Attitudes of Lower Court Judges in Germany and the Netherlands* (Eleven Publishers 2012).

37 *Åkerberg Fransson* (n 27).

38 *Melloni* (n 6), para. 60; Case C-112/13 *A v B and Others* [2014] ECLI:EU:C:2014:2195, para. 44.

for national (constitutional) courts to uphold domestic rights catalogues in situations within the remit of Union law.

Yet, a different approach might also have its benefits. When it comes to scrutinising the compliance of national measures that give effect to, or seek to derogate from, EU law with fundamental rights, allowing national (constitutional) courts to take the lead would enable the CJEU to make strategic use of its finite judicial resources. The active involvement of national constitutional courts in establishing the meaning of fundamental rights at the Union level has further been defended with reference to their mandate and concomitant experience in safeguarding individual rights and freedoms:

> Courts might have different approaches to the law as a consequence of their respective institutional roles and their position in the legal system. One of the main functions of constitutional courts is precisely the protection of rights and the review of legislation in light of fundamental rights. In contrast, the ECJ is a court of general jurisdiction. It was set up to secure that 'in the implementation of the common market the law is observed', and it might possess a bias favouring the success of the integration process.[39]

This line of thinking appeals to the importance of infusing the process of defining the content and scope of fundamental rights with bottom-up legitimacy and support, a point to which we return below.

3.3 Justifying some Measure of Flexibility in Enforcing Higher National Fundamental Rights Standards in Situations that Fall within the Scope of EU Law

Having unpacked the rationales underlying the Court's approach as regards Article 53 of the Charter, this sub-section seeks to identify potential problems that may arise from an undue emphasis on uniformity and commonality in the understanding of fundamental rights.

One of the problems is that too strong an insistence on the primacy and unity of EU law may perversely result in a lowering of the protection guaranteed to fundamental rights in the Member States. *Melloni* itself is illustrative in this regard: Spain (or more accurately: its *Tribunal Constitucional*) is prevented from enforcing the higher protection for the right to a fair trial provided under its constitution and make the execution of EAWs in case of *in absentia* rulings conditional on the availability of a

---

[39] Aida Torres Pérez 'The Dual System of Rights Protection in the European Union in Light of US Federalism' in Elke Cloots, Geert De Baere and Stefan Sottiaux (eds), *Federalism in the European Union* (Hart Publishing 2012) 127.

retrial. There are other examples of Member States guaranteeing more extensive protection to fundamental rights under their national constitutions than what appears to be on offer under the Charter. One can refer, for example, to the right to reputation in Ireland, the right to a good administration in Portugal or the natural rights of the human person and family in Luxembourg.[40] More seriously, writing pre-Charter, Anneli Albi has identified instances where constitutional courts in Central and Eastern Europe have deemed it necessary to downgrade the level of protection they afford to domestic fundamental rights situations coming within the scope of Union law in order to ensure respect for the doctrine of primacy.[41] Such a judicial approach by national highest courts can be commended as EU-friendly and celebrated for recognising the importance of openness, accommodation and respect insisted on in the constitutional pluralism literature. Yet, it should be acknowledged that, from the perspective of affected individuals, the potential of a reduction in the degree of fundamental rights protection is worrisome.

To be sure, if and when the CJEU chooses a high level of protection for the rights guaranteed under Union law, the prospect of national courts and authorities having to accept a lower level of protection than would be available as a matter of domestic constitutional law in situations coming within the scope of Union law becomes more remote. So too does the poignancy of EU law accommodating flexibility in the domain of fundamental rights. However, such a state of affairs is not so likely to occur. One reason for this is that so far the Court's case law does not suggest a strong judicial willingness to provide very extensive protection for Charter rights.[42] Yet, even if this were to change, the fact remains that the CJEU should not (and will not) systematically emulate the Member State that offers the highest protection for a given fundamental right, i.e., adopt a 'maximalist' approach when deciding on the meaning of Charter rights. Since they encapsulate the views of a particular national society,

---

40 Leonard Besselink, 'The Protection of Fundamental Rights post-Lisbon: The Interaction between the EU Charter of Fundamental Rights, the European Convention on Human Rights (ECHR) and National Constitutions' (2012) FIDE General Report, 5–6.

41 Anneli Albi, 'From the *Banana* Saga to a Sugar Saga and Beyond: Could the Post-Communist Constitutional Courts Teach the EU a Lesson in the Rule of Law?' (2010) 47 CML Rev 791.

42 *Melloni* is a case in point: the CJEU was content to peg the EU level of protection for the fundamental rights in question to that available under the ECHR, which however acts as a minimum standard of rights protection within Europe.

domestic rights standards may not be suitable for unquestioning duplication in the Union context, not to mention that this would result in the challenging issue of what the CJEU would do in situations where country A offers a very high level of protection to a particular fundamental right, while country B accords a very high level of protection to a competing fundamental right.[43] Reduced levels of fundamental rights protection at the national level will always remain a problematic possibility under the Court's interpretation of Article 53 as set out in *Melloni*. Depending on the extent of the discrepancy between the protection available under domestic and Charter standards, the result may be more resistance or even outright conflict between the fundamental rights guardians at the national and Union level in the years to come.

Second, too strong an insistence on uniformity concerning the substantive content and scope of fundamental rights is liable to create legitimacy problems for the Union. Fundamental rights have competing conceptions: they often raise 'questions of political morality'[44] and can thus be said to lack a single, fixed interpretation. According to Jeremy Waldron, reasonable people who share a general commitment to rights protection often disagree on matters of rights, including the precise meaning and scope of any particular right.[45] Examples abound: for example the fundamental rights to be enjoyed by criminal suspects, the reach of a right to equal treatment regardless of sexual orientation or the permissibility of affirmative action policies.[46] In negotiating the substantive content and scope of rights, diverging views have to be considered and merged, either through political discourse or the judicial process. Regardless of the result arrived at when these negotiations are concluded, fundamental rights will only be

---

[43] See Joseph HH Weiler, *The Constitution of Europe – 'Do the New Clothes have an Emperor?' and Other Essays on European Integration* (Cambridge University Press 1999) 110–12.

[44] Ronald Dworkin, *Freedom's Law: The Moral Reading of the American Constitution* (Harvard University Press 1996) 75.

[45] Jeremy Waldron, 'The Core of the Case Against Judicial Review' (2006) 115 *Yale Law Journal* 1348, 1367.

[46] These issues have all been the subject of legislative and/or judicial debate within the EU: see for instance the Commission's Proposal for a Council Directive on implementing the principle of equal treatment between persons irrespective of religion or belief, disability, age or sexual orientation COM(2008) 426; the Resolution of the Council of 30 November 2009 on a Roadmap for strengthening procedural rights of suspects or accused persons in criminal proceedings [2009] OJ C295/1 and Case C-450/93 *Kalanke v Freie Hansestadt Bremen* [1995] ECLI:EU:C:1995:322 and the follow-up in Case C-409/95 *Helmut Marschall v Land Nordrhein Westfalen* [1997] ECLI:EU:C:1997:533.

truly effective – in the sense of intrinsically deemed worthy of respect and protection – when their meaning and reach is perceived by their addressees to reflect a fair balance or compromise between the different views that exist in the community in which the right will have to be administered. In other words, the social legitimacy of fundamental rights is closely linked to these rights expressing the collective will in or of the community in question.

This raises the question what, in the Union setting, can be considered to be the 'community' whose moral and political disagreements have a bearing on the negotiation of fundamental rights standards. This, in some sense, is reminiscent of the earlier demos/no demos debate and the contribution, if any, of the provisions on Union citizenship in polity- and identity-building.[47] While limited space prevents a detailed consideration of this issue here, the following remarks are nevertheless warranted. According to Article 2 TEU, both the Union and its Member States are committed to upholding the triumvirate of the rule of law, democracy and human rights, and, as regards the latter value, explicit mention is made of human dignity, equality and non-discrimination and the rights of persons belonging to minorities. Yet, this strong commitment to fundamental rights should not blind us to the fact that, as mentioned earlier, differences remain among the Member States and their constituent communities (and within each of these) as to the 'correct' meaning and application of rights. By way of example, the Irish understanding of the right to life is quite far removed from the Dutch view; same-sex couples are accorded more comprehensive equal treatment with heterosexual couples in France than in Poland.

In light of this reality, and bearing in mind that decisions on the content and scope of rights are intimately linked to historical, sociological and political factors, it may be premature to regard the Union, its Member States and their citizens as a single community for the purposes of negotiating universal fundamental rights standards. Rather, the existing state of affairs would offer support for some measure of flexibility or room for differentiation in making choices in this regard, in order to

---

[47] See e.g., Dieter Grimm, 'Comments on the German Constitutional Court's Decision on the Lisbon Treaty: Defending Sovereign Statehood against Transforming the European Union into a State' (2010) 5 EuConst 353; Samantha Besson, 'Deliberative demoi-cracy in the European Union: Towards the Deterritorialization of Democracy' in Samantha Besson and José L Marti (eds), *Deliberative Democracy and its Discontents: National and Post-National Challenges* (Ashgate 2006); Kalypso Nicolaides, 'We, the Peoples of Europe …' (2004) 83 *Foreign Affairs* 97.

ensure concordance with moral and political considerations that as yet are often still domestic in reach. Such an approach would be particularly apposite in fields such as criminal law or asylum law, where government regulation and intervention tends to provoke strong sentiments. The political and social legitimacy of Union measures in these non-economic areas may be compromised when there is only a light-touch review of the compatibility of these measures with EU fundamental rights and national measures giving effect to the Union instruments cannot be checked for compliance with domestic fundamental rights standards offering more protection than the EU standards.

4. TOOLS FOR (MORE) DIFFERENTIATION AND FLEXIBILITY IN THE FUNDAMENTAL RIGHTS DOMAIN

Having identified several reasons that militate in favour of some measure of flexibility and room for differentiation in the domain of fundamental rights, this section explores various techniques and tools that the EU institutions, and in particular the CJEU, can use to accommodate diversity in national constitutional values.[48]

An obvious way for the Court to accommodate national value diversity centres on the approach taken to the interpretation of Article 53 of the Charter. A relevant factor in deciding whether or not to allow Member States to enforce their own (higher) fundamental rights standards when Union law and the Charter are applicable should be the degree of attention towards fundamental rights that the European rules in question exhibit. The Court's first authoritative reading of Article 53 was given in a case where the intention of the Union legislature was to harmonise the degree of protection to be afforded to the fundamental rights in question: the relevant provision of the Framework Decision, according to the judges, 'reflect[ed] the consensus reached by all the Member States regarding the scope to be given under EU law to the procedural rights enjoyed by persons convicted in absentia who are the subject of a

---

[48] For reasons of space, the discussion that follows will not address modalities of judicial decision-making such as deferring the application of the proportionality test to national courts (compare Case C-368/95 *Vereinigte Familiapress Zeitungsverlags- und vertriebs GmbH v Heinrich Bauer* [1997] ECLI: EU:C:1997:325) or the explicit recognition of a margin of appreciation doctrine in CJEU case law.

European arrest warrant'.[49] There would thus appear to be room for the Court to develop a bifurcated approach to Article 53, whereby Member States are granted more leeway to apply domestic rights standards in situations where the Union measure at stake does not enshrine a shared understanding of the meaning and reach of fundamental rights.[50]

A willingness to embrace such an appeal can perhaps be detected in the later decision in *Jeremy F*, which incidentally also concerned the EAW Framework Decision, although neither the referring court nor the CJEU made reference to Article 53 of the Charter.[51] In this case, the referring court wished to know whether national legislation could give persons subject to decisions pertaining to their surrender to another Member State under an EAW the right to appeal such decisions with suspensive effect. This case in essence also raised the question whether Member States can provide protection for fundamental rights that might not be available under EU law.

In its ruling, the CJEU started by pointing out that the Framework Decision is silent on this issue. Referring to the concern to uphold fundamental rights evident in this instrument and to European case law holding that the right of access to court does not require countries to provide for an appeal procedure,[52] it concluded that the Framework Decision left 'the national authorities a discretion as to the specific manner of implementation of the objectives it pursues', including as regards the procedural issue that was the subject of the preliminary reference.[53] Indeed, 'provided that the application of the Framework Decision is not frustrated [...] it does not prevent a Member State from applying its constitutional rules relating inter alia to respect for the right to a fair trial'.[54] In this particular case, the Court held that Member States would not undermine the system put in place by the Framework Decision if any right under national law to bring a suspensive appeal would be exercised in accordance with the time limits expressly mentioned in this

---

49 *Melloni* (n 6), para. 62.

50 A comparable approach was adopted by AG Bot in his Opinion in *Melloni* ibid., paras 124–127.

51 *Jeremy F* (n 18).

52 *Marturana v Italy* App. No 63154/00 (ECtHR, decision of 4 March 2008), para. 110 and case law cited there; Case C-69/10 *Brahim Samba Diouf v Ministre du Travail, de l'Emploi et de l'immigration* [2011] ECLI:EU:C:2011:524, para. 69.

53 *Jeremy F* (n 18), para. 52.

54 Ibid., para. 53.

Decision. It would be good if the CJEU would, at the earliest opportunity, clarify its interpretation of Article 53 in cases like *Jeremy F*, where the Union legislature has not addressed the standard of fundamental rights protection and explicitly recognise that Member States have more room for the application of divergent national rights standards in such situations.[55]

To be clear, we are not advocating greater flexibility and accommodation of value diversity in the review of Union measures for their compatibility with fundamental rights. Subjecting rules of EU law to domestic fundamental rights scrutiny could bring about the confusing situation where such rules are considered valid in some Member States and invalid in others. This would clearly be problematic in light of the principles of legal certainty and equality. When the conformity of Union law with fundamental rights guaranteed by the Charter or general principles is in doubt, there are accordingly good reasons to respect the Court's appeal to the need for uniformity that it originally made in *Foto-Frost*.[56] At the same time, and going back to a point made earlier, the Court does have a role to play in reducing the risk of national (constitutional) courts enforcing domestic fundamental rights standards vis-à-vis EU acts by subjecting such acts to a sufficiently robust review, thereby signalling that it takes its task of keeping the Union legislature in check seriously.

Additionally, or alternatively, the Court can practise restraint in finding that particular situations involving actions taken by national authorities fall within the Charter's scope of application. Finding that the conduct of Member State authorities in a given scenario is not governed by the fundamental rights enshrined in the Charter means that there is simply no need to determine where to strike the balance between showing respect for national constitutional diversity and safeguarding core tenets of Union law. This would moreover not be a novel technique, having famously been used by the Court in the older pre-Charter case of *Grogan* to avoid

[55] For an argument along similar lines that also emphasises the importance of discretion on the part of Member States as the justification for the application of (higher) national fundamental rights standards, see Weiler (n 43) 123–8 and De Witte (n 31) 1533–4.

[56] Case C-314/85 *Firma Foto-Frost v Hauptzollamt Lübeck-Ost* [1987] ECLI: EU:C:1987:452, especially para. 15.

having to adjudicate the compatibility of the Irish abortion regime, including its constitutional foundations, with the Treaty's free movement rules.[57]

The question when Member States are required to act in accordance with the Charter – and hence possibly subjected to the conditions set out in *Melloni* – was addressed in *Åkerberg Fransson*.[58] The case concerned criminal proceedings brought against a Swedish fisherman for tax evasion, including the failure to declare value-added tax (VAT). Several governments and the Commission had argued that the Court lacked jurisdiction to hand down a preliminary ruling, relying on the fact that the Charter states in Article 51(1) that it is binding on the Member States 'only insofar as they implement EU law' and that the Swedish legislation at issue had not been adopted in furtherance of the country's obligations under EU law. The Court disagreed and, in line with the Explanations to the Charter, found that this instrument applies in all cases coming within the scope of EU law, including those when Member States seek to derogate from, or restrict the exercise of, the market freedoms.[59]

As this pronouncement continues the approach developed in pre-Charter case law,[60] it cannot be considered unexpected. Yet, the Advocate General had a different view on this matter and, in light of the focus of this chapter, his Opinion merits attention. AG Cruz Villalón puts forward a more nuanced approach to the interpretation of Article 51 of the Charter. He suggests that the decisive criterion for the applicability of the Charter to a national measure should be the existence of a 'specific interest' on the part of the EU to verify the legitimacy of such acts in light of the Charter and other rules of Union law. It is clear that this approach could be seen as a minor revolution when it comes to the Charter's applicability to Member State measures, which may explain the Court's refusal to follow the direction proposed by the Advocate General. Also, should the Advocate General's approach be followed, one may readily expect a series of preliminary questions concerning the precise meaning of the phrase 'significant interest'.

---

57 Case C-159/90 *The Society for the Protection of Unborn Children Ireland Ltd v Stephen Grogan and others* [1991] ECLI:EU:C:1991:378.

58 *Åkerberg Fransson* (n 27).

59 See also *Cruciano Siragusa v Regione Sicilia* (n 27), paras 24–26; Case C-390/12 *Robert Pfleger and Others* [2014] ECLI:EU:C:2014:281, paras 35–36; *Hernández v Reino de España* (n 27), para. 37.

60 See notably Case C-5/88 *Hubert Wachauf v Bundesamt für Ernährung und Forstwirtschaft* [1989] ECLI:EU:C:1989:321; Case C-260/89 *ERT v Dimotiki Etairia Pliroforissis and others* [1991] ECLI:EU:C:1991:254.

Yet, while his approach is not without problems, the Advocate General is correct in acknowledging the need for some degree of judicial caution when deciding on the reach of Union human rights law:[61] this is a call that ought to be heeded, in particular bearing in mind the centripetal tendencies that 'federal' rights documents are prone to generate.[62]

Leaving aside the interpretation of the Charter's general provisions, Article 4(2) TEU must also be considered, which requires the Union to respect the national identities of its Member States 'inherent in their fundamental structures, political and constitutional'.[63] The Court had already cited this provision when assessing whether Member States could justifiably derogate from the Treaty's free movement provisions.[64] In *Melloni*, the CJEU made no reference to Article 4(2) TEU, in all likelihood because this provision was not mentioned in the request for a preliminary reference and the agent for Spain stated during the hearing that the relevant case law of the *Tribunal Constitucional* did not pertain to the country's national identity. Nevertheless, in future cases, this provision can conceivably be relied upon to accommodate constitutional value diversity.

To be sure, not every case that involves questions regarding the protection of national fundamental rights and liberties will *ipso facto* implicate a country's identity.[65] However, there will be instances where a

---

[61] In this context, note also the judgment in Case C-256/11 *Murat Dereci and others v Bundesministerium für Inneres* [2011] ECLI:EU:C:2011:734 in which the CJEU refused to accept that cases involving Union citizens who had not made use of their free movement rights are within the scope of EU law, including the Charter.

[62] See e.g., Koen Lenaerts, 'Federalism and Rights in the European Community' in Ellis Katz and George A Tarr (eds), *Federalism and Rights* (Rowman & Littlefield Publishers 1996).

[63] On this provision, see e.g., Alejandro Saiz Arnaiz and Carina Alcoberro Liivina (eds), *National Constitutional Identity and European Integration* (Intersentia 2013); Leonard Besselink, 'National and Constitutional Identity before and after Lisbon' (2010) 6 *Utrecht Law Review* 36; Armin von Bogdandy and Stephan Schill, 'Overcoming Absolute Primacy: Respect for National Identity under the Lisbon Treaty', (2011) 48 CML Rev 1417.

[64] Case C-208/09 *Ilonka Sayn-Wittgenstein v Landeshauptmann von Wien* [2010] ECLI:EU:C:2010:806; Case C-391/09 *Malgožata Runevič-Vardyn en Łukasz Paweł Wardyn v Vilniaus miesto savivaldybės administracija e.a.* [2011] ECLI:EU:C:2011:291. See also the pre-Lisbon ruling in Case C-36/02 *Omega Spielhallen- und Automatenaufstellungs-GmbH v Oberbürgermeisterin der Bundesstadt Bonn* [2004] ECLI:EU:C:2004:614.

[65] This is rightly acknowledged by AG Bot in his Opinion in *Melloni* (n 6), para. 142.

Member State (or its principal constitutional guardian) considers that the application or implementation of Union measures affects the protection of domestic fundamental rights that it considers an integral part of its national identity. For example, the right to informational privacy is considered to be part of Germany's national identity.[66] For Slovenia the same can be said about the protection of national heritage and in Belgium linguistic rights are said to be covered by the national identity concept.[67] Article 4(2) TEU provides the CJEU with a legal device to deal with claims that a Member State's identity in the form of a particular conception of fundamental rights is at stake, including by allowing Member States to rely on their own standard of rights protection in situations involving national measures adopted in the execution of or derogation from Union law.

In the wake of *Melloni*, a question that remains is whether Member States may also invoke Article 4(2) TEU to rely on their higher standards of fundamental rights when the EU rule to be applied gives expression to a common understanding of the right(s) concerned under Union law. One could argue that this should not be possible and that, in such situations, it is the responsibility of the Member State whose identity is affected to raise this matter during deliberations on the Union rule in Council. Yet, it is submitted that this would be too strict an approach, in particular when the EU measure in question has been adopted by QMV, which means that Member States can be outvoted.

This leads to a final point, namely the role of the European legislature in signalling to the Court that there may be room for Member States to enforce their domestic fundamental rights standards. The Framework Decision on racist and xenophobic speech and crime is instructive in this regard.[68] The aim of this legal instrument is to put in place a common approach across the Member States in sanctioning a range of intentional actions with racist or xenophobic overtones by means of criminal law. Article 7 of the Framework Decision deals with constitutional rules and fundamental principles, the second paragraph of which explicitly allows Member States to adopt and enforce national fundamental rights standards:

---

[66] BVerfG, 1 BvR 256/08 (2010), para. 218.

[67] See Besselink (n 40) 6.

[68] Council Framework Decision 2008/913/JHA of 28 November 2008 on combating certain forms and expressions of racism and xenophobia by means of criminal law [2008] OJ L328/55.

> This Framework Decision shall not have the effect of requiring Member States to take measures in contradiction to fundamental principles relating to freedom of association and freedom of expression, in particular freedom of the press and the freedom of expression in other media as they result from constitutional traditions or rules governing the rights and responsibilities of, and the procedural guarantees for, the press or other media where these rules relate to the determination or limitation of liability.

The EAW Framework Decision does not contain a similar 'safeguard clause' and in *Melloni* the Court refused to read such a provision into this instrument. If and when Member States desire the possibility of applying (higher) domestic standards of fundamental rights in a particular field, it would accordingly appear sensible for them to ensure that clauses along the lines of Article 7(2) of the Racism and Xenophobia Framework Decision are included in the relevant Union measures.[69] It can be expected that the CJEU will in turn be (more) accommodating of national fundamental rights diversity in the implementation of such EU rules, also bearing in mind the deference generally shown by the Luxembourg judges to the policy decisions of the European legislature.

5. CONCLUSION

In recent years, the co-existence of multiple fundamental rights regimes in Europe has attracted considerable academic attention. An important question that arises concerns the relationship between the various human rights catalogues.[70] This chapter has explored the substantive interplay between two such catalogues, viz. the Charter of Fundamental Rights and

---

[69] It is also possible for the Court to construe discretionary or flexibility clauses found in existing EU instruments – such as art. 3(2) of Regulation (EU) 604/2013 of the European Parliament and of the Council of 26 June 2013 establishing the criteria and mechanisms for determining the Member State responsible for examining an application for international protection lodged in one of the Member States by a third-country national or a stateless person (recast) [2013] OJ L180/31 – as encompassing fundamental rights 'safeguard clauses'. In this regard, see also Case C-528/11 *Zuheyr Frayeh Halaf v Darzhavna agentsia za bezahntsite pri Ministerskia savet* [2013] ECLI: EU:C:2013:342, in which the CJEU clarified that the discretion of a Member State to examine asylum applications even though it is not responsible to do so under the criteria set out in Regulation 604/2013 'is not subject to any particular condition'.

[70] Other scholars have for instance focused on the practical implications of this phenomenon for individuals seeking redress for alleged encroachment of

domestic bills of rights, in the wake of the CJEU's ruling in *Melloni* as to the meaning to be given to Article 53 of the former instrument. Its main finding is that while the significance attributed by the Court to the classic doctrines of primacy and the *effet utile* of Union law is understandable, it would be preferable to see a judicial approach more accepting of flexibility and differentiation in the fundamental rights domain. More particularly, Member States should be given sufficient space to enforce the additional protection offered by their own rights standards as compared to that available under the Charter whenever the administration of EU rules is at stake. There are several tools available to achieve this objective, some of which have already made a tentative appearance in the case law. A firm commitment to continue to use or introduce these techniques in future judgments would be welcome, not in the least because doing so may positively contribute to the political and social legitimacy of the ongoing integration process.

REFERENCES

Albi A, 'From the *Banana* Saga to a Sugar Saga and Beyond: Could the Post-Communist Constitutional Courts Teach the EU a Lesson in the Rule of Law?' (2010) 47 CMLR 791–829.

Anderson D, and Murphy C, 'The Charter of Fundamental Rights' in Biondi A, Eeckhout P and Ripley S (eds), *EU Law After Lisbon* (Oxford University Press 2012) 155–79.

Arnull A, 'Protocol (No 30) on the Application of the Charter of Fundamental Rights of the European Union to Poland and the United Kingdom' in Peers S, Hervey T, Kenner J and Ward A (eds), *The EU Charter of Fundamental Rights – A Commentary* (Hart Publishing 2014) 1595–612.

Avbelj M and Komárek J (eds), *Constitutional Pluralism in the European Union and Beyond* (Hart Publishing 2012).

Besselink L, 'National and Constitutional Identity before and after Lisbon' (2010) 6 *Utrecht Law Review* 36–49.

Besselink L, The Protection of Fundamental Rights post-Lisbon: The Interaction between the EU Charter of Fundamental Rights, the European Convention on Human Rights (ECHR) and National Constitutions' (2012) FIDE General Report.

Besson S, 'Deliberative Demoi-cracy in the European Union: Towards the Deterritorialization of Democracy' in Besson S and Marti JL (eds), *Deliberative Democracy and its Discontents: National and Post-National Challenges* (Ashgate 2006) 181–214.

their rights, see e.g., Catherine Van de Heyning, *Fundamental Rights in the EU: Lost in Complexity?* (doctoral thesis, University of Antwerp 2011).

Brkan M, 'L'arrêt Melloni: nouvelle pierre dans la mosaïque de la protection des droit fondamentaux dans l'Union européenne' (2013) 1 *Revue des affaires européennes* 139–46.

Craig P, *The Lisbon Treaty: Law, Politics, and Treaty Reform* (Oxford University Press 2010).

Davies G, 'Constitutional Disagreement in Europe and the Search for Pluralism', in Avbelj M and Komárek J (eds), *Constitutional Pluralism in the European Union and Beyond* (Hart Publishing 2012) 269–84.

de Boer N, 'Addressing Rights Divergence under the Charter: *Melloni*' (2013) 4 CMLR 1083–103.

de Visser M, 'Dealing with Divergences in Fundamental Rights Standards' (2013) 4 *Maastricht Journal of European and Comparative Law* 576–88.

de Visser M, *Constitutional Review in Europe – A Comparative Analysis* (Hart Publishing 2014).

De Witte B, 'Article 53' in Peers S, Hervey T, Kenner J and Ward A (eds), *The EU Charter of Fundamental Rights – A Commentary* (Hart Publishing 2014) 1523–38.

Dworkin R, *Freedom's Law: The Moral Reading of the American Constitution* (Harvard University Press 1996).

Eleftheriadis P, 'The European Constitution and Cosmopolitan Ideas' (2001) 7 *Columbia Journal of European Law* 21–40.

Gerards J, 'Advisory Opinions, Preliminary Rulings and the New Protocol No.16 to the European Convention on Human Rights – A Comparative and Critical Appraisal' (2014) 21 *Maastricht Journal of European and Comparative Law* 630–51.

Grimm D, 'Comments on the German Constitutional Court's Decision on the Lisbon Treaty: Defending Sovereign Statehood against Transforming the European Union into a State' (2010) 5 EuConst 353–73.

Halberstam D, 'Constitutional Heterarchy: The Centrality of Conflict in the European Union and the United States' in Dunnoff JL and Trachtman JP (eds), *Ruling the World? Constitutionalism, International Law, and Global Governance* (Cambridge University Press, 2009) 326–55.

Iglesias Sanchez S, 'The Court and the Charter: The Impact of the Entry into Force of the Lisbon Treaty on the ECJ's Approach to Fundamental Rights' (2012) 49 *Common Market Law Review* 1565–611.

Jacqué J-P, 'The Accession of the European Union to the European Convention on Human Rights and Fundamental Freedoms' (2011) 48 *Common Market Law Review* 995–1023.

Keller H and Stone Sweet A (eds), *A Europe of Rights: The Impact of the ECHR on National Legal Systems* (Oxford University Press 2008).

Kumm M, 'The Jurisprudence of Constitutional Conflict: Constitutional Supremacy in Europe before and after the Constitutional Treaty' (2005) 11 *European Law Journal* 262–307.

Lenaerts K, 'Federalism and Rights in the European Community' in Katz E and Tarr GA (eds), *Federalism and Rights* (Rowman & Littlefield Publishers 1996) 139–71.

Liisberg JB, 'Does the EU Charter of Fundamental Rights Threaten the Supremacy of Community Law?' (2003) 38 *Common Market Law Review* 1171–99.

Lock T, 'EU Accession to the ECHR: Implications for Judicial Review in Strasbourg' (2010) 35 *European Law Review* 777–99.

MacCormick N, 'The Maastricht Urteil: Sovereignty Now' (1995) 1 *European Law Journal* 259-–66.

Martinico G and Pollicino O (eds), *The National Judicial Treatment of the ECHR and EU Laws: A Comparative Constitutional Perspective* (Europa Law Publishing 2010).

Möstl M, 'Preconditions and Limits of Mutual Recognition' (2010) 47 *Common Market Law Review* 405–36.

Nicolaides K, 'We, the Peoples of Europe …' (2004) 83 *Foreign Affairs* 97–110.

Nowak T, Amtenbrink F, Hertogh M and Wissink M, *National Judges as European Union Judges: Knowledge, Experience and Attitudes of Lower Court Judges in Germany and the Netherlands* (Eleven Publishers 2012).

Saiz Arnaiz A and Alcoberro Liivina C (eds), *National Constitutional Identity and European Integration* (Intersentia 2013).

Torres Pérez A, 'Spanish Constitutional Court, Constitutional Dialogue on the European Arrest Warrant: The Spanish Constitutional Court Knocking on Luxembourg's Door' (2012) 8 EuConst 105–27.

Torres Pérez A, 'The Dual System of Rights Protection in the European Union in Light of US Federalism' in Cloots E, De Baere G and Sottiaux S (eds), *Federalism in the European Union* (Hart Publishing 2012) 110–30.

Torres Pérez A, '*Melloni* in Three Acts: From Dialogue to Monologue' (2014) 10 EuConst 308–31.

Van de Heyning C, *Fundamental Rights in the EU: Lost in Complexity?* (doctoral thesis, University of Antwerp 2011).

von Bogdandy A and Schill S, 'Overcoming Absolute Primacy: Respect for National Identity under the Lisbon Treaty', (2011) 48 *Common Market Law Review* 1417–53.

Voßkuhle A, 'Multilevel Cooperation of the European Constitutional Courts: Der Europäische Verfassungsgerichtsverbund' (2010) 6 EuConst 175–98.

Waldron J, 'The Core of the Case Against Judicial Review' (2006) 115 *Yale Law Journal* 1348–406.

Weiler JHH, *The Constitution of Europe – 'Do the New Clothes have an Emperor?' and Other Essays on European Integration* (Cambridge University Press 1999).

PART II

Policy-specific aspects

8. Differentiated integration in EMU

Stefaan Van den Bogaert and Vestert Borger

1. INTRODUCTION

Economic and Monetary Union (EMU) is often regarded as the paradigm of differentiated integration in the EU. The straightforward explanation is that, up to today, only 19 of the 28 Member States have exchanged their national currencies for the euro. The remaining Member States have not adopted the single currency yet, and they may very well not all do so in the foreseeable future. But differentiation is a concept that covers multiple realities within EMU, reaching far beyond the mere *differentiation in terms of membership* of the euro area. In a desperate effort to contain the damage caused by the debt crisis and subsequently to strengthen the economic set-up of EMU, the Union and the Member States have pulled out all the stops and have taken decisive action, thereby giving rise to three other forms of differentiation: in *participation*, in *objectives and instruments* and in *law*.

Differentiation in participation is closest to that in membership, the difference being that it does not run along the lines of Member States within and outside the euro area. Given that states take part in rescue and structural reform measures to varying degrees and in differing compositions, it no longer suffices merely to distinguish between the 'ins' and the 'outs'. These measures, in turn, equip the Union and its Member States with a larger set of tools to conduct economic policy, thereby giving rise to *differentiation in terms of objectives and instruments*. Since Member States at times have ventured out of the safe confines of the EU Treaties to put in place these tools, in particular by concluding *inter se* agreements, the crisis has led to *differentiation in law* as well. To each of these forms of differentiation, old and new, we will look in turn.

2. DIFFERENTIATION IN TERMS OF MEMBERSHIP AND PARTICIPATION

2.1 Membership of the Euro Area

Within the Economic and Monetary Union, differentiation is to be found first and foremost in terms of *membership*. Currently, not all Member States of the EU have adopted the euro as the Union's single currency and have consequently become members of the euro area. It cannot be completely ruled out that at some point in the future there will be a complete overlap between the EU and the euro zone; however, as things stand now, this scenario seems rather unlikely.

EU Member States cannot simply decide overnight to accede to the euro area and to substitute the national currency with the euro. In order to be able to participate in the single currency, Member States must fulfil certain requirements. These requirements are both of a legal and economic nature. Legally speaking, Member States must ensure that their national legislation is compatible with the Union Treaties and the Statute of the European System of Central Banks (ESCB) and of the European Central Bank (ECB). In particular, this means respect must be had for the independence of the ECB and national central banks (NCBs) in the performance of their tasks.[1] Better known are the economic criteria, also called the 'convergence criteria'. They are laid down in Article 140(1) TFEU and are further specified in Protocol No. 13. In essence, they boil down to the following:

- the achievement of a high degree of price stability: the average rate of inflation, observed over a period of one year before the examination, must not exceed by more than 1.5 per cent that of, at most, the three best-performing Member States;
- the sustainability of the government financial position: the annual government budget deficit should not exceed 3 per cent of GDP and the total government debt should not exceed 60 per cent of GDP;[2]
- the observance of the normal fluctuation margins provided for by the exchange-rate mechanism of the European Monetary System (ERM II) for at least two years prior to examination;
- the durability of convergence achieved by the Member States, in particular in terms of interest rates: observed over a period of one

---

1 Arts 130, 131 and 140(1) TFEU.

2 On the meaning of excessive deficits see text to note 19 *infra*.

year before examination a Member State's long-term nominal interest rate levels may not exceed by more than 2 per cent that of, at most, the three best performing Member States in terms of price stability.

In addition to these central criteria, Article 140(1) TFEU makes clear that Member States' economic performance is also assessed in relation to the integration of markets, the situation and development of the balance of payments on current account and the development of unit labour costs.

Following the procedure and the timetable set out in the Treaty, the Council, meeting at the level of heads of state and government, decided on 3 May 1998 that 11 of the then 15 EU Member States satisfied the necessary conditions for the adoption of the single currency on 1 January 1999: the six founding Member States, Belgium, Luxembourg, the Netherlands, Germany, France, and Italy, as well as Spain, Portugal, Ireland, Austria and Finland.[3] Only the UK, Sweden, Denmark and Greece remained on the sidelines: the first three voluntarily, the last unwillingly. In July 2000, one and a half years after the introduction of the euro as an accounting currency, but still before the physical euro coins and banknotes would enter into circulation on 1 January 2002, the Council also allowed Greece entry into the euro zone.

Since the introduction of the euro, the EU has further enlarged from 15 to currently 28 Member States. At the same time, euro-area membership has increased from 12 to 19. This is not surprising. Adoption of the euro is a condition for EU membership. The new Member States are committed to work towards the introduction of the euro. At the time of their accession in 2004, 2007 or 2013, the 13 new Member States did not meet the criteria for entry to the euro area. In their Treaties of Accession, they were allowed the time to make the necessary adjustments. In the meantime, seven of the new Member States have managed to fulfil the convergence criteria and have adopted the euro: Slovenia adopted the single currency on 1 January 2007, Cyprus and Malta on 1 January 2008, Slovakia on 1 January 2009, Estonia on 1 January 2011, and Latvia on 1 January 2014. Until now, Lithuania was the latest Member State to join the euro zone on 1 January 2015.

For the time being, the six remaining new Member States – Poland, Czech Republic, Hungary, Romania, Bulgaria and Croatia – do not meet the convergence criteria. They are still considered as 'Member States

[3] Council Decision (EC) 98/317 of 3 May 1998 in accordance with art. 109j(4) of the Treaty [1998] OJ L139/30.

with a derogation'. At least once every two years, or at the request of the Member States with a derogation, their progress and compliance vis-à-vis the legal and economic criteria is monitored by the Commission and the ECB. Their reports set in motion a procedure which may eventually lead to the Council deciding to abrogate a Member State's derogation and to irrevocably fix the rate at which the euro shall be substituted for its currency.[4]

Until that time, the Member States with a derogation are subject to a specific legal regime set out in Articles 139–144 TFEU.[5] This has a number of important legal consequences. For example, when Member States with a derogation incur excessive deficits, they cannot be coerced into remedying them.[6] Moreover, when a Member State with a derogation encounters balance of payment difficulties, or is in danger of ending up in such a situation, it may qualify for the granting of mutual assistance by the Council.[7] During the last couple of years, Hungary, Latvia and Romania have benefited from such assistance.

Besides the 19 euro-area Member States and the six Member States with a derogation, three Member States that originally remained outside the euro area – Denmark, the UK and Sweden – find themselves in special situations. The first two states enjoy special legal status, put in place to overcome ratification problems with the Treaty of Maastricht, which are regulated in Protocols annexed to the Union Treaties.[8] Denmark obtained an exemption clause from EMU. As a result of this exemption, and unlike Member States with a derogation, Denmark will not have to introduce the euro unless it requests that its exemption be abrogated.[9] For the remainder, however, its legal position is similar to that of Member States with a derogation. The UK's position is more difficult. Like Denmark, it is not obliged to introduce the euro, unless it notifies the Council of its intention to do so.[10] However, unlike Denmark, the UK's legal position differs substantially from Member States with a derogation in other respects as well. The Protocol governing its status

---

4 Art. 140(1)–(3) TFEU.

5 See also Chapter IX of Protocol No. 4 on the Statute of the ESCB and of the ECB.

6 Art. 139(2)(b) TFEU.

7 Arts 143–144 TFEU.

8 Protocol No. 15 on certain provisions relating to the United Kingdom of Great Britain and Northern Ireland; Protocol No. 16 on certain provisions relating to Denmark.

9 Para. 2 of Protocol No. 16, ibid.

10 Para. 4 of Protocol No. 15, ibid.

sets out, in great detail, which of the Treaty provisions on EMU apply to it and which do not. One of the most eye-catching differences is that, unlike Member States with a derogation, the UK is not subject to the requirement in Article 130 TFEU to secure the independence of its central bank.

Conversely, Sweden does not benefit from a special legal status. Officially, it is therefore considered as a Member State with a derogation, meaning that it is under a Treaty obligation to adopt the euro once it complies with the convergence criteria. However, in a popular referendum held on 14 September 2003, 55.9 per cent of voters made it clear they were against membership of the currency union. As a consequence, the Swedish government decided not to adopt the euro for the time being. Most political parties in Sweden appear to believe that euro-area membership would be beneficial to the country, but they remain committed to respecting the popular opinion, which, if one may believe the polls, remains negative. For now, the EU *de facto* accepts that Sweden is staying outside the euro zone of its own will.

What all Member States outside the currency union have in common, however, is that they do not participate in the Euro Group, an informal meeting of the finance ministers of the euro area, the ECB and the Commission.[11] Similarly, they do not participate in meetings of the Euro Summit. This body, which has received specific recognition in the Treaty on Stability Coordination and Governance (TSCG),[12] consists of the euro area Heads of State and Government and the presidents of the Commission and the ECB. Both the Euro Group and the Euro Summit aim at discussing questions related to the governance of the currency union. During the last years, they have been central in combating the financial and sovereign debt crises.

2.2 Participation in Economic Governance

So far, we have primarily distinguished between the Member States that are 'in' and those that are 'out' in terms of euro-area membership.

---

[11] Art. 137 TFEU and Protocol No. 14 on the Euro Group.

[12] Art. 12 of the Treaty on Stability, Coordination and Governance in the Economic and Monetary Union, Brussels, 2 March 2012 (hereinafter 'TSCG'). Note, however, that art. 12(3) TSCG makes clear that Contracting Parties that have not (yet) adopted the single currency shall participate in Euro Summit meetings concerning competitiveness, the global architecture of the euro area and the fundamental rules that will apply to it in the future, as well as in discussions on specific issues of implementation of the TSCG.

However, as a result of the crisis, it no longer suffices merely to differentiate among Member States along these lines. A vast number of legal and political measures has been taken to combat the crisis and to strengthen the EU's economic governance system. Some of them apply only to the 'ins', others to 'ins' and 'outs', and some to a group of states existing of 'ins' but some 'outs' as well. As a result, the system of economic governance has developed into a patchwork of measures, cutting across the traditional distinction between those states that have adopted the euro and those that have not. Three examples serve to illustrate this development.

A measure that only applies to euro-area Member States is the European Stability Mechanism (ESM). This permanent assistance fund has been established on the basis of an international treaty which only the euro-area Member States have signed.[13] The situation already becomes less straightforward with the 'six-pack', a set of five Union regulations and one directive that tighten budgetary discipline and create a system to prevent and detect other macro-economic imbalances.[14] Some of these legislative instruments apply to 'ins' and 'outs', whereas others (in particular those regulating sanctions) only apply to the states belonging to the euro area. The TSCG, containing the so-called fiscal compact with the 'balanced budget rule', makes it even more difficult. It has been concluded by 'ins' and 'outs', except for the UK and the Czech Republic. However, part of its content only applies to those Contracting Parties that have adopted the euro.[15]

These three measures are only some of the most obvious examples of how, as a result of the crisis, Member States participate in economic governance initiatives to varying degrees and in different compositions. Whereas the setup of EMU was already far from straightforward at its inception, with different legal regimes applying to Member States within and outside the euro area, this development risks complicating matters even further.

---

[13] Treaty establishing the European Stability Mechanism, Brussels, 2 February 2012 (hereinafter 'ESM Treaty').

[14] Regulation (EU) 1173/2011 [2011] OJ L306/1; Regulation (EU) 1174/2011 [2011] OJ L306/8; Regulation (EU) 1175/2011 [2011] OJ L306/12; Regulation (EU) 1176/2011 [2011] OJ L306/25; Council Regulation (EU) 1177/2011 [2011] OJ L306/33; Directive 2011/85/EU [2011] OJ L306/41.

[15] See art. 14(5) TSCG.

3. DIFFERENTIATION IN POLICY GOALS AND INSTRUMENTS

The differentiation in participation that has been described above is not a self-fulfilling mechanism. It takes place for a reason. This reason, in very general terms, is the need to strengthen the EMU, both in the short term and in the long run. Measures aimed at achieving this goal engender a second form of differentiation: that in policy *goals* and *instruments*. In order to grasp this second form of differentiation fully, it is necessary first to examine the essential features of the Treaty framework governing the EMU as it stood before the crisis.

3.1 The Original EMU Treaty Framework: Focus on Price Stability

The original Treaty framework on EMU was greatly inspired by the goal of safeguarding *price stability*. In fact, this was not only a goal of EMU but of the Union as such. Telling in this regard is Article 3(3) TEU, which states that the Union shall work for the sustainable development of Europe based, inter alia, on price stability. Article 119(3) TFEU, the starting provision of the Title on economic and monetary policy in the TFEU, similarly declares that the Union's activities in this field shall be based on the guiding principle of stable prices.[16] When looking at the subsequent specific Treaty provisions on EMU, the focus on price stability first and foremost becomes apparent from the fact that the primary objective of the monetary policy of the ESCB is price stability.[17] Yet, it is not confined to the realm of monetary policy but also underlies many provisions of the economic policy chapter, which is of particular concern in this chapter.

To maintain price stability, national governments must display budgetary prudence. Several provisions of the economic policy chapter in the TFEU are focused on bringing precisely this about, most notably Articles 123–126 TFEU. These provisions can be divided into two groups: those

---

[16] Next to sound public finances and monetary conditions and a sustainable balance of payments.

[17] Art. 127(1) TFEU and art. 2 of Protocol No. 4 on the Statute of the ESCB and of the ECB. As long as not all Member States have joined the currency union, this goal only applies to the Eurosystem, which consists of the ECB and the national central banks of the Member States belonging to the currency union (art. 282(1) TFEU). Member States with a derogation, as art. 139(2)(c) TFEU makes clear, are not subject to this goal. The same goes for Denmark and the UK. See §4 of Protocol No. 15 (n 8) and Protocol No. 16 (n 8).

that try to entice Member States to prudent budgetary policy through the instrument of *public discipline* and those that use the instrument of *market discipline*.[18]

On the one hand, Article 126 TFEU is a representative of the instrument of public discipline. Its first paragraph obliges Member States to avoid excessive deficits. Article 1 of Protocol No. 12 further clarifies what is to be understood as excessive. The reference value for government deficits is set at 3 per cent of GDP, the one for debts at 60 per cent of GDP.[19] Paragraphs 126(2)–126(12) TFEU set out the excessive deficit procedure on the basis of which the Commission and the Council examine compliance with these reference values. This procedure is further elaborated upon in the corrective part of the Stability and Growth Pact (SGP)[20] and may result in the imposition of sanctions by the Council.[21]

On the other hand, Articles 123–125 TFEU focus on market discipline. What these articles have in common is that they try to ensure that a Member State displays budgetary prudence by subjecting it to the disciplining force of the markets. They do so by ruling out several other possible financing channels, thereby aiming to achieve that Member

---

[18] See also Stefaan Van den Bogaert and Vestert Borger, 'Twenty Years after Maastricht: The Coming of Age of the EMU?' in Maartje de Visser and Anne Pieter van der Mei (eds), *The Treaty on European Union 1993-2013: Reflections from Maastricht* (Intersentia 2013) 451, 454–5.

[19] In addition to the obligation to avoid excessive deficits, Member States are also under an obligation to achieve so-called Medium Term Budgetary Objectives (MTOs), which may diverge from the requirement of a budget that is close to balance or in surplus position. For Member States belonging to the euro area or those participating in ERM 2, the MTO ranges between –1 per cent of GDP and balance or surplus. See art. 2a of Regulation (EC) 1466/97 on the strengthening of the surveillance of budgetary positions and the surveillance and coordination of economic policies [1997] OJ L209/1, as last amended by Regulation (EU) 1175/2011 [2011] OJ L306/12. The Contracting Parties to the TSCG have further tightened their MTO obligations in art. 3 by lifting the lower limit to –0.5 per cent of GDP.

[20] Regulation (EC) 1467/97 on speeding up and clarifying the implementation of the excessive deficit procedure [1997] OJ L209/6, as last amended by Regulation (EU) 1177/2011 [2011] OJ L306/33.

[21] The sanctioning possibilities for Member States belonging to the euro area have been enhanced with the entry into force of the six-pack. As far as the excessive deficit procedure is concerned, this has been done most notably through the introduction of 'reverse qualified majority voting' and the possibility to impose sanctions at an earlier stage of the procedure. See Regulation (EU) 1173/2011 [2011] OJ L306/1.

States have to finance themselves on the markets just like private entities.[22] Article 123 TFEU prohibits overdraft facilities or other credit facilities with the ECB or national central banks in favour of, inter alia, national authorities. Moreover, it excludes the possibility that the ECB or national central banks purchase their debt instruments directly. Article 124 TFEU contains a prohibition on privileged access, which means that it forbids any measures, not based on prudential considerations, establishing privileged access to financial institutions for, inter alia, national authorities. Article 125 TFEU, to conclude, contains a prohibition on bail-outs by determining that neither the Union nor a Member State shall be liable for or assume the financial commitments of other national authorities.

The ultimate consequence of these three prohibitions for fiscally negligent Member States, or so it was thought by many before the start of the crisis,[23] was that they would be left to their own devices if things came to the crunch, possibly even leading to a sovereign default. In other words, if a Member State was no longer able to finance itself on the markets, or only at unsustainable rates, it would have to face the consequences itself and would, in principle, not be bailed out by the Union (including the ECB) or other Member States. The only counterweight in this regard, at least as far as Member States in the euro area are concerned,[24] was provided by Article 122(2) TFEU; this provision allows the Union to grant financial assistance to a Member State that is in difficulty, or is threatened with severe difficulties, caused by 'exceptional occurrences' beyond its control.

3.2 Enlarging the Focus: Financial Stability of the Union

The sovereign debt crisis has exposed several weaknesses of this original Treaty set-up. This chapter will focus on those related to financial

---

[22] Fabian Amtenbrink, Leendert Adrie Geelhoed and Suzanne Kingston, 'Economic, Monetary and Social Policy' in Paul Joan George Kapteyn et al. (eds), *Kapteyn & VerLoren van Themaat – The Law of the European Union and the European Communities* (Kluwer Law International 2008) 881, 907–9.

[23] Jean-Victor Louis, 'Guest Editorial: The No-bailout Clause and Rescue Packages' (2010) CMLR 979–80.

[24] Member States with a derogation as well as the UK and Denmark can also benefit from balance of payments assistance on the basis of art. 143 TFEU.

stability.[25] Views about the exact meaning of financial stability differ and the notion is therefore difficult to define.[26] Schoenmaker, however, explains that it is closely related to systemic risk, which he defines as 'the risk that an event will trigger a loss of economic value or confidence in a substantial portion of the financial system that is serious enough to have significant adverse effects on the real economy'.[27] During the debt crisis this risk was, and to a lesser certain extent still is, omnipresent. The risk posed by a Greek default, the first state to run into trouble on the markets at the end of 2009, as well as that of other states in the periphery of the euro area, for financial stability was enormously high.

The original Treaty system of EMU, however, was not up to the challenge of facing this financial stability risk, both at the level of *goals* as well as *instruments*. In terms of policy goals, the system was strongly focused on price stability, but it paid relatively little attention to financial stability.[28] Illustrative in this regard is that financial stability does not feature among the guiding principles in Article 119(3) TFEU that need to be taken into account by the Union and the Member States when conducting economic and monetary policy.[29] A similar neglect of financial stability becomes apparent from the system's *instruments*. They were also strongly targeted at budgetary discipline and price stability, but they were not necessarily apt for maintaining financial stability, especially in times of crisis. Exemplary in this regard are the instruments focusing on market discipline, in particular the prohibitions on monetary financing and bail-out. Leaving a Member State on its own – the essential idea behind these prohibitions – proved not to be a viable option when the crisis erupted in 2010. The risk that the crisis would spread from one

---

[25] For a much more elaborate overview of the shortcomings of the EMU governance system see e.g., Jean-Pisany Ferry, *The Known Unknowns and Unknown Unknowns of EMU* (Bruegel Policy Contribution 2012/18, 2012).

[26] See also Rosa Maria Lastra, 'Systemic Risk, SIFIs and Financial Stability' (2011) *Capital Markets Law Journal* 197, 207–8.

[27] Dirk Schoenmaker, 'The Financial Trilemma' (2011) *Economics Letters* 57, 57.

[28] See also Vestert Borger, 'How the Debt Crisis Exposes the Development of Solidarity in the Euro Area' (2013b) EUConst 7, 25.

[29] The only reference to financial stability could be found in art. 127(5) TFEU which states that: 'The ESCB shall contribute to the smooth conduct of policies pursued by the competent authorities relating to the prudential supervision of credit institutions and the stability of the financial system.'

state to another, thereby affecting the currency union at large, was (feared to be) too high.[30]

Be that as it may, this neglect of financial stability is now in the process of being remedied. The result of this process is a further differentiation in terms of policy goals and instruments, which means that, at both levels, the predominant focus on price stability is exchanged for one that also takes financial stability into account. One measure, the ESM, already referred to above,[31] is particularly illustrative of this form of differentiation. Interestingly, in *Pringle* the Court was asked to rule upon the compatibility of this permanent assistance mechanism with Union law. Let us see how it dealt with this task and approached the issue of differentiation in EMU.

The ESM was not the first assistance instrument that was put in place during the crisis to help out financially distressed Member States in the euro area. As a first response to the crisis, on 2 May 2010, euro-area Member States established the Greek Loan Facility (GLF), a set of pooled bilateral loans, worth €110 bn, that was administered by the Commission.[32] Shortly after the launch of the GLF, and faced with the fact that the crisis had not beed confined to Greece, the Union and the Member States decided to establish two temporary rescue facilities, the *European Financial Stabilisation Mechanism* (EFSM) and the *European Financial Stability Facility* (EFSF).[33] The EFSM is a Union law instrument, stemming from a Regulation based on the emergency clause in Article 122(2) TFEU,[34] with a firepower of €60 bn. The EFSF is not based on Union law. Instead, it forms a 'Special Purpose Vehicle' (SPV) with an effective lending capacity of €440 bn, moulded in the form of a public company (Société Anonyme) under Luxembourg private law.[35]

---

[30] Mark Mink and Jakob de Haan, 'Contagion during the Greek Sovereign Debt Crisis' (2013) *Journal of International Money and Finance* 102, 103.

[31] See text to *supra* note 13.

[32] See also Alberto de Gregorio Merino, 'Legal Developments in the Economic and Monetary Union During the Debt Crisis: The Mechanisms of Financial Assistance' (2012) CMLR 1613, 1616–18.

[33] These decisions were taken on 9 May 2010. See Decision 9614/10 of the representatives of the governments of the euro-area Member States Meeting within the Council of the European Union, 9 May 2010 Brussels. See also Conclusions of the (Ecofin) Council, 9602/10, 9 May 2010, Brussels. See also De Gregorio Merino (n 32) 1618–24.

[34] Regulation (EU) 407/2010 establishing a European financial stabilisation mechanism [2010] OJ L118/1.

[35] Most of the governing arrangements concerning the EFSF are laid down in a framework agreement concluded between the EFSF and the euro-area

Given the temporary nature of these assistance facilities, awareness quickly grew that a permanent assistance mechanism would have to be put in place. At its meeting of 28–29 October 2010, the European Council decided to create a permanent crisis resolution mechanism. It entrusted its president Van Rompuy with the task of consulting the Member States 'on a limited treaty change required to that effect, not modifying Article 125 TFEU'.[36] At its next meeting on 16–17 December 2010, the European Council decided to launch the simplified Treaty revision procedure laid down in Article 48(6) TEU, thereby aiming to add a third paragraph to Article 136 TFEU, a provision specifically targeted at the euro area.[37] This third paragraph reads:

> The Member States whose currency is the euro may establish a stability mechanism to be activated if indispensable to safeguard the stability of the euro area as a whole. The granting of any required financial assistance under the mechanism will be made subject to strict conditionality.[38]

From this text the differentiation in policy goals and instruments becomes clearly apparent. In terms of policy goals, this provision aims at the stability of the euro area as a whole. In terms of instruments, by providing for the possibility of establishing a stability mechanism, this provision shifts away from the no-bail-out clause's focus on market discipline, recognizing that different instruments are needed to safeguard financial stability in times of crisis.

On 25 March 2011, the European Council adopted Decision 2011/199 adding this third paragraph to Article 136 TFEU.[39] The Decision entered into force on 1 May 2013 after all Member States had approved it in accordance with their national constitutional requirements. It should be noted that this date was well beyond the initially envisaged date of 1 January 2013.[40] While the amendment procedure of Article 48(6) TEU was taking place, the Member States of the euro area started working on a separate international treaty in order to establish the permanent stability

---

Member States as its shareholders. This Framework Agreement is available at <http://www.efsf.europa.eu/about/index.htm> accessed 31 March 2014.

[36] European Council Conclusions, Brussels, 28–29 October 2010, para. 2.

[37] European Council Conclusions, Brussels, 16–17 December 2010, para. 2.

[38] Ibid., Annex I.

[39] European Council Decision (EU) 2011/199 amending art. 136 on the Treaty on the Functioning of the European Union with regard to a stability mechanism for Member States whose currency is the euro [2011] OJ L91/1.

[40] This date is later than the envisaged one of 1 January 2013 set out in art. 2. This delay was due to ratification problems in the Czech Republic.

mechanism. This treaty was concluded by the euro-area Member States on 2 February 2012. It entered into force on 27 September 2012,[41] directly after the German Constitutional Court, the *Bundesverfassungsgericht* (*BVerfG*), had rejected applications for temporary injunctions aiming to prevent the German ratification of the treaty.[42] The ESM was officially inaugurated on 8 October 2012.[43] Given that it is based on an international treaty, the ESM operates as an organization under public international law. It has an effective lending capacity of €500 bn.[44] Assistance can be granted in various ways: via precautionary assistance, loans, primary and secondary market support facilities, and the indirect recapitalization of financial institutions.[45]

In *Pringle*, the Court of Justice of the EU was asked to rule upon the compatibility of the ESM with Union law. The case reached the European Court via preliminary questions asked by the Irish Supreme Court.[46] Like the *BVerfG*, the Irish Court too had to rule on complaints

---

41 It was initially planned that the ESM Treaty would enter into force as of July 2012. However, art. 48(1) ESM Treaty prescribes that the treaty will only enter into force once the instruments of ratification or approval have been deposited by Contracting Parties whose capital subscription represents no less than 90 per cent of the ESM's authorized capital stock. Given that Germany's contribution to the capital stock amounts to 27 per cent, the Treaty could not enter into force before Germany had ratified it.

42 BVerfG, 2 BvR 1390/12. The *BVerfG* made ratification subject to two conditions, to be ensured by declarations under international law upon ratification of the ESM Treaty. First, the amount of Germany's payment obligations under the ESM Treaty cannot exceed its maximum subscription to the authorized capital stock without the consent of the *Bundestag*. Second, the ESM Treaty's provisions on the inviolability of documents, professional secrecy and immunities of persons cannot stand in the way of the comprehensive information of the *Bundestag* and *Bundesrat*. The declaration ensuring these conditions was also adopted by the euro-area Member States on 27 September 2012. It should be noted that the *BVerfG* rendered its judgment in the principal proceedings on 18 March 2014. It declared the constitutional complaints and the *Organstreit* proceedings against, inter alia, the ESM Treaty inadmissible or unfounded. See BVerfG, 2 BvR 1390/12.

43 See Press release, 'European Stability Mechanism (ESM) is inaugurated' (8 October 2012), available at <www.esm.europa.eu/press/releases/20121008_esm-is-inaugurated.htm> accessed 10 July 2014.

44 Recital 6 ESM Treaty. With a view to achieving this lending capacity, the authorized capital stock is set at €700 bn. See art. 8(1) ESM Treaty.

45 See arts 14–18 ESM Treaty. The list of instruments can be reviewed by the Board of Governors. See art. 19 ESM Treaty.

46 Case C-370/12 *Thomas Pringle v Government of Ireland, Ireland, the Attorney General* [2012] ECLI:EU:C:2012:756.

against the ESM. One of the questions it asked of its European counterpart was whether the ESM Treaty was in conformity with the no-bail-out clause in Article 125 TFEU.[47]

From a legal point of view, arguably the soundest reasoning, theoretically speaking, would be to say that Article 136(3) TFEU constitutes an exception to the no-bail-out clause that clears the way for the ESM Treaty by allowing Member States to establish this assistance mechanism.[48] In other words, by limiting the scope of application of the no-bail-out clause, Article 136(3) TFEU makes it possible for the differentiation in policy instruments and goals to take place. However, for two reasons it was difficult for the Court to follow this reasoning. First, in the run up to the adoption of Decision 2011/199, the European Council had made it clear that any Treaty amendment should not modify the no-bail-out clause.[49] Although the Court is obviously not bound by such statements, it will surely have taken note of it. Second, and perhaps more important, the ESM Treaty entered into force on 27 September 2012 and thus before Decision 2011/199. Consequently, Article 136(3) TFEU was not yet operative at that time. If Article 136(3) TFEU were to constitute an exception to the no-bail-out clause, the establishment of the ESM before the entry into force of Decision 2011/199 would have amounted to a violation of Union law.

The Court, perhaps because of these reasons, adopted a different reasoning which consisted of three steps.[50] First, it looked at the text of Article 125 TFEU. Given that it only speaks about '*being liable for* or *assuming the commitments* of other Member States', the Court stated that the provision does not intend to prohibit the Union or the Member States from granting any form of assistance whatsoever to another Member State.[51] Second, it turned to the purpose of the no-bail-out clause in order to determine which forms of financial assistance would be compatible

---

[47] For extensive analyses of the European Court's judgment in the *Pringle* case see, among others, Vestert Borger, 'The ESM and the European Court's Predicament in *Pringle*' (2013) GLJ 113–40; Bruno de Witte and Thomas Beukers, 'The Court of Justice Approves the Creation of the European Stability Mechanism outside the EU Legal Order: *Pringle*' (2013a) CMLR 805–40; Stanislas Adam and Francisco Javier Mena Parras, 'The European Stability Mechanism Through the Legal Meanderings of the Union's Constitutionalism: Comment on Pringle' (2013) EL Rev. 848–65; Chris Koedooder, 'Pringle Judgment: Economic and/or Monetary Union' (2013) Fordham Int'l L.J. 111–46.

[48] See also Borger (n 47) 129–37.

[49] See text to note 36 *supra*.

[50] See also Borger (n 47) 129-132.

[51] *Pringle* (n 46), paras 130–132.

with the provision. This purpose, according to the Court, was to stimulate budgetary discipline on the side of Member States by subjecting them to the forces of the market.[52] Third, and this is crucial for the issue of differentiation, the Court then reasoned that the objective of budgetary discipline only constitutes an intermediate one, contributing in turn to the attainment of a higher objective: *financial stability* of the currency union.[53] Consequently, Article 125 TFEU does not prohibit the granting of assistance by one or more Member States to another Member State, provided that: (1) the latter remains responsible for its commitments to its creditors; (2) it is subject to conditions such as to prompt the receiving state to budgetary prudence; and (3) it is only granted if indispensable for the safeguarding of the financial stability of the currency union.[54] Given that the ESM Treaty complies with these conditions, the Court found that it does not violate the no-bailout clause.[55]

Paradoxically, with this reasoning the Court has approved of the recent differentiation in policy goals and instruments by denying its novelty. By reading the *objective* of financial stability into the no-bail-out clause, the Court can reach the conclusion that Member States have always had the possibility to establish an assistance *instrument* like the ESM. As a result, conclusion and ratification of the ESM Treaty is not dependent on the entry into force of Decision 2011/199 which integrates Article 136(3) into the TFEU.[56] Given the difficulties surrounding the Court in *Pringle*, it could hardly have adopted a different reasoning. This reasoning does have as a consequence, however, that instead of symbolizing the recent differentiation in EMU, Article 136(3) TFEU is reduced to a provision that merely makes explicit an assistance possibility that, according to the Court, has always been there.

Recently, the Court pronounced itself again on the issue of differentiation in policy goals and instruments in *Gauweiler*.[57] On 14 January 2014, the *BVerfG* decided to ask preliminary questions about the compatibility of the ECB's Outright Monetary Transactions Programme (OMT-programme) with Union law.[58] The ECB announced the technical

---

52 Ibid., para. 135.
53 Ibid.
54 Ibid., paras 136–137.
55 Ibid., paras 138–147.
56 Ibid., para. 185.
57 Case C-62/14 *Gauweiler ao v Deutscher Bundestag* [2015], ECLI:EU:C:2015:400.
58 BVerfG, 2 BvR 2728/13, 14 January 2014.

features of this programme on 6 September 2012[59] after its president Mario Draghi had already said on 26 July 2012 that, within its mandate, the ECB would do whatever it takes to preserve the euro, adding the words: 'and believe me, it will be enough'.[60] With the programme, the ECB aims to combat tensions in euro area government bond markets with a view to safeguarding an appropriate monetary policy transmission and the singleness of this policy. A crucial feature of the OMT-programme is that it enables the ECB to intervene on the secondary markets for euro-area government bonds, provided that the Member State whose bonds are purchased is subject to an EFSF/ESM macroeconomic adjustment programme or a precautionary programme. Although the programme has not yet been incorporated into Union law,[61] its mere announcement immediately had effect on the markets, considerably bringing down interest rates for government bonds of peripheral euro-area Member States.

Without entering into the details of the case,[62] it can be observed that one of the issues that the Court was asked to address concerned the relationship between the OMT-programme and the prohibition of monetary financing in Article 123 TFEU. As stated above, this provision prohibits the ECB from purchasing government bonds from Member States directly ('primary market intervention'). However, the preamble to Regulation 3603/93, which specifies definitions for the prohibition in Article 123 TFEU, indicates that interventions on the secondary market

---

[59] ECB Press release, 'Technical features of Outright Monetary Transactions', 6 September 2012, available at <www.ecb.europa.eu/press/pr/date/2012/html/pr120906_1.en.html> accessed 10 July 2014.

[60] Verbatim of the remarks made by Mario Draghi at the Global Investment Conference in London, 26 July 2012, available at <www.ecb.europa.eu/press/key/date/2012/html/sp120726.en.html> accessed 10 July 2014.

[61] According to the *BVerfG*, the fact that the OMT-programme had (and still has) not (yet) been laid down in Union law should not prevent the Court from dealing with its questions on substance. Given that the *BVerfG* had the obligation to grant preventive legal protection, the Court's answers to its questions were relevant to the constitutional proceedings even if the OMT-programme could not (yet) be qualified as an 'act' within the meaning of art. 267(1)(b) TFEU. See BVerfG, 2 BvR 2728/13, 14 January 2014, paras 34–35, 101.

[62] In its Order, the *BVerfG* had not only set out the questions it asked to the Court, but it had also given its own, very critical, analysis of the OMT's compatibility with Union law. For a thorough discussion of this analysis see Thomas Beukers, 'The Bundesverfassungsgericht Preliminary Reference on the OMT Program: "In the ECB We Do Not Trust. What About You?"' (2014) GLJ 343–68; V. Borger, 'Outright Monetary Transactions and the Stability Mandate of the ECB: *Gauweiler* (2016) CMLR 139–196.

are also not without limits.[63] Its seventh recital states that purchases on the secondary market must not be used to circumvent the objectives of the prohibition. This raises the question as to what exactly these objectives are. Interestingly, and contrary to its approach to the no-bail-out clause in *Pringle*, this time the Court was not prepared to link the monetary financing prohibition to the objective of financial stability. The goals pursued by the prohibition on monetary financing have therefore not experienced a similar development as a result of the crisis as those of the no-bail-out clause.[64] Whereas the latter is now aimed at the higher and ultimate objective of financial stability, the former is still geared towards the goals the Treaty drafters attributed to it when the Treaty on European Union was signed more than 20 years ago.

4. DIFFERENTIATION IN LAW

In the field of EMU, differentiation does not stay confined to membership, participation and policy goals and instruments. Closely linked to these kinds of differentiation is differentiation in the law itself, manifesting itself in a tendency of the Member States to give further shape to economic governance not only within the confines of the Union Treaties but also outside them. This is not a new phenomenon: throughout the European integration process, Member States have made use of other cooperation vehicles, in particular international treaties which they can conclude as subjects of international law.[65] However, as a result of the crisis these legal instruments have gained renewed importance due to their pivotal importance for the stability of the currency union.

4.1 About EFSF, ESM and TSCG

In the early days of the debt crisis, back in May 2010, the euro-area states first resorted to cooperation outside the Union Treaties when they decided to establish the EFSF, a special-purpose vehicle based on

---

[63] Regulation (EC) 3603/93 specifying definitions for the application of the prohibitions referred to in arts 104 and 104b(1) of the Treaty [1993] OJ L332/1.

[64] See for more detail Borger (n 62) 188–191.

[65] For an analysis of such treaties concluded between all or some Member States see Bruno de Witte, 'Chameleonic Member States: Differentiation By Means of Partial and Parallel International Agreements' in Bruno de Witte, Dominik Hanf and Ellen Vos (eds), *The Many Faces of Differentiation in EU Law* (Intersentia 2001) 231–67; Allan Rosas, 'The Status in EU Law of International Agreements Concluded by EU Member States' (2011) 34 Fordham Int'l L.J. 1304–45.

Luxembourg private law.[66] Despite not having its legal basis in the Union legal order, the EFSF is nevertheless closely related to it. Not only does the EFSF aim to strengthen one of the Union's most important projects, EMU, by safeguarding financial stability in the euro area,[67] several EU institutions are also involved in its functioning.[68] Moreover, since the entry into force of the 'two-pack', consisting of two Union legislative instruments aimed at tightening budgetary discipline and increasing surveillance of euro-area states dealing with financial stability risks,[69] this close relationship has only been strengthened. One of these instruments, Regulation 472/2013, requires that Member States requesting financial assistance from the EFSF (or the ESM, see *infra*) implement macro-economic adjustment programmes in order to address financial stability risks emanating from them.[70] As a result, the policy conditionality attached to financial assistance is brought back into the sphere of the Union legal order.[71]

Important as the EFSF may have been, it is merely a temporary assistance instrument. It could only provide assistance to financially distressed euro-area Member States until 30 June 2013.[72] As of 1 July

---

66 See text to note 35 *supra*.

67 See point 1 of the preamble to the EFSF Framework Agreement which is available at <http://www.efsf.europa.eu/about/index.htm> accessed 31 March 2014.

68 The Commission, the ECB and the Court are involved in the functioning of the EFSF. See in particular arts 2(1)(a), 3(1) and 16(2) EFSF Framework Agreement. Given that these tasks bear great resemblance to the ones that are assigned to these institutions by the ESM Treaty, they will be discussed in greater detail in relation to the ESM. See text to note 75 *infra*.

69 Regulation (EU) 472/2013 of 21 May 2013 on the strengthening of economic and budgetary surveillance of Member States in the euro area experiencing or threatened with serious difficulties with respect to their financial stability [2013] OJ L140/1; Regulation (EU) 473/2013 of 21 May 2013 on common provisions for monitoring and assessing draft budgetary plans and ensuring the correction of excessive deficit of the Member States in the euro area [2013] OJ L140/11.

70 See art. 7 of Regulation 472/2013. Member States receiving assistance on a precautionary basis are subject to 'enhanced surveillance'. See art. 2(3) of Regulation 472/2013.

71 See also De Witte and Beukers (n 47) 836. The exact relationship between the conditionality attached to EFSF or ESM assistance and the macro-economic adjustment programmes that need to be adopted on the basis of Regulation 472/2013 is a complicated one and will not be discussed further in this chapter.

72 See points 2(5)(b), 2(11) and 11(2) of the EFSF Framework Agreement.

2013, the EFSF may no longer engage in new financing programmes or enter into new loan facility agreements and may only continue with ongoing programmes. One could therefore argue that the EFSF's relevance for the structural development of the Union is limited. Yet, this argument does not hold true for two other instruments aiming to strengthen the economic underpinnings of the single currency: the ESM and the TSCG.

Similar to the EFSF, the ESM and the TSCG aim to strengthen the EMU, while not being based on Union law[73] but rather on so-called partial *inter se* agreements – treaties concluded between some of the Member States.[74] And they too rely heavily on Union institutions for their proper functioning. The European Commission, the ECB and the Court of Justice are involved in the operation of the ESM. The Commission and the ECB negotiate the memorandum of understanding (MoU), detailing the policy conditionality attached to financial assistance,[75] sign it on behalf of the ESM[76] and monitor subsequent compliance with it by the receiving state.[77] The Court is tasked with deciding on any disputes concerning the interpretation or application of the ESM Treaty arising between ESM members or between the ESM and a member.[78]

With regard to the TSCG, the involvement of the institutions becomes especially apparent from the balanced budget rule in the fiscal compact. The Commission has to propose the common principles underlying the automatic correction mechanism that the Contracting Parties need to incorporate into their national (constitutional) law.[79] Moreover, it is

---

73 See in this regard art. 1(1) TSCG which states: 'By this Treaty, the Contracting Parties agree, *as Member States of the European Union*, to strengthen the economic pillar of the economic and monetary union … .'

74 See also De Witte (n 65) 232.

75 Art. 13(3) ESM Treaty.

76 Only the Commission has to sign the MoU. See art. 13(4) ESM Treaty.

77 Art. 13(7) ESM Treaty. Both institutions are also tasked, upon receipt of a request for assistance of an ESM member, with assessing the existence of any financial stability risks, the respective member's public debt position, as well as the latter's financing needs. See art. 13(1) ESM Treaty. Moreover the ESM Board of Governors can only grant financial assistance through secondary market interventions on the basis of an analysis of the ECB recognizing the risk of exceptional financial market circumstances and risks to financial stability. See art. 18(2) ESM Treaty.

78 The Court, however, only comes into play if a prior decision of the ESM Board of Governors on the matter is contested by an ESM member. See art. 37(2) and (3) ESM Treaty.

79 Art. 3(2) TSCG.

invited in due time to present reports on the implementation of the balanced budget rule and the corresponding automatic correction mechanism into national law by the Contracting Parties.[80] If it concludes in its report that a Contracting Party has failed to comply with its implementation duties, the matter needs to be brought to the Court by one or more Contracting Parties.[81] The Court's judgment shall be binding on them.[82]

Unlike the EFSF, however, the ESM and the TSCG are of considerable structural significance due to their longer life span. The ESM forms the successor to the EFSF and, as such, is of a permanent nature.[83] The TSCG's existence is, admittedly, not intended to be permanent, but neither is it *a priori* limited like the EFSF. Article 16 TSCG provides that within five years, at most, of the entry into force of the treaty, the Contracting Parties should undertake an effort to incorporate its substance, including the fiscal compact, into the legal framework of the Union. At the same time, however, there is no guarantee that the Contracting Parties will succeed in this task. It can therefore not be excluded that the TSCG will govern the budgetary policies of its Contracting Parties for a longer period than the envisaged five-year period.

4.2 Relationship with the EU Legal Order

Initiatives like the ESM and TSCG create an interesting paradox. On the one hand, they strengthen the single currency by introducing reforms to its economic foundation. On the other hand, however, they do so by going outside the legal framework within which this currency is embedded. This urges the question as to how one should assess the relationship between such *inter se* initiatives and the Union. For many reasons, this chapter cannot provide a definite assessment of this relationship. What we can do, however, is make a start with it, focusing on its *legal* dimension. Two issues stand out in this respect: first, how does Union

---

80 Art. 8(1) TSCG.

81 Art. 8(1) TSCG. A Contracting Party that, independent of the Commission's report, considers that another Contracting Party has failed to comply with its implementation duties may also bring the matter before the Court.

82 In case a Contracting Party considers that another Party has not taken the required measures to comply with the Court's judgment, it may bring the case before the Court and request the imposition of financial sanctions in accordance with the criteria established by the Commission in the framework of art. 260 TFEU. See art. 8(2) TSCG.

83 See also recital 1 ESM Treaty.

law control the functioning of *inter se* instruments like the ESM and the TSCG?; second, and building on the first, is it possible for Union institutions – and if so, to what extent – to be involved in the operation of such instruments? Each of these issues will be considered in turn. Where possible, reference will be made to the ESM, the TSCG and the *Pringle* case to illustrate their practical relevance.

The first issue requires looking at the doctrine of pre-emption and the principles of primacy and loyal cooperation. *Inter se* instruments like the ESM and TSCG are not rooted in the Union legal order. The latter does, however, exert considerable influence on their establishment and functioning in several ways.[84] The first channel of influence is the doctrine of pre-emption. This doctrine plays a role in delimiting competences and defining the areas in which Member States may resort to *inter se* instruments.[85] Evidently, Member States cannot make use of such instruments in areas that belong to the exclusive competence of the Union.[86] Yet, even in areas that do not belong to the exclusive competence of the Union, the doctrine of pre-emption puts limits on the ability of Member States to resort to *inter se* cooperation. Article 2(2) TFEU makes clear that in areas of shared competence, Member States can only act to the extent that the Union has not exercised its competences.[87]

Even if Member States are not *a priori* barred from resorting to *inter se* instruments due to pre-emption, they do not have carte blanche to act as they wish. Two other channels of influence limit Member States' space to move in the context of such initiatives: the principles of primacy and loyal cooperation. According to the principle of primacy, Member States must respect Union law, regardless of whether they are acting on their own or together in the context of an *inter se* instrument.[88] In this respect, Member States may want to incorporate a conflict rule within the instrument itself, indicating that Union law will have priority over the

---

[84] See also Vestert Borger and Armin Cuyvers, 'Het Verdrag Inzake Stabiliteit, Coördinatie en Bestuur in de Economische en Monetaire Unie: de juridische en constitutionele complicaties van de eurocrisis' (2012) SEW 370, 374; Thomas Beukers, 'The Eurozone Crisis and the Legitimacy of Differentiated Integration' (EUI Working Papers 2013) 3.

[85] See De Witte (n 65) 240.

[86] See also art. 2(1) TFEU.

[87] See in this regard in relation to the TSCG also Paul Craig, 'The Stability, Coordination and Governance Treaty: principle, politics and pragmatism' (2012) ELR 231, 239.

[88] De Witte (n 65) 244; Rosas (n 65) 1319.

inter se instrument in case of conflict.[89] The TSCG forms a case in point. Article 2(2) of the treaty provides that the TSCG shall only apply insofar as it is compatible with Union law. Obviously, however, primacy of EU law is not dependent on a conflict rule like the one in the TSCG as it follows from the nature of the Union legal order itself.[90] The *Pringle* case provides an excellent example of the practical relevance of the principle of primacy of Union law for *inter se* instruments. In its judgment, the Court held that the ESM treaty is in conformity with EU law, inter alia, Article 125 TFEU.

In addition, when making use of *inter se* agreements, Member States have to comply with the principle of loyal cooperation which is enshrined in Article 4(3) TEU. It provides, among other things, that Member States shall facilitate the achievement of the Union's tasks and, moreover, that they refrain from any measure which could jeopardize the Union's objectives. Like the principle of primacy, the applicability of the principle of loyal cooperation flows from the Union legal order itself and is not dependent on any specific confirmation by the Member States in an *inter se* instrument. Again, however, the Contracting Parties to the TSCG have explicitly referred to their duty of loyal cooperation in Article 2(1) TSCG.

It has been argued that the principle of loyal cooperation not only governs the conduct of Member States when *making use* of partial *inter se* instruments, but that it may also bar them from *resorting* to such instruments altogether when recourse to the enhanced cooperation procedure in Article 20 TEU is open.[91] However, in our opinion, the better view is that Member States are free to decide whether to make use of the enhanced cooperation procedure or an *inter se* instrument. If they were to be deprived of this freedom of choice, the principle of loyal cooperation would be endowed with a pre-emptive capacity, thereby indirectly shifting the division of competences between the Union and the Member States in favour of the former. An interesting question is whether this judgment changes in cases where Member States intend to involve Union institutions in their cooperation. Would Member States in such cases be obliged to make use of the enhanced cooperation procedure in the Union Treaties instead of *inter se* instruments? This is a complex legal issue which has been touched upon in the *Pringle* case. Before specifically

---

89 De Witte (n 65) 244–5.

90 See also Steve Peers, 'The Stability Treaty: Permanent Austerity or Gesture Politics?' (2012) EUConst 404, 409–10.

91 See e.g., Vlad Constantinesco, 'Les clauses de "coopération renforcée"' (1997) RTD eur 751, 755.

addressing it, regard should be had to the second issue, that of the involvement of Union institutions in *inter se* instruments.

As shown above, the Union institutions are extensively chartered by the TSCG and the ESM Treaty. The Court's involvement is based on Article 273 TFEU,[92] which provides that it shall have jurisdiction in any dispute between Member States which relates to the subject matter of the Treaties if the dispute is submitted to it under a special agreement between the parties.[93] But what about the involvement of non-judicial institutions like the Commission and the ECB? At first sight, it seems to run counter to the Union Treaties, in particular Article 13(2) TEU, which provides that each institution shall act within the limits of the powers conferred on it in the Treaties. This wording appears to rule out the possibility that Union institutions are exercising powers not provided for by the Union Treaties. However, in two cases from the early 1990s, *Bangladesh* and *Lomé*,[94] the Court made clear that, Article 13(2) TEU notwithstanding,[95] Union institutions can be involved in the operation of *inter se* instruments. In *Bangladesh* the Court approved of the Commission's involvement in the steering of a humanitarian aid scheme. Similarly, in *Lomé* it accepted its chartering by the Member States for the sake of administering the seventh European Development Fund. Admittedly, however, these tasks were relatively modest and of an administrative nature. In the context of the TSCG and ESM Treaty, the role played by the Union institutions is much more considerable. Would that also be permissible?

In *Pringle* the Court ruled that it is permissible as far as the chartering of the Commission and the ECB by the ESM Treaty is concerned, while at the same time it clarified the limits to such borrowing of Union

---

[92] Recital 16 and art. 37(3) ESM Treaty; recital 15 and art. 8 TSCG.

[93] For the Court's interpretation of art. 273 TFEU in the context of the ESM treaty see *Pringle* (n 46), paras 170–177.

[94] Joined Cases C-181/91 and C-248/91 *Parliament v Council and Commission* [1993] ECR I-3685 (*Bangladesh*); Case C-316/91 *Parliament v Council* [1994] ECR I-625 (*Lomé*).

[95] Note in this regard that in the opinion in *Lomé* AG Jacobs already argued that the main aim of art. 13(2) TEU (ex. Art. 4(1) EEC) is to define the constitutional position of the Union institutions vis-à-vis the Member States, by making clear that the institutions only have those powers that are expressly or impliedly conferred on them by the Treaties. Consequently, it does not intend to rule out the possibility that Member States themselves decide to involve Union institutions in their *inter se* cooperation. See opinion AG Jacobs, *Lomé* [1994] ECR I-625, para. 83.

institutions. According to the Court, the tasks performed by the institutions in the context of *inter se* instruments may not 'alter the essential character of the powers conferred on those institutions' by the Union Treaties.[96] De Witte and Beukers argue that a way to understand this limit is to distinguish between 'powers' and 'tasks'.[97] Powers are fixed by the Treaties. This does not rule out the possibility, however, that additional 'tasks' are attributed to institutions by *inter se* instruments as long as they 'fit' within their existing competences and do not affect the position of other institutions.[98]

Seen from this perspective, we submit that the Commission's involvement in the fiscal compact is also in conformity with Union law. Its tasks of monitoring compliance with the balanced budget rule, devising the common principles for the automatic correction mechanism and overseeing implementation of the balanced budget rule and the corresponding mechanism in national (constitutional) law appear to be consistent with, or even subsumed by, its competences under the Union Treaties.[99]

Let us now return to the issue of enhanced cooperation. Is a group of Member States required to use this option if they want to involve Union institutions in their *inter se* initiative? In *Pringle* the Court was confronted with this issue. The applicant in the main proceeding had argued that the euro-area Member States should have established enhanced

---

[96] *Pringle* (n 46), para. 158. It is important to stress that the criterion of preserving the 'essential character' of the power of Union institutions is a *substantive* one. It does not tell us anything about the *procedure* leading up to the decision to make use of the institutions in an *inter se* instrument. In particular, it leaves unanswered the question whether all Member States, even those not participating in the instrument, need to consent to the chartering of the institutions. Such consent is present in case of the ESM (see recital 10 ESM Treaty), but it is lacking as regards the TSCG. The Court, however, did not address this procedural issue in its *Pringle* judgment. For the view that consent by all Member States is not necessary see Steve Peers, 'Towards a New Form of EU Law?: The Use of EU Institutions outside the EU Legal Framework' (2013) EUConst 37, 54; Borger and Cuyvers (n 84) 384. For a different view see Paul Craig, 'Pringle and Use of EU Institutions outside the EU Legal Framework: Foundations, Procedure and Substance' (2013) EUConst 263, 271–3.

[97] De Witte and Beukers (n 47) 846.

[98] Note in this regard that protection of the institutional balance is precisely one of the aims pursued by art 13(2) TEU. See also Jean-Paul Jacqué, 'The Principle of Institutional Balance' (2004) CMLR 383, 384; Borger and Cuyvers (n 84) 383.

[99] See also Peers (n 96) 51; Borger and Cuyvers (n 84) 383–4. For a much more critical view of the permissibility of the Commission's role see Craig (n 87) 241–5.

cooperation between them in order to be able to make use of Union institutions. He pointed out that the *Bangladesh* and *Lomé* cases predated the introduction of the enhanced cooperation procedure by the Treaty of Amsterdam. The introduction of this procedure, so he reasoned, provides evidence of a desire among the Member States to rule out the possibility of using Union institutions in (partial) *inter se* instruments.

In its judgment the Court avoided giving a final judgment on this issue. It simply pointed out that Article 20(1) TEU makes clear that enhanced cooperation can only take place when the Union has a competence in the area concerned by that cooperation. However, the Union does not have a specific competence for the establishment of a stability mechanism like the ESM. In these circumstances, according to the Court, Article 20 TEU does not preclude euro-area Member States from resorting to an *inter se* instrument like the ESM.[100] That still leaves the question as to what would happen if the Union *does* have a specific competence to act in the area of envisaged cooperation. Would Member States then be required to make use of the enhanced cooperation procedure if they would like to involve the Union institutions? Advocate General Kokott argued in her opinion that even in this case Member States remain free to choose between using enhanced cooperation or an *inter se* instrument.[101] She made clear that she was not persuaded by the argument that the introduction of the rules on enhanced cooperation had aimed at restricting the possibility of making use of the Union's institutions outside the scope of the Union Treaties. We subscribe to this view. Member States are allowed to use Union institutions in their *inter se* cooperation, even if they could have resorted to enhanced cooperation, provided that this fits with the essential character of their powers under the Union Treaties.[102] In fact, and in line with Peers,[103] we would submit that, in light of the principle of loyal cooperation, Member States may be *required* to involve Union institutions in such initiatives. When *inter se* cooperation is closely linked to a policy area of the Union, as in the case of the ESM and the

---

[100] *Pringle* (n 46), paras 167–169.

[101] Opinion AG Kokott in *Pringle* (n 46), paras 174–175. See also Peers (n 96) 48.

[102] For a different view see Craig (n 96) 273–4; M. Klamert, *The Principle of Loyalty in EU Law* (Oxford University Press 2014) 295–6. The latter argues that 'extra-Union cooperation has limits if it is used to circumvent the carefully balanced framework provided by the enhanced cooperation procedure under the EU Treaties'.

[103] Peers (n 96) 71–2.

TSCG, involvement of the Union institutions may be imperative in order to ensure consistency with Union law and policy.[104]

5. CONCLUSION

When thinking of the concept of differentiation in the context of Union law, EMU is unquestionably one of the first areas that springs to mind for the simple reason that not all Member States have adopted the euro as their currency. But this chapter has aimed at showing that the importance of differentiation for EMU reaches far beyond this issue of membership, manifesting itself in participation, policy goals and instruments as well as in law. Considering these various manifestations of differentiation, a complex picture emerges of a myriad of legal norms, adopted both inside and outside the formal treaty framework, not invariably applicable to all Member States, and created to achieve a plurality of aims, in particular price and financial stability.

Often this variety and complexity is seen as worrisome, entailing the risk of disintegration of the euro area and even of the Union. Although these concerns should be recognized, differentiation has an important positive dimension to it as well. Differentiation is not something static. Rather, it evolves and develops over time. This dynamism shows itself in all the forms of differentiation discussed in this chapter. Membership of the euro area has increased from 11 at the kick-off of the euro in 1999, to 19 at present, and this number will increase further. The ESM is illustrative of how the Union's focus on price stability has been enriched by instruments and goals geared to financial stability. And whereas the Treaty on Stability, Coordination and Governance currently has an existence outside the Union Treaties, it specifically envisages the possibility of being incorporated into them during the coming years. What this shows, first and foremost, is that the Union possesses a unique transformative capacity, allowing it to adapt to the challenges of its time. The debt crisis constitutes a prime example of such a challenge and, until now, the Union and its Member States have withstood it successfully.

---

[104] See in this regard also Jean-Claude Piris, *The Future of Europe: Towards a Two-Speed EU?* (Cambridge University Press 2012) 140–41. See also opinion AG Kokott in *Pringle* (n 46), para. 199. Assessing the compatibility of the ESM treaty with the principle of loyal cooperation, she considered it impossible to discern in what way this principle would be adversely affected. Rather, she argued, the involvement of the Commission and the ECB in the operation of the ESM 'seem to be evidence to the contrary'.

REFERENCES

Adam S and Mena Parras FJ, 'The European Stability Mechanism through the Legal Meanderings of the Union's Constitutionalism: Comment on Pringle' (2013) 38(6) *European Law Review* 848–65.

Amtenbrink F, Geelhoed LA and Kingston S, 'Economic, Monetary and Social Policy' in PJG Kapteyn et al. (eds), *Kapteyn & VerLoren van Themaat – The Law of the European Union and the European Communities* (Kluwer Law International 2008) 881–1086.

Beukers T, 'The Eurozone Crisis and the Legitimacy of Differentiated Integration', EUI Working Papers (2013).

Beukers T, 'The Bundesverfassungsgericht Preliminary Reference on the OMT Program: "In the ECB We Do Not Trust. What About You?"' (2014) 15(2) *German Law Journal* 343–68.

Borger V, 'The ESM and the European Court's Predicament in *Pringle*' (2013a) 14 *German Law Journal* 113–40.

Borger V, 'How the Debt Crisis Exposes the Development of Solidarity in the Euro Area' (2013b) 9(1) EUConst 7–36.

Borger V, 'Outright Monetary Transactions and the Stability Mandate of the ECB: *Gauweiler*' (2016) *Common Market Law Review* 139–96.

Borger V and Cuyvers A, 'Het Verdrag Inzake Stabiliteit, Coördinatie en Bestuur in de Economische en Monetaire Unie: de juridische en constitutionele complicaties van de eurocrisis' (2012) 10 SEW 370–90.

Constantinesco V, 'Les clauses de "coopération renforcée' (1997) 4 *Revue Trimestrielle de Droit européen* 751–67.

Craig P, 'The Stability, Coordination and Governance Treaty: Principle, Politics and Pragmatism' (2012) 37(3) *European Law Review* 231–48.

Craig P, '*Pringle* and Use of EU Institutions outside the EU Legal Framework: Foundations, Procedure and Substance' (2013) EUConst 263–84.

de Gregorio Merino A, 'Legal Developments in the Economic and Monetary Union During the Debt Crisis: The Mechanisms of Financial Assistance' (2012) 49(5) *Common Market Law Review* 1613–45.

De Witte B, 'Chameleonic Member States: Differentiation By Means of Partial and Parallel International Agreements' in De Witte B, Hanf D and Vos E (eds), *The Many Faces of Differentiation in EU Law* (Intersentia 2001) 231–67.

De Witte B and Beukers T, 'The Court of Justice Approves the Creation of the European Stability Mechanism outside the EU Legal Order: *Pringle*' (2013) 50(3) *Common Market Law Review* 80–40.

Ferry J-P, 'The Known Unknowns and Unknown Unknowns of EMU' (2012) 18 *Bruegel Policy Contribution* 1–10.

Jacqué J-P, 'The Principle of Institutional Balance' (2004) *Common Market Law Review* 383–91.

Klamert M, *The Principle of Loyalty in EU Law* (Oxford University Press 2014).

Koedooder Chr, '*Pringle* Judgment: Economic and/or Monetary Union' (2013) 37(1) *Fordham International Law Journal* 111–46.

Lastra RM, 'Systemic Risk, SIFIs and Financial Stability' (2011) 6(2) *Capital Markets Law Journal* 197–213.

Louis JV, 'Guest Editorial: The No-bailout Clause and Rescue Packages' (2010) *Common Market Law Review* 971–86.

Mink M and de Haan J, 'Contagion during the Greek Sovereign Debt Crisis' (2013) 34 *Journal of International Money and Finance* 102–13.

Peers S, 'The Stability Treaty: Permanent Austerity or Gesture Politics?' (2012) EUConst 404–41.

Peers S, 'Towards a New Form of EU Law?: The Use of EU Institutions outside the EU Legal Framework' (2013) EUConst 37–72.

Piris J-C, *The Future of Europe: Towards a Two-Speed EU?* (Cambridge University Press 2012).

Rosas A, 'The Status in EU Law of International Agreements Concluded by EU Member States' (2011) 34 *Fordham International Law Journal* 1304–45.

Schoenmaker D, 'The Financial Trilemma' (2011) 111 *Economics Letters* 57–9.

Van den Bogaert S and Borger V, 'Twenty Years after Maastricht: The Coming of Age of the EMU?' in de Visser, M and van der Mei, AP (eds), *The Treaty on European Union 1993–2013: Reflections from Maastricht* (Intersentia 2013) 451–71.

9. Differentiated integration in the field of economic and monetary policy and the use of '(semi-)extra' Union legal instruments – the case for '*inter se* Treaty amendments'

Christoph Herrmann

1. INTRODUCTION

The European integration process has gone through rough waters in recent times. Part of the strategy chosen to cope with the problems labelled 'euro crisis' or – more suitably – 'European Sovereign debt crisis' has been the recourse to legal instruments entirely (extra) or partly (semi-extra) outside the framework of the EU legal order: bilateral loans by Eurozone Member States to Greece;[1] the establishment of the European Financial Stability Facility (EFSF) as a special purpose vehicle under Luxembourg private law,[2] regulated by a framework agreement of the EFSF shareholders, which is governed by English private law;[3] the establishment by the 17 euro area Member States of the ESM as an international financial institution under public international law;[4] and the conclusion by 25 EU Member States of the Treaty on Stability, Coordination and Governance (TSCG) in the Economic and Monetary Union

[1] See Greek loan facility agreement, 8 May 2010.

[2] Treaty document <http://www.efsf.europa.eu/attachments/efsf_articles_of_incorporation_en.pdf> accessed 23 April 2015).

[3] EFSF framework agreement, <http://www.efsf.europa.eu/attachments/20111019_efsf_framework_agreement_en.pdf> accessed 23 April 2015.

[4] Treaty establishing the European stability mechanism, 8 October 2012 <http://www.esm.europa.eu/pdf/esm_treaty_en.pdf> accessed 23 April 2015.

(EMU), also under public international law.[5] Furthermore, the International Monetary Fund (IMF) has been greatly involved in the political decisions taken at Union level as well as in the respective Member States in distress.[6] Where 'true' EU law instruments were used – namely with the six-pack and the two-pack[7] – they only apply to euro area Member States and arguably stretch their legal basis considerably. Most recently, the Member States agreed to base the financing mechanism of the single resolution mechanism (SRM) on an intergovernmental agreement[8] instead of Article 114 TFEU – as the rest of the SRM.[9]

For the many European lawyers who only discovered their interest in the field of monetary law in recent times, this may come as a surprise and as a threat to the integration process and to the integrity of the Union's legal framework. However, recourse to extra-Community legal instruments and the heavy reliance on an international monetary law framework has existed for a long time in Europe. With the level of constitutionality achieved at the EU level, this may seem awkward and it may be the right time to integrate EMU more fully into the general EU legal framework. However, what it needs to achieve this is an additional amendment procedure (Article 48a TEU *new*) designed explicitly to serve the needs of the euro area and making amendments to some rules of

---

[5] Treaty document available at <http://www.consilium.europa.eu/european-council/pdf/Treaty-on-Stability-Coordination-and-Governance-TSCG/> accessed 23 April 2015.

[6] See an overview at <http://www.imf.org/external/np/exr/facts/europe.htm> accessed 23 April 2015.

[7] See <http://ec.europa.eu/economy_finance/articles/governance/2012-03-14_six_pack_en.htm> accessed 23 April 2015 for detailed information on six-pack and two-pack acts.

[8] See Agreement on the Transfer and Mutualisation of Contributions to the Single Resolution Fund, Brussels, 14 May 2014, (OR. en), 8457/14, LIMITE, EF 121, ECOFIN 342, <http://register.consilium.europa.eu/doc/srv?l=EN&f=ST%208457%202014%20INIT> accessed 23 April 2015.

[9] See Regulation (EU) No 806/2014 of the European Parliament and of the Council of 15 July 2014 establishing uniform rules and a uniform procedure for the resolution of credit institutions and certain investment firms in the framework of a Single Resolution Mechanism and a Single Resolution Fund and amending Regulation (EU) No 1093/2010, OJ [2014] L225/1 and Directive 2014/59/EU of the European Parliament and of the Council of 15 May 2014 establishing a framework for the recovery and resolution of credit institutions and investment firms and amending Council Directive 82/891/EEC, and Directives 2001/24/EC, 2002/47/EC, 2004/25/EC, 2005/56/EC, 2007/36/EC, 2011/35/EU, 2012/30/EU and 2013/36/EU, and Regulations (EU) No 1093/2010 and (EU) No 648/2012, of the European Parliament and of the Council, OJ [2014] L173/190.

EMU – those listed in Article 139 TFEU[10] – dependent only on the consent and ratification by all euro area Member States.[11] We will develop this argument on the basis of the past experience with differentiation in EMU-related matters (2) and the present use of (semi-)extra EU legal instruments during the euro crisis (3) and will try to look at possible advantages of an inter-se amendment procedure for certain provisions of EU law (4).

2. THE PAST – DIFFERENTIATION AND EXTRA-COMMUNITY MEASURES AS THE STANDARD MODEL OF THE EUROPEAN MONETARY CONSTITUTION

International economic transactions require mechanisms to deal with cross-border payments. The principle legal questions – absent a generally accepted international means of payment and with the existence of national currencies – are: (1) Can cross-border payments be made at all and can the national currency be traded against foreign currencies for that purpose (freedom of payments and convertibility)?; (2) if the answer to (1) is yes: at what rate of exchange are these transactions to take place; are they determined by market conditions or set by public authorities?; (3) can capital be transferred freely into other jurisdictions?; and finally, (4) how can international liquidity (in foreign currencies) be secured and what happens if a country is running out of foreign reserves? All these questions need to be addressed in an international economic system based on free trade and investment. This is all the more the case in a 'common market' or 'internal market' as was the goal of the EU from the very beginning with the establishment of the EEC in 1958.[12]

However, hardly any of the questions were addressed in the EEC Treaty. This was partly because, monetary integration – to some extent – had already taken place prior to the foundation of the Communities,

---

[10] OJ [2012] L326/13 (consolidated version).

[11] A different proposal with a similar goal is the "Euro area flexibility clause" that was proposed by Beukers at the beginning of 2014, see Thomas Beukers, 'Flexibilisation of the Euro Area: Challenges and Opportunities' (2014) EUI Working Paper MWP 2014/01.

[12] See art. 2 of the Treaty establishing the European Economic Community, 25 March 1957; see also Case C-10/73 *Rewe-Zentral AG v Hauptzollamt Kehl* [1973] ECLI:EU:C:1973:111, where the ECJ held that separate currencies are alien to a true common market.

within the framework of the OEEC,[13] which paved the way for the conclusion of a cross-border payments system, leading to the European Payments Union (EPU) in 1950,[14] which was then replaced by the European Monetary Agreement (EMA) of 1955, which also established the European Fund.[15] The Bank for International Settlements (BIS), founded originally in 1930 to administer the German reparations payments, was tasked with the execution of the payment agreements. The international monetary relations of the founding Member States of the Communities were – furthermore – governed by the Articles of Agreement of the IMF, to which all the Member States had acceded prior to the establishment of the Communities.[16]

Against this backdrop, the EEC Treaty only briefly referred to monetary matters. This reference, however, addressed questions (1) (in Article 106 EECT) and (4) (Articles 108, 109 EECT). Questions (2) and (3) were also addressed, but rather in soft language. Together with the fixed exchange-rate system of the time, a complete monetary legal framework for the intra-EEC monetary relations existed, but it was based largely on non-EEC legal instruments. Generally, no true competencies were transferred to the EEC. First initiatives towards monetary integration in the 1960s led to more cooperation of the Member States in the field of exchange rates and international monetary policy as well as the introduction of monetary support mechanisms, but they did not alter the Treaty framework.[17]

This picture did not change significantly when the Bretton Woods system of fixed exchange rates broke up between 1971 and 1978. As in recent times, short-term crisis management dominated over long-term political integration strategies. The legal bases used were not always entirely clear (or even sufficient) and the EEC and the Member States

---

[13] Convention for European economic cooperation, 16 April 1948 <http://www.cvce.eu/content/publication/1999/1/1/769de8b7-fe5a-452c-b418-09b068bd748d/publishable_en.pdf> accessed 23 April 2015.

[14] Agreement on the establishment of a European Payments Union, 19 September 1950 <http://www.cvce.eu/obj/agreement_on_the_establishment_of_a_european_payments_union_19_september_1950-en-7b471fa9-af0b-427d-a657-017de6a3e1de.html> accessed 23 April 2015.

[15] European Monetary Agreement, 5 August 1955 <http://www.cvce.eu/obj/european_monetary_agreement_paris_5_august_1955-en-58d18d59-c3b0-4bdc-9756-d23dd322382d.html> accessed 23 April 2015.

[16] See list of Members with accession dates: <http://www.imf.org/external/np/sec/memdir/memdate.htm> accessed 23 April 2015.

[17] See Christoph Herrmann, *Währungshoheit, Währungsverfassung und subjektive Rechte* (Mohr Siebeck 2010) 195 et seq.

resorted to hybrid constructions of a mixed semi-extra Community legal nature in order to compensate for the insufficient powers of the Community.[18] This finding is similarly true for the 'snake in the tunnel', for the Regulation establishing a European Monetary Cooperation Fund[19] and the European Monetary System.[20] Article 102a(2) of the EECT, inserted by the Single European Act in 1986/1987,[21] tried to set a legal limit to the use of such instruments. However, even later on, the creative use of Community and non-Community legal instruments was necessary in order to adapt the legal framework to the actual economic needs, e.g., when the bands in the EMS were widened from 2.25 to 15 per cent and when the ERM II[22] was established, once again, on a dubious legal basis.[23]

Whereas the original Treaty framework of the 1950s had been based on a uniform integration approach, the accessions of the 1970s,[24] as well as the break-up of the Bretton Woods system, led to differentiated integration, in particular with regard to exchange-rate policies. The differentiated system of today is the aftermath of those times of trouble.[25]

3. THE PRESENT – THE EURO SOVEREIGN DEBT CRISIS AND DIFFERENTIATED INTEGRATION

3.1 Differentiation in the General Legal Framework of EMU

Of the many areas of European Union law, the Economic and Monetary Union is certainly the field where differentiated integration is most relevant and complex. The economic concept underlying the convergence criteria presupposed that not all EU Member States would enter stage three of the EMU – as the introduction of the euro was labelled then – at the same time. Until all Member States have introduced the euro as their legal tender on the basis of Article 140 TFEU (if ever), some will be

---

[18] Ibid., 202 et seq.

[19] OJ [1973] L89/2.

[20] OJ [1978] L379/2.

[21] OJ [1987] L169/20.

[22] OJ [2006] C73/21.

[23] See <http://ec.europa.eu/economy_finance/emu_history/legalaspects/part_c_1.htm> accessed 23 April 2015 for a chronological overview.

[24] UK, Denmark and Ireland, 1 January 1973, OJ [1972] L73/3.

[25] For a full account of differentiated integration in the field of EMU see Jochen Beutel, *Differenzierte Integration in der Europäischen Wirtschafts- und Währungsunion* (De Gruyter 2006).

'Member States with a derogation' (Article 139(1) TFEU, the so-called 'pre-ins'), to which some of the key provisions of EMU do not apply (fully) (cf. Article 139(2) TFEU) and which are exempted from decisions that are to be taken thereunder. In return, they may still receive medium-term balance of payments assistance under Articles 143 and 144 TFEU.

In addition to the 'pre-ins' (which are expected to introduce the euro as the currency of the Union as a monetary union, cf. Article 3(4) TEU), the real 'outs' (the UK and Denmark) are not even under an obligation to introduce the single currency.[26] The 'ins', i.e., the Member States of the euro area, have surrendered their monetary sovereignty and are subject to stricter legal obligations, in particular with a view to the surveillance of their budgetary and economic policies. Furthermore, they gather without the 'pre-ins' and 'outs' in the Eurogroup in order to discuss matters of interest for the euro area and prepare the decision-making of the ECOFIN council of ministers, where the others participate but have no right to vote under Article 139(4) TFEU. A particular legal basis with an uncertain scope (Article 136(1) TFEU) allows for measures to strengthen the coordination and surveillance of the budgetary discipline between euro area Member States and for economic policy guidelines addressed only to them. The relationship between this specific form of closer cooperation and the general provisions on 'enhanced cooperation', however, remain unclear. Presumably, Article 20 TEU[27] and Article 326 through Article 334 TFEU could still also be used in the realm of EMU.

3.2 Insufficiencies of the Pre-Crisis European Monetary Constitution; Unavailability of and Limits to Existing Mechanisms of Differentiated Integration

When the crisis broke out finally in the spring of 2010, it became obvious that the EU did not have in place the legal instruments necessary to cope with a sovereign debt crisis. Financial assistance mechanisms for euro area Member States were not in place nor could they be established – arguably – on the basis of the Treaties. The intensity of economic policy coordination and budgetary surveillance was limited and could not be easily extended. Moreover, it is the legal framework of EMU which makes a sovereign default all the more likely, as it effectively confines

[26] Protocol 15 and 16, OJ [2012] C326/284 and C326/287 (consolidated version).

[27] OJ [2012] L326/13 (consolidated version).

the financing of Member States to raising taxes or issuing debt instruments, but it prevents monetary financing from happening (see in particular Article 123 TFEU).

The medium-term financial assistance, available to non-euro area Member States, could not be used for Greece or other euro area Member States (and would not have sufficed). Other than Article 122(2) TFEU, no legal basis foresaw the granting of financial assistance of any kind to euro area Member States threatened by a default and Article 122(2) TFEU could only have been used (as later with the enacting of the EFSM Regulation[28]) by the EU, which would not have had the financial means (legally) or the necessary credibility for the required rescue operations. With no EU competencies existing, it was for the Member States to act quickly and forcefully and so they did, together with the IMF as the usual troubleshooter in times of financial crisis. The latter was possible, since the euro area Member States – despite having transferred their monetary sovereignty to the EU, which arguably also includes the external dimension – remain members of the IMF in their own right, including drawing on resources of the IMF (even though it raises legal difficulties under IMF law if a member draws in its own currency).[29]

What was also made visible by the crisis was the insufficiency of the governance framework of EMU, in particular the lack of 'bite' in the excessive deficit procedure. However, despite realizing that the framework of Article 126 TFEU and the Stability and Growth Pact was insufficient, there was no easy consensus regarding how to amend it. Legally, the ideal solution would have been to replace Protocols No. 12 and No. 13[30] on the basis of Article 126(14) TFEU and Article 6 of Protocol No. 13 by means of secondary legislation. These protocols flesh out much of the content of the excessive deficit procedure and they can be changed without going through the cumbersome procedure of a formal Treaty amendment. However, unanimity is still required, even if Member States are not bound by all the rules of Article 126 TFEU.

This simplified amendment procedure, however, would have required unanimity in the Council, where the 'outs' and 'pre-ins' would have had a full voting and veto right. Instead, a solution based on Article 136(1) TFEU was chosen. Coordination was strengthened only for the euro area Member States. The problems of this specific provision are to be found

---

[28] Council Regulation (EU) No 407/2010 of 11 May 2010 establishing a European financial stabilisation mechanism, OJ [2010] L118/1.

[29] On this see Charlotte Gaitanides, 'Intervention des IWF in der Eurokrise: mandatswidrig?' (2011) 14 Neue Zeitschrift für Verwaltungsrecht 848 et seq.

[30] OJ [2012] C326/279 and C326/281 (consolidated version).

in the legal constraints – unclear and controversial as they are – which are imposed by the phrase 'in accordance with the relevant procedure from among those referred to in Articles 121 and 126, with the exception of the procedure set out in Article 126(14) TFEU'. Many commentators argue that Article 136(1) TFEU cannot be used to introduce fines earlier or for a reversal of qualified majority voting in the Council when deciding under Article 126 TFEU.[31] Even if one does not fully agree with these limitations, it is obvious that Article 136(1) TFEU is not designed to substantially alter the provisions of Articles 121 and 126 TFEU. The differentiation allowed by Article 136(1) TFEU is thus limited.

Similar limitations do – of course – apply to enhanced cooperation, which is subject to the general condition that it must comply with the Treaties and Union law (Article 326(1) TFEU), i.e., it cannot alter Treaty provisions or secondary legislation. Obviously, it is useless if deficiencies are determined in the existing legal framework of the EU. It is equally useless where no Union competencies exist, as a non-exclusive competence of the Union is another condition for enhanced cooperation (Article 20(1) TEU)) to be put in place. It is not designed to overcome the principle of conferral nor is it possible to use Article 326 TFEU and Article 352 TFEU in conjunction, as they presuppose entirely contrary situations with regard to the competencies of the Union.[32]

If one had a 'Euro area flexibility clause', i.e., a provision similar to Article 352 TFEU, allowing for action to be taken by the Euro area only (like Article 136 TFEU or enhanced cooperation)[33] where no obvious competence of the EU exists – which would also require prior treaty amendment – the situation would not change either. Such a clause could overcome the difficulties in relation to the principle of conferral but not with regard to substantive insufficiencies in the Treaty provisions.[34]

---

[31] See Thomas Beukers, 'The Eurozone Crisis and the Legitimacy of Differentiated Integration' (2013) EUI Working Papers MWP 2013/36; Ulrich Häde, 'Art. 136 AEUV – eine neue Generalklausel für die Wirtschafts- und Währungsunion?' (2011) 7 Juristenzeitung 333 et seq.; Christoph Ohler, 'Die zweite Reform des Stabilitäts- und Wachstumspaktes' (2010) 25 Zeitschrift für Gesetzgebung 330 et seq.

[32] But see Beukers (n 11), 2, and Michael Schwarz, 'A Memorandum of Misunderstanding – The Doomed Road of the European Stability Mechanism and a Possible Way Out: Enhanced Cooperation' (2014) 51 CMLR 389 (404 et seq.) who are both obviously of the view that the two instruments could be used in combination.

[33] This proposal is made by Beukers (n 11).

[34] This is also conceded by Beukers, ibid., 9.

3.3 Instrumentalizing Public International Law for Eurozone Purposes

Given the problems with the available Treaty instruments or their mere non-existence, the Member States resorted to extra-union legal instruments. Because of their permanent nature and public international law character, the Treaty establishing the European Stability Mechanism (TESM)[35] and the Fiscal Pact (TSCG)[36] are of particular interest here.

The TESM establishes the ESM as an international financial institution, enjoying legal personality under public international law (Article 32 TESM). Its Contracting Parties, which can only be euro area Member States, become Members of the ESM (Articles 1 and 2 TESM). The capital subscription of the Members is determined in accordance with their capital share in the ECB. The purpose of the ESM, to mobilize funding and provide stability support to ESM Members, closes the lacuna in the TEU and TFEU and compensates for the lack of competencies on the part of the EU. Despite the separate legal personality of the ESM and its special organs, the institutions of the EU – in particular the Commission and the ECB – are involved in ESM action in many ways.[37] Even the Court of Justice of the European Union (CJEU) is tasked with the settlement of disputes arising under the TESM (Article 37(3) TESM). The links between the ESM and the EU are thus very close. As a consequence, the German Constitutional Court held that the information obligation resting upon the Federal Government under Article 23 German Basic Law also applied to the ESM Treaty (and the Fiscal Pact) as a 'matter of the European Union'.[38] Despite the obvious links with the EU, there is no conflict clause subjugating the ESM to EU law nor an intention pronounced in the TESM to transfer it into the closer EU legal framework. However, the new Article 136(3) TFEU mentions the ESM and ensures – albeit merely declaratory – its compliance with EU law.[39]

---

35 <http://www.esm.europa.eu/pdf/ESM%20Treaty%20consolidated%2013-03-2014.pdf> accessed 23 April 2015.

36 <http://www.consilium.europa.eu/european-council/pdf/Treaty-on-Stability-Coordination-and-Governance-TSCG/> accessed 23 April 2015.

37 See e.g., arts 4, 5, 6 and 13 TESM.

38 BVerfG, Judgment of 12 September 2012, 2 BvR 1390/12 etc., para. 215 (available in English at <http://www.bundesverfassungsgericht.de/SharedDocs/Entscheidungen/EN/2012/09/rs20120912_2bvr139012en.html> accessed 23 April 2015).

39 See European Council Decision of 25 March 2011 amending art. 136 of the Treaty on the Functioning of the European Union with regard to a stability mechanism for the Member States whose currency is the euro, OJ [2011] L91/1.

Whether it could also have constitutive effects, with the result that it legalizes action by the ESM that would otherwise have been illegal under the Treaties, remains to be seen in the future.

Whereas the TESM falls into an area where the EU arguably had no competencies – confirmed by the CJEU in its November 2012 *Pringle* judgment[40] – the Fiscal Pact comes much closer to EU law and should originally have been adopted by Treaty amendment. Not only that, 25 of the 28 Member States have signed (and ratified) the Fiscal Pact, even though not all of its rules are applicable to all Contracting Parties. Most of its provisions refer to the EU, EU law, EU institutions etc. in one way or the other. Conceptually, the Fiscal Pact is confirming, reaffirming, strengthening or adding to legal obligations already existing under pure EU law. Being an agreement under public international law, it cannot of course alter provisions of the EU Treaties; nevertheless, it goes beyond the Treaties in some respects in a way which would not have been feasible under EU law itself, e.g., the *pactum de contrahendo* in Article 7 TSCG, which obliges the Member States to vote in a certain way when it comes to decision-making in the Council under Article 126 TFEU. The TSCG, in fact, reverses the qualified majority voting rule applicable under the latter provision, something which could not have been done under Article 136(1) TFEU. The binding force may not be as strong as under EU law (especially as this obligation is not subject to the CJEU jurisdiction under Article 8 TSCG); but it is still binding under public international law. Again, the Commission is entrusted with tasks under the TSCG, as is – albeit more limited – the CJEU. Given the more obvious overlaps with EU law, the TSCG does not only contain a conflict clause (ensuring the primacy of EU law over the TSCG; Articles 2 and 3(1) TSCG), but it also envisages the use of Article 136(1) and enhanced cooperation insofar as possible as well as the future transfer of the TSCG into EU law (Articles 10 and 16 TSCG).

In particular the TSCG, with its peculiar entry-into-force provision (Article 14 TSCG), according to which ratification of the TSCG by euro area and non-euro area Member States has a different effect and different parts of the TSCG enter into force at different points in time[41] leads to

---

40 Case C-370/12 *Pringle* [2012] ECLI:EU:C:2012:756, para. 95.

41 Art. 14 TSCG reads:

> 1. This Treaty shall be ratified by the Contracting Parties in accordance with their respective constitutional requirements. The instruments of ratification shall be deposited with the General Secretariat of the Council of the European Union ('the Depositary').
>
> 2. This Treaty shall enter into force on 1 January 2013, provided that twelve

further forms of differentiated integration. In theory, there could – at present – be up to five euro area Member States not fully bound by the TSCG. As a corollary, they would also be exempted from using the funds mobilized by the ESM. At the same time, not all 'outs' or 'pre-ins' are Contracting Parties to the TSCG.[42] It is obvious that the determination of the individual legal obligations of EU Member States becomes less and less transparent as a result.

3.4 Differentiation without Legal Limits? Harmonious Interpretation of Disharmony

The excessive use of non-EU legal instruments for the purposes of the integration process is obviously not the best solution. However, given the practical needs of crisis politics, it was the second best and first-best possible when a Treaty amendment could not be achieved (as in the case of the TSCG) or may not even have been useful (as arguably in the case of the ESM).

The Member States, when using public international law instruments, cannot of course circumvent their EU law obligations. EU law has to

---

Contracting Parties whose currency is the euro have deposited their instrument of ratification, or on the first day of the month following the deposit of the twelfth instrument of ratification by a Contracting Party whose currency is the euro, whichever is the earlier.
3. This Treaty shall apply as from the date of entry into force amongst the Contracting Parties whose currency is the euro which have ratified it. It shall apply to the other Contracting Parties whose currency is the euro as from the first day of the month following the deposit of their respective instrument of ratification.
4. By derogation from paragraphs 3 and 5, Title V shall apply to all Contracting Parties concerned as from the date of entry into force of this Treaty.
5. This Treaty shall apply to the Contracting Parties with a derogation, as defined in Article 139(1) of the Treaty on the Functioning of the European Union, or with an exemption, as referred to in Protocol (No 16) on certain provisions related to Denmark annexed to the European Union Treaties, which have ratified this Treaty, as from the date when the decision abrogating that derogation or exemption takes effect, unless the Contracting Party concerned declares its intention to be bound at an earlier date by all or part of the provisions in Titles III and IV of this Treaty.

[42] E.g. The United Kingdom of Great Britain and Northern Ireland.

prevail, in all circumstances.[43] Both the TESM and the TSCG were possible, since the EU has no exclusive powers in the fields governed by the two treaties. They fall squarely into the realm of economic policy and not monetary policy. Hence, the Member States only had to ensure that they do not impose legal obligations contrary to substantive EU law or make sure that in case of conflict, EU law did prevail. With regard to monetary policy, the situation would be quite different.

The use of the institutions was, however, more delicate, as the extra-union use of institutions had only been cleared for situations where all Member States agreed to such use.[44] In case of the Fiscal Pact – contrary to the ESM – they did not. The CJEU, however, did not attach any significance to the consent of the Member States when assessing the legality of the tasking of the Commission and ECB under the ESM Treaty. Instead, it considered it decisive that the tasks entrusted to the Commission and the central bank outside the actual EU law framework did not alter the essential character of the powers conferred on those institutions by the Treaties.[45] Given the role of the Commission and the ECB under the EMU provisions as well as the possibilities offered under Article136(1) TFEU and the enhanced cooperation provisions, it would have been odd to prevent Member States from using EU institutions outside the Treaty just because of the lack of consent of non-participating Member States.

4. THE FUTURE – A CALL FOR DIFFERENTIATED TREATY AMENDMENT PROCEDURES

What lessons are to be learned from the experience with differentiated integration and the use of non-EU-law instruments in the distant past and in more recent times? The answer is: one should think of differentiation not only at the level of primary law (as in Articles 139 et seq. TFEU and the Protocols on the UK and Denmark) or secondary law (as in Article 136(1) TFEU, enhanced cooperation or a ‘euro area flexibility clause’). One should think about differentiated integration on the level of Treaty amendment. *In concreto*, the introduction of a new Article 48a TEU (by use of the ordinary Treaty amendment procedure) should be considered.

---

[43] Case C-22/77 *Commission v Council (AETR)* [1971] ECLI:EU:C:1971:32, paras 15 et seq.; Case C-45/07 *Commission v Greece* [2009] ECLI:EU:C:2009:81, para. 17.

[44] *Pringle* (n 40), para. 158.

[45] Ibid., para. 162.

This new provision would provide for amendments to be made to the provisions listed in Article 139(2) TFEU (which do not apply to the non-euro area Member States) by agreement and ratification *by the euro area Member States only (inter se* Treaty amendment). An amendment would be effectuated by analogy to Article 48(6), but with a limitation of voting rights in the European Council (as in Article 139(4) TFEU) and the need for ratification limited to the euro area Member States (one could even imagine to test entry-into-force with super-qualified majorities and less than full ratification). For the Member States with a derogation, the application of these new provisions would depend on the abrogation of their derogation by the Council in accordance with Article 140 TFEU. Of course, the ratification of the amendment by the Member State with a derogation would be a further condition for the abrogation to become effective.

The possible amendments would be limited to the provisions explicitly listed. The CJEU could – in line with its *Pringle* reasoning on its jurisdiction – intervene if the amendments affected other provisions of the Treaties.

What is the benefit of such an amendment? Euro area Member States could, for example, change the voting rules for the excessive deficit procedure (the phases not applicable to Member States with a derogation) without asking the others; they could have introduced the ESM Treaty into EU law instead of resorting to an international law agreement; they could have intensified economic coordination beyond the limits of Article 136(1) TFEU; and they could have reformed the banking supervision primary law framework of the EMU. In none of these cases, would the question have arisen whether these changes are compatible with the EMU Treaty articles, but only the question would arise whether they violate other provisions of primary law not subject to this *inter se*-amendment procedure. This would arguably be an easier test to pass. The question also would not have arisen whether the institutions, including the CJEU, may legitimately be tasked with the administration and adjudication of these rules. The EU legal order, based on the Treaties, is less flexible than national constitutions and most international agreements. At the same time, it is much more precise in terms of legal rules that govern the action by the institutions and the Member States. This combination is fatal whenever the precise-but-hard-to-change rules turn out to be inadequate: they cannot be used effectively, but they may not be changed due to national vetoes. This is – of course – an already well-known problem of the EU legal order.[46] Most proposals in the past dealing with the matter rather opted for super-qualified majorities for the adoption and ratification of amendments. Theoretically, I would immediately subscribe to this idea, in particular in relation to major treaty reversals (with a 'take it (the amendment) or leave it (the EU)' approach). However, it is politically unrealistic that this may ever be agreed upon by the 28 Member States. My proposal is less ambitious but maybe more realistic. Given that there is only a theoretical obligation to join the euro area, which cannot be enforced, the prerogatives of the 'outs' would not be impaired in the same way. They could still decide not to join the amended euro area if they do not agree with what the older euro area members have changed. For the constitutional deadlock in which the euro area finds itself right now, it seems to be the only proposal which is innovative and radical enough to make things better in any way and also realistic enough to have at least a minimum chance of being realized.

5. CONCLUSION AND SUMMARY

The euro crisis has put differentiated integration back on the agenda of the European Union, and it has done so with an entirely different urge and intensity. Practically no response to the crisis consists of an ordinary one-for-all EU legal instrument and most of the responses had to be created with other legal raw material altogether. This fact is undoubtedly a threat to the unity of the EU legal order. It may seem contradictory to answer a call for unity by offering more flexibility. However, if one accepts that recourse to full unity is unlikely as the interests of the Member States inside and outside the euro area are too far apart, it may be the only feasible way to bring the legal and constitutional framework of the Euro area under the full umbrella of the Treaties back again and this would certainly constitute a major step forward!

---

[46] See the discussion by Bruno De Witte, 'Entry into Force and Revision' in De Witte B (ed.), *Ten Reflections on the Constitutional Treaty* (Robert Schuman Centre for Advanced Studies 2003) 206 et seq.; Steven Peers, 'The Future of EU Treaty Amendments' (2012) 31 *Yearbook of European Law* 17 et seq. (in particular 87 et seq. and 104 et seq.).

REFERENCES

Beukers T, 'The Eurozone Crisis and the Legitimacy of Differentiated Integration', EUI Working Papers, MWP 2013/36.

Beukers T, 'Flexibilisation of the Euro Area: Challenges and Opportunities', EUI Working Paper, MWP 2014/01.

Beutel J, *Differenzierte Integration in der Europäischen Wirtschafts- und Währungsunion* (De Gruyter 2006).

De Witte B, 'Entry into Force and Revision', in De Witte B (ed.), *Ten Reflections on the Constitutional Treaty* (Robert Schuman Centre for Advanced Studies 2003) 203–19.

Gaitanides C, 'Intervention des IWF in der Eurokrise: mandatswidrig?' (2011) 14 Neue Zeitschrift für Verwaltungsrecht 848–52.

Häde U, 'Art. 136 AEUV – eine neue Generalklausel für die Wirtschafts- und Währungsunion?' (2011) 7 *Juristenzeitung* 333–40.

Herrmann C, *Währungshoheit, Währungsverfassung und subjektive Rechte* (Mohr Siebeck 2010).

Ohler C, 'Die zweite Reform des Stabilitäts- und Wachstumspaktes' (2010) 25 *Zeitschrift für Gesetzgebung* 330–45.

Peers S, 'The Future of EU Treaty Amendments', (2012) 31 *Yearbook of European Law* 17–111.

Schwarz M, 'A Memorandum of Misunderstanding – The Doomed Road of the European Stability Mechanism and a Possible Way Out: Enhanced Cooperation', (2014) 51 CMLR 389–423.

10. European Banking Union and the EU single financial market: more differentiated integration, or disintegration?

Eilís Ferran[*]

1. INTRODUCTION

The European Banking Union (EBU) has been formed inside the EU Single Market and applies only to a subset of the EU Member States, namely the Member States that use the euro (whose participation in EBU is compulsory) and other Member States that choose to opt in. EBU is expected to play an integration-deepening role within the euro area.[1] In the long run, its differentiated, optionality-based approach to Member States outside the euro area could also widen EU integration by serving as a staging post for adoption of the euro by laggard Member States. On the other hand, the advance of integration within the euro area, and prospectively beyond as well, could result in those Member States that remain on the outside of EBU becoming increasingly marginalized within the EU, and the unity of the Single Market could be jeopardized as a result.

There is an existing body of scholarship on the causal relation between integration and differentiation. Questions examined include whether

* I am particularly grateful to Michael Waibel for insightful comments on an earlier draft. The usual disclaimer applies.

[1] Herman Van Rompuy, Towards a Genuine Economic and Monetary Union, 26 June 2012; Herman Van Rompuy, Towards a Genuine Economic and Monetary Union, 5 December 2012; Jean-Claude Juncker, Completing Europe's Economic and Monetary Union, 22 June 2015; European Commission, 'A Blueprint for a Deep and Genuine Economic and Monetary Union: Launching a European Debate', COM(2012) 777; European Commission, 'Building a Capital Markets Union' COM(2015) 63.

differentiated arrangements have centripetal or centrifugal effects on initially unwilling outsiders and whether the institutional flexibility in differentiated integration leads to a 'positive dynamic of integration, to a negative dynamic of disintegration, or to uneasy and lasting divisions within the Union?'[2] EBU now provides an important new context for the examination of the effects of differentiation on integration, and for the deepening of theory-based approaches to these issues. The purpose of this chapter is to contribute to the analysis of the issues by examining the impact of EBU on the Single Market from a legal standpoint. The legal framework for EBU contains a variety of procedures and safeguards to encourage participation in EBU and to protect the integrity of the Single Market. These measures have assumed considerable significance at the political level as examples of the solutions that can be found to ease tensions and reconcile the different interests of Member States inside and outside the euro area.[3] Since legal devices are meant to perform such a critical role in holding things together, the strength of the glue merits close attention.

2. THE EUROPEAN BANKING UNION: THE KEY FEATURES AND ISSUES

2.1 Component Parts of EBU

EBU comprises a Single Supervisory Mechanism (SSM) and a Single Resolution Mechanism (SRM) which includes a Single Resolution Fund (SRF). The intended third pillar of EBU is a Single Deposit Guarantee Scheme (SDGS). The legal framework for the institutional architecture of the SSM and the SRM, which comprises EU and public international law instruments, is now in place but the establishment of a SDGS is not being

---

[2] Alkuin Kölliker, 'Bringing Together or Driving Apart the Union: Towards a Theory of Differentiated Integration' (2001) 24 *West European Politics* 125. See also Alkuin Kölliker, *Flexibility and European Unification: The Logic of Differentiated Integration* (Rowman and Littlefield 2006); Jan-Emmanuel de Neve, 'The European Onion? How Differentiated Integration is Reshaping the EU' (2007) 29 *Journal of European Integration* 503; Kenneth Dyson and Angelos Sepos (eds), *Whose Europe? The Politics of Differentiated Integration* (Palgrave Macmillan 2010); Kenneth Dyson and Martin Marcussen, 'Transverse Integration in European Economic Governance: Between Unitary and Differentiated Integration' (2010) 32 *Journal of European Integration* 17.

[3] Viviane Reding, The United Kingdom and the EU – Inevitably Drifting Apart?, Mackenzie Stuart Lecture, Cambridge, 17 February 2014.

actively pursued at present.[4] In its supervisory capacity the European Central Bank (ECB) works closely with the other authorities that are part of the European System of Financial Supervision, in particular the European Banking Authority (EBA). The EBA, which was established in 2011 and which is based in London, is an independent EU Authority with a mandate to ensure effective and consistent prudential regulation and supervision across the European banking sector. The EBA does not itself have direct responsibility for the supervision of banks.

The ECB is the institutional hub of the SSM. Within the SSM the ECB is in overall charge of bank prudential supervision in the EU Member States that participate in EBU and it is directly responsible for the prudential supervision of the most significant banks and bank groups. The ECB assumed its supervisory tasks in full on 4 November 2014.[5] A

---

[4] Council Regulation (EU) No 1024/2013 of 15 October 2013 conferring specific tasks on the European Central Bank concerning policies relating to the prudential supervision of credit institutions [2013] OJ L287/63 (SSM Regulation); Regulation (EU) No 1022/2013 of the European Parliament and of the Council of 22 October 2013 amending Regulation (EU) No 1093/2010 [2013] OJ L287/5; Regulation (EU) No 806/2014 of 15 July 2014 of the European Parliament and of the Council for the resolution of credit institutions and certain investment firms in the context of a Single Resolution Mechanism and a Single Bank Resolution Fund and amending Regulation (EU) No 1093/2010 [2014] OJ L225/1 (SRM Regulation); Intergovernmental Agreement on the Transfer and Mutualisation of Contributions to the Single Resolution Fund (May 2014) (SRF Intergovernmental Agreement); Council Implementing Regulation (EU) 2015/81 of 19 December 2014 specifying uniform conditions of application of Regulation (EU) No 806/2014 of the European Parliament and of the Council with regard to ex ante contributions to the Single Resolution Fund [2015] OJ L15/1; Commission Delegated Regulation (EU) 2015/63 of 21 October 2014 supplementing Directive 2014/59/EU of the European Parliament and of the Council with regard to ex ante contributions to resolution financing arrangements [2015] OJ L11/44.

[5] Supporting arrangements that needed to be put in place included: Memorandum of Understanding between the Council and the ECB on practical aspects of the exercise of democratic accountability of the supervisory tasks of the ECB vis-à-vis the Council (5687/14, January 2014); Inter-institutional Agreement covering practical aspects of the exercise of democratic accountability of the supervisory tasks of the ECB vis-à-vis the European Parliament [2013] OJ L320/1; Regulation (EU) No 468/2014 of the European Central Bank of 16 April 2014 establishing the framework for cooperation within the Single Supervisory Mechanism between the European Central Bank and national competent authorities and with national designated authorities [2014] OJ L141/1 (SSM Framework Regulation); Regulation (EU) No 469/2014 of the European Central Bank of 16 April 2014 amending Regulation (EC) No 2157/1999 on the powers of the

key part of the preparatory work was the ECB's 'comprehensive assessment', a health check of significant banks' balance sheets and risk profiles that aimed to address legacy issues.[6] The comprehensive assessment – which consisted of the asset quality review (AQR) and a forward-looking stress test of the bank – found a capital shortfall of €25 billion at 25 banks.[7] Twelve of the 25 banks had already covered their capital shortfall by the time of the announcement of the results and the others were given up to nine months to cover the capital shortfall.

At the heart of the SRM is a new EU agency, the Single Resolution Board (SRB), which is due to become fully functioning from 1 January 2016.[8] The SRB's core responsibility is to draw up and to execute resolution schemes for significant banks and cross-border banking groups in the participating Member States. It also has responsibilities for resolution planning, including the development of so-called 'living wills'. Constructing the SRB presented considerable design challenges because the required elements for an effective resolution regime tested the boundaries of Treaty bases for the establishment of agencies and of delegation to agencies under EU law. The need for secure resolution funding in the form of the SRF also gave rise to legal complications as well as acute political sensitivities that were only resolved by recourse to an intergovernmental agreement outside EU law. The structure that was finally adopted has certain weaknesses that make it vulnerable to legal challenge.[9] However, the fortuitous timing and results of Case C-270/12 *United Kingdom v European Parliament and Council*, on delegation to agencies and the use of Article 114 in the case of the short-selling intervention powers conferred on the European Securities and Markets Authority by Article 28 of the Short Selling Regulation,[10] and Case

European Central Bank to impose sanctions (ECB/1999/4) [2014] OJ L141/51; Council Regulation (EU) 2015/159 of 27 January 2015 amending Regulation (EC) No 2532/98 concerning the powers of the European Central Bank to impose sanctions [2015] OJ L27/1.

[6] SSM Regulation, art. 33(4); ECB, Aggregate Report on the Comprehensive Assessment October 2014.

[7] ECB's In-depth Review Shows Banks Need to Take Further Action, ECB Press Release 26 October 2014.

[8] SRM Regulation, art. 42.

[9] Press reports in July 2014 indicated that a group of German academics were launching a challenge at the German Constitutional Court to the SRM and also aspects of the SSM.

[10] Regulation (EU) No 236/2012 of the European Parliament and of the Council of 14 March on short-selling and certain aspects of credit default swaps [2012] OJ L86/1. The case is reported at [2014] 2 CMLR 44.

C-370/12 *Pringle v Ireland*[11] on the interrelationship between intergovernmental agreements between Member States and EU law and institutions, have increased legal certainty in these areas. On balance, it is possible to be cautiously optimistic about the capacity of the SRM to withstand challenge, to help stabilise the euro area and to make a contribution towards the reversal of the trend towards EU financial market disintegration.[12]

2.2 EBU and the EU Regulatory and Supervisory Framework

The pan-EU (or EU28) single rulebook in banking – of which the core elements are the Capital Requirements Regulation (CRR), the Capital Requirements Directive IV (CRDIV), the Bank Recovery and Resolution Directive (BRRD) and the recast Deposit Guarantee Schemes Directive – provides the regulatory framework for EBU.[13] Formally, the EU28 regulatory framework applies as much to the ECB and the SRB as it does to the national supervisory and resolution authorities of the Member States that are not in the EBU. This follows axiomatically from the principle of the EU legal order that the law must apply uniformly. However, needs and preferences that arise within EBU are likely over time to have spillover effects and to exert an increasingly strong influence over the contents of regulation at the EU28 level. A similar

---

[11] [2013] 2 CMLR 2.

[12] Eilís Ferran, 'European Banking Union: Imperfect, But It Can Work' in Danny Busch and Guido Ferrarini, *European Banking Union* (OUP 2015).

[13] Regulation (EU) No 575/2013 of the European Parliament and of the Council of 26 June 2013 on prudential requirements for credit institutions and investment firms and amending Regulation (EU) No 648/2012 [2013] OJ L176/1 (CRR); Directive 2013/36/EU of the European Parliament and of the Council of 26 June 2013 on access to the activity of credit institutions and the prudential supervision of credit institutions and investment firms, amending Directive 2002/87/EC and repealing Directives 2006/48/EC and 2006/49/EC [2013] OJ L176/338 (CRDIV); Directive 2014/59/EU of the European Parliament and of the Council of 15 May 2014 establishing a framework for the recovery and resolution of credit institutions and investment firms and amending Council Directives 77/91/EEC and 82/891/EC, Directives 2001/24/EC, 2002/47/EC, 2004/25/EC, 2005/56/EC, 2007/36/EC and 2011/35/EC and Regulations (EU) No 1093/2010 and (EU) No 648/2012 [2014] OJ L173/190 (BRRD); Directive 2014/49/EU of the European Parliament and of the Council of 16 April 2014 on deposit guarantee schemes [2014] OJ 173/149. CRR/CRDIV constitute the revamped EU prudential regulation framework, implementing the Basel III international standards. BRRD puts in place a (minimum) harmonization regulatory regime for intervention in distressed banks and some other financial firms.

trajectory can be predicted for supervisory policies, practices and procedures. This trend has implications for the EBA as the EU28 independent agency with the remit to prepare EU-wide technical standards and guidance, and to promote pan-EU convergence of supervisory practices. The ECB will put its own stamp on supervision within EBU, which could be a mixed blessing for the EBA: on the one hand, this convergence-promoting work across a significant part of the EU should alleviate the burden on the EBA but, at the same time, it is likely to result in pressure on the EBA to promote an EU-wide model that is very heavily influenced by the ECB's approach. These tensions are at the heart of the debate surrounding the potential threat of EBU to the unity of the Single Market (Part 4 below).

2.3 Other Linked Elements

The European Stability Mechanism (ESM) is the permanent stability mechanism for euro area Member States, constituted by means of an intergovernmental treaty.[14] Subject to strict conditionality, the ESM can provide financial support to member countries that are in financial difficulties. There is also the possibility for the ESM to be used to support direct bank capitalization and this forms a direct link between the ESM and EBU because a supervisory upgrade was identified as a necessary precondition for the unlocking of ESM funding for direct bank recapitalization.[15] The capacity for the ESM to engage in direct bank recapitalization became operational in December 2014.[16] Aid from public sources must comply with the State Aid regime set out in the Commission's framework for support measures in favour of banks. The ESM does not extend beyond the euro area. The mix of EU and public international law, seen in relation to the ESM and elsewhere (the Treaty on Stability, Coordination and Governance (where recourse to international law was in part a stratagem to bypass opposition from the UK) and, as discussed later in this chapter, in the context of the SRF (as a response to German concerns about mutualization), gives rise to its own distinctive set of risks to EU unity and method from a constitutional and institutional perspective.[17]

---

[14] Treaty Establishing the European Stability Mechanism (T/ESM 2012/en 1).

[15] Euro Area Summit Statement, 29 June 2012.

[16] ESM Direct Recapitalisation Instrument adopted by the ESM Board of Governors on 8 December 2014.

[17] Edoardo Chiti and Pedro Gustavo Teixeira, 'The Constitutional Responses to the Financial and Public Debt Crisis' (2013) 50 CML Rev 683; Jonathan

3. EBU AND DIFFERENTIATED INTEGRATION

3.1 Placing EBU into Theories on Integration and Differentiation

Theories on integration and differentiation focus on the degree of compatibility of national preferences, international independencies and transnational interactions, compliance problems associated with lack of coordination, autonomy costs, the strength of supranational actors, the extent of an ideational consensus, and the character of the issue area and its relevance for national identities.[18] Differentiated integration is more likely where these factors are unevenly distributed.[19] Within the EU, differentiated integration, as a response to preference heterogeneity among Member States, the varying capacity of the EU Institutions to influence different policy areas, and the political sensitivity of the issues, comes in many forms and can be categorized according to its temporal, territorial or sectoral scope, although these categories are not mutually exclusive.[20] EBU is most obviously an example of functional, sector-specific differentiated integration but it is also territorial and temporal in that EBU will comprise the euro area to start with but has the capacity to expand to include other Member States as well.

3.2 The Appeal of Participation in EBU for Member States that Do not Use the Euro as their Currency

Unlike adoption of the euro, which for most Member States is mandatory on satisfaction of the convergence criteria, EBU participation is optional for EU Member States so long as they do not use the euro as their currency. Non-euro Member States can choose to participate in the SSM

Tomkin, 'Contradiction, Circumvention and Conceptual Gymnastics: The Impact of the Adoption of the ESM Treaty on the State of European Democracy' (2013) 14 *German Law Journal* (online).

[18] Dirk Leuffen, Berthold Rittberger and Frank Schimmelfennig, *Differentiated Integration: Explaining Variation in the European Union* (Palgrave Macmillan 2013); Katharina Holzinger and Frank Schimmelfennig, 'Differentiated Integration in the European Union: Many Concepts, Sparse Theory, Few Data' (2012) 19 *Journal of European Public Policy* 292; Kölliker, 'Bringing Together' (n 2).

[19] Leuffen et al (n 18) 105.

[20] Alexander CG Stubb, 'A Categorization of Differentiated Integration' (1996) 34 *Journal of Common Market Studies* 283.

by entering into a close cooperation agreement with the ECB,[21] which carries with it automatic participation in the SRM as well.[22]

In principle non-euro Member States that are important hosts to foreign banks headquartered in the euro area would have much to gain from improved management of interdependencies within EBU. They could expect to be major beneficiaries of a supranational system of supervision that is more impartial and more conscious of cross-country spillovers. Moreover, domestically-owned banks of Member States outside EBU could be at a competitive disadvantage if the quality of their domestic banking supervision is deemed to be inferior to that within the SSM as this could result in higher funding costs.[23] Opting in would, moreover, spread the blame for supervisory failure. That there is considerable interest in exploring the opt-in possibility is evident, for example, in the work of the 'Vienna Initiative', which brings together public and private sector stakeholders of EU-based cross-border banks active in emerging Europe. This group includes non-euro Member States that acceded to the EU from 2004 and which are obliged to enter the euro area when they satisfy the convergence criteria. As hosts for foreign banks' branches or subsidiaries that have become systemic within the host economy, these countries have faced problems that were not fully recognized when the home-host principle for supervision was established.[24] The Vienna Initiative working group on EBU and Emerging Europe has acknowledged that opting in would give other EU countries 'essentially' the same benefits as euro area members with respect to

---

[21] SSM Regulation, art. 7; Decision of the European Central Bank of 31 January 2014 on the close cooperation with the national competent authorities of participating Member States whose currency is not the euro (ECB/2014/5) [2014] OJ L198/7.

[22] SRM Regulation, art. 4.

[23] Zsolt Darvas and Guntram B Wolff, 'Should Non-Euro Area Countries Join the Single Supervisory Mechanism?' Hungarian Academy of Sciences Discussion Papers (MT-DP 2013/23). ECB supervision may enhance the opting-in Member State's reputation as a banking centre by reducing the risk of supervision being tainted by national bias; and, in addition, the ECB has the prestige and presence to attract high calibre supervisory staff and can recruit from a much broader pool of talent than is likely to be available to most Member State supervisory authorities: Gerard Hertig, Ruben Lee and Joseph A McCahery, 'Empowering the ECB to Supervise Banks: A Choice-Based Approach' (2010) 7 *European Company and Financial Law Review* 171.

[24] Katharina Pistor, 'Governing Interdependent Financial Systems: Lessons from the Vienna Initiative' (2012) 2 *Journal of Globalization and Development*, art. 4.

mitigation of home-host problems, quality and consistency of supervision, and reversal of fragmentation.[25]

However, there are also off-setting reservations about how EBU would actually work in Member States that have their own currencies and interest rate policies, and whose domestic banks do not have access to Eurosystem liquidity provision. The complexities of the calculations make it easily understandable why, for example, the Polish finance minister, Mateusz Szczurek, has indicated that Poland is in no particular rush to join.[26] The two Vienna Initiative non-euro Member States that have so far signalled an intention to become part of EBU – Romania and Bulgaria – are among the weaker EU economies, and they have their own reasons to seek participation. Romania, an economy that suffered badly in the aftermath of the global financial crisis but is now recovering after a severe austerity programme, was the first to signal an intention to join. Potential 'first mover' reputational advantages of being willing to submit its banking sector to ECB supervision may have been part of the motivation. The governor of its central bank has explained that the domination of its domestic banking system by euro area banks makes especially appealing the capacity of EBU participation to act as a mechanism for removing incentives for deleveraging on the part of banks with foreign capital, to eliminate possibilities of jurisdictional arbitrage and to create a more competitive market.[27] Doubts about the ability of domestic Romanian mechanisms, resources and instruments to cope on their own with the contagion effects of crisis have also been mentioned.[28] The weaknesses of domestic arrangements have also been a major factor in the case of Bulgaria, where a major banking crisis, with ramifications including the resignation of the Prime Minister, have propelled it towards EBU.[29]

---

[25] <http://vienna-initiative.com/wp-content/uploads/2013/05/VI2-BU-WG-April-2013_final.pdf> accessed 2 April 2015.

[26] 'Financial Services: Supervisors Prepare for Capital Shortfall in European Banks' Europolitics 29 January 2014 (online).

[27] Mugur Isarescu, Relations between euro and non-euro countries within the Banking Union, 17 July 2014. Speech by Mr Mugur Isarescu, Governor of the National Bank of Romania, before the Unicredit 15th International Advisory Board, Rome, 10 July 2014.

[28] Ibid.

[29] Georgi Kantchev, 'Caught in Indecision, Bulgarian Government is Urged to Solve Banking Crisis' *The New York Times*, 4 August 2014 (online). Hertig et al. (n 23) presciently noted the 'lemons' issue but concluded that it was in fact a benefit of a choice-based approach because it would be in the wider interests of the EU for the ECB to be the supervisor of weaker banks.

Non-euro Member States that have major banks with a significant cross-border presence in euro area Member States also have reason to look closely at the option to participate. This point is particularly relevant to the Nordic-Baltic region, which is characterized by a high degree of financial market integration and long-standing cross-border collaboration in financial supervision.[30] The assets of the six largest banks (Danske Bank, DNB, Handelsbanken, Nordea, SEB, and Swedbank) comprise around 90 per cent of the total assets of all of the region's publicly-listed banks with most of their business concentrated within the Nordic-Baltic region. Banking systems in the Baltic countries are dominated by large Nordic banks (in Estonia and Lithuania, for example, the banking systems are more than 90 per cent foreign owned) and Baltic banks are also heavily dependent on funding from their Nordic parent banks. Finland, Estonia and Latvia have been in the euro area for some time and Lithuania joined in 2015. Denmark and Sweden are EU Member States but do not use the euro (Denmark has an opt out and Sweden has not met the convergence criteria), while Norway also has its own currency and is outside the EU (but in the Single Market as a member of the EEA). IMF staff have pointed out that, in principle, EBU membership for Denmark and Sweden could smooth the process of regulatory coordination, financial supervision, and cross-border bank resolution for the region.[31] But the devil is in the detail as the attitude of regional politicians and officials has made clear: as EBU has become more concrete, significant sections of Danish opinion have begun to warm to the idea of joining,[32] although,

---

[30] This paragraph draws extensively on IMF, Nordic Regional Report, IMF Country Report no 13/274, September 2013.

[31] Ibid.

[32] In February 2014, Lars Rohde, governor of the National Bank of Denmark, recommended that Danish interests would be served better through participation in EBU. Politicians and banks remained hesitant. Some sections (Liberal Alliance, Danish People's Party, Red-Green Alliance) claimed that Danish entry into EBU would be equivalent to participation in the euro area and that it would therefore have to be preceded by a referendum: Folketinget, Opinion on European Commission Proposal For Bank Resolution – COM(2013) 520, 11 September 2013. However, in April 2015 the Danish Ministry of Justice presented a report that concluded that joining the SSM would involve no loss of sovereignty and thus would not require a referendum. A statement by the Economy and Business Ministers that accompanied publication of the report declared that it would be an advantage for Denmark to join the strengthened bank union.

for now, Sweden appears to be settled in the out camp.[33] Darvas and Wolff make reference to different perceptions about Danish and Swedish supervisory practices in this context.[34] This argument touches, again, on the important point that the quality of existing national arrangements will be an important factor in determining whether there are net gains from opting into EBU. Also relevant is survey data indicating that Sweden is among the Member States that are most in favour of leaving or reducing the EU's powers in general.[35] But Denmark, like Poland, has made it clear that caution is likely to prevail until the terms of entry (and exit) are completely clear.[36]

3.3 Differentiated Participation Terms: A Work in Progress

A Member State that does not use the euro has to participate in EBU on different terms from euro area Member States. This differentiation is inevitable because of the euro's legal framework and institutional architecture, and is a consequence of political conditions in which Treaty change cannot be countenanced and developments must be fitted into the existing framework. Whereas participation in EBU is directly prescribed by EU law for euro area Member States, for non-euro Member States it is facilitated by EU law but constituted by a voluntary agreement.[37]

One of the key areas of substantive difference is with respect to participation in the governance of the SSM.[38] Driven by the ECB's established legal framework, its new Supervisory Board cannot have formal decision-making powers and, instead, those powers are exercised by the Governing Council of the ECB. The ECB founding statute limits membership of the Governing Council to members of the Executive Board of the ECB and the governors of the national central banks of the Member States whose currency is the euro. Accordingly, non-euro

---

[33] The Swedish general, county and municipal elections in September 2014 saw a swing to the left. A change of government is not expected to result in a change of policy regarding remaining outside EBU.

[34] Darvas and Wolff (n 23) 11.

[35] Ipsos European Pulse, 16 March 2014.

[36] 'Vestager Says Bridge Financing Key to Banking Union Call' *Bloomberg News*, 17 January 2014; 'Bank-Union Red Lines Drawn Around Danish Mortgage Finance System' *Bloomberg News*, 6 May 2015.

[37] A choice-based approach to ECB supervision had been canvassed in the academic literature prior to the emergence of EBU: Hertig et al. (n 23).

[38] The issues discussed in this paragraph are analysed in more detail in Eilís Ferran and Valia S G Babis, 'The European Single Supervisory Mechanism' (2013) 13 *Journal of Corporate Law Studies* 255.

Member States that participate in EBU are formally excluded from the key formal decision-making forum. The ingenious workaround for this issue provided by the SSM Regulation[39] is that: (i) the Supervisory Board, in which non-euro Member States can participate, is responsible for preparing draft decisions; (ii) draft decisions are deemed to be adopted unless the Governing Council objects in accordance with prescribed procedures (in effect, a reverse voting procedure); and (iii) a disagreement mechanism allows a non-euro Member State to say that it will not be bound by a decision to which it objects and, ultimately, to exit EBU through termination of the close cooperation agreement by the ECB. This structure, and other safeguards in the SSM Regulation, appears to go as far as is legally possible to place euro and non-euro Member States on an equal footing with respect to governance arrangements and whilst the outcome is not ideal for non-euro participating Member States, it is expedient.

There are also inequality of treatment risks as between non-euro and euro area Member States in the crisis management context. A non-euro Member State that opts to join the SSM will automatically also be part of the SRM. This bundled arrangement is necessary because supervision and resolution support each other and both have to be at the same level.[40] The governance issues that pertain to the SSM are not replicated in the SRM context because the Single Resolution Board is an EU agency established under TFEU, Article 114 in which all participating Member States are on an equal footing. The complications in the crisis management context principally concern financial support for ailing banks and financial support in the resolution of those that have failed.

That the private sector should bear the costs of bank deterioration and failure is at the heart of post-crisis thinking on bank recovery and resolution. This is the philosophy that is reflected in both the Commission's Banking Communication on the criteria for State Aid and the BRRD, which together form the EU framework within which the SRM and the national regimes of non-participating Member States will operate. Specific aspects of this philosophical approach are that the recovery plans that banks are required to maintain in preparation for a deterioration in their financial situation shall not assume any access to or receipt of extraordinary public financial support,[41] and that authorization for State Aid will be subject to the precondition that all measures to limit such aid

---

[39] Arts 26(8) and 7(7)–(8), and elaborated further in SSM Framework Regulation, Pt IX.

[40] SRM Regulation, Recital 11.

[41] BRRD, art. 5(3).

to the minimum necessary have been exploited to the maximum extent.[42] The BRRD bail-in tool gives resolution authorities wide powers to write down or to cancel the claims of the unsecured creditors of a failing institution, to convert debt claims to equity, and to change the terms of debt instruments,[43] and there are powers, both in resolution and independently of resolution action, for the write down or conversion of capital instruments as well.[44] The obligation on the private sector to meet the costs of failure is also reflected in the European System of Financing Arrangements, an industry-funded bank resolution funding structure established by the BRRD. The System comprises mandatory national funding arrangements that are to be prefunded by annual industry contributions.[45] Each bank's contribution is to be proportional to its liabilities (less own funds and guaranteed deposition), adjusted in proportion to its risk profile.[46] Bail-in of at least 8 per cent of a bank's total liabilities including own funds must be imposed before a resolution fund is tapped for a contribution in respect of losses that cannot be passed on to other creditors.[47]

Within the SRM, the national resolution funds of the participating Member States are to be consolidated into a Single Resolution Fund (SRF), to which access will be subject to BRRD-derived criteria.[48] The establishment of the SRF was the single most contentious issue for the euro area Member States in the SRM negotiations, mainly because of German-led opposition to the centralization of control and the mutualization of financial responsibility for bank failure. The uneasy bifurcated

---

[42] Communication from the Commission on the application, from 1 August 2013, of State aid rules to support measures in favour of banks in the context of the financial crisis ('Banking Communication') 2013/C 216/01 [2013] OJ C216/1, para. 29.

[43] BRRD, arts 37, 43–56. And see also SRM Regulation, art. 27.

[44] BRRD, arts 59–62; SRM Regulation, art. 21; Commission Delegated Regulation (EU) 2015/63, [2015] OJ L11/44; Council Implementing Regulation (EU) 2015/81 [2015] OJ L15/1. And see Banking Communication, para. 41.

[45] BRRD, arts 99–103; SRM Regulation, arts 67–70. Additional ex-post contributions can also be called for: BRRD, art. 104; SRM Regulation, art. 71.

[46] BRRD, art. 103; SRM Regulation, art. 70; Commission Delegated Regulation (EU) 2015/63, [2015] OJ L11/44, arts 4–13.

[47] BRRD, art. 44(5); SRM Regulation, art. 27(7). Under BRRD, art. 44(8) there is an alternative threshold of 20 per cent of the risk weighted assets of the institution concerned in certain circumstances, but this does not apply in the SRM context: SRM Regulation, art. 27(11).

[48] SRM Regulation, art. 27 and arts 67–74; Council Implementing Regulation (EU) 2015/81 [2015] OJ L15/1.

compromise that was eventually devised to overcome German objections treats the requirement for banks to make contributions to resolution funding as an obligation that remains with Member States, and it is then for the Member States to transfer the contributions raised at national level into the SRF in accordance with the criteria, modalities and conditions set out in an Intergovernmental Agreement between all the Member States apart from the UK and Sweden.[49] At the outset the SRF is to be divided into national compartments but these compartments are to be mutualized over an eight-year transitional period.

The SRM Regulation and the SRF Intergovernmental Agreement in combination govern the position of non-euro Member States with respect to the SRF. These arrangements are a vital part of the differentiated aspect of EBU because the costs and financial implications of participation are bound to feature heavily in the deliberations of any Member State that is considering its options. The terms of both entry and of exit are important: while it may be true that exit is a highly theoretical possibility,[50] having negotiated for an explicit EBU exit mechanism (another respect in which participation in EBU is different from membership of the euro area),[51] it is only to be expected that Member States will want to know exactly how it is meant to work financially before they take the plunge, and also that national public opinion will require the terms to be demonstrably fair and balanced. The overriding principle that has been adopted is one of equality between the original participants and those that join later.[52] So far as entry terms are concerned, this essentially means that the joining Member State must transfer into the SRF an amount equal to the amount it would have transferred if it had been an original participant.[53] On exit, the Member State will recoup an amount that is sufficient to permit the establishment and funding of a national resolution fund up to the BRRD-required level.[54] The SRB is to determine entry and exit amounts in agreement with the relevant Member State. SRB decisions may be referred to the CJEU.[55] But the decision on the modalities

---

49 SRM Regulation, art. 67(4); SRF Intergovernmental Agreement, art. 3.

50 Remarks by Eurogroup President Jeroen Dijsselbloem at the Ecofin press conference of 18 February 2014 on the Special ministerial meeting on the IGA on the Single Resolution Fund.

51 SSM, art. 7.

52 SRF Intergovernmental Agreement, Recital 23.

53 Ibid., art. 8(1).

54 Ibid, art. 8(5); SRM Regulation, art. 4(3).

55 SRM Regulation, art. 86; SRF Intergovernmental Agreement, art. 14. Case C-370/12 *Pringle v Ireland* ECLI:EU:C:2012:756, [2013] 2 CMLR 2 on

of recoupment may not be immediate, conditions may be associated, and distributions may be spread over a period of time. These aspects of the process may introduce an unwelcome, but perhaps not decisive, degree of unpredictability and uncertainty for a non-euro Member State that is considering its options.

On the surface, a potentially more serious stumbling block is the position with regard to access to public sector support funds. Notwithstanding the emphasis on the private sector absorption of the costs of failure, the need for 'last resort' public sector support, on a temporary or 'bridge' basis, cannot be ruled out. The Commission's Banking Communication is predicated on a continuing need for State Aid, and this possibility is also envisaged by the BRRD.[56] At present bailout responsibilities default to national Treasuries, although euro area Member States, but not Member States that do not use the euro, have the possibility of applying to the ESM for bridge financing. Non-euro Member States are therefore in a different position from euro area Member States because they and their banks do not have access to the ESM. While the SRF Intergovernmental Agreement envisages the development during the transitional period of a common backstop that ensures equivalent treatment across all EBU participants,[57] until that backstop is in place, there will be a gap so far as non-euro Member States are concerned. The stringency of the conditions for accessing ESM financing[58] may mean

the role of EU Institutions in relation to intergovernmental agreements is relevant here. Since the SRF Intergovernmental Agreement and the SRM Regulation are closely entwined, any question about the interpretation or application of the Agreement is likely also to concern the interpretation or application of EU law (*Pringle*, para. 174) and thus to involve the subject matter of the EU Treaties for the purposes of TFEU, art. 273. *Pringle* notwithstanding, recourse to intergovernmental agreements remains controversial as, among other things, a potential risk to constitutional balance in the EU: Matthias Ruffert, 'The European Debt Crisis and European Union Law' (2011) 48 CML Rev 1777; Mark Dawson and Floris De Witte, 'Constitutional Balance in the EU after the Euro-crisis' (2013) 76 MLR 817; Piet Eeckhout and Michael Waibel, 'The United Kingdom' in Fabian Amtenbrink (ed), *Constitutional and Institutional Aspects of the Economic Governance within the EU* (Djøf 2014) 487.

[56] BRRD, arts 56–58.

[57] SRF Intergovernmental Agreement, Recital 13. The Five Presidents Report of June 2015) identified the establishment of a credible common backstop as a priority: Juncker, Completing Europe's Economic and Monetary Union (n 1) 11.

[58] In particular the thresholds attaching to direct bank access to ESM financing (bail-in of private investors, exhaustion of available SRF financing, capital contribution by ESM Member State but indirect bank capitalization ruled

that the disadvantage is more apparent than real, especially for those non-euro Member States with national economies that are sufficiently strong to make a need to seek external support a remote possibility, particularly given the further consideration that if bail-in works as planned, the circumstances in which a need to access public support should be much reduced anyway.[59] But optics matter.

Political leaders can be expected to be reluctant to risk the public opprobrium that could result from an attempt to take their country into a controversial arrangement on real, or perceived, disadvantageous terms. So the question then is whether enough has been done to reassure non-euro Member States that the terms of entry into (and exit from) EBU are certain, predictable and fair. On the SSM-governance front, the indications are that concerns about unequal treatment are receding. Equal participation in the governance of the SSM was indeed a major issue during negotiations in the period leading up to political agreement on the SSM text, as can be seen from remarks by the then Danish economics minister Margrethe Vestager that being overruled by the ECB would be unacceptable and that: 'Therefore, Denmark demands, as a critical condition, that we have the right to be exempt from the supervision council's decisions should we judge that to be best for Denmark.'[60] But the arrangements that have since been put in place have been good enough to satisfy Mugur Isarescu, the Governor of the Romanian National Bank, with regard to the adequacy of the representation of non-euro Member States in the SSM decision-making processes.[61] However, equal access to public sector bridge financing, as well as to central bank liquidity support, remain more open issues. Margrethe Vestager has identified bridge financing as the factor that will 'drive' Denmark's decision on whether to join EBU.[62] Mugur Isarescu has singled out access to euro liquidity as one particular issue where equal treatment of euro area and non-euro area members of EBU is still not ensured.[63]

---

out (because of its impact on the sovereign balance sheet)) are very high ('too high' according to the IMF: 2014 art. IV Consultation with the Euro Area Concluding Statement of the IMF Mission (19 June 2014) para. 10).

[59] The European Commission has suggested that if bail-in at 8 per cent had been available, the sums generated would have been sufficient to cover most of the bank losses that triggered publicly-funded bailouts during the crisis.

[60] Quoted in article at n 36.

[61] See n 27.

[62] See n 36.

[63] See n 27.

3.4 Will Non-euro Member States Join EBU? Beyond the Terms of Participation

Fair participation terms are a necessary but not sufficient precondition to the exercise of the option to participate in EBU. The wide-ranging political calculations by non-euro Member States on whether there are net welfare gains from participation in EBU can be expected to include many other considerations. The policy preferences of private stakeholders are perceived to play an important role in shaping financial regulation in general, and their attitudes towards EBU can be expected to be highly influential. In particular, powerful industry players such as major banks are typically able and willing to devote considerable resources towards seeking to shape financial regulatory policy to suit their preferences. Banks based in non-euro Member States with significant euro area cross-border business are likely to be among those most predisposed towards joining EBU. For them, there is potentially much to be gained from the streamlining afforded by supervisory consolidation within EBU. Opting in could significantly reduce duplication and inconsistency risks that currently exist. Consider, for example, the 2014 asset quality review by the ECB and the EU-wide stress test exercise under the auspices of the EBA. The asset quality review was part of the comprehensive assessment that the ECB conducted prior to taking up its supervisory responsibilities.[64] It applied at the level of the highest level of consolidation within the euro area and therefore caught significant subsidiaries of non-euro Member States' banking groups (as well as subsidiaries of US or other third-country-headquartered bank groups). Danske Finland, DNB Estonia, HSBC France, Nordea Finland, SEB Estonia, SEB Germany, SEB Latvia, Swedbank Estonia, Swedbank Latvia and the Royal Bank of Scotland Netherlands were among the non-euro Member State banks included. The EBA stress test meanwhile was conducted by the national competent authority and applied at the highest level of consolidation in the EEA.[65] While the EBA worked closely with the ECB and national supervisory authorities in devising the stress test methodology, the fit in practice between the asset quality review and the stress test exercise was not perfect in every respect and in the case of UK banks the position was further complicated by the decision of the UK authorities to conduct an additional UK-only test as well as the EU-wide tests.

---

[64] See nn. 6–7.

[65] EBA, Main Features of the 2014 EU-wide Stress Test, 31 January 2014.

If the 'badge of quality' associated with being under the supervision of the ECB really does translate into being able to raise finance on more favourable terms, this will be another reason for banks outside the euro area to lobby their government to join EBU. They may be joined in this opinion by central bankers and national supervisors, another group whose views can exert considerable influence at the political level.[66] This suggestion is supported by the example of Romania, where the governor of the national bank has been a prominent advocate of joining EBU.

General public opinion is another key consideration, but it may pull in a different direction from that favoured by the industry and/or supervisors. Theoretical study on EU integration and differentiated integration in the area of monetary policy has identified deeply-rooted public scepticism towards the EU as the most convincing explanation for the formal or de facto opt outs from monetary union maintained by Denmark, Sweden and the UK.[67] This thesis is also supported by relatively low levels of public support for the euro in Poland and the Czech Republic.[68] Referendum requirements or political undertakings give public opinion added bite.[69] The thesis is not watertight – it is challenged by the example of Latvia which became a member of the euro area in 2014 despite reports of popular opposition[70] – but it is quite compelling. Since participation in EBU is a step closer to adoption of the euro, and has even been presented by some as being equivalent to being in the euro area,[71] those attitudes are likely to carry across. The benefits of EBU in terms of supervisory consistency, cost of capital and so forth, are difficult to convey in terms that have obvious mass appeal – except, perhaps in a crisis situation such as that experienced in Bulgaria, where exigencies can override normal objections. This suggests that, in general, EBU is unlikely to be a gamechanger that leads to an upturn in mass-level public opinion towards Europe in non-euro Member States. This view derives support from the UK's position where despite being both the headquarters for major international banks that have extensive cross-border operations and the host of subsidiaries and branches of euro area banking groups, there is no chance of the UK giving the option of joining EBU

---

[66] See n 32, (noting the recommendation of Lars Rohde, governor of the National Bank of Denmark on Danish interests and EBU participation).

[67] Leuffen et al. (n 18) 176–8.

[68] Ibid.

[69] Ibid.

[70] As noted in Alan Dashwood, 'The United Kingdom in a Re-formed European Union' (2013) EL Rev 737, 739.

[71] See comments in n 31 above.

serious consideration over any realistic time horizon. This stance reflects widespread ambivalence towards the EU in general, and a climate of opinion in which pragmatic calculations on the mutual benefits of the UK-EU relationship, which tend to command support among finance and business groups, moderate but do not trump more negative views.[72] It is also consistent with UK banks having less to gain from EBU because of the quality of their national financial regulatory system.

4. EBU AND DISINTEGRATION

4.1 Disintegration Risks

Instead of stimulating a surge in pro-European views, the advent of EBU could further harden negative attitudes. Moreover, the situation could become progressively worse if some non-euro Member States are pulled towards the centre by EBU, as that could leave those left on the outside increasingly isolated: centripetal and centrifugal forces could be in play at the same time. The critical junction for potential centrifugal effects is where the EBU and the UK meet. The concentration of EU financial market activity in the UK, London's role as a gateway to Europe and euro-denominated transactions, adamant British opposition to joining EBU, and distaste elsewhere in Europe for the UK serving as a major 'offshore' euro-denominated financial centre in the euro area's own backyard combine to form a potent cocktail.[73]

---

[72] The CityUK, UK and the EU: A Mutually Beneficial Relationship (December 2013) includes a report on a survey of business leaders indicating that nearly 90 per cent agreed on the benefits of EU membership and 84 per cent wanted the UK to remain a member.

[73] The UK is the largest net exporter of financial services and markets in the world: HM Treasury, Review of the Balance of Competences between the United Kingdom and the European Union – The Single Market: Financial Services and the Free Movement of Capital (Summer 2014), para. 3.7. The EU is the biggest single market for UK exports of financial services generating a surplus of £15.2bn (33 per cent of the UK's total trade surplus in financial services in 2012): The CityUK, ibid. Financial services is a major source of FDI into the UK and nearly half of total FDI in the UK comes from the EU: The CityUK, ibid. The UK has a major share of EU business across a range of financial services and markets (OTC derivatives (74 per cent), foreign exchange turnover (78 per cent), management of hedge fund assets (85 per cent), private equity fund (57 per cent), international insurance premiums (54 per cent) and fund management

EBU is but one of many issues that are currently fuelling heated political debate about the UK's membership of the EU ahead of the referendum on membership to be held before the end of 2017 but it is an issue that generates particular concern because of the importance of financial services for the UK economy. Fears that EBU could place potentially intolerable strain onto the UK's already fragile relationships with other Member States and EU Institutions are not wholly without foundation.[74] The UK's failure to prevent the imposition of a mandatory maximum base pay/bonus ratio in CRDIV[75] (a historic overruling of Europe's financial powerhouse on a substantial matter of financial services policy, of which aspects were challenged unsuccessfully before the Court of Justice[76]) and its legal challenges to various other recent developments in EU financial regulation (the use of enhanced cooperation for the adoption of the financial transaction tax,[77] the scope of the discretionary authority conferred on the European Securities and

assets (50 per cent) and related professional services add further to its position as a global leader: The CityUK, ibid. See also HM Treasury, ibid, Ch. 3 in general.

[74] For a helpful summary of the state of play on the 'ins' and 'outs' of the UK's participation in the legal framework of EMU and also a summary of current UK legal concerns see Eeckhout and Waibel (n 55).

[75] CRDIV, art. 94.

[76] Case C-507/13 *UK v European Parliament and Council* [2014] ECLI:EU: C:2014:2481. The UK decided to drop the case after a negative opinion from Advocate General Jääskinen delivered on 20 November 2014.

[77] The basis of the challenge is TFEU, art. 327 (extraterritorial effects failing to respect the competences, rights and obligations of non-participating States), extraterritoriality in breach of customary international law, and TFEU, art. 332 (causing costs to be incurred by non-participating States): Case C-209/13 *UK v Council of the EU* [2013] ECLI:EU:C:2014:283. The Council Legal Service gave an Opinion that is favourable to the UK's position by accepting that 'deemed residency' of financial institutions in non-participating States amounts to the exercise of jurisdiction over entities outside the zone, in contravention of customary international law, and that the proposals therefore go beyond what is allowable under enhanced cooperation. The Opinion also suggests that the different treatment of cross-border transactions within and outside the zone would be discriminatory. But the UK lost its first challenge to the Commission's decision to authorize enhanced cooperation: Judgment of the Court (Second Chamber) of 30 April 2014 [2014] 3 CMLR 48. This challenge did not address the substance of the proposed tax, which is still to be settled. The UK's action in applying to the CJEU as a precautionary matter was, in effect, ruled to be premature.

Markets Authority (ESMA) by the Short Selling Regulation,[78] and the ECB's now-abandoned plans to require euro area clearing of transactions in euro denominated products[79]) all contribute to the febrile atmosphere into which EBU has been born. The use of intergovernmental agreements (eg for the ESM and the SRF) has also begun to attract concern on the grounds that this could be a way for relevant Member States to agree measures outside the Treaty framework in a way that denies non-contracting Member States an opportunity to shape those measures, notwithstanding their close association with EU regulation.[80] Rather than being just another example of deviations from the uniformity of an 'ever closer union', which across the EU as a whole is neither a recent nor a rare phenomenon,[81] for the UK EBU could be part of a new and extreme type of differentiation initiative with a latent destructive capacity.[82]

4.2 Legal Safeguards in EBU that Address Disintegration Risks

The design of EBU, in which participation is theoretically open to all,[83] and the political reality that over any realistic short- to medium-term time horizon the UK is going to remain always on the outside, are uneasy

---

78 Case C-270/12 *UK v Council of the EU, European Parliament*, [2014] ECLI:EU:C:2014:18. The action sought to annul Regulation (EU) 236/2012 art. 28, which empowers ESMA to impose short selling restrictions in exceptional circumstances. The judgment of the Court was to dismiss the action in its entirety.

79 Case T-93/13 *United Kingdom v ECB* [2015] ECLI:EU:T:2015:290; Case T-45/12 *United Kingdom v ECB* [2015] ECLI:EU:T:2015:289; Case T-496/11 *United Kingdom v ECB* [2015] ECLI:EU:T:2015:133. In its judgement on 4 March 2015 in case T-496/11 the EU General Court annulled the Eurosystem Oversight Policy Framework published by the ECB in so far as it set a requirement for CCPs involved in the clearing of securities to be located within the eurozone. Thereafter the UK government confirmed that, in light of the agreements reached between the Bank of England and the ECB it was withdrawing Cases T-45/12 and T-93/13.

80 HM Treasury (n 73) para. 3.113.

81 Neil Walker, 'Sovereignty and Differentiated Integration in the European Union' (1998) 4 *European Law Journal* 355, 374. Dashwood (n 70) 738 notes that '[d]ifferentiation, in the sense that not all Member States are subject to the same rules or accept the same commitments, is and always has been a central organising principle of the Union's constitutional order'.

82 Matej Avbelj, 'Differentiated Integration – Farewell to the EU-27?' (2013) *German Law Journal* 191.

83 SRM Regulation, Recital 17 optimistically notes that the SRM 'could potentially' extend to the entire internal market.

bedfellows. The legal framework that supports EBU cannot be viewed as a permanent solution to this problem. That would require a much more fundamental constitutional re-ordering, which could, as Alan Dashwood has argued, involve the establishment of new executive and parliamentary organs as well as Treaty changes.[84] However and notwithstanding recent high level political acknowledgement of the potential need for Treaty change,[85] since the degree of centralization that would need to occur for demands for an ambitious new constitutional settlement to gain traction is unlikely to materialize in the foreseeable future,[86] the legal safeguards have been inserted into the EBU framework to support differentiation and address disintegration risks merit being regarded as much more than fleeting stopgap measures. A lot is resting on these special safeguards, which go beyond the now broadly standard provisions and structures, such as supervisory colleges (which are coordination structures to bring together the supervisors of a banking group), in EU financial services legislation that are intended to provide for consistency, openness, consultation and cooperation between national authorities within the European System of Financial Supervision.

One level of unity-protecting measures contains high-level expressions of principle. Article 1 of the SSM Regulation declares that: 'No action, proposal or policy of the ECB shall, directly or indirectly, discriminate against any Member State or group of Member States as a venue for the provision of banking or financial services in any currency.' The SSM Regulation also requires the ECB to respect the balance between participating and non-participating Member States in home/host matters.[87] These sentiments are repeated in the SRM Regulation, which includes, inter alia, express wording that: 'no action, proposal or policy of the Board, the Council, the Commission or a national resolution authority shall discriminate against entities, deposit holders, investors or other creditors established in the European Union on grounds of their nationality or place of business'; 'every action, proposal or policy of the Board, the Commission and the Council or of a national resolution authority in the framework of the SRM shall be undertaken with full regard and duty of care for the unity and integrity of the internal market'; and 'when making decisions or taking actions, in particular regarding entities in both participating and non-participating Member States, possible negative

---

[84] Dashwood (n 70) 755–6.

[85] George Osborne and Wolfgang Schäuble, 'Protect Britain's Interests in a Two-Speed Europe', *Financial Times*, 28 March 2014, 13.

[86] Dashwood (n 70) 755–6.

[87] SSM Regulation, art. 17(3).

effects on non-participating Member States, including on entities established in those Member States, shall be considered'.[88]

On a second level are more functional provisions that require the taking of prescribed steps or which regulate the way in which decisions are taken. This category includes requirements for memoranda of understanding between bodies within EBU and relevant authorities in non-participating Member States,[89] the obligation to invite national resolution authorities of non-participating Member States to SRB executive sessions when deliberating on a group that has subsidiaries or significant branches located there,[90] and the commitment by the participating Member States to reimburse non-participating Member States for the amount that State has paid in own resources in respect of the application of the Union budget to meet non-contractual liabilities and costs in relation to tasks under the SRM Regulation.[91] Amid high poltical controversy and to assuage the UK yet again, the strategy of formally insulating non-euro Member States from financial exposure to the euro area was taken a step further in July 2015 when, in the context of the Greece negotiations, the Commission and the Council jointly agreed that any future use of instruments for the purpose of safeguarding the financial stability of a Member State whose currency is the euro would be made conditional upon arrangements being in place to ensure that no financial (direct or indirect) liability would be incurred by the non-participating Member States.[92] In order to reflect this principle, the Commission made a proposal for the appropriate changes to a Regulation governing the existing European Financial Stabilisation Mechanism[93] and has committed not to bringing forward any proposal for the use of the EFSM without a mechanism for the protection of the non-participating Member States being assured.

The adjustments to the operations and governance of the EBA are of particular importance.[94] As noted earlier, the EBA is the EU28 agency

---

88 SRM Regulation, Recital 12 and art. 6.

89 SSM Regulation, art. 3(6); SRM Regulation, art. 32.

90 SRM Regulation, art. 53.

91 SRM Regulation, Recital 99 and SRF Intergovernmental Agreement, Recital 21 and art. 15.

92 Joint Declaration by the Commission and the Council on the use of the EFSM, 16 July 2015.

93 Council Regulation (EU) 2015/... of ..., [2015] ... amending Regulation (EU) No 407/2010 establishing a European financial stabilisation mechanism.

94 Regulation (EU) No 1022/2013 of the European Parliament and of the Council of 22 October 2013, [2013] OJ L287/5 amending Regulation (EU) No

that is responsible for, amongst other things, preparing the binding technical standards that fill in the details of EU banking regulation, and for issuing EU-wide guidance.[95] The EBA also has powers in the supervisory realm, including a 'hard' power in certain circumstances and under prescribed conditions to settle disagreements between supervisors on cross-border matters. The ECB, as supervisor, is a 'competent authority' for the purposes of being subject to the EBA's powers to settle disagreements with binding effect.[96] The SRB will also be a competent authority and will be subject to the EBA's power to make binding determinations where applicable.[97] The EBA's tasks now include the development and maintenance of an EU supervisory handbook on the supervision of financial institutions, setting out supervisory best practices for methodologies and processes.[98] The EBA Handbook will provide the pan-EU frame that the ECB must keep within in establishing supervisory practices with EBU, including its own Supervisory Manual.[99]

The EBA must act independently, objectively and in a non-discriminatory manner.[100] This broad exhortation has been reinforced by adjustments to the EBA's internal decision-making processes specifically to address the risk of EBU domination through consistent outvoting by the participating Member States of non-participating Member States. The most notable modification at this juncture (the attention on this aspect

---

1093/2010 establishing a European Supervisory Authority (European Banking Authority) as regards the conferral of specific tasks on the European Central Bank pursuant to Council Regulation (EU) No 1024/2013. The amended version is referred to hereafter in these notes as the EBA Amended Regulation. Also notable is the requirement for the Management Board to include at least two representatives of non-participating Member States: EBA Amended Regulation, art. 45. The changes to EBA internal governance are discussed further in Ferran and Babis (n 38).

[95] EBA Amended Regulation, arts 10–16.

[96] EBA Amended Regulation, art. 4(2); SSM Regulation, art. 4(1).

[97] SRM Regulation, Recital 118 and arts 3, 5 and 95. The Council and the Commission are also competent authorities for certain purposes: SRM Regulation, art. 95.

[98] EBA Amended Regulation, art. 8.

[99] The ECB should not replace the tasks of the EBA to develop draft technical standards and guidelines, ECB's guidelines, recommendations and decisions should be in compliance with regulatory and implementing technical standards developed by the EBA and adopted by the Commission, and the ECB may adopt its own regulations only to the extent necessary to organise or specify the modalities for carrying out its supervisory tasks: SSM Regulation, Recital 32 and art. 4(3).

[100] EBA Amended Regulation, art. 1(5).

can be explained in part by the fact that the bulk of the EBA's work to date has been regulatory rather than supervisory) is that EBA decisions on quasi-legislative/regulatory matters (the development of binding technical standards, the issuance of guidance) are now to be made on the basis of qualified majority voting in the Board of Supervisors, with the innovation being that this must include at least a simple majority from members of participating Member States and a simple majority from members of non-participating Member States.[101] The ECB representative on the Board of Supervisors is not entitled to vote (but in practice the ECB can be expected to play a significant role in shaping the views of the members from the participating Member States).[102] The 'double lock' is not a permanent arrangement because it is to be reviewed when the number of non-participating Member States reaches four.[103] This caveat is understandable because it would be fanciful to expect the overwhelming majority of Member States to give a permanent veto to a tiny minority. It could be said that the 'fix' merely postpones the problem for the UK but a more optimistic assessment is that in a highly dynamic situation, it is a reasonable interim compromise. Since only a few non-euro Member States appear to be actively seeking to join EBU the double lock voting mechanism could be in place for quite some time yet. Indeed, it is possible that the favourable weighing that the double lock gives to the views of non-participating Member States could be a 'minus' factor in a non-euro Member State's evaluation of the pros and cons of opting into EBU.[104]

4.3 Differentiated Integration, Economic Incentives and Public Preferences

Worries about threats to the unity of the Union have always swirled around the arrangements for the single currency.[105] However, there is no *a priori* reason to treat the advent of EBU as a development that makes

---

[101] Ibid., art. 44.

[102] The ECB can contribute to the development of technical standards, including by drawing the EBA's attention to a potential need to prepare draft standards amending existing standards: SSM Regulation, art. 4(3).

[103] EBA Amended Regulation, art. 81a.

[104] Eddy Wymeersch, 'The Single Supervisory Mechanism or 'SSM', Part One of the Banking Union' (2014) European Corporate Governance Institute (ECGI) – Law Working Paper no 240/2014. Available at SSRN: <http://ssrn.com/abstract=2397800> 69–70, accessed 2 April 2015.

[105] Chiara Zilioli and Martin Selmayr, *The Law of the European Central Bank* (Hart Publishing 2001) 1.

the UK's exit from the EU inevitable. In EU relations as a whole there is nothing fundamentally new about the UK being the awkward partner,[106] and weighty scholarly support can be found for looking to the solutions forged in the EBU context, especially the dual voting mechanism, as positive examples of what can be done to accommodate UK concerns within the overall EU structure.[107]

An effective transition from law 'on the books' to 'law in action' is never guaranteed, but the existence of multidirectional economic incentives to make EBU differentiation work in the short to medium term bodes well and allows for a cautiously optimistic short- to medium-term prognosis. The European financial services market is of crucial importance to the UK's economic interests and London's continuing prominence as a global finance centre depends in part on its popularity among global businesses as an entry point to the EU Single Market.[108] It is also very much in the economic interests of the UK for the euro area to be secure and stable, and supported by strong fiscal discipline.[109] At the wider geopolitical level, the UK's membership of the EU enhances its international statute and influence. There are thus strong arguments for the UK to remain committed to constructive dialogue within the EU.[110] From the other side, the potentially quite threatening prospect of the inclusion of the UK's supersize banking industry in arrangements that envisage the (eventual) mutualization of the financial burdens of bank failure provides a strong case from the standpoint of the Member States that participate in EBU for the UK to remain on the outside of EBU.[111] At the same time, it is economically advantageous to keep the UK in the Single Market and the EU because the EU as a whole benefits from its global strength in finance, as well as its capabilities in other areas such as diplomacy and defence.[112] These considerations imply that there are

---

[106] Stephen George, *An Awkward Partner: Britain in the European Community* (3rd edn, OUP 1998).

[107] Dashwood (n 70) 748–9.

[108] HM Treasury (n 73) paras 3.84 and 3.88 (mutual benefits for the UK and the EU).

[109] Ibid., paras 3.102–3.103.

[110] The CityUK (n 72) provides supporting statistical data. Previous studies point in the same direction: eg, Stephen Booth, Christopher Howarth, Mats Persson and Vincenzo Scarpetta, Continental Shift: Safeguarding the UK's Financial Trade in a Changing Europe (Open Europe, December 2011).

[111] Dirk Schoenmaker and Arjen Siegmann, 'Winners of a European Banking Union' <http://www.voxeu.org/article/winners-european-banking-union> accessed 2 April 2015.

[112] Dashwood (n 70) 756.

powerful constraints against behaviour, such as caucus voting, that could change the calculation for the UK so markedly that it would be better off outside the EU.

What, though, of mass public opinion and its power to carry the day on contentious integration issues? British public opinion is represented in the media as becoming increasingly anti-EU and feedback loops between political actions and public opinion may reinforce these sentiments and modes of behaviour. However, survey data indicates that the most popular option for Britons is to stay in the EU but to reduce its powers or, putting it another way, differentiation is preferred to disintegration.[113] The negotiations over EBU in fact allowed the UK's political leaders to act in ways that were well-attuned to the public mood: on the one hand, they could play to more populist anti-EU sentiments by claiming that they had won concessions to protect British interests, and, on the other, they could also simultaneously present their actions as being in accord with the preferences of pro-EU industry and business groups to remain within the EU and exert influence from the inside. It is possible that growing British public discontent with other EU policy areas could propel the UK towards the exit, but so long as the economic incentives operate properly, EBU should not add to that pressure.

5. CONCLUSION

European Banking Union provides an important new context in which to examine how differentiation affects integration. This chapter has conducted such an examination primarily from a legal standpoint but also drawing upon the work of political economists that seeks to understand the nature of differentiated integration. It has focused on two issues in particular: (1) the short- to medium-term appeal of EBU participation for Member States that do not use the euro (centripetal effects); and (2) the potential over the same time horizon for EBU to lead to disorderly break-up of the EU (centrifugal effects). On (1), EBU pushes the boundaries of legal technology with a view to maximizing the functional equivalence between euro Member States, whose participation is compulsory, and the non-euro Member States that choose to participate in EBU via a close cooperation agreement. The early indications that some non-euro Member States do want to join EBU notwithstanding certain lingering differences between their position and that of euro area

113 Ipsos European Pulse, March 2014.

Member States, provide an encouraging sign as to the value of those efforts. But while fair participation terms are necessary, they are not a sufficient precondition to exercise of the option to participate in EBU. Each non-euro Member State will make its own wide-ranging political calculations on whether there are net welfare gains from EBU and in doing so will take due account of the policy preferences of private and public stakeholders, which may pull in different directions. The full extent of the centripetal effect of EBU is therefore hard to predict, but it is certainly a new force to be reckoned with. On (2), the chapter arrives at a cautiously optimistic prognosis. The legal safeguards in EBU to address disintegration risks are not a permanent solution to the problem of the UK being intent upon remaining outside deeper integration in the monetary and economic sphere but nor are they merely fleeting or stopgap measures. The chapter identifies compelling economic incentives for all Member States to make these safeguards work and to resist destructive behaviour. So long as the economic incentives work properly, self-interest should limit the mass appeal of calls to use EBU as a reason to exit the Single Market.

REFERENCES

Avbelj M, 'Differentiated Integration – Farewell to the EU-27?' (2013) *German Law Journal* 191–212.

Booth S, Howarth Chr, Persson M and Scarpetta V, Continental Shift: Safeguarding the UK's Financial Trade in a Changing Europe (Open Europe, December 2011).

Chiti E and Teixeira PG, 'The Constitutional Responses to the Financial and Public Debt Crisis' (2013) 50 *Common Market Law Review* 683–708.

Darvas Z and Wolff GB, 'Should Non-Euro Area Countries Join the Single Supervisory Mechanism?' Hungarian Academy of Sciences Discussion Papers (MT-DP 2013/23).

Dashwood A, 'The United Kingdom in a Re-formed European Union' (2013) *European Law Review* 737–56.

Dawson M and De Witte F, 'Constitutional Balance in the EU after the Euro-crisis' (2013) 76 *Modern Law Review* 817–44.

de Neve J-E, 'The European Onion? How Differentiated Integration is Reshaping the EU' (2007) 29 *Journal of European Integration* 503–21.

Dyson K and Marcussen M, 'Transverse Integration in European Economic Governance: Between Unitary and Differentiated Integration' (2010) 32 *Journal of European Integration* 17–39.

Dyson K and Sepos A (eds), *Whose Europe? The Politics of Differentiated Integration* (Palgrave Macmillan 2010).

Eeckhout P and Waibel M, 'The United Kingdom' in F Amtenbrink, *Constitutional and Institutional Aspects of the Economic Governance within the EU* (Djøf 2014).
Ferran E, 'European Banking Union: Imperfect, But It Can Work' in Danny Busch and Guido Ferrarini, *European Banking Union* (OUP 2015)
Ferran E and Valia SG Babis, 'The European Single Supervisory Mechanism' (2013) 13 *Journal of Corporate Law Studies* 255–85.
George S, *An Awkward Partner: Britain in the European Community* (3rd edn, OUP 1998).
Hertig G, Lee R and McCahery JA, 'Empowering the ECB to Supervise Banks: A Choice-Based Approach' (2010) 7 *European Company and Financial Law Review* 171–215.
Holzinger K and Schimmelfennig F, 'Differentiated Integration in the European Union: Many Concepts, Sparse Theory, Few Data' (2012) 19 *Journal of European Public Policy* 292–305.
Isarescu M, Relations between euro and non-euro countries within the Banking Union, 17 July 2014.
Isarescu M, Speech before the Unicredit 15th International Advisory Board, Rome, 10 July 2014.
Juncker J-C, Completing Europe's Economic and Monetary Union, 22 June 2015.
Kantchev G, 'Caught in Indecision, Bulgarian Government is Urged to Solve Banking Crisis' *The New York Times*, 4 August 2014 (online).
Kölliker A, 'Bringing Together or Driving Apart the Union: Towards a Theory of Differentiated Integration' (2001) 24 *West European Politics* 125–51.
Kölliker A, *Flexibility and European Unification: The Logic of Differentiated Integration* (Rowman and Littlefield 2006).
Leuffen D, Rittberger B and Schimmelfennig F, *Differentiated Integration: Explaining Variation in the European Union* (Palgrave Macmillan 2013).
Osborne G and Schäuble W, 'Protect Britain's Interests in a Two-Speed Europe', *Financial Times*, 28 March 2014, 13.
Pistor K, 'Governing Interdependent Financial Systems: Lessons from the Vienna Initiative' (2012) 2 *Journal of Globalization and Development* (online).
Reding V, The United Kingdom and the EU – Inevitably Drifting Apart?, Mackenzie Stuart Lecture, Cambridge, 17 February 2014.
Ruffert M, 'The European Debt Crisis and European Union Law' (2011) 48 *Common Market Law Review* 1777–806.
Schoenmaker D and Siegmann A, 'Winners of a European Banking Union', available at <http://www.voxeu.org/article/winners-european-banking-union>.
Stubb ACG, 'A Categorization of Differentiated Integration' (1996) 34 *Journal of Common Market Studies* 283–95.
Tomkin J, 'Contradiction, Circumvention and Conceptual Gymnastics: The Impact of the Adoption of the ESM Treaty on the State of European Democracy' (2013) 14 *German Law Journal* (online).
Van Rompuy H, Towards a Genuine Economic and Monetary Union, 26 June 2012.
Van Rompuy H, Towards a Genuine Economic and Monetary Union, 5 December 2012.

Walker N, 'Sovereignty and Differentiated Integration in the European Union' (1998) 4 *European Law Journal* 355–88.
Wymeersch E, The Single Supervisory Mechanism or 'SSM', Part One of the Banking Union (21 February 2014).
Zilioli C and Selmayr M, *The Law of the European Central Bank* (Hart Publishing 2001).

11. The financial transaction tax project

Pieter Van Cleynenbreugel and Wouter Devroe

1. INTRODUCTION

In the aftermath of the financial crisis, states and international organisations have actively been looking for new ways to ensure that the financial sector effectively contributes to the rebuilding of a scattered economy.[1] One of the most popular proposals voiced in that regard comprises the introduction of a tax on (speculative) transactions in financial instruments engaged in by financial institutions. This financial transaction tax would require every financial institution to pay a levy amounting to a small percentage of the value underlying those transactions.

This chapter analyses the European Union's proposal for a Directive establishing a common financial transaction tax (FTT). The proposal is controversial in its own right, as it relies on extended establishment criteria to determine who should pay the envisaged tax. In addition, the proposal emerges from an enhanced cooperation initiative by only 11 Member States willing to implement a common taxation scheme. The regulatory developments concerning the enhanced cooperation FTT mechanism, as outlined in section 2, point to the emergence of a 'fast-track' European integration scheme that complements other schemes of differentiated and flexible integration mechanisms pervading post-crisis EU law and governance. In section 3, it will be submitted that such a fast-track project directly affects the role and scope of fiscal diversity and regulatory competition as central values underlying the European integration project in general and the EU internal market in particular. At the same time, however, EU law does not seem to exclude the adoption of this and similar fast-track integration projects.

[1] See Commission Press Release IP/11/1085 of 28 September 2011, 'Financial Transaction Tax: Making the financial sector pay its fair share'.

2. FROM COMMISSION PROPOSAL TO CONTESTED ENHANCED COOPERATION INITIATIVE

This section outlines the proposals for an EU-wide financial transaction tax. It briefly summarises the process leading to the adoption of the current proposal for a Directive (2.1), prior to discussing the contents and scope of that proposal (2.2).

2.1 Enhanced Cooperation in Action

The proposal for an EU-wide FTT emerged from discussions conducted at global level immediately after the crisis. The Group of 20 Leading Economies (the G20) initially discussed the development of a global financial transaction tax scheme but failed to reach an agreement in that regard.[2] In parallel with those (eventually stillborn) initiatives, the European Commission proposed its own EU-wide tax scheme on 28 September 2011, following up on a preliminary 2010 Communication.[3] The proposal provided for the adoption of an EU Directive imposing a common financial transaction tax. It particularly aimed to counter potentially disparate regulatory developments across Member States, which individually sought to impose financial transaction taxes on particular transactions.[4] The Directive would indeed require that Member States no longer maintain or introduce taxes on financial transactions other than the FTT.[5]

The Commission based its proposal on Article 113 TFEU, which enables the Council, acting *unanimously* in accordance with a special legislative procedure and after consulting the European Parliament and

---

[2] See G20 Cannes Summit Final Declaration, 'Building our Common Future: Renewed Collective Action for the Benefit of All' <https://www.g20.org/>, para. 82, accessed 24 March 2015.

[3] The 2011 Proposal for a Council Directive on a common system of financial transaction tax and amending Directive 2008/7/EC, COM(2011) 594 final can be found at <http://ec.europa.eu/taxation_customs/resources/-documents/taxation/other_taxes/financial_sector/> accessed 24 March 2015 (hereinafter referred to as 2011 Proposal). See also the Communication from the Commission to the European Parliament, the Council, the European Economic and Social Committee and the Committee of the Regions – Taxation of the Financial Sector, COM(2010) 549 final. Most policy documents relating to the FTT can be found on that website. If no particular reference is given in subsequent footnotes, the references can be found there.

[4] 2011 Proposal, 2.

[5] Ibid., art. 12.

the Economic and Social Committee, to adopt provisions for the harmonisation of legislation concerning *indirect taxation*. Contrary to EU-determined value-added tax (VAT), which is calculated on the basis of the value added during a particular production or delivery stage and where the value-added taxes already paid at an earlier stage of the production or distribution process will be deducted from the actual tax amount due,[6] the proposed FTT is meant to be a particular kind of 'sales tax'. A sales tax is levied at every point of 'buying and/or selling', i.e. at the point of every transaction without any possibility of taking previously paid transaction taxes into account.[7]

At the June and July 2012 Council meetings, it became clear that the then 27 Member States could not reach a unanimous agreement on the desirability, scope and relevance of an EU-wide FTT.[8] As a result, it appeared highly unlikely that a common FTT would effectively be adopted by means of an EU Directive in the upcoming years. The United Kingdom and Sweden were particularly vocal in opposing the adoption of the envisaged EU-wide FTT Directive.[9] Responding to those difficulties, both France and Italy proceeded by proposing the adoption of their own national financial transaction tax regimes.[10] At the same time, 11 Member States (France and Italy, but also Belgium, Germany, Estonia, Greece, Spain, Austria, Portugal, Slovenia and Slovakia) asked the

---

[6] VAT is presently governed by Council Directive 2006/112/EC of 28 November 2006 on the common system of value added tax, [2007] OJ L347/1. See on deductions in particular, arts 168 and 169 of the Directive.

[7] For that analogy, see Robert Pollin, 'A U.S. Financial Transaction Tax: How Wall Street Can Pay for its Mess' (2012) 21 *New Labour Forum* 96, 97.

[8] See for that information the Commission's 2012 Proposal for a Council Decision authorising enhanced cooperation in the area of financial transaction tax, COM(2012) 631 final, 3 (hereinafter Commission 2012 authorisation proposal).

[9] See Rebecca Cristie and Jim Brunsden, 'EU Transaction Tax Debate Highlights Euro-Area Disagreement', *Bloomberg Business Week*, 8 November 2011 <www.businessweek.com> accessed 24 March 2015.

[10] See *EUobserver.com*, 'France Launches Financial Transaction Tax', 2 August 2012. The provision can be found in art. 235 ter ZD Code général des impôts, available at <www.legifrance.gouv.fr> accessed 24 March 2015. See art. 1, paras 491–500 LEGGE 24 dicembre 2012, n 228 <www.gazzettaufficiale.it> accessed 24 March 2015. For background on the Italian FTT regime, see <http://www.borsaitaliana.it/azioni/notiziedettaglio/iftt.en.htm> accessed 24 March 2015.

Commission to continue the FTT harmonisation process on the basis of enhanced cooperation.[11]

According to Article 20 TEU, Member States that wish to establish enhanced cooperation among them, within the framework of the Union's non-exclusive competences, may make use of the EU institutions and exercise those competences by applying the relevant provisions of the Treaties. Article 329 TFEU adds that those Member States willing to embark upon this process have to file a request to the Commission, specifying the scope and objectives of the enhanced cooperation proposed. In order to initiate such a procedure, at least nine Member States have to join the request. Between 28 September 2012 and 23 October 2012, 11 Member States effectively made such requests, enabling the Commission to submit a proposal to the Council on 25 October 2012.[12]

Following submission of a Commission proposal, the Council is called upon to consider the adoption of a decision authorising enhanced cooperation among the participating Member States. The Council is only entitled to authorise enhanced cooperation after obtaining consent from the European Parliament.[13] On 12 December 2012, the Parliament effectively consented to the FTT proposal by the Commission. The Parliament specifically held that the possibility of raising harmonised FTT on the territories of the participating Member States seemed to affect 'neither the ability of non-participating Member States to maintain or introduce similar taxation at a national level, nor the conditions for raising such taxes on their territories'.[14] As a result, it agreed on the enhanced cooperation envisaged. In the wake of the Parliament's consent, the Council adopted Decision 2013/52/EU on 22 January 2013, authorising enhanced cooperation concerning the FTT between the 11 Member States.[15] Such a decision, which has to be taken unanimously by the participating Member States only, allows for EU legislation to be developed according to the EU Treaties' procedures and requirements.[16] The Council's authorisation decision enabled the Commission to adopt an

---

[11] Commission 2012 authorisation proposal, 3.

[12] Ibid.

[13] See art. 329 TFEU.

[14] European Parliament legislative resolution of 12 December 2012 on the proposal for a Council decision authorising enhanced cooperation in the area of the creation of financial transaction tax <www.europarl.europa.eu> accessed 24 March 2015.

[15] Council Decision of 22 January2013/52/EU of 2013 authorising enhanced cooperation in the area of financial transaction tax, [2013] OJ L22/11.

[16] Arts 20(3) and (1) TEU.

adapted proposal on 14 February 2013.[17] That proposal is presently being considered for legislative adoption.

On 18 April 2013, the UK initiated annulment proceedings – on the basis of Article 263 TFEU – against the Council decision authorising enhanced cooperation.[18] According to the UK, the decision authorising enhanced cooperation was in breach of Article 327 TFEU, which states that enhanced cooperation shall respect the competences, rights and obligations of those Member States which do not participate in it. By authorising the adoption of a proposed Directive that would directly affect and limit the taxing powers of non-participating Member States, the UK considered that its own rights and obligations under the Treaties were being infringed.[19] It additionally maintained that the decision violated Article 332 TFEU, arguing that it would have to bear expenditure associated with the enhanced cooperation mechanisms.[20] That provision requires that such expenditure will only be borne by the participating Member States, unless all Member States decide otherwise. Such a decision did not accompany the FTT proposal.

The Court of Justice dismissed the objections by the UK against the initiation of enhanced cooperation procedures and effectively allowed the project to proceed in a Second Chamber judgment delivered on 30 April 2014. The Court stated that its review of an authorisation decision is only related to 'the issue of whether that decision is valid as such in the light of, inter alia, the provisions, contained in Article 20 TEU and in Articles 326 TFEU to 334 TFEU, which define the substantive and procedural conditions relating to the granting of such authorisation'.[21] Above all, it was held that such a review 'should not be confused with the review which may be undertaken, in the context of a subsequent action for annulment, of a measure adopted for the purposes of the implementation of the authorised enhanced cooperation'.[22] As the principles of taxation challenged by the UK were not in any way constituent elements of the authorisation decision under scrutiny in this case, they could not support

[17] Proposal for a Council Directive implementing enhanced cooperation in the area of financial transaction tax, COM(2013) 71 final (hereinafter referred to as 2013 Commission Proposal).

[18] Case C-209/13 *United Kingdom v Council* [2014] ECLI:EU:C:2014:283, para. 13.

[19] Ibid., paras 19–20, also referring to customary international law arguments in that regard.

[20] Ibid., para. 33.

[21] Ibid., para. 34.

[22] Ibid., para. 36.

a plea for the annulment of the authorisation decision. The same was true for the expenditure implications, as they would only be clear once the measures were in operation.[23] The substantive law objections made by the UK could therefore not be invoked at this stage. The Court did not however exclude that the UK could effectively launch a potentially successful action for the annulment of the actual Directive once it was effectively adopted.

In the immediate wake of the judgment, ten of the 11 original Member States firmly expressed their commitment to proceed with legislative discussions on the proposed FTT Directive.[24] At the 6 May 2014 Council meeting, a state of play and outlook for the future was discussed.[25] It was maintained that technical discussions on the scope of the tax, as well as the relationship between the proposed Directive and the EU financial regulation framework, needed to be clarified in the months to come.[26] Specific attention was also paid to reflecting on additional categories of transactions exempted from the tax, as well as to the progressive introduction of the tax for similar transactions rather than the immediate introduction and imposition of a fully-fledged generally applicable tax across the participating Member States.[27] Above all, the notes expressed a willingness to proceed with the enhanced cooperation harmonisation attempt but also acknowledged that more technical discussions were needed.[28] Once those technical discussions result in an agreement among the participating Member States, the Directive can be adopted and published in accordance with the procedure referred to in Article 113 TFEU.[29] On the basis of this state of play, the actual introduction of a harmonised 'enhanced cooperation' FTT was expected to take place in January 2016 at the earliest.[30] Throughout 2016, however, no progress

---

23 Ibid., para. 38.

24 See Alex Barker, 'Eurozone Divided over Financial Transaction Tax Deal', *Financial Times*, 6 May 2014 <www.ft.com> accessed 24 March 2015. Slovenia did not sign the agreement, as it was without a government at that stage, see 'UK, Sweden Attack FTT Statement by Euro Nations', <www.euractiv.com> accessed 24 March 2015.

25 See Council Interinstitutional File 2013/0045 (CNS) <www.consilium.europa.eu> accessed 24 March 2015 (hereinafter referred to as 2014 FTT State of Play).

26 Ibid., para. 9.

27 Ibid., para. 11.

28 Ibid., paras 12 and 15.

29 Ibid., para. 14.

30 See Barker (n 24). After talks failed in December 2014, ten Member States have restarted debates aiming at 1 January 2016 and 1 January 2017 for the

has been made in this regard. The only development worth mentioning is that in March 2016 Estonia decided no longer to join the enhanced cooperation initiative.[31] As a result, only 10 Member States remain committed to proceed with the adoption of an EU-wide FTT.

2.2 The Proposed FTT Directive in a Nutshell

The technical discussions on the scope of the FTT revolve around the Commission's 14 February 2013 revised proposal for a Directive. The proposal's aims are essentially threefold: (1) to avoid fragmentation in the internal market for financial services, bearing in mind the increasing number of uncoordinated national tax measures being put in place; (2) to ensure that financial institutions make a fair contribution to covering the costs of the recent crisis and to ensure a level playing field with other sectors from a taxation point of view; and (3) to create appropriate disincentives for transactions that do not enhance the efficiency of financial markets thereby complementing regulatory measures aimed at avoiding future crises.[32] A fourth – yet less direct – aim of the proposal was to extend the EU's own resources and to diminish national contributions to its budget. Although the 2011 proposal was more outspoken on the budgetary scope,[33] the 2013 enhanced cooperation proposal also refers to the FTT as a means to finance the EU's own resources.[34] The 2013 proposal indeed envisages that a part of the FTT revenue generated by the Member States could be transferred to the EU's 'own resources' pool.[35]

The proposal envisages charging financial institutions a levy of 0.1 per cent or (in the case of derivative contracts) 0.01 per cent[36] of the consideration paid or of the market price on every financial transaction concluded by them.[37] In order for the EU tax to be imposed, at least one

introduction of (parts of the) FTT package, see Mark Deen and Rebecca Christie, 'Europe Financial Transaction Tax gets new push from 10 Countries', *Bloomberg Business*, 27 January 2015, <http://www.bloomberg.com> accessed 4 November 2016.

31 Council State of Play document of 3 June 2016 on Enhanced cooperation in the area of Financial Transaction Tax, <http://data.consilium.europa.eu/doc/document/ST-9602-2016-INIT/en/pdf> accessed 4 November 2016.

32 2013 Commission Proposal, 4.

33 Ibid., 3

34 Ibid., 14.

35 Ibid., 15.

36 Ibid., art. 9(2).

37 Ibid., art. 6.

party to the transaction will need to be established in a participating Member State. In addition, a financial institution established in the territory of a participating Member State would necessarily also have to be a party to the transaction, acting either for its own account or for the account of another person or in the name of a party to the transaction.[38] Member States' tax authorities would be responsible for levying and charging the tax at the time of occurrence of the financial transaction.[39] Every financial institution that is a party to the transaction, acting in the name of a party or having the transaction carried out on its account, would be liable to pay the tax.[40] This means that if two credit institutions established in participating Member States are involved in the transaction, each of them would have to pay the tax. FTT would be payable only in the participating Member State in which the financial institution is (considered to be) established.[41] A Member State established in another participating Member State (Germany), yet concluding a transaction with an Italian insurance fund in Italy, would thus have to pay the tax in Germany.

In order to capture as many financial transactions and financial market operators as possible, the proposal defined financial transactions and financial institutions in a broad-brushed fashion.[42] As soon as a different party assumes the risk attached to a financial instrument and a financial institution is involved in the process, the transaction will fall within the proposed Directive's scope.[43] A financial transaction is defined as: (a) the purchase and sale of a financial instrument (a wide definition in its own right, which includes shares, bonds, units in collective investment undertakings, money market instruments, instruments traded over-the-counter or on regulated markets …[44]), before netting and settlement; (b) the transfer between entities of a group of the right to dispose of a financial instrument as owner and any equivalent operation implying the transfer of the risk associated with the financial instrument; (c) the conclusion of derivative agreements before netting or settlement; (d) exchange contracts

38 Ibid., art. 3(1).
39 Ibid., art. 11(1).
40 Ibid., art. 10(1) and (2).
41 Ibid., art. 10(1), final sentence.
42 Ibid., art. 2(2) and (8).
43 Ibid., 8.
44 The proposal in that regard consistently refers to more specific definitions provided for in instruments of EU secondary legislation, see ibid., art. 2(8) for examples.

relating to financial instruments; and (e) repurchase agreements,[45] reverse repurchase agreements or securities lending and borrowing agreements.[46] Primary market transactions – the raising of capital in return for newly emitted shares – and spot currency transactions (agreements to buy and sell different currencies at exchange rates determined at a specific day (spot date) in the near future) are excluded from the Directive.[47]

Financial institutions have also been defined widely and include credit institutions, investment firms, insurance undertakings, undertakings for the collective investment in transferable securities, regulated markets, pension funds, and alternative investment funds.[48] The European Central Bank, national central banks, as well as international financial organisations or the European stability mechanisms are to be excluded from the scope of the Directive.[49]

The 2013 proposal particularly defines the concept of 'establishment in a Member State' widely, in an attempt to avoid tax-induced relocation to non-participating Member States. In order for the Directive to apply, a link between the economic substance of the transaction and the territory of any Member State was to be present or had at least to be so presumed.[50] To that extent, a cascade of establishment criteria for financial institutions was proposed, both for financial institutions and for non-financial institutions.

A financial institution is considered to be established in a Member State if it is authorised there, has its registered seat or permanent address there or operates a branch which concludes transactions there.[51] If the institution has been authorised or is entitled to operate in another country and provides cross-border services as a financial institution in regard to the territory of an FTT Member State, it will equally be deemed to be established in that Member State in relation to transactions covered by

---

[45] See art. 3(1)(m) Directive 2006/49/EC of the European Parliament and of the Council of 14 June 2006 on the capital adequacy of investment firms and credit institutions (recast), [2006] OJ L177/201.

[46] The 2011 Commission proposal only referred to points a, b and c, yet it included repurchase agreements sub a, in addition to purchase and sale transactions.

[47] 2013 Commission Proposal, art 3(4)(a).

[48] Member States and central counterparties are excluded from the definition, see 2013 Commission Proposal, art. 3(2).

[49] Ibid., art. 3(4)(b), (c) and (d).

[50] Ibid., 10.

[51] Ibid., art. 4(1)(a), (c), (d) and (e).

the authorisation or entitlement.[52] In addition, the proposed Directive also deems a financial institution to be established in a Member State if it is a party to or acting in the name of someone else for a financial transaction with a financial institution or another person established in that participating Member State.[53] As a result, the FTT proposal relies on a supplementary presumption that a financial institution concluding a transaction with a resident counterparty also resides in the participating Member State for the purposes of levying the FTT.[54] This would imply that a Canadian pension fund with no branch in the EU could nevertheless be taxed in, for example, France if it were to purchase financial instruments from a France-based credit institution. The French credit institution would equally be taxed on the same transaction, as it also fulfils the establishment criteria by virtue of its establishment in a participating Member State.[55]

In addition to the establishment principles outlined above, the 2013 proposal also introduces an 'issuance' principle to counter tax avoidance. According to the proposal, a financial institution is then deemed to be established in a participating Member State when it is party, acting either on its own account or on account of another person, or is acting in the name of a party to the transaction, to a financial transaction in a structured product or one of the financial instruments *issued in the territory of a participating Member State*.[56] As a result of that principle, a situation in which a Russian credit institution established in Russia sells German securities to a Chinese credit institution established in China would be covered by the proposal and would effectively amount to both parties being taxable in Germany.[57]

A person which is not a financial institution is deemed to be established within a Member State if its registered seat or, in case of a natural

---

[52] Ibid., art. 4(1)(b); this situation occurs, inter alia, when the financial institution relies on its European 'passport' to provide cross-border services in a particular Member State, without however being established or having a subsidiary in that Member State, see ibid., 10.

[53] Ibid., art. 4(1)(f).

[54] This rule only comes into play if no other condition outlined above could first be established, see ibid., art. 4(4).

[55] On the basis of ibid., art. 4(1)(c).

[56] Ibid., art. 4(1)(g).

[57] For this and other similar examples, the Commission drafted a specific memorandum on 'How the FTT Works in Specific Cases and other Questions and Answers' <http://ec.europa.eu/taxation_customs/resources/documents/taxation/other_taxes/financial_sector/ftt_examples.pdf> accessed 24 March 2015.

person, if its permanent address or usual residence is located in that State, or it has a branch in that State, in respect of financial transactions carried out by that branch.[58] The 2013 proposal particularly added that a person is also established in a participating Member State if it is party to a financial transaction in a structured product or one of the financial instruments issued in the territory of a participating Member State.[59] As a result, the purchase of German securities by a Danish housing corporation from a Chinese credit institution would also fall within the scope of the proposed Directive. Both parties would be deemed to be established in Germany, yet only the Chinese credit institution would have to pay the FTT, as the tax is only imposed on financial institutions.

In cases where establishment in a participating Member State has been determined, a financial institution would still be able to escape the imposition and payment of the tax if it can prove that the economic substance of the transaction considered does not have a link with the territory of the Member State concerned.[60] The Commission refrained from providing clear guidance as to how such proof should be delivered and what standard is required to rebut the establishment or issuance principles. As a result, any transaction that fulfils the criteria outlined here will in principle be subject to FTT payable at the time of transaction by the financial institutions involved in the transaction. The proposal additionally contains an anti-abuse clause to avoid artificial tax constructions to be set up.[61] In doing so, the participating Member States would ensure that all relevant transactions remain subject to the tax. Finally, the proposal does not affect existing EU law provisions on mutual assistance that seek to ensure that the FTT dues can also be easily recovered across non-participating Member States.[62]

3. REGULATORY DIFFERENTIATION IN THE SERVICE OF 'FAST-TRACK' EUROPE?

The adoption of an FTT on the basis of enhanced cooperation between 11 Member States directly invites one to reflect upon the nature and

58 2013 Commission Proposal, art. 4(2)(a) and (b).

59 Ibid., art. 4(2)(c).

60 Ibid., art. 4(3).

61 Ibid., art. 13.

62 Ibid., 14, referring to instruments pertaining to mutual assistance between Member States. No special regime for enforcement in third countries is considered in the proposal, a reference to existing OECD documents notwithstanding.

scope of enhanced cooperation and on the extent to which such cooperation can be operationalised in the service of the internal market. This section submits that the EU's FTT proposals incorporate a particular 'fast-track' interpretation of EU integration through enhanced cooperation (3.1). While the Court of Justice seemingly removed initial constitutional objections against such fast-track developments in its 30 April 2014 judgment, the current FTT proposals *prima facie* remain difficult to square with the acknowledgment of fiscal diversity and regulatory autonomy in EU free movement law (3.2). This section outlines those objections and the ways in which they have been addressed throughout legal and policy discussions accompanying the FTT proposal. It will be submitted that no clear legal or constitutional limits can be found to impede the introduction of a fast-track FTT regime. The introduction of such a regime would nevertheless significantly transform the balance between harmonisation and regulatory competition traditionally underlying EU internal market integration.

3.1 From 'Two-speed' to 'Fast-track' Europe

The willingness of 11 Member States to implement a common FTT in the absence of harmonisation among all Member States confirms a preference for a 'multi-speed' Europe to be developed more intensely. According to multi-speed or differentiated integration theory, European integration should proceed at different speeds, depending on the policy area concerned and the incentives or willingness of political actors involved.[63] Legislative or regulatory action by the EU's 28 Member States (EU28) should still comprise the bulk of activities taking place within the formal framework developed by the EU Treaties. In addition, however, several 'speedier' integration initiatives could be developed or remain in place in the shadows of those Treaties, allowing for a core group of Member States to move ahead with the European integration project.[64] Those initiatives seek to establish more detailed or enhanced

[63] See for background, Matej Avbelj, 'Differentiated Integration – Farewell to the EU-27?' (2013) 14 *German Law Journal* 191, 194 for an overview of techniques in that regard.

[64] The framework of differentiated integration sketched here is obviously more nuanced, see for different perspectives, Bruno De Witte, Dominik Hanf and Ellen Vos (eds), *The Many Faces of Differentiation in EU Law* (Intersentia 2001).

legal norms, which do not replace but complement the 'classical' EU legal standards.[65]

The provisions on enhanced cooperation are peculiar in that regard since they allow for explicit reliance on the procedures, institutions and legal instruments provided in the EU Treaties in order to adopt speedier integration measures.[66] As such, it has been argued that enhanced cooperation initiatives promote a 'two-speed' Europe approach. Enhanced cooperation instruments comprise EU law instruments that address only a 'core' group of participating Member States, without affecting the rights, prerogatives and obligations of non-participating Member States.[67] The latter continue the integration process at regular speed, whereas the participating Member States not only participate in the regular speed process but also and supplementarily ensure that they can operate at a faster integration pace in particular complementary and discrete policy domains.

Earlier enhanced cooperation initiatives in relation to the EU internal market exemplify that two-speed approach. First, a Regulation outlining common rules relating to the law applicable to divorce and legal separation has been established on the basis of enhanced cooperation.[68] The Regulation – an initiative emerging from originally 15 Member States – sought to develop a set of uniform conflict of laws rules governing legal separation and divorce in transnational settings.[69] In doing so, the Regulation essentially sought to replace variegated national

---

65 See for an overview of such measures from a political science point of view, Douglas Webber, 'The Politics of Differentiated Integration in the European Union: Origins, Decision Making and Outcomes' (2012) Monash University European and EU Centre Working Paper 2012/1 <http://artsonline.monash.edu.au/europecentre/files/2012/08/Working-Papers-2012-01.pdf> accessed 24 March 2015.

66 See on the role and specificity of those provisions already José Maria de Areilza, 'The Reform of Enhanced Co-operation Rules: Towards Less Flexibility?' in De Witte et al (n 63), 27–40.

67 See art. 327 TFEU.

68 See Council Decision 2010/405/EU of 12 July 2010 authorising enhanced cooperation in the area of the law applicable to divorce and legal separation, [2012] OJ L189/12.

69 See recitals 11 and 14 of Council Regulation 1259/2010 of 20 December 2010 implementing enhanced cooperation in the area of law applicable to divorce and legal separation, [2010] OJ L343/10. The 15 original Member States are Belgium, Bulgaria, Germany, Greece, Spain, France, Italy, Latvia, Luxembourg, Hungary, Malta, Austria, Portugal, Romania, and Slovenia, according to recital 6. Lithuania and Greece subsequently requested to join the enhanced cooperation regime in accordance with art. 328 TFEU.

conflict of laws standards on this topic, without however directly affecting or replacing the national conflict of laws provisions entertained by non-participating Member States. Transnational couples seeking divorce or legal separation could obtain rights from the Regulation if and to the extent that a court in a participating Member State is called upon to hear the particular action.[70] Other Member States could retain their own conflict of laws standards and their national judges would not have to apply the Regulation's principles. Secondly, enhanced cooperation also resulted in proposals for the establishment of a unitary patent among participating Member States.[71] The Regulation thus adopted seeks to ascertain that the uniform protection of patented inventions across the participating Member States would result in a simplification for patent applicants by extending the scope of protection of their intellectual property right.[72] Once again, the laws of non-participating Member States remain in force, yet more uniform protection standards and rights protected only within the participating Member States have been provided for.[73]

It can be submitted that the FTT proposal does not entirely fit the two-speed Europe logic illustrated above. Whereas the FTT also establishes an additional layer of regulation particularly tailored to the needs of a 'core' group of 11 Member States, the envisaged FTT project does not merely supplement existing EU rules and standards. More than any previous proposal, the FTT also directly *interferes* with rules and standards that have not been the subject of (full) harmonisation at the supranational level. By adopting broad 'establishment' criteria in order to impede intra-Union tax avoidance, the proposed Directive denies the regulatory competition among Member States' legal systems that is a hallmark of EU internal market integration in the absence of (EU28) legislative harmonisation. To the extent that the European Union – implying all 28 Member States – did not directly intervene through the

---

[70] As apparent from art. 10 Council Regulation 1259/2010. For an assessment of the system, see Jan-Jaap Kuipers, 'The Law Applicable to Divorce as a Test Ground for Enhanced Cooperation' (2012) 18 *European Law Journal* 201–29.

[71] See Council Decision 2011/167/EU of 10 March 2011 authorising enhanced cooperation in the area of the creation of unitary patent protection [2011] OJ L76/53. In this case, 25 Member States – all except for Spain and Italy at that time – requested the authorisation.

[72] See art. 5 Regulation 1257/2012 of the Parliament and of the Council of 17 December 2012 implementing enhanced cooperation in the area of the creation of unitary patent protection, [2012] OJ L361/1.

[73] Recital 7, Regulation 1257/2012.

adoption of secondary legislation, Member States have always remained free to adopt and design national legislation, as long as such legislation is compatible with the Treaty's free movement entitlements.[74] The EU11's proposal partially *forecloses* such competition by subjecting everyone conducting a transaction that remotely relates to a participating Member State's territory (by virtue of the extended establishment criteria or the issuance of particular instruments) to the tax rules. By foreclosing competition that normally prevails in the absence of EU-wide harmonisation, the FTT proposal effectively precludes other Member States from engaging in meaningful regulatory competition under the auspices of EU law. A direct consequence of this approach is that the FTT proposal is capable of imposing pecuniary *obligations* on financial institutions, rather than granting them new rights under EU law, as the divorce and patent enhanced cooperation initiatives did. In both the divorce Directive and the unitary patent proposals, enhanced cooperation resulted in more rights being granted to citizens and businesses falling within the scope and the enhanced cooperation instruments.

Non-participating Member States and financial institutions established in those Member States are as a result restricted in the policies they want to adopt, despite not directly participating in the enhanced cooperation framework. Not unlike a 'fast-track' waiting line, through which some customers are allowed to skip the regular waiting lines and which results in an additional restriction of non-fast-track waiting customers' movements, the FTT proposal cuts short the ability to move forward without being constrained by others imposing obligations that affect or even impede such moving forward. Two-speed Europe applied in the FTT context thus essentially results in slowing down non-fast-track Member States.

3.2 Treaty Objections against 'Fast-track' Enhanced Cooperation

The FTT Directive proposal indicates that the fast-track approach to enhanced cooperation is considered to fall within the ambit of the Treaty. Two particular types of objections can nevertheless *prima facie* be voiced against such a fast-track interpretation. This subsection identifies and addresses those objections and assesses their validity from an EU law point of view. Firstly, the enhanced cooperation provisions do not explicitly allow for fast-track proposals to be developed. Open-ended

---

[74] For an assessment of the relationship between regulatory competition and harmonisation, see Simon Deakin, 'Legal Diversity and Regulatory Competition: Which Model for Europe?' (2006) 12 *European Law Journal* 440–54.

interpretations of the provisions' conditions and requirements nevertheless support the conclusion that no meaningful impediments for the creation of fast-track mechanisms can be found in that regard (3.2.1). Secondly, the system of free movement law and its tolerance of diverse national tax regimes would at first sight be difficult to reconcile with the FTT proposal that would not cover the entire Union territory. Relying on analogous reasoning from the Court's case law on Member States' tax powers in the internal market, the Commission seemingly found a convincing argument in favour of a common FTT framework (3.2.2).

3.2.1 Inherent 'enhanced cooperation' objections

The Treaty provisions on enhanced cooperation seemingly introduce constitutional limits on the scope and extent of enhanced cooperation initiatives. In practice, however, the Court of Justice has consistently refrained from reading clear judicially-sanctioned limits on enhanced cooperation into those provisions. Case law on Article 20 TEU and Article 327 TFEU is exemplary in that regard.

Article 20(1) TEU states that enhanced cooperation measures should 'aim to further the objectives of the Union, protect its interests and reinforce its integration process'. To the extent that this is not the case, the Council should not authorise enhanced cooperation. In its *United Kingdom v Council* judgment however, the Court did not feel obliged to test whether the authorisation decision concerned a project that actually furthers the objectives of the Union and would reinforce the integration process along the way. The Court only stated that the substantive principles the UK put forward did not comprise 'constituent elements' of the authorisation decision.[75] It could thus be argued that – even though the Court reviews the substantive and procedural conditions underlying the adoption of a Council authorisation decision[76] – it did not at this stage seem willing to investigate the actual proposal. In its 2013 *Spain and Italy v Council* judgment, the Court had already held that the mere fact that a unitary patent would guarantee more uniformity, and thus integration, compared to the previous situation, was sufficient to meet the threshold posited in that provision.[77] A cursory look at the objectives of the authorisation decision thus seems to be the most the Court is willing to do in this context.

---

75 *United Kingdom v Council* (n 18), para. 36.

76 Ibid., para. 34.

77 Joined Cases C-274/11 and C-295/11 *Spain and Italy v Council* [2013] ECLI:EU:C:2013:240, para. 63.

The Court essentially confirmed that position in relation to Article 20(2) TEU, which refers to enhanced cooperation being a 'last resort' mechanism. In the abovementioned *Spain and Italy v Council* judgment, the Court of Justice held that the Union's interests and the process of integration would not be protected if 'all fruitless negotiations could lead to one or more instances of enhanced cooperation, to the detriment of the search for a compromise enabling the adoption of legislation for the Union as a whole'.[78] To the extent however that the Council can reasonably argue that the adoption of an EU28 proposal would not be likely in the foreseeable future,[79] the Court considers any authorisation decision to fall within the scope of Article 20(2) TEU. The authorisation decision will have to make clear whether and why this is the case in a particular setting.

Article 327 TFEU states that enhanced cooperation initiatives need to respect the competences, rights and obligations of those Member States that do not participate in it. The extent to which the Court is willing to review such respect for the competences, rights and obligations of non-participating Member States has also been rather limited. In *Spain and Italy v Council*, the Court maintained that Article 327 does not impede the adoption of rules by those taking part in this cooperation 'with which those non-participating States would not agree if they did take part in it'.[80]

In its September 2013 Opinion on the legality of the FTT proposal's extended establishment principle, however, the Council legal service argued that '[r]egardless of the decision of these Member States not to participate in the enhanced cooperation, their financial markets would be burdened with the tax' as a result of the extended establishment principles.[81] Such burdening would suffice to consider the rights of those Member States to be infringed and the boundaries of enhanced cooperation to be crossed. In its own legal opinion, the Commission countered this argument by stating that the extended establishment principle 'has no impact on the freedom of non-participating Member States to exercise their own tax competence in whatever manner they see fit'.[82] As a result, their rights would not be affected. Whereas the Council

---

[78] Ibid., para. 49.

[79] Ibid., para. 54.

[80] Ibid., para. 82.

[81] Interinstitutional file 2013/0045 (CNS) <www.consilium.europa.eu> accessed 24 March 2015, para. 36 (hereinafter Council legal opinion).

[82] Commission Opinion on the legality of the 'counter-party principle' laid down in art. 4(1)(f) of the Commission Proposal for a Council Directive

apparently considers a fast-track FTT initiative to fall outside the scope of Article 327 TFEU, the Commission proposes a wider reading of that provision, which would effectively enable the creation of such an FTT. The disagreements between both institutions will have to be addressed throughout the regulatory process anticipating the adoption of the FTT enhanced cooperation Directive.

On the basis of the above, it can be submitted that Article 20 TEU and Article 327 TFEU above all provide political rather than legal guidance. The Court's deferential judgments and the Council's and Commission's different legal opinions highlight that the Treaty provisions on enhanced cooperation do not readily offer clear guidance on the limits of (fast-track) enhanced cooperation. As long as the Court defers those matters to the responsible institutions, however, those provisions do not even seem to provide any limits whatsoever to the development of fast-track integration mechanisms such as the FTT.

3.2.2 'Internal market' objections

In addition to the inherent objections emerging from the Treaty requirements underlying enhanced cooperation, Article 326 TFEU, second sentence, additionally incorporates an 'internal market' limit: enhanced cooperation is neither to undermine the internal market or economic, social and territorial cohesion nor to constitute a barrier to or discrimination in trade between Member States, distorting *competition between them*. Enhanced cooperation is meant to support the internal market, not to frustrate it, and to support the regulatory competition process inherent to the internal market in the absence of harmonisation. In order for an enhanced cooperation FTT regime to be compatible with the internal market, it should thus stay within the boundaries of that provision and the system of internal market governance at large.

According to the Court in *Spain and Italy v Council*, the mere fact that enhanced cooperation sought to introduce a unitary patent applicable in the participating Member States, and not in the Union, was not sufficient to maintain that the internal market or the economic, social and territorial cohesion of the Union would be damaged.[83] Even though Article 26(2) TFEU states that the internal market comprises an 'area' in which free movement is ensured, that provision would not seem to preclude more specific 'core' areas to be constructed as parts of that market. Such core

implementing enhanced cooperation in the area of FTT – COM(2013) 71 final of 14 February 2013, 1 (hereinafter Commission legal opinion).

[83] *Spain and Italy v Council* (n 76), para. 75.

areas would not discriminate against non-participating legal systems, as the latter always have the opportunity to join the enhanced cooperation scheme.[84]

The Commission's legal opinion concerning the extended establishment principle in the FTT proposal confirms that position. The Commission maintained that: '[t]he fact that non-participating Member States are not allocated taxing rights by the proposed harmonised system cannot be regarded as discrimination since they will not participate in it and will therefore be outside the system's scope'.[85] In the field of tax law, this appears to be confirmed by the case law of the Court, which claims that divergences between the legislation of different Member States are inherent in the exercise of their tax sovereignty and do not infringe fundamental freedoms.[86] To the extent that Member States effectively join forces to adopt a harmonised indirect taxation system, such divergences would effectively be diminished between the Member States.[87] As a result, the internal market would benefit from the allocation of financial transaction taxation powers at EU level, as it would allow for a more uniform allocation of such powers. The Council legal service, on the contrary, maintained that the proposed FTT would significantly impede the free movement of capital and/or services.[88]

That interpretation – based on analogous reasoning from the Court's case law on taxation in relation to free movement rights – is nevertheless flawed in two respects. First, that case law only relates to Member States adopting tax measures, not the EU. Although the proposed FTT would be adopted under the banner of enhanced cooperation, it would still comprise an EU legislative act binding upon the participating Member States, without being a part of the Union's *acquis*.[89] Such measures cannot however be equated with a national tax measure scrutinised on its compatibility with EU free movement rights. This is where the opinion of the Council legal service falls short. The Council failed to demonstrate how an instrument of EU secondary legislation – adopted on the basis of Treaty provisions and procedures – could in reality amount to having an

---

[84] Ibid., para. 83.

[85] Commission legal opinion, 2.

[86] For a recent illustration, see Case C-337/08 *X. Holding BV* [2013] ECLI:EU:C:2010:89, para. 62.

[87] See for that argument Federico Fabbrini, 'Taxing and Spending in the Eurozone: Legal and Political Challenges Related to the Adoption of the Financial Transaction Tax' (2014) 39 EL Rev 155, 170.

[88] Council legal opinion, paras 40–41.

[89] See art. 20(4) TEU.

effect equivalent to that of a duty imposed by a *Member State* in contravention of the free movement of capital and/or services and whether EU law should indeed make that equation in this regard. Secondly, the effective 'allocation of taxing powers' argument developed in the case law relates to the justification for an established restriction on the free movement of capital and/or services. In order to develop that argument, a restriction has to be established first. In the case of the FTT proposal, an EU Directive – albeit only binding in the participating Member States and financial institutions 'established' there – potentially restricts or at least regulates the free movement of capital across participating Member States, towards non-participating Member States and to third countries. In maintaining that the proposal could have an impact on capital movement, the Council failed to appreciate that every harmonising measure has such effect. The Commission basically acknowledged this in its own opinion.[90] At the same time, however, the latter also did not address the fact that the FTT Directive would only bring about harmonisation across 10 of 28 Member States.

The real question – which neither the Commission nor the Council addressed – is whether an EU legislative instrument resulting from enhanced cooperation and in principle only binding on participating Member States, can be allowed to have spill-over effects in non-participating Member States, just like any EU28 harmonisation Directive might produce spill-over effects in third countries.[91] If that would not be the case, enhanced cooperation could not be relied upon as a tool to speed up the internal market integration process by foreclosing some forms of regulatory competition by non-participating Member States. That question nevertheless remains unanswered so far.

4. CONCLUSION

This chapter analysed the EU's financial transaction tax project as an example of 'fast-track' enhanced cooperation provided for under the Treaties. It outlined the different stages and addressed the scope of the Court's rubber stamping of the enhanced cooperation authorisation in this regard. If implemented in its current proposed format, the FTT would be

---

90 Commission legal opinion, 2–3.

91 See on those general tensions underlying free movement law, Alexandre Saydé, 'One Law, Two Competitions: An Enquiry into the Contradictions of Free Movement Law' (2011) 13 *Cambridge Yearbook of European Legal Studies* 365–413.

imposed on any financial institution 'established' in a participating Member State. The Directive itself outlines very generous establishment criteria, also in order to capture transactions substantially related with – but not conducted in – the territory of a participating Member State.

The proposed FTT Directive directly challenges the EU's internal market governance model based upon regulatory competition in the absence of harmonisation of laws across all 28 Member States. Although 'internal market' objections that have arisen during the FTT drafting and negotiation processes reflect genuine threats to the EU's internal market project, the arguments outlined here do not impose insurmountable obstacles that would prevent the adoption of an EU-wide FTT. As no clear guidance on the legality of spill-over effects produced by a measure grounded in enhanced cooperation has been provided so far, the internal market objections identified will most likely not posit meaningful limits on the FTT proposal's adoption and implementation. Only once such a proposal has been adopted will the Court have the opportunity to rule on the objections outlined here and the role of enhanced cooperation mechanisms in the service of more intense EU internal market integration. The proposal's extended establishment criteria effectively foreclose regulatory competition between peripheral and participating Member States in the interest of the EU as a whole. The adoption of those criteria implicitly amounts to a core group of Member States being competent or at least capable to determine and constrain the future and regulatory freedom of non-participating Member States. It will be for the Council, upon deliberation, and for the Court of Justice, upon review, to assess whether that fast-track model should indeed be considered the way forward in EU (financial) market integration and to what extent a core group should be considered capable of indirectly structuring peripheral Member States' legal regimes as a matter of EU secondary legislation.

REFERENCES

Avbelj M, 'Differentiated Integration – Farewell to the EU-27?' (2013) 14 *German Law Journal* 191–212.

Barker A, 'Eurozone Divided over Financial Transaction Tax Deal' (2014) *Financial Times*, 6 May 2014 <www.ft.com>.

Cristie R and Brunsden J, 'EU Transaction Tax Debate Highlights Euro-Area Disagreement' (2011) *Bloomberg Business Week*, 8 November 2011 <www.businessweek.com>.

de Areilza JM, 'The Reform of Enhanced Co-operation Rules: Towards Less Flexibility?' in De Witte B, Vos E and Hanf D (eds), *The Many Faces of Differentiation in EU Law* (Intersentia 2001) 27–40.

De Witte B, Hanf D and Vos, E (eds), *The Many Faces of Differentiation in EU Law* (Intersentia 2001).

Deakin S, 'Legal Diversity and Regulatory Competition: Which Model for Europe?' (2006) 12 *European Law Journal* 440–54.

Fabbrini F, 'Taxing and Spending in the Eurozone: Legal and Political Challenges Related to the Adoption of the Financial Transaction Tax' (2014) 39 EL Rev 155–75.

Kuipers J-J, 'The Law Applicable to Divorce as a Test Ground for Enhanced Cooperation' (2012) 18 *European Law Journal* 201–29.

Pollin R, 'A U.S. Financial Transaction Tax: How Wall Street Can Pay for its Mess' (2012) 21(2) *New Labour Forum* 96–9.

Saydé A, 'One Law, Two Competitions: An Enquiry into the Contradictions of Free Movement Law' (2011) 13 *Cambridge Yearbook of European Legal Studies* 365–413.

Webber D, 'The Politics of Differentiated Integration in the European Union: Origins, Decision Making and Outcomes' (2012) Monash University European and EU Centre Working Paper 2012/1 <http://artsonline.monash.edu.au/europecentre/-files/2012/08/Working-Papers-2012-01.pdf>.

12. Differentiated integration or uniform regime? National derogations from EU internal market measures

Ellen Vos and Maria Weimer[1]

1. INTRODUCTION

The creation of one internal market in which products may freely circulate has been central to the EU's integration project from its very start. Article 26(2) TFEU thus stipulates that this internal market will embrace 'an area without internal frontiers in which the free movement of goods, persons, services and capital is ensured'. Over the years, this internal market has evolved on the basis of various features of different integration models such as host country control, home country control and harmonisation.[2] The latter relates particularly to the rules established with regard to the creation of the internal market. The attractiveness of harmonisation lies in the fact that EU rules can also take into account interests other than purely economic ones, such as the protection of human health and the environment, as is expressly stipulated in Article 114(3) TFEU.[3] Inevitably, however, there is a tension between harmonised rules and respect for diversity. In politically sensitive matters, it may therefore appear difficult to find a compromise and to adopt EU-wide measures. Moreover it may appear difficult within the internal

[1] We would like to thank Giulia Giardi (Maastricht University) for helping us with the empirical research carried out.

[2] Jukka Snell, 'The Internal Market and the Philosophies on Market Integration' in Catharine Barnard and Steve Peers (eds), *European Union Law* (Oxford University Press 2014) 304–5.

[3] See Bruno De Witte, 'The Competence to Protect. The Pursuit of Non-market Aims through Internal Market Legislation', in Philip Syrpis (ed.), *The Judiciary, the Legislature and the Internal Market* (Cambridge University Press 2012) 25–46.

market measures to offer the appropriate level of protection of, for example, environment and human health.[4]

On the other hand, it is also true that the possibility for Member States to create and/or maintain diverse conditions has for a long time been part of the EU integration process. Accordingly, EU law provides for several mechanisms of legal differentiation and flexibility. These mechanisms allow Member States to derogate from the harmonised European rules under certain circumstances in order to respond to new health or environmental risks or other individual national or regional policy needs at the national level. Examples are the 'opt-out' clauses of Article 114(4) and (5) TFEU as well as various so-called 'safeguard clauses' laid down in EU secondary legislation in the fields of EU environmental and health and safety policy.[5] The use of these mechanisms by the Member States, however, has created difficulties in the past as well as disagreement between the invoking Member State and the EU institutions with regard to the interpretation of the legal conditions and their fulfilment in each and every particular case. Especially in the field of consumer health and environmental protection, the bone of contention has often been the availability and interpretation of the scientific data with regard to the existence of health and environmental risks at the national level. Hence, the authority of scientific expertise in the use of legal differentiation mechanisms, together with the question of how far scientific evidence should be an exclusive factor in granting more regulatory flexibility at the national level, are key issues to be considered.

This chapter will take stock of these developments examining the dynamics of legal differentiation in EU's internal market law in an empirically informed way. In particular, it will address the question of how far the actual use of the different available derogation mechanisms of Article 114 TFEU and secondary law safeguard clauses points to the existence of processes of differentiated integration or whether it triggers follow-up regulatory developments at EU level. In other words, we aim to analyse whether, considering both the way EU law frames and approves of national derogation and safeguard clauses and the way scientific evidence is being used in this process, we can today observe a trend towards more harmonisation and less flexibility in the use of these mechanisms or whether, on the contrary, more legal differentiation is provided for. Before examining the current derogation practice under the

---

[4] Moreover the EU measures may prove inflexible, rigid and difficult to change. Snell (n 2) 304.

[5] See art. 114(10) TFEU. See section 6 of this chapter.

mechanisms provided for in Article 114 TFEU and the safeguard clauses (sections 5 and 6), we will first discuss the origins of these mechanisms (section 2) and briefly delineate their requirements (sections 3 and 4).

2. INTERNAL MARKET LAW IN THE FACE OF DIVERSITY

At the end of the 1960s the EU had already envisaged the use of harmonisation to achieve its internal market ambitions with the adoption of its harmonisation programme of 1969.[6] At the same time, it pursued the home country control model. Importantly, the Treaty requires Member States to refrain from creating barriers to trade. Article 34 TFEU thus prohibits Member States from imposing quantitative restrictions on imports or measures having equivalent effect. It was however particularly in the 1980s, when the landmark ruling of the Court of Justice of the EU (CJEU) in *Cassis de Dijon* highlighted the mutual recognition principle,[7] that the home state control model gained in importance. Cumbersome and slow decision-making by the EU institutions, together with the development of the mutual recognition principle by the Court, pushed the European Commission, endorsed by the Council,[8] to adopt a New Approach to harmonisation and technical standards in 1985.[9]

This approach took mutual recognition as its main principle while identifying approximately 300 measures to be adopted in line with the harmonisation model, particularly on issues involving health and safety. Over the years, the Court has always been careful to avoid situations in which regulatory gaps could arise. It has been quite tolerant in allowing Member States, in line with the justification grounds of Article 36 TFEU, to derogate from the obligation to allow foreign products on their markets which would not conform to their own strict health and safety standards, particularly in cases of scientific uncertainty. This led to a surge in the host state control model in cases of health protection measures, which led

[6] Council resolution drawing up a programme for the elimination of technical barriers to trade, (1969) OJ C76/1.

[7] Case C-120/78 *Rewe-Zentrale AG v Bundesmonopolverwaltung für Branntwein* [1979] ECLI:EU:C:1979:42.

[8] Council Resolution on a New Approach to Technical Harmonisation and Standards (1985) OJ C136/1.

[9] COM(85) 19 final, 31 January 1985.

in turn to situations of justified trade barriers blocking the free movement of products. Harmonisation measures were necessary to lift such trade barriers.[10]

The introduction of a new Treaty provision, then Article 100A EEC, now Article 114 TFEU, allowed for internal market measures to be adopted by qualified majority voting (QMV) and this was essential for the success of the 1985 New Approach. It was also clear that in order to get agreement on the introduction of QMV for internal market measures by the Single Act, Member States needed to be reassured that they would not be outvoted on measures that would reduce existing levels of health and environmental protection.[11] In that manner, the former Article 100A(4), now Article 114(4 and 5) TFEU, provided for the possibility of Member States opting out of harmonisation measures in order to adhere to stricter levels of protection.[12] While some welcomed this provision as establishing, within the Treaty, the legitimate importance of national regulatory measures and the concept of shared competences,[13] others expressed their fears that opt-outs would damage the uniformity of the EU legal order and that it would compartmentalise the single market.[14]

After the failure of the application of the mutual recognition principle in the manner the New Approach had envisaged,[15] the harmonisation model has become increasingly popular. Although the Single Act also

---

[10] See e.g. Ellen Vos, 'Differentiation, Harmonisation and Governance', in Bruno De Witte, Dominik Hanf and Ellen Vos (eds), *The Many Faces of Differentiation in EU Law* (Intersentia 2001) 145–79.

[11] See Claus Gulmann, 'The Single European Act – Some Remarks from a Danish Perspective' (1987) 24(1) CML Rev. 31–40 and Ludwig Krämer, 'The Single European Act and Environmental Protection: Reflections on Several New Provisions in Community Law' (1987) 24 CML Rev. 659–88, at 681.

[12] See Claus-Dieter Ehlermann, 'Increased Differentiation or Stronger Uniformity?' EUI Working Paper RSC 95/21, Florence 1995 at 389 ff. See also AG Saggio in Case 319/97 *Kortas* [1999] ECLI:EU:C:1999:272, para. 17.

[13] Stephen Weatherill, 'Beyond Preemption? Shared Competence and Constitutional Change in the European Community', in David O'Keeffe and Patrick M Twomey (eds), *Legal Issues of the Maastricht Treaty* (Chancery Law Publishing 1994) 23.

[14] See Pierre Pescatore, 'Some Critical Remarks on the "Single European Act"' (1987) 24 CML Rev. 9–18.

[15] See e.g. Case C-188/84 *Commission v France* [1986] ECLI:EU:C:1986:43. See special issue of the Hanse Law Review Gert Brüggemeier, Josef Falke, Christian Joerges and Hans-W Micklitz, 'European Product Safety, Completion of the Internal Market and the New Approach to Technical Harmonisation and Standards – Reissued' (2010) 6(2) *Hanse Law Review* 107–14.

embraced the concept of diversity in other provisions,[16] for the purpose of this contribution we will look at the derogation mechanisms provided for in Article 114 TFEU to see how they have impacted the internal market.[17]

3. DEROGATION THROUGH THE 'OPT-OUT' CLAUSES: ARTICLE 114(4) AND (5) TFEU

The anchoring of opt-out clauses in Article 114 TFEU seems to reflect a diversity principle even within harmonised areas of EU law, which therefore enjoys a constitutional status. As pointed out above, this mechanism was a political/strategic reply to Member States unwilling to reduce their health and safety protection levels within the EU framework. Opting out of harmonisation measures under Article 114(4) and (5) TFEU comes close to what has been termed 'variable geometry', in which unattainable or unavoidable differences are admitted and which allows a separation between a 'hard core' and lesser-developed integrative units.[18] Article 114(4) TFEU gives a limited minimum harmonisation facility for internal market measures that, in the opinion of the opting-out Member State, fail to provide for appropriately stringent levels of protection.[19]

Yet, this constitutional principle of diversity is not unlimited. It must fulfil various requirements; most notably national rules may not constitute arbitrary discrimination or distort the functioning of the internal market and, as such, they are subjected to the Commission's technocratic oversight. Paragraphs (4) and (5) of Article 114 TFEU distinguish between national measures which exist at the moment of the adoption of

---

16 Such as then art. 8c EEC that expressly obliged the Commission to take account of the differences in the development of certain economies and then art. 130t EEC that introduced the concept of minimum harmonisation techniques relating to environmental policy.

17 See, already, James Flynn, 'How Will Article 100A (4) Work? A Comparison with Article 93' (1987) 24(4) CML Rev. 689–707; Kay Hailbronner, 'Der "nationale Alleingang" im Gemeinschaftsrecht am Beispiel der Abgasstandards für Pkw' (1989) 16 EuGRZ 101–22; Pierre Pescatore, 'Die 'Einheitliche Europäische Akte'. Eine ernste Gefahr für den Gemeinsamen Markt' (1986) 21(2) EuR 153–69.

18 See Ehlermann (n 12).

19 On different models of differentiation in harmonised areas see Vos (n 10).

a harmonisation measure (para. (4)) and national measures which are introduced after the adoption of a harmonisation measure (para. (5)). Paragraph (4) lists the criteria for the possibility of maintaining the already existing national measures, namely, the protection of the interests laid down in Article 36 TFEU and the protection of the environment or working environment. Importantly, under Article 114(4) TFEU, it is not possible to maintain national provisions that are less protective than the provisions laid down in the relevant EU harmonisation measure.[20]

Stricter limitations are applied to the introduction of national measures after harmonisation. Paragraph (5) only allows Member States to adopt new national measures based on new scientific evidence due to a problem that has arisen after the adoption of a harmonisation measure and is specific to that Member State. The justification grounds are more restrictive than those that may be resorted to under paragraph 4: only the protection of the environment or the working environment. The introduction of new measures for reasons of health protection is therefore not allowed.[21] Where a problem relating to health protection is signalled by a Member State in a field regulated by harmonisation measures, that Member State needs to bring the matter to the attention of the Commission. The Commission in turn has to examine immediately whether it is necessary to propose appropriate measures to the Council (para. (8)). This seems to suggest that after harmonisation, health protection is a matter for the EU institutions.

The notification procedure to the Commission is laid down in paragraphs (6)–(7). Where a Member State deems it necessary to apply its national measure based on one of the justification grounds, it must notify the Commission before the time-limit for the implementation of the Community measures involved expires. Paragraph (6) stipulates that the Commission must 'approve' or 'reject' the national provisions, after having verified whether or not they are a means of arbitrary discrimination or a disguised restriction on trade and whether or not they

---

[20] Commission Decision 1999/835/EC on the Danish derogation concerning the limitation to the placing on the market and use of creosote, (1999) OJ L329/82, para. 112.

[21] Nicolas De Sadeleer, *EU Environmental Law and the Internal Market* (Oxford University Press 2014) 364–5 and 374; Isidora Maletić, *The Law and Policy of Harmonisation in Europe's Internal Market* (Edward Elgar Publishing 2013) 75.

constitute an obstacle to the functioning of the internal market. The Commission must fully satisfy the obligation to state reasons. It cannot merely state that the national derogation is compatible with the requirements for opting out laid down in Article 114 TFEU without stating the reasons on the basis of which the Commission considered that all conditions are fulfilled.[22] Where the Commission fails to adopt a decision within six months, the national provisions are deemed to have been approved.[23] A decision that has been adopted by the Commission but not notified to the derogating Member State does not interrupt the time-limit.[24] The six-month period may be formally extended with another six months if the complexity of the risk assessment so requires.[25]

The Commission has a wide discretion to make complex technical evaluations in the Article 114 procedures. The evidence relied upon must be factually accurate, reliable and consistent; that evidence must contain all the relevant information and must be capable of substantiating the conclusions drawn from it;[26] and it must observe the fundamental guarantees of an administrative procedure, in particular 'the obligations to examine carefully and impartially all the relevant elements of the individual case and to give an adequate statement of the reasons for its decision'.[27] Quite remarkably, within this procedure, Member States do not have a right to be heard.[28] In *Danish Additives*[29] and in *Upper*

---

[22] As the Court held in Case C-41/93 *Commission v France* [1994] ECLI:EU:C:1994:196, para. 36, now codified in art. 114(6) TFEU.

[23] Case T-69/08 *Poland v Commission* [2010] ECLI:EU:T:2010:504, para. 71. See Maletić (n 21) 81 and De Sadeleer (n 21) 369.

[24] *Poland v Commission* ibid., para. 62.

[25] See e.g. Cases C-439/05 and C-454/05 *Land Oberösterreich and Austria v Commission* [2010] ECLI:EU:C:2007:510, para. 40 and *Poland v Commission*, ibid., para. 60.

[26] Case C-405/07 *Netherlands v Commission (Dutch emissions)* [2008] ECLI:EU:C:2008:613, para. 55.

[27] Ibid., para. 56 with reference to Case C-269/90 *Technische Universität München* [1991] ECR I-5469, para. 14; Joined Cases C-258/90 and C-259/90 *Pesquerias De Bermeo and Naviera Laida v Commission* [1992] ECLI:EU:C:1992:199, para. 26; and Case C-525/04 P *Spain v Lenzing* [2007] ECLI:EU:C:2007:689, para. 58.

[28] See e.g. Case C-3/00 *Denmark v Commission* [2003] ECLI:EU:C:2003:167, para. 49.

[29] Ibid., para. 50.

Austria[30] the CJEU found that the Commission is not obliged to grant the Member State a right to be heard before adopting its decision under either paragraph (4) or (5). Hereby the Court emphasised the intention of the drafters of the Treaty to conclude the derogation procedure swiftly in the interest of the notifying Member States and the proper functioning of the internal market.[31]

As rightly observed by Maletić, such a reading of the Article 114 procedures requires an extensive degree of diligence and foresight on the part of the notifying Member State. Not only does it oblige the Member State to anticipate all possible counter-arguments to its notification, Member States are also prevented from commenting on the observations submitted to the Commission by other Member States as a reaction to the notification. It should be added that a denial of the right to be heard might in some cases be counter-productive to the purpose of speeding up the opt-out procedure.[32] It follows, moreover, that the rejection of the right to be heard seems to be in conflict with an understanding of the Article 114 opt-out procedures as a mechanism for regulatory learning.

When a Member State is authorised to maintain or introduce derogating national provisions, the Commission must immediately examine whether the relevant harmonisation measure should be adapted accordingly (para. (7)). If the Commission or a Member State considers that another Member State is making improper use of this provision, it may bring the matter directly before the CJEU (para. (9)).

---

30 *Land Oberösterreich* (n 25), para. 44.

31 Ibid., paras 37–41; see also Advocate General Sharpston's opinion, para. 137.

32 For example, a lengthy judicial procedure before the EU courts could in some cases be avoided if the Member State is given the right to be heard and thereby to correct a mistake made by the Commission in its assessment. As Wennerås observes on the *Danish Additives* case, 'if Denmark had been allowed to comment on the flawed interpretation of the SCF's 1995 opinion, there is a possibility that the Commission would have recognized its error and instead have approved the Danish provisions'. Pål Wennerås, 'Fog and Acid Rain Drifting from Luxembourg over Art. 95(4) EC: Case C-3/0 Kingdom of Denmark v. the Commission of the European Communities Danish Food Case' (2003) 12(6) *European Energy and Environmental Law Review* 169–78, at 175. Similarly, one could argue that in the *Dutch Emissions* case an action for annulment could have been avoided if the Netherlands had been given the right to comment on the Commission decision, which erroneously stated that the 2004 air quality assessment report was not submitted to it.

4. DEROGATION THROUGH THE 'OPT-OUT' CLAUSES: NUMBER OF APPLICATIONS, APPROVALS AND REJECTIONS

Overall we can conclude that the notification procedure is being interpreted strictly and is in fact 'narrowly construed'.[33] Our analysis of the derogation practice reveals a rather modest application of the derogation mechanisms. From 1987 until 2014, a total number of 34 derogations were sought by various Member States under both Article 114(4) and (5) TFEU (see Table 12.1 below). A close examination of the derogation requests reveals that there are considerable differences in the derogation practices under Article 114 paragraphs 4 and 5. Derogation under paragraph (4) were sought in 22 cases,[34] 16 of which were approved by the Commission. Four notifications were rejected, one was withdrawn and one was declared inadmissible. In contrast, under Article 114(5), derogations were sought in 12 cases, only one of which was approved. Eight notifications were rejected, one was withdrawn and one was declared inadmissible. It shows that the Commission is more willing to approve pre-existing measures than to allow for new measures to be introduced after harmonisation. Overall, our analysis reveals a varied picture in terms of the functioning of opt-outs as mechanisms of differentiation in EU internal market law. Importantly, in its decision-making the Commission, following established EU case law,[35] has always stressed the necessity to interpret the legal requirements for derogation narrowly, given the exceptional nature of the opt-out clauses and the fact that they challenge the attainment of a fundamental Treaty objective, the integration of the market for goods. The practice followed by both the Commission and the Court shows that derogation from EU harmonisation measures will not be permitted easily.[36]

---

[33] *Kortas* (n 12), para. 23.

[34] The three requests that were made under the old art. 100A EEC also considered the requests to maintain legislation and therefore, for the purpose of our statistical analysis, we have added these three requests to the number of requests made under the new art. 114(4) EEC post Amsterdam.

[35] See *France v Commission* (n 22), paras 23–30 and *Kortas* (n 12).

[36] See Stephen Weatherill, *Cases and Materials on EU Law*, 9th edition (Oxford University Press 2010) at 587; Maletić (n 21) 118.

Table 12.1 Overview of the number of Member State notifications and Commission decisions made under Article 114 (4) and (5) TFEU between 1987 and 2014

Member State	**Old Article 100a (4)**			**Article 114 Paragraph 4**					**Article 114 Paragraph 5**				
	A	R	Total	A	R	W	I	Total	A	R	W	I	Total
Austria	–	–	–	2	–	–	–	2	–	1*	1	–	2
Belgium	–	–	–	–	–	–		–	–	1	–	–	1
Cyprus	–	–	–	–	–	–	–	–	–	–	–	1	1
Czech Republic	–	–	–	–	–	1	–	1	–	–	–	–	–
Denmark	1	–	1	3	1*	–	–	4	–	–	–	–	–
Finland	–	–	–	1	–	–	–	1	–	–	–	–	–
France	–	–	–	–	–	–	–	–	–	1	–	–	1
Germany	1*	–	1	2	2	–	–	4	–	2*	–	–	2
Poland	–	–	–	–	–	–	–	–	–	1*	–	–	1
Portugal	–	–	–	–	–	–	–	–	–	–	–	–	1†
Sweden	–	1‡	1	2	–	–	–	2	–	1	–	–	1
The Netherlands	–	–	–	4*	–	–	–	4	1	1*	–	–	2
United Kingdom	–	–	–	–	–	–	1	1	–	–	–	–	–
	A	R		A	R	W	I		A	R	W	I	
	2	1		14	3	1	1		1	8	1	1	
Total n. derogations sought**			3					19					12

Notes:
A – Approved.
R – Rejected.
W – Withdrawn.
I – Declared inadmissible.
* Matter taken before CJEU).
† Pending before Commission.
‡ Case before CJEU related to the matter, but not seeking annulment of Commission Decision.
**Where same measures notified twice or renewal of already notified derogation sought, calculated as single instance.
Total disaggregated number of Commission Decisions: 39.
Total derogations sought (aggregated): 34.
Total approved: 17.
Total rejected: 12.
Total withdrawn: 2.
Total declared inadmissible: 2.
Pending: 1.

5. DEROGATION THROUGH THE 'OPT-OUT' CLAUSES IN PRACTICE: MAIN FINDINGS

Our findings reveal important insights into the way the derogation mechanisms under Article 114 TFEU work. We would like to highlight six important findings of our analysis of the derogations practice in relation to: (i) the role of science; (ii) the precautionary principle; (iii) the relevance of international developments; (iv) proportionality; (v) burden of proof; and (vi) the level of risk management. The consequences of the derogation mechanisms for the internal market as a whole will be discussed in section 7.

5.1 Role of Science

The role that scientific evidence plays in the derogation procedure is crucial. As the Court phrased it in the *Upper Austria* cases: 'First of all, it should be pointed out that the lawfulness of national measures notified under Article 95(5) EC is closely linked to the assessment of the scientific evidence put forward by the notifying Member State.'[37] The same holds true for measures notified under paragraph 4, although it does not formally refer to scientific evidence. The Court's observation indicates that science plays a dual role in the notification procedure: first, scientific evidence must be produced at the national level in order to demonstrate that the derogation is justified; and second, this evidence is reviewed at the EU level by a scientific committee or EU agency as requested by the Commission.

That it is crucial for the Commission to have scientific evidence produced by national authorities reviewed by another (EU) body flows from the Court's case law in *France v Commission*. In this case, the Commission had merely confined itself to indicating to the content of the German provisions, taking notice of the evidence submitted by the German authorities, and referring to the dangers of PCP as revealed by these authorities. The Court however reprimanded the Commission for not having properly explained 'the reasons of fact and law on account of which the Commission considered that all the conditions contained in Article 100a(4) were to be regarded as fulfilled in the case in point'[38] and annulled the Commission's approval for lack of argumentation. Subsequently the Commission resorted to an internationally recognised expert,

---

[37] *Land Oberösterreich*(n 25) para. 56.

[38] *France v Commission* (n 22) para. 36.

Professor Rappe of the Swedish Institute of Environmental Chemistry, who confirmed that the German derogation was justified by the specific circumstances relating to health protection and the environment in Germany. This led the Commission to approve again of the German derogation.[39]

The reproach by the Court in *PCP* has been key for the Commission's practice and its reliance on an assessment by scientific bodies created at the EU level. Soon after the *PCP* case, the Commission thus started to involve its own scientific bodies in reviewing scientific evidence submitted by national authorities. In general, the outcome of that re-evaluation determined the further outcome of the procedure. Our analysis thus confirms the authoritative role played by EU bodies and their scientific opinions as observed in other areas of risk regulation.[40] In the creosote cases, the Commission resorted to the Scientific Committee for Toxicology, Ecotoxicology and the Environment (CSTEE) (now renamed SCHER: Scientific Committee on Health and Environmental Risks), that it had created in the 1980s.[41] In all derogations that were notified by the various Member States in those cases, this Committee confirmed the evidence submitted by the Member States that these substances were harmful to human health or the environment. This subsequently led the Commission to approve all derogations[42] and to amend the relevant EU legislation (see section 5.2). A similar situation occurred in relation to the Austrian, Finnish and Swedish derogations to the EU legislation on cadmium in fertilisers which were approved by the Commission on the

---

39 Commission Decision 94/783/EC concerning the prohibition of PCP notified by the Federal Republic of Germany (1994) OJ L316/43–48.

40 See e.g. Michelle Everson and Ellen Vos (eds), *Uncertain Risks Regulated* (Cavendish 2009).

41 The Scientific Advisory Committee examined the toxicity and ecotoxicity of chemical compounds established by Commission Decision 78/618/EEC, as last amended by the Act of Accession of Austria, Finland and Sweden (1978 OJ L198/17) was replaced by the Scientific Committee on Toxicity, Ecotoxicity and the Environment, Commission Decision of 23 July 1997 setting up Scientific Committees in the field of consumer health and food safety, OJ L237 of 28.08.97.

42 See Commission Decision on the Danish derogation 1999/835/EC (1999) OJ L329/82; Commission Decision on the Dutch derogation 1999/832/EC (1999) OJ L329/25 and Commission Decision 1999/834/EC on the Swedish derogation (1999) OJ L329/63.

basis of an opinion by the Committee highlighting risks to the environment and public health resulting from the use of cadmium-containing fertilizers.[43]

The Commission is not formally bound by the scientific opinion produced by the EU bodies. Yet it must take sufficient account of such opinions. In the *Danish Additives* case of 2003, the Court thus found that the Commission had failed to take sufficient account of the EU's former Scientific Committee on Food (SCF) (now EFSA) opinion; an opinion the Danish authorities had referred to in order to support their derogation request.[44] Subsequently, in the *Dutch Emissions* case, the Court reaffirmed the Commission's obligation to take account of all available scientific evidence. In this case, the Court stressed the obligation of the Commission, in its decisions in the field of the environment, to take into account *all* available new scientific and technical data based on the first indent of what is now Article 191(3) TFEU.[45] This seems to imply that the Commission can base its assessment under Article 114 (4*) et seq* on various scientific sources including national and international studies.

In the *Danish Additives* case the Court moreover opened up a degree of flexibility for Member States that seek to derogate on the basis of different standards than those adopted at the EU level.[46] The Court took an 'unusually expansive approach'[47] to the scientific evidence that may be submitted by a derogating Member State and ruled that:

> in the light of the uncertainty inherent in assessing the public health risks posed by, inter alia, the use of food additives, divergent assessments of those risks can legitimately be made, without necessarily being based on new or different scientific evidence.[48]

This flexibility was however somewhat neutralised by the Court's strong emphasis on the burden of proof placed on Germany (see section 5.5) and its strict interpretation of the requirements. Moreover, the Court's lenient approach does not cover requests for derogations under Article 114 (5). In the *Upper Austria* case the Court confirmed that the Commission had discretion in choosing experts in order to assess

---

[43] Commission Decision 2006/349/EC for Austria (2006) OJ L 129/31; Commission Decision 2006/348/EC for Finland (2006) OJ L 129/25; Commission Decision 2006/347/EC for Sweden, (2006) OJ L 129/19.

[44] *Denmark v Commission* (n 28) paras 110–114.

[45] *Dutch Emissions* (n 26) para. 61.

[46] See Maletić (n 21) 115.

[47] Ibid.

[48] *Denmark v Commission* (n 28), paras 63–64.

whether the evidence submitted complied with the prerequisite of 'new scientific evidence' under paragraph (5). In this case the Commission had asked EFSA to assess the scientific evidence that Austria had submitted. Where EFSA came to the conclusion that the evidence in the so-called Müller report, which the Austrian authorities relied on, did not contain 'new or uniquely local scientific information on the environmental or human health impacts of existing or future GM crops or animals',[49] the Commission subsequently rejected the request.[50] The approval of this practice by the Court again confirms the predominant role of scientific opinions adopted by EU committees or agencies and will make it difficult for Member States to fulfil the criteria posed by this provision.[51]

5.2 Precautionary Principle

Closely linked with the role of science is the application of the precautionary principle in the notification procedure. As indicated above, in the *Danish Additives* case the Court appeared to be quite favourable towards a certain degree of respect for regulatory diversity within the derogation procedure of Article 114 (4) and alluded to the relevance of the precautionary principle and scientific uncertainty.[52] Also, various Commission decisions contain precautionary language in response to the invocation of the principle by the derogating Member States.[53] Hereby

---

[49] *Land Oberösterreich* (n 25), para. 65.

[50] Commission Decision 2003/653/EC relating to national provisions on banning the use of genetically modified organisms in the region of Upper Austria notified by the Republic of Austria pursuant to Article 95(5) of the EC Treaty, 2003, L230/34.

[51] See also Maletić (n 21) 130.

[52] *Denmark v Commission* (n 28), paras 63–64.

[53] See in the 'creosote' cases, e.g. Commission Decision 1999/835/EC on the Danish derogation, 1999 OJ L329/82 stating at para. 110 that 'national measures aiming at reducing the probability of prolonged dermal exposure to creosote, either through direct contact with creosote or wood treated with creosote, are justified in the light of the precautionary principle'. The three other decisions on derogation requests for creosote contain similar statements. See Commission Decision on the Dutch derogation 1999/832/EC (1999) OJ L329/25 and Commission Decision 1999/834/EC on the Swedish derogation (1999) OJ L329/63. See also Commission Decision 2006/372/EC on a Dutch derogation request on the regulation of limit values for the emissions of particulate matter by diesel vehicles, (2006) OJ L142/16 paras 25–31; Commission Decision 2007/395/EC approving a Dutch derogation aiming to maintain more stringent national provisions on short-chain chlorinated paraffins, (2007) OJ L 148/17, paras 36–45.

we can observe that when scientific evidence, assessed by an EU scientific committee or agency, confirms scientific uncertainty, the Commission tends to refer to the precautionary principle when approving the national derogations.

Yet, at the same time, both the Commission and the Court have been very restrictive in allowing the precautionary principle to be applied in the context of the derogation mechanisms of Article 114(5) TFEU, in particular in relation to the criteria of new scientific evidence and new problems. Hence recourse to the precautionary principle does not appear to mitigate the stringent criteria of Article 114(5).[54] In the *Upper Austria* cases, Advocate General Sharpston expressed this by stressing that, however pertinent the precautionary principle may be in relation to new evidence concerning a new situation, 'no amount of precaution' could make that evidence or situation new and that in this manner the novelty of the situation and the evidence was a 'dual criterion which must be satisfied before the precautionary principle comes into play'.[55]

5.3 Relevance of International Developments

The assessment of scientific evidence submitted by the derogating Member States by the Commission seems less important when there are clear international obligations that Member States (and the EU) need to adhere to. In several cases, the Commission allowed for differentiated regimes to be maintained, taking into account obligations from international agreements, without submitting the national derogation to review by EU bodies. For example, in the case of the EU framework aiming to achieve the Union's targets under the Kyoto Protocol for the reduction of greenhouse gases, Austria[56] and Denmark[57] were allowed, for the purposes of environmental protection, to maintain lower targets for the level of so-called fluorinated gases than those set out in an EU regulation.[58] In these cases, the Commission found that both the Danish and Austrian measures were already contributing to the overall objective of the Kyoto Protocol to reduce greenhouse gases and went further than the EU

---

[54] See Maletić (n 21) 128.

[55] Opinion of AG Sharpston in *Land Oberösterreich* (n 25), para. 134.

[56] Commission Decision 2008/80/EC concerning national provisions notified by the Republic of Austria on certain fluorinated greenhouse gases, 2008 OJ L24/45.

[57] Commission Decision 2007/62/EC concerning national provisions notified by Denmark on certain industrial greenhouse gases, 2007 OJ L32/130.

[58] Regulation (EC) No 842/2006, 2006, OJ L161/1.

regulation which aimed to result in significant F-gases emission reductions throughout the EU, principally in those Member States where appropriate measures for reducing F-gases emissions were not yet in place. In this manner, the EU would adopt more stringent measures at a later stage. To this end, Regulation 842/2006 had already recognised that Member States would be able to maintain more stringent national measures until 2012.[59] Denmark, for example, had already had strict measures in place 50 years earlier and applied for a derogation. The Commission examined the Danish order and concluded that it met needs based on grounds of environmental protection proportionality and did not constitute an arbitrary discrimination or disguised restriction on trade. Herewith the Commission allowed Denmark to be a forerunner in fulfilling international obligations. In 2014 the EU adopted new more stringent requirements in Regulation No 517/2014.[60]

Also, in the case of so-called short-chain chlorinated paraffins (SCCPs), the Commission approved a Dutch derogation aiming to maintain more stringent national provisions on the SCCPs than laid down in Directive 76/769/EEC,[61] in particular taking account of new developments at EU and international level. When assessing the Dutch notification of 2006,[62] the Commission was well aware of novel scientific insights. First, a UK risk assessment had indicated new risks for certain applications of SCCP, which the Commission intended to send to the SCHER committee for review. Second, the EU had notified SCCPs as candidates under the UNECE Protocol and the Stockholm Convention on Persistent Organic Pollutants (POPs) respectively. Given that the outcomes of these processes could lead to further restrictions at EU level and that the precise scope of any such further restrictions was unclear at that moment, the Commission considered it necessary to apply the

---

[59] See art. 9(3)(a) of Regulation (EC) No 842/2006, 2006, OJ L161/1.

[60] European Parliament and Council Regulation No 517/2014 on fluorinated greenhouse gases and repealing Regulation (EC) No 842/2006, 2014, OJ L150/195.

[61] Directive 76/769/EEC, this was repealed by Regulation (EC) No 1907/2006 of the European the Registration, Evaluation, Authorisation and Restriction of Chemicals (REACH).

[62] A first Dutch notification of 2003 was approved only insofar as they did not apply to the use of SCCPs as constituents of other substances and preparations in concentrations lower than 1 per cent intended for use as plasticisers in paints, coatings or sealants, and flame retardants in rubber or textiles. See Commission Decision 2004/1/EC concerning national provisions on the use of short-chain chlorinated paraffins notified by the Kingdom of the Netherlands under Article 95(4) of the EC Treaty, 2004 OJ L1/20.

precautionary principle. It thus authorised the Dutch provisions this time in their entirety without further review until new EU measures taking full account of the latest scientific data would be adopted.[63] In 2010 the Commission decided that the Netherlands could maintain its legislation until 1 June 2013 and called for a re-examination of the restriction of SCCPs laid down in the REACH regulation.[64] Finally, pushed by new international obligations flowing from the Stockholm Convention, the Commission amended its rules on persistent organic pollutants in 2012 and widened the scope of the restriction on the use of SCCPs by prohibiting their production, placing on the market, and use, except for two exempted uses.[65]

5.4 Proportionality

Member States that wish to derogate must prove that their provisions are not a means of arbitrary discrimination or a disguised restriction on trade between the Member States and do not constitute an obstacle to the functioning of the internal market (Article 114(6) TFEU). An important aspect of the procedure of national derogations therefore has been for the Commission to analyse whether the national derogating measures go beyond what is necessary to attain the objective foreseen and hence to apply the proportionality principle. A good example is the Commission's assessment of the German derogation request on pharmacovigilance under Directive 2000/38 introducing a new EU-wide electronic data system of pharmacovigilance.[66] According to the German authorities, their existing stricter obligation requirements would attain the highest possible level of protection for the population in their use of medicinal

---

[63] Commission Decision 2007/395/EC concerning national provisions on the use of short-chain chlorinated paraffins notified by the Kingdom of the Netherlands under Article 95(4) of the EC Treaty 2007 OJ L148/17, paras 36–45.

[64] Commission Decision 2010/226/EU on the re-examination of the restriction concerning short-chain chlorinated paraffins (SCCPs) listed in Annex XVII to Regulation (EC) No 1907/2006 of the European Parliament and of the Council.

[65] Commission Regulation 519/2012 amending Regulation (EC) No 850/2004 of the European Parliament and of the Council on persistent organic pollutants as regards Annex I, 2014, OJ L363/67.

[66] Commission Directive 2000/38/EC amending Chapter Va (Pharmacovigilance) of Council Directive 75/319/EEC on the approximation of provisions laid down by law, regulation or administrative action relating to medicinal products 2000 OJ L139/28.

products. The Commission, however, rejected the notification, emphasising that the system of information sharing chosen under the EU Directive would adequately protect public health. It stated that 'maintaining the previous obligations to report would place an unnecessary and unjustifiable burden on the respective marketing authorization holders'.[67] Moreover, the Commission deemed its assessment of the appropriateness of the EU system to be supported by the fact that Germany 'is the only Member State which does not restrict the obligation to report adverse reactions occurring in non-member countries to those which are unexpected, but extends this obligation to adverse reactions which are expected'.[68]

In the *Dutch emissions* case, the Commission carried out a similar strict analysis. Here it recognised the need for further reductions of emissions but emphasised the grave consequences for the vehicle manufacturers who would have to adapt their production or restrict the models on the Dutch market.[69] It concluded that the envisaged national measure was not the least restrictive to achieve the desired environmental and health protection and would constitute a disproportionate barrier to the functioning of the internal market.[70] Hence, in this case, the Commission gave more weight to the disruption of the internal market than the potential benefits of the measure. This suggests the application of the most onerous version of the proportionality principle.[71]

5.5 Burden of Proof

Our analysis reveals a strong emphasis by both the Commission and the Court on the burden of proof that is being placed on the Member States that wish to derogate when faced with challenges to the Commission's rejections of derogations. We have already set out above that in the *Danish additives* case the Court's lenient approach towards the permissible scientific data that could be submitted by the derogating Member State was counterbalanced by its strict adherence to the burden of proof

[67] Commission Decision 2001/571/EC, on the national provisions notified by Germany in the field of pharmacovigilance, 2001, L202/46, para. 24.

[68] Ibid., para. 29.

[69] Commission Decision 2006/372/EC concerning draft national provisions notified by the Kingdom of the Netherlands under Article 95(5) of the EC Treaty laying down limits on the emissions of particulate matter by diesel-powered vehicles (OJ 2006 L142, p. 16).

[70] Ibid., para. 62.

[71] Maletić (n 21) 145.

placed on that State. The latter had to prove that the national provisions ensure a level of health protection which is higher than the EU harmonisation measure and that they do not go beyond what is necessary to achieve that objective.[72] In *Toys*, the General Court again emphasised the burden of proof on Germany that wished to maintain its existing legislation upholding stricter limits on values for lead, barium, arsenic, antimony, mercury, nitrosamines, and nitrosatable substances in toys. The Court ruled that Germany had failed to demonstrate that the national measure provided a higher level of protection than the EU harmonising measure and that it did so in a proportionate manner.[73]

5.6 EU Rather Than National Norms and Provisions

Closely linked to the above is our, rather unsurprising, finding that both the Commission and the Court seem to prefer the EU harmonisation measures to the notified national derogation measures. Therefore, an important aspect in the assessment of derogation requests has been the question whether the national measure was based on evidence already available prior to EU harmonisation and whether the EU took this evidence into account in the preparation of the EU harmonising measure. Hence, all notifications rejected under Article 114(4) suggest a presumption in favour of the risk management choice made at EU level by both the Commission and the Court.[74]

The central role assigned to the Commission as the risk manager within Article 114 opt-outs by the Court in its case law is crucial. In the *PCP* case the Court held that Member States cannot unilaterally apply national measures which deviate from the norm set by harmonisation measures adopted in the field concerned.[75] The centrality of the Commission's role as a risk manager was further underlined by the Court in the *Kortas* case[76] and was confirmed in the *Dutch Emissions* case of 2008. In the latter case, the Court held that the primary responsibility for the assessment of the merits of a request for derogation rests on the

[72] *Denmark v Commission* (n 28), para 64.

[73] Case T-198/12 *Germany v Commission* ECLI:EU:T:2014:251. In this case Germany challenged Commission Decision 2012/160/EU that only in part and temporarily approved the derogation.

[74] See also ibid., 139 ff.

[75] *France v Commission* (n 22), para. 30.

[76] *Kortas* (n 12).

Commission, which must itself properly take account of all the relevant evidence and explain the essential considerations that led to adopting its decision.[77]

It thus seems that, in cases of divergent risk management choices regarding differences in the appropriate level of protection based on the same risk assessment, there is a clear preference for the EU norms adopted either by the legislator or, in the case of new evidence, the Commission. This conclusion is substantiated by the Commission's assessment in 2003 of the German derogation request on the use of azodyes,[78] which sought to impose a higher level of protection by also banning azodyes in materials other than textiles and leather. To support its notification, Germany relied on the same SCTEE scientific opinions but interpreted them differently with regard to the risks posed by the use of azodyes in other materials. The Commission held that the new EU legislation already took these opinions into account and had opted for a regime to impose restrictions only where sufficient data has clearly shown the existence of risks (namely for textiles and leather).[79] Since Germany failed to prove 'the existence of a known risk to human health going beyond the risk already identified by the Community legislature',[80] the Commission rejected the request, even considering the lack of scientific data with regard to the use of azodyes in other materials than textiles and leather. Hence, the risk management choice taken by the EU legislature seems to have been decisive in this case.

Also the Commission's scrutiny of Denmark's request to derogate from the EU Additives Directive[81] relied on a similar reasoning. In this case, Denmark relied in particular on the risks pointed out by several scientific opinions of the EU's former Scientific Committee on Food (SCF) (now EFSA). The Commission, while acknowledging these risks, stressed that the EU Directive already took into consideration all the questions raised by the SCF and rejected the request. Hereby it stressed the 'responsibility

[77] *Netherlands v Commission* (n 26), para. 67.

[78] European Parliament and Council Directive 2002/61/EC amending for the nineteenth time Council Directive 76/769/EEC relating to restrictions on the marketing and use of certain dangerous substances and preparations (azocolourants), 2002, OJ L243/15.

[79] Commission Decision 2003/829, concerning national provisions on the use of azodyes notified by Germany under Article 95(4) of the EC Treaty 2003 OJ L311/46, para. 41.

[80] Ibid., para. 46.

[81] European Parliament and Council Directive 95/2/EC on food additives other than colours and sweeteners, 1995, OJ L61/1.

incumbent on a legislator, whether Community or national, with regard to risk management'.[82] Hence, according to the Commission, Denmark's responsibility as a risk manager in this case was much more restricted than the responsibility of the EU legislature. Yet, in 2003, the Commission's decision was annulled by the Court for having failed to duly to take into account an opinion of the EU Scientific Committee for Food, which affected the scientific basis of the EU harmonisation measure and which was favourable to Denmark's submission.[83]

This judgment influenced the subsequent Commission approach to a new Danish derogation request for nitrites in meat. Here Denmark wished to derogate from Directive 2006/52/EC, which amended the previous EU framework in the light of a new EFSA opinion and the Court's *Danish Additives* judgment.[84] This time, although still considering that the EU Directive provided for an adequate response to the challenge of reconciling two health risks,[85] the Commission acknowledged the possibility of Denmark choosing a different level of protection for a limited period of time. It submitted that it was necessary 'to evaluate the specific choices made by the Danish regulator and the experience made with these rules, which have been in force for a considerable period of time' and that 'the Danish legislation is compatible with the relevant scientific opinions of the Union's scientific bodies'.[86] Subsequently, the Commission has continued to extend its approval of the Danish derogation for its provisions on nitrates in meat,[87] while requiring EFSA to re-evaluate the use of nitrites by the end of

---

[82] Commission Decision 1999/830/EC on national provisions notified by Denmark concerning the use of sulphites, nitrites and nitrates in foodstuffs, 1999 OJ L329/1.

[83] *Denmark v Commission* (n 28) para. 114.

[84] See para. 10 of Commission Decision 2010/561/EC concerning national provisions notified by Denmark on the addition of nitrite to certain meat products, 2010, OJ L247/55.

[85] Namely, the presence of nitrosamines in meat products, on the one hand, and the microbiological safety of meat products, on the other hand, see paras 49–50 of Commission Decision 2010/561/EC, ibid.

[86] Commission Decision 2008/448/EC (2008) OJ L157/98, paras 51–52.

[87] Commission Decision 2008/448/EC allowed first for a derogation of two years. Subsequently the Commission, in its Decision 2010/561/EC, approved of the Danish derogation for a period of five years, most recently, Commission Decision (EU) 2015/826 approved the provisions until 22 May 2018, 2015 OJ L130/10.

2015.[88] It is likely that after such a re-evaluation of these substances, the Commission will either adjust the EU legislation or ensure that the Danish provisions will be in line with the EU rules. Therefore, the Court's lenient ruling and the Commission's cooperative practice towards the Danish provisions on nitrates in meat seem to be rather an exception to the practice of derogations under Article 114(4) and are rooted in the complexities and uncertainties as to the use of nitrates in meat. It seems therefore very likely that after 22 May 2018 – the date until which the Danish derogating provisions have been approved – and EFSA's opinion – that was due by the end of 2015 but has not been adopted yet – either the EU or Danish legislation will be amended.

6. DIFFERENTIATION THROUGH SAFEGUARD CLAUSES

6.1 Article 114(10) and Safeguard Clauses in EU Legislation

The Treaty instructs the European institutions to provide for safeguard clauses in measures that deal with the protection of human health and safety and the environment. Member States may thus derogate from the obligation to ensure free movement of goods that comply with the rules laid down in EU harmonisation measures if a specific product legitimately produced in accordance with the EU rules causes a danger to, inter alia, human health or the environment. Thus paragraph (10) of Article 114 TFEU stipulates that harmonisation measures shall, in appropriate cases, include a safeguard clause which enables the Member States to take provisional measures for one or more of the non-economic reasons referred to in Article 34 TFEU, which are subjected to an EU control procedure.[89]

The safeguard clause requires Member States to notify the Commission of any stricter national provision they want to maintain or adopt and complements the notification procedures for non-(fully) harmonised

---

[88] Commission Regulation 257/2010 setting up a programme for the re-evaluation of approved food additives in accordance with Regulation (EC) No 1333/2008 of the European Parliament and of the Council on food additives, 2010 OJ L80/19.

[89] In practice, the inclusion of such clauses in directives was already common prior to the Single European Act, which introduced this possibility into the Treaty. See the survey carried out by Ludwig Krämer, *EEC Consumer Law* (Story-Scientia 1986) points 242–246.

areas. It aims to prevent dangerous products from circulating in the EU market. At the same time, the inclusion of safeguard measures reflects a recognition of the constitutional obligation of most Member States to ensure the health and safety of their citizens.[90] Hence, where a Member State has good grounds for believing that a product which satisfies the requirements set out in a specific directive nonetheless poses a hazard to safety or health, it may temporarily prohibit this product or attach special conditions to its circulation. The final say in this procedure is left to the Commission, often together with a committee composed of national representatives. These cases generally lead the Commission to consider whether a revision of the relevant provisions in the harmonisation measure is necessary. Practice shows that in situations where Member States rely on the safeguard clause, resort to science and reasoning in terms of science has also become crucial. As will be discussed below (section 6.2.), in relation to the authorisation of GMOs, comitology has given the Member States an instrument to enforce the maintenance of national derogations against the will of the Commission.

In addition, we also observe a recent trend of a disappearance of safeguard clauses from some of the EU food legislation. While this seems unconstitutional and in conflict with the rationale underlying Article 114(10) TFEU, our analysis reveals that the safeguard clauses in such measures are replaced by the emergency procedures of the General Food Law that empower the Commission (and the Member States only in a second stage) to take measures at once.[91] This would indicate a shift from the power of Member States to act as risk managers to the Commission as the central risk manager as we already signalled above. This shift may in turn cause tension in relation to the constitutional obligations of some Member States to protect the health and safety of their citizens.

6.2 From Safeguard to Opt-out Clause Laid Down in a Directive: The Case of GMOs

Our analysis reveals that it has appeared virtually impossible to find information on the use of safeguards, which has led us, for the time being, to limit our research to the food sector. Here it seems that

---

[90] See Hans W Micklitz, Thomas Roethe and Stephen Weatherill (eds), *Federalism and Responsibility. A Study on Product Safety Law and Practice in the European Community* (Graham & Trotman 1994).

[91] Articles 50 and 53, 54 of European Parliament and Council Regulation 178/2002, 2002, OJ L31/1, as lastly amended by Regulation (EU) No 652/2014, 2014 OJ L189/1.

relatively few derogations have been requested.[92] Most derogation requests concerned the notifications in the framework of the safeguards clauses laid down in the GMO Deliberate Release Directive[93] (13 notifications). These cases are exemplary in demonstrating the limits of scientific expertise when resolving politically sensitive regulatory issues. In the GMO case science, although frequently invoked by both Commission and Member States, has so far not been able to resolve the regulatory deadlock,[94] for which the EU has been condemned by a WTO panel.[95] Rather, this deadlock led the Commission in 2010 to propose an amendment to the Deliberate Release Directive so as to include a new and highly unusual opt-out clause in this Directive.[96] After five years of discussion, the reform finally entered into force in April 2015.[97]

The new so-called 'flexible approach' to GMO cultivation embodied in the now-amended Deliberate Release Directive is an exceptional example of a process in which a persistent invocation of both Article 114 opt-outs and safeguard clauses has resulted in a new differentiated regulatory regime. Moreover, for the first time, the Commission has proposed to give back to Member States decision rights previously exercised at the EU level and thereby to allow for less harmonisation across the Union.[98] According to the now agreed amendment of Directive 2001/18, a new

---

92 A mere 16 invocations were done under Directives 90/220, 2001/18, 2002/53, and Regulation 178/2002.

93 European Parliament and Council Directive 2001/18/EC on the deliberate release into the environment of genetically modified organisms and repealing Council Directive 90/220/EEC, 2001 OJ L106/1.

94 Maria Weimer, 'Applying Precaution in EU Authorization of Genetically Modified Products – Challenges and Suggestions for Reform' (2010) 16(5) *European Law Journal* 624 and Maria Weimer, 'Risk Regulation and Deliberation in EU Administrative Governance' (2015) 21(5) *European Law Journal* 622.

95 Maria Lee, *EU Regulation of GMOs* (Edward Elgar 2008); Denise Prévost, 'Opening Pandora's box: The Panel's Findings in the EC-Biotech Products Dispute' (2007) 34(1) *Legal Issues of Economic Integration* 67–101.

96 Maria Weimer, 'What Price Flexibility? – The Recent Commission Proposal to Allow for National "Opt-outs" on GMO Cultivation under the Deliberate Release Directive and the Comitology Post-Lisbon' (2010) 1(4) *European Journal of Risk Regulation* 345; and Weimer 2015 (n 94).

97 European Parliament and Council Directive 2015/412 amending Directive 2001/18/EC as regards the possibility for the Member States to restrict or prohibit the cultivation of genetically modified organisms (GMOs) in their territory, 2015, OJ L68/1.

98 For a more detailed discussion of the nature and problems of this reform see Weimer 2015 (n 94).

Article 26b[99] entitled 'Cultivation' shall be inserted, laying down the procedure for the adoption by a Member State of measures restricting or prohibiting the cultivation of a GMO previously authorised at EU level in all or part of its territory. The most unusual feature of this new legal basis for GMO opt-outs consists in the nature of the grounds for 'opting-out.' In contrast to the traditional opt-out (Article 114) and safeguard measures discussed above, which have been provided for by the EU legislator in order to allow for a better protection of public health and the environment, the GMO 'opt-out' excludes these grounds from the permissible grounds on which Member States may rely when banning GMOs. Quite the contrary, Member States have to base their opt-outs on grounds which do not conflict with the scientific risk assessment of health and environmental risks conducted by the EFSA. The new Article 26b(3) states that Member States may adopt opt-out measures:

> provided that such measures are in conformity with Union law, reasoned, proportional and non-discriminatory and, in addition, are based on compelling grounds such as those related to: (a) environmental policy objectives; (b) town and country planning; (c) land use; (d) socio-economic impacts; (e) avoidance of GMO presence in other products without prejudice to Article 26a; (f) agricultural policy objectives; (g) public policy.

The amendment emphasises that the assessment of potential risks for human and animal health and the environment of the deliberate release of GMOs is fully harmonised. Therefore, the Member States should only use grounds related to environmental policy objectives which do not conflict with the EU assessment of risks.[100]

The rationale behind this framing is to grant the Member States more regulatory autonomy when it comes to GMO cultivation, but only for the purpose of responding to so-called 'other legitimate factors' involved in GMO cultivation. The EU centralised authorisation procedure with its harmonised risk assessment and EFSA's epistemic authority[101] ought to

---

[99] Moreover, an art. 26c is inserted concerning 'Transitional measures.'

[100] See recitals (6) and (14) of Directive 2015/412, amending Directive 2001/18/EC as regards the possibility for the Member States to restrict or prohibit the cultivation of genetically modified organisms (GMOs) in their territory, 2015, OJ L68/1.

[101] See Maria Weimer and Gaia Pisani, 'Expertise as Justification – The Contested Legitimation of the EU 'Risk Administration' in Maria Weimer and Anniek de Ruijter (eds), *Regulating Risks in the European Union – The Co-production of Expert and Executive Power* (forthcoming with Hart Publishing).

be preserved, however. This also shows that the persistent invocation of opt-out and safeguard clauses in the GMO case has *not* led to a differentiation in terms of different levels of public health and environmental protection across the Union (as was sometimes the case in other areas, see discussion above). In other words, it has not led to the acceptance by the EU, most notably the Commission, of scientific pluralism including different evaluations of scientific evidence on GMOs. Instead, national bans and restrictions on GMOs have led to opening up the 'scientific risk' framing of the GMO regulatory regime by providing the Member States with a legal basis to act upon other concerns surrounding the issue of GMO cultivation (e.g. agricultural, land use and even more abstract public policy[102] concerns).

Interestingly, the GMO case also signals an important difference between Article 114 opt-outs and safeguard clauses in terms of their impact on differentiation versus harmonisation. The resistance to GMO authorisation on the part of several Member States was mainly channelled through the invocation of the safeguard clause laid down in Article 23 of the Deliberate Release Directive. This was unsurprisingly due to the fact that comitology, as the applicable procedure, provided for a forum in which Member States could voice their opposition to a Commission decision rejecting the safeguard measure. In this way comitology allowed for a certain mitigation of (EU) science as the sole basis for the Commission decision bringing concerns other than science and divergent national evaluations of scientific evidence into the discussion surrounding GMOs. This leads us to assume that the gradual disappearance of safeguard clauses in EU secondary legislation involving foodstuffs is likely to result in strengthening the role of the Commission as the central EU risk manager at the expense of a more multi-level approach.[103]

---

[102] On the invocation of ethical and religious arguments against GMOs, see Case C-165/08 *Commission v Poland* [2009] ECLI:EU:C:2009:473.

[103] See Maria Weimer, 'The Right to Adopt Post-Market Restrictions of Genetically Modified Crops in the EU – A shift from De-Centralised Multi-Level to Centralised Governance in the Case of GM Foods', Case note on Court of Justice of the European Union, Joined Cases C-58/10 to C-68/10 Monsanto SAS and Others (2012) 3 *European Journal of Risk Regulation* 445.

7. CONCLUDING REMARKS AND REFLECTIONS ON THE IMPACT OF THE DEROGATION MECHANISMS ON THE INTERNAL MARKET

Overall, in the case of opt-out notifications we can observe the following pattern in the practice of Commission decision-making. First, EU scientific opinions seem to play a crucial role in determining whether or not the Commission approves a national derogation under both Article 114(4) and (5). The Commission does not simply consider the evidence submitted to it by the notifying Member State, but it typically sends it to EFSA or a relevant EU scientific committee for re-evaluation. Where the EU scientific bodies confirm the scientific justification invoked by the notifying Member State, the Commission authorises the derogation. Hereby, in several cases, the Commission has relied on the precautionary principle or has invoked scientific uncertainty as an argument to approve the notification – only in accordance with the advice of EU scientific bodies, however. Another important factor of a successful notification seems to be whether a re-evaluation of a risk assessment with regard to a particular substance or product is already on-going at the EU level. Moreover, international developments and institutions provide an important context, which the Commission takes into account in its decisions. This was the case with the Kyoto Protocol in the fluorinated gases cases and with WHO guidelines in the short-chain chlorinated paraffins case. Finally, it can be noted that those cases in which derogations resulted in the adjustment of rules at the EU level were characterised by the fact that several (more than two) Member States filed a notification.

The modest application of the derogation possibilities under Article 114(4) and (5) shows that the initial fears that the opt-out mechanism would lead to a fragmented internal market have not materialised.[104] Member States have in only a few cases enforced their national positions on health and safety issues notwithstanding a common approach adopted at EU level. And, of the 38 cases that were notified, 17 derogations were approved. Notably, in approximately 50 per cent of the latter cases, the derogations have led to an adjustment of the EU framework to set a higher level of protection. In the other 50 per cent of derogation approvals, the situation is less straightforward. In five cases the approval of derogations did not immediately lead to any further action at the EU level. The Danish provisions on nitrates in meat have been controlled by the Commission renewing its approval of these derogation measures three

104 See e.g. Pescatore (n 14).

times. As indicated above, currently EFSA will re-evaluate the use of these substances, which in all likelihood will subsequently lead to either an amendment of EU legislation or the discontinuation of the Danish derogation measures. The other four cases seem rather atypical cases of compliance with the Kyoto Protocol where the Commission did not submit the national derogation request for scientific review at the EU level but rather approved the national derogation. In these cases, the derogation was approved for a limited period. Both new scientific insights at the EU and international level have led the Commission after ten years to revise the relevant EU measures and to expand the restriction on the use of SCCPs. In the other cases, derogations were granted in the light of or until the completion of the revision of EU legislation. Hence, it seems that, where differentiation has been permitted by the Commission, the permission was of temporary nature until a revised EU framework would be established.

Therefore in the case of approved notifications, both Article 114(4) and (5) seem to be an important mechanism of regulatory adjustment and learning in the fields of public health and environmental protection at the EU level. In some cases the successful invocation of an opt-out has ultimately triggered a process of further harmonisation at EU level aiming to remove the regulatory disparities among the Member States. In such cases the Commission was more tolerant in allowing a derogation, especially in cases in which many Member States filed a notification to derogate from the same harmonisation measure, such as in case of PCP, creosote and cadmium, thus threatening the internal market laws on these substances. Hereby, it seems that it is not coincidental that the approval of the derogations resulted in the adjustment of the EU rules at the higher level of protection, pushed for by the derogating Member States. The Commission's line of argumentation in these cases clearly shows the importance of avoiding what it deems as unnecessary burdens on traders.[105]

Moreover, the emphasis on the relevance of choices made in other Member States refutes the logic of differentiation. Rather, a 'one size fits all' approach becomes apparent. Our study shows that the opt-out mechanism can be seen as failing to realise the promise of regulatory diversity and instead ultimately strengthens the uniformity of regulatory requirements in the EU internal market. Hence, the practice does not confirm the view that opt-out and safeguard clauses constitute a means of

---

[105] For a similar reasoning see Commission Decision 2003/829 on azodyes recital 46 (n 79).

differentiated integration in EU internal market law. Rather they can be regarded as mechanisms increasing the uniformity of regulatory requirements in the EU internal market and thereby serving as means of further harmonisation. This happens mainly in two ways. First, the strict interpretation by both the Commission and EU courts of the legal requirements for a Member State to invoke an opt-out or safeguard clause successfully prevents more frequent invocation of these derogation mechanisms. Secondly, where these mechanisms are actually being invoked successfully, this ultimately triggers a process of further harmonisation at the EU level to remove the regulatory disparities among the Member States. In these cases, the derogation clauses could be characterised as a kind of learning process indicating the need to provide other EU legal solutions and could act as a catalyst for better regulation and protection at the EU level.[106] The ultimate result, however, is a uniform EU framework rather than the acceptance of regulatory differences.

An example of this is the strengthening of the role of the European Commission as a central risk manager of crisis situations and emergencies with regard to food safety. However, as the GMO case shows, persistent national derogations might also indicate the need to provide for more regulatory autonomy at the national level. The recent 'flexible approach' of the Commission to GMO cultivation, which followed a year-long national non-compliance with EU rules in this field, is a case in point. It exemplifies the tension between the creation of one internal market on which all products that conform to the EU rules may freely circulate on the one hand and the possibility, and right, of Member States to adhere to the values that they highly regard and wish to uphold on the other. The complexities of decision-making on GMOs illustrate a strong reliance of the Commission on scientific expertise (also pushed by the WTO), which has been accompanied by a continuous 'battle of the experts'.[107] Persistent invocation of derogations by several Member States has in this case led to a new differentiated regulatory regime, as well as to the creation of a novel type of opt-out to be invoked on grounds other than public health and environmental safety. Consequently, GMO derogations have *not* led to a differentiation in terms of different levels of public health and environmental protection across the Union,

[106] See also Maletić (n 21) 186.

[107] See Denise Prévost, 'The Role of Science in Mediating the Conflict between Free Trade and Health Regulation at the WTO: The EC – Biotech Products Dispute' in Marjolein Van Asselt, Ellen Vos and Michelle Everson (eds), *Trade, Health And The Environment: The European Union Put To The Test* (Routledge Explorations in Environmental Studies 2013) 161–212.

given that the EU-wide scientific assessment remains fully harmonised. Instead, they resulted in opening up the 'scientific risk' framing of the GMO regulatory regime by allowing the Member States to act upon other concerns surrounding the issue of GMO cultivation.

Lastly, we need to reflect on what the low number of invocations of the opt-out clauses (and the safeguard clauses) really tells us. Does this mean that Member States are satisfied with the level of protection of the non-market values and that they feel no need to opt out of the general harmonisation schemes? This is not necessarily the case. First, the opt-out procedure is important in the negotiations of a harmonisation measure and gives Member States an important tool to push for a level of protection that is satisfactory to all Member States. In addition, analysis of the practice and case law on the opt-out procedures reveals that both the Commission and the Courts have an extremely rigid reading of the procedure while the grounds for invocation are very limited. This may conflict with the practical operation of the procedure discouraging Member States from appealing to appeal to it. As the GMO case exemplifies, it requires a rethinking of the ways in which the paradigm of uniformity may be combined with a respect for diversity, which eventually will impact on the implementation of international legal (trade) regimes. This entails a profound reflection on what ultimately should be the 'soul' of the internal market[108] and more generally of the EU.

REFERENCES

Brüggemeier G, Falke J, Joerges C and Micklitz H-W, 'European Product Safety, Completion of the Internal Market and the New Approach to Technical Harmonisation and Standards – Reissued' (2010) 6(2) *Hanse Law Review* 107–14.

De Sadeleer N, *EU Environmental Law and the Internal Market* (Oxford University Press 2014).

De Witte B, 'The Competence to Protect. The Pursuit of Non-market Aims through Internal Market Legislation' in Syrpis P (ed), *The Judiciary, the Legislator and the Internal Market* (Cambridge University Press 2012) 25–46.

Ehlermann CD, 'Increased Differentiation or Stronger Uniformity?' EUI Working Paper RSC 95/21, Florence 1995.

---

[108] Stephen R Weatherill, 'Maximum versus Minimum Harmonization: Choosing between Unity and Diversity in the Search for the Soul of the Internal Market' in Niamh Nic Shuibhne and Lawrence W Gormley (eds), *From Single Market to Economic Union: Essays in Memory of John A Usher* (Oxford University Press 2012) 175.

Everson M and Vos E (eds), *Uncertain Risks Regulated* (Cavendish 2009).
Flynn J, 'How Will Article 100A (4) Work? A Comparison With Article 93' (1987) 24 CML Rev 689–707.
Gulmann C, 'The Single European Act – Some Remarks from a Danish Perspective' (1987) 24 CML Rev 31–40.
Hailbronner K, 'Der "nationale Alleingang" im Gemeinschaftsrecht am Beispiel der Abgasstandards für Pkw', (1989) 16 EuGRZ 101–22.
Krämer L, *EEC Consumer Law* (Story-Scientia 1986).
Krämer L, 'The Single European Act and Environmental Protection: Reflections on Several New Provisions in Community Law' (1987) 24 CML Rev. 659–88.
Lee M, *EU Regulation of GMOs* (Edward Elgar Publishing 2008).
Maletić I, *The Law and Policy of Harmonisation in Europe's Internal Market* (Edward Elgar Publishing 2013).
Micklitz HW, Roethe Th and Weatherill S (eds), *Federalism and Responsibility. A Study on Product Safety Law and Practice in the European Community* (Graham & Trotman 1994).
Pescatore P, 'Die 'Einheitliche Europäische Akte'. Eine ernste Gefahr für den Gemeinsamen Markt' (1986) 21 EuR 2 153–69.
Pescatore P, 'Some Critical Remarks on the "Single European Act"' (1987) 24 CML Rev 9–18.
Prévost, D, 'Opening Pandora's box: The Panel's Findings in the EC-Biotech Products Dispute' (2007) 34(1) *Legal Issues of Economic Integration* 67–101.
Prévost D, 'The Role of Science in Mediating the Conflict between Free Trade and Health Regulation at the WTO: The EC – Biotech Products Dispute' in Van Asselt M, Vos E and Everson M (eds), *Trade, Health And The Environment: The European Union Put To The Test* (Routledge Explorations in Environmental Studies 2013) 161–212.
Snell J, "The Internal Market and the Philosophies on Market Integration' in Barnard C and Peers S (eds), *European Union Law* (Oxford University Press 2014) 300–24.
Vos E, 'Differentiation, Harmonisation and Governance' in De Witte B, Hanf D and Vos E (eds), *The Many Faces of Differentiation in EU Law* (Intersentia 2001) 145–79.
Weatherill S, 'Beyond Preemption? Shared Competence and Constitutional Change in the European Community' in O'Keeffe D and Twomey PM (eds), *Legal Issues of the Maastricht Treaty* (Chancery Law Publishing 1994) 13–33.
Weatherill S, *Cases and Materials on EU Law*, 9th edition (Oxford University Press 2010).
Weatherill S, 'Maximum versus Minimum Harmonization: Choosing between Unity and Diversity in the Search for the Soul of the Internal Market' in Nic Shuibhne N and Gormley LW (eds), *From Single Market to Economic Union: Essays in Memory of John A Usher* (Oxford University Press 2012) 174–99.
Weimer M, 'What Price Flexibility? – The Recent Commission Proposal to Allow for National "Opt-outs" on GMO Cultivation under the Deliberate Release Directive and the Comitology Post-Lisbon' (2010) 1(4) *European Journal of Risk Regulation* 345–52.

Weimer M, 'Applying Precaution in EU Authorization of Genetically Modified Products – Challenges and Suggestions for Reform' (2010) 16(5) *European Law Journal* 624–657.

Weimer M, The Right to Adopt Post-Market Restrictions of Genetically Modified Crops in the EU – A Shift from De-Centralised Multi-Level to Centralised Governance in the Case of GM Foods', Case note on Court of Justice of the European Union, Joined Cases C-58/10 to C-68/10 Monsanto SAS and Others (2012) 3 *European Journal of Risk Regulation* 445–51.

Weimer M, 'Risk Regulation and Deliberation in EU Administrative Governance' (2015) 21(5) *European Law Journal* 622–40.

Weimer M and Pisani G, 'Expertise as Justification – The Contested Legitimation of the EU 'Risk Administration' in Weimer M and de Ruijter A (eds), *Regulating Risks in the European Union – The Co-production of Expert and Executive Power* (forthcoming with Hart Publishing).

Wennerås P, 'Fog and Acid Rain Drifting from Luxembourg over Art. 95(4) EC: Case C-3/0 Kingdom of Denmark v. the Commission of the European Communities Danish Food Case' (2003) 12(6) *European Energy and Environmental Law Review* 169–78.

13. Flexibility in EU environmental law and policy: a response to complexity, or fig leaf for expediency?

Suzanne Kingston

> (T)he EC must take care to leave national, regional and local bodies as much freedom of discretion as possible. Harmonisation must be aimed at only to the extent necessary for a minimum level of protection of the whole EC and for the free circulation of goods as well as undistorted competition …
>
> The diversity in geographical and natural situations, and between the tasks of the different regions, may sometimes require the application of different standards.
>
> European Commission, Proposal for an EEC Environmental Action Programme (SEC (72)666), at p. 6.

1. INTRODUCTION

Flexibility has been embedded in the EU's environmental law and policy from its very beginnings. Despite the urgent tone of the UN's 1972 Stockholm Conference which influenced the Community's first steps towards a formal policy on the environment,[1] the above excerpt from the Commission's proposal for the EEC's first Environmental Action Programme shows that Brussels considered from the outset that, whatever

[1] See the Declaration of the United Nations Conference on the Human Environment (Stockholm, 1972). The recognition of flexibility in the above extract from the Commission proposal of the same year may be contrasted, for instance, with the absolutism of Principle 1 of that Declaration: 'Man has the fundamental right to freedom, equality and adequate conditions of life, in an environment of a quality that permits a life of dignity and well-being, and he bears a solemn responsibility to protect and improve the environment for present and future generations ….' Such absolutism has however disappeared in subsequent UN Declarations, in favour of the notion of sustainability and the principle of Common But Differentiated Responsibility (CBDR), discussed further below.

kind of environmental policy the Community would eventually end up with, it could not be a 'one-size-fits-all' policy.

It is no surprise, therefore, that long before the idea of 'constitutional' flexibility found its way into the Treaty for other areas, in the sense of enhanced cooperation and opt-out Protocols for certain Member States, we had already seen a significant level of flexibility written into the Treaty in terms of environmental protection. As discussed below, such flexibility was striking from the very first inclusion of an environmental chapter in the EEC Treaty with the Single European Act. Since then, as the scope and volume of EU environmental legislation has grown vastly (such that, on average, 80 per cent of all national environmental law is now derived from EU law),[2] so too has the reliance on flexibility mechanisms in EU environmental policy. The environmental sphere has also been one of the EU's first-movers in the use of 'new governance' techniques, moving away from traditional top-down regulation to participatory, adaptive and experimental techniques.

In this sense, therefore, environmental policy can be viewed as a regulatory guinea pig in the EU's flexibility experiments and, in considering whether flexibility can deliver a coherent effective policy outcome, one might naturally look to the environmental experience for an answer. Are the flexibility mechanisms in use really increasing the effectiveness of the EU's environmental policy, viz. better achieving a '*high level of protection*' of the EU's environment? Or are they being used instead of less flexible, but more effective, mechanisms where 'flexibility' is more politically palatable than compulsory, definite obligations?

This chapter considers the use of flexibility in EU environmental law, and the coherence of that use. It maps the meanings of what we might consider to be flexible mechanisms in EU environmental law, and considers how they have been employed to date. It concludes with a critical discussion of justifications for flexibility in the environmental field, and the limits of flexibility.

---

[2] See, for instance, Commissioner Dimas in European Environment Bureau, EU Environmental Policy Handbook (Brussels 2005), at 3; Government of the Netherlands, 'EU legislation' <http://www.government.nl/issues/environment/roles-and-responsibilities-of-central-government/eu-legislation> accessed 5 November 2014.

2. MAPPING MEANINGS AND USAGE OF FLEXIBILITY IN EU ENVIRONMENTAL LAW AND POLICY

As is highlighted in many of the chapters in this volume, the concept of flexibility can mean many different things. In the environmental context, we can distinguish three distinct manifestations of flexibility: flexibility of implementation; flexibility of enforcement; and flexibility of (substantive) standards. The common theme running throughout is the idea that, subject to respect for Treaty obligations, differences between States or even between environmental actors should be taken into account, and that there may not necessarily be a single policy and/or legal solution appropriate for the entire EU.

2.1 Flexibility of Implementation

A first sense of flexibility in EU environmental policy is flexibility in implementation, understood as the idea that Member States should be given discretion or leeway in deciding how to implement EU environmental norms, including by using a wider category of policy tools including Framework Directives and co-Regulation.

This strategy was famously championed by the Commission's 2001 White Paper on European Governance[3] and, as discussed below, has been used liberally in the environmental context, especially in recent years. In principle, if used correctly, it has the benefit of simplifying EU legislation by cutting down on the level of detail required in favour of broader, target-based provisions. This simplification agenda has since been picked up on in the EU's 'Better' or 'Smart' Regulation Strategy, where it has often been combined with the separate drive towards cost-benefit analysis of regulatory burdens (including from environmental legislation), particularly in the EU's Regulatory Fitness and Performance Programme (REFIT).[4] Proponents of flexibility of implementation would also argue that it has the benefit of enabling Member States to mould their implementation strategies to fit local conditions, by choosing what they

[3] COM(2001) 428.

[4] See, as regards environmental regulation, the Action Programme for Reducing Administrative Burdens in the EU – Final Report, SWD(2012) 422, where the Commission released an action plan to reduce the costs for the seven most burdensome pieces of environmental legislation for business by around €300 million per annum. Specific burdens were identified in the fields of waste and chemicals, particularly REACH.

consider to be the best way of achieving the relevant legislative obligations in the context of the State at issue.

In the environmental context, this kind of flexibility of implementation has been widely used, and its incidence is certainly increasing.

An obvious example is the form of EU environmental legislation that has been preferred in recent years. While EU environmental legislation has long tended to take the form of Directives rather than Regulations, the EU has used Framework Directives to tackle environmental topics that are particularly important and complex. The Water Framework Directive[5] and the Waste Framework Directive are good examples.[6] In principle, these Framework Directives seek to achieve a coherent EU-level policy while still leaving room for manoeuvre for Member States. The reason for this is expressed in recital 13 of the Preamble to the Water Framework Directive, which notes that:

> There are diverse conditions and needs in the Community which require different specific solutions. This diversity should be taken into account in the planning and execution of measures to ensure protection and sustainable use of water in the framework of the river basin. Decisions should be taken as close as possible to the locations where water is affected or used. Priority should be given to action within the responsibility of Member States through the drawing up of programmes of measures adjusted to regional and local conditions.

In this sense, the use of Framework Directives is aimed at ensuring that the principle of subsidiarity is complied with as far as possible in these complex fields of legislation, in recognition of the fact that Member States rather than the Commission will be best placed in many instances to draw up detailed programmes suitable for their own jurisdiction. This is coupled with relatively broadly worded aims set out in the legislation (see, for instance, Article 4 of the Water Framework Directive). Aside from such flexibility of implementation, however, the environmental Framework Directives also go further in some circumstances, to expressly entitle Member States to adopt less stringent standards, as will be mentioned below.

In diametric opposition to this embrace of flexibility, however, is the declaration in the EU's Seventh Environmental Action Programme

---

[5] Directive 2000/60/EC of the European Parliament and of the Council of 23 October 2000 establishing a framework for Community action in the field of water policy OJ [2000] L327/1.

[6] Directive 2008/98/EC of the European Parliament and of the Council of 19 November 2008 on waste and repealing certain Directives OJ [2008] L312/3.

(EAP), which sets out the key priorities of the EU's environmental policy from 2013–20, that, in the interest of improving implementation, EU environmental legislation will by preference henceforth be in the form of Regulations (at §63):

> As a general rule, where legal obligations are sufficiently clear and precise and where a harmonised application in all Member States is deemed the most effective way of achieving Union objectives, those legal obligations will be enshrined in regulations, which have direct and measurable effects and lead to fewer inconsistencies in implementation.[7]

What this will actually mean in practice is debatable, however, particularly given that the Seventh EAP also states, in its operative part (Article 2(4)), that, '[a]ll measures, actions and targets set out in the 7th EAP shall be proposed and implemented in accordance with the principles of smart regulation'.

This would seem to condition the validity of all environmental measures on compatibility with the principles of smart regulation, a proposition that in principle favours flexibility. The clear tensions here are just one manifestation of the battle currently taking place for what some might characterise as the soul of the EU's environmental policy, and its relationship with other EU policies. The increasing moves to monetise (i.e., place a monetary value on) environmental benefits and degradation in taking policy decisions is central to this battle.[8] Thus, making environmental legislation subject to smart regulation principles might seem unremarkable until one considers, for instance, that it might mean that environmental legislation which is considered (in the first instance, by the Commission) to place an undue financial burden upon industry would not be acceptable. This, indeed, is the spectre raised by one of the current REFIT projects, announced in February 2014, which considers the compatibility of the EU's flagship nature conservation legislation, the 1976 Wild Birds Directive and the 1992 Habitats Directive, with the principles of smart regulation. A brief glance at the mandate for this fitness check suffices to confirm that this could have far-reaching implications. The mandate makes clear that the future of the EU's nature legislation will be dependent on its passing a test of '*fitness for purpose*'

---

[7] Decision No 1386/2013/EU of the European Parliament and of the Council of 20 November 2013 on a General Union Environment Action Programme to 2020 'Living well, within the limits of our planet' OJ [2013] L354/171.

[8] See, for instance, among the voluminous literature on this controversy, Editorial, 'Ecosystem Services and Capitalism: A Valuation or Devaluation of Nature?' (2014) 5(2) *Journal of Human Rights and the Environment* 1.

based on the aim of seeking to ensure the '*best possible cost/benefit ratio for EU regulation*'.[9] Yet, as discussed further below, such a measurement of success is in the environmental context inevitably controversial and value-laden. It is certainly far from the neutral, objective assessment that the Commission has liked to cast itself as carrying out.

Aside from this debate about the specificity (and ensuing regulatory burden) of EU environmental legislation, the drive for flexibility in implementation is also evident in the embrace of so-called 'new' modes of governance and 'new' policy instruments in EU environmental policy, especially in the past ten years. As is well known, for around the first 20 years of its existence, Community environmental policy relied almost exclusively on what we might call traditional regulatory techniques, relying primarily on hierarchical proscriptions by law-makers (e.g., the imposition of environmental standards by law, or the banning of environmental hazardous substances by law) to be enforced by public authorities (e.g., agencies or courts). These techniques, variously called hierarchical, direct, or command-and-control regulation, were supplemented in the 1990s by an increasing reliance upon market mechanisms to achieve environmental aims. Such market-based instruments, including emissions trading and environmental taxes and charges, now play a vital role in the EU's regulatory mix.[10]

A further important part of this mix in contemporary EU environmental policy is the increasing use of instruments aimed at encouraging the individuals and organizations (voluntarily) to get involved in achieving the EU's environmental policy goals. These instruments may be viewed as forming part of the development of network-based governance, i.e., reliance on non-hierarchical, societal-driven methods of achieving policy aims.[11] In the case of corporations, one example is the emphasis on corporate social responsibility, a trend generally embraced by the EU and Member State governments, but regarded with deep suspicion by some environmentalists. At EU level, the European Commission has developed a CSR agenda, which is largely based on soft-law, non-binding

---

[9] Commission, Fitness Check Mandate for Nature Legislation, 25 February 2014, 1, <http://ec.europa.eu/environment/nature/legislation/fitness_check/docs/Mandate%20for%20Nature%20Legislation.pdf> accessed 6 November 2014.

[10] See Suzanne Kingston, *Greening EU Competition Law and Policy* (Cambridge University Press 2012) Ch. 2, and Suzanne Kingston, 'Developments in EU Law: Environment' (2010) 59 ICLQ 1129.

[11] See, Andrew Jordan and Adriaan Schout, *The Coordination of the European Union: Exploring the Capacities of Network Governance* (Oxford University Press 2006).

efforts such as enhancing the visibility of CSR and disseminating good practices. However, it has also led to measures with more teeth, including a 2014 Directive on disclosure of non-financial and diversity information by large companies and groups.[12] This will oblige companies falling within its scope to disclose information on policies, risks and outcomes as regards, among other things, environmental matters. However, companies are left with significant flexibility as to the manner in which they choose to disclose relevant information (for instance, they may follow UN, European or national guidelines, depending on their preference).

One outcome of the current EU CSR agenda has been an emphasis on improving self- and co-regulation processes. In the environmental context, an important technique for achieving this has been the use of voluntary environmental agreements, i.e., agreements entered into by private parties aimed at achieving environmental objectives.[13] These may include self-regulatory arrangements, where the agreement is put in place solely by market actors on a voluntary basis, whether in the form of binding agreements or gentlemen's agreements. Alternatively, co-regulation may be used, i.e., where legislative or regulatory act entrusts attainment of environmental aims to non-state actors.[14]

The European Commission has signalled its cautious approval and encouragement of the use of environmental agreements in Communications of 1996 and 2002, and has formally recognized voluntary agreements on a number of occasions, normally by adopting a Recommendation confirming the content of the industry's engagement, or simply acknowledging the environmental agreement by exchange of letters. The Commission has stressed, however, that such action can '*never*' mean that it forgoes its right of initiative.[15]

---

[12] The Directive was adopted by the Council on 29 September 2014. See Council Press Release PRESSE 481, 29 September 2014.

[13] Communication on Environmental Agreements COM(2002) 412.

[14] See the EU's definition included in the *Interinstitutional Agreement on better law making* [2003] OJ C321/4, at para. 18.

[15] Communication on Environmental Agreements COM(2002) 412, at 5. See, for example, the recommendations issued acknowledging a voluntary agreement on the labelling of detergents in 1989 (Commission Recommendation 89/542/EEC OJ [1989] L291/55), and the recommendations acknowledging voluntary agreements between associations of European, Japanese and Korean car manufacturers on the reduction of carbon dioxide emissions from passenger cars (Commission Recommendation 1999/125 OJ 1999 L40/49, Commission Recommendation 2000/303 OJ [2000] L100/45 and Commission Recommendation 2000/304 OJ [2000] L100/57).

More broadly, the emphasis on improving environmental governance in Europe, in particular by means of the principles of access to information, participation and access to justice in environmental matters, provided for in the 1998 UNECE Aarhus Convention, can also be viewed as part of the effort to get non-governmental individuals and organizations involved in environmental protection. This 'enabling' of civil society, through the increased recognition of environmental rights, now forms an important part of the regulatory toolkit for improving environmental protection within the EU and Europe more broadly. One might also include initiatives such as the EU's ecolabel regulation;[16] the EU's organic farming Regulation, which sets down requirements for organic production;[17] and the energy class rating system, which identifies refrigerators, freezers and other household equipment which are particularly economical in terms of electricity consumption,[18] as new governance instruments aimed at nudging European consumers towards environmentally friendlier behaviour.

Viewed together with the EU's embrace of market-based instruments, all of this represents a change in the architecture of EU environmental governance, from a state-centred approach to a more pluralist harnessing of business and society in pursuit of the EU's environmental aims.[19] The EU's continued commitment to flexibility of implementation in this sense has been reaffirmed in its Seventh EAP.[20] However, it is obvious that the

---

[16] Regulation (EC) No 66/2010 of the European Parliament and of the Council of 25 November 2009 on the EU Ecolabel OJ [2010] L27/1. Medicinal products and certain hazardous chemicals are excluded from the system.

[17] Council Regulation (EC) No 834/2007 of 28 June 2007 on organic production and labelling of organic products and repealing Regulation (EEC) No 2092/91 OJ [2007] L189/1.

[18] Ratings range from A++ rating to G. See Directive 2010/30/EU of the European Parliament and of the Council of 19 May 2010 on the indication by labelling and standard product information of the consumption of energy and other resources by energy-related products OJ [2010] L153/1. See also, Regulation (EC) No 106/2008 of the European Parliament and of the Council of 15 January 2008 on a Community energy-efficiency labelling programme for office equipment OJ [2008] L39/1.

[19] See further, Andrew Jordan, Rüdiger Wurzel and Anthony Zito, 'Policy Instrument Innovation in the European Union: A Realistic Model for International Environmental Governance?' in Gerd Winter (ed.), *Multilevel Governance of Global Environmental Charge: Perspectives from Science, Sociology and the Law* (Cambridge University Press 2006).

[20] The Seventh EAP states (at (33)):

> An appropriate mix of policy instruments would enable businesses and consumers to improve their understanding of the impact of their activities on

success of such instruments will be judged on whether, aside from whatever increase in environmental democracy new governance may represent, they ultimately deliver the goods in terms of improved environmental effectiveness.

2.2 Flexibility in Enforcement?

Linked to this idea of flexibility of implementation is the far more radical idea of flexibility in enforcement of obligations flowing from EU environmental law, which (although not termed as such) can be discerned in certain recent important EU environmental policy documents.

Perhaps the most important such example is the EU's Seventh EAP, which sets out the key priorities of the EU's environmental policy from 2013–20. One of these priorities is improving the enforcement of EU environmental law, on which the EU does not have a particularly good record. The EAP uses the broader term 'implementation', but it is clear that much of the problem identified is really concerned with the issue of enforcement, rather than (for instance) non-transposition of EU obligations into national law. The idea of flexibility in enforcement as outlined below is also evidently quite different from the idea of flexibility in the methods or instruments that Member States use to implement EU law.

In this context, the EAP raises a vision of targeting under-enforcement by means of flexible approaches, involving contracts tailored to the circumstances of individual Member States to deal with their specific challenges:

> Implementation challenges specific to an individual Member State will be targeted for assistance, similar to the tailored approach followed in the European Semester process. For instance, partnership implementation agreements involving the Commission and individual Member States will be drawn up, addressing issues such as where to find financial support for implementation and better information systems to track progress. With a view to maximising the effectiveness of this approach, Member States should, as appropriate and in accordance with their administrative arrangements, encourage participation by local and regional authorities … .

A little more detail on the Commission's vision on the matter was provided by the 2012 Commission Communication on improving the

---

the environment and to manage that impact. Such policy instruments include economic incentives, market-based instruments, information requirements as well as voluntary tools and measures to complement legislative frameworks and to engage stakeholders at different levels.

delivery of benefits from EU environment measures,[21] which formed a precursor of the implementation aspect of the Seventh EAP. The Communication noted that:

> Implementation agreements that commit, without prejudice to the provisions of the Treaties and the Commission's role as guardian of the Treaties, Member States to actions having either the preventive aim of strengthening the capacity to deliver effective implementation or, where appropriate, the remedial aim of resolving specific problems through targeted action. Partnership implementation agreements could proactively direct EU assistance towards improved implementation structures within Member States and might be linked to other initiatives in this Communication, such as effective information systems, complaint-handling mechanisms and inspections. They could also, on a case by case basis, endorse Member State remedial plans to resolve specific problems through targeted and adequately-resourced programmes of work featuring milestones, guarantees of transparency and other safeguards.

This concept of flexibility broadly follows on from the 2001 White Paper on Governance, which floated the idea that 'target-based, tripartite contracts' could be concluded between Member States, regions and localities, and the Commission, with environmental policy a leading candidate. This was followed by a 2002 Commission Communication on 'A framework for target-based tripartite contracts and agreements between the Community, the States and regional and local authorities',[22] and led to a number of regulatory experiments in this field, of which the Lombardy Tripartite Agreement on Sustainable Mobility is perhaps the best known. Signed in 2004, the Lombardy Agreement was the first of its kind in Europe, concluded between the Commission, the Italian government and the region of Lombardy in Italy, with the aim of improving regional sustainable mobility by, for instance, reducing the volume of traffic in certain zones, improving the public transport offering, and increasing the use of less polluting motor fuels. However, the agreement was not particularly successful in achieving its goals, and only lasted for one of its four planned phases, due among other things to a lack of budgetary and technical commitment from its signatories.[23]

---

21 COM(2012) 95.

22 COM(2002) 709.

23 Martino Mazzoleni, 'The First Tripartite Agreement in the EU: An Actor-centred Analysis of an Experimental Multi-level Interaction' (2006) 16 *Regional and Federal Studies* 263–79. For the text of the agreement, see <http://ec.europa.eu/governance/docs/texte_convention_tripartite_en.pdf> accessed 6 November 2014.

It would seem that the partnership implementation agreements of the Seventh EAP bear some relationship to the tripartite agreement experiments. However, they are envisaged to be bipartite (with no region necessarily involved, although this will be 'encouraged') and exclusively focused on 'implementation', for which we can presumably read, areas of environmental law with which the Member State at issue is systematically failing to comply. For instance, in the wake of the CJEU's finding that Ireland had been systematically failing to enforce the Waste Framework Directive (in the Court's terms, a 'general and persistent breach' of the Directive),[24] Ireland entered into an agreement with the Commission following bilateral meetings, entailing the development of a road map of outstanding deliverables to satisfy the judgment, the provision of a time line for each item, and publication of the details on the Irish government's website.[25]

While the Irish Waste Framework Directive example is typically seen as a success, the idea that some kind of network of partnership implementation agreements might be developed more generally by the Commission, across subject areas and States, raises serious questions about the nature of the Commission's role in enforcing EU environmental law, particularly in circumstances where (contrary to the Irish case) there has been no CJEU judgment on the matter. Of course it is clear that the Commission has discretion whether to engage in enforcement action against Member States under Article 258 TFEU and Article 260(2) TFEU. One might argue, therefore (as the Commission has indeed done),[26] that the Commission is perfectly entitled to set its enforcement priorities and decide how it wishes to promote enforcement. However, the notion of implementation agreements as currently expressed by the Commission goes potentially much further than this. On the basis of the 2012 Communication cited above, for instance, the notion could extend to situations where, in specific cases of (alleged) breach, Member States' remedial plans would be 'endorsed' by the Commission. It seems clear that, in the absence of a CJEU judgment on the matter, it would exceed

---

24 Case C-494/01 *Commission v Ireland* [2005] ECLI:EU:C:2005:250.

25 See also, for instance, the statement of Irish Water, the newly created utility in Ireland, that it is to seek to enter into a partnership implementation agreement with the Commission in relation to the Water Framework Directive (where Ireland has also regularly been found in breach).

26 See especially, Commission Communication on implementing European Community Environmental Law, COM(2008) 773 (setting out the key priorities in terms of environmental enforcement, following on from its 2007 Communication, '*A Europe of Results – Applying Community Law*').

the Commission's institutional competence to enter into any agreement that purported to definitively assess the compatibility of Member States' actions with EU law, or indeed to bind the EU institutions (viz. including the CJEU) to accept such compatibility. In such cases, flexibility of enforcement reaches its limits.

2.3 Flexibility of Standards

A final notion of flexibility also visible in the White Paper is the idea that different standards might be appropriate for different States or geographic regions of the Union, because of the need to take account of what the 1972 Commission Proposal for the First Environmental Action Plan, cited at the top of this contribution, expressed as the 'diversity in geographical and natural situations, and between the tasks of the different regions.' Put simply, this type of flexibility recognizes that differences in the very subject matter being regulated (i.e., the local environment) may justify not only differences in the way in which environmental laws are implemented and enforced, but also *differences in the substantive levels of environmental protection required by law.*

From the beginning, the Treaty has made specific provision enshrining, at a constitutional level, the possibility for Member States to take unilateral action to achieve a higher level of environmental protection, where the conditions set out in the Treaty are satisfied (the so-called environmental safeguard or guarantee provisions). Here, the test determining whether a Member State's greener laws are compatible with the Treaty depends in the first instance on whether the area is occupied or not by EU legislation.

2.3.1 Flexibility where EU legislation exists

In the case where harmonizing EU legislation exists in the field, adopted on the basis of the internal market legal basis provision of Article 114 TFEU, Article 114(4) enables Member States to maintain a national provision that already existed at the time of adoption of the EU harmonization measure, where, 'a Member State deems it necessary to maintain national provisions on grounds of major needs referred to in Article 36, or relating to the environment or the working environment …' where such provisions are notified to the Commission, along with the grounds for maintaining them.[27]

[27] Contrast the version of this provision as originally introduced by the Single European Act, as art. 100a(4),

Article 114(5), inserted by the Treaty of Amsterdam, enables Member States to introduce different national provisions for the first time after the EU harmonizing legislation has been adopted, subject to compliance with stricter conditions than applicable to Article 114(4), if:

> … a Member State deems it necessary to introduce national provisions based on new scientific evidence relating to the protection of the environment or the working environment on grounds of a problem specific to that Member State arising after the adoption of the harmonization measure … .

Here, the Member State is obliged to notify the Commission of the 'envisaged' national provision (i.e., prior to their adoption) as well as the grounds for introducing them.

Both Article 114(4) and (5) are subject to the procedural provisions contained in Articles 114(6)–(9) (as inserted by the Treaty of Amsterdam), which set a period of six months for the Commission to approve or reject the measure and, where a measure has been authorized, oblige the Commission to consider proposing an adaptation to the relevant EU legislation.

The application of these provisions has been dealt with elsewhere in this volume.[28] In the environmental context, however, it is worth observing that the standard required of Member States to satisfy the test for new national environmental provisions is certainly a high one. In contrast to the far more permissive notion for legacy environmental provisions that the Member State must 'deem it necessary' to maintain such provisions on grounds 'relating' to the environment (Article 114(4)),[29] for new provisions Member States must prove that:

> If, after the adoption of a harmonization measure by the Council acting by a qualified majority, a Member State deems it necessary to *apply* national provisions on grounds of major needs referred to in Article 36, or relating to protection of the environment or the working environment, it shall notify the Commission of these provisions. The Commission shall confirm the provisions involved after having verified that they are not a means of arbitrary discrimination or a disguised restriction on trade between Member States. (emphasis added).

[28] See Ch. 12 Ellen Vos and Maria Weimer.

[29] Or other relevant objective of public interest: note the narrower scope of justifications permitted for art. 114(5) as compared to art. 114(4).

- There is 'new scientific evidence' relating to the protection of the environment (i.e., since the adoption of the EU harmonizing measure) which justifies the measure; and
- The problem is 'specific to that Member State'.

It is also important to recall that, in putting forward legislative proposals pursuant to Article 114(1) TFEU concerning 'health, safety, environmental protection and consumer protection', the Commission is already obliged to take 'as a base a high level of protection, taking account in particular of any new development based on scientific facts' (Art. 114(3) TFEU). In *Denmark v Commission*, in holding that Article 114(5) will be narrowly interpreted, the CJEU noted that, in contrast to Article 114(4), the Community legislature by definition could not have taken the national measures at issue into account when passing the relevant harmonizing legislation.[30] In *Netherlands v Commission*, the CJEU emphasized that, although the Commission enjoyed a wide discretion in assessing whether the conditions of Article 114(5) are made out, this does not exclude a relatively intensive judicial review of the Commission's decision, particularly as the administrative procedure of Article 114(5) does not include a right to be heard as such.[31]

It is also worth observing that, in contrast to Article 193 TFEU considered below, Article 114(5) does not specify that the national provisions envisaged must result in more stringent (as opposed to merely different) levels of environmental protection, as long as such difference is justified by new scientific evidence and meets the specificity criterion. This raises the possibility that Article 114(5) could extend not only to environmental safeguard measures, but also potentially to derogation measures.

To these internal market safeguard clauses must be added the specific environmental safeguard clause contained in Article 193 TFEU, which provides:

> The protective measures adopted pursuant to Article 192 [i.e., the environmental legal basis] shall not prevent any Member State from maintaining or introducing more stringent protective measures. Such measures must be compatible with the Treaties. They shall be notified to the Commission.

---

[30] Case C-3/00 *Denmark v Commission* [2003] ECLI:EU:C:2003:167, para. 58.

[31] Case C-405/07 P *Netherlands v Commission* [2008] ECLI:EU:C:2008:613, paras 54–56.

It is clear that the test set out in Article 193 TFEU for the introduction of new, greener national provisions is far less prescriptive than Article 114(5) TFEU and therefore, one might reasonably suppose, far easier for Member States to satisfy. There is no requirement for new scientific evidence; there is no requirement to demonstrate a problem specific to one Member State. Further, as the CJEU has held, failure to notify the Commission of the relevant measures, or to obtain the Commission's agreement to them, does not render such measures invalid.[32] However, as with the other conditions for these safeguard clauses, the burden of proving this lies on the Member State.[33]

Until recently, Article 193 had been dealt with relatively rarely by the CJEU, suggesting that Member States may not be relying on it (in comparison, for instance, to the quite frequent reliance on the internal market safeguard clauses). Recently, however, the CJEU has dealt with a number of cases clarifying the scope of this provision and its use where there is relevant EU environmental legislation. Many of these cases have focused on the question whether the relevant existing EU environmental legislation can be interpreted to allow a higher level of environmental protection on the part of Member States. This will be so where, as properly interpreted, the legislation achieves minimum but not exhaustive harmonization.

To date, these cases show that the CJEU has typically interpreted the level of harmonization achieved by a given environmental Directive to be minimum in nature, relying on the terms of the Directive as well as Article 193 TFEU to conclude that Member States are in principle free to enact more stringent measures in furtherance of the overall aim of a high level of protection of the environment. In *Fornasar*,[34] the CJEU held that the EU Hazardous Waste Directive 91/689 did not preclude Member States from unilaterally classifying additional categories of waste as hazardous, reasoning that (para. 46):

> the Community rules do not seek to effect complete harmonisation in the area of the environment. Even though [present Article 191] of the Treaty refers to certain Community objectives to be attained, both [present Article 193 TFEU] and Directive 91/689 allow the Member States to introduce more stringent protective measures. Under present Article 191] of the Treaty, Community

[32] See Case C-2/10 *Azienda Agro-Zootecnica Franchini* [2011] ECLI:EU: C:2011:502, para. 53.

[33] See, e.g., Joined Cases C-439/05 and C-454/05 *Land Oberösterreich and Austria v Commission* [2010] ECLI:EU:C:2007:510.

[34] C-318/98, ECLI:EU:C:2000:337.

> policy on the environment is to aim at a high level of protection, taking into account the diversity of situations in the various regions of the Community.

Similarly, in *Deponiezweckverband Eiterköpfe*,[35] the CJEU interpreted the Landfill Directive in the light of the principles of the EU's environmental policy set out in what is now Article 191(2) TFEU, to conclude that the Directive did not achieve complete harmonization, but permitted Member States to adopt stricter landfill rules in compliance with Article 193 TFEU (citing *Fornasar*). The CJEU also rejected the contention that Article 193 TFEU in itself included any proportionality test, emphasizing that it 'falls to the Member States to define the extent of the protection to be achieved' in cases falling under this Article (para. 61). By contrast, the proportionality principle would be applicable insofar as Article 193 TFEU was being used to assess whether the national measures complied with other Treaty provisions, as is required by Article 193 TFEU. For instance, proportionality is evidently highly relevant when assessing compatibility of *prima facie* restrictive measures under Article 34 TFEU on the free movement of goods, considered below.

Most recently, in *Azienda Agro-Zootecnica Franchini*,[36] the CJEU considered the question of the circumstances in which Member States were entitled to take more protective measures as compared to the EU's nature conservation legislation (namely, the Habitats and Birds Directives).[37] That case concerned Italian measures which restricted *a priori* the building of wind turbines on land situated within protected areas to cases where those turbines were intended for self-consumption only. Wind turbines intended for other use were refused authorization, even without carrying out any appropriate assessment of the project's environmental impacts as is provided for in the Habitats and Birds Directives. In holding that such measures were compatible with the Directives, the CJEU noted that, contrary to the Birds Directive, the Habitats Directive did not contain any express provision authorizing more stringent measures. However, Article 193 TFEU could be relied upon, despite the fact that the Italian measures had not been notified to or approved by the Commission in advance.

---

[35] Case C-6/03 *Deponiezweckverband Eiterköpfe v Land Rheinland-Pflaz* [2005] ECLI:EU:C:2005:222.

[36] See *supra* n 32.

[37] Council Directive 92/43/EEC of 21 May 1992 on the conservation of natural habitats and of wild fauna and flora, OJ [1992] L206, 7 and Council Directive 79/409/EEC of 2 April 1979 on the conservation of wild birds, OJ [1979] L103, 1.

The CJEU went on to consider whether, as required by Article 193 TFEU, the Italian measures complied with other TFEU provisions. On that point, the applicants had submitted in this regard that the objective of developing new and renewable forms of energy, as established for EU policy by Article 194(1)(c) TFEU, should take precedence over the environmental protection objectives pursued by the Habitats and Birds Directives. The CJEU's response was clear (paras 56–57):

> Suffice it to observe in that connection that Article 194(1) TFEU states that European Union policy on energy must have regard for the need to preserve and improve the environment.
>
> Moreover, a measure such as that at issue in the main proceedings, which prohibits only the location of new wind turbines not intended for self-consumption on sites forming part of the Natura 2000 network, with the possibility of exemption for wind turbines intended for self-consumption with a capacity not exceeding 20 kW, is not, in view of its limited scope, liable to jeopardise the European Union objective of developing new and renewable forms of energy.

It is evident, however, that the CJEU's review would be far more intensive in case of alleged incompatibility with the free movement provisions, for instance, where the Treaty's rules are much more precise, and do not have the same commonality of purpose as the TFEU's energy and environment provisions.

Aside from Article 114(4)/(5) and Article 193 TFEU, which enshrine (in principle pro-environmental) flexibility tests in the Treaty, it is important to note the separate phenomenon whereby, in the case of certain EU environmental legislation, the legislation itself provides for or permits different standards for different States or actors (sub-constitutional flexibility). In the case of legislation based on Article 114(1) TFEU, this possibility is expressly provided for in Article 114(10) TFEU, which provides:

> The harmonisation measures [adopted on the basis of Article 114(1) TFEU] shall, in appropriate cases, include a safeguard clause authorising the Member States to take, for one or more of the non-economic reasons referred to in Article 36, provisional measures subject to a Union control procedure.

Perhaps the best-known examples of express safeguard clauses in EU environmental legislation are those contained in EU legislation regulating genetically modified organisms (GMOs). The CJEU has held these safeguard clauses to be an expression of the precautionary principle, and therefore must be interpreted in the light of this principle.[38] For instance, Article 23 of Directive 2001/18/EC[39] provides:

> Where a Member State, as a result of new or additional information made available since the date of the consent and affecting the environmental risk assessment or reassessment of existing information on the basis of new or additional scientific knowledge, has detailed grounds for considering that a GMO as or in a product which has been properly notified and has received written consent under this Directive constitutes a risk to human health or the environment, that Member State may provisionally restrict or prohibit the use and/or sale of that GMO as or in a product on its territory.
>
> The Member State shall ensure that in the event of a severe risk, emergency measures, such as suspension or termination of the placing on the market, shall be applied, including information to the public. ...

In such cases, Member States have an obligation to inform the Commission and other Member States immediately, providing inter alia reasons and the environmental risk assessment, with the Commission to take a decision on the matter within 60 days, to which time period is added, for instance, the time necessary to consult the Scientific Committee as provided for in Article 30(2) of that Directive.

It is unsurprising that, given the wide divergence of views at political but also citizen level on GMOs and their safety within the EU, numerous Member States have chosen to make use of this safeguard clause to ban the use and/or sale of certain GMO products within their territory (at the time of writing, Austria, France, Greece, Hungary, Germany and Luxembourg apply the clause). In 2010, for instance, Eurobarometer data showed that 80 per cent of Latvian respondents and 78 per cent of Greek respondents considered that GM food was not good, compared to 39 per cent in Ireland and 40 per cent in the United Kingdom. While derogating Member States must provide scientific evidence justifying their approach, it is clear that Member States' stances on GMOs are also influenced by other factors, including culture and social acceptability. The same Eurobarometer poll indicated, for instance, that factors such as religion can play a significant role in attitudes of EU citizens to GMOs.[40]

---

38 Case C-236/01 *Monsanto* [2003] ECLI:EU:C:2003:431.

39 Directive 2001/18/EC of the European Parliament and of the Council of 12 March 2001 on the deliberate release into the environment of genetically modified organisms and repealing Council Directive 90/220/EEC OJ [2001] L106/1.

40 Eurobarometer Special Report no 341 on Biotechnology, October 2010.

While the reasons for such flexibility as to GMOs may be clear on an internal level, it has caused major problems for the EU on the world stage, most notably in the context of the WTO, where the EU's GMO system has been found to contravene WTO rules and to be unjustified by the precautionary principle. In *EC-Biotech*, the WTO Panel found that the EC's application of its GMO rules, including Member States' actions in taking safeguard measures prohibiting the import and marketing of specific GMO products within their territory, contravened the WTO's SPS Agreement.[41] In particular, the WTO Panel held that no adequate scientific risk assessment had been carried out for the purposes of Article 5.1 of the SPS Agreement in taking the impugned safeguard measures. In June 2014, political agreement was finally reached within the EU to replace the EU's current GMO legislation with a new settlement which, at least as envisaged at present, looks set to increase flexibility for Member States to ban cultivation of certain GMO products on their territory.[42]

The above discussion has dealt only with EU environmental legislation authorizing (or not prohibiting) *higher* standards of environmental protection. However, it is important to note that there are very many examples of EU environmental legislation expressly permitting *lower* standards of environmental protection, i.e., derogations from the general rules. Indeed, it is fair to say that, the more sensitive the subject matter (which environmental regulation increasingly is, insofar as it is perceived as a restriction on economic activity and growth), the greater the derogations contained in the legislation.

To take just a couple of examples, the EU's flagship legislative instrument for dealing with climate change, the Emissions Trading Scheme Directive, contains multiple derogations for Member States as well as for particular industries which, it is argued, might be particularly

---

[41] DS291 European Communities – Measures Affecting the Approval and Marketing of Biotech Products.

[42] See the Statement by Commissioner Borg following the Council's political agreement to allow the prohibition of GMO cultivation, Brussels, 12 June 2014. In the terms announced, flexibility will be present on two levels. First, a Member State will be able, before the authorization of a GMO, to request an applicant company, via the Commission, to specify in the application that the GMO cannot be cultivated on all or part of its territory. Secondly, even after authorization, the Member State in question will be able to opt out of cultivating an EU authorized GMO on its territory, which opt-out may be based on a wide range of factors, including environmental or agricultural policy objectives, town and country planning, land use, socio-economic impacts, avoidance of GMO presence in other products, or public policy.

heavily hit by the economic consequences of putting a price on carbon, or (in the case of industries) where there is a risk that the companies at issue might decide to leave the EU (the so-called 'carbon leakage' scenario).[43] Similarly, the Water Framework Directive, discussed above, permits Member States to adopt less stringent measures for specific bodies of water where they are (Article 4(5)), 'so affected by human activity … or their natural condition is such that the achievement of these objectives would be infeasible or disproportionately expensive', and where certain conditions are met, including that the 'environmental and socioeconomic needs served by such human activity cannot be achieved by other means, which are a significantly better environmental option not entailing disproportionate costs'; that the best environmental outcome 'possible' is achieved; and that no further deterioration occurs, subject to periodic review of compliance with these conditions.

These cases of 'downward' flexibility have generally very little to do with achieving effective environmental protection, but are rather typically aimed at protecting the effectiveness of other EU policies (for instance, in the ETS carbon leakage example, the EU's economic competitiveness policy). In other cases, they are merely added for reasons of political expediency to get the measure through (as, for instance, with the manifold derogations from the EU's Energy Taxation Directive).[44]

2.3.2 Flexibility in the absence of EU legislation

In principle, the flexibility left to Member States in the absence of any relevant harmonizing EU legislation might be thought to constitute the broadest flexibility of all in terms of permitting Member States to make their own choices about the appropriate level of environmental protection. However, these choices remain, of course, subject to compatibility with the Treaty provisions themselves, including the EU free movement, internal taxation and State aid rules.

---

[43] Directive 2009/29/EC of the European Parliament and of the Council of 23 April 2009 amending Directive 2003/87/EC so as to improve and extend the greenhouse gas emission allowance trading scheme of the Community OJ [2009] L140/63. See the discussion in Suzanne Kingston, 'Surveying the State of EU Environmental Law' (2013) 62 ICLQ 965–82.

[44] Council Directive 2003/96/EC of 27 October 2003 restructuring the Community framework for the taxation of energy products and electricity OJ [2003] L283/51.

While space does not permit a detailed consideration of this topic here,[45] it will be recalled that the CJEU has generally sought to adopt a broadly pro-environment stance in many of the cases where national environmental measures have conflicted with EU internal market law. Many of these cases have concerned conflicts with the Article 34 TFEU prohibition on restrictions on the free movement of goods, where the CJEU has accepted environmental protection as a mandatory requirement justifying indistinctly applicable restrictions on free movement of goods[46] resulting from national legislation. This trend in the CJEU's case law began with its 1989 *Danish Bottles* judgment, just after *ADBHU* and came hot on the heels of the 1986 SEA's insertion of explicit environmental aims for the Community into the Treaty.[47] The CJEU has also in certain cases accepted environmental justifications for distinctly applicable[48] Member State measures which restrict the free movement of goods. Such judgments, which include the *Walloon Waste*; *Dusseldorp*, *Aher-Waggon*; *PreussenElektra*; and *Inn Valley* judgments,[49] arguably go against the CJEU standard internal market case law, according to which the only acceptable justifications for distinctly applicable measures are those set out in Article 36 TFEU, where environmental protection does not as such feature.[50] However, the judgments are consistent with the obligation contained in Article 11 TFEU that environmental protection requirements be integrated into the definition and implementation of all other EU policies and activities.[51]

---

[45] See, for previous discussion by the present author, Suzanne Kingston, *Greening EU Competition Law and Policy*, *supra* n 10, Chs 3 and 12.

[46] That is, restrictions applicable equally in law to domestic goods and goods from other EU States.

[47] Case C-302/86 *Commission v Denmark* [1988] ECLI:EU:C:1988:421, Case C-240/83 *ADBHU* [1985] ECLI:EU:C:1985:59.

[48] That is, restrictions which apply differently in law to domestic goods and goods from other EU States.

[49] Case C-379/98 *PreussenElektra* [2001] ECLI:EU:C:2001:160; Case C-2/90 *Commission v Belgium* [1992] ECLI:EU:C:1992:310; Case C-320/03 *Commission v Austria (Inn Valley)* [2005] ECLI:EU:C:2005:684.

[50] This has led some commentators to call for the express recognition of environmental protection as equivalent to the express art. 36 TFEU derogations. See the Opinion of AG Jacobs in *PreussenElektra* and the Opinion of AG Geelhoed in *Inn Valley*, ibid. The possibility of inserting environmental considerations into art. 36 TFEU as an express ground for derogating from the principle of free movement of goods was considered and rejected by the authors of the Treaty of Amsterdam.

[51] See generally, Kingston *supra* n 45.

3. THE LIMITS OF FLEXIBILITY?

Against this narrative of increasing flexibility in EU environmental policy, it is worth pausing to note the evidence that, even as flexibility is embraced in some contexts, it is clear that it has its limits.

A first limit is where a Member State's efforts to adopt (what in its opinion is a) higher level of environmental protection conflicts with principles that are (more?) fundamental to the EU's legal order. In *PFOS*, for instance, the CJEU ruled that Sweden had breached its duty of loyal cooperation by unilaterally proposing to list a substance in an Annex to the Stockholm Convention on Persistent Organic Pollutants, in circumstances where the EU had delayed in taking any action (due inter alia to a conflict of views) and Sweden had decided to take matters into its own hands.[52] This is also apparent in the *MOX* case, where Ireland was held to have breached EU law by suing the UK before the International Tribunal of the Law of the Sea for breach of the provisions of the UN Convention of the Law of the Sea in relation to pollution of the Irish Sea with radioactive waste.[53]

A second limit of flexibility is where it has been proved not to work. For instance, the EU gave up its efforts to rely on the voluntary agreements between car manufacturers where it became clear over time that these were ineffective, leading to the present reliance on the very non-flexible legal form of a Regulation.[54]

Further, environmental flexibility plays notably little role in cases where the EU is dealing with third countries, and it considers that it has the power (and wishes) to apply its own environmental standards. In such cases, the EU has not hesitated to place its own specific and non-flexible environmental requirements on third countries and actors based in third countries, with obvious examples including the EU's ban on import of seal products; the inclusion of third-country airlines in the EU ETS (which was ultimately unsuccessful due to the pushback of third countries); and the inclusion of environmental conditionality clauses in development agreements.

---

[52] Case C-246/07 *Commission v Sweden* [2010] ECLI:EU:C:2010:203.

[53] Case C-459/03 *Commission v Ireland* [2006] ECCLI:EU:C:2006:345.

[54] Regulation (EC) No 443/2009 of the European Parliament and of the Council of 23 April 2009 setting emission performance standards for new passenger cars as part of the Community's integrated approach to reduce CO_2 emissions from light-duty vehicles OJ [2009] L140/1, as amended.

4. DISCUSSION: JUSTIFYING FLEXIBILITY IN EU ENVIRONMENTAL LAW AND POLICY

It is clear from the above mapping exercise that flexibility is an increasingly prevalent and accepted concept, at constitutional and sub-constitutional levels, in EU environmental law. It is also clear that flexibility in EU environmental law now goes far beyond the idea that Member States should be left a wide discretion in implementing EU legislation or that a broader set of policy instruments should be used, but extends in some cases to flexibility of substantive standards (the possibility to adopt higher, but also lower, standards) and even, perhaps most controversially, to a certain flexibility of enforcement.

This increasing reliance on flexibility begs the question whether, and in which circumstances, it is really justified. Are there particular features of EU environmental law and/or policy that provide particular justification for such use of flexibility mechanisms, and what are the limits of these justifications?

It is not difficult to identify a variety of features suggesting that, by its very nature, EU environmental policy is a prime candidate for flexibility-based approaches. Some of these are obvious. Geographies and environmental conditions differ tremendously across the EU's territory, which comprises more than 10 million km^2, and with population densities ranging from over 1,300/km^2 in Malta to only 18/km^2 in Finland.[55] Each Member State (and region) has its own particular environmental challenges, in part dictated by physical geographies and in part by varying pressure on natural resources placed by human populations.

Perhaps less obvious is the diversity in what we might term environmental philosophies within the EU. It is obvious that Member States' differences in preferences as to environmental protection levels reflect some pretty fundamental differences as to where environmental values and priorities should stand in comparison to other social and economic priorities.[56] By and large, the constitutional environmental obligations set out in the EU Treaties are broadly worded enough to accommodate most of these values. The Treaties are certainly based on an anthropocentric philosophy of the environment, whereby the value of the environment is

---

55 Source: Eurostat, Population Density (Inhabitants per km^2), 2012 figures.

56 See generally, John Dryzek, *The Politics of the Earth: Environmental Discourses* (2nd edn., Oxford University Press 2005) and Duncan Liefferink et al, 'Leaders and Laggards in Environmental Policy: A Quantitative Analysis of Domestic Policy Outputs' (2009) 16 *Journal of European Public Policy* 677–700.

viewed primarily in terms of its value to humans.[57] However, they contain no explicit hierarchy of the EU's goals.

The closest thing to any kind of express environmental philosophy in the Treaties is probably the aim of sustainable development contained in Article 3(3) TEU,[58] which is premised on the belief that the goals of economic growth and environmental and social protection can be pursued at the same time.[59] Even this goal is extremely open-textured, however, and leaves room for a wide spectrum of Member State views as to the relative importance of environmental protection compared to, for instance, economic goals or social protection. These views might legitimately differ, for instance, depending on the relative level of economic prosperity of the Member State at issue (as, for instance, the lower standard for certain Member States permitted by the EU ETS Directive recognizes).[60] Similarly, views differ markedly between (and within) Member States on such basic issues as the extent to which environmental goods and bads can be monetized or economized and, linked to this, the extent to which cost-benefit analysis is acceptable in the case of sensitive areas of environmental regulation such as nature conservation.[61] These

---

[57] See, for instance, the expression of the EU's goals in environmental policy, which include protecting human health.

[58] Art. 3(3) TEU provides that the EU shall work towards, 'sustainable development of Europe based on balanced economic growth and price stability, a highly competitive social market economy, aiming at full employment and social progress, and a high level of protection and improvement of the quality of the environment'.

[59] Contrast, for instance, the Community's first Environmental Action Programme (Declaration of the Council of the European Communities and of the representatives of the Governments of the Member States meeting in the Council of 22 November 1973 on the programme of action of the European Communities on the environment OJ [1973] C112/1), which notes that

> When they met in Paris on 19 to 20 October 1972, the Heads of State or Government of the Member States declared that 'economic expansion is not an end in itself: its first aim should be to enable disparities in living conditions to be reduced. It must take place with the participation of all the social partners. It should result in an improvement in the quality of life as well as in standards of living. As befits the genius of Europe, particular attention will be given to intangible values and to protecting the environment so that progress may really be put at the service of mankind.

[60] This reason for diverse obligations is present in international environmental law in the form of the principle of CBDR.

[61] For instance, the UK has embraced the notion of (putting a price on) ecosystem services, but this has not been done to the same extent in other Member States. See the UK National Ecosystem Assessment (June 2011).

are fundamental issues in taking choices about how EU environmental policy should look.

Linked to diversity of values, a further justification for flexibility-based approaches in EU environmental policy is the inherent scope for reasonable differences in scientific opinion in the field. It is clear that uncertainty, risk, and the limits of scientific knowledge form an inevitable part of environmental policy-making, and that different States may have varying opinions on, and appetites for, potential environmental risks. The safeguard provisions in EU GMO legislation, discussed above, form a good example – albeit one which has caused the EU problems when set in the context of the WTO's chosen level of acceptable risk and its (very different) approach to the precautionary principle.

The inherent scientific uncertainty underlying environmental policy-making forms part of why, in the scientific literature, the environment is viewed as a classic example of a complex system, in the sense of a system composed of many interacting variables, where it is not possible to distinguish simple causal links between these variables.[62] This polycentric nature of environmental problems means that, using Fuller's metaphor of a spider's web, 'a pull on one strand will distribute tensions after a complicated pattern throughout the web as a whole'.[63] All of this suggests that it is reasonable for the EU to be open to differences of opinion on policy effectiveness and instruments, and new governance and/or experimental methods, as discussed above. In this sense, flexibility within EU environmental policy forms one response to the natural complexity and indeterminacy of the subject matter.

These reasons certainly justify *some* degree of flexibility in the EU's environmental policy. However, it hardly needs to be said that maintaining the integrity and the effectiveness of the EU's environmental policy ultimately demands clarity about what the essential, non-derogable core of EU environmental policy is, and its relationship with other policies. Here, as in the case of conflicts with fundamental principles of the EU's legal order, flexibility must reach its limits. Forty years on from the emergence of the Community's own environmental policy, and despite the large body of EU environmental law now on the books, it is

---

[62] See James Ladyman, James Lambert and Karoline Wiesner, 'What is a Complex System?' (2013) 3 *European Journal of Philosophy of Science* 33; Simon A Levin, 'Ecosystems and the Biosphere as Complex Adaptive Systems' (1998) 1 *Ecosystems* 431.

[63] Lon L Fuller and Kenneth I Winston, 'The Forms and Limits of Adjudication' (1978) 92 *Harvard Law Review* 353, 395.

remarkable how many of the existential questions of that policy's identity have yet to be answered fully.

REFERENCES

Dryzek J, *The Politics of the Earth: Environmental Discourses* (2nd edn., Oxford University Press 2005).

Editorial, 'Ecosystem Services and Capitalism: A Valuation or Devaluation of Nature?' (2014) 5(2) *Journal of Human Rights and the Environment* 1.

Fuller LL and Winston KI, 'The Forms and Limits of Adjudication' (1978) 92 *Harvard Law Review* 353–409.

Jordan A and Schout A, *The Coordination of the European Union: Exploring the Capacities of Network Governance* (Oxford University Press 2006).

Jordan A, Wurzel R and Zito A, 'Policy Instrument Innovation in the European Union: A Realistic Model for International Environmental Governance?' in Winter G (ed.), *Multilevel Governance of Global Environmental Charge: Perspectives from Science, Sociology and the Law* (Cambridge University Press 2006) 470–92.

Kingston S, 'Developments in EU Law: Environment' (2010) 59 *International and Comparative Law Quarterly* 1129–41.

Kingston S, *Greening EU Competition Law and Policy* (Cambridge University Press 2012).

Kingston S, 'Surveying the State of EU Environmental Law' (2013) 62 *International and Comparative Law Quarterly* 965–82.

Ladyman J, Lambert J and Wiesner K, 'What is a Complex System?' (2013) 3 *European Journal of Philosophy of Science* 33–67.

Levin SA, 'Ecosystems and the Biosphere as Complex Adaptive Systems' (1998) 1 *Ecosystems* 431–6.

Liefferink D, Arts B, Kamstra J and Ooijevaar J, 'Leaders and Laggards in Environmental Policy: A Quantitative Analysis of Domestic Policy Outputs' (2009) 16 *Journal of European Public Policy* 677–700.

Mazzoleni M, 'The First Tripartite Agreement in the EU: An Actor-centred Analysis of an Experimental Multi-level Interaction'(2006) 16 *Regional and Federal Studies* 263–79, available at: <http://ec.europa.eu/governance/docs/texte_convention_tripartite_en.pdf>.

14. The perils of differentiated integration in the field of asylum

Nadine El-Enany*

1. INTRODUCTION

Since the EU has expanded, both in size and competence, differentiation in the levels of willingness to integrate and in political, socio-economic and cultural terms has become an increasingly prominent feature.[1] According to Monar, differentiation in relation to immigration and asylum matters 'has emerged primarily in order to allow for the pursuit of a "deepening" of integration in circumstances in which the full participation of some countries is not possible'.[2] Maria Fletcher has observed that for the EU, as a 'flexible and evolving legal order', there is 'a fine line between the stagnating impact of accommodating too little and the fragmenting impact of accommodating too much diversity'.[3] Fletcher has argued that CJEU judgments along with Lisbon's opt-in/-out protocols suggest that the EU places 'a more explicit emphasis on incentivising maximum participation and disincentivising a "pick and choose" and "free rider" mentality to flexibility'.[4] This chapter argues

* The author would like to thank Bruno De Witte and Liam Thornton for comments on earlier drafts of this paper. Research for this paper took place before the Brexit referendum of June 2016.

[1] Walter Van Gerven, *The Economic Union: A Policy of States and Peoples* (Hart Publishing 2005) 28–9 and 31–2 cited in Maria Fletcher, 'Schengen, the European Court of Justice and Flexibility under the Lisbon Treaty: Balancing the United Kingdom's "Ins" and "Outs"' (2009) 5(1) *European Constitutional Law Review* 73.

[2] Jörg Monar, 'The "Area of Freedom, Security and Justice": "Schengen" "Europe", Opt-outs, Opt-ins and Associates' in Kenneth Dyson and Angelos Sepos (eds), *Which Europe? The Politics of Differentiated Integration* (Palgrave 2010) 289.

[3] Fletcher (n 1) 72.

[4] Ibid.

that the field of asylum should be entirely free from differentiated integration arrangements. As a field of law which directly affects the rights of individuals in a context in which their physical survival and psychological wellbeing is at risk, the field of asylum law is unlike other competences of the EU where there is scope for differentiated integration.

The chapter's focus is the UK, a Member State with a flexible opt-in approach in relation to asylum and immigration matters. The chapter identifies a distinction between formal differentiation and informal flexibility, both of which can be conceived of as differentiation that is provided for in the field of asylum. Formal differentiated integration entails the official agreements concluded with the UK, Ireland and Denmark, which either enable or exclude the participation of these countries in asylum matters to predetermined degrees. These formal arrangements have serious consequences for the integrity of the EU's asylum system. Under the current arrangements, in practice the UK is permitted to cherry-pick in a highly selective manner, for instance participating in the Dublin system but refusing to be bound by the legally enforceable minimum standards legislation which arguably comprises one of the few safeguards that could mitigate the potential for harm in the 'one chance of asylum' rule.

Informal flexibility describes the EU's tolerance of the uneven or mal-implementation of agreed asylum standards. At Tampere in 1999, the European Council agreed 'to work towards establishing a Common European Asylum System [CEAS], based on the full and inclusive application of the Geneva Convention, thus ensuring that nobody is sent back to persecution, i.e. maintaining the principle of non-refoulement'.[5] In its effort to create a CEAS, whereby the same minimum standards of protection and procedures apply in the field of asylum to participating Member States across the EU, the EU has adopted a series of directives. These directives contain numerous discretionary clauses leaving Member States wide scope in implementing diverse standards of protection. The most recent EU legislation to be adopted in this field has neither sufficiently improved this situation, nor has the European Commission adopted an enforcement approach in relation to the asylum directives which is as vigilant as the enforcement approach it has adopted in other

[5] Tampere European Council Presidency Conclusions 1999, para. 13.

legal fields[6] in which Member States have failed to properly implement their provisions or the Court judgments relating to them. The EU's tolerance of this situation suggests that it has acquiesced to a scope for flexibility outside the formally agreed differentiated integration arrangements.

The chapter begins by examining the current status of formal differentiated integration in the field of asylum. It then turns to consider the scope for informal flexibility and the harmful consequences of the interplay between the uneven and mal-implementation of asylum measures and the Dublin system.

2. FORMAL DIFFERENTIATED INTEGRATION IN THE FIELD OF ASYLUM

The current state of play in relation to formal differentiated integration in the field of asylum is as follows: the UK, Ireland and Denmark are not participating in the second-phase asylum directives on qualification, reception conditions and procedures, which apply to all other Member States.[7] However, the UK and Ireland continue to be bound by the first-phase qualification and procedures directives and the UK remains bound by the first-phase reception conditions directive. All Member States are bound by the recast Dublin and Eurodac measures, as are some associated countries.[8] Denmark is the only Member State not bound by the rules on the refugee fund and the asylum support office.[9]

---

[6] See for example, Jonas Tallberg, *Making States Comply: The European Commission, The European Court of Justice, and the Enforcement of the Internal Market* (Lund University Press 1999) 109.

[7] Directive 2011/95/EU of the European Parliament and of the Council of 13 December 2011 on standards for the qualification of third-country nationals or stateless persons as beneficiaries of international protection, for a uniform status for refugees or for persons eligible for subsidiary protection, and for the content of the protection granted (recast) OJ L337/9 20.12.2011; Directive 2013/33/EU of the European Parliament and of the Council of 26 June 2013 laying down standards for the reception of applicants for international protection (recast) OJ L180/96 26.6.2013; Directive 2013/32/EU of the European Parliament and of the Council of 26 June 2013 on common procedures for granting and withdrawing international protection (recast) OJ L180/60 29.6.13.

[8] Norway, Iceland, Switzerland and Liechtenstein.

[9] The associated countries are negotiating an agreement with the EU to participate in the asylum support office. See Proposal for a Council Decision on the conclusion of the Arrangement with the Republic of Iceland on the

In a Protocol to the 1999 Treaty of Amsterdam, the UK, Ireland and Denmark secured opt-outs from EU treaty provisions on immigration, asylum and civil law. Unlike Denmark, which cannot opt-in, the British and Irish opt-outs allow for these countries to choose whether or not to participate in the discussions on legislation in this area. While the UK has cooperated closely on asylum and refugee policy with the other EU Member States for many years, the latest developments in British policy suggest that a new period characterising the UK's attitude towards the Common European Asylum System has dawned. Maria Fletcher has argued that, since the introduction of opt-ins and -outs 'into the EU governance armoury at the Maastricht Treaty, the United Kingdom ... has exploited the ... mechanism as a tool of diversity management to the greatest extent'.[10] In practice, with regard to asylum, until recently, the UK has opted out of nearly all proposals concerning visas, borders and legal migration, but it has opted into all proposals concerning asylum and civil law and nearly all proposals concerning illegal migration.[11] Tony Blair, in an interview on 25 October 2004, described the UK's position as follows:

> With the Treaty of Amsterdam seven years ago, we secured the absolute right to opt in to any of the asylum and immigration provisions we wanted to in Europe. Unless we opt in, we are not affected by it. And what this actually gives us is the best of both worlds.[12]

After years of having regularly opted in, the approach of the UK and Ireland has changed and their participation in common policies on illegal migration and asylum policy has become more selective, which has been criticised by former Justice and Home Affairs Commissioner Vitorino, who has argued that opt-outs in this area 'undermine burden-sharing'.[13] Not only did the UK government's recent opt-outs go against the advice of the House of Lords European Union Committee,[14] as well as the

---

modalities of its participation in the European Asylum Support Office COM(2013) 0875 final.

[10] Fletcher (see p. 383) 74.

[11] The Irish practice has been almost identical to that of the UK.

[12] 'Government pledges to opt out of common EU asylum system' by Nigel Morris and Stephen Castles in Luxembourg, *The Independent,* Tuesday, 26 October 2004.

[13] Ibid.

[14] House of Lords European Union Committee, 'Asylum directives: scrutiny of the opt-in decisions' (1st Report of Session 2009-10, HL Paper 6, 4 December 2009).

UNHCR,[15] but they have been widely criticised by lawyers, NGOs and academics.[16] One of the principal reasons for these objections is that the new directives do contain provisions, however limited, which are designed to at least marginally improve the protection of asylum seekers, as discussed below. Furthermore, Immigration Law Practitioners' Association (ILPA) has noted that the second-phase instruments are intended in part to 'strengthen the homogeneity and consistency of the determination of claims for international protection across the European Union'.[17] The UNHCR stated that, in its view, 'the proposed recast Directives would contribute to, rather than undermine, the objective of swift and fair decision-making in the Member States of the European Union, and would contribute to the reduction of secondary movements between Member States'.[18]

The UK having distanced itself from any further formalisation of asylum norms at EU level by opting out of the latest phase of asylum directives is problematic for a number of reasons. First, its continued participation in the Dublin Regulation while opting out of the (nevertheless aspirational) level playing field that forms the justification for the mutual recognition of asylum decisions is to be questioned, if not in practice, then in principle. The Dublin Convention was signed in 1990,[19] limiting the number of claims for protection that an individual could make to one, and establishing a system for the allocation of responsibility for asylum applicants between Member States. The Convention came into force in 1997. The Dublin Regulation is now the central binding instrument for the implementation of the 'safe third country' concept, which assumes that all EU countries are safe for the purposes of returning asylum seekers, and incorporates the Dublin Convention into

---

15 UNHCR, 'Briefing to the House of Lords on the adoption and application of the proposed EU Asylum Procedures and Qualifications Directives' (UNHCR, London, January 2010). Available at: <http://www.unhcr.org.uk/info/briefings/responding_to_policy/documents/LordsBriefingonEUDirectives.pdf>, accessed 24 May 2013.

16 See for example, ILPA, 'Immigration Law Practitioners' Association briefing for House of Lords Debate 12 January 2010 on the UK opt-in to the draft EU Asylum Procedures Directive and Qualifications Directives'. Available at: <http://www.ilpa.org.uk/briefings/10%2001%2012%20HL%20Debate%20Procedures%20&%20Qualification%20Directives.pdf> accessed 24 May 2013.

17 Ibid., 2.

18 See UNHCR (n 15), 2.

19 Convention determining the state responsible for examining applications for asylum lodged in one of the Member States of the European Communities, 15 June 1990 [1997] OJ C254/1.

EU legislation.[20] The rules for the determination of responsibility for hearing the claims of asylum seekers are premised on the notion that responsibility lies with the first Member State with which an asylum applicant establishes contact, whether due to the issuance of a transit visa, the legal presence of a close family member or, in the absence of these, the first physical contact with the territory.[21] Even if the UK's treatment of asylum seekers is of a standard high enough for it to be considered a so-called safe country for asylum seekers, its refusal to agree to the legally enforceable safeguards that underlie the Dublin system raises questions as to whether the EU should in principle tolerate such cherry-picking in a sensitive area of law that directly affects the lives of vulnerable individuals.

The UK opted out of the revised asylum measures at a very early stage in the legislative process. Although the proposals did not meet the UK's restrictive preferences at the time it opted out, the measures were yet to be negotiated and ultimately were watered down by the Council, despite the European Parliament's efforts to the contrary. One of the reasons the UK 'exited' rather than remained 'loyal'[22] to the European asylum legislative project is because of the importance of the notion of discretion in the historical evolution of its asylum regime. While it considers that the Dublin and Eurodac regulations contribute to its ability to offer asylum, it sees the limitation of discretion entailed in the asylum directives, their rights-enhancing nature and the potential for the increased judicialisation of asylum as posing a challenge to its discretionary purview over its protection regime. The UK considered that some of the proposed elements put its ability to reduce the number of asylum seekers on its territory, to deter 'false applicants' and to control its borders in jeopardy. In respect of border control, we have seen the UK's reticence most clearly in its opt out of Schengen. The UK's treatment of the second phase of asylum directives suggests that it is unwilling to

---

[20] Regulation No 604/2013 of the European Parliament and of the Council of 26 June 2013 establishing the criteria and mechanisms for determining the Member State responsible for examining an application for international protection lodged in one of the Member States by a third-country national or a stateless person (recast) OJ L180/31 29.6.2013. See further, Nadine El-Enany, 'EU Asylum and Immigration Law under the Area of Freedom, Security, and Justice' in Anthony Arnull and Damian Chalmers (eds), *The Oxford Handbook of European Union Law* (Oxford University Press 2015).

[21] Regulation No 604/2013, ibid., arts 7–15.

[22] Albert O Hirschman, *Exit, Voice, and Loyalty: Responses to Decline in Firms, Organizations, And States* (Harvard University Press 1970).

consider change that is not in line with its domestic policy agenda. This attitude is compounded by its flexible opt out which allows the UK to retreat from European cooperation as and when it pleases.

Despite the UK's rejection of the possibility of further legislative cooperation on asylum at the EU level, it has declared itself an active promoter of European collaboration, so long as this is confined to 'practical cooperation'.[23] This is however neither a comparable nor adequate alternative to legislation which guarantees visible and enforceable standards of protection. The Commission has insisted that practical cooperation methods 'are insufficient, on their own, to adequately and comprehensively address the problems which flow from the ambiguities and possibilities for derogations in the legislation itself'.[24] While the other Member States must, whatever the extent of their discomfort with the proposed directives, sit down around the negotiating table, the position of the UK is different. For the UK, having an opt out means that, in instances where it is inclined to be restrictive, it neither has to justify its asylum regime choices as reasonable, sensible, moral, or defensible, nor must it compromise on its individual preferences.

3. DISCRETION AND IMPROPER IMPLEMENTATION AS INFORMAL FLEXIBILITY

Since the emergence of the EU asylum regime, there have been increasing pressures for reform, originating both from within the EU governance framework and outside it. The failings of the first round of asylum directives were seen to have various effects, ranging from inbuilt inefficiency to curtailing the rights of those seeking asylum in the EU. In 2008, the Commission released a Policy Plan,[25] which was the product of

---

[23] See for example, evidence given by James Brokenshire MP, then Parliamentary Under-Secretary of State and Minister for Crime Prevention, Home Office, to the House of Lords European Union Committee, House of Lords European Union Committee, *The Treaty of Lisbon: An Impact Assessment: Vol. I Report* (10th Report, Session 2007–2008), 125–6.

[24] European Commission, Staff Working Document Accompanying the Proposal for a Directive of the European Parliament and of the Council on minimum standards for the qualification and status of third country nationals or stateless persons as beneficiaries of international protection and the content of the protection granted (Recast) – Impact Assessment SEC (2009) 1371, 4.

[25] Communication from the Commission to the European Parliament, the Council, the European Economic and Social Committee and the Committee of

a public consultation in the form of a Green Paper presented in 2007.[26] The objective of the Green Paper was to identify 'the possible options for shaping the second phase of the CEAS', which was set out in the 2004 Hague Programme as being the creation of a common asylum procedure and a uniform status for those granted refugee status or subsidiary protection.[27] The European Council 2010 Stockholm Programme, which followed the Tampere Programme (1999–2003) and the Hague Programme (2004–09) expressed a commitment to achieve the CEAS by 2012 and noted that '[i]t is crucial that individuals, regardless of the Member State in which their application for asylum is lodged, are offered an equivalent level of treatment', but that '[t]here are still significant differences between national provisions and their application … Common rules, as well as a better and more coherent application of them, should prevent or reduce secondary movements within the Union, and increase mutual trust between Member States'.[28] However, the 2010 Stockholm Programme was concerned primarily with ensuring the 'security' of the Union from perceived threats,[29] such as irregular migration. The European Council reiterated the Union's goal of preventing or reducing 'secondary movements' of asylum seekers[30] and described the Dublin system as the 'cornerstone in building the CEAS'.[31]

According to the 2009 Lisbon Treaty, the initial Tampere objectives of creating a 'uniform status of asylum' to be 'valid throughout the Union' are legal obligations.[32] In its 2008 Policy Plan, the Commission reported on three trends it identified through statistical analysis and which were to inform developments in asylum policy. The first trend was that the

Regions on the 'Policy Plan on Asylum: An Integrated Approach to Protection Across the EU' of 17 June 2008 COM(2008) 360.

[26] European Commission 'Green Paper on the future Common European Asylum System' Brussels, 6.6.2007 COM(2007) 301 final.

[27] The Hague Programme, *Strengthening Freedom, Security and Justice in the European Union*, Presidency Conclusions, Brussels 4/5 November 2004.

[28] The Stockholm Programme, An Open and Secure Europe – Serving and protecting Citizens, OJ C115/1 4.5.2011.

[29] See Tony Bunyan, 'Commission Action Plan on the Stockholm Programme: A Bit more Freedom and Justice and a lot more Security' (Statewatch 2011).

[30] European Council, The Stockholm Programme – An Open and Secure Europe Serving and Protecting Citizens OJ C115/1 2010.

[31] Ibid.

[32] Art. 78 TFEU. See Steven Peers, 'The Second Phase of the Common European Asylum System: A Brave New World – or Lipstick on a Pig?' (Statewatch, 8 April 2013) 1.

Member States, bar 'some border States', were 'under less pressure than in the recent past', leading the Commission to conclude that the time was right for working to improve the quality of protection standards in the EU.[33] Secondly, the Commission reported that, despite the achievement of some level of legislative harmonisation at the EU level, 'a lack of common practice, different traditions and diverse country of origin information sources are, among other reasons, producing divergent results'. According to the Commission, the differing implementation records of the Member States were working against the principle of providing equal access to protection in the Union as well as creating secondary movements.[34] Finally, the Commission found that where individuals are granted protection, an increasing number received subsidiary protection or another form of protection based on national law rather than refugee status according to the 1951 Refugee Convention. As a result, the Commission highlights the importance of paying particular attention to subsidiary and other forms of protection during the second phase of the CEAS.[35] While subsidiary protection has been dealt with in the new directives, the problems associated with national forms of protection remain.

Along with the trends identified by the Commission in its Policy Plan it also reports on several shortcomings in relation to the first phase of CEAS legislative instruments. In view of these problems, coupled with the concern that the minimum standards delimited in the first-phase directives had failed to fulfil the objective of creating a level playing field, the Commission expressed its intention to put forward proposed amendments to the existing directives as well as to consider the possibility of new instruments.[36] With regard to the Reception Directive, it identified a number of problems 'largely due to the discretion allowed to Member States in a number of key areas'. Thus, the Commission states that the amended version 'should contribute to achieving a higher degree of harmonisation and improved standards of reception, so as to limit the scope of such issues to drive secondary movements'.[37] The wide discretion left to the Member States is identified as a general problem in

---

33 Communication from the Commission to the European Parliament, the Council and the European Economic and Social Committee and the Committee of the Regions: Policy Plan on Asylum, An integrated approach to protection across the EU. Brussels 17.6.2008 COM(2008) 360 final, s. 1.2.

34 Ibid.

35 Ibid.

36 Ibid., s. 3.

37 Ibid., s. 3.1.

relation to the first round of asylum directives. The first Procedures Directive was referred to in the Policy Plan as allowing for 'diverse procedural arrangements', which along with 'qualified safeguards' result in 'different results when applying common criteria' for identifying those in need of protection. This was said to harm 'the very objective of ensuring access to protection under equivalent conditions across the EU'.[38] In support of its intention to significantly amend the directive, the Commission referred to the TFEU as well as the Hague Programme, which both call for the establishment of a common asylum procedure.[39] With regard to the first Qualifications Directive, the Commission reports on the significant variation in the recognition of protection needs of applicants from the same countries of origin.[40] According to the Commission, this is in part due to 'the wording of certain provisions' of the Qualifications Directive.[41]

In part to deal with these problems, the Commission proposed a set of 'recast' legislative proposals in 2008.[42] The five principal measures comprising the CEAS were updated as part of the second phase of the system's evolution.[43] Progress made with regard to protection differs to a

---

38 Ibid., s. 3.2.

39 Ibid.

40 Ibid., s. 3.3.

41 Ibid.

42 Recasting is a legislative technique used in the EU context whereby, in cases where a substantive amendment needs to be made to an existing legal act, the Commission can propose a single legal act for adoption, which introduces the desired amendment while also codifying that amendment with the unchanged provisions of the earlier act and repealing that act. See European Parliament, Council and Commission, Interinstitutional Agreement on a more structured use of the recasting technique for legal acts of 28 November 2001 (2002/C 77/01) OJ C77/1 28.3.2002.

43 Directive 2011/95/EU of the European Parliament and of the Council of 13 December 2011 on standards for the qualification of third-country nationals or stateless persons as beneficiaries of international protection, for a uniform status for refugees or for persons eligible for subsidiary protection, and for the content of the protection granted (recast) OJ L337/9 20.12.2011; Directive 2013/33/EU of the European Parliament and of the Council of 26 June 2013 laying down standards for the reception of applicants for international protection (recast) OJ L180/96 26.6.2013; Directive 2013/32/EU of the European Parliament and of the Council of 26 June 2013 on common procedures for granting and withdrawing international protection (recast) OJ L180/60 29.6.13; EU Regulation No 604/2013 of the European Parliament and of the Council of 26 June 2013 establishing the criteria and mechanisms for determining the Member State responsible for examining an application for international protection lodged in one of the

minimal extent between each of the second-phase measures. In general, any progressive change to the first-phase directives is largely the result of the influence of the European Parliament, whose success in having its amendments adopted varied across the second-phase instruments.

The Qualifications Directive saw improvements in relation to the rules on qualification as a refugee. For instance, the definition of 'family members' has been expanded to include children who are not dependants[44] and allows for the possibility of protection where authorities fail to protect against persecution by non-State actors.[45] While the second-phase directive improves the situation as regards differential treatment between those granted subsidiary protection compared to those with refugee status, Member States are still able to discriminate in this regard in relation to granting residence permits and access to social security.[46]

Noteworthy aspects regarding improvements made to the Reception Conditions Directive relate to the delimiting of measures on detention, accommodation and access to employment for asylum seekers. In relation to employment, asylum seekers are to be granted access to the labour market after nine months of waiting for a first-instance decision on their asylum claim.[47] The rules on accommodation have been altered to insist that Member States 'take appropriate measures to prevent assault and gender-based violence, including sexual assault and harassment' when accommodating asylum seekers.[48] The directive has been marginally improved through a reduction in grounds for detention[49] and enhancing

---

Member States by a third-country national or a stateless person (recast) OJ L180/31 29.6.2013; EU Regulation No 603/2013 of the European Parliament and of the Council of 26 June 2013 on the establishment of 'Eurodac' for the comparison of fingerprints for the effective application of Regulation (EU) No 604/2013 establishing the criteria and mechanisms for determining the Member State responsible for examining an application for international protection lodged in one of the Member States by a third-country national or a stateless person and on requests for the comparison with Eurodac data by Member States' law enforcement authorities and Europol for law enforcement purposes, and amending Regulation (EU) No 1077/2011 establishing a European Agency for the operational management of large-scale IT systems in the area of freedom, security and justice (recast) OJ L180/1 29.6.2013.

[44] Qualifications Directive, art. 2(j).

[45] Ibid., art. 6(c).

[46] Ibid., arts 24(2) and 29(2).

[47] Reception Conditions Directive, art. 15(1).

[48] Ibid., art. 18(4).

[49] Ibid, art. 8.

conditions[50] and reducing the possibilities for Member States to reduce or withdraw reception conditions.[51] However, as Peers has pointed out, 'the revised directive does not improve the reception conditions for asylum seekers very significantly and, while Member States face some restrictions as regards the detention of asylum-seekers, they still retain a great degree of discretion', e.g. with regard to detaining asylum seekers, in relation to giving them access to social security and 'due to limits on legal aid', it will be 'difficult in practice to challenge any of these decisions'.[52]

The Procedures Directive has seen a number of developments, including improvements in relation to access to asylum procedures. For instance, the directive introduced a three-day time limit for registering new claims.[53] There is a time limit of six months for a decision to be made on a claim, but this can be extended up to 21 months under certain conditions.[54] The directive introduces a right to an effective remedy where an application for refugee status is refused.[55] However, several problems with the directive remain. For example, it is not clear whether the shortened list of circumstances in which Member States may accelerate asylum procedures is non-exhaustive.[56] If so, as Peers has noted, 'the reduction in the list is irrelevant'.[57] A new optional exception has been added to the rules on legal aid that are applicable to appeals whereby Member States may deny legal aid to 'applicants who are no longer present on their territory'.[58]

Mal-implementation plagued the initial directives and, in view of the marginal alterations made in the recast versions, it is likely to persist as a problem in relation to the second-phase directives. There will, therefore, continue to be a need for the CJEU to clarify Member State obligations under the directives. The Council's unwillingness to be bound in a discretion-free manner to minimum standards of protection, which meet international and human rights obligations, necessitates court rulings on the interpretation of EU asylum provisions. Considering the protracted and difficult nature of the recent round of negotiations, reliance on the

---

50 Ibid., art. 10.
51 Ibid., art. 20.
52 Peers (n 32) 5.
53 Procedures Directive, art. 6(1).
54 Ibid., art. 31(3), (4) and (5).
55 Ibid., art. 46(1).
56 Ibid., art. 31(8).
57 Peers (n 32), 15.
58 Procedures Directive, art. 21(2).

Court is the only remaining route towards uniform standards of protection across the Union. Since the agreement on the Lisbon Treaty, the CJEU has enjoyed general jurisdiction over the whole of the Area of Freedom, Security and Justice. The preliminary reference procedure is no longer limited to national courts or tribunals against whose decisions there is no judicial remedy, but it is available to all national courts.[59] Arguably, the activity of the Court of Justice in this area has led to some limited legal protection for the rights of individuals. This has primarily taken place through the CJEU's interpretation of substantive provisions of EU law. However, thus far, uniformity and a complete application of the asylum directives have not been achieved through the extension of the Court's jurisdiction.[60] According to Peers, the problem of mal-implementation:

> [...] should have been ameliorated somewhat by the increased jurisdiction for the Court of Justice on asylum matters following the Treaty of Lisbon, but the increase in its case load has only been modest and reportedly a number of Member States' authorities and courts are finding ways to refuse to implement the Court's judgments properly.[61]

The lack of sufficient reform as well as the issue of improper implementation is relevant to the subject of differentiated integration. A harmonisation project demands at least a basic level of commitment among Member States to pull together to create a level playing field. However, in the field of asylum, what we see is Member States purporting to be in support of a harmonisation project, but reluctant to make alterations to their domestic legal frameworks or to cede any significant measure of control to the supranational institutions. We have seen that Member States are not only dispassionate about adopting exception and discretion-free minimum standards, but they are also reticent about implementing court judgments where they uphold an interpretation of the law or seek to enforce a law that is undesirable to Member States. This suggests that if there were more opportunities for Member States to be accommodated through formal differentiated integration measures we could find that more Member States would follow the example of the UK. According to Peers, reducing 'divergences in application of the EU rules' and ensuring 'their correct implementation' is likely to require the

---

59 See House of Lords European Union Committee, *The Treaty of Lisbon: An Impact Assessment*(n 23), 125–6.

60 See Anthony M. Collins, 'Recent Developments in Asylum and Immigration Law before the Court of Justice' (2009) 9 *ERA Forum* 581–90.

61 Peers (n 32) 8.

adoption of 'further legislation harmonizing standards' as well as 'new methods of ensuring its implementation, for example a vigorous enforcement policy by the Commission, the creation of a common asylum court or joint processing of applications'.[62]

Although it is the case that a higher degree of harmonisation is needed, it seems that Member States will not be willing to embark on a further legislative project in the near, or perhaps even distant, future. Having only just emerged from an arduously long and fraught legislative process, we can safely assume that the level of harmonisation currently in place is the level at which the EU will rest for some time to come. It is evident that cooperation in this field will remain an uphill struggle in light of the divergence of the views of the Member States, the Commission and the European Parliament on what is to be considered a sufficient level of harmonisation.

Despite the fact that the second-phase directives have now been agreed upon, the preceding years of negotiation and prolonged stalemate are nevertheless revealing for the level of cooperation in the EU on asylum matters. As mentioned above, the changes brought in by the new directives are overall not significant despite the long wait. The Commission was forced to withdraw its more ambitious earlier proposals for new directives due to general unwillingness among Member States to enhance asylum standards. Instead, for the most part, we have seen watered-down versions adopted in their place with the legislative process following the usual pattern: the Council watered down the Commission's semi-ambitious proposal, followed by the European Parliament's insertion of some protective measures, some of which were ultimately accepted and some rejected by the Council.

4. THE INCOMPATIBILITY OF DIFFERENTIATED INTEGRATION WITH THE DUBLIN SYSTEM

At the heart of a harmonisation project is the necessity for the limitation of the discretion of participating Member States to legislate differently in a specific area, and this is particularly important with regard to the EU's asylum project because of the persistence of Dublin's 'one chance of asylum' rule. In view of this, it is questionable whether any level of formal differentiated integration or informal flexibility should be tolerated. The dreadful effects of the interaction between the Dublin system

62 Ibid.

and a context of differing levels of reception conditions became apparent in the case of *MSS v Belgium and Greece,* a landmark case as the first in which the European Court of Human Rights (ECtHR) held that the transfer of an asylum seeker between two EU countries under the Dublin rules was in violation of a series of Convention rights by both the sending and receiving state. Unlike the case of *TI v UK*,[63] in which the Court ruled that the transfer in question was lawful because the asylum seeker would have the opportunity to make a new asylum claim in Germany and receive effective protection, this was not the case in respect of a transfer from Belgium to Greece. The *MSS* case concerned an Afghan asylum seeker whose first contact with the Union was Greece but who claimed asylum in Belgium. The Belgian authorities returned the individual to Greece in accordance with the Dublin II Regulation, requesting that Greece accept responsibility for the applicant. Upon arrival, the individual was placed in a detention centre close to Athens airport, locked in a small space with 20 other detainees, with access to toilets only with the guards' permission, was not allowed out into the open air, was given very little food and forced to sleep on a filthy mattress or on the bare floor.[64] Upon his release, the applicant was not provided with accommodation by the authorities and so, having no means of subsistence, lived in a park in central Athens.[65] The Court held that both the conditions in which the applicant was detained and his living circumstances outside detention amounted to a breach of Article 3 of the Convention. The applicant had received no assistance from the Greek authorities despite its obligations under the EU Reception Directive. The Greek authorities were also held to be in breach of Article 13 in conjunction with Article 3 as a result of their failure to properly examine the applicant's asylum claim and the risk he faced in being deported to Afghanistan without a full examination of the merits of his case or access to an effective remedy. Belgium was also held liable for a breach of Convention Article 3 as well as Article 13 in conjunction with Article 3. The Court considered that the deplorable conditions facing asylum seekers in Greece were well known to the Belgian authorities, citing for example a letter sent to the Belgian Minister for Migration and Asylum Policy by the UNHCR two months prior to the individual's return to Greece in which the deficiencies of the asylum procedure in Greece were

---

63 *TI v United Kingdom* [2000], Application No. 43844/98 ECHR.

64 *MSS v Belgium and Greece* [2011] Application No. 30696/09, para. 34.

65 Ibid., para. 37.

set out and a recommendation made to suspend transfers to Greece.[66] *MSS v Belgium and Greece* differed from *KRS v UK*[67] in that, at the time the latter case was decided, there was, according to the ECtHR, an 'absence of proof' that Greece was not complying with its obligations under the Reception Directive and Article 3 of the ECHR. The Court therefore decided on 'the information available at the time' to both the UK and itself that sending individuals back to Greece was not in violation of the Convention. In *MSS v Belgium and Greece*, the Court drew upon a wealth of documents produced by the UNHCR, the European Commissioner for Human Rights, Amnesty International, Human Rights Watch, Pro-Asyl and the European Council on Refugees and Exiles, the Greek Helsinki Monitor, and the Greek National Commission for Human Rights in order to conclude that Greece was not a safe destination country for asylum seekers for the purposes of the Convention and that, in returning an individual there, Belgium was in violation of a number of its provisions.[68]

The ECtHR noted in the *MSS* judgment the problematic way in which the Dublin II Regulation functioned. It drew attention to the high proportion of non-EU nationals entering the Union through Greece.[69] Asylum seekers fingerprinted there under the Eurodac system are liable to be returned to Greece for processing. Although Greece was criticised for not having a proper and functioning asylum procedure or adequate detention and accommodation facilities, the ECtHR expressed concern that Greece was under significant pressure. It stated the following:

> … States which form the external borders of the European Union are currently experiencing considerable difficulties in coping with the increasing influx of migrants and asylum seekers. The situation is exacerbated by the transfers of asylum seekers by other Member States in application of the Dublin Regulation. The Court does not underestimate the burden and pressure this situation places on the States concerned, which are all in the present context of economic crisis.

The Court considered that the Dublin system aggravated the situation by increasing pressures on border states such as Greece. Indeed, as part of

66 Ibid., para. 16.
67 *KRS v. United Kingdom* [2008] Application no. 32733/08
68 *MSS v Belgium and Greece* (n 64), paras 343 and 348.
69 Ibid., para. 125.

the reform package prepared by the Commission and proposed in 2008, it had put forward a proposal to redraft the Dublin Regulation.[70]

The case of *MSS* influenced the Court of Justice of the European Union judgment in the case of *NS*.[71] The *NS* case dealt with an Afghan asylum seeker's challenge of a decision taken by UK authorities to return him to Greece in accordance with the Dublin Regulation. The Court held that an asylum seeker cannot be returned to a country where there is a serious risk his or her rights under the EU Charter of Fundamental Rights will be violated, which may require setting aside the Dublin rules on the allocation of responsibility for asylum claims between Member States. While it was asserted that the EU's obligations under the ECHR and the Refugee Convention meant that the Dublin rules did not in principle breach the Charter where a country such as Greece failed to comply with its human rights obligations, leading to a situation of a serious risk of breach of an individual's rights under the Charter, transfer under the Dublin regulation would be incompatible with the Charter. The overloading of the Greek asylum system created a serious risk of breach of Articles 1 (right to dignity), 4 (freedom from torture and inhuman and degrading treatment or punishment), 18 (respect for the rules of the Refugee Convention), and 19(2) (*non-refoulement*) of the Charter. Therefore, the UK's irrebuttable presumption that all Member States are safe for asylum seekers is in breach of the EU Charter, while a rebuttable presumption would be permissible (para. 178). Breaches of a Member State's obligations under EU law, which do not violate human rights obligations, would not however demand a suspension of the Dublin rules. However, Steve Peers has noted that, '[g]iven the close connection between the EU asylum legislation and fundamental rights obligations, it will not always be easy to establish whether a Member State is "merely" breaching EU legislation, or is also breaching the Charter'.[72]

While the Court of Justice agreed with the ECtHR that the operation of the Dublin Regulation should be limited in the case of systematic deficiencies in the asylum systems of receiving Member States amounting to a real risk of a breach of Article 3 ECHR and the corresponding provision, Article 4, in the Charter of Fundamental Rights, it made clear

[70] COM(2008) 820 final/2; The ECtHR made reference to the Commission's proposal in paras 77 and 78 of its judgment in *MSS v Belgium and Greece* (n 64).

[71] Joined Cases C-411/10 and *NS and Others v Secretary of State for the Home Department* and C-493/10 *ME and Others v Refugee Applications Commissioner and Minister for Justice, Equality and Law Reform* [2011] ECLI: EU:C:211:865.

[72] Peers (n 32) 2-3.

that this was exceptional and that not all infringements of fundamental rights will affect Member States' other obligations under the Dublin Regulation.[73] Since this case, the ECtHR has amplified its standard of protection, insisting that states parties to the ECHR make an individual assessment of the level of human rights protection in the receiving EU countries when implementing Dublin transfers.[74] In its recent Opinion that the agreement on the EU's accession to the ECHR was incompatible with primary EU law, the CJEU argued that the principle of mutual trust, as exemplified by the Dublin system, does not allow for an individual assessment of another country's behaviour, except in the narrowly defined circumstances of the *NS* case. Bruno de Witte and Šejla Imamovic have argued that the Court's argument 'boils down to a claim that EU law should be allowed to give *less protection* than the Convention requires to certain rights in certain circumstances: namely, to the rights at stake in mutual recognition situations in the area of freedom, security and justice'.[75]

The European Council on Refugees and Exiles (ECRE) has stated that 'the Dublin system's harmful effects go beyond those caused by the currently imperfect CEAS' and calls for the system to be dismantled and replaced with one based on free choice of the asylum applicant as to which state examines their claim.[76] The disastrous effects of the interplay between the workings of the Dublin system in a context of differing levels of reception conditions was made clear in the case of *MSS v Belgium and Greece*. Different levels of protection across the Member States 'produce an "asylum lottery" in the EU'.[77] ECRE reports that 2005 recognition rates for Chechens varied from approximately 0 per cent in Slovakia to 90 per cent in Austria. The problem is also significant in the case of Iraqis with 2007 recognition rates showing an 87.5 per cent success rate in Cyprus, 85 per cent in Germany, 82 per cent in Sweden, 30 per cent in Denmark, 13 per cent in the UK and 0 per cent in Slovenia and Greece.[78] With these figures in mind, depriving asylum seekers the

---

[73] Cases *NS* and *ME* (n 71), paras 82–83.

[74] *Tarakhel v Switzerland* (2015) 60 EHRR 28.

[75] Bruno De Witte and Šelja Imamovic, 'Opinion 2/13 on Accession to the ECHR: Defending the EU Legal Order against a Foreign Human Rights Court' (2015) 40 *European Law Review* 702.

[76] ECRE, Comments on the European Commission Proposal to recast the Dublin Regulation (April 2009) 3 and 4.

[77] Ibid.

[78] ECRE, 'Five years on Europe is still Ignoring its Responsibilities towards Iraqi Refugees' (March 2008), 15.

choice of where to seek asylum in the EU on the premise that they receive the same treatment across the Member States seems ludicrous. ECRE has warned that, 'Lack of equal protection can create a real risk of *refoulement*, and thus of failing to conform to international legal obligations'.[79] The contribution of the Dublin system to the pressure on border states creates the risk that these states will work to limit access to their territories or to asylum procedures.[80] There is also the danger that asylum seekers will try to avoid being transferred or even escape the asylum system altogether.[81] In this way the Dublin system can transform 'a visible flow of asylum seekers into a covert movement of irregular migrants that is even more difficult for states to count and control'.[82] Jonathan Aus has noted the 'immediate reaction' of asylum seekers seeking protection in Nordic countries to Eurodac, which as discussed above is designed to complement the Dublin System by requiring the fingerprinting of all asylum seekers on entry in order to enable transfers, has been to 'deliberately *cut or burn their fingertips* … A member of the *Swedish Migration Board* reported "scars from knives and razors, or entire [fingerprint] patterns that are entirely destroyed because they've used acid or some other kind of product to destroy their hands"'.[83]

The Dublin system is indefensible in a context which lacks full harmonisation. It is simply not compatible with a system that does not include the following: *all* Member States participating in Dublin Regulation sign up to providing the same high level of protection to all asylum applicants (including with regard to reception, procedures and recognition rates, etc.); all Member States actually provide this protection *in practice*. Neither of these conditions is satisfied at present. The UK has opted out of the second phase of asylum directives but has opted in to the Dublin and Eurodac regulations. Implementation remains a serious problem across the board, with Greece providing an example of a country simply unable to deal with the volume of applicants it receives.

---

[79] ECRE, 'Sharing Responsibility for Refugee Protection in Europe: Dublin Reconsidered' (March 2008) 16.

[80] ECRE, 'The Way Forward Towards Fair and Efficient Asylum Systems in Europe' (September 2005) 13.

[81] ECRE (n 79) 16.

[82] Gil Loescher, 'Forced Migration in the Post-Cold War Era' in Bimal Ghosh (ed.), *Managing Migration: Time for a New International Regime?* (Oxford University Press 2000).

[83] Jonathan P. Aus, 'Eurodac: A Solution Looking for a Problem?' (2006) 10 *European Integration Online Papers* 12 (emphasis in original).

Despite the case law of the European courts, the focus in amending the Dublin Regulation was to enhance the efficiency of the system, rather than increase protection standards. This is despite the fact that the system has long been in need of a complete overhaul, or indeed abolition, considering its effect of placing a hugely disproportionate burden on the Southern European States, which are struggling to manage arrivals and facing significant economic challenges. The Dublin system has led 'to significant human rights abuses',[84] acknowledged by the European courts. In spite of this, a 'radical reform of Dublin rules was never seriously considered'.[85] Minor improvements include the rules on detention, which ban the detention of an asylum seeker merely because the Regulation is applicable.[86] An exception is stipulated in cases where there is a 'significant risk of absconding' enabling Member States to detain an asylum seeker where there are 'reasons in an individual case, which are based on objective criteria defined by law, to believe that an applicant or a third-country national or a stateless person who is subject to a transfer procedure may abscond'.[87] In such cases, detention must be 'proportional and other less coercive alternative measures cannot be applied effectively'[88] and detention must 'be for as short a period as possible'.[89]

The revised Dublin Regulation codifies the decision of the Court of Justice of the European Union in *NS* and *ME*[90] with regard to the suspension of transfers,[91] but the Commission failed to have its proposed formal procedure for suspension adopted. Nevertheless, the European Parliament was successful in influencing changes to the new rules on a mechanism for early warning and crisis management, which includes an express reference to the fundamental rights of asylum seekers.[92] Peers has noted that, had the Commission's proposal to suspend the Dublin system in instances of human rights abuse been successful, this would 'not have fixed the underlying illness, but only treated the symptoms' and yet 'even that proposal was rejected by the Council'.[93] The result is that

---

84 Ibid., 8.
85 Peers (n 32) 6.
86 Dublin Regulation, art. 28(1).
87 Ibid., art. 2(n).
88 Ibid., art. 28(2).
89 Ibid., art. 28(3).
90 *NS* and *ME* (n 71).
91 Dublin Regulation, art. 3(2).
92 Ibid., art. 33.
93 Peers (n 32) 8.

'[a]ny significant change in the Dublin rules will therefore remain – as with the first-phase Regulation – in the hands of the courts'.[94]

The Eurodac Regulation, which obliges that the fingerprints of all asylum seekers and individuals who cross the external borders of Member States irregularly be taken, principally for the purpose of enabling the operation of the Dublin system, has seen a number of changes in the second-phase instrument. The most significant amendment is that national law enforcement agencies as well as Europol are granted access to the database.[95] Peers has warned that this 'risks stigmatising large categories of foreign citizens, including those whose refugee and subsidiary protection status has been recognised'.[96]

5. CONCLUSION

This chapter has argued that differentiated integration, neither in the form of official agreements, nor in the form of informal flexibility, should be tolerated in the field of asylum. Formal differentiated integration arrangements have enabled the UK to adopt a cherry-picking approach to participation in the CEAS. While the UK has opted into the Dublin system, it has opted out of the second-phase directives which comprise legally enforceable minimum standards designed to reduce differences in protection standards across the Union. However, the asylum directives, by allowing Member States a wide scope of discretion in interpretation and application, are themselves a cause of informal flexibility. There remain vast differences in practice between Member States in their treatment of asylum seekers, for instance in relation to their recognition as refugees. This is compounded by the Commission's lack of vigilance as regards enforcement of the directives coupled with Member States' unwillingness to implement the CJEU rulings properly. Asylum is a field which directly affects the lives of vulnerable individuals and is heavily regulated by international and human rights norms. In view of this, it has been argued that there should be no provision for formal and informal flexibility. This tension, created by the existing formal and informal flexibility arrangements, puts in question the integrity of the CEAS in its accommodation of a situation of no equivalence of protection across Member States despite the persistence of the Dublin 'one chance of asylum' rule.

---

94 Ibid.

95 Eurodac Regulation, arts 5, 6, 7, 19–21, 33 and 36.

96 Peers (n 32) 10.

REFERENCES

Aus J P, 'Eurodac: A Solution Looking for a Problem? (2006) 10 *European Integration Online Papers* 12.

Bunyan T, 'Commission Action Plan on the Stockholm Programme: A bit more freedom and justice and a lot more security' (Statewatch, 2011).

Collins A M, 'Recent Developments in Asylum and Immigration Law before the Court of Justice' (2009) *ERA Forum* 581–90.

De Witte B and Imamovic Š, 'Opinion 2/13 on Accession to the ECHR: Defending the EU Legal Order against a Foreign Human Rights Court' (2015) 40 *European Law Review* 683–705.

El-Enany N, 'EU Asylum and Immigration Law under the Area of Freedom, Security, and Justice' in Arnull A and Chalmers D (eds), *The Oxford Handbook of European Union Law* (Oxford University Press 2015) 86–91.

Fletcher M, 'Schengen, the European Court of Justice and Flexibility Under the Lisbon Treaty: Balancing the United Kingdom's "Ins" and "Outs"' (2009) 5(1) *European Constitutional Law Review* 71–98.

Ghosh B (ed.), *Managing Migration: Time for a New International Regime?* (Oxford University Press 2000).

Hirschman AO, *Exit, Voice, and Loyalty: Responses to Decline in Firms, Organizations, And States* (Harvard University Press 1970).

Loescher G, 'Forced Migration in the Post-Cold War Era', in Ghosh B (ed.) *Managing Migration: Time for a New International Regime?* (Oxford University Press 2000) 190–219.

Monar J, 'The "Area of Freedom, Security and Justice": "Schengen" "Europe", Opt-outs, Opt-ins and Associates' in Dyson K and Sepos A (eds), *Which Europe? The Politics of Differentiated Integration* (Palgrave 2010) 279–92.

Peers S, 'The Second Phase of the Common European Asylum System: A Brave New World – or Lipstick on a Pig?' (Statewatch, 8 April 2013).

Tallberg J, *Making States Comply: The European Commission, The European Court of Justice, and the Enforcement of the Internal Market* (Lund University Press 1999).

Van Gerven W, *The Economic Union: A Policy of States and Peoples* (Hart Publishing 2005).

15. Between flexibility and disintegration in EU criminal law

Ester Herlin-Karnell*

1. INTRODUCTION

The idea of flexibility seems to provide an attractive European model to aim for, not least to avoid the accusation of a 'one-size' fits all approach to the highly complicated project of an EU of 28 Member States. Yet, as this chapter will try to show, as much as the notion of flexibility seems to be an attractive concept, it is also a rather vague one. Specifically, this chapter sets out to explore the notion of 'flexible' integration in the concrete area of EU criminal law. The phenomenon of EU criminal law is traditionally meant to capture cross-border criminality where the EU is taking multilateral Member State action to combat particularly serious criminality such as terrorism, organized crime and cyber-crime related criminality. However, in recent years, the EU has acquired a more freestanding competence to legislate on criminal law proper. With the Lisbon Treaty, the EU gained certain EU competences in criminal law, either when there is a cross-border dimension or if harmonization of criminal law at the EU level would be needed for the effective implementation of an area that has already been subject to harmonization (Article 83 TFEU).

Despite its novel nature in an EU context, or perhaps exactly because of it, criminal law offers a good example of limits, and varied meaning, to the concept of flexibility as a tool for European integration. But what then does it mean to refer to flexibility in EU criminal law? In answering this question, arguably we first need to know what flexibility means in EU law proper. While the notion of flexibility is far from a new concept and traditionally it has been defined as the possibility of one or more

* I would like to thank Andrea Ott for her useful comments on this chapter, with the usual disclaimer. The research for this chapter was supported by a VENI grant from the Dutch Research Council (NWO).

Member States choosing to remain outside the scope of certain activities pursued within the Union's legal framework or conversely to move forward by heading a selective group of '*Avant garde*' States wanting to go further through experiments of integration processes than others, the very notion of flexible integration poses some pertinent questions in the current financial (and constitutional) crisis of the EU. Indeed, while Deirdre Curtin was right in her early assessment and prediction of a Europe consisting of 'bits and pieces',[1] in connection with the creation of the intergovernmental pillars and its exclusion from the Community method, what seems to be emerging in contemporary EU law is a Court-led era of differentiation.[2] Flexibility as a concept can be found throughout the Treaty and could be said to represent codified pluralism.[3] When discussing the concept of 'flexibility' in terms of differentiation, the starting point is often the enhanced cooperation mechanisms as the most clear-cut example of flexible integration.[4] In short, the classic notion of 'enhanced cooperation' means that some Member States go further than other States. The concept accepts that there is room for action outside the EU model and that not all Member States have to be in the same boat, while still respecting each other through the fundamental loyalty principle of the Article 4(3) Treaty of the European Union. Moreover, the concept of enhanced or closer cooperation is an expression

---

[1] Deirdre Curtin, 'The Constitutional Structure of the Union: A Europe of Bits and Pieces' (1993) 30 CML Rev 17.

[2] Gráinne de Búrca, 'Legal Principles as an Instrument of Differentiation?' in Bruno De Witte, Dominik Hanf and Ellen Vos (eds), *The Many Faces of Differentiation in EU Law* (Intersentia 2003) 131.

[3] On differentiation, see Andrea Ott, 'EU Constitutional Boundaries to Differentiation: How to Reconcile Differentiation with Integration?' in Andrea Ott and Ellen Vos (eds), *Fifty Years of European Integration: Foundations and Perspectives* (T.M.C. Asser Press 2009) 113; Ester Herlin-Karnell and Theodore Konstadinides, 'The Rise and Many Expressions of Consistency in EU Law: Legal and Strategic Implications for European Integration' (2013) *Cambridge Journal of European Legal Studies* 139. On the notion of flexibility see e.g. Curtin (n 1) 17; Alexander Stubb, 'A Categorization of Differentiated Integration' (1996) 34 *Journal of Common Market Studies* 283; Bruno De Witte, 'Old-fashioned Flexibility: International Agreements between Member States of the European Union' in Gráinne de Búrca and Joanne Scott (eds), *Constitutional Change in the EU, From Uniformity to Flexibility?* (Hart Publishing 2000) 31.

[4] E.g. Stephen Weatherill, 'If I'd Wanted You to Understand I Would Have Explained it Better: What is the Purpose of the Provisions on Closer Co-operation Introduced by the Treaty of Amsterdam?' in David O'Keeffe and Patrick Twomey (eds), *Legal Issues of the Amsterdam Treaty* (Hart Publishing 1999) 21.

of flexibility since it offers an alternative model of multi-speed integration. The phenomenon of a 'two-speed' Europe is most evidently manifested in the Treaty of Prüm[5] and the Schengen *acquis,*[6] whereby some Member States sought to go further than those less 'integrative' Member States by establishing the 'highest possible' standard of cooperation. Such cooperation has been taking place especially by means of the exchange of information, particularly in combatting terrorism, cross-border crime and illegal migration.[7] Specifically, I have chosen to refer to the notions of flexibility and differentiation interchangeably without implying a second-class 'two-tier' Europe or making any actual substantive distinction between a two-speed Europe and a multi-speed Europe. Yet, it seems fair to believe that what is actually happening is a multi-speed Europe.[8] A recent example of the possible use of the multi-speed concept of enhanced cooperation is that of the establishment of a European Public Prosecutor,[9] which sparked a yellow card procedure in the Member States because of its highly controversial nature. In spite of this, the Commission proposed a new measure that does not seem to capture all the requirements expressed by the Member States. If this remains the case, we would then have the first test case of enhanced cooperation in a criminal law context.[10]

This chapter is structured in three parts. The first part will set out the framework for how to understand a multi-speed Europe with regard to criminal law and procedure by first setting the scene of criminal law and thereafter assessing the notion of flexibility and enhanced cooperation. The second part looks more specifically at the prospect of enhanced

---

5 Convention between Belgium, Germany, Spain, France, Luxembourg, the Netherlands and Austria, signed in Prüm, Germany on 27 May 2005.

6 1985, The Schengen Agreement, [2000] OJ L239.

7 See generally House of Lords European Union Committee, 18th Report of Session 2006-07 'Prüm: An Effective Weapon against Terrorism and Crime?' (2007), <http://www.publications.parliament.uk/pa/ld200607/ldselect/ldeucom/90/90.pdf>, accessed 1 June 2011.

8 Paul Craig, 'Review of Piris Two-Speed Europe' (2012) 37 EL Rev 800.

9 Proposal for a Council Regulation on the establishment of the European Public Prosecutor's Office, COM(2013) 0534 final – 2013/0255 (APP).

10 See Katalin Ligeti (ed.), *Toward a Prosecutor for the European Union*, Volume 1 (Hart Publishing 2012); Gerard Conway, 'The Future of a European Public Prosecutor in the Area of Freedom, Security and Justice' in Maria Fletcher, Ester Herlin-Karnell and Claudio Matera (eds), *The European Union as an Area of Freedom, Security and Justice*, (Routledge 2015, forthcoming); Marianne L. Wade, 'A European Public Prosecutor: Potential and Pitfalls' (2013) 59 *Crime, Law & Social Change* 439.

cooperation in the tangled landscape of opt-outs/opt-ins in the EU area of freedom security and justice (AFSJ). The specific case of the emergency brake for triggering the enhanced cooperation mechanism will not be dealt with extensively, but the focus here is rather on the tension between flexibility and disintegration as such and where the emergency brake will be only briefly described.[11] The third section looks at the concept of differentiation as it may be identified in the concept of mutual recognition as such. Furthermore, the notion of mutual recognition has always been the main source of integration in criminal law matters and is considered a less sharp integration tool. Yet, as will be shown, in the recent cases of *Melloni*[12] and *De Silva Jorge*,[13] the Court of Justice seems to have opted for a fairly static interpretation of trust in the context of the European Arrest Warrant (EAW) and it is rather the principle of effectiveness that continues to play a prominent role in the Court's case law with regard to the shaping of criminal law. The chapter concludes with some observations on the wider impact of the Charter of Fundamental Rights.

2. THE STATE OF PLAY: INTEGRATION AND CRIMINAL LAW

The purpose of the EU, as stated in the Treaty, is to create an ever-closer Union among the people of Europe. Within this integration progression and aspiration, EU criminal law is still a relatively novel EU area, which is rapidly emerging as part of the development of the AFSJ. In 2009 the Lisbon Treaty confirmed that previously nationally dominated area of criminal law now belonged to the EU supranational level through the rearrangement of the Treaty structure. Prior to that, most cooperation in that field was based on intergovernmentalism and the Court only had a very limited jurisdiction before the Treaty changes made by Lisbon.[14] A great deal has been written about the constitutionalization process of EU criminal law, which will not be reiterated here.[15] The crucial provisions

---

[11] On the emergency brake, see e.g. Ester Herlin-Karnell, *The Constitutional Dimension of European Criminal Law* (Hart Publishing 2012) Ch. 4.

[12] Case C-399/11, Criminal proceedings against *Stefano Melloni*, ECLI: EU:C:2012:600, Opinion of AG Bot delivered on 2 October 2012.

[13] Case C-42/11, *Joao Pedro Lopes Da Silva Jorge,* ECLI:EU:C:2012:517.

[14] See former art. 35 TEU.

[15] E.g. Sarah Summers et al, *The Emergence of EU Criminal law* (Hart Publishing 2014); Samuli Mettinen, *EU Criminal Law* (Routledge 2013); Maria

for criminal law are to be found in Chapter 4 of title V of the TFEU and more specifically in Articles 82 TFEU (procedural criminal law) and 83 TFEU (substantive criminal law). These provisions must, however, be read in the light of Chapter I of Title V of TFEU, which sets out the general goals to be achieved in this area. More specifically, Article 67 TFEU stipulates, inter alia, that the Union shall constitute an AFSJ with respect for fundamental rights and the different legal systems and traditions of the Member States. Therefore the project of EU criminal law is part of the bigger venture of establishing an AFSJ.

Apart from the general abolition of the former Third Pillar and also the specific EU competences with regard to criminal law, there are several important novelties that need to be considered; for example, the emergency brake provisions (where Member States can pull the brake if the proposed legislation is a sensitive matter in the national legal criminal law system) as well as the notion of expedited procedures for persons in custody. Article 267 TFEU provides that if a question is raised in a case pending before a court or tribunal in a Member State with regard to a person in custody, the Court of Justice of the European Union shall act with a minimum of delay.[16] However, despite the reformation of the Court of Justice's jurisdiction introduced by the Lisbon Treaty, the Court of Justice still does not have the power to review the validity or proportionality of operations carried out by the police or other law enforcement agencies of a Member State or the exercise of responsibilities incumbent upon Member States with regard to the maintenance of law and order and the safeguarding of internal security (Article 276 TFEU). That by itself indicates a degree of fragmentation in the landscape of EU criminal law.

Today not only is the concept of EU criminal law – and the AFSJ more broadly – still the fastest expanding field in contemporary EU integration, but it is also a very sensitive field, dealing with the most delicate legal issues such as the fight against crime, security, fundamental rights protection and justice cooperation. The Stockholm programme, which entered into force in conjunction with the Lisbon Treaty and which drew up an important vision for the future of AFSJ, had already come to an end in 2014. The EU is currently negotiating the new AFSJ agenda (of

---

Fletcher et al, *EU Criminal Law* (Edward Elgar Publishing 2008); Valsamis Mitsilegas, 'The Transformation of Criminal Law in the Area of Freedom, Security and Justice' (2007) 26 *Yearbook of European Law* 1; Herlin-Karnell (n 11).

[16] The procedure is governed by art. 23a of the Protocol on the Statute of the Court of Justice and art. 104b of its Rules of Procedure.

some sort) and, for the first time, the AFSJ and the new multi-annual programme is placed in the wider context of the future of Europe. Yet, perhaps the most complex issue for the future, and notably not discussed much by the Commission in its vision on how to shape Europe in 2020, is that of the flexibility mechanisms within the AFSJ.[17]

This chapter seeks to place recent developments in EU criminal law in the context of the likelihood of an increased use of 'flexibility' provisions in EU integration through criminal law.

3. CRIMINAL LAW AND FLEXIBILITY: A FRAGMENTED CHAPTER

As noted in the introduction, flexibility as a legal concept, albeit with political connotations, is by no means new in EU law.[18] As for criminal law, however, the flexibility mechanism of enhanced cooperation has not been used yet. Moreover, flexibility is most evidently exemplified in the 'one step backwards, two steps forwards' mechanisms, that is the emergency brake and accelerator procedure. More specifically, the provisions of Articles 82(2) and 83(1) and (2) stipulate in their respective paragraph 3 the possibility of applying a so-called 'emergency brake' if the law in question would affect fundamental aspects of a Member State's criminal justice system. If such an emergency brake scenario occurs, a Member State may request that the measure be referred to the European Council. In that case, the ordinary legislative procedure is suspended and, after discussion and 'in case of a consensus, the European Council shall, within four months of this suspension, refer the draft back to the Council, which shall terminate the suspension of the ordinary legislative procedure'. In short, the Lisbon Treaty contains an emergency brake that permits Member States to pull this brake if the legislation in question would affect fundamental aspects of criminal law legislation. Whether or not a single Member State pulls the emergency brake, the Lisbon Treaty provides for the possibility of enhanced cooperation for the remaining Member States.[19] It also means that there

---

17 COM(2010) 2020 final.

18 Giorgio Gaja, 'How Flexible is Flexibility under the Amsterdam Treaty?' (1998) 35 CML Rev 855.

19 Arts 82 and 83 TFEU state respectively: in case of disagreement, and if at least nine Member States wish to establish enhanced cooperation on the basis of the draft directive concerned, they shall notify the European Parliament, the Council and the Commission accordingly. In such a case, the authorization to

is no obligation, as set out in Article 329 TFEU, to address a request to the Commission, specifying the scope and objectives of the enhanced cooperation in question. Neither is there an obligation (as Article 20(2) TFEU of the Lisbon Treaty reads) that the Council as a last resort shall adopt the decision at issue. In addition, there is no obligation to consult the European Parliament. This raises two questions. First, it is possible to argue that the mere fact that the Member States do not need to show the last resort requirement as stated in Article 20(2) TFEU can be regarded as being in disharmony with the sensitive character of criminal law as the *ultimo ratio*. Secondly, there is a risk that such cooperation could result in varying views on what it means exactly to refer to freedom, security and justice in multi-speed Europe.[20]

In fact, the establishment of enhanced cooperation, particularly under the regime provided by the Lisbon Treaty, appears to be slightly biased if we consider the general principle of loyalty (Article 4(3) TFU). How could the 'last resort' solution requirement, as set out in Article 20(2) TEU of the Lisbon Treaty, be reconciled with the peculiarities within criminal law if a Member State has pulled the emergency brake? This would confront it with principles of criminal law policy. At issue here is the fact that it may not always be in the EU's interest to move forward and in this regard the possible disharmony with subsidiarity comes to the fore as well as the criminal law principle that any criminalization must be the last resort as a means of control.

The core of the issue in the present context is the obligation of loyalty as set out in Article 4(3) TEU. Accordingly, one may ask – in the framework of the Lisbon Treaty and as already implied above – whether it would be the Member State that pulled the emergency brake in criminal law that would be under a loyalty obligation rather than the other Member States. This poses two immediate questions: first, whether 'moving forward' is always the best alternative and, second, whether it really is feasible to treat criminal law as one EU policy among others. It is submitted that criminal law does not suit the traditional pattern of EU law making, as law making requires a more sophisticated approach in which the aspiration of uniformity or consistency is not enough to take precedence over fundamental principles of criminal law. Indeed, the whole question links to the wider debate on subsidiarity, Article 5(3)

---

proceed with enhanced cooperation referred to in art. 20(2) of the Treaty on European Union and art. 329 of this Treaty shall be deemed to be granted and the provisions on enhanced cooperation shall apply.

20 Draws on Herlin-Karnell (n 11) Ch .4.

TFEU and its function in the AFSJ and EU criminal law. The point is that the aspirations of moving forward by using the enhanced cooperation mechanisms might clash with the idea of criminal law as the last resort.

Clearly, the emergency brake raises as many issues as it attempts to solve. Furthermore, although the Lisbon Treaty abolished the previous pillar structure, it provides for two Treaties (TFEU and TEU) where all issues on external relations are confined to the TEU. In the context of EU criminal law cooperation, this raises some interesting issues. In the field of anti-terrorist financing, for example, there is no clear dividing line between internal and external security, despite the Lisbon Treaty's attempt to draw one, which makes it difficult to pin down just what the *acquis communautaire* – post Lisbon – entails and hence where the boundaries of enhanced cooperation lie.

Imagine the following scenario: nine Member States wish to go further by establishing enhanced cooperation regarding a security related measure on, for example, the need to combat cyber-crime-related criminality, despite the fact that the emergency brake has been pulled. It is clear that such a measure would also have an external impact regarding the fight against terrorism. It confirms the many internal, external and hybrid layers that interact here and how complex this area is with regard to exact constitutional structures.

But it does not only raise issues about the internal and external security divides. The point is that paying insufficient attention to accompanying regulation regarding the adequate protection of the individual in criminal law proceedings, as well as respect for the principles of criminalization, risks making the current pursuit of effectiveness (as both a competence and an enforcement issue) and the development of criminal law within the EU, counterproductive. In other words, there could be a scenario where not all Member States opt for the adoption of a legal safeguard measure while they are bound by the fundamental rights granted by the Charter.

It is also necessary for the EU to consider the principle of proportionality here. The concept of loyalty has previously dictated the exercise and establishment of enhanced cooperation in this area, which meant that it was never used in practice. It is likely, therefore, that what will emerge in this area is something similar to a proportionality test: a balancing act between the Member States and the EU. Yet, regardless of the possible merits of a proportionality test, the strong political dimension in this area means that not all Member States may decide to participate in an instrument.

3.1 A European Public Prosecutor?

An interesting example of the possible future use of the enhanced cooperation provision in the EU criminal law context is that of the controversial establishment of a European public prosecutor. According to Article 86 TFEU, a European Public Prosecutor (EPP) shall be established to counter fraud against the EU's budget. The prosecutor will be responsible for investigating, prosecuting and bringing to judgment, where appropriate in liaison with Europol, the perpetrators of and accomplices in offences against the Union's financial interests, as determined by the regulation provided for in Article 86 TFEU. The establishment of an EPP has however met with some serious opposition. Moreover, considering the fact that at present 11 Member States have voted against the proposal through the yellow card procedure, it appears as if the enhanced cooperation mechanism will be the only avenue available. The Commission's proposal has essentially remained intact, notwithstanding the fact that the yellow-card subsidiarity procedure has been used twice since the procedure's inclusion in the Lisbon Treaty.[21] The main argument as presented by the Commission, is that Eurojust and Europol have a general mandate to facilitate exchange of information and coordinate national criminal investigations and prosecutions, but they lack the power to carry out acts of investigation or prosecution themselves. According to the Commission, action by national judicial authorities often remains slow, prosecution rates are, on average, low and results obtained in the different Member States of the Union are as a whole unequal. Based on this track record, the judicial action undertaken by Member States against fraud may currently not be considered effective, equivalent or deterrent as required under the Treaty. As pointed out by Peers, however, there is a fundamental flaw in the creation of an EPP. The point is that it is difficult to separate, on the one hand, rules relating to investigations and prosecutions (at the EU level) and, on the other hand, trials (Member State level). According to Peers, the Commission should have considered other possibilities of more limited measures to achieve the same objectives, such as the harmonization of the national prosecution rules in this area.[22]

It should be pointed out that there has been a debate as to whether such a Prosecutor should have a wider criminal law mandate than that of the

---

[21] See Conway (n 10).

[22] Steve Peers, *EU Justice and Home Affairs Law* (Oxford University Press 2011) 858–60.

financial sphere.[23] Article 86(4) provides the opportunity for a future European Council to adopt a decision amending the competences of such a prosecutor to include serious crimes with a cross-border dimension in the broader sense. As for the UK, the European Union Act 2011 would require a referendum in the UK before it could agree to the UK accepting an EPP into UK law, although there are no indications that the UK government wishes to opt-in to the proposed EPP.[24] Whether Eurojust would simply be transformed into an EPP or would be used to assist the formation of an EPP is an open question on the basis of the phrasing in Article 86(1). As noted by Conway, it is also an open question whether it would be useful to continue Eurojust as a separate prosecution branch. And, if an EPP is adopted by only some (nine at least for the enhanced cooperation to be triggered) Member States, Eurojust would automatically remain for the non-participating Member States.[25] This confirms that the result would be a messy landscape of flexibility.

4. THE OPT OUTS/OPT INS: POLITICS AND CONSTITUTIONAL CHALLENGES

Another way of flexible integration in criminal law matters is that of the opt-out and opt-in regimes. As is well known, the UK, Ireland and Denmark have negotiated a unique approach to the AFSJ project. This poses challenges not only for those trying to analyse the current state of play but also for national courts as well as the Court of Justice when applying EU constitutional principles. These Member States have the opportunity to opt out of criminal law cooperation provisions, as provided for by the Lisbon Treaty and Protocol No. 21.[26] They can later opt in under the conditions set out in the Protocol. Yet, in some areas, such as anti-money laundering and counter-terrorist finance, opt outs are less

---

[23] Jörg Monar, 'Justice and Home Affairs in the EU Constitutional Treaty. What Added Value for the "Area of Freedom, Security and justice"?' (2005) 1 *European Constitutional Law Review* 226.

[24] Conway (n 10).

[25] The European Commission accompanied its 2013 proposed Regulation on an EPP with a proposed Regulation to reform Eurojust: *Proposal for a Regulation of the European Parliament and of the Council on the European Union Agency for Criminal Justice Cooperation* (Eurojust), Brussels, 17.7.2013, COM(2013) 0535 final – 2013/0256 (COD).

[26] See Peers (n 22); Alicia Hinarejos, John R Spencer and Steve Peers, 'Opting out of Criminal Law: What is Actually Involved?' (2012) Centre for European Law Cambridge, working paper 2012/1.

likely because of the international obligations beyond EU law and because the UK has been one of the leading proponents of further cooperation in this field. In addition, the Transitional Protocol No. 36 contains specific rules which apply only to the UK and in which the UK had to decide by 2014 whether it wished to participate at all in the remaining third pillar measures and if it accepted the jurisdiction of the Court in this area.[27] The consequence of any opt out (that is not participating in a measure) is that the Court of Justice will not have jurisdiction to monitor it. An opt out also applies to any international agreement concluded by the Union in relation to the cooperation in question. In other words, an opt out has serious consequences for the EU endeavour of ensuring consistency across its policies.

Needless to say any opt-out decision is bound to be a political decision and will be the cause of further complexity in the legal discussion of the AFSJ. For example, one could ask how the Court will develop the rights of relevance for criminal law such as that of *ne bis in idem*, legality and fair trial as recognized in the Charter to cover situations where the UK has opted out, for example a measure on legal safeguards (e.g. Articles 47–50 of the Charter). Arguably, the opt-out area offers a fascinating yet complicated test case of which constitutional principles apply exactly and how they work in the AFSJ. The opt-out area and the concept of a multi-speed Europe is a testing ground for the AFSJ and the scope and function of the classic EU constitutional principles in this field.

As indicated above, the UK and Ireland have negotiated a complete 'smorgasbord' – or pick-and-choose – approach to the AFSJ project. These Member States have the opportunity to opt out of criminal law cooperation provisions, as provided for by the Lisbon Treaty and Protocol No. 21. They can later opt in under the conditions set out in the said Protocol. Yet, in the area of, for example, the fight against money laundering and financial crime, it appears less likely that the UK and Ireland would remain outside EU cooperation, given that it is not only the EU which initiated these initiatives (that is, the international obligations as the guidelines set by the Financial Action Task Force on which the EU Directives are based, compliance 'threat' would remain) and that (at least) the UK has been one of the leading proponents of further cooperation against money laundering across the EU. Indeed, it raises

---

27 See House of Lords, '13th Report of Session 2012-13, EU Police and Criminal Justice Measures: The UK's 2014 Opt-out Decision'. See Jean-Claude Piris, *The Lisbon Treaty. A Legal and Political Analysis* (Cambridge University Press 2010) 199–200; Craig (n 8) 341.

some delicate questions about the delimitation of EU internal and external powers with regard to the EU's strategy to counter terrorism effectively.

In addition, closely related to the notion of differentiation within EU criminal law is the Schengen example, which demonstrates that the Court can effectively police the Member States' level of participation in a given policy area by 'gate-keeping' their preferences which amount to non-unitary integration.[28] The Schengen *acquis,*[29] where some Member States have sought to go further than other less 'integrative' Member States by establishing the 'highest possible' standard of cooperation, is one of the first examples of a flexible style of integration method in AFSJ-related matters. Such cooperation has been taking place especially by means of the exchange of information and particularly in combatting terrorism, cross-border crime and illegal migration.[30] The UK is not part of the Schengen *acquis*, but it may make a request to the Council for authorization to participate in part or all of the Schengen provisions and, in addition, to contribute to the adoption of measures based on the Schengen *acquis* (Articles 4 and 5 of the Schengen Protocol). The Council has to decide on such a request by unanimity unless the legislative proposal in question is built on the pre-existing Schengen *acquis*, to which the UK has secured an opt out. Such was the case in *UK v Council*,[31] where the UK sought the annulment of Regulation 2007/2004 adopted in 2004 with a view to establishing the external border control agency Frontex.[32] The UK was not included in the adoption of the challenged Regulation that was built on the provisions of the pre-existing Schengen *acquis*. In yet another case, the UK again sought the annulment of a Regulation on the standards for security features and biometrics in passports and travel documents issued by Member States. As in the previous case, the UK

---

[28] See also Maria O'Neil, 'EU Cross-border Policing Provisions: The View from One of the Schengen Opt Out States' (2010) 18 *European Journal of Crime, Criminal Law and Criminal Justice* 73–89

[29] 1985, The Schengen Agreement, [2000] OJ L239.

[30] See generally House of Lords European Union Committee (n 7).

[31] Case C-77/05 *UK v Council* [2007] ECLI:EU:C:2007:803; Case C-137/05 *UK v Council* [2007] ECLI:EU:C:2007:805.

[32] Council Regulation (EC) No 2007/2004 of 26 October 2004 establishing a European Agency for the Management of Operational Cooperation at the External Borders of the Member States of the European Union [2004] OJ L349/1.

was excluded from participating in the adoption of the Regulation.[33] In both cases, the Court upheld the Council's discretion to refuse to allow the UK to take part in the adoption of these Regulations.[34] These judgments can be characterized as consistency-driven.[35] This is interesting in the area of criminal law mutual recognition, as will be explored below. The Court seems more concerned with upholding the effectiveness of EU law than consistency as such.

4.1 The Curious Case of Denmark

Denmark offers a unique test case for the practicality of the AFSJ project. Protocol No. 22, as attached to the Lisbon Treaty, grants Denmark a special position by granting it the right to remain outside the project.[36] This Protocol means that Denmark participates in Schengen-related measures and Pre-Lisbon third pillar instruments on the basis of international law, which continue to be binding and applicable to Denmark as before. Denmark may however notify the other Member States that it wishes to join the EU criminal law/AFSJ venture. Likewise, amendments of pre-Lisbon instruments do not apply to Denmark and the old version will still apply to Denmark. Notoriously, ever since the Maastricht Treaty, Denmark has had some serious objections to the EU project. The well-known referendum in connection with the entry into force of the Maastricht Treaty was perhaps the trendsetter in relation to later referenda in France, the Netherlands and Ireland. As a brief historic account, it is worth recalling that, in accordance with the Danish Protocol attached to the previous Amsterdam Treaty, Denmark was exempted from almost all measures adopted within the framework of former Title IV of the old EC Treaty. In addition, Denmark had special rules in place regarding the Schengen *acquis*.[37] These rules are now transferred to and bundled together in one document under the regime provided by Lisbon, namely Protocol No. 22. When the Lisbon Treaty was being negotiated, the

---

33 Council Regulation (EC) No 2252/2004 of 13 December 2004 on standards for security features and biometrics in passports and travel documents issued by Member States [2004] OJ L385/1.

34 Ibid.

35 Herlin-Karnell and Konstadinides (n 3) 139.

36 This section is partly based on Esther Herlin-Karnell, 'Denmark and the European Area of Freedom, Security and Justice: A Scandinavian Arrangement'(2013) 5(1) *Amsterdam Law Forum* 95.

37 See generally Peers (n 22) 674.

Danish government set out to hold a referendum on the Danish opt outs, but such plans were ultimately abandoned.[38]

In short, the Danish position is as follows. As for AFSJ measures, which build upon the Schengen *acquis* and also fall within the scope of Title V of the TFEU, Denmark has six months to decide whether to apply each measure in its national law.[39] Unlike the UK and Ireland, it does not have the possibility to opt in later. According to Article 8 in the Protocol No. 22, at any time Denmark may, in accordance with its constitutional requirements, inform the other Member States that it no longer wishes to avail itself of all or part of this Protocol. As noted by Suominen, this means that Denmark could decide to opt in to the whole 'thing' unlike the UK and Ireland, which are opting in or out with respect to each new criminal law measure.[40] Therefore, Denmark is out unless it 'buys' the whole concept. Yet, at present Denmark is not participating in any of the criminal law cooperation set out in Articles 82–86 TFEU. Denmark is excluded unless the measures in question also build upon the Schengen *acquis*. The relationship between Denmark and all other Member States in the EU (except the UK and Irish opt-outs) is based on intergovernmental cooperation and Council of Europe Treaties such as, most prominently, the European Convention of Human Rights standards (which will create an interesting situation when the EU accedes and the Convention rights are of course already binding the EU).[41]

Arguably, the Danish approach of rejecting the whole AFSJ threatens the consistency of the practicability of the operation of criminal law mutual recognition as the judicial system is largely based on mutual recognition in this area. Nevertheless, others have argued that the approach as adopted by Denmark strengthens sovereignty without undermining uniformity in the AFSJ. Specifically, Adler-Nissen argues that differentiated integration is not a threat to the notion of 'an ever closer Union', but rather it offers an innovation quite consistent with the *doxa*

---

[38] See Report of the Danish Institute for International Studies, 'The Danish Opt Outs from the European Union: developments since 2000' Folketing (Danish Parliament) available at: <http://www.eu-oplysningen.dk/emner_en/forbehold/> (accessed 16 January 2014).

[39] Peers (n 22) 674.

[40] Annika Suominen, 'EU Criminal Law Cooperation before and after the Lisbon Treaty – Aspects and Comments Especially in Relation to the Norwegian Position' (2012) 6 *Tidskrift utgiven av juridiska föreningen Finland* 573–604.

[41] Ibid.

of integration'.[42] It could be argued that this is a confirmation of the CJEU's approach as demonstrated in *Spain and Italy v Council,*[43] albeit in the context of enhanced cooperation and not in the specific context of criminal law. But there is one important difference. Exporting the 'bits and pieces' approach to the AFSJ also runs the risk of undermining fundamental rights protection and thereby lowering the standard of human rights protection in the EU where it is most needed. For example, how will mutual recognition work, if at all, if all Member States are not participating? Clearly, this challenges the very point of it.[44]

5. MUTUAL RECOGNITION AS AN EXPRESSION OF DIFFERENTIATION IN CRIMINAL LAW

As mentioned above, the concept of mutual recognition is the backbone of much of EU criminal law cooperation. As such, the concept of mutual recognition is based on trust. It seems, however, difficult to uphold 'trust' unless all Member States are participating in the cooperation with regard to legal safeguards. The key question here is to what extent the concept of mutual recognition could function adequately without the participation of all the Member States. Before the Lisbon Treaty there was very little power within the former third pillar to enact legislation to harmonize national criminal law and therefore mutual recognition remained the dominant theme.[45] Does mutual recognition then offer a differentiated approach with regard to criminal law? Recent case law on the EAW seems to give a negative answer to this question by rather emphasizing the importance of the full effectiveness of EU law.

One of the most drastic examples of mutual recognition in the context of criminal law is that of the European Arrest Warrant that abolished dual criminality for 32 crimes and has been hotly debated since its adoption in 2002.[46] The operation of this measure raised a debate as to the extent to which national courts could insist on a higher level of fundamental rights

---

[42] Rebecca Adler-Nissen, 'Opting Out of an Ever Closer Union: The Integration Doxa and the Management of Sovereignty' (2011) 34(5) *West European Politics* 1092.

[43] Allan Rosas and Lorna Armati, *EU Constitutional Law* (Hart Publishing 2010) 108–10. Joined Cases C-274/11 and C-295/11, *Spain and Italy v Council*, ECLI:EU:C:2013:240 judgment of 16 April 2013.

[44] See further Herlin-Karnell and Konstadinides (n 3) 139.

[45] See former arts 29–31 TEU.

[46] 2002/584/JHA [2002] OJ L190/1, on the European Arrest Warrant.

protection than that granted by the EAW. In the recent case of *Stefano Melloni,*[47] on the validity of the amendments made to the EAW by Framework Decision 2009/299/JHA,[48] and addressing the application of the principle of mutual recognition to trial *in absentia* which was guaranteed by the Spanish Constitution, AG Bot provided an interesting account of the relationship between the EAW and the Charter of Fundamental Rights. The Advocate General focused on Article 53 of the Charter, which provides for the highest relevant human rights standard to be applied. Specifically, the Charter stipulates that:

> nothing in the Charter shall be interpreted as restricting or adversely affecting human rights and fundamental freedoms as recognized, in their respective fields of application, by Union law and international law and by international agreements to which the Union or all the Member States are party, including the European Convention for the Protection of Human Rights and Fundamental Freedoms, and by the Member States' constitutions.

In doing so, he argued that the Charter is not, in any event, a primacy-restricting measure and does not empower the Member States to 'opt-out' from EU law in a system based on trust. The Court of Justice agreed and held that such an interpretation of Article 53 of the Charter would undermine the principle of the primacy of EU law. Specifically, the Court stated that, where an EU legal act calls for national implementing measures, national authorities and courts remain free to apply national standards of protection of fundamental rights, provided that the level of protection provided for by the Charter, as interpreted by the Court, and the primacy, unity and effectiveness of EU law are not thereby compromised.[49] It could be argued however that Article 53 of the Charter does not hinder the EU from adopting a higher standard. As pointed out by Leczykiewicz, while the immediate effects could be restricted to the particular EU legislative act in question, the judgment sends a very worrying message about the way in which the Court of Justice sees its role as a constitutional review court.[50] It seems to confirm a very low threshold for fundamental rights protection in the context of the EAW and the fundamentals of mutual recognition.

---

[47] *Melloni* (n 12), Opinion of AG Bot.

[48] Framework Decision, 2009/299/JHA, [2009] OJ L81/24.

[49] Case C-399/11, Criminal proceedings against *Stefano Melloni*, ECLI:EU:C:2013:107, judgment of 26 February 2013, at para. 60.

[50] Dorota Leczykiewicz, 'Melloni and the Future of Constitutional Conflict in the EU' (2013) UK Constitutional Law Association, available at: <http://ukconstitutionallaw.org> (last accessed 6 November 2013)

Moreover, in the recent case of *Da Silva Jorge*, the Court of Justice stretched the reach of the classic effectiveness test to the EAW.[51] In *Da Silva Jorge*, the Court of Justice also emphasized the importance of the full effectiveness of the operation of the EAW in the context of the possibility of opting-out from this measure under certain circumstances. In *Da Silva Jorge*, the Advocate General focused his Opinion on the need to recognize clearly the limits to mutual recognition in criminal law matters and concluded that trust is a highly differentiated concept. However, the Court instead relied chiefly on the doctrine of indirect effect, following the developments in the sphere of remedies and thus shifted its jurisprudence on EU criminal law more towards the doctrine of effectiveness.[52] Therefore if, at present, mutual recognition does not seem to allow for any flexibility in terms of extended protection in the context of the EAW, what then is the impact of the Charter of Fundamental Rights more specifically?

5.1 The Wider Impact of the Charter

A further question is of course the wider impact of the Charter of Fundamental Rights in a multi-speed Europe. How much will its legally binding status change the current state of play? As pointed out by the House of Lords Select Committee, the ECHR is widely considered as providing the benchmark for minimum human rights standards. Thus, some of the rights set out in the Charter correspond directly to those in the ECHR.

Yet, any reference to ensuring the correct implementation of EU legislation and rhetorical commitments to the Charter mean nothing without the Commission committing itself to bringing about more infringement actions in such cases.[53] In respect of due process rights, Article 49 of the Charter provides a requirement of legality and proportionality in a more extensive way than the ECHR. Also, Article 47 of the Charter guarantees the right to an effective remedy, as noted above, while Articles 48–49 stipulate the presumption of innocence and the right of

---

[51] *Lopes Da Silva Jorge* (n 13).

[52] Ibid. The Court cited e.g. Case C-282/10, *Maribel Dominguez*, judgment of 24 January 2012. On effectiveness, see e.g. Armin von Bogdandy, 'Founding Principles', in Armin von Bogdandy and Jürgen Bast (eds), *Principles of European Constitutional Law* (Hart/Beck/Nomos 2010) ch 1.

[53] Steve Peers, 'The Next Multi-year EU Justice and Home Affairs Programme: Views of the Commission and the Member States' (2014), available at: <statewatch.org> (accessed 10 September 2015).

defence.[54] The latter provision also makes clear that the severity of penalties may not be disproportionate to the criminal offence. It is therefore likely that the binding status of the Charter will both be of significant symbolic importance and have a substantive impact on criminal law. The future will show how far reaching the Charter is in light of the limitations set by Article 51 of the Charter and its insistence on an implementation measure to trigger its application in the Member States.[55] In any case, it always applies to the EU institutions in all their activities and that is very important. Several important instruments have recently been adopted in this area, such as the Directive on the Right of Access to a Lawyer.[56]

Furthermore, in the *Radu* case, concerning the question whether arresting someone breaches that person's right to liberty in EU law, AG Sharpston went as far as to suggest that the Charter should constitute the template for deciding on the extent of mutual recognition.[57] According to AG Sharpston, the attribution of binding force to the Charter of Fundamental Rights is an expression of a political move towards enhancing the visibility of human rights and merely confirms the human-rights oriented approach which had already been enshrined in the Framework Decision in question (EAW in this case) prior to the entry into force of the Treaty of Lisbon.[58] The Court of Justice in its recent judgment did not elaborate on this aspect.[59]

It seems clear that this is an area in which any potential 'opt outs' from legal safeguards will be problematic with regard to due process guarantees and where the reach of the Charter of Fundamental Rights could become the turning point as regards the general application of fundamental rights beyond title V of the TFEU.

---

54 In her opinion delivered on 18 October in C-396/11 *Radu* ECLI:EU:C:2012:648, para. 103, AG Sharpston discusses the boundaries of art. 49 of the Charter by stipulating that it would be interesting to explore the boundaries of these provisions within the context of art. 3 ECHR, where the ECtHR has held that a grossly disproportionate sentence could amount to ill-treatment contrary to art. 3 ECHR. The Court did not elaborate on this issue.

55 See Case C-617/10 *Åkerberg Fransson* [2013] ECLI:EU:C:2013:105, for a liberal interpretation of the scope of the Charter.

56 Directive 2013/48/EU.

57 *Radu* (n 54).

58 Ibid.

59 Case C-396/11 *Radu* ECLI:EU:C:2013:39, judgment of 29 January 2013.

6. CONCLUDING REMARKS

EU criminal law offers a good test case not only for the usefulness of the emergency brake provision as an expression of flexibility but also as to the limits to the concept of flexibility (depending on what this term is taken to mean in practice). As argued above, flexibility in the context of the emergency brake means that the EU could always move forward by establishing automatic enhanced cooperation. I have argued that the classic loyalty obligation could then result in a revised burden of proof; that the Member State that pulled the brake sooner or later would have to catch up with the other Member States and that it is likely that what will emerge in this area is something similar to a proportionality test. Moreover, one could imagine and hope that 'flexibility' should be identified in the national identity provision of Article 4(2) TEU with regard to criminal law. Yet, recent case law in the context of mutual recognition and the operation of the EAW seem to focus more on keeping up the effectiveness of the EU enforcement machinery. There is however scope for allowing a degree of flexibility through a strict interpretation of rights as interpreted by the Charter.

The UK and Ireland opt outs pose a threat to the consistency of the AFSJ project at the same time as these opt outs reflect a broader objection to the EU project being too 'centralized'. Denmark offers another example of real limits to the benefits of differentiation. The extensive opt out granted to Denmark in terms of Protocol No. 22, which grants Denmark a special position with respect to the whole AFSJ, is highly unfortunate because, regardless of the merits from a sovereignty perspective, it could lead to too much fragmentation in fundamental rights protection as Denmark remains outside the CJEU's jurisdiction.

At the end of the day, the question of how best to tackle EU flexibility in criminal law goes to the core of the rule of law and citizens' rights. As argued elsewhere,[60] there may be conflicting values at issue here: on the one hand, ensuring consistency with Union action and, on the other hand, respecting fundamental principles of criminal law and the adequate safeguards of the individual. As explained, the establishment of enhanced cooperation in criminal law means that the last resort criteria (as stipulated in Article 20 TEU) does not have to be demonstrated by the Member States, as it will be considered as granted automatically in the

[60] Ester Herlin-Karnell, 'Enhanced Cooperation and Conflicting Values: Are New Forms of Governance the Same as Good Governance?' in Martin Trybus and Luca Rubini (eds), *Treaty of Lisbon and the Future of European Law and Policy* (Edward Edgar Publishing 2012) 146.

area of criminal law. Yet, too much flexibility in criminal law is likely to constitute a challenge to the legality principle and the possibility for citizens to claim (and know) their rights in cross-border criminal proceedings.

REFERENCES

Adler-Nissen R, 'Opting Out of an Ever Closer Union: The Integration Doxa and the Management of Sovereignty' (2011) 34(5) *West European Politics* 1092–113.

Conway G, 'The Future of a European Public Prosecutor in the Area of Freedom, Security and Justice' in Fletcher M, Herlin-Karnell E and Matera C (eds), *The European Union as an Area of Freedom, Security and Justice* (Routledge 2016, forthcoming) XXX.

Craig P, 'Review of Piris Two-Speed Europe' (2012) 37 EL Rev 800.

Curtin D, 'The Constitutional Structure of the Union: A Europe of Bits and Pieces' (1993) 30 CML Rev 17–69.

De Búrca G, 'Legal Principles as an Instrument of Differentiation?' in De Witte B, Hanf D and Vos E (eds), *The Many Faces of Differentiation in EU Law* (Intersentia 2003) 131–44.

De Witte B, 'Old-fashioned Flexibility: International Agreements between Member States of the European Union' in De Búrca G and Scott J (eds), *Constitutional Change in the EU. From Uniformity to Flexibility?* (Hart Publishing 2000) 31–58.

Fletcher M et al, *EU Criminal Law* (Edward Elgar Publishing 2008).

Gaja G, 'How Flexible is Flexibility under the Amsterdam Treaty?' (1998) 35 CML Rev 855–70.

Herlin-Karnell E, *The Constitutional Dimension of European Criminal Law* (Hart Publishing 2012).

Herlin-Karnell E, 'Enhanced Cooperation and Conflicting Values: Are New Forms of Governance the Same as Good Governance?' in Trybus M and Rubini L (eds), *Treaty of Lisbon and the Future of European Law and Policy* (Edward Edgar Publishing 2012) 146–59.

Herlin-Karnell E, 'Denmark and the European Area of Freedom, Security and Justice: A Scandinavian Arrangement' (2013) 5(1) *Amsterdam Law Forum* 95–105.

Herlin-Karnell E and Konstadinides T, 'The Rise and Many Expressions of Consistency in EU Law: Legal and Strategic Implications for European Integration' (2013) *Cambridge Journal of European Legal Studies* 139–67.

Hinarejos A, Spencer J and Peers S, 'Opting Out of Criminal Law: What is Actually Involved?' (2012) Centre for European Law Cambridge, working paper 2012/1.

Leczykiewicz D, 'Melloni and the Future of Constitutional Conflict in the EU' (2013) UK Constitutional Law Association, <http://ukconstitutionallaw.org>.

Ligeti K (ed.), *Toward a Prosecutor for the European Union*, Volume 1 (Hart Publishing 2012).

Mettinen S, *EU Criminal Law* (Routledge 2013).
Mitsilegas V, 'The Transformation of Criminal Law in the Area of Freedom, Security and Justice' (2007) 26 *Yearbook of European Law* 1–32.
Monar J, 'Justice and Home Affairs in the EU Constitutional Treaty. What Added Value for the "Area of Freedom, Security and Justice"?' (2005) 1 *European Constitutional Law Review* 226–46.
O'Neil M, 'EU Cross-border Policing Provisions: The View from One of the Schengen Opt Out States' (2010) 18 *European Journal of Crime, Criminal Law and Criminal Justice*, <http://uaces.org/documents/papers/0901/o_neill.pdf>.
Ott A, 'EU Constitutional Boundaries to Differentiation: How to Reconcile Differentiation with Integration?' in Ott A and Vos E (eds), *Fifty Years of European Integration: Foundations and Perspectives* (T.M.C. Asser Press 2009) 113–38.
Peers S, *EU Justice and Home Affairs Law* (Oxford University Press 2011).
Peers S, 'The Next Multi-year EU Justice and Home Affairs Programme. Views of the Commission and the Member States' (2014) <statewatch.org>.
Piris JC, *The Lisbon Treaty. A Legal and Political Analysis* (Cambridge University Press 2010).
Rosas A and Armati L, *EU Constitutional Law* (Hart Publishing 2010).
Stubb A, 'A Categorization of Differentiated Integration' (1996) *Journal of Common Market Studies* 283–95.
Summers S et al, *The Emergence of EU Criminal Law* (Hart Publishing 2014).
Suominen A, 'EU Criminal Law Cooperation before and after the Lisbon Treaty – Aspects and Comments Especially in Relation to the Norwegian Position' (2012) 6 *Tidskrift utgiven av juridiska föreningen Finland* 573–604.
von Bogdandy A, 'Founding Principles' in von Bogdandy A and Bast J (eds), *Principles of European Constitutional Law* (Hart/Beck/Nomos 2010) 11–54.
Wade ML, 'A European Public Prosecutor: Potential and Pitfalls' (2013) 59(4) *Crime, Law & Social Change* 439–86.
Weatherill S, 'If I'd Wanted you to Understand I Would Have Explained it Better: What is the Purpose of the Provisions on Closer Co-operation Introduced by the Treaty of Amsterdam?' in O'Keeffe D and Twomey P (eds), *Legal Issues of the Amsterdam Treaty* (Hart Publishing 1999) 21–40.

16. Foreign policy between opt-outs and closer cooperation

Panos Koutrakos

1. INTRODUCTION

The legal framework which governs the foreign and security policy of the European Union (EU) provides an intriguing case study of flexibility. On the one hand, it has provided fertile ground for an impressive range of structures of flexibility, both formal and informal, which have emerged in different ways and for different reasons over the course of the development of Common Foreign and Security Policy (CFSP) as a distinct strand of the Union's external action. On the other hand, flexibility has been inherent in the conduct of the policy as a matter of practice and quite independently from the legal mechanisms set out in the Union's primary rules.

This chapter will argue that there is a density of rules and procedures governing flexibility which has developed independently from the *ad hoc* arrangements prevailing in the area of security and defence as a matter of practice. This phenonemon illustrates a heavily proceduralized emphasis on law which is justified by neither prior experience, nor subsequent practice. The analysis is structured as follows. First, it will examine the typology of flexibility mechanisms set out in the rules which govern the CFSP and the Common Security and Defence Policy (CSDP). Secondly, it will explore the central position of flexibility in the design and application of the CFSP/CSDP system and its impact on the conduct of the Union's security and defence policy. Finally, it will reflect on the qualitative differences which characterize flexibility in this area compared to other strands of EU action.

2. FLEXIBILITY AS AN INHERENT CHARACTERISTIC OF CFSP/CSDP

Flexibility has been inherent in the very design of the legal set of rules which governs CFSP/CSDP. This was apparent quite early on, since its inception as a distinct legal framework within the Union's constitutional structure.

2.1 The General Opt-out for Denmark

The Single European Act (SEA) incorporated in primary law the first sets of rules on foreign policy. These were laid down in Article 30 SEA and governed the European Political Cooperation, the precursor to CFSP.[1] As these rules were of a somewhat loose wording and aimed merely to formalize prior institutional practice, the issue of an opt-out was not raised.

Things changed when the EU was established at Maastricht and the CFSP was introduced as a formal part of its constitutional structure. The formalization of CFSP was accompanied by an express opt-out for Denmark. The opt-out originates in a Decision of the Heads of Government and State adopted in Edinburgh in December 1992 following the rejection of the Maastricht Treaty by referendum in Denmark. It should be recalled that the Maastricht Treaty provided for the first time for the CFSP and set out a tighter set of rules to govern this policy in the form of the much maligned second pillar.[2] The opt-out was then formalized in a Protocol annexed to the Amsterdam Treaty and has been retained in every amendment of the Union's primary rules.

The Danish opt-out is set out in its current form in Protocol 22 on the Position of Denmark Article 5, of which reads as follows:

> With regard to measures adopted by the Council pursuant to Article 26(1), Article 42 and Articles 43 to 46 of the Treaty on European Union, Denmark does not participate in the elaboration and the implementation of decisions

---

[1] On EPC, see Simon Nuttall, 'European Political Co-operation and the Single European Act' (1985) 5 *Yearbook of European Law* 203 and Stelios Perrakis, 'L'incidence de l'Acte Unique Européen sur la Cooperation des Douze en Matière de Politique Etrangére' (1988) 34 *Annuaire Français de Droit International* 807.

[2] On the Maastricht rules on CFSP, see Panos Koutrakos, *Trade, Foreign Policy and Defence in EU Constitutional Law* (Hart Publishing 2001) 18–26.

> and actions of the Union which have defence implications. Therefore Denmark shall not participate in their adoption. Denmark will not prevent the other Member States from further developing their cooperation in this area. Denmark shall not be obliged to contribute to the financing of operational expenditure arising from such measures, nor to make military capabilities available to the Union.
>
> The unanimity of the members of the Council, with the exception of the representative of the government of Denmark, shall be necessary for the acts of the Council which must be adopted unanimously.
>
> For the purposes of this Article, a qualified majority shall be defined in accordance with Article 238(3) of the Treaty on the Functioning of the European Union.

The material scope of the opt-out is defined in two ways: the first is in relation to measures adopted by the Union, namely general guidelines defined by the European Council and measures adopted in the context of CSDP; the second way is in relation to the effect of EU measures, namely the defence implications of EU decisions and actions. Article 5 of the Protocol only refers to guidelines defined by the European Council. This by no means suggests that the scope of the opt-out is confined to them. On the one hand, this choice is explained by the express reference in Article 26(1) first subparagraph TEU to the possibility that such measures may have defence implications. On the other hand, Article 26(2) first subparagraph TEU bestows on the Council the responsibility for the definition and implementation of CFSP by means of decisions and on the basis of the general guidelines defined by the European Council.

Another question raised by the wording of the first indent of Article 5 of the Protocol is about the choice of words which refer to the CSDP provisions: while all provisions of Section 2 of Title V TEU are mentioned, that is the CSDP-specific part of the CFSP set of rules, these provisions are not mentioned as a whole. Instead, reference is made expressly to Article 42 TEU and then to Articles 43–46 TEU. The unnecessarily cumbersome wording of the above rules notwithstanding, Article 5 of the Protocol exempts Denmark from the ambit of any CFSP measure with any defence implications. The opt-out refers to decision-making, implementation and financing of any such measures.

2.2 *Ad hoc* Opt-outs: Constructive Abstention

In addition to the permanent opt-out granted to Denmark, EU law also provides for the possibility of an opt-out for individual Member States on an *ad hoc* basis. This takes the form of constructive abstention which aims to render the unanimity rule, pursuant to Article 31(1) first subparagraph TEU, more workable. It is set out in Article 31(1) second subparagraph TEU and reads as follows:

> When abstaining in a vote, any member of the Council may qualify its abstention by making a formal declaration under the present sub-paragraph. In that case, it shall not be obliged to apply the decision, but shall accept that the decision commits the Union. In a spirit of mutual solidarity, the Member State concerned shall refrain from any action likely to conflict with or impede Union action based on that decision and the other Member States shall respect its position. If the members of the Council qualifying their abstention in this way represent at least one third of the Member State comprising one third of the population of the Union, the decision shall not be adopted.

The provision for constructive abstention has been part of the CFSP rules since the Amsterdam Treaty[3] and its function is to ensure that decision-making is not rendered hostage to a lone dissenter or a small minority of dissenters. It has only been invoked once, by Cyprus in February 2008 in the context of the launching of EULEX Kosovo under Joint Action 2008/124/CFSP.[4] The political sensitivity underpinning this incident is apparent: Cyprus did not and has not recognized Kosovo as it objects to setting an international precedent which might be deemed relevant to the self-proclaimed Republic of Northern Cyprus.[5] However, it did not wish its political objections to the issue of recognition to prevent the Union from engaging in a mission which would contribute to the peace and stabilization in the Balkans.

2.3 Security Opt-outs: Acknowledging National Choices about Defence

Opt-outs, whether general or *ad hoc,* introduce flexibility by enabling specific Member States not to participate at all in a host of or specific policy initiatives. There is another form of flexibility which is indirect in the ways in which it manifests itself. It is about the acknowledgment of

---

[3] See art. 23(1) second subparagraph TEU (Amsterdam).

[4] [2008] OJ L42/92. The text of the declaration by Cyprus is set out in Marise Cremona, 'Enhanced Cooperation and the Common Foreign and Security Policies of the EU' (2009) EUI Working Papers Law 2009/21, 15.

[5] For political reasons, four other Member States (Spain, Greece, Slovakia, and Romania) have also not recognized Kosovo.

the fundamental defence choices made by Member States. This is illustrated by the second subparagraph of Article 42(2) TEU, which reads as follows:

> The policy of the Union in accordance with this Section shall not prejudice the specific character of the security and defence policy of certain Member States and shall respect the obligations of certain Member States, which see their common defence realized in the North Atlantic Treaty Organization (NATO), under the North Atlantic Treaty and be compatible with the common security and defence policy established within that framework.

There are six EU Member States which are not NATO members, namely Austria, Finland, Sweden, Ireland, Malta and Cyprus.[6] However, it is not just their special status that Article 42(2) TEU seeks to protect. The broad wording of this provision suggests a 'catch-all clause'[7] which aims to accommodate the security and defence considerations prevailing in different Member States. In fact, these qualifications are significant because they tell us something about the general tenor of the CSDP, that is, its inherently limited function, its narrow reach, and the centrality of the Member States whose right to make the fundamental choices about their defence is not called into doubt.

This central aspect of the character of the policy is underlined further by Declarations 13 and 14 concerning the common foreign and security policy annexed to the Lisbon Treaty.

The former reads as follows:

> The Conference underlines that the provisions in the Treaty on European Union covering the Common Foreign and Security Policy, including the creation of the office of High Representative of the Union for Foreign Affairs and Security Policy and the establishment of an External Action Service, do not affect the responsibilities of the Member States, as they currently exist, for the formulation and conduct of their foreign policy nor of their national representation in third countries and international organisations.

---

6 Following the adoption of the Nice Treaty, the Irish Constitution was amended in order to include the following clause: '[t]he State shall not adopt a decision taken by the European Council to establish a common defence pursuant to Article 1.2 of the [Nice] Treaty … where that common defence would include the State' (art. 29.4.9). On the origins and differences of the neutral status of these countries, see Eileen Denza, *The Intergovernmental Pillars of the European Union* (Oxford University Press 2002) 347–50.

7 Ben Tonra and Patrick Keatinge, *European Security and Defence Policy and the Lisbon Treaty* (The Institute of International and European Affairs 2009), para. 28.

> The Conference also recalls that the provisions governing the Common Security and Defence Policy do not prejudice the specific character of the security and defence policy of the Member States.
>
> It stresses that the European Union and its Member States will remain bound by the provisions of the Charter of the United Nations and, in particular, by the primary responsibility of the Security Council and of its Members for the maintenance of international peace and security.

Declaration 14 reads as follows:

> In addition to the specific rules and procedures referred to in paragraph 1 of Article 24 of the Treaty on European Union, the Conference underlines that the provisions covering the Common Foreign and Security Policy including in relation to the High Representative of the Union for Foreign Affairs and Security Policy and the External Action Service will not affect the existing legal basis, responsibilities, and powers of each Member State in relation to the formulation and conduct of its foreign policy, its national diplomatic service, relations with third countries and participation in international organisations, including a Member State's membership of the Security Council of the United Nations.
>
> The Conference also notes that the provisions covering the Common Foreign and Security Policy do not give new powers to the Commission to initiate decisions nor do they increase the role of the European Parliament.
>
> The Conference also recalls that the provisions governing the Common Security and Defence Policy do not prejudice the specific character of the security and defence policy of the Member States.

The largely repetitive wording of the above Declarations focuses on the role of Member States in designing and carrying out their foreign policy as fully sovereign subjects of international law. It also expressly maintains that 'the specific character of the security and defence policy of the Member States' would not be undermined by the CSDP provisions of the Lisbon Treaty. This illustrates a different type of flexibility, broader in its scope and wider in its implications as it touches upon the very core of CSDP. It is also more pervasive as it permeates the whole range of the Union's actions and underpins the specific ways in which the CSDP is carried out.

This type of flexibility ought to be understood in the context of the broader position of CSDP within the Union's constitutional order. The Lisbon Treaty approaches foreign, security and defence policy on the basis of a bifurcated approach. On the one hand, in the light of the arrangements introduced by the Lisbon Treaty and the ensuing revamping of the Union's external policies, CFSP appears integrated within the system governing the EU's external action: the much-maligned pillar structure is abolished and a set of principles and objectives are set out in Article 24 TEU and apply both to CFSP and all other strands of EU external action (economic, trade and political). So strong is the emphasis on the appearance of integration that the term 'external action' has been chosen to cover all strands of EU external relations, including CFSP/CSDP, hence conveying a sense of unity and common perspective. Therefore, the current constitutional arrangements stress the substantive integration of CFSP within the broader contours of EU external action.

On the other hand, the language of integration in which certain provisions about the constitutional position and conduct of CFSP are couched ought to be assessed against the clear indications of the distinct nature of the policy. First, the CFSP rules are not set out in the TFEU along with the provisions governing all the other strands of external action. Instead, they are laid down in the TEU. In fact, along with CSDP it is the only substantive policy whose provisions are set out in TEU. Secondly, the Union's competence in the area of CFSP is distinguished from the other EU competences and is not included in Article 2 TFEU and, therefore, may not be characterized as either exclusive, shared, coordinating, supporting or supplementing. Instead, it is listed separately in Article 2(4) TEU. Similarly, Article 24(1) subparagraph 2 TEU states that the common foreign and security policy 'is subject to specific rules and procedures'. Thirdly, Article 40 TEU, which refers to the relationship between the CFSP rules and the rest of the primary rules governing the Union's action, underlines further the distinct legal position of CFSP rules. Therefore, the whole logic of the institutional and normative underpinnings of CFSP/CSDP underline their distinct nature within the EU constitutional framework.[8]

3. ENHANCED COOPERATION IN CFSP/CSDP

The main provision for enhanced cooperation is set out in Article 20 TEU and the arrangements about its application in Articles 362–364 TFEU. Their analysis is beyond the scope of this chapter.[9] For the purposes of this analysis, suffice it to point out that the scope of the application of this mechanism to CFSP is broader under the Lisbon Treaty in two ways. The first is about its relationship with existing policy initiatives. Under

---

[8] This point is elaborated on in Panos Koutrakos, *The EU Common and Security Policy* (Oxford University Press 2013) 25–35.

[9] See, for instance, the chapter in this book by Peers.

the pre-existing rules, enhanced cooperation was confined to measures adopted in order to implement a joint action or a common position.[10] This restriction is now removed. The second way in which the scope of enhanced cooperation is broadened is in relation to security and defence policy. The pre-Lisbon provision exempted this area,[11] but this restriction is not repeated in Article 20 TEU. By broadening the scope of enhanced cooperation in relation to CFSP/CSDP activities, the Lisbon Treaty appears to render the latter closer to the mainstream of EU activities. It also appears to suggest an understanding of CFSP/CSDP as a policy space which is closer to other EU policies in conceptual terms than the previous constitutional arrangement had suggested. In doing so, Article 20 TEU reflects the language of integration in which the constitutional constellation laid down in the Lisbon Treaty is couched. A case in point is the elaboration of a set of principles and objectives common to all strands of EU external action set out in Article 21(1)–(2) TEU.[12] As enhanced cooperation aims 'to further the objectives of the Union', and given the single set of objectives of what the EU does in the world, the normalization of the position of CFSP/CSDP within the scope of application of Article 20 TEU reflects the overhaul of EU external action carried out at Lisbon.

Furthermore, the procedure for the establishment of enhanced cooperation in CFSP is somewhat distinct from that which applies to other policies.[13] The Member States which wish to establish such cooperation between them are to address their request to the Council, rather than the Commission, and they are not required to specify the scope and objectives of the enhanced cooperation proposed.[14] The request is to be forwarded both to the High Representative of the Union for Foreign Affairs and Security Policy and to the Commission: the former gives an opinion on the consistency of the establishment of enhanced cooperation with the EU's CFSP, and the latter gives an opinion on its consistency with other EU policies. The consent of the European Parliament is not required. Instead, the request for the establishment of enhanced cooperation is to be forwarded to it for information.

---

[10] See art. 26(b) TEU (Nice).

[11] Ibid. See Thomas Jaeger, 'Enhanced Cooperation in the Treaty of Nice and Flexibility in the Common Foreign and Security Policy' (2002) 7 *European Foreign Affairs Review* 297.

[12] See art. 21(3) TEU.

[13] See art. 329(2) TFEU.

[14] This is a requirement which applies to the other policy areas under art. 329(1) TFEU.

Finally, the conditions for the participation of a Member State in an enhanced cooperation mechanism already in progress are also set out separately.[15] The intention to participate is notified to the Council, the High Representative, and the Commission. However, no specific role for the Commission is laid down. It is for the Council to confirm the participation of the Member State having consulted the High Representative and after noting, where necessary, that the conditions of participations are fulfilled. In cases where it takes the view that the conditions for participation of the requesting Member State are not fulfilled, the Council 'indicates the arrangements to be adopted to fulfil those conditions and shall set a deadline for re-examining the request for participation'.[16] The High Representative may propose transitional measures which may be necessary for the application of acts already adopted in the context of enhanced cooperation. Such measures are adopted by the Council. In this context, it appears that it is the role of the Council, acting by unanimity of the participating Member States,[17] rather than that of the Commission which is central. This reflects the distinct character of CFSP and its position within the broader constitutional landscape: the Union's primary rules may well be couched in the language of integration, but the distinctiveness of CFSP/CSDP is actually reinforced.

4. FORMALIZATION OF FLEXIBILITY PURSUANT TO THE LISBON TREATY

One of the innovations introduced at Lisbon is the formalization of flexibility, that is the establishment of mechanisms which would authorize an *ad hoc* group of Member States to undertake CSDP actions on behalf of the Union. There are two such mechanisms.

4.1 Member States Acting on Behalf of the Union

According to Article 42(5) TEU, the 'Council may entrust the execution of a task, within the Union framework, to a group of Member States in order to protect the Union's values and serve its interests'. This would be done in accordance with the standard voting requirement, namely unanimity, pursuant to Article 42(4) TEU, and following a proposal by the High Representative or an initiative by a Member State.

---

[15] Art. 331(2) TFEU.
[16] Art. 331(2) subpara. 2 TFEU.
[17] Art. 331(2) subpara. 3 TFEU.

The delegation of this role is governed by Article 44 TEU which reads as follows:

1. Within the framework of the decisions adopted in accordance with Article 43, the Council may entrust the implementation of a task to a group of Member States which are willing and have the necessary capability for such a task. Those Member States, in association with the High Representative of the Union for Foreign Affairs and Security Policy, shall agree among themselves on the management of the task.
2. Member States participating in the task shall keep the Council regularly informed of its progress on their own initiative or at the request of another Member State. Those States shall inform the Council immediately should the completion of the task entail major consequences or require amendment of the objective, scope and conditions determined for the task in the decisions referred to in paragraph 1. In such cases, the Council shall adopt the necessary decisions.

It follows from the above that there are two substantive conditions which need to be met: the first is subjective and requires that the Member States involved are willing to implement the task in question; the second condition is objective, and requires that the Member States involved have the necessary capability for such a task. The wording of Article 44(1) TEU makes it clear that these conditions must be met cumulatively.

The management of the task is for the relevant Member States to agree among themselves in association with the High Representative. It is not clear what the role of the High Representative is in this context. As the Member States act in order to protect the Union's interest, they may not decline to consult with the High Representative. In any case, the expertise of the latter (assisted by the resources of the European External Action Service) on the management of CSDP tasks would make her advice invaluable for the Member States concerned. However, the High Representative may not dictate how a task should be managed under Article 44 TEU.

The above provision suggests a degree of close interaction between Member States and EU institutional bodies in the context of actions undertaken by Member States on behalf of the Union. In fact, there is a reasonably tight framework which provides for adequate supervision. In any case, the subject-matter of such actions distinguishes the legal and policy context set out in Article 44 TEU from other areas of EU law where Member States act as trustees of the Union's interests.[18] The

[18] For an analysis of such areas, see Marise Cremona, 'Member States as Trustees of the Union Interest: Participating in International Agreements on

applicable criteria for assessing the effectiveness of the procedures governing management and accountability for tasks delegated to Member States allow room for political flexibility and independent action by those actually involved.

4.2 Permanent Structured Cooperation

The Treaty provides a mechanism for permanent structured cooperation. In accordance with Article 42(6) TEU, this is open to Member States 'whose military capabilities fulfil higher criteria and which have made more binding commitments to one another in this area with a view to the most demanding missions'. However, rather than merely outlining the relevant criteria, the drafters of the Treaty seek to define them. In a Protocol attached to the Lisbon Treaty, the commitments on military capabilities are set out in detail. In Article 1, a Member State wishing to participate in a structured cooperation mechanism is required to:

> (a) proceed more intensively to develop its defence capacities through the development of its national contributions and participation, where appropriate, in multinational forces, in the main European equipment programmes, and in the activity of the Agency in the field of defence capabilities development, research, acquisition and armaments (European Defence Agency), and
> (b) have the capacity to supply by 2010 at the latest, either at national level or as a component of multinational force groups, targeted combat units for the missions planned, structured at a tactical level as a battle group, with support elements including transport and logistics, capable of carrying out the tasks referred to in Article 43 of the Treaty on European Union, within a period of 5 to 30 days, in particular in response to requests from the United Nations Organisation, and which can be sustained for an initial period of 30 days and be extended up to at least 120 days.

In Article 2, the Protocol requires the participating Member States to:

> (a) cooperate, as from the entry into force of the Treaty of Lisbon, with a view to achieving approved objectives concerning the level of investment expenditure on defence equipment, and regularly review these objectives, in the light of the security environment and of the Union's international responsibilities;

Behalf of the European Union' in Anthony Arnull, Catherine Barnard, Michael Dougan and Eleanor Spaventa (eds), *A Constitutional Order of States: Essays in European Law in Honour of Alan Dashwood* (Hart Pubishing 2011) 435.

(b) bring their defence apparatus into line with each other as far as possible, particularly by harmonising the identification of their military needs, by pooling and, where appropriate, specialising their defence means and capabilities, and by encouraging cooperation in the fields of training and logistics;
(c) take concrete measures to enhance the availability, interoperability, flexibility and deployability of their forces, in particular by identifying common objectives regarding the commitment of forces, including possibly reviewing their national decision-making procedures;
(d) work together to ensure that they take the necessary measures to make good, including through multinational approaches, and without prejudice to undertakings in this regard within the North Atlantic Treaty Organization, the shortfalls perceived in the framework of the 'Capability Development Mechanism';
(e) take part, where appropriate, in the development of major joint or European equipment programmes in the framework of the European Defence Agency.

Member States fulfilling the criteria and having made the above commitments may notify their intention to engage in permanent structured cooperation to the Council and the High Representative. In accordance with Article 46(2) TEU, the decision to establish such cooperation rests with the Council which is expected to take it within three months following notification by a qualified majority and following consultation with the High Representative.

Once permanent structured cooperation has been established, any decision and recommendation by the Council on its management is taken unanimously on the basis of the votes of the representatives of the participating Member States under Article 46(6) TEU, unless otherwise provided for in Article 46 TEU.

There are certain principles which appear to govern the permanent structured cooperation mechanism. First, the principle of openness: provided that the criteria and requirements set out in Article 46(1) TEU and Articles 1 and 2 of the Protocol are met, any Member State may participate in the mechanism, either *ab initio* or at a later stage. In the latter case, following a notification from the relevant State to the Council and the High Representative, the former will adopt the decision confirming the participation of the Member State by qualified majority of the participating Member States and after consulting the latter.[19]

The second principle is that of continuity: every participating Member State must fulfil the criteria and make the necessary commitments

[19] Art. 46(3) subpara. 2 TEU.

throughout their participation. According to Article 46(4) TEU, if at any point it ceases to do so, the Council may suspend the participation of the Member State concerned by a qualified majority of the members representing the participating Member States, with the exception of the Member State in question. In this respect, Article 3 of the Protocol on Permanent Structured Cooperation provides for the involvement of the European Defence Agency (EDA). In accordance with this provision, the role of EDA is broad: it contributes to the regular assessment of participating Member States' contributions regarding capabilities in general, and in particular these made in accordance with the criteria elaborated upon on the basis of amongst others, Article 2 of the Protocol. However, its impact is limited, at least as a matter of law: while it is entrusted with reporting at least once a year, its assessment 'may serve as a basis for Council recommendations and decisions adopted in accordance with Article 46 of the Treaty on European Union'.[20]

Third, the free will of the Member States is an essential precondition for their participation: any participating Member State may withdraw by notifying its intention to do so to the Council. The latter has no power to approve or to veto this. In accordance with Article 46(5) TEU, it can only 'take note that the Member State in question has ceased to participate'.

The procedural arrangements governing the establishment of and participation in permanent structured cooperation suggest the willingness of the drafters of the Treaties to facilitate recourse to this mechanism. This is consistent with overall tenor of the Lisbon Treaty. After all, it is at Lisbon that the possibility of enhanced cooperation is extended for the first time to the area of security and defence policy. From a pragmatic point of view, this is sensible, given that the defence capabilities of Member States differ widely and only in the case of a handful of them are they robust enough to carry out their internal security function and be deployed in different areas in the context of multinational operations simultaneously.

On the other hand, once the permanent structured cooperation mechanism has been established, the applicable procedure reverts to the one which governs all CSDP decisions, that is, unanimity. The logic of the functioning of enhanced cooperation, therefore, is that of the conduct of CSDP generally: the direction and pace of development relies entirely upon Member States.

As for the definition of the capabilities criteria mentioned in Article 46(1) TEU and set out in Article 2 of the Protocol on Permanent

[20] Art 3 of Protocol on Permanent Structured Cooperation.

Structured Cooperation, the relevant primary rules are not particularly illuminating. Their interpretation is subject to a dynamic, incrementally evolving process. Both Articles 2 and 3 of the Protocol suggest that they need to be further elaborated and defined in greater detail. This is realistic given that requirements related to military capabilities may vary depending on factors as diverse as technical and operational needs, geopolitical environment, activities of international security organizations, financial conditions, and political commitment. Treaties are unsuited to defining with any degree of precision such requirements. On the other hand, the vagueness of the relevant provisions is such as to render their application entirely a matter to be determined on the basis of factors as inherently fluid as political will, and as constantly evolving as economic realities.

Considerable vagueness characterizes, therefore, the legal rules on permanent structured cooperation. Viewed as a way of enabling the Union to shape its security and defence identity more efficiently, one might have hoped that the mechanism of permanent structured cooperation would have provided a clearer yardstick as to quite how the Member States might rely upon it. The relevant legal provisions appear to acknowledge that their contribution to the Union's foreign affairs is merely to set out the broad parameters within which the Member States and the Union's institutional actors may determine how to proceed, at what pace and in which direction. In this respect, there was some discussion amongst Member States during the Belgian Presidency in the latter part of 2010, and a German-Swedish proposal for closer military cooperation.[21] However, neither has given rise to any progress under the legal umbrella provided by the TEU on permanent structured cooperation.

5. DIFFERENTIATION IN CFSP/CSDP AS A PARADOX

The analysis so far has suggested that flexibility and differentiation are an inherent characteristic of the legal framework which governs CFSP/CSDP. In their various forms, the different permutations of interests which are expected to be addressed, and the variety of actors involved, make this policy area an ideal canvass in which the Member States may

21 For a discussion of these developments, see Sven Biscop and Jo Coelmont, 'CSDP and the "Ghent Framework": The Indirect Approach to Permanent Structured Cooperation?' (2011) 16 *European Foreign Affairs Review* 149. [The chapter was finalized in April 2014].

experiment with the legal management of flexibility. The drafters of the Treaties appear to accept this as they provide legal formulas which would seek to address a wide range of manifestations of flexibility.

The wide range of mechanisms set out in EU law and practice is a main characteristic of flexibility in CFSP/CSDP. This may be due to the fact that this policy area appears ideally suited for the application of flexibility mechanisms because of the nature of their subject-matter. As foreign policy and security and defence lie at the core of national sovereignty, their conduct is in greater need of being attuned to the different interests which Member States have in the area of high politics. This is all the more so in the light of the wide range of diverse Member States – small and large, north and south, new and old, rich and poor. While apparent in decision-making in any policy area, the differences to which this diversity gives rise emerge more starkly in foreign policy. In doing so, they introduce a factor which is inherently intangible, and yet central to policy-making. This dimension was set out succinctly by Advocate General Jacobs, as he then was, in a different context in Case C-120/94 *Commission v Greece*:[22]

> Because of differences of geography and history each of the Member States has its own specific problems and preoccupations in the field of foreign and security policy. Each Member State is better placed than the Community institutions or the other Member States when it is a question of weighing up the dangers posed for it by the conduct of a third State. Security is, moreover, a matter of perception rather than hard fact. What one Member State perceives as an immediate threat to its external security may strike another Member State as relatively harmless.

This inherently indeterminate dimension of the subject-matter of CFSP/CSDP may explain why it may be viewed as fertile ground for flexibility.

The second characteristic is the gradual formalization and proceduralization of flexibility which is apparent in this policy area. Emerging gradually over the years, the Treaties' provisions examined in this chapter intend to provide for legal solutions which would enable groups of Member States to do together within a set EU framework what they may otherwise choose to do beyond the EU structure altogether.

The third noteworthy feature of flexibility in this area has to do with the broader context of foreign policy in the EU. Coalitions of States have always been active in a manner considerably more direct than we

---

[22] Case C-120/94 *Commission v Greece* [1996] ECLI:EU:C:1996:116, para. 54. For an analysis of this context, see Panos Koutrakos, 'Is Article 297 EC a "Reserve of Sovereignty"?' (2000) 37 CML Rev 1339.

encountered in other policy areas. For instance, in the 1990s there were bi-annual meetings between the leaders of the UK, France, Spain, Italy and Germany and the Turkish Prime Minister. Another prominent example of groups of Member States cooperating closely beyond the framework of the Union's primary rules was provided by the Contact Group in former Yugoslavia.

However, the effort to cater for such a range of flexibility mechanisms in legal terms is also characterized by certain problems. First, there is already considerable flexibility and enhanced cooperation within the CSDP as a matter of practice. A case in point is the existence of battlegroups. This is an initiative focused on the swift deployment of 'effective, credible and coherent' rapid reaction units.[23] Declared operational on 1 January 2007, battlegroups consist of 1,500 troops each of which should be deployable at 15 days' notice and sustainable for at least 30 days (potentially extended to 120 days) either as a stand-alone force or as a part of a larger operation. The idea is that the EU should have two battlegroups on standby call at all times and that both should rotate every six months. This would enable the Union to carry out two simultaneous operations for a period of up to four months. Each battlegroup is led by a Member State which acts as the lead nation and provides the assets either on its own or with the contribution of other States. This initiative developed from the bottom up, an expression of the concern of the Member State that small, tangible forces would contribute effectively to the conduct of CSDP. No primary rules were required, and the absence of a detailed procedural framework for their establishment by no means prevented the establishment of battlegroups.

Second, in the area of defence in particular, a lot hinges on practical considerations: the defence capabilities of Member States, their willingness to deploy them, their ability to pay for them, the political capital which such choices would entail for the government of the day. In this respect, it is noteworthy that these practicalities appear to be acknowledged by the Member States. A case in point is the establishment of the European Defence Agency, an intergovernmental agency which specializes in the area of defence capabilities development, research, acquisition and armaments.[24] And yet, everything about the Agency reminds us of the limits of primary legal rules in the area. It was established prior to the

---

[23] Headline Goal 2010, Annex I to the Presidency Report on ESDP (European Council, Brussels 17–18 June 2004).

[24] Art. 42(3) TEU.

entry into force of the Lisbon Treaty,[25] and its work has been limited in effect and marred by disagreements among Member States, not least on issues related to the budget of the Agency.

The relevant legal framework illustrates the rather strong belief of its drafters that the provision of legal rules and procedures is a necessary feature of flexibility in CFSP/CSDP. The formalization of flexibility in primary law has been viewed as introducing a set of rules of considerable complexity which may prevent the emergence of initiatives by Member States beyond the EU framework altogether.[26] This view is entirely consistent with the broader tenor of the EU's approach to security and defence: a conviction that a tighter legal framework with a strong institutional and procedural dimension would enhance the effectiveness of the policy. This is the process-oriented approach which underpins the current rules on CFSP.[27]

This view ignores two factors. The first factor is practice. Practice of CFSP/CSDP does not suggest a reduced appetite for Member States to act in parallel to or even independently from EU initiatives. The experience in Libya is a case in point. It is recalled that, in March 2011, a coalition of various States initiated a military operation against Libya under the authorization of United Nations Security Council Resolution (2011) 1973.[28] This operation aimed to enforce a no-fly zone and a naval blockade. It led, controversially but inevitably, to strikes against forces remaining loyal to Gaddafi. The operation was not carried out by the EU, but a number of individual States and was led by the UK and France, while the US were content, for political reasons, to play second fiddle. It is worth noting that Germany abstained at the UN Security Council vote on SC Resolution 1973, in the company of China and Russia. It is also interesting that British Prime Minister David Cameron, French then President Nicolas Sarkozy and US President Barack Obama wrote an article about the operation in which there was not a single reference to the European Union.[29]

---

[25] Joint Action 2004/551/CFSP [2004] OJ L245/15, repealed by Council Decision 2011/411/CFSP [2011] OJ L183/16.

[26] See Ramses A Wessel, 'Differentation in EU Foreign, Security, and Defence Policy: Between Coherence and Flexibility' in Martin Trybus and Nigel White (eds), *European Security Law* (Oxford University Press 2007) 247–8.

[27] This argument is put forward in Koutrakos (n 8) above.

[28] The Member States which participated in the coalition right from the start were Belgium, Denmark, France, Italy, Spain and the UK. They joined forces with Canada, Norway, Qatar, and the United Nations.

[29] *The Times*, 15 April 2011, at 25.

The second factor is the profound role of the practicalities of an effective security policy: on the one hand, the political will of national governments to commit troops and capabilities, personnel and resources; on the other hand, the perilous state of defence industries. These are intrinsically linked: the Member States have shown little interest in addressing together the issue of their capabilities in a politically sensible and economically rational manner.[30]

These two factors have something else in common too: they are impervious to legal formulas. The increased legalization which characterizes the Union's approach to security and defence is of questionable relevance when it comes to addressing these factors. This observation also applies to the duty which Article 42(3) TEU imposes on Member States. This provision requires that Member States 'make civilian and military capabilities available to the Union for the implementation of the common security and defence policy, to contribute to the objectives defined by the Council'. This is coupled with the duty on Member States to 'undertake progressively to improve their military capabilities'.[31] These provisions appear to enhance the ability of the Union to carry out CSDP missions. And yet, their function is bound to be rhetorical at best. The choices of Member States about their capabilities are determined on the basis of multifarious factors extraneous to the legal provisions set out in the Treaty, including, but by no means confined to, internal political developments, economic exigencies, the geopolitical environment and the security approach of actors such as the US. The premise that a primary law provision would marginalize such factors and affect the political assessment of national authorities ignores the realities of security and defence policy.

The record of the Union's military operations and civilian missions illustrate clearly the inherent limits of heavily proceduralized rules in the area introduced in the Treaties. While the range and territorial scope of the Union's activities is broad, the overall size of the operations and missions is rather small, their mandate narrow and the terrain in which they are deployed largely safe. A characteristic which all military operations share is the unwillingness of the Member States to provide the troops necessary for deployment. Furthermore, considerable time and energy is spent in coordination and turf wars between the personnel

---

30 See Koutrakos (n 8) above Ch. 9.

31 Art. 42(3) subpara. 2 TEU.

deployed in CSDP operations and missions and other EU actors both on the ground and in Brussels.[32]

Finally, there is another consideration which raises questions as to the role of the legal rules on flexibility in CFSP/CSDP. It does not follow that the ability to act faster by relying upon fewer Member States would necessarily render the Union's position more credible and influential on the international scene. As Monar points out:

> [a] majority decision on a foreign policy matter is totally different in character from a majority decision on an EC legal act: adopted against the will of some Member States it would lose much or even most of its international credibility and could be easily subverted by signals from the opposing Member States through its national diplomatic channels.[33]

6. CONCLUSION

The analysis in this chapter suggested that differentiation and flexibility are prevalent in CFSP/CSDP as a wide range of arrangements which have been relied upon by the Member States as a matter of practice co-exist with an array of legal mechanisms set out in primary law. The latter lay down a heavily proceduralized framework which illustrates the conviction of the drafters of the Treaties that more constitutional law in this area will make for a more effective security and defence policy.

This approach is entirely consistent with the general tenor of the Union's approach to CSDP, which is distinctly process-oriented and heavily legalized. It also gives rise to a paradox: while CFSP/CSDP is a policy area most suitable for accommodating differentiation in a wide range of mechanisms, it is also least amenable to a process-oriented management of differentiation. The CSDP practice has questioned further the relevance of existing primary rules on differentiation. All in all, there is a disjunction between the range and density of the rules and procedures governing flexibility and the conduct of CSDP on the ground. In this heavily politicized area, it appears that there is, after all, such a thing as too much law.

---

32 See the analysis in Koutrakos (n 8) above, in Chs 5–6.

33 Jörg Monar, 'The European Union's Foreign Affairs System after the Treaty of Amsterdam: A "Strengthened Capacity for External Action?"' (1997) 2 *European Foreign Affairs Review* 418.

REFERENCES

Biscop S and Coelmont J, 'CSDP and the "Ghent Framework": The Indirect Approach to Permanent Structured Cooperation?' (2011) 16 *European Foreign Affairs Review* 149–67.

Cremona M, 'Enhanced Cooperation and the Common Foreign and Security Policies of the EU' (2009) EUI Working Papers Law 2009/21.

Cremona M, 'Member States as Trustees of the Union Interest: Participating in International Agreements on Behalf of the European Union' in Arnull A, Barnard C, Dougan M and Spaventa E (eds), *A Constitutional Order of States: Essays in European Law in Honour of Alan Dashwood* (Hart Pubishing 2011) 435–57.

Denza E, *The Intergovernmental Pillars of the European Union* (Oxford University Press 2002).

Jaeger T, 'Enhanced Cooperation in the Treaty of Nice and Flexibility in the Common Foreign and Security Policy' (2002) 7 *European Foreign Affairs Review* 297–316.

Koutrakos P, 'Is Article 297 EC a "Reserve of Sovereignty"?' (2000) 37 *Common Marlet Law Review* 1339–62.

Koutrakos P, *Trade, Foreign Policy and Defence in EU Constitutional Law* (Hart Publishing 2001).

Koutrakos P, *The EU Common and Security Policy* (Oxford University Press 2013).

Monar J, 'The European Union's Foreign Affairs System after the Treaty of Amsterdam: A "Strengthened Capacity for External Action?"' (1997) 2 *European Foreign Affairs Review* 413–36.

Nuttall S, 'European Political Co-operation and the Single European Act' (1985) 5 *Yearbook of European Law* 203–32.

Perrakis S, 'L'incidence de l'Acte Unique Européen sur la Cooperation des Douze en Matière de Politique Etrangére' (1988) 34 *Annuaire Français de Droit International* 807–22.

Tonra B and Keatinge P, *European Security and Defence Policy and the Lisbon Treaty* (The Institute of International and European Affairs 2009).

Wessel RA, 'Differentation in EU Foreign, Security, and Defence Policy: Between Coherence and Flexibility' in Trybus M and White N (eds), *European Security Law* (Oxford University Press 2007) 225–48.

Index